WITHDRAWN

WITHDRAWN

# Personality

## A Behavioral Analysis

# Personality
# A Behavioral
# Analysis Second Edition

### ROBERT W. LUNDIN
*The University of the South*

Macmillan Publishing Co., Inc.
New York

Collier Macmillan Publishers
London

Earlier edition entitled *Personality: An Experimental Ap-
proach* © 1961 by Robert W. Lundin. Earlier edition entitled
*Personality: A Behavioral Analysis* copyright © 1969 by
Robert W. Lundin.

Macmillan Publishing Co., Inc.
866 Third Avenue, New York, New York 10022

Collier-Macmillan Canada, Ltd., Toronto, Ontario


Library of Congress Cataloging in Publication Data

Lundin, Robert William
  Personality: a behavioral analysis.

  Bibliography: p.
  1. Personality.  I. Title.  [DNLM: 1. Personality.
BF698 L962p 1974]
BF698.L83 1974        155.2        73-3890
ISBN 0-02-372670-9

Printing: 1 2 3 4 5 6 7 8    Year: 4 5 6 7 8 9 0

*To Margaret*

# Preface to the Second Edition

Since the publication of the first edition of this book in 1969, the amount of experimental data to support a behavioral approach to personality has increased at an almost staggering rate. After reviewing over 500 studies, I have deleted about 22 references and selected 42 new references which further support the behavior principles outlined in this book. Quite a few of the new studies have been drawn from the area of behavior modification; thus Chapter 18, on behavior therapy, has been considerably expanded, whereas other studies have become integral parts of other chapters. The studies were deleted not because they were necessarily poor, but because they do not seem to be as appropriate to the general thesis of the book as they were five years ago. The new studies are almost completely devoted to experiments with human subjects.

The overall size of the edition is not appreciably larger than the first edition. It is my hope that this latest edition with its new studies will enhance the general interest of the student, since the new references appear to me to show greater application to human affairs outside the laboratory.

As in the first edition, any errors of fact or omission are my own responsibility.

R. W. L.

# Preface to the First Edition

This book, *Personality: A Behavioral Analysis*, is based on a book published in 1961 called *Personality: An Experimental Approach*.

The past eight years have seen tremendous strides in the application of behavior principles to the study of personality. In 1961 the number of operant conditioning studies involving human subjects was relatively small. At that time the development of a new approach to the study of personality based on behavior theory had to depend in part on studies from the animal laboratory as an extrapolation to human responding. Now the situation has changed considerably. Of approximately one hundred new references in *Personality: A Behavioral Analysis*, the vast majority involve experimentation with human subjects—normal as well as disturbed and retarded children and adults. Some studies previously cited have been deleted where more appropriate substitutes could be made. I hope the reader will find many of these new references both exciting and interesting.

In making the revision, I have allowed major changes in the addition of new material as well as deletion and rearrangement of other material. Chapter 1 has been expanded to devote more attention to alternate viewpoints. In the early chapters in which basic behavior principles are set down, I have stressed studies involving human subjects. Chapters 11 ("Punishment"), 15 ("Neurotic Behavior"), and 16 ("Psychotic Behavior") have been considerably altered and expanded in keeping with recent experimental literature. A new chapter on behavior therapy (Chapter 18) has been added. Other experiments in this area have been appropriately placed in other chapters to describe relevant principles.

It is my earnest hope that this revision has placed the study of personality more firmly within the framework of behavior theory and drawn it closer to experimental psychology. If there are any errors of fact, or glaring omissions, the responsibility is entirely my own.

R. W. L.

# Contents

# 1 The Study of Personality

HISTORICALLY, THE STUDY OF PERSONAL-
ity developed somewhat apart from the field of
experimental psychology. As a systematic investigation, it arose as part of the clinical tradition of
observation, beginning with such French physicians
of the nineteenth century as Charcot and Janet.
These men were particularly interested in the study
and treatment of abnormal personalities and more
especially in a common disorder of the time, hysteria. A little later the Viennese physician Sigmund
Freud took up the study of man's personality again
in order to understand and treat his failings. Freud
attracted many men about him, some of whom
agreed with his ideas and some of whom, like Carl
Jung and Alfred Adler, eventually broke away and
developed their own theories and methods. Regardless of later developments, the first really comprehensive study of personality from a psychological
standpoint began with Freud and the various other
psychoanalytical schools as an effort to understand the basic nature of man as well as those
deviations and peculiarities of his conduct which
we designate as abnormal or psychopathological.

Most all the early personality theorists were
physicians who combined their theories of personality with the practice of psychotherapy as a means
of treating mental disorders. Their observations,
although lacking the controls of the modern experimental laboratory, were often very astute, and we

1

have been able to learn much from them. Freud was a pioneer and a genius, and his ideas have had a profound influence on modern psychology. Unfortunately psychoanalysis has suffered from too much theorizing based on conjecture and not enough observation. Often the ideas developed to account for man's behavior had little or no reference to events existing in time and space. Thus the early study of personality has distinguished itself from other branches of psychology by being more speculative and less subject to careful controls, that is, based more on intuition than experience. The experimental laboratory was seldom called upon for supporting evidence, so that carefully measured observations were not the rule. As psychology has advanced from an introspective analysis of the so-called mind to a science of behavior, there has arisen a need for the study of personality to become an integral part of scientific psychology. It must be lifted out of the sphere of the mystical psyche and placed on firm ground.

The earlier psychoanalysts, like Freud, have taught us much, but modern experimental psychology has now reached the point where it must accept the study of personality as a part of the science of psychology, no longer leaving it to the exclusive domain of the physicians and psychotherapists. Of course clinical observation is still helpful in understanding individual personality, but we must not rely on case histories alone as the source of our data.

The recent movement in *behavior therapy* in all its aspects (see Chapter 18) over the past decade has dealt with many clinical problems in an experimental manner and has added tremendously to an experimental approach to the study of personality.

Our aim is to present a systematic approach to the study of personality, based on data obtained as much as possible from controlled observations. Such an approach is called *behavioristic*, which means simply that the data for study *are* observable behavior. Through careful and systematic observation and experimentation, it is possible to develop a set of principles which can adequately explain human conduct. Psychology is then no longer left in the realm of the mind or spirit but becomes a science of the behavior of organisms, behavior which takes place within the physical dimensions of space and time. We thus leave the study of man's soul or spirit to the theologians and limit our analysis to those events which can be empirically observed.

## What Is Personality?

For many students, before they begin the study of psychology, the meaning of the word "personality" may be somewhat vaguely associated with the idea of social attractiveness. To say that one *has* personality is generally considered to be a compliment, implying a high degree of acceptability by some group. The exact meaning of the word is seldom clear to those who use it, but if pressed to explain further what they mean by personality, they may describe it as charm, good manners, verbal facility, and physical attractiveness.

Commercial establishments that advertise "personality improvement" courses attempt (particularly for the female of the species) to improve physical features, posture, and hair style, as well as to present a set of rather superficial rules on how to get along successfully with others. These rules may include: smiling, not criticizing, appealing to others' interests, speaking in a soft voice, and so forth. For the scientific psychologist this kind of interpretation is often referred to as the *layman's definition*, although it is certainly not his exclusive domain. Such an explanation does not consider the actual behavior of the individual so much as it does the *effects* which personality as a stimulus object has on others. An attempt is made to describe a particular stimulus object instead of the responses of a behaving organism. Those features and characteristics of an individual which are considered to be attractive in our cultural tradition make up the personality. More technically, this conception is referred to as a *stimulus definition*.[1]

Allport[2] has made perhaps the most exhaustive survey of definitions of personality, some fifty in number, beginning with the etymology of the word "persona," which originally denoted the theatrical mask worn in the Greek drama and later used by the Romans. In extending the concept of "persona," it came to mean external appearance (not the true self).[3] This idea was later embodied in more modern personality theories of Carl Jung.[4] We cannot go into Jung's highly complex system of personality at this time except in mentioning that "persona" was at the outer edge of the self, a mask worn by the person in response to the demands of social convention. It was the role given him by his culture, the part he was expected to play in life; in other words, his public personality. This concept accounted for only a small segment of the entire personality, the great majority being relegated to more "inner" self.

From our earlier description of the layman's interpretation, we see the modern conceptualization of the early idea of the mask. When one is to meet an important person or wants to make a favorable impression, he must try to "turn on the personality" so as to exhibit behavior which will be attractive to others. The external characteristics become quite real and sometimes operate to conceal his more implicit or covert reactions (what he is thinking about the whole situation).

If we look into the history of philosophy for a moment, we observe

---

[1] G. W. Allport, *Personality: A psychological interpretation* (New York: Holt, 1937).

[2] Ibid., p. 41.

[3] Ibid., p. 27.

[4] C. G. Jung, *Symbols of transformation*, vol. 5 of *Collected works* (London: Kegan Paul, 1956).

that personality has been often associated with what we call *thinking* or *reasoning*. According to Leibnitz, personality referred to "a substance gifted with understanding." [5] On the other hand, the British empiricist John Locke emphasized the idea of "a thinking, intelligent being, that has reason and reflection and can consider self as itself." [6]

### PSYCHOLOGICAL DEFINITIONS

A variety of definitions proposed by psychologists has been classified by a number of authors under the headings of *omnibus, integrative, hierarchial,* and *adjustmental.*[7]

**1.** *Omnibus.* The founder of behaviorism, John Watson, proposed an interpretation of personality which would fall into this first group. He considered personality to be the *sum total of one's behavior.*[8] Such a description simply enumerated all possible responses. Bunched together, these responses constitute personality. Critics of this interpretation claim that the view lacks any order or organizing principle.

**2.** *Integrative.* This approach stresses some organizational function. Personality is not haphazard but possesses some core or unifying principle. Exactly what the integrating function is may or may not be stated explicitly. It could be a basic drive or need, or simply the fact that as coordinated beings we organize our behavior instead of operating as separate unconnected reflexes.

One definition proposed by Norman Cameron, the behavior pathologist, would fit into this class. Personality is:

> . . . the dynamic organization of interlocking behavior systems that each of us possesses, as he grows from a biological newborn to a biosocial adult in an environment of other individuals and cultural products.[9]

Cameron stresses the fact that we begin life as purely biological organisms but enter into an environment which is already *an organization* of other human beings. We each must learn the patterns of satisfaction, denial, delay, and punishment that operate in our society from infancy on. These patterns become a related set of behaviors.

[5] G. W. Leibnitz, *Hauptschriften zur Grundlegung der Philosophie,* E. Cassirer, ed., vol. 2, 1906, p. 184.

[6] J. Locke, *An essay concerning human understanding,* Book 11 (London: A. and J. Churchel, 1694), ch. 27, sec. 9.

[7] G. W. Allport, op. cit., pp. 41 ff.; C. S. Hall and G. Lindzey, *Theories of personality,* 2nd ed. (New York: Wiley, 1970), pp. 8 ff.

[8] J. B. Watson, *Behaviorism* (New York: Norton, 1930).

[9] N. Cameron, *The psychology of behavior disorders* (Boston: Houghton Mifflin, 1947).

**3.** *Hierarchial.* These hierarchial definitions have in common some idea of demarcation of functions or layers of traits or characteristics. Two of the most famous ones in this class are represented by William James[10] and Sigmund Freud.[11]

James treated the *self* (he seldom used the word "personality") as consisting of layers viewed from within. First of all there was the *material self*, consisting of the body, one's possessions, family, and friends. The *social self* represented other's impressions of one (personality as a stimulus object). One could have as many social selves as there were persons or groups who recognized him. The third level, or *spiritual self*, served to organize opposing tendencies or traits, and the fourth layer, the *pure ego*, was really not separate from the spiritual self. It was the "I," or knower, as opposed to the "me," or self as known. It constituted the other side of the spiritual self and pure ego represented opposite sides of the same coin.

Finally, Freud's conception of personality as being structured into the *id, ego,* and *super ego* also fits into this class of definition. We shall have reason to discuss this matter in more detail in a later section.

**4.** *Adjustmental.* A final class of definitions considers personality in terms of *adjustment.* Here the emphasis is placed on characteristics or behaviors which enable a person to adjust or get along in his environment. This is a kind of *mental hygiene* approach. Personality in this concept is circumscribed by those acts we perform which help us keep our equilibrium or stay in harmony with our surroundings. When these efforts fail, we end up with what is called a *maladjusted personality.*

## Personality and Learning Theory

Thus far we have said nothing about an acceptable definition of personality for this book. The approach to personality taken here considers the psychology of personality from the viewpoint of *learning theory.* A complete understanding of this approach will be gained as the reader proceeds through subsequent chapters and learns about the basic principles of man's conduct. Our definition is really based on much fact and little theory, but tradition influences the relation of the word "theory" to it. We believe that there is no reason to assume that the study of personality proposes any new problems peculiar to itself (most personality theories do). The psychology of personality is that

[10] W. James, *Principles of psychology,* 2 vols. (New York: Holt, 1890).
[11] S. Freud, *An outline of psychoanalysis* (New York: Norton, 1949; first German ed., 1940).

branch of the general field of learning which studies in particular those processes most significant to *human* adjustment. Among others these include how learning operates in early development, the importance of motivation, the effects of aversive conditions, conflict and its consequences (maladaptive behavior, neuroses, and psychoses), and the role of learning in therapy.

Because there are a number of theories currently popular in psychology, it is important that we designate just what particular approach we are to follow. Ours is certainly not the first attempt to formulate the study of personality in terms of a theory of behavior. In 1950 Dollard and Miller made a significant step forward when they attempted to apply the learning theory of Clark L. Hull to the study of personality in their book *Personality and Psychotherapy*.[12] Since that time psychologists have become increasingly aware of the importance of learning for the study of personality.

In 1938 B. F. Skinner published what has turned out to be a very significant book in which he described a good deal of his own research using animals as subjects. This book, *The Behavior of Organisms*, set off a whole new era in psychology.[13] Skinner developed experimental techniques which many psychologists have followed, so that today his approach to psychology is one of the most widely accepted. The term *reinforcement theory* has often been applied because of the great emphasis placed on reinforcement, or the consequences of an act, in determining the future probability of that act's occurring again. More recently, the term *behavior theory* has become popular. In this book we propose to develop an approach to personality based on Skinner's approach to psychology.

Skinner's early experimental work dealt mostly with lower organisms —in particular, rats and pigeons. However, during the past decade and a half, psychologists and people in related fields have become increasingly aware that the principles Skinner developed in the animal laboratory apply, for the most part, equally well to human behavior. This is not mere speculation but, as many of the studies reported in this book will demonstrate, the principles apply to a great variety of species including humans.

WHAT DOES THIS APPROACH STRESS?

First of all, as we have already implied, this approach emphasizes the process of learning. Because the vast majority of man's behavior is

---

[12] J. Dollard and N. E. Miller, *Personality and psychotherapy* (New York: McGraw-Hill, 1950).

[13] B. F. Skinner, *The behavior of organisms* (New York: Appleton-Century-Crofts, 1938).

learned, an understanding of personality comes first from an observation of *how* and under *what* conditions behavior is learned. Learning involves certain lawful relationships which one needs to understand. Although our behavior may be lawful, each one of us develops under a different set of environmental conditions; hence, as adults, we end up with a different or *unique* kind of behavior equipment. The unique kind of behavior patterns acquired over the long period of an individual's development is the behavior peculiar to him and constitutes *his* personality. Thus an understanding of the conditions under which one develops behavior is necessary. This is the problem of *stimulus control*. Although there are biological foundations for behavior which are set at conception (some of us are destined to be taller or shorter, blonde or brunette, to have weaknesses or strength), most of the individual differences among people arise out of the different histories of development each person has had. Therefore the process of behavior acquisition is important, particularly in studying the disturbances in behavior. We shall investigate conditions in infancy and childhood which contribute to the specific kind of adult personality one happens to be. The problems of biological limitations and potentialities as well as the environmental (stimulus) conditions which contribute to the uniqueness of behavior also need to be understood.

Finally, since responses do not come in isolated packages, the problem of relatedness is important. Actually, responses are connected to each other in chains wherein one response may operate as a stimulus to the next. Furthermore, responses which we learn under one set of conditions may generalize to others. Very few of us have "split" personalities of the Dr. Jekyll and Mr. Hyde type. Our behavior is ordinarily integrated. We do not usually exhibit responses that are out of keeping with the environmental circumstances.

When a personality does get excessively out of step with his environmental demands, we call him *psychopathological*. Here the uniqueness has gone too far. Nevertheless the basic principles of learning still apply. The differences lie in the unusual kind of reinforcement history and peculiar developmental circumstances this individual has had. With these facts in mind one may come out with a working definition of personality as follows:

*Personality is that organization of unique behavior equipment an individual has acquired under the special conditions of his development.*

### PERSONALITY AND SCIENTIFIC INVESTIGATION

One of the main problems in the scientific study of personality is that it deals with humans, by and large, when conditions are such that the investigator is not able to control all the possible variables affecting the behavior under observation. In the light of this difficulty, some psychologists simply set up highly complicated theories with vast numbers of assumptions and slim facts, relying on their conjectures and intuitions. These personality theorists have gotten into insurmountable difficulty by relying on assumptions, which cannot be tested. Of course this difficulty is not peculiar to the personality theorist alone; many other theorists suffer like difficulties. However, the problem is not without resolution. Through controlled investigations, using humans and animals as subjects, proper environmental controls can be developed, and an understanding of the basic principles of personality can be achieved. This has been demonstrated in many careful experiments, some of which we shall examine in this text. By using empirical investigations as evidence, it is possible to develop a psychology of personality based on observable facts. These observations consider the way behavior is learned, the conditions under which it is learned, and circumstances which alter it. With this knowledge at our hands, we are then in a position to understand how a unique personality comes to be, what he is, and what environmental conditions are operating to control him.

## Alternate Theories of Personality

For the most part, the remainder of this volume will be devoted to a *reinforcement or behavioral theory of personality*. From time to time reference to other approaches has to be made for purposes of comparison and criticism. It is therefore appropriate at this point to survey briefly a few of the other approaches that have shared the field. These tend to fall into two main groups: (1) those which stress structure and measurement of personality, and (2) those which stress the development process.

**1.** *Structural Theories.* Perhaps the first of the structural theories goes back to about 400 years B.C. to the Greek physician Hippocrates, who proposed four temperaments based on the four humors of the body. These in turn were based on the four cosmic elements proposed by the Greek philosopher Empedocles about fifty years earlier. The relationships between the elements, their characteristics, the humors, and temperaments can most clearly be understood by reference to the following table:

| Elements | Properties | Humors | Temperament |
|---|---|---|---|
| Earth | Cold, Dry | Black Bile | Melancholic |
| Air | Warm, Moist | Blood | Sanguine |
| Fire | Warm, Dry | Yellow Bile | Choleric |
| Water | Cold, Moist | Phlegm | Phlegmatic |

If the humors were mixed in proper proportions, a well-balanced personality resulted. When the humors were out of balance, the personality type became that of the dominant humor. For example, an overbalancing of blood produced a sanguine person (cheerful, optimistic), whereas an abundance of phlegm produced a phelgmatic person (calm, stolid).

A more recent type of personality theory, also based on temperamental characteristics as well as body type, is that of Sheldon and Stevens.[14] Their theory assumes that a relationship exists between body-build and personality, although they are not the first to advance this idea. The earlier *physiognomists*, who thought they could "tell" personality by examining its physical features, thrived on this philosophy (red heads are hot tempered, shifty eyes mean deceit, receding hairlines indicate intelligence). A little later a slightly more scientific conception appeared in the ideas of Kretschmer,[15] which influenced Sheldon strongly. Kretschmer observed (or at least thought he did) that short, fat people (pyknic type) were inclined to be a cheerful, jolly disposition, and if they became insane, would become manic or depressive. On the other hand, the tall, thin person (leptosome type) was inclined to be withdrawn and shy, and if he became insane, would develop dementia praecox, a disorder in which the individual characteristically withdraws from reality and becomes extremely seclusive.

Sheldon improved on Kretschmer's ideas in two ways. First of all he used photographs (instead of incidental observations) of several thousand college students and identified them on the basis of three types of build. Secondly, these types could be rated on a continuum from 1 to 7 instead of being classified as an either/or proposition. Sheldon's three body types were *endomorphy*, *mesomorphy*, and *ectomorphy* (see Figure 1–1). The *endomorph* had a highly developed viscera and digestive tract and therefore would tend to be short and fat when found in the extreme form. The *mesomorph* was characterized by a predominance of bone and muscle. He would be strong and tough. The *ectomorph* was likely to have a tall, slender frame and fragile features. His muscles tended to be underdeveloped. Every individual (each of us) could be rated on *each* of these three types by using a series of numerals and by rating on the scale of 1 to 7, in the order of endomorphy, mesomorphy, and ectomorphy. For example, the most extreme endomorph would be represented by $7 - 1 - 1$; most extreme mesomorph, by $1 - 7 - 1$; and most extreme ectomorph, by $1 - 1 - 7$. Of course these extreme types are seldom found to exist in their pure form. Most of us will fall somewhere

---

[14] W. H. Sheldon, and S. S. Stevens, *The varieties of human physique, an introduction to constitutional psychology* (New York: Harper & Brothers, 1940).

W. H. Sheldon, and S. S. Stevens, *The varieties of human temperament, a psychology of constitutional differences* (New York: Harper & Brothers, 1942).

[15] E. Kretschmer, *Physique and character* (New York: Harcourt, Brace, 1925).

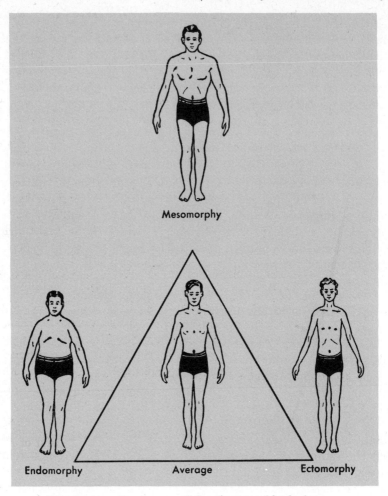

**Figure 1–1.** Continuum of distribution of body form among male population with illustrations of extreme development and an average individual. Endomorphy corresponds to the viscerotonic type, mesomorphy to the somatotonic type, and ectomorphy to the cerebrotonic type. Drawn from photographs in W. H. Sheldon and S. S. Stevens, *The Varieties of Human Physique*, New York: Harper and Bros., 1940. (Drawing reproduced here from L. C. Steckle, *Problems of Human Adjustment*, New York: Harper and Bros., 1949, p. 99. Reproduced by permission of the publishers.)

in between. For example, an individual who is predominantly meso-morphic but shows some slight endomorphic characteristic and lacks in ectomorphy would be rated maybe 2 − 6 − 1.

Correlated with the three physical types were the three dimensions of temperament (personality): *viscerotonia, somatotonia,* and *cerebrotonia.* *Viscerotonia* was typified by relaxation, love of comfort, and an extraverted disposition. This was supposed to be highly related to endomorphy. *Somatotonia* was described as energetic, active, and aggressive. It correlated with mesomorphy. Finally, *cerebrotonia* was likened by the traits of inhibition, restraint, and withdrawal and was related to ectomorphy. Sheldon's original study reported high correlations between the body types (called *somatotypes*) and the characteristics of temperament. He came about his evaluation of the temperamental side by using clinical ratings, but he did not take the proper precautions to allow for raters' biases. For example, a rater characterizing a subject who was quite endomorphic could easily rate him as viscerotonic if that was what the rater was looking for—and *knew* what he was looking for. Thus the rater had a preconceived notion of what the theory was supposed to prove. This weakness plus the fact that other investigators have failed to substantiate Sheldon's findings to any great degree reflect upon the usefulness of the theory.[16]

Moreover, Sheldon has assumed a direct or innate (inborn) connection between the two classes of physique and temperament. However, relationships that do exist can be better explained in terms of learning. We realize that physique can set certain limitations on learning and in that sense can be a secondary determinant of behavior. A strong muscular boy can more easily develop behavior described as self-confident because of his success in athletics and the approval of his classmates. On the other hand, a weak, delicate child has a better than average chance of withdrawing from contacts with other children because of the attitudes which prevail to some extent in our society today against the weak and fragile child.

**2.** *Factor Theories.* The basic rationale underlying factor theories is a set of specified variables (or factors) that are used to account for the broad complexity of behavior. These variables have usually been accumulated from extensive studies of behavior involving many subjects and using a variety of measures which permit some kind of quantitative scoring. The essential idea of factor analysis was introduced by an English psychologist, Spearman, and revised by Thurstone in America. Spearman[17] suggested that if we give two related tests of ability to a person, we may

---

[16] I. L. Child, The relationship of somatotype to self-ratings on Sheldon's Temperamental traits, *Jour. Pers.*, **18** (1950), 440–453.

D. W. Fiske, A study of relationship to somatotypes, *Jour. Appl. Psychol.*, **28** (1944), 504–519.

[17] C. Spearman, "General intelligence," objectively defined and measured, *Amer. Jour. Psychol.*, **15** (1904), 201–293.

find two kinds of factors: first a general one that is important to both tests and then a specific one that may be unique to each test. Thurstone[18] suggested that a series of multiple factors could better account for the behaviors being measured. The factors are usually discovered by giving a person a series of tests and ratings, or using some other device for analysis. The subject is asked to answer a variety of questions in a "yes" or "no" manner or according to what he likes or dislikes. On the basis of his answers to these questions, evaluations are made as to what kind of personality he is. It is assumed that the one taking the test answers truthfully and consistently and that he is able fairly well to evaluate himself.

After the results are in, a number of complex mathematical operations are performed. In general, factor analysis depends on the *correlation coefficient*. If two things vary together, they are said to be positively correlated, and if they vary inversely, they are negatively correlated. If they do not seem to vary at all, as in a chance or random manner, the correlation will be zero. The degree to which this variation occurs can be expressed by a numerical figure from $-1.00$ as a perfect negative correlation through 0.00 to 1.00, to a perfect positive correlation. Now, after a person answers these numerous questions, the items are all intercorrelated in an attempt to find common factors which can be isolated and labeled and then given as major dimensions of the personality. If certain items are answered similarly, it may be that the answers correlate very highly and have something in common. If the factor can be identified by a name, a trait has been discovered. The technique is used to study how many factors may be needed to account for a given number of relationships between tests.

The British personality theorist Eysenck[19] has identified what he feels to be the three primary dimensions or factors of personality: introversion-extraversion, neuroticism, and more recently, psychoticism. Among the many other investigators who have used this technique (Guilford, Thurstone, Cattell), some of the following factors have been frequently identified: anxiety, introversion, cleverness, shyness, self-confidence, depression, neuroticism.

One of the most obvious difficulties with such an approach is that it uses most often as its basic data paper-and-pencil personality tests. Question: "Do you cross the street to avoid meeting people?" The response is supposed to be an indication of introversion if one answers "Yes." However, it may depend on how one feels at the moment, maybe the subject has just met his worst enemy. Often the questions are difficult to answer in a definite manner, but if the answer spaces are all blanks, there is no test. Besides being somewhat unreliable, these tests measure

---

18 L. L. Thurstone, Primary mental abilities, *Psychometric Monog.*, No. 1, 1938.
19 H. J. Eysenck, *Dimensions of personality* (London: Routledge and Kegan Paul, 1947).

only the rather superficial aspects of behavior. Such a piecemeal analysis can only reach a small segment of the behavior it is attempting to analyze. Furthermore, its predictability is limited. It assumes a commonness of personality (we all take the same test) and fails to reveal any of the uniqueness of behavior of which we spoke earlier.

## Traits and Trait Organization

Of the many personality theories which abound in psychology today, a large number makes use of the concept of traits. In many theories the organization of these traits constitutes *the personality*. The factor and structural theories discussed earlier exemplify the importance of traits and their organization for understanding an individual personality. One of Carl Jung's first achievements was the introduction of the traits of introversion and extraversion into psychology as dimensions of personality. He considered these to be attitudes or orientations of the psyche. If one were extraverted, he would be oriented toward the outside world, whereas one whose attitude was introverted showed an orientation toward the inner self, emphasizing introspection, inner thought, and self-analysis.

Having discovered a number of traits, the trait psychologist typically makes use of a series of adjectives which describe what he has found. A particular individual may be characterized as "quiet, thoughtful, intelligent, and pedantic." These words are, of course, merely descriptive terms which apply to a number of different behavioral characteristics. In a sense, each term stands for a generalization, a different group of responses, each of which purports to have some degree of similarity.

An example of one widely recognized trait theory is that of Gordon Allport. He considers traits to be the most fundamental aspect of the personality structure. This interpretation defines a trait as an enduring predisposition of a person to act in a particular way when certain classes of stimuli are presented. Some traits are very central to an individual's makeup. Others are more specific or superficial. The particular way in which an individual's traits are ordered constitutes his uniqueness. As he develops psychologically, his trait pattern becomes more unique and stabilized. Sometimes there is one dominant or cardinal trait which emerges to govern all others. In such a case this trait controls the personality and renders the other less important traits consistent and subservient to it.

Some time ago Allport and Odbert[20] made a study of the exhaustive

    [20] G. Allport and A. S. Odbert, Trait names: A psychological study, *Psychol. Monog.*, **47** (1936), 1–171.

number of words in the English language that could be used to distinguish one person from another. They came up with a total number of 17,953.

Raymond B. Cattell[21] has been one of the most prominent trait theorists in this country. He has reduced the number to 171 different trait names. He was able later to reduce the number still further to 35 "trait clusters" in which various traits correlated highly with each other. Cattell lists his clusters in dimensions such as the following:

Intelligence vs. mental defect
Dominance vs. submission
Surgency vs. melancholy
Sensitive vs. tough poise
Trained vs. boorish
Adventurous vs. withdrawn
Wise vs. foolish
Affectionate vs. cold
Honesty vs. dishonesty

An illustration of a cardinal trait around which the rest of personality is organized is *authoritarianism*. This trait has been extensively studied by Adorno and Frenkel-Brunswick,[22] who consider it to be the core around which the entire personality organization of some people is built. The authoritarian personality is described as having great concern with authority, both in his own exercise of it as well as his deference to superior authority. Other characteristics include extreme conventional behavior, exploitation of other people, a general lack of self-understanding, and a rigidity of thinking. These authors suggest that the development of such a personality organization stems from severe discipline in childhood, extensive stress on rules and regulations, and the insistence of complete obedience by the parents. Although the child may submit, strong hostility is aroused in him. This may be displaced or suppressed, but the resentment may be later expressed in the authoritarian ways of adulthood.

### THE USEFULNESS OF TRAITS

A trait has been traditionally explained as some relatively enduring characteristic of behavior which manifests itself in a variety of ways, still keeping some common similarity among the behaviors. If a person has the trait of generosity, for example, he would be generous in a number of different situations. He could be generous with his family, friends, church, and community. The ways in which his generosity expresses

---

[21] R. B. Cattell, The description of personality principles and findings in factor analysis, *Amer J. Psychol.*, **58** (1945), 69–90.

[22] T. W. Adorno, E. Frenkel-Brunswick, D. J. Levinson, and R. N. Sanford, *The authoritarian personality* (New York: Harper & Brothers, 1950).

itself may differ from one situation to another. He may be generous with his pocketbook, his praise, or his affection. Traits are often signified by dimensions along which people vary in the amount of the trait established. These can be measured by ratings, questionnaires, or the observation of individuals in a series of standard situations.

In the evaluation of the concept of traits for the study of personality, we must ask ourselves whether or not they are helpful in the functional analysis of behavior. Many students of personality have, as might have been expected, answered the question definitely in the affirmative. They give as evidence the many studies of factor analysis, including the development of numerous measures which attempt to sample behaviors and to give an estimation of the degree of any trait or group of traits that a given individual possesses. To be valuable, traits should be indicative, according to the aim of psychology, of future behavior, on the basis of the known measure. Of course such a technique has its limitation.

Skinner[23] has suggested that we can predict much better on the basis of a *single response* rather than on a trait configuration. A trait is at best a measure of a *variety of behaviors* which appear to have some common descriptive characteristic, whereas a single response can be more readily identified and measured. It is easier to predict a single response than multiple reactions, which could include many behaviors emitted in a variety of situations. One expression of the trait of dominance could be given in the presence of some person (as a stimulus) who is responding in an acquiescent manner, but the response may be quite different if emitted in the presence of an equally dominant figure. Dominance, therefore, obviously depends on what the specific situation is in which the person makes his response.

Traits are, then, not the causes of behavior but merely descriptive terms applied to a general class of responses which appear to have something in common. The fewer traits we define, the more generalized we shall have to be, and the less accurate our predictions will be. The typical personality test purports to measure a group of general traits by taking a sample among many different possibilities, and on the basis of this sample, attempts to describe a vast amount of an individual's behavioral attitudes. The test will have certain limitations in meeting the predictive aim of psychology as a science. Whenever a prediction is made, it will always be within a wide range of probability, and the chances of being right may often be only as frequent as the possibilities of being wrong.

A functional analysis of personality as represented by the viewpoint set forth in this book recognizes the limitations of the concept of traits. As a predictor of future behavior, a trait is based on many responses in the past history of the organism, which have had multiple causes. Their effectiveness as predictors is impaired by the multiple variables, which

---

[23] B. F. Skinner, *Science and human behavior* (New York: Macmillan, Inc., 1953).

are largely unknown to the analyst. A functional analysis of behavior would preferably consider a specific response of the organism and then, from the variables known to the investigator, predict which experience has led to the emission of that response.

### THE MEASUREMENT OF TRAITS

The clinical psychologist who has had experience in the sampling of traits by using the many available measures is witness to the fact that such sampling is not without merit. In the field of intelligence, for example, much time and effort have been put into the development of a number of standard measures which exist today. By giving a test such as the *Stanford-Binet Scale*[24] or the *Wechsler Adult Intelligence Scale,*[25] one is able to discover a great deal about an individual's potentiality for future occupations. Let us suppose that, on the basis of the Binet test, a child's IQ is measured at 70. If accurately given, we can predict certain things from the test, such as that he will not succeed in college, and that the kinds of vocations open to him are going to be very limited. Indeed he may have to be cared for within the walls of an institution for mental defectives. On the other hand, a child with a measured IQ of 165 gives a very different story. He will have great potentiality for academic learning. Whether or not this will become an actuality will depend on a number of other variables not under the control of the test or test administrator. Such a measure of intelligence attempts to sample a vast number of behavior variables which have been found to have more than a chance relationship with success in school and certain specified occupations.

Of special interest to the students of personality have been the various measures called *personality inventories, projective techniques,* and *personal ratings.* The typical personality inventory consists of a number of statements or questions to which the individual must give a specified response such as "Agree," "Disagree," "Like," "Dislike," "Yes," or "No," depending on the particular system employed. The score on a particular trait is based on the answers to several items, all of which are intended to reveal the degree of a particular trait in question. A single inventory may give a measure of a dozen or more traits at the same time. For example, in the *Allport-Vernon-Lindzey Study of Values*[26] a series of statements is presented, to which the subject must indicate preference.

---

[24] L. M. Terman and M. Merrill, *Measuring intelligence* (Boston: Houghton Mifflin, 1937).

[25] D. Wechsler, *Wechsler adult intelligence scale manual* (New York: The Psychological Corp., 1954).

[26] G. W. Allport, P. E. Vernon, and G. Lindzey, *A study of values manual of directions,* rev. ed. (Boston: Houghton Mifflin, 1951).

The items are selected on the basis of their apparent relevance to one or more of six values: theoretical, economic, aesthetic, social, political, and religious.

Another personality inventory which has achieved great popularity in the field of clinical psychology is the *Minnesota Multiphasic Personality Inventory*[27] (abbreviated MMPI). This consists of 550 simple statements to each of which the subject must answer "True," "False," or "Cannot say." Such diverse topics range from bodily complaints ("I frequently have aches and pains all over") to fears ("I am afraid of closed places") or social and moral issues ("I do not blame a person who takes advantage of someone who lays himself open to it"). The test is scored on a number of standard scales that are intended to measure various degrees of behavioral deviation like depression, paranoia, or hysteria. The test has been widely used by clinical psychologists in the diagnosis of personality disturbances.

The test was standardized on a group of 700 individuals representing a cross section of the Minnesota population obtained from students and visitors to the University Hospitals. This is intended to represent the normal population (although some have objected to this sample as being representative of a normal population). The scales were then developed by contrasting this normal group with individuals diagnosed with various kinds of abnormality from the psychiatric division of the University Hospitals.

In interpreting the results of the MMPI, the individual scores are compared with the average and distributions of scores around the average. Abnormally high scores are given attention, but the whole profile is taken into consideration. The general shape of the profile is then interpreted by a psychologist experienced in the nuances of the test. For example, certain types of profiles are more common among abnormal people.

The inventories have, of course, their limitations, as we have already suggested. They can take only samples of behavior, which may be inadequate. There is, furthermore, the problem of interpretation. The series of trait scores will mean different things to different examiners, depending on the background and experience of each. There is also the matter of falsification. A sophisticate in the use of such devices can make the score come out according to his own liking if he happens to know the objectives of a particular test situation or circumstance. Some psychologists complain that the inventories are "superficial" and do not measure the "deeper-lying" aspects of personality. To overcome this last criticism, the measures known as *projective techniques* have been applied.

---

[27] S. R. Hathaway and J. C. McKinley, *Minnesota multiphasic personality inventory manual* (New York: The Psychological Corp., 1951).

## Developmental Approaches

The approach to personality which has had a most profound influence on our thinking in the field of personality has been that of psycho-analysis, represented in the main by the writings of Sigmund Freud. Since we shall make considerable reference to Freud for purposes of comparison throughout this book, some introduction to this view may be worth considering at this point. Even though we are interested in an experimentally oriented approach to personality, we cannot afford to ignore the psychoanalytic theory.

A brief presentation of such a complex system is difficult without running the risk of being superficial and unfair. The problem is further complicated by the slight variations in theory among the so-called ortho-dox analysts as well as among those who have strayed farther from the beaten path of Freud's theories, often calling themselves neoanalysts or neo-Freudians. Our account here will be based on the writings of the founder and acknowledged leader of psychoanalysis. This brief summary will suffice for now, and we shall have reason to take up other aspects of Freud's theory in later sections of this book.

### PSYCHOANALYSIS

Calvin Hall, in his *Primer of Freudian Psychology*[28] has suggested a threefold division of Freud's theory[29] of normal personality into *organization*, *dynamics*, and *development*.

1. *Organization.* The topography of the personality is divided into three main parts, the *id, ego,* and *superego.* This is further complicated by a threefold division into *consciousness, preconsciousness,* and *unconsciousness* (Figure 1–2).

The id's function is to provide a discharge of energy. This fulfills the primary or basic principle of life, called the *pleasure principle.* (Some people say that the reinforcement theory has merely substituted rein-forcement for pleasure.) If pleasure is not achieved, tension results, which one feels as pain or discomfort. The id is the source of all energy which runs the personality, and as such, is the seat of the instincts. It is unorganized, unreasonable, illogical. Freud called it the "spoiled child of the personality." Either the id is able to discharge its energy or it is frustrated in its attempts by the ego. The id is entirely unconscious, having no contact with reality except through the ego. One may liken the id to the primitive or animal nature of man.

---

[28] C. S. Hall, *A primer of Freudian psychology* (New York: World, 1954).
[29] S. Freud, *The standard edition of the complete psychological works,* ed. J. Strachey (London: Hogarth Press, 1953).

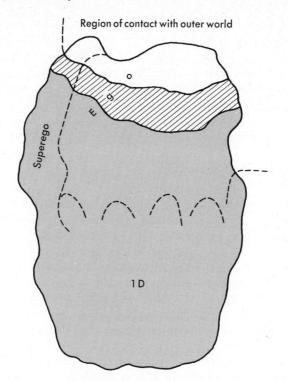

**Figure 1–2.** The psychoanalytic conception of personality elaborated from Freud's diagram of *The ego and the id.* The heavily shaded portions represent the unconscious mind; the lightly shaded area is the preconscious or foreconscious, and the unshaded area represents consciousness. In relation to these three levels of awareness are the three structures of the personality: the id, ego and superego. The id is entirely unconscious and gains contact with the outer world only through the other structures. (From W. Healy, A. F. Bronner, and A. M. Bowers, *The Structure and Meaning of Psychoanalysis.* New York: Alfred A. Knopf, Inc., 1930. Reproduced by permission of the publisher.)

The ego is considered the executive of personality. It is partly conscious and partly unconscious. In infancy it is small and weak, but through the process of *identification* (matching of conscious and unconscious images) it grows in stature to be the controlling system in the mature personality. The ego is practical; it is the *reality principle.* Through its efforts, the ego discharges the id energy in a way that is sensible and in keeping with the demands of society. It discovers a way, a plan of action that will reduce the tension, keep the id satisfied and the personality out of trouble. The ego is a complex organization of psychological processes (thinking, remembering, perceiving, etc.), the processes which serve reality and act as intercessors between the id and the external world.

The *superego* is the moral branch of the personality. It really represents a person's moral code, being developed through the child's assimilation of his parents' standards of proper conduct. It is made up of two subsystems, the *conscience* and *ego ideal*. The *ego ideal* represents the concepts of what is right or good, and it rewards the ego when it is good. The *conscience* corresponds to one's conception of what is wrong or bad, and it punishes the ego when it is naughty. These two systems are really simply two sides of the same coin.

In a highly moralistic and guilt-ridden person, the superego has taken over control and the ego is subservient to it. Conflict often arises between the superego and the id via the ego. The ego may try to satisfy the impulses of the id, but it is then punished by the superego for so doing.

**2.** *Dynamics.* Psychoanalysis emphasizes force and energy in the operation of the personality. The energy is called *psychic energy* and operates the three systems. It is derived from the biological functions of the body, but Freud never tells exactly how the physical energy is converted into the psychic. The psychic energy does the psychological work, and without it the psychological process would be vacant and static. The energy used has its source in the id with the instincts. Freud recognized two main groups of instincts, the *life* and *death instincts*. The life instinct includes the impulses that operate for the preservation of life. Freud emphasized, in particular, the sex instinct among them. The form of energy that the life instinct takes is called *libido*. The death instinct operates less obviously. The ultimate goal of the death instinct is the return to inorganic matter. The most obvious expression of the death instinct is in its derivatives—destructiveness and aggression. Freud did not mention the death instinct in his early writings, and it was only after World War I that he was convinced of its existence.

Although all the psychic energy originates in the id, it is distributed among the other systems through the process of development. The ego saps the energy from the id (through identification) for its work, and similarly the superego depletes the ego. Under normal conditions the ego has the balance of power in the control of psychic energy. The dynamics of personality involve the changes and transfer of energy among the systems, and the norm of conduct is determined by which system has the preponderance of energy. If an individual is impulsive and obviously wish-fulfilling, his id has control; if he is practical and realistic, it will be the ego; and if he is conscience-ridden and highly moralistic, it will be the superego.

Because each system has energy, it can operate against the other. There are, therefore, urging as well as checking forces, called *cathexes* and _anticathexes_. When a cathexis (urging) is checked by an anticathexis (restraining), the process is referred to as _repression_. Much of this anticathexis is done by the ego on the id. The instinctual impulses of the id "want out," but the ego says "No"! Forgetting an unpleasant memory is a good example of this process. The memory is repressed by the ego into the id. This process also serves to relieve the ego of the anxiety or pain that the unpleasant memory may give it. When the repression is lifted, the memory will be recalled. Frequently during sleep, the anticathexes of the ego are lifted or relaxed, and the repressions may come out in the form of dreams but usually in disguised forms, as the anticathexes of the ego are only partially lifted. An even simpler example of cathexis versus anticathexis is the urge to grab a piece of food if one is hungry but which is checked because one is out in polite company.

One of the most important jobs of the ego is to deal with the threats and dangers that beset a person. These cause anxiety and are painful to him. One solution, of course, is problem solving, which the ego uses if it can. Sometimes, however, realistic solutions are impossible. To protect itself, the ego may attempt to shunt off the anxiety by building up some sort of defense. Such methods may attempt to deny the danger (repression), falsify it, or distort the threat. These mechanisms do not solve the problem, but they often allow the ego to save face and free itself from painful anxiety. A more thorough discussion of Freud's theory of anxiety and defense mechanisms will be found in chapters 12 and 14.

**3.** _Development_. Freud placed great emphasis on the developmental processes of personality. He believed the individual goes through three principal stages. First was the _infantile_; this is subdivided into the oral, anal, and phalic substages, the entire infantile period lasting up to about five or six years of age. Next comes the _latent_ period, lasting from about six until puberty. Finally the individual reaches the genital stage, continuing from puberty to maturity.

Perhaps of greatest importance is the infantile period. During this phase the libido energies are localized at various regions of the body, known as _erogenous zones_. During the _oral_ period, the pleasure of the id is derived from mouth activity—putting things in, sucking, biting, spitting. The kinds of experiences at this period may have profound influences on later personality traits. Such personalities become the prototypes of these early experiences: acquisitiveness (taking in), aggressiveness (biting), contemptuousness (spitting out). Activities in adult life, such as smoking, chewing gum, drinking from a beer can (instead of a glass), are means we still use to discharge the libido energy; they are carryovers from our infancy, and in this sense we are still in oral period. The heavy smoker, obviously, had never satisfied his sucking impulses and in all probability was weaned too early.

Another zone which when stimulated gives satisfaction is that of the *anus*. Here explusion gives relief of tension, or holding on has its pleasurable consequences as the feces stimulates the walls of the intestines. The kind of toilet training a child has may leave a strong mark on his later personality. Frustrations and conflicts in this period may leave scars. If *retention* is stressed too much, the adult may be thrifty, parsimonious, or even downright stingy. On the other hand, if the mother rewards the child generously for his movements, he may grow to value them too highly. Generosity or philanthropy may result from this experience.

The third important pleasure zone of the body is the *genitalia*. Stroking these organs (masturbation) gives pleasure to the child. This portion of the infantile period is called the *phallic* period. Many symbols (called phallic) are reminiscent of this period and represent the genital organs (church steeples, umbrellas, canes, pencils, or other long pointed objects represent the male organ, while enclosures such as boxes, suitcases, and rooms may represent the female organ).

During the phallic period the *Oedipus complex* emerges. The boy develops a strong attachment for his mother, with the unconscious desire to have intercourse with her. Coupled with this is his castration anxiety or fear that his father will deny him of the one thing which would make this possible. He thus becomes a rival with his father for his mother's affections and hates him. For the girl the attachment is for the father, an unconscious desire to bear him a child. She believes her mother has denied her the male organ and feels castrated. The envy she has for this lost object is called *penis envy*. As the boy realizes the impossibility of his desire and becomes disappointed with his mother, he identifies with his father, represses the Oedipus complex, and the problem is solved. A somewhat similar situation occurs in the girl. There is one basic difference, however. In the girl the penis envy *brings on* the Oedipus complex, while its counterpart (the castration anxiety) in the boy helps resolve the complex.

During the latency period sexual energies are generally repressed, and with the onset of puberty and the *genital* period the sexual desires are again awakened, and the person begins to cathect energy on members of the opposite sex. Here the sexual urges can be directed eventually to their proper fulfillment, that of reproduction.

**4.** *Psychoanalytic Therapy.* The aim of Freud's therapy was based on the idea that a disturbed person suffers from a lack of proper energy available to the ego, which would enable it to handle the demands of the id. Frequently, the energy is still used in cathecting infantile objects. Furthermore the ego is using up so much energy in defending itself from internal and external threats it has none left over for realistic problem solving. Much of the energy is used up in repression because the ego cannot stand the unconscious threats of the id. Freud employed several techniques for discovering the unconscious material which was causing the personality so much difficulty. Two principal methods used were *free association* and *dream analysis*. The free association method requires the patient to lie down and relax on a couch and then relate anything and everything that comes into his mind. The patient is encouraged to tell everything, no matter how painful or trivial it may seem. The analyst then interprets the material (since it usually comes out in disguised form). As the patient becomes relaxed, resistances are broken down and the person tells the analyst everything.

The patient also brings his dreams to the analytic session. He may use them as a point of departure for his free associations, or the analyst may use them as a key to the understanding of the patient's unconscious. Because the dreams are disguised, the analyst must interpret them in symbolic form. The dream, as the patient reports it, is the *manifest form*, and the underlying significance of the dream, as interpreted, becomes the *latent form*. By interpreting the dream to the patient, the analyst may be able to break down the patient's resistances by revealing to him the infantile origin of his complexes.

The theory of dreams plays a large part in Freud's psychology. These manifestations provide one of the chief means of understanding the unconscious, which is in effect the greater portion of the personality. Dreams are basically wish-fulfilling devices. Through the proper interpretation of the symbols expressed in the dream, the analyst can get an idea of the basic determinants of personality which lie in the id.

**5.** *Evaluation of Freud.* There is no doubt of Freud's genius or his influence on many aspects of our thinking. Whether or not one agrees with the observations and interpretations of psychoanalysis, its influence cannot be denied. The fields of art and literature, medicine, and psychology illustrate this. The plays of Eugene O'Neill, such as *Strange Interlude* or *Mourning Becomes Electra*, illustrate Freudian concepts. Surrealistic art is full of Freudian symbolism. Much of the teaching of modern psychiatry has a strong psychoanalytic flavor to it, and we shall see Freud's influence as we progress in our study of personality. Some of Freud's concepts are scientifically untenable; others, if interpreted in the proper perspective, can be valid and useful.

One of the basic difficulties scientific psychology has had with the Freudian approach is the *unreliability of the data*. Freud based his theory on his own observations of people (which, though uncontrolled, were often very astute), the free associations of neurotic people, and reports of their dreams. Much of these data is not publicly verifiable and would not be acceptable to most scientists.

A second major difficulty is the *untestability of Freud's hypotheses.*

Such concepts as ego, superego, and psychic energy lack any empirical validity. His concepts are so vague that they are quite difficult to accept. They are what is referred to in psychological theory as *mentalistic*. His concepts refer to mind, psyche, or some nonexistential reference, in contrast to a behavioristic approach which confines its explanations only to the realm of observable and publicly verifiable facts. Some of Freud's ideas must be discarded as useless. Others bear reappraisal. It is often possible for the behavioral scientist to translate some of these loose terms into meaningful concepts which can be defined in terms of observational variables.

Many of Freud's concepts cannot be proved. The hypotheses must remain as such. To illustrate, consider the apparatus or structures of the mind. Freud thought of the mind as some realm not necessarily having physical dimensions but yet capable of a kind of geographical breakdown (see Figure 1–2) into the three spheres of ego, superego, and id. The mentalistic constructs were interrelated in various ways; they might exchange energy (nobody really knew how) or oppose each other. Nevertheless Freud and some of his followers thought of this hypothetical topography as being real. According to Skinner:

> One may take the line that metaphorical devices are inevitable in the early stages of any science and that although we may look with amusement upon "essences," "forces," "phlogistons," and "ethers," of the science of yesterday, these nevertheless were essential to the historical process. It would be difficult to prove or disprove this. However, if we have learned anything about the nature of scientific thinking . . ., it is possible to avoid some of the mistakes of adolescence. Whether Freud could have done so is past demonstrating, but whether we need similar constructs in the future prosecution of a science of behavior is a question worth considering.[30]

Although there are many differences between Freud's theory and those of a reinforcement theory of personality, some common ground is worth noting. Neither theory proposes hypothetical dimensions along which personality must vary (as the type theorist does). Both agree that, whether or not it is valid, talk about the existence of a given behavior will depend on the individual's previous history of experiences. Both psychoanalytic and reinforcement (behavior) theory stress the *developmental approach to personality*. Although the Freudians do not say this in so many words, the importance of past learning in personality is undeniable. The importance of the first six years in the development of the adult personality is of utmost importance. Furthermore, certain experiences, particularly in childhood, can operate as variables in a person's environment which will exert inexorable control over his later adult activity.

---

[30] B. F. Skinner, Critique of psychoanalytical concepts and theories, *Scient. Month.*, **79** (1954), 300–305 (p. 301).

# Heirs to Freud

## CARL JUNG'S ANALYTICAL PSYCHOLOGY

Jung made a dramatic break with Freud in 1912. Prior to that time Freud had hoped that Jung would be the heir apparent to carry on the psychoanalytic system as Freud was then developing it. Jung's basic difference from Freud involved the nature of the libido theory. Although various interpretations have been given, the real variance was the fact that Jung believed that Freud was simply placing too much emphasis on the sex instinct as the source of psychic energy. This difference was not based on any virtuous morality but on the fact that Jung believed the source of the psychic energy which ran the personality was much more general in nature, arising out of the metabolic processes of the body.

Jung's conception of the personality structure is much more complex than Freud's threefold division of personality into the ego, superego, and id. For Jung the structure was divided into consciousness and unconsciousness. The ego resided in consciousness with the persona or mask, which really amounted to one's public personality—that is, the superficial nature that he presented to the outside world. The ego and persona have direct contact with external reality. In the center of the structure was the *self*, both conscious and unconscious, the integrating principle of unity. In the unconscious lay the shadow which consisted, among other things, of man's animal nature.

Perhaps Jung's most notable contribution was the concept of the *collective unconscious*, in which resides our ancestral past. Jung thought of the unconscious as being divided into layers–the top layer being the personal unconscious—and consisting of any one individual's own past and forgotten personal experiences. But as one dips deeper and deeper into the collective unconscious, he encounters the collective experiences of all mankind, particular experiences that have been encountered over and over through countless generations. Eventually these take the form of *archetypes*, or universal thought forms. Jung was not trying to suggest that these were merely inherited ideas but simply dispositions to react selectively to environmental stimuli. Fear of snakes is easy to acquire because snakes have been a constant threat to countless past generations. Nor is it difficult to know God, because the worship of some kind of deity or deities goes back to primitive times, for example, the sun god.

Jung also developed a kind of personality categorization. There were two basic attitudes referred to before, introversion and extraversion, plus the four types: thinking, feeling, intuition, and sensing, making a total of eight basic types of men. One could be a thinking introvert or a thinking extravert, a sensing introvert or sensing extravert, and so on. A serious researcher who cares little for social interactions would probably be classified as a thinking introvert, whereas an outgoing person who derives full satisfaction from the fulfillment of his sensory capacities would be a sensing extravert.

Concerning personality development, Jung did not divide it into as many stages as Freud. He regarded the first part of life up to the ages of 35 to 40, as the rising of the sun from dawn to noon, constituting the biological stage. During this period one grows, is concerned with keeping alive, courtship, marriage, and the begetting of children. Some people never go beyond this stage in their development. They go to work, come home for dinner, watch television, go to bed, day in and day out. For the more mature the spiritual stage is yet to come. After the age of 40, the spiritual stage of man's nature comes into full fruition. One way to achieve the spiritual self is through religion, although Jung did not suggest that this was the only rout. The ultimate attainment of selfhood or unity among all the systems was the ultimate goal of life. All the systems of the personality attain their full being through the individuation process, but there is the transcendent function that holds them all together in the principle of unity.

### ALFRED ADLER'S INDIVIDUAL PSYCHOLOGY

Adler parted company with Freud about a year before Jung. In his early writings he stressed the importance of aggression or power as being man's fundamental driving force. Later on he widened his conception and stressed the basic need for superiority. This developed out of a basic feeling that he observed in all mankind, namely the need to compensate or make up for inferiority. Originally he had noted that when one of the senses was deficient—for example, vision—another sense tended to make up or compensate for that defect (one's hearing would be enhanced, for example). Eventually he broadened his theory to include the recognition that because of the helplessness of infancy, which must be made up for, we compensate for our basic inferiority in many psychological ways. Finally, Adler broadened his theory of striving for superiority to include the concept of an unselfish social interest. This included cooperation, social relations, and the individual's need to help society toward a goal of greater perfection. Social interest was a latent, inborn tendency, but it had to be cultivated. Some people, such as neurotics, drunks, prostitutes, perverts, and criminals, lack social interest. These people have inhibited this basic tendency to reach fruition.

Often the particular ways in which one goes about compensating for his inferiority, securing superiority, and social interest constitute what Adler called the *style of life*. The style of life is set when one is very young, in about the fifth year. All aspects of one's life and one's particular ways of behaving center around one's style of life. It includes all aspects of behavior that are oriented toward the aim of achieving the life's goal. Because the style of life is pretty well set early in life, it is difficult, although not impossible, to change. This changing of an unfortunate style of life is where psychotherapy comes in. People who have personality problems have developed what Adler called a *faulty style of life*. He cites the neglected, the pampered, or inferior styles of life as examples.

In regard to the direction of one's life, Adler believed that our present conduct is determined by future goals. This is a teleological rather than a causal concept in which the present is determined by the past. This is a distinct difference from Freud who, being a determinist, stressed the nature of causality, namely that one's present behavior is the result of past experiences. Furthermore, in speaking of the final goals that guide our behavior, Adler stressed the fact that they were mere fictions that do not necessarily conform with reality. This is the concept called *fictional finalism*. Some of these fictions that man lives by might include such aphorisms as "honesty is the best policy," "all men are created equal," "evil acts will always be punished," and so on. Belief in such fictions is not necessarily a bad thing, as they serve to help us cope more successfully with the vicissitudes of life.

Adler also considered *degrees of activity* as a primary aspect of the human personality. His description of degrees of activity was given by example. A boy who runs away from home or starts a fight in the streets would have a high degree of activity as compared with one who simply stays at home or reads a book, the latter involving a lower degree of activity.

If we combine degrees of activity with *social interest* mentioned above, we can get a certain personality typology. It will be recalled that social interest was the ultimate striving in which superiority is fulfilled through one's involvement with other people in his work or the betterment of society or love. Although the potentiality for social interest is inherent in all of us, not all people achieve it. Adler mentioned that drunkards, prostitutes, criminals, neurotics, and psychotics lacked social interest.

A person with a high social interest and a high degree of activity becomes the *socially useful person*. It is impossible to have high social interest and a low degree of activity, for high social interest and high degree of activity go hand in hand. However high degree of activity and *low* social interest result in the *ruling person*. He is out for his own self-interests, not others. Such people might be tyrants or despots. Low degree of activity and low social interest result in either the *getting person* (take all and give nothing) or the *avoiding person* (to be found in the recluse).

Finally, Adler thought his concept of the *creative self* to be one of his finest discoveries. It is only inferred and not known directly. It is not known by itself but in its effects. It is the mediator of the stimulating influences from the environment and the reactions between an individual and his environment. It becomes a kind of "free will." Unlike Freud's complete determinism Adler, in his concept of the creative self, gives man a freedom to act in the ways in which he chooses so that it is possible for him to be master of his own fate.

### LATER THEORISTS SHOWING FREUDIAN INFLUENCES

*Karen Horney.*   Horney was not one of the original Freudian group, although she was trained in Berlin in the traditional Freudian theory and analysis. Her basic theory falls within the Freudian framework, and consequently she has often been called a neo-Freudian. Many of her basic ideas are expressed in an early work, *The Neurotic Personality of Our Time.*[31] This work has had a considerable impact on later Freudian theorizing. One of her most important concepts is the *basic anxiety* we all feel from being isolated and helpless in a hostile world. Many environmental conditions contributes to this insecurity: parental dominance, indifference, parental inconsistency, lack of respect for the child's needs, disparaging attitudes, overprotection, isolation, and so forth. The needs that we develop are not only of a biological nature. Actually, the more important needs are acquired and arise out of our social contacts. Among them, and typically important, is the need for security. Sometimes our needs become so excessive that they become neurotic. They are characterized by their overpowering nature and insatiability.

The directions that our needs take can be moving *toward others* (compliant type), *away from others* (detached type), and *against others* (hostile type). In the neurotic, these needs come in conflict with each other and create our *inner conflicts*. Unlike the normal, the neurotic has been unable to reconcile these opposing tendencies. Frequently a *vicious circle* develops. For example, one may have a strong neurotic need for affection. When this need is blocked, anxiety is created. Consequently one strives harder and is more demanding in his cravings for the comfort of others. When this need in turn becomes blocked, more anxiety results, and the vicious circle continues.

Unlike Freud, Horney stressed factors in one's social environment that mold personality and may cause difficulties as well. We are caught up in cultural conflicts that involve opposing value systems. For example, we teach our children to stand up for their rights, but we tell them they must not be "pushy." Or we are anxious for our children to become mature adults, but we are fearful of giving them independence.

Like Freud, Horney stressed unconscious conflicts, repression, resistance, transference in therapy, and the practice of free association and dream analysis in therapy.

---

31 K. Horney, *The neurotic personality of our time* (New York: Norton, 1937).

*Erich Fromm.* Fromm has deviated more widely from the traditional Freudian system. Perhaps his most important work is *Escape from Freedom*[32] in which he emphasized his basic theory. In later works he has elaborated and added a number of other ideas. Fromm's main theme is expressed in the title of the early work. As we all have developed from childhood to adulthood, we have gained greater freedom and independence, but in gaining greater freedom we have become lonely and isolated. This loneliness produces a situation in which we would like to escape from freedom. One mode of escape would be to submit to social authority and utter conformity.

In developing this concept, Fromm traces the history of mankind. In the beginning, man was part of nature, the cosmos. He was an animal and part of it. During the Middle Ages the peasant had the security of living under his lord. He worked the land and was protected by his master. Furthermore, the all-powerful Church gave him security. In the later Middle Ages the guilds and crafts were formed, giving man greater freedom because he could work more independently with less reliance on one superior to him. With the rise of our present industrial society and democratic systems man has gained greater and greater freedom and has consequently become more lonely. Prior to World War II Hitler and his principles appealed to the German people because he offered them greater security and an escape from their loneliness. Likewise, other totalitarian states have offered a freedom from loneliness. Man faces the inevitable conflict of being part of the social order and separate from it. Our present-day democracy offers no solution. Man has great independence, but there are strong pressures toward conformity. Personality problems arise from a failure of society to permit man's greatest development. No society has yet developed which meets man's needs. Such a society is possible, however—a society in which man will have productive relationships with other men, will be a brother to his fellow men, but at the same time be allowed the ultimate fulfillment of his creative capacities and attain a sense of self. Such a society will fulfill the needs of belonging and love and at the same time allow man his individuality and independence.

## ROGER'S SELF THEORY

Like the various psychoanalysts we have studied, Rogers began his career as psychotherapist, and his theory of personality grew out of his experiences in working with people in a therapeutic setting.[33] The method he developed has enjoyed considerable popularity over the years;

---

[32] E. Fromm, *Escape from freedom* (New York: Holt, Rinehart and Winston, 1941).

[33] C. R. Rogers, *Counseling and psychotherapy* (Boston: Houghton Mifflin, 1942).

it is known as *non-directive*, or *client-centered*, therapy (see Chapter 17). In this the therapist plays a passive role reflecting back in a verbal manner the feelings and experiences that his client expresses. Thus the concept of *experience* becomes very important to the theory. Experience consists of everything that a person is aware of or what is going on within him. All of our experiences constitute the *phenomenal field*. This becomes a person's own frame of reference and can only be known by him. How a person is going to behave, then, depends on his phenomenal field or what might be called his subjective reality, and not merely his objective reality.

Gradually a portion of the phenomenal field emerges, which Rogers identifies as the *self*.[34] The self consists of conceptions of the "I" or "me" and perceptions of the "I" or "me" to other people and various aspects of life. Subsequently there is the ideal self, which is what the person would like to be.

There is a striving force within the self, and that is to be *actualized*. This involves growth, not only physical but psychological. This kind of growth, or self-actualization, is a very important goal in Roger's psychotherapy. As part of the self-actualization concept, there is a need to regard one's self positively.

The individual and his self are subject to environmental influences, particularly the social as separated from the physical environment. Sometimes a person develops a distortion of his self-concept in the process of development. One may have experiences that are incompatible with self-concept. Thus the self as perceived will influence other experiences. For example, the perception of the self as being bad will affect how one is going to perceive other aspects of the world.

One of the basic aims of Roger's therapy is to bring about an agreement between one's own concept of his self and his experiences. A warm, accepting attitude on the part of the therapist should allow an individual to perceive and evaluate these experiences which are inconsistent with his own concept of his self. It may be that one must reevaluate and revise his concept of his self in order to assimilate those diverse experiences. Roger's theory stresses *reality as one perceives it*, the subjective nature of the experiences and the basic striving for self-actualization.

## Summary

In this chapter we have briefly traced the history of personality, beginning with the original interpretation of the term *persona* as mask. We have considered the layman's approach, which looks on personality from

34 C. R. Rogers, *On becoming a person* (Boston: Houghton Mifflin, 1961).

the point of view of one's social attractiveness, and the psychological view of personality, which considers the behavioral or response side. Psychological definitions fall into various classes, depending on what aspects of the concept are being emphasized. These definitions may be omnibus (which lumps all behavior together), integrative (where some organizing principle is stressed), hierarchical (which stresses divisional relationships), or adjustmental (where personality consists of those aspects of an individual which direct him toward keeping on an even keel, or in equilibrium). A more useful definition, based on the learning theory of reinforcement, considers personality as being the unique behavior equipment which one has acquired through a history of learning. Such a view of personality considers it to be a part of the general field of learning, dealing in particular with those learning processes that are involved in man's adjustment to his environment.

Alternative theories of personality were considered. These tend to fall into two classes: First, those which stress the structures or types of personality, some based on the asumption that all people have a commonness of traits which can be measured along a variety of dimensions. They fail, however, to consider any unique or specific characteristics of the personality. The other type of theory stresses the developmental processes. In this latter class falls the present approach, as well as that of psychoanalysis.

# 2   Scientific Method and Personality

IN THE YEAR 1913 THERE BEGAN TO TAKE
place what may be called a major revolution in
psychology. All the excitement was started by the
publication of an article by John Watson, in which
he threw the mind and other unobservables out of
psychology.[1] Of course, any drastic change that
takes place in the history of a subject does not come
without preparation. Psychological laboratories had
already been in operation for some time, and those
who worked in them believed they were taking a
very systematic and careful approach toward the
analysis of the mind. Wilhelm Wundt was credited
with starting the first psychological laboratory in
Leipzig, Germany, in 1879; so, in this sense, Wundt
is the founder of modern experimental psychology.
He in turn leaned heavily on the earlier work of
Weber and Fechner, who had developed psycho-
physical methods in an attempt to study directly
the relationships between mind and body. Wundt's
psychology was based on the analysis of the con-
tents of the mind, or what he referred to as "immediate experience," that is, experience dependent on
the experiencing individual. This is the experience
that each of us gains from the world about us. The
experience is different for every person. The other
kind of experience was "mediate experience," the

---

[1] J. B. Watson, Psychology as the behaviorist views it, *Psychol. Rev.*, **20** (1913),
158–177.

subject matter of physics and the other sciences, which is independent of the experiencing individual. This is the public world of natural fact. Wundt thought of the mind as being made up of two kinds of elements: sensations and feelings. These had certain qualities and could be added together as compounds. Much of his experimentation had to do with sense-organ physiology and the corresponding mental events of experience.[2]

Wundt, along with one of his pupils, Edward Titchener, developed a school of psychology known as *structuralism*. Their aim was the analysis of experience or consciousness. The approach was purely academic or "ivory tower," since it had nothing to say about any applications or problems of man's conduct. It was pure psychology. For them, the mind was the datum of psychology and the methods were those of *introspection* (looking into oneself and analyzing self-experiences into their basic elements). Not just anybody could do this, but one had to be a trained introspectionist so as not to miss any of the subtle nuances of mental life.

There were other psychologists who differed with Wundt's and Titchener's approaches. William James[3] considered psychology to be the study of mental life. He thought of it as a flowing stream, ever changing, rather than a static compound that could be broken down into basic elements. James likened this stream of mental thought to the flights and perchings of a bird, ever changing. The job of the psychologist was to catch a moment of this passing experience and study it.

Developing alongside these approaches were, of course, Freud and his followers, of whom we have already spoken. Their interest was in treating sick minds. An analysis of the mind or personality simply grew out of their clinical observations. All these approaches had one thing in common—they were dealing with the concept of "mind" in some fashion or other. This mind might be connected in some way with the body (they never said exactly how; for example, Freud converted physical energy into psychic energy), or the two, mind and body, might run parallel, always beside each other but never interacting. In other words, something happens in the mind, and a corresponding event occurs in the body.

Such was the tradition of psychology in which John Watson found himself. He had been trained at the University of Chicago in a school of psychology known as *functionalism*. This had stemmed from William James' psychology, and the approach was also mentalistic. It considered psychology to be the study of mental functions, rather than the static states accepted by the structuralists. The functionalists were also strongly influenced by the evolutionary theory of Darwin, which stressed the

---

[2] W. Wundt, *Grundzuge der Physiologischen Psychologie*, 2nd. ed. (Leipzig: Engelmans, 1880).

[3] W. James, *Principles of psychology*, 2 vols. (New York: Holt, 1890).

idea of survival. They translated this survival concept into adjustment and believed the mind operated to aid the organism in its fight for survival. For example, man has the capacity (or function) of reason which gives him great advantage over the lower animals by enabling him to cope with his enemies and find the goals necessary to survival. The functionalists had added the study of behavior to the purely mental phenomenon. This, of course, was a step in the right direction.

Watson realized the uselessness of trying to study mind, spirit, or consciousness, or whatever names happened to be attached to the mental phenomenon. He likened this to the phenomenon of spiritualism and observed that if psychology were ever to be a science, it must limit itself to events that can be objectively observed. He noted that in all the other sciences, the facts of observation are objective and verifiable, they are public rather than private, and if valid events, they can be reproduced.[4] His approach was simple, and the *behaviorism* that he propounded became a flourishing school in the early part of this century. Of course it was not without its critics, who cried, "mechanistic, inhuman, atheistic," and so forth. For some of the more theologically minded psychologists (in particular the Thomists), this was pure heresy. Watson's behaviorism was a far cry from the behaviorism of today. His analysis was straight-forward, however. He said behavior was the activity of the muscles and the glands. He distinguished the striped muscles such as those used in walking, gesturing, or talking from the smooth muscles of the stomach, bladder, and intestine. He also spoke of the glands of both internal secretion (adrenals, thyroid, etc.) and the duct glands (salivation, per-spiration) as being of concern to the psychologist.

Watson was much impressed with the Russian physiologist Ivan P. Pavlov, who had discovered a new method of study, the *conditioned reflex*. Pavlov's early work[5] had been concerned with the conditioning of the salivary response in the dog. When a bell was rung and the dog then presented with meat, he obviously salivated. Later on, however, the dog salivated to the mere ringing of the bell. The reflex had been con-ditioned and brought out by the presentation of a new stimulus, the bell, previously inadequate for the elicitation of that response. Watson stressed this process of conditioning as being the way in which much of our early behavior was acquired.[6]

He also distinguished between overt and implicit responses. The overt ones, such as walking, were easily distinguishable. The implicit ones were

[4] J. B. Watson, *Psychology from the standpoint of a behaviorist* (Philadelphia: Lippincott, 1919).

[5] I. P. Pavlov, *Conditioned reflexes*, trans. G. V. Anrep (London: Oxford University Press, 1927).

[6] J. B. Watson, The place of the conditioned reflex in psychology, *Psychol. Rev.*, **23** (1916), 89–116.

more subtle and harder to observe. Thinking fell into this latter class. The earlier mentalists had simply considered thinking to be an attribute or one of the mind's functions. Watson, on the other hand, reduced thinking to the status of subvocal talking. He observed that a child thinks (talks) out loud. Through conditioning, he is made to talk to himself.[7] Some of these early observations have more recently been substantiated by controlled experimental investigation using finely refined instrumentation. Jacobson[8] gave his subjects training in progressive relaxation, then placed electrodes in the region of certain muscles, and asked his subjects to engage in activities of thinking and imagining. He found a corresponding electrical effect in the muscles specifically involved in the imagined activity (lift your arm or imagine you are smoking a cigarette). Another experiment of Max[9] used deaf mutes. When these subjects were given problems to solve (in their heads), he found an exaggerated degree of implicit finger and arm movements not found in subjects who had learned to talk. While perhaps primitive by our present-day standards. Watson's methods considered psychology as an empirical science dealing with observable events. This attitude has left its mark on psychology today.

A second influence of Watson on modern psychology was the aims set for psychology, that is, the *prediction* and *control* of behavior (particularly human). If one were to make progress in his science, he believed, he must aim at a degree of control over the material with which he works. Watson felt that through systematic observation and experimentation, the laws and principles that governed man's behavior could be discovered. We are still working today toward this aim. By knowing the laws and the circumstances under which the behavior occurs (the given stimuli and environmental situations), one is in a better position to predict the probability of a given response occurring in the future.

These two aims are still the objectives of psychology today.[10] Hopefully, we have gone a long way in understanding man's behavior and have discovered many of the laws controlling his conduct. Hence we are closer to the basic aims now than psychology was forty years ago. The reader can judge for himself as he proceeds through the chapters of this book.

The ideas that Watson set forth in the early part of this century were considered very revolutionary at that time. The mentalists had been and

---

[7] J. B. Watson, *Psychological care of infant and child* (New York: Norton, 1928).

[8] E. Jacobson, The electrophysiology of mental activities, *Amer. Jour. Psychol.*, 44 (1932), 677–694.

[9] L. W. Max, Experimental study of the motor theory of consciousness, IV. Action current responses in the deaf, during awakening, kinesthetic imagery and abstract thinking, *Jour. Comp. Psychol.*, 24 (1937), 301–344.

[10] B. F. Skinner, *Science and human behavior* (New York: Macmillan, Inc., 1953).

still are reluctant to give up their cherished concept of mind, for such an appeal is the easy way out. If something needs explaining, simply attribute it to the mind. This same attitude is also shared by telepathists. If a person appears to have extraordinary luck in calling cards, better than chance, they say he has "extra-psychic" or "extrasensory" powers. It is much easier to say this than to attempt an explanation of the event on the basis of some observable relationships. When we are ignorant of the causes of an event, it is simple to add some hypothetical explanation and thus solve the problem. One has to chuckle when the extrasensory perceptionists claim that the nonbelievers in their work are usually very poor at calling the cards. That is, these skeptics lack the power (extrasensory perception).

Some of Watson's ideas have prospered, others have fallen by the wayside. As the science of psychology has progressed, it is natural for change to occur. As new discoveries are made, old ideas may have to be abandoned. The student should not be misled into thinking that the behaviorism of today is the same that Watson fostered over fifty years ago. Nonetheless those people who are ignorant of the progress of psychology will often lift their eyebrows when someone speaks of himself as being a behaviorist. In today's terminology a behaviorist is any one who believes that psychology is the study of observable behavior and that the way to understand that behavior is through the methods of careful observation and experimentation. No scientifically minded person can object to that.

## Some Problems in the Study of Psychology as a Science

One of the most common objections to the scientific analysis of behavior is that *it cannot be done.* One may be asked, "How can you possibly attempt to analyze such a complex thing as the human spirit?" The implication here is that the data of psychology are inaccessible and incapable of analysis. These critics would be content to leave psychology in the hands of the theologians and arm-chair philosophers where it remained for centuries before any experimentation was attempted. The problem of psychology is not its *inaccessibility* but its complexity.[11] First of all, behavior is changing and is not a static state that can be viewed through a microscope for hours on end. It is a process rather than a thing. One solution to this problem, suggested by Skinner and his associates, is to take a simple event (such as a rat pressing a bar or a pigeon pecking a key) and then examine all the possible variables

[11] Ibid., p. 15.

involved in this operation.[12] This can also be done with humans. For example, Lindsley has developed a plunger technique (like that used on a candy or cigarette machine) as a response to study in his analysis of adult psychotic behavior (see Chapter 16).

A second criticism commonly levied against scientific psychology is that behavior is really not lawful and can therefore never be predicted. The implication here is that when we deal with humans endowed with *free will*, our prediction and control break down.[13] Man, after all, has freedom of choice. As you read through the pages of this book, ask yourself, from time to time, does he really? If one does not wish to get involved in the problems of free will, it will be easier to say that behavior is frequently spontaneous or capricious. The final answer to this objection will be found in the discovery that behavior *is* lawful and predictable; that it can be brought under stimulus control. "The proof of the pudding is in the eating," and the evidence thus far accumulated contradicts this contention that behavior is free of control and therefore impossible to predict.

## Scientific Method and Psychology

Since psychology studies behavior, it is therefore concerned with the relationships of the behavior to conditions that control it. The variables about which psychology is concerned are the behavior itself as well as those which lie outside the organism in what is commonly called the environment and the organism's environmental history.[14]

Science distinguishes between two sets of variables, called *dependent* and *independent*. Some theorists also add *intervening* variables, and a word will be said of these shortly. The phenomena that the scientist studies are the *dependent variables*. In psychology the dependent variables are the aspects of the behavior which we attempt to predict and control. In a very simple laboratory experiment in which an animal (say, a rat) presses a lever in order to get food, a dependent variable is the bar-pressing behavior or some measure of it, that is, the frequency, force, or time it takes to make the response. Or let us say we want to study the consumption of alcoholic beverages among college students, a matter of concern for most college administrators. The drinking behavior would be the dependent variable, that is, its frequency, kinds of bever-

---

[12] C. B. Ferster, The use of the free operant in the analysis of behavior, *Psychol. Bull.*, **50** (1953), 263–274.

[13] Skinner, op. cit., p. 17.

[14] Ibid., p. 31.

ages consumed, or amount of consumption on any given occasion. The behavior must be described in physical terms. Precise observation under the proper controls will enable us to give an accurate description of the nature of the events we are studying.

The *independent* variables refer to the events from which the prediction is made. These refer to antecedent conditions (often called *causes*). We manipulate these events (if we are using the method of experimentation) and observe the changes that occur in our *dependent* variables. These independent variables are the external conditions of which the behavior is a function. Relationships between the two, *independent* and *dependent*, result in the discovery of principles and constitute the data of psychology.

Suppose we wish to study the effect of various degrees of food deprivation on the rate of bar-pressing behavior of our rats. We could deprive rats of food for various amounts of time, say, 12, 24, 48, or 72 hours prior to the start of an experiment. We would then observe the effect of these various degrees of deprivation on our rate of bar pressing. The deprivation becomes our independent variable, for this is the thing we manipulate or vary in order to observe the effects on the dependent variable, response rate.

In our human example we observed the behavior of drinking to be our dependent variable. Those antecedent conditions which led to the drinking would be the independent variables. Since this is not an experiment, these conditions may be many; for example, the past history of contact with alcoholic drinks, degree of deprivation or satiation (how long since the last drink), how much had been drunk in a given prior period of time or whether the subjects happened to be teetotalers. All these variables would enter in the prediction, and thus, in knowing these facts and others, would be in a position to predict the probability of a person's taking a drink at the present moment. The old adage "you can lead a horse to water but you can't make him drink" holds true only if one knows that the horse has been satiated with water. Had the horse been deprived for twenty-four hours and then led to the trough, our prediction that he would drink would doubtless come true.

Some further examples of the relationship between independent and dependent variables may help to make the point clear.

Suppose that a manufacturer wants to find out the relationship between the number of pretzels eaten and amount of beer drunk in a given period of time. He finds that the more pretzels eaten (antecedent condition, independent variable) the more beer is drunk (resulting condition, dependent variable). In this instance the more pretzels eaten the greater the amount of beer consumption. The amount of beer consumed is *dependent* on the number of pretzels eaten.

A psychologist wishes to see if there is any relation between the sex of a monkey (male or female) and his ability to solve a mechanical problem. He finds, curiously enough, that the females do better. Thus the sex of the animal is the independent variable and the performance, the dependent variable. Performance is related, among other things, to the animal's sex.

If predictions go wrong, it is not that the behavior was necessarily capricious or free from control but that there may have been variables operating in the situation about which we either had no knowledge or were not under our control. This problem frequently arises in the study of human behavior because we cannot lock a person in a closet and control all variables until we are ready to experiment with him, nor do we know his entire past history. In any event, behavior is just as lawful even though we do not have the adequate controls that can be arranged in the experimental laboratory.

It is clear, therefore, why the psychologist likes to use laboratory experimentation whenever possible. Here the variables can be known and properly controlled; the result can thus demonstrate the most meaningful relationships. It is equally clear why many psychologists prefer to use lower organisms, such as the rat, pigeon, or monkey as their subjects. All conditions can be known and properly controlled: the hereditary origins, previous learning, appropriate stimuli, and other relevant things. It is through such experimentation that psychology advances and becomes an exact science. Of course humans too can be legitimate subjects for experimentalists through proper instrumentation in the measurement of the response and through careful manipulation of the variables that are relevant.

Laboratory experimentation is not the only method of gathering data available to the psychologist. Clinical observation is likewise employed and of special importance in understanding personality. Standard practices of interviewing are available to the trained psychologist, and methods of testing allow him to observe behavior that is crucial to his analysis. When our clinical observations and experimentation substantiate each other, we are in an excellent position to develop principles that aid us in achieving our eventual goal of understanding behavior.

As we have made brief reference to in the previous chapter, many of the more traditional clinical problems are now being handled through various methods of behavior therapy, or what has become known as *behavior modification*. In this instance a particular response or series of responses that are to be altered are identified. Let us take a common example of a person who has a phobia (intense fear) of snakes. By a method called *desensitization* (see Chapter 18 for a detailed description), the subject is first taught deep relaxation. He is then asked to imagine snakes in various degrees of intensity (looking at them in a cage or imagining they are crawling about him). Progressively, if he can imagine the snake and relax at the same time, the snake phobia is gradually eliminated since complete relaxation is incompatible with intense anxiety.

In many cases the procedure works, and under proper supervision the person is rid of his snake phobia. This method is at some variance with the more traditional clinical procedures of "talking out," as used by psychoanalysis.

A practical example of the combination of the two methods of experimentation and clinical observation is in the study of the effects of drugs on behavior. After a given drug has been developed, it may be administered to laboratory animals. Many psychologists are currently employed in research sponsored by pharmaceutical houses. Their job is to develop a variety of behavioral situations that are similar to those encountered by humans. The behavior of the animal is observed under the given set of conditions, with and without drugs, and proper measures are taken. Perhaps we want to study how a rat goes about escaping from an electric shock. This aversive condition has its corollary in many human acts. We may not always be trying to escape from shocks, but we may wish to evade people, undesirable situations, and the like. Having observed a basic rate or baseline of behavior without the drug, it is then administered (independent variable) and the changes in behavior are carefully noted (dependent variable). These observations are made over a period of time. Perhaps the drug depresses the escape behavior so that the animal "ignores" the shock. This is certainly a change from his previous behavior of running to a safe place whenever he received it. Since all other conditions were the same, we may conclude that the change in the rat's behavior is a function of the administration of the drug. When the drug has been determined safe, it can then be tried out on humans who may be suffering from some condition from which they are trying to escape. The effects may be similar. The results at the human level may take the form of verbal reports from the subject in an interview situation or observations of other people concerning the changes in his behavior after the drug. This has been the kind of technique used in testing many of the tranquilizing drugs developed today in the control of behavior disorders. It would be a dangerous thing to develop new drugs without first considering the effect they may have on laboratory animals. Since we already know that escape behavior is often the same in rats and man, this kind of experimentation is not only possible but useful.

THE PSYCHOLOGICAL EXPERIMENT

Outside the laboratory in human affairs, a particular kind of behavior will be a function of a number of independent variables. For example, a person's academic performance as measured by grades (dependent variable) could be a function of many independent variables: previous behavior learned in other academic situations (high school performance), living conditions including roommates, quality of his teachers, how many courses he is taking, his social life, and so forth. All of these may be operating, in part, either to facilitate or to interfere with his academic performance. Some would be more important than others, and our casual observations might be quite inadequate in giving us the appropriate answers.

Thus, if we are really interested in finding out direct functional relationships, certain matters (potential independent variables) must be *controlled* so that in a well-designed experiment any variables that might affect the dependent variable must either be *the* independent variable (the one we manipulate or change) or a control (also called controlled variables). These may be handled in one of two ways. They may be controlled by *eliminating* them or *equating* them. Thus, in the first instance of eliminating, we may refer back to the earlier example on page 38 in which the experimenter wished to find the relationship between number of hours of food deprivation (independent variable) and the rate of bar pressing to get food (dependent variable). Certain factors that we would wish to control would be the sex of the animals used (only males), the age of our animals (old rats might be slower than young ones), living conditions outside the experiment such as temperature, light, and so forth, weight of the animals (fat rats might work more slowly), genetic strain (some breeds are more active than others). These potential independent variables or controls which might affect our results are eliminated, so that the one independent variable, amount of deprivation, is the only one operating. Of course, in more complicated experiments it is possible to manipulate more than one independent variable, but this is not a book on experimental design and such procedures need not be discussed here.

Sometimes the variables may be controlled by equating them. For example, let us suppose we wanted to observe the relationship between college board scores (SAT) (independent variable) and academic performance as measured by grade point average. In this instance we might divide our group of students into lowest, middle, and highest on their college board scores. To control for sex we should have an equal number of females (or males), say 50 per cent in each of the groups. It would be improper to have all males in the lowest group and all females in the highest. This kind of equating would have to be done in selecting the subjects before we did our study.

Sometimes our language can involve us in inferring faulty relationships. Suppose we take three groups of students which will constitute our independent variable. We give Group I Scotch and soda; Group II, gin and soda; and Group III, bourbon and soda. As a result, we note that, given equal amounts, all students exhibit drunken behavior. Since, from a verbal point of view, the common element is soda, we might fallaciously conclude that the cause of drunkeness was "soda." The terms of the other three drinks are different. The hidden factor was, of course, alcohol contained in all three spirits, and this was the variable that led to the drunken behavior.

There are, of course, many kinds of designs we might follow in experimenting with behavior, both human and infrahuman. Some of these are very complicated and often end up as nothing more than "intellectual games" that psychologists can play with each other or by themselves. Our own inclination is to follow rather simple procedures, as we feel these usually yield the most valid resutls.

*Experimental and Control Groups.*   As an introduction to the practical aspects of experimentation, let us describe two basic procedures that the reader will frequently encounter as he learns how psychologists study various aspects of behavior. First, let us consider the use of experimental and control groups. Actually the procedure is quite simple. We take two groups of organisms, human or otherwise, and match them in as many respects as possible. We then alter one element in the experimental group, which becomes our independent variable, usually some aspect of the environment that we change in one group and not the other. If all other variables are appropriately controlled, we can say that the behavioral changes that occurred in our experimental group were the result of the manipulation of that independent variable.

As an example, let us describe a simple experiment by Skinner[15] to show the effects of punishment on response rate (see also chapter 11 and Figure 9–2). He took two groups of rats, matched in age, genetic background, sex, and so on. Both groups were trained to press a lever on the side of their cage to receive a pellet of food. After both groups had been working at a steady rate, Skinner then withheld the food. This process is known as *extinction* (see Chapter 3). In the control group he simply allowed the animals to continue to press the lever until their rate gradually died out. In the experimental group, however, he introduced the independent variable; that is, each time the rat pressed the bar he was punished for the first ten minutes of their extinction. Then the punishment was terminated. The effect was a temporary suppression of the rate. But after a while, when the punishment had ceased, the rate began to recover, and eventually the experimental group gave out as many responses as had the control group. On the basis of these findings Skinner could legitimately conclude that the effect of introducing the independent variable, punishment, was to cause a temporary suppression in their rate. These same results have subsequently been demonstrated

[15] B. F. Skinner, *The behavior of organisms* (New York: Appleton-Century-Crofts, 1938).

using humans as subjects. However, had Skinner not used a control group—a group that had not received the punishment—he could have no way of knowing for sure that the effect of the punishment was only a temporary suppression in the rate.

*Using the Organism as Its Own Control.* Another very popular technique in experimentation is to use the same organism as its own control. In other words, as organism acts both as the control and the experimental group. This technique has an added advantage in that any differences resulting from uncontrolled aspects of the experimental situation are ruled out, or at least act equally in the experimental and control situation. In explaining how this works, let us return to our example of using drugs as the independent variables. First, as in the previous example, let us condition one or more animals to press a lever for food. We will then find that, rather shortly, our animal will be responding at a very regular and steady rate, which we call *the baseline rate*, and acts in the same way as our control group world. Then, after our control baseline rate of responding has been established, we then introduce the independent variable (the drug) and observe if any changes occur. If we give the animal some stimulating drug such as dexedrine we will find that the rate may be doubled and continue at that rate so long as the drug is in effect. We can conclude that the effect of the drug was to double the response rate because all other conditions were the same. On the other hand, if we were to inject our animal with a tranquilizer such as reserpine, we would find that our rate would drop possibly as much as 50 per cent over the original baseline rate. This technique also is very useful in human experimentation where there are so many complex variables to contend with, such as differences in the past history of subjects. With animals we can use the subjects who are considered "experimentally naïve," that is, those who have never before been used as experimental subjects and whose past experiences have been limited to living in a cage since birth with only food and water. It is possible to use human subjects who are "experimentally naïve" to the extent that they are not knowledgeable about the principles of psychology or the design of the experiment they are going to participate in. However, each human organism has had different experiences that could affect his reactions to the new experimental stimuli. Consequently, using the organism as its own control makes it possible for an experiment to be carefully executed.

INTERVENING VARIABLES

In attempting to give a more precise explanation of what happens between the independent and dependent variables, some psychologists make use of what are called *intervening variables*. These are nothing more than hypothetical concepts or constructs which are not subject to direct observation or analysis.

We can diagram our relationships as follows:

| Independent Variable | Intervening Variable | Dependent Variable |
| --- | --- | --- |
| (Antecedent condition) | (Hypothetical concept) | (Response) |

In our simple example of drinking among college students or our study of the effects of food deprivation in the rat, we could set up an intervening variable as follows:

| Independent Variable | Intervening Variable | Dependent Variable |
| --- | --- | --- |
| Deprivation of Drink or Food | Drive-Hunger or Thirst | Behavior (Drinking or Eating) |

The concept of "drive" (thirst or hunger) is merely an inferred state. We have no direct knowledge of it and lack any way of measuring it. We could, of course, ask a person, "How thirsty are you?" He might reply, "Very," or "not so very." This is very vague and adds little to our understanding.

Consider another example. We observe that a person plays the piano with measured ability. We ask, "Why does he play so well?" The most obvious answer is that he has had a past history of musical training and experience. But some may prefer to add that he also has talent. Here the hypothetical talent is our intervening variable.

| Independent Variable | Intervening Variable | Dependent Variable |
| --- | --- | --- |
| History of Music Lessons | "Talent" | Proficiency in Piano Playing |

In the first example, the intervening variable referred to some hypothetical internal state of "drive." In the second, the intervening is equally hypothetical, referring to some "internal capacity." Some psychologists feel that the use of intervening variables (even in learning theory) add something more to the understanding of the events they are studying. This is particularly true when the independent variables are not all known or under control. They therefore assume these hypothetical entities and give them as part of the explanation. *We do not share their opinion.*

In the final analysis of behavior, is it not simpler to say a man drinks because he has been deprived of water for six hours rather than to say because he is thirsty? Such statements as "thirsty" are perfectly acceptable in common parlance but cannot be allowed in scientific analysis. The idea of "thirst" or "drive" tells us nothing that a knowledge of the organism's history of deprivation does not tell us better. Likewise, to explain a man's ability in terms of some unknown "talent" is less acceptable than his known history of music lessons and practice. If by talent one *means* his ability to play the piano with a given degree of proficiency, that is another matter, and then talent is equated with behavior. In our example this is not the case.

THE PROBLEM OF CAUSATION

There are psychologists (and other scientists alike) who find the use of the terms *cause* and *effect* troublesome. They feel the appeal is to animistic or mystical referents. There is implied "force" between the antecedent event and the present condition. Such conceptions are frequently used in theological explanations (quite properly)—but we are scientists, not theologians.

The fact of the matter is that predictions involve some idea of relationships. Skinner suggests that all we mean by *cause* is a change in the independent variable; and by *effect*, some change in the dependent variable.[16] A functional relationship is established which is perfectly acceptable to science. If we limit our conception of cause and effect to this kind of explanation, which remains at the level of observation, we shall stay out of any mentalistic difficulty. Unfortunately, in the earlier stages of psychology (and even today) psychologists gave as causes of behavior some intervening variable or hypothetical construct which was at best only a partial explanation and in effect no explanation at all.

1. *Hereditary Causes.* "Do you believe that intelligence is caused by heredity or environment?" is a question frequently asked of a psychologist. If one said "heredity," he would be guilty of substituting some biological limitation or potentiality for his independent variable. Biological capacity is *not* the cause of behavior. It may set limits within which behavior operates. (Humans can play tennis, rats cannot.) Such limitations or potentialities are worth considering and must often be taken into account. We do not inherit genes for intelligence per se. We do inherit a physical structure, which in some cases may limit the kinds of behavior that can be acquired. But intelligence, as such, refers to behavior of a certain kind, and this behavior, like most others (excluding reflexes), is learned (see Chapter 8).

Likewise, behavior is not caused by physique. Sheldon, in relating body build to temperament (behavior), never made clear which was the cause and which the effect. Assuming that any relationship does exist, the best that can be said for physique is that it may limit the acquisition of certain kinds of behavior. A small frail boy is not likely to make a

---

[16] Ibid., p. 23.

good football player, whereas a heavy muscular one may. Physical features can operate to the advantage or disadvantage in the playing of certain sports, but they are not the cause.

**2. *Neural Causes.*** The behavior of thinking is an activity which psychologists frequently study. What is the cause? A common explanation is that thinking is caused by some activity in the brain and nervous system. A common causal explanation of behavior is in the complex activity of the nervous system. Needless to say, without a nervous system we would be operating at the level of some lower phylum like the jellyfish. The nervous system is necessary for certain kinds of psychological activity, but it is not the cause of it. We often speak of a "nervous breakdown," or after a hard day at work we may say "our nerves are shot." We do not really mean this. In the earlier history of psychology the term *neurasthenia* referred to a behavior disorder in which the person complained of chronic fatigue, hypersensitivity to external stimuli, insomnia, and so forth. The term actually meant "weak nerves," and the sufferer was prescribed a cure of complete rest so that his nerves could recover. Today we no longer accept such an explanation but realize that the so-called "nervous breakdown" is a disturbance in behavior resulting from a highly complex set of conditions in a person's environment and life history. The actual disturbance is learned.

We are not denying that the nervous system exists or that activity goes on there when one behaves. The problem is that we do not have, first of all, the necessary equipment or instrumentation at hand to study the nervous system so that sufficient knowledge of it would enable us to predict a specific instance of behavior from it.[17] If one is interested in studying, to the degree that he is able, those correlated conditions which occur neurologically when observable behavior takes place, all well and good. This adds to his general knowledge, but is of limited use in the prediction and control of behavior.

We do not mean to imply that it is inappropriate for psychologists to do experiments that involve the nervous system. For example, we can infuse alcohol directly into an animal's brain, or take out part of that brain, or electrically stimulate the brain and then observe the effect these experimental operations have on some behavioral measure. In all these instances, infusion, removal, or stimulation of the brain become the independent variables and the resulting changes in behavior are the dependent variables. Note, however, that the results we observe are attributed directly to the observed experimental operation we performed, that is, what we did to the organism. The results are attributed to the independent variables and not to some internal neural traces or causes. What we did to the organism and the resulting changes in his behavior

17 Ibid., p. 28.

that we observed can be precisely described as empirical, observable events.

**3.** *Mental Causes.* One of the most common fallacies applied by psychologists, and in particular those who have concerned themselves with the field of personality, is attributing the cause of some event to the hypothetical entity of "mind," "psyche," or "inner spirit." These explanations were the vogue prior to the beginning of behavioristic psychology. They have taken many forms, old and new. We recall the "consciousness" of Wundt, the psychic "inner springs of action" of McDougall,[18] or the elaborate personality structures of Freud and Jung. Modern mentalists are not so naïve or so primitive as to use a simple term like "mind." They now try a more subtle approach. The topological theory of personality set forth by Lewin[19] advances more indirect psychic causes such as "inner tensions" in the personality structure, or "forces" or "vectors" which operate from without. These serve in some hypothetical way to direct the person toward some goal or away from some purpose that is aversive.

The Freudian conception of mental apparatus also well illustrates the point. Psychic energy is exchanged among the subsystems. They conflict, but nonetheless serve in one way or another to direct activity. Freud's terminology was indeterminate because he did not clearly define his dependent variables. He referred to vague terms such as "libido," "cathexis," or "psychic" energy. For instance, let us say a man had done wrong and consequently suffered feelings of remorse and guilt. Freud explained this by saying that the doer's ego was punished by the superego, giving him the guilt. The punishment may take the form of some physical act: The man trips and falls. What caused it? Because he was bad, the superego made him do it. On the other hand, if the man was especially good on a particular day, the superego might reward him by allowing an indulgence or by pouring on him feelings of pride. Freud recognized quite clearly that the superego developed from one's conception of what his parents believed to be right and wrong; some prior events therefore influenced the present state. However, Freud fell short in his explanation by stopping at the hypothetical middle point (intervening variable) instead of going back to the environment and environmental history of the individual (independent variable). These intermediate causes and variables add nothing to our understanding of behavior. They only serve to confuse the issue, and if persistently relied upon, only delay the development of the scientific study of personality.

Some psychologists argue that such hypothetical constructs or inner causes are necessary at the present developmental stage of psychology

---

[18] W. McDougall, *Outline of abnormal psychology* (New York: Scribner, 1926).
[19] K. Lewin, *Principles of topological psychology* (New York: McGraw-Hill, 1936).

as a science. Because all the facts are not known, such hypotheses are supposed to serve to connect observations into an organized and systematic explanation. However, Skinner does not share this opinion:

> But it is possible that the most rapid progress toward an understanding of learning may be made by research that is not designed to test theories. . . . An acceptable scientific program is to collect data and relate it to the manipulable variables, selected for study through a common sense exploration of the field.[20]

### THE PROBLEM OF DETERMINISM

When we understand the principle of cause and effect as applied to behavior, we realize that the resulting behavior is determinable and not in any way free or spontaneous. When we are able to realize which variables determine the response and how to manipulate the variables properly, then we are in a position to predict with absolute certainty whether or not a given response will occur. Since this is a difficult analysis to apply to humans, we frequently must be satisfied with a degree of probability. The greater our control of the variables, the more accurate will be our prediction. The problem is not whether behavior is partially free and partially determinable, but that it is matter of knowing and controlling the conditions of which that behavior is a function.

> When all relevant variables have been arranged, an organism will or will not respond. If it does not, it can not. If it can, it will. To ask whether someone *can* turn a handspring is merely to ask whether there are circumstances under which he will do so. A man who *can* avoid flinching at gun fire is a man who will not flinch under certain circumstances . . . when all relevant variables have been taken into account it is not difficult to guarantee the result.[21]

In speaking about the prediction of a man coming to the table before a meal, Skinner suggests:

> Before we can predict that he will come to the table as surely as we predict that he will salivate, we must have information about all relevant variables —not only those which increase the probability of the response but also those which increase the probability of competing responses. Since we ordinarily lack anything like adequate knowledge of all these variables, it is simpler to assume that the behavior is determined by the guest's will—that he will come if he wants to and wills to do so. But the assumption is of

---

[20] B. F. Skinner, Are theories of learning necessary? *Psychol. Rev.*, **57** (1950), 193–216 (p. 215).

[21] B. F. Skinner, *Science and human behavior* (New York: Macmillan, Inc., 1953), p. 122.

neither theoretical nor practical value, for we still have to predict the behavior of the "will." If many variables are important, many variables must be studied.[22]

Like the behaviorist, Freud was also a complete determinist. Some consider his application of the principle of cause and effect to human behavior to be one of his greatest contributions to psychology. Freud placed great emphasis on the previous history of the individual, to explain his present condition. Unfortunately he lacked the kinds of quantitative proofs ordinarily acceptable to science to substantiate his hypothesis. He accounted for behavior as being determined, which previously had been accountable in terms of spontaneity, or free will. Regrettably, he got involved in his inner determiners (personality apparatus). This inner apparatus had a damaging effect on his theory, since it became the main event for study and little was left for the behavior itself.[23]

The behaviorist as determinist has been recently criticized by some scientists and philosophers for maintaining a position contrary to the Heisenberg principle of indeterminism as stated in modern physics, which notes that the movement and measurement of atoms is not predictable, that is, indetermined. We would maintain that we are concerned with behavior on a molar (much larger) scale, and we are not in the least concerned with the movement of atoms, whether or not they are determined. As the physicist can also predict on a molar scale the speed and distance of the movement of a billiard ball if he knows the force of the push as well as other relevant variables influencing that movement, so too can the psychologist predict behavior with great accuracy if he knows all the relevant variables involved. If this were not so, there could be no laws of behavior and psychology, as the science of behavior would return to its superstitious ancestry.

OPERATIONISM

As psychology advances as a science, the need for what is called *operationism*, or an operational approach, is increased. By this is meant "the general point of view toward the data and concepts of natural science (including psychology), which holds that the concepts of a science are defined by the experimental operations involved in investigation and measurement." [24]

Analysis will reveal that if the concept under consideration can be

[22] Ibid., p. 123.
[23] B. F. Skinner, Critique of psychoanalytical concepts and theories, *Scient. Month.*, **79** (1954), 300–305.
[24] W. S. Verplanck, A glossary of some terms used in the objective science of behavior, *Psych. Rev.* (sup. 6, past. 11) **64** (1957), p. 23.

defined in terms of the experimental operations, it will be acceptable. If it involves some mentalistic entity which cannot meet such analysis, it must be rejected.

Events that are described in terms of observations are capable of being operationally defined. The meaning of the concepts, therefore, has reference to events which are publicly observable. If a so-called unobservable event can be legitimately translated into one which can be tested and verified, it will be acceptable to science. The definitions of the events must be brought into definite contact with reality or observable data. Such definitions specify the operations in which the variables and concepts can be measured.

However, we must be on our guard against the notion that one can establish the existence of a thing merely by performing a set of operations. We must not fall into the trap of taking some mentalistic concept, reducing it to some verbal statement, and calling it *operational*. Only those events that have reference to observables are capable of having operational meaning.[25]

Take the term *motivation*, for example. This term means many different things to different people (see Chapter 6): "inner springs of action," "drive," "death instinct," "psychic force," "vector," and so forth. In their original state these terms are not capable of operational analysis and not allowable in an empirical science. However, if by motivation we mean the *operations of depriving or satiating an organism of some substance* such as water or food for a given period of time, the definition of motivation then takes on operational meaning. We have now stated our concept in terms of the observable, measurable, and verifiable operations. Likewise, personality must be defined operationally in order to be useful. To say that it is the "inner self," "spirit," "controlling will," "inner nature of man," or an "organization of psychic structures" is meaningless. On the other hand, if by personality we mean the behavior unique to an individual which has resulted from a history of contacts with observable stimuli, we are on safe ground.

Likewise, our earlier examples of giving drugs, infusing alcohol, cutting and stimulating the brain are all described as experimental operations. We describe as precisely as we can what we are doing, measure our results, and attribute these results to the experimental operations we have performed. Only in this way can psychology, and in particular the study of personality, become a legitimate scientific investigation. If hypothetical constructs, intervening variables, and other "unmeasurables" and unobservable fictions persist, psychology can never progress in its discovery of the basic principles of behavior and might as well regress to its origins, namely philosophical speculation.

---

[25] J. R. Kantor, *Interbehavioral psychology* (Bloomington, Ind.: Principia Press, 1958), p. 135.

## Summary

The proper approach of the psychologist to the study of personality is by the methods of science. An understanding of behavior will be found in proper measurements and in the investigation and control of the conditions which precede the behavior. Stimuli in the environment and environmental history of the organism constitute the independent variables, and the resulting behavior verifies the dependent variables. The functional relationships between these two sets of variables can be referred to as cause-effect relationships. However, we should not be led into interpreting intervening or limiting conditions as the causes. Limiting conditions, neurological functions, and hypothetical mental constructs have commonly and improperly been attributed as the causes of behavior by those who fail to go back to the environmental antecedents. The most proper safeguard against mentalistic thinking in the analysis of personality is to see that one's referents are capable of operational definition. An operational approach to the study of personality assures it the proper place as a scientific study.

# 3 Conditioning and Extinction

## Respondent Behavior

BEHAVIOR FALLS INTO TWO CLASSES: that which is learned or conditioned and that which is unlearned or unconditioned. In humans the amount of unlearned behavior is very limited, being confined to a group of responses, largely physiological in nature, called *reflexes*. These reflexes are naturally elicited if certain appropriate agents called *stimuli* are presented. In their original state, the reflexes are said to have survival value; we cough to dislodge mucus so that breathing is easier, sneeze when an irritant gets into our nostrils, or wink when some foreign matter blows into our eyes. Glandular activity is also included among these reflex functions. Salivation aids digestion, and we perspire in warm weather to reduce body temperature to its proper level. The infant automatically eliminates when his bladder becomes full and sucks to receive nourishment. Although important, these unlearned reflexes constitute a limited portion of our behavioral repertoires. Some reflexes present at birth, such as gasping or sucking, gradually disappear during maturation and are replaced by learned responses.

In lower forms the repertoire of unlearned behavior may constitute a larger portion of the organism's behavior. Instincts, for example, constitute a pattern of reflexes highly stereotyped in nature, demonstrated to be universal in the species. They are set off by a specific set of stimuli in the environment. Among these we may include migration and nest building as well as certain forms of maternal and copulatory behavior.

## CONDITIONING OF RESPONDENT BEHAVIOR

A simple reflex may be elicited by the presentation of a stimulus, called *unconditioned* (US), which means that it has the properties of calling out a response without prior learning. Through the process of stimulus substitution, other stimuli may also serve to elicit this reflexive behavior. These neutral stimuli, which acquire the properties of drawing out a response, become *conditioned stimuli* (CS). The Russian physiologist Ivan P. Pavlov was the first to demonstrate this phenomenon experimentally. By pairing a neutral stimulus with one that naturally caused the response, an *unconditioned reflex* (UR) became a *conditioned reflex* (CR). This change occurred when the conditional stimulus (CS) was *followed by* the unconditioned one (US).

Through repeated pairings of these two stimuli the substitute stimulus was able to elicit the response independently. Pavlov first studied this process while working with the digestion. He found he was able to condition the salivary reflex, which he called the *psychic secretion*. In a typical experimental procedure which involved no small degree of careful control, a normal dog was placed in a harness in the experimental chamber where all external conditions were properly controlled. A small opening, called a fistula, was made in the dog's cheek. When the fistula was healed, a glass tube was placed in the opening which could draw off the saliva when it was secreted. Thus the amount of secretion could be carefully measured. The dog was then exposed to the pair of stimuli, the food as an unconditioned stimulus, and a tone as the conditioned stimulus. After several pairings of these stimuli, in which the tone immediately preceded the food, the tone was tested alone. If the dog salivated, the reflex was said to be conditioned. The stimulus response relationship can be represented by the following paradigm:

Unconditioned stimulus (US)⎯⎯⎯⎯⎯⎯⎯⎯⟶Response (UR and CR)
     (food)                              (salivation)
Conditioned stimulus (CS)⎯⎯⟋
     (tone)

By this procedure the tone acquired the property of eliciting a secretion. Pavlov also studied the effect of the time interval between the two stimuli. He established a *delayed conditioned reflex*, whereby the CS (tone) was presented for a period of time prior to the US (food). This was more difficult to develop. When it occurred, the organism did not respond immediately when the CS was presented but waited until the approximate time interval had passed. One can see here that the animal was able to "tell time" with considerable accuracy.

A variation of the delayed CR technique was the "trace" CR. Instead of having the tone sustained continuously during the period of delay, the tone was presented only at the beginning of the interval, then followed merely by the passage of time until the unconditioned stimulus was presented.[1]

The study of conditioned responses of this sort is not limited to dogs. Experimental literature demonstrates that conditioning has been established in a variety of species, including worms, cockroaches, sheep (Figure 3–1), and man. Hardly a species has been studied in which some conditioned response was not established. In humans many reflexes—including eye-wink, knee jerk, pupillary reflex, and hand flexion (withdrawal to a painful stimulus)—have been conditioned. Frequently the process of conditioning involves groups of responses which are under the control of a single stimulus. An example is the smooth muscle

**Figure 3–1.**   The apparatus used for conditioning sheep at the Cornell University Behavior Farm Laboratory. In this instance the CS is the ticking of the metronome (left) and the US is an electric shock applied to the hind foot. The response to be conditioned is the foot withdrawal to the ticking of the metronome. (From H. S. Liddell, Conditioning and emotions, *Scientific American*, **190**, no. 1 [1954], 48–57, p. 49. Copyright © 1954 by Scientific American, Inc. All rights reserved.)

[1] I. P. Pavlov, *Conditional reflexes*, trans. G. E. Anrep (London: Oxford University Press, 1927).

and glandular responses which are functions of the autonomic nervous system. These responses can include changes in heart rate, blood pressure, adrenal secretion, perspiration, salivation, and stomach and bowel activities.

Many of these changes are involved in what we commonly refer to as "emotional responses." The emotion, of course, is not limited to these reflexive changes alone, but the process of conditioning may be intimately involved. We are all aware of losing our appetites when bad news comes to us, or of wanting to vomit when some repulsive individual enters our environment. Our angers and fears involve reactions of this sort. They have been acquired through the conditioning of these reflexive behaviors. When we say that a person "makes our blood boil," what we really mean is that some physiological changes have taken place which include elevation of heart rate and blood pressure, increased muscular tension, and adrenal secretion. These changes result from the presentation of that person as a stimulus. Possibly the individual, originally a neutral stimulus, has become associated with certain painful stimuli at an earlier time. Now that individual's mere presence automatically puts us into the "emergency state." The process is involved in the child's fear of the doctor or dentist. The man in the white coat (CS) drills his teeth or sticks him with a needle, both painful stimuli. Later, the sight of the doctor or the sound of the drill puts him into a state of terror.

A classical experiment on the conditioning of emotional responses in a child, reported in 1920 by Watson and Raynor,[2] illustrates more precisely how the process works. Their subject was an 11-month-old infant named Albert. Prior to the experiment it had been determined that he had never seen any animals. When tested, Albert showed only approach reactions to rabbits, cats, dogs, and white rats. Watson's procedure was to present a tame white rat to Albert and immediately strike an iron bar with a hammer, causing a loud noise to occur. Just as Albert's hand touched the rat, the iron bar was struck behind his head. Albert jumped and fell forward, burrowing his face in a mattress. On the second trial, Albert jumped violently, fell forward, and began to whimper. After several combined stimulations of this sort, the rat was presented alone, and the infant began to cry, turned sharply to the left, and fell over. In seven pairings of the two stimuli, a strong conditioned response had been set up.

Another interesting observation in the experiment is that the fear generalized (see Chapter 5) to other furry animals. Later tests indicated that Albert showed fear reactions to a rabbit, a dog, a fur coat, and even a Santa Claus mask. In adults, similar fears at the sight of dogs, rats, strangers, or of the dark may have been learned in precisely this manner.

[2] J. B. Watson and R. Raynor, Conditioned emotional reactions, *Jour. Exp. Psychol.*, **3** (1920), 1–14.

What the original unconditioned stimulus was is not always known; it might have been a screaming mother, an attack by an animal, or some other sudden and intense stimulus. One thing is certain, the response was learned sometime in the past, perhaps in infancy or childhood, and not inherited, as some may think.

According to Watson and Raynor:

> Unfortunately, Albert was taken from the hospital. . . . Hence, the opportunity of building up an experimental technique by means of which we could remove the conditioned emotional response was denied us. Our own view, expressed above . . . is that these responses in the home environment are likely to persist indefinitely, unless an accidental method for removing them is hit upon.[3]

An accidental kind of respondent conditioning probably accounts for a peculiar form of sexual behavior we call a *fetish*. In this unusual condition, a person develops a sexual excitement when certain inanimate objects are presented to him such as a shoe, boot, article of clothing, or lock of hair. (Read Alexander Pope's famous poem, *The Rape of the Lock*, and see if you do not think he is describing a fetish.)

Rachman[4] has demonstrated experimentally how such sexual fetishes can be developed. In the experiment the unconditioned stimuli (US) consisted of photographic slides of attractive naked girls. The conditioning stimulus (CS) was a slide of a pair of black knee-length boots. The CS was presented for 15 seconds followed by one of the six slides of nude women. The response to be conditioned was sexual arousal as manifested by an increase in volume of the penis. The volume change was measured by an instrument called a phallo-plethysmograph. The instrument consisted of an extensible rubber tube containing mercury. As the length of the tube increased, the length of the mercury thread was extended giving the measure of the change in penis size. Such a sexual arousal response is clearly of the respondent (reflexive) variety. In all three subjects the response was conditioned between 30 and 65 trials. Generalization took place in that the response was also elicited to both high- and low-heeled boots. It would seem unfair (and perhaps unethical) to leave the men in such a condition and therefore the response was extinguished (see next section) during which the boots were presented in the absence of the nude pictures. The experiment gives clear evidence that such fetishes are conditioned. In all probability most fetishes are developed in this way, except under more casual and accidental contingencies of stimulus pairing.

[3] Ibid, p. 14.
[4] S. Rachman, Sexual fetishism: An experimental analogue, *Psychol. Rec.*, **16** (1966), 293–296.

A variety of more favorable responses can be conditioned as well. The functions of symbols and insignia to inspire patriotism, and music and art to set the occasion for worship are likewise learned. A salesman buys his customer a lunch before presenting his sales pitch, or the lover sends his sweetheart candy and flowers to dispose her emotions toward him.

Counterconditioning is sometimes applied to get rid of certain undesirable responses, previously acquired. The procedure involves the conditioning of incompatible reactions so that one set of responses is replaced by another. A child who fears the doctor or dentist is given a lollipop before the "shot," or comic books to read in the dentist's office.

One of the "cures" for drinking involves this process. A person has previously acquired the drinking habit. He is then presented with his beloved beverage (CS) along with some substance called an *emetic* (US) which has the properties of causing nausea. The vomiting response (UR) is unlearned and is naturally called out by the noxious substance. Through pairing of the nauseating substance with the liquor, eventually the liquor takes on the function of eliciting nausea (CR). Here an avoidance response can be acquired in place of the approach response of drinking the alcoholic beverages.

A great deal of research has been done using this method in the treatment of alcoholism as well as a number of other behavior disorders. It is another form of behavior therapy (see Chapter 18). It is frequently necessary for the individual to undergo many treatment sessions of this sort. Furthermore, "follow-up" treatments are often necessary, for example, six months later. The method is not always successful, as the rates of relapse vary.

Quarti and Renaud[5] report a technique for treating constipation by respondent conditioning. The apparatus they used generates a mild electric current that is reported as "almost pleasurable." The subject is stimulated by two electrodes applied to each side of the lumbar spine and secured to the abdomen by a strap. This constitutes the CS. The subject is instructed to take his usual laxative so as to produce one bowel movement a day. Prior to the time of elimination the subject puts on the apparatus and begins the stimulation. He stops the stimulation as soon as evacuation is complete. Gradually the subject can reduce the quantity of laxative. Once conditioning has occurred (usually after 20 to 30 trials) the electrical stimulus alone can produce defecation. The second step involves what is called *higher order conditioning.* In this situation another stimulus is presented as the CS, in which the subject

[5] C. Quarti and J. Renaud, A new treatment of constipation by conditioning: A preliminary report. In C. M. Franks, ed., *Conditioning techniques in clinical practice and research* (New York: Springer, 1964), pp. 219–227.

goes to the toilet at the same time each day, preferably after breakfast in order to benefit from the morning gastrocolic response. The chosen hour now becomes the CS so that eventually the person can abandon the apparatus (electrical stimulation) entirely.

The responses, both unconditioned and conditioned, which we have discussed so far fall into a class of behavior called *respondent*. They differ both in their nature and acquisition from a larger class of behavior, called *operant*, which we shall study in the next section. At this point all that one needs to remember is that the unlearned as well as the conditioned responses (acquired through the process similar to that experimentally demonstrated by Pavlov) constitute a distinct class of responses. These are represented by the term *respondent*.

### EXTINCTION OF RESPONDENT BEHAVIOR

Pavlov also demonstrated a process opposite to that of conditioning, called *extinction*. Once a conditioned respondent has been formed, it is possible to eliminate the response by presenting the conditioned stimulus *without* the reinforcing unconditioned stimulus. In this way the response becomes weakened and eventually dies out. It should be realized, however, that the conditioned or learned response is the one that becomes extinguished and *not* the unconditioned one. How soon the extinction will occur depends generally on the degree of the previous conditioning. A response conditioned by many pairings of the two stimuli will take many more responses to extinguish than one developed only through a few successive trials. After the response appears to be extinguished when tested a few days later, it will usually reappear, a condition called *spontaneous recovery*. What really happens is that the response in question simply was not completely extinguished during the first session of the experiment.

Extinction, too, has its practical application. If a conditioned fear has been established, the procedure is to present the feared object without the unconditioned stimulus. Jones, using a child named Peter as subject,[6] introduced the feared animal, a rabbit (the fear having previously been acquired), into a room while the child was eating. At first it was presented at a considerable distance from the child. Each day the animal was moved a little closer to the point where the child would tolerate its presence. In one instance the experimental procedure was delayed when the child was accidentally scratched by the animal, thus reinforcing the fear that the experimenters were attempting to extinguish. By repeated contacts with the rabbit in the absence of any fear reinforcer, the response was eventually eliminated. Of course the process of extinction

[6] M. C. Jones, A behavior study of fear: The case of Peter, *Jour. Genet. Psychol.*, **31** (1924), 508–515.

in this instance was not solely responsible for the elimination of the fear. The activity of eating, as well as the presence of a reassuring adult, contributed to the counterconditioning of the responses which were in opposition to the fear.

She also found that the extinction process had its effect on other fears that Peter had toward a variety of furry animals. They were likewise eliminated.

Because the conditioned respondents do not disappear through "disuse" or the mere passage of time, but only through extinction or counterconditioning, people are encouraged to extinguish a fear immediately after it has been acquired, if at all possible. This is why a person who has been involved in an automobile accident is encouraged to resume driving as soon as he is able. Likewise, an aviator is made to fly again immediately after a minor crash. We hear frequently that the man thrown from a horse should immediately resume his mount if he is capable. In all these instances the fear may have been aroused through one-trial conditioning, and thus by resuming the activity, the fear can be quickly extinguished.

A major step in the treatment of behavior disorders involves the extinction process. Take stuttering, for example, where anxiety and embarrassment have been generated by persons who have laughed at or been impatient with the speaker. Frequently the stuttering is merely a by-product of the anxiety, and once the anxiety is extinguished, the stuttering will also die out. Even a nonstutterer may find himself speechless or gasping for words in an intensely emotional situation. People have been known to stammer only when asked their names or addresses following an accident.

The Freudian technique of the *abreaction* involved this process.[7] A person suffering from some phobia (intense fear) was encouraged to recall, either through free association or hypnosis, the events that precipitated the fear. Frequently this was difficult to do because the patient was aware of his fear but could not recall the events which led to its acquisition. However, through continued therapy as the facts came to light, the patient was able to "relive" the event which he supposedly had forgotten. As he recalled the event, trembling and other emotional behavior involved the physiological reactions (which frequently accompany the fear) were exhibited. In continuing to relive this incident, the fear became extinguished by exhibiting the conditioned response in the absence of the conditioning situation. More recently, various drugs, often called *truth serums*, are administered, enabling a person to recall events that have operated in the acquisition of his earlier fears.

[7] J. Breuer and S. Freud, Studies in hysteria. In *Standard edition*, vol. 11 (London: Hogarth 1955; first German ed., 1895).

## Operant Behavior

Thus far we have dealt with respondent behavior, although operant behavior was also involved in our discussion of some emotional reactions. Reflexes and conditioned reflexes fall in the class of respondent behavior and are certainly important to the psychologist. Of greater concern is that class of behavior called *operant*. This includes the largest proportion of our response equipment. Since it involves so much of our behavior, a study of it is not new to the psychologist. In the earlier days it was called *voluntary* or "willed" behavior in contrast to the involuntary or unwilled behavior we have discussed in the preceding section. The term *operant* has been substituted first of all because the organism, in his responding, *operates on the environment* or does something to it. I pick up a book, speak to a friend, or turn off the light. We avoid the use of the terms *voluntary* or *willed* because, in actuality, that is not the case. All our responses are under some form of stimulus control. The problem is to discover what the stimuli are and under what conditions the response develops, rather than to assume that the willed behavior is spontaneous or capable of unpredictable assertion.

The experimental technique used in the early study of operant behavior is credited with having its origin in the animal experiments of Edward Thorndike.[8] Thorndike used a variety of species in his experiments, but one illustration will suffice. (See Figure 3–2.) A cat, deprived of food, was placed in a problem box and left there until he accidentally released a mechanism, such as pressing a pedal. This opened the door of the chamber, allowing the cat to escape and eat a bit of food available outside. He was then put back in the box by the experimenter and the door again locked. The procedure was then repeated until the animal had learned the task by easily opening the door. Thorndike noted the reduction in time taken per trial for the animal to escape from the box. He also observed that despite the general decrease in overall time taken, there was considerable irregularity between trials. Eventually, when the method of escape was swift and regular, the problem was determined as solved. Thorndike designated this process of solution as "trial and error" learning; that is, through repeated trials and accidental successes, the task was eventually acquired.

### THE LAW OF EFFECT

Thorndike explained the trial-and-error process by considering that an association was built up between some aspect of the stimulus situation

[8] F. S. Keller and W. N. Schoenfeld, *Principles of psychology* (New York: Appleton-Century-Crofts, 1950), chapter 3.

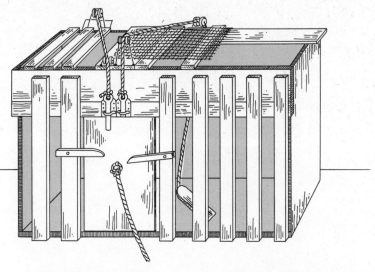

**Figure 3–2.** Thorndike's puzzle box. When the cat pushed the appropriate pedal, the door opened so he could escape and receive food. (From E. L. Thorndike, *Animal Intelligence,* New York: Macmillan Inc., 1911, Fig. 1, p. 30. Reproduced by permission.)

and the specific movement that led to the opening of the door. Furthermore, the pleasurable consequences of getting out and receiving food served to "stamp in" the connection between the stimulus and response.

> Of several responses made to the same situation, those which are accompanied or closely followed by satisfaction to the animal will, other things being equal, be more firmly connected with the situation.[9]

Here then was a basic principle to account for the formation of associations.

Thorndike was not the first to speak of associations in learning or the pleasurable or satisfying consequences of an act as an explanation for its acquisition. Aristotle had written about the laws of association and had accounted for them by means of similarity, contrast, and contiguity. Association had been the principal concern of the British philosophers Hobbes, Locke, Berkeley, Hume, and the Mills in formulating their theories of how ideas stick together. Later, Wundt thought of association as the glue that made the elements of consciousness attract each other and thus form compounds.

Nor was the idea of pleasure or satisfaction as a governing principle a

[9] E. L. Thorndike, *Animal intelligence: Experimental studies* (New York: Macmillan, Inc., 1911), p. 244.

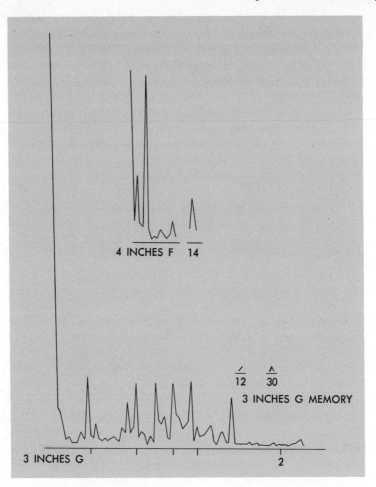

**Figure 3–3.**   Record of the time it takes a cat to escape
from the puzzle box shown in Figure 3–2. The time is
plotted on the vertical axis and number of trials on the
horizontal axis. Notice the irregularity in time to escape
from trial to trial along with the eventual reduction when
the cat had solved the problem. (From E. L. Thorndike,
*Animal Intelligence,* New York: Macmillan Inc., 1911,
Fig. 6, p. 45. Reproduced by permission.)

new innovation by Thorndike. The search for pleasure was mentioned by
Plato as an important motive. The first of the British empiricists, Thomas
Hobbes, mentioned in his *Leviathan* the importance of seeking pleasure
and avoiding pain as the governing principle of social conduct. We are
already familiar with Freud's pleasure principle as the aim of the life
instincts.

   What Thorndike did was to subject the association and pleasure hypothesis to experimental test. His experiments, extending over a half-century, obtained an empirical verification of the laws of learning. Besides the *law of effect*, he also formulated the *law of exercise*.[10] (The law of exercise makes learning a function of the number of repetitions of the stimulus-response connection.) Thorndike later abandoned the law of exercise and made his law of effect the central principle in the learning process.

What constitutes a *satisfying state?* For Thorndike it meant that which the animal did nothing to avoid but something which it did to attain and preserve. In the light of modern behavioristic psychology. Thorndike's principle offers certain difficulties. How do you know the animal is really satisfied? How can such mental states influence the physical response? Here again the old mind-body problem comes into the picture. If one is to allow the law of effect, a more operational interpretation is necessary.

OPERANT CONDITIONING

In the early 1930s, B. F. Skinner[11] described a technique which has become the prototype today for the experimental analysis of behavior. He used an apparatus which consisted of an experimental chamber (often referred to as a *Skinner box*). At one end was a lever or bar which could be pressed down with a certain force by the animal. Below the lever was a food tray into which a pellet of food could be presented to a hungry animal whenever it made the response of pressing the lever downward. Every time the lever was pressed, a food magazine was activated, and the pellet was dropped. At the same time, a record was made on a rotating kymograph drum. The record was cumulative in the sense that each time a response was made, the needle of the cumulative recorder made a step upward, never downward (see Figure 3–4). This is known as a *cumulative response curve* to which each response is added to the next while the kymograph drum moves slowly forward to indicate the passage of time. If no response is made, the pen merely moves in a straight line across the paper. Skinner's early experiment involved (1) a period of adjustment in which the animal was placed in the experimental chamber 2 hours a day for two weeks; (2) a tray-approach training in which the click of the magazine which delivered the food served as a stimulus for the response and movement toward the tray; and (3) the actual training in bar pressing.

After the animal was placed in the cage in step 3, sooner or later he pressed the bar in the process of his activity around the chamber, and the

10 Ibid., p. 243.
11 B. F. Skinner, On the rate of formation of a conditioned reflex, *Jour. Gen. Psychol.*, 7 (1932), 274–285.

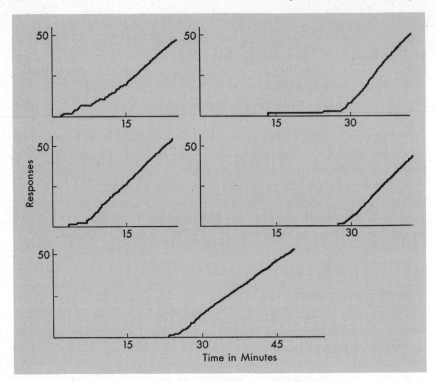

**Figure 3–4.** Typical cumulative response curves obtained from rats on the first day of conditioning to the bar press under a schedule of regular or continuous reinforcement (crf). Each response was reinforced with a pellet of food. Note the regularity of the response rates. Once the bar has been pressed and the response reinforced, conditioning is usually "instantaneous." (From B. F. Skinner, *The Behavior of Organisms*, p. 68. Copyright 1938, D. Appleton-Century Co., Inc. Reproduced by permission of Appleton-Century-Crofts, Inc.)

food pellet was dropped in the cup below. At the same time the response was recorded. A second response soon followed, and before long the animal was responding at a maximal rate of pressing and eating. Skinner observed that his conditioning was different from that used by Pavlov, both in the kind of behavior conditioned and the experimental procedure used. He proposed a distinction between the two types of conditioning, which he called Type S and Type R. Type S referred to the original Pavlovian procedure (also called *classical conditioning*) in which a neutral stimulus serves to elicit some reflexive act after a series of pairings. The reinforcement in Pavlov's experiment was always related to the neutral stimulus. Type R was designated as operant conditioning because the organism did something to secure his reinforcement; in this case, pressing a bar to get food.

Such a sequence can be designated by the paradigm.[12]

$$(s) \longrightarrow R \text{ (bar pressing)} \longrightarrow S \text{ (food)} \longrightarrow R \text{ (eating)}$$

Respondent conditioning involves a response elicited by a given stimulus. In this sense, it is "pulled out." In operant conditioning, we do not know the original stimulus that causes the response. Once it occurs, however, we are in a position to bring the response under control. We "set the occasion" for the response. In operant conditioning a response already present is strengthened. We shall see later how, through a series of carefully differentiated steps, it is possible to shape or bring into existence a response which has not previously been part of the organism's repertoire.

In both respondent and operant behavior we are interested in strengthening a response. In respondent, the response is strengthened by pairing the reinforcer with a given neutral stimulus. In operant conditioning, the reinforcement is contingent on the response (no bar press, no food). Thus, one way of distinguishing between operant and respondent behavior is on the basis of the controlling stimuli which strengthen the response. In respondent behavior the stimulus comes before the response (food before salivation), whereas in operant behavior it follows the response increasing the probability that the response will occur again. In setting up such a contingency, a response followed by reinforcement is strengthened; that is, the probability of future occurrence is increased. Therefore *rate of response*, the number of responses emitted in a given unit of time, is the most common measure used.

*Operant Level.*   Many experimental procedures involving operant conditioning make use of what is called the determination of the *operant level*. This means the rate of responding, such as bar pressing, prior to any training where the food is located or the introduction of reinforcement. For example, if a "naive" rat is placed in the operant conditioning chamber for an hour, the chances are that he may press the bar quite "by accident" several times. However, when the reinforcement of food is introduced, the rate will markedly increase indicating that the food is functioning as a reinforcer to strengthen the behavior.

Many of our responses, of course, have an operant level of zero. They have to be trained or shaped out by a method of successive approximations to the final desired response. (See Chapter 5.) In animal experimentation using operant conditioning techniques during the past twenty years, pigeons have been a popular organism to use. In this case the response to be conditioned is usually pecking a key or disc placed

---

[12] F. S. Keller and W. N. Schoenfeld, *Principles of psychology* (New York: Appleton-Century-Crofts, 1950), p. 48.

on one side of the cage. The point here is that such a response has an operant level of zero. That is, we might have to wait a lifetime before the bird emitted that response. Therefore, successive approximations to the final desired response have to be shaped out. This will be made clear in Chapter 5.

The selection of the response to be studied is somewhat arbitrary.[13] The basic point under consideration is that through using some simple response under controlled conditions, the basic principles of behavior can be experimentally studied. In Skinner's initial experiments the control of the response was gained by manipulating the food reinforcement when the response was made. At this point we see in Figure 3–4 how the rate of bar pressing can be drastically increased by the simple presentation of a food pellet to a deprived animal, once the response has been made. Later we shall see how the response can be controlled by a variety of other stimuli and experimental conditions.

THE PRINCIPLE OF REINFORCEMENT

Up to this point we have used the term *reinforcement* without bothering to explain it. We observed earlier that Thorndike spoke of the "satisfying consequences" of an act. In order to avoid the mentalistic involvements in the terms *satisfaction* or *pleasurable*, we define a reinforcer in operational terms.

> Positive reinforcer refers to those stimuli which strengthen responses when presented (e.g., food strengthens bar-pressing behavior).[14]

Here reinforcement merely consists in presenting some stimulus when a response is made. If, as the result of this operation, we observe that the rate increases, we designate that stimulus as a positive reinforcer.

In Chapter 9 we shall deal in detail with the problem of *negative reinforcement* and the escape response. It may be well for purposes of comparison, however, to consider what this term means. Negative reinforcers are designated as those stimuli "which strengthen (behavior) when they are removed." [15] In this instance a response is strengthened by the removal of some aversive stimulus such as a bright light or an electric shock. The process can be quite simply demonstrated experimentally by presenting an electric shock to the floor of the animal's cage. When a prescribed response is made that indicates a need for strengthening, turn off the shock immediately. If this procedure is continued, eventually the response will be made immediately following

---

13 B. F. Skinner, op. cit.
14 F. S. Keller and W. N. Schoenfeld, op. cit., p. 61.
15 Ibid.

the presentation of the aversive stimulus. In negative reinforcement something is taken away; a stimulus is removed and by its removal the response is strengthened. Contrariwise, in positive reinforcement something is added, and by its addition the response is likewise strengthened. What constitutes a reinforcer can be discovered only by subjecting it to an experimental test. Observe the frequency of a response and present the reinforcer. If there is an increase we may consider the stimulus as having a reinforcing function.

Of course, for practical purposes, a survey of those events which may be reinforcing is helpful. In experiments with animals, food or some form of liquid has been most frequently used as positive reinforcers, and shock, bright light, or loud noise as negative reinforcers. However, an experiment by Olds and Milner illustrates an ingenious technique whereby shock to the brain of the animal can operate as a positive reinforcer.

The reinforcement was presented by applying an electrical stimulation to various areas of a rat's brain. Electrodes were permanently im-

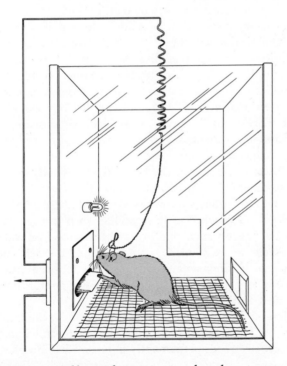

**Figure 3–5.** Self-stimulating circuit; when the rat presses the treadle, it triggers an electric stimulus to its brain and simultaneously records the response. (From J. Olds, Pleasure centers in the brain, *Scientific American*, **195** [1956], 108–113, p. 114. Copyright © 1956 by Scientific American, Inc. All rights reserved.)

planted in various areas and the tests begun. In their initial experiment,[16] Olds and Milner left a rat alone, and once the bar press occurred, a shock was given for about 1 second. Depending on the area of the brain involved, the response rate varied from 200 to 5,000 bar presses per hour. They found the best results occurred when the electrodes were placed in areas of the hypothalamus and certain midbrain nuclei. Some rats stimulated their brains more than 2,000 times per hour over a period of 24 hours. In some of the lower parts of the midline system, the opposite effect occurred. The animal pressed the bar and never went back again. This had a punishing effect. They also found so-called neutral areas in which the animal did nothing to obtain or avoid the stimulation.

Furthermore the reinforcing effects of the shock appeared to be far more rewarding than food. They found that food-deprived rats ran faster to reach an electric stimulator than they did to reach food. In fact the deprived rats often ignored available food in favor of the "self-stimulator." [17] The interpretation of these findings, according to the authors, is that there are certain positive and negative reinforcing areas in the brain, the so-called pleasure or pain centers.

A more recent investigation by Olds[18] showed that the rats do not become satiated with "self-stimulation," as is ordinarily the case with most primary positive reinforcers like food or water. In these latter cases, after an organism has "had his fill" (see Chapter 7), his response rate drops off, and the stimulus of water or food ceases to maintain its reinforcing function. However, Olds found that his rats would continue to stimulate themselves to the point of exhaustion, showing no satiation effects. The animals were observed to respond continuously for 48 hours without any reduction in rate.

A few differences between the behavior of animals under the intercranial self stimulation (ICS) technique and other forms of reinforcement are noted. First, the animals do not seem to satiate. As indicated above, they do not get "filled up," so to speak, as an organism would if continued long enough on such reinforcements as food or water. Furthermore, they seem to extinguish very quickly if the self-stimulation is stopped. Ordinarily, animals and humans alike will continue to respond (sometimes for long periods of time) when the reinforcement is withdrawn (see next section).

The technique has been tried on many species including humans. In this instance society does not ordinarily allow us to drill a hole in a man's head and insert electrodes permanently in his brain. However, in the case

---

[16] J. Olds and P. Milner, Positive reinforcement produced by electrical stimulation of the septal area and other regions of the rat brain, *Jour. Comp. Physiol, Psychol.*, **47** (1954), 419–427.

[17] J. Olds, Pleasure centers in the brain, *Scientific Amer.*, **195** (1956), 108–116.

[18] J. Olds, Satiation effects on self-stimulation of the brain, *Jour. Comp. Physiol. Psychol.*, **51** (1958), 675–678.

of people who are hopelessly psychotic, the technique is sometimes permitted. The patients can go around stimulating themselves and report that it is an excellent antidote for depression. It has been suggested, in all seriousness, that perhaps the time will come when we will all go about with self-stimulating devices attached to our brains to cheer ourselves up when we feel discouraged.

In human affairs, positive and negative reinforcers are equally important in the control of behavior. We work for food, and drink or stay out of the hot sun, and close the door when the noise outside becomes too intense. The number of reinforcers available to human individuals is in all probability far greater than in animals. When we consider the various fields of human endeavor—art, music, literature, sports, religion, business, industry, education, entertainment, government, and the like—we become aware of the vast variety available. We work for money, study for diplomas, worship for salvation, or perform for the approval we get from others. When we speak of an "interest" in a job or hobby, we mean that engaging in this behavior "pays off"; it is reinforcing. There are consequences in the act which are positive. Skinner interprets the strength of a reinforcer as being related to what "one gets out of life." [19] The person who attends the movies frequently, is a baseball fan, or an addict of jazz can be observed to find something reinforcing in these activities. Some measurement of the reinforcing function of a performer to an audience can be made in the number of tickets sold to see him, or the number of people who turn on their TV sets to watch his show.

Individuals differ as to what events reinforce them. Each of us has a unique set of interests or events which prove to be reinforcing to him. Some love music, others sports, and still others just prefer to watch TV for hours on end. The man who enjoys his job is finding more reinforcement in its activity than the man who simply "punches the clock." Of course even the clock puncher is getting a positive reinforcement when he receives his weekly pay check. Those special events that for each of us operate as reinforcers constitute part of our unique personality equipment.

## PRIMARY AND SECONDARY REINFORCERS

Some of the reinforcers that we have discussed so far are primary; others are designated as *conditioned* or *secondary* (see Chapter 6). The property to reinforce of the latter group has been acquired in the life history of one's development. We share them in common to the degree that we have shared similar conditions of training and experience. The functions of conditioned reinforcers have developed through association

[19] B. F. Skinner, *Science and human behavior* (New York: Macmillan, Inc., 1953), p. 74.

with the reinforcer, which we refer to as *primary*. Reinforcers such as food, water, or sexual contact are designated as primary because they have *biological importance*.

The relationship between the conditioned and primary reinforcers can be clearly understood if we take the example of money (conditioned reinforcer) and food (primary reinforcer). Food has obvious biological importance to the man deprived of it. In our society we exchange money for food. Once this association is established, *money* takes on a reinforcing function all its own. Money is a very important secondary reinforcer because of the tremendous variety of responses it reinforces. It is also intimately related to a variety of primary reinforcers. It buys our food, pays our water bills, enables us to keep clothes on our body, pays the rent so that we may have shelter from the noxious elements.

*Why is a reinforcer reinforcing?* A deprived rat will press a bar to receive food or water or even a member of the opposite sex. He will avoid shock, bright light, or loud noise if possible. The reinforcing value of these events has been experimentally demonstrated. At the human level, if we do not eat or drink or avoid extremes of heat or cold, we eventually expire.

Freud suggested the achievement of the "pleasure principle" as the primary goal of the id, the life instincts operated for the preservation of man. Of special importance was the sex instinct, and when various zones of the body (called erogenous) were stimulated (mouth, breasts, genitalia), sexual excitement was aroused. There was a time in the history of man when sexual behavior was even more important for the survival of the species than it is today. Death rates were extremely high because of famine, pestilence, and disease.

Stimuli associated with the primary reinforcers also take on reinforcing functions. Those associated with the sexual zones can take on the function of sexual arousal in their own right. Pornographic pictures or even legitimate art objects operate here. Furthermore, other tactual stimuli may generate reinforcement even though they may not be primarily associated with the sexual area. Other forms of sensory stimulation can be reinforcing: hearing, smelling, and tasting. The apparent importance of these forms of reinforcement can be experimentally demonstrated when humans are deprived of them (see Chapter 7).

The point we are making should be clear by now; a biological explanation is about as far as we can go in our final analysis of finding out why a reinforcer is reinforcing. Even so, this explanation may be of little help. It need not inhibit our analysis of behavior, however. The fact is that once a reinforcing function is demonstrated, these stimuli can then be used to reinforce an individual. This is sufficient information to put us in a position when the prediction and control of his acts are possible. One of the first problems of control is to find out precisely what events are reinforcing to a person and then to present them or without them, as we desire, in order to manipulate that person's behavior. We have the added advantage of knowing that many people share the same reinforcers, primary and secondary. Most of us respond favorably to attention, approval, and affection. The expression "money talks" is more true than many of us would like to believe. Few people, other things being equal, will turn down a job that pays more or will refuse an increase in salary when it is offered.

SOME APPLICATIONS OF OPERANT CONDITIONING TO HUMANS

Throughout this book you will read of many experimental examples of the application of operant conditioning. Often they are applied to training or "shaping" new behaviors (Chapter 5). Likewise, these techniques are receiving widespread uses in psychotherapy in a particular form called *behavior therapy* (Chapter 18). In this instance reinforcement principles are applied to correct or modify undesirable behavior. At this point, we would like to introduce a few examples from various areas of psychology where conditioning with positive reinforcement has been applied to demonstrate its usefulness.

A significant study reported by Fuller[20] illustrates what can be done in order to achieve learning even when the subject is a vegetative idiot. The subject in his experiment was eighteen years old. Prior to conditioning, his behavior had been described as follows:

He lay on his back and could not roll over; he could, however, open his mouth, blink, and move his arms, head, and shoulders to a slight extent. He never moved his trunk or legs. The attendant reported he never made any sounds; but in the course of the experiment, vocalizations were heard. He had some teeth but did not chew. He had to be fed liquids and semi-solids all his life. While being fed, he sometimes choked and coughed vigorously.[21]

The response selected to condition was the movement of the right arm to a vertical or nearly vertical position. The right arm was selected because it had been observed that, prior to experimentation, he moved it about a third more frequently than the left. Warm milk solution served as the reinforcement, administered by mouth through a syringe.

Before the experiment began, the subject was deprived of food for 15 hours. When he made even the slightest movement of his arm, a small amount of the solution was injected into his mouth. This process was continued until he lifted his arm higher toward the vertical level desired.

[20] P. R. Fuller, Operant conditioning in a vegetative human organism, *Amer. Jour. Psychol.*, **62** (1949), 587–590.
[21] Ibid.

By the end of the fourth experimental session, the subject was making definite and discrete movements at the rate of three per minute. The rate at the end of the conditioning sessions was three times greater than that during the first session. The response was well differentiated. A period of extinction followed, during which the response rate was reduced to zero after 70 minutes.

The subject's physicians had not thought it possible for him to learn anything, for according to them, he had not done so for the first eighteen years of his life. The experimenter was of the opinion that, if time had been permitted, other responses could have been conditioned and discriminations learned.

Here we observe in a human, whose personality is as close to zero as one will find, the process of learning taking place through the proper manipulation of reinforcement. When the right conditions are present, behavior can be learned that was not thought possible. On the basis of this kind of evidence, one should be convinced that much can be done with what have been referred to as hopeless mental defects. Even though we do not imply that they can be normal, it would seem that through proper training and use of these techniques, that many persons previously thought helpless could be trained to be useful citizens.

More recently, Rice and McDaniel[22] have shed further light on the problems involved in conditioning vegetative idiots. They have pointed out the problems in finding an appropriate reinforcer in a conditioning situation such as that described by Fuller. In one of their patients chocolate ice cream was an effective reinforcer for strengthening the arm-raising response. On one occasion they ran out of chocolate ice cream and substituted lime sherbet, whereupon the subject vomited it all back. It turned out that the subject had come down with a virus infection, which they presumed had caused the rejection. However, upon the patient's recovery, they again tried the sherbet, but the previously stable response rate of 30 responses per 45 minutes fell to 3. Chocolate ice cream was again reintroduced at the next session, and soon the rate returned to the pre-sherbet level. Another subject responded well to a recorded piece of music, a particular Tommy Dorsey record. When other records were substituted they failed to act as reinforcers. Precisely why certain reinforcers operate as they do and others fail with these severely retarded mental defects remains to be seen.

Azrin and Lindsley[23] have applied positive reinforcement to the conditioning of cooperative responses among young children. Twenty children, ages seven to twelve, were matched into ten teams. Two

[22] H. K. Rice and M. W. McDaniel, Operant behavior in vegetative patients, *Psychol. Rec.*, **16** (1966), 279–281.

[23] N. H. Azrin and O. R. Lindsley, The reinforcement of cooperation between children, *Jour. Abn. Soc. Psychol.*, **52** (1956), 100–102.

children in each team were seated on opposite sides of a table, and each child was presented with three holes and a stylus in front of him (Figure 3–6). If the children happened to place their styli in holes opposite each other (cooperative response), a red light flashed on, and a single jelly bean was delivered, available to either child. Other arrangements of the styli (uncooperative responses) yielded no reinforcement. All teams learned the cooperative response within 10 minutes of experimentation in the absence of specific instructions. Almost immediately eight teams divided the candy in some manner. In the other two teams, one child took all the candy as it was delivered until the other child refused to cooperate. When verbal agreement had been reached, these members also divided the candy.

The results of the experiment indicate that cooperative responses can be developed and eliminated, using only a single reinforcement for two people in a manner similar to that for individual conditioning. The reinforcing stimulus need not be delivered to each member of the team for the cooperative response to take place. Rate of cooperation also increased with the frequency of reinforcements and gradually decreased with extinction. During the reinforcement period the cooperative responses were maintained at a stable rate but occurred in periodic bursts during extinction (similar to that found in the rat when extinction is followed by regular reinforcement). When conditioning was again attempted after extinction, there was an almost immediate restoration of the previous rate of cooperative responding.

A final example of conditioning that could be called an example of *behavior therapy* will complete our illustrations. Many examples of

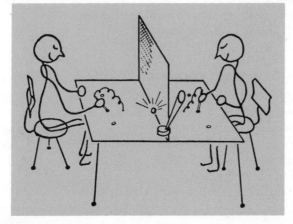

**Figure 3–6.** Apparatus used for the reinforcement of cooperation between children. (From N. H. Azrin and O. R. Lindzey, The reinforcement of cooperation between children, *Journal of Abnormal and Social Psychology*, **52** [1956], 100–102, p. 101.)

operant conditioning with human subjects involve a very specific response, such as a bar press, plunger pull, press of a telegraph key, etc. This is done intentionally for purposes of proper experimental control and discrete analysis of the response rate. However, Mertens and Fuller[24] have suggested that perhaps a larger sample of behavior might also be conditioned. In their study they selected the shaving response with an electric shaver, using a very regressed psychotic patient as subject (see Chapter 16, "Psychotic Behavior"). As a criterion for a "good shave" they used a rating scale in which time to shave is considered as well as other characteristics of what might constitute a good clean shave, including shaving in the right places (for example, not eyebrows). To ensure proper reinforcement, each subject was presented with a tray of possible stimuli from which to choose (gum, fruit, cigarettes, money, pastry, candy, etc.). Sometimes it was necessary to shape out the proper responses by reinforcing approximations to correct shaving. Some subjects had to be coaxed and instructed, but none was forced. Results showed that the technique was generally successful. Indices of improvement included the following factors: (1) reluctance to come to the shaving room was reduced; (2) in 51 days of training, almost all subjects accepted shaving as part of their general hospital routine; (3) increased shaving skills were evidenced by decreases in bizarre shaving responses such as shaving the head or eyebrows. The experiment is all the more significant when one considers that these were severely disturbed men who, prior to the experimental procedure, had shown great resistance to shaving.

The literature on behavior therapy and behavior modification abounds with examples of the use of positive reinforcement (either primary or secondary) to establish more desirable behavior patterns. Many of these will be cited throughout this book.

### EXTINCTION OF OPERANT BEHAVIOR

Like respondent behavior, the withholding of the reinforcement has a weakening effect on the response. After a response is strengthened through successive presentation of the reinforcing stimulus, it may be withheld. For a while the organism continues to respond, but eventually the rate becomes slower and slower, and the loss of strength is measured by the falling off of the rate.

If we consider that a line with a slash in it (————/————) means *is not followed by*, then the paradigm for extinction would read:

$$R \text{————}/\text{————} S^R$$
$$\text{(bar press)} \qquad \text{(food)}$$

---

[24] G. C. Mertens and G. B. Fuller, Conditioning of molar behavior in "regressed" psychotics, *Jour. Clin. Psychol.*, **19** (1963), 333–337.

A response (bar press) is made, but it is not followed by the stimulus (food), consequently the process of extinction is taking place.

Typical extinction curves following conditioning with regular reinforcement are illustrated by Figure 3–7. Note that the extinction rate is not regular but is typified by bursts and depressions of responses. These may be interpreted as emotional in character. Although the curves represent the extinction of a rat's bar-pressing behavior, it has its human corollary. When we have been accustomed to receiving regular reinforcement for some act and then fail to get it, do we not often respond in an angry or aggressive manner? We are used to having our telephone calls answered. When the party on the other end fails to answer, we hang up and try later. If the call is especially urgent, we may slam down the receiver and utter a variety of verbal exclamations of anger and disgust. Suppose a drawer, which usually opens, sticks because of damp weather. We try again and again. If it still resists, we may kick it or bang it, although these efforts may in no way facilitate the drawer's responding. Children's behavior also illustrates the character of this kind of extinction. The child who receives candy regularly asks for it again and again. When it is withheld or refused after several tries, he may throw a temper tantrum.

*Resistance to extinction* has frequently been used as a measure of response strength. It has been found in animals that, up to a point, a response which has had a longer history of reinforcement shows greater resistance to extinction as measured by the number of responses emitted in the extinction process.[25] This is what we easily observe in our everyday affairs as well. We seek out the people whom we like the best because they reinforce us more often. The fellow who usually lends us money is the one we ask; even though at some time he begins to refuse, the more we succeed, the more likely we shall continue to try.

Response strength has also been shown to be positively related to the amount of reinforcement given for each response. Guttman[26] used various amounts of sucrose solution (sweet) in water as the reinforcements for bar pressing with rats as subjects. Four groups were conditioned with 4, 8, 16, and 32 per cent sucrose solution. Each group was observed under conditioning and extinction situations. The time required to condition rats to execute 300 responses decreased as the concentration increased. Furthermore, in extinction, he found that the resistance, measured in terms of number of responses in the initial 15 minutes of extinction, increased with the increased degree of concentration used.

Ordinarily we work better when the pay is good than when it is a

[25] S. B. Williams, Resistance to extinction as a function of the number of reinforcement, *Jour. Exp. Psychol.*, **23** (1938), 506, 522.

[26] N. Guttman, Operant conditioning, extinction and periodic reinforcement in relation to concentration of sucrose used as a reinforcing agent, *Jour. Exp. Psychol.*, **46** (1953), 213, 234.

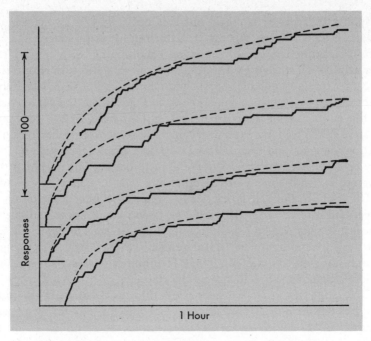

**Figure 3–7.** Cumulative response curves of extinction
following regular or continuous reinforcement. Typical
response curves for four different rats, following
conditioning with regular reinforcement. Each animal had
received about 100 reinforcements during the original
conditioning procedure. Note the irregularity of responding,
characterized by "bursts" and "depressions" in the
response rate. (From B. F. Skinner, On the rate of
extinction of a conditioned reflex, *Journal of General
Psychology,* **8** [1933], 114–129, Fig. 1, p. 115.)

mere pittance. We prefer restaurants which serve man-sized meals rather
than little tea-room tidbits. A cordial "hello" is more reinforcing than a
subdued grunt of recognition.

*Extinction in Human Affairs.* Personality development involves the
continuous processes of conditioning and extinction. People whom we
have liked in the past at some time may cease to reinforce us (maybe
their money goes to their heads) and are sought out less frequently.
Those who are seldom at home are less likely to be called upon. We are
used to receiving a reply when we speak to people. Those who choose
to ignore our salutation are likewise ignored. You may recall the requests
of people for a match, a pencil, or the use of your phone. Actually the
granting of these simple requests is usually reinforced by the words
"thank you" or some other act of recognition. However, you become
reluctant to grant these requests to individuals who accept without

delivering any reinforcement in return. When they persist, you eventually may refuse. They are described as rude or lacking good manners.

Like respondent extinction, operant extinction can also be used to eliminate unfortunate behavior or bad habits if the contingencies can be arranged appropriately. The complaining housewife can be made to rid herself of her complaints if one can tolerate and ignore them. By listening or giving in to her tirades, the husband is only reinforcing to greater strength the behavior which he finds annoying. The spoiled behavior of the indulged child is intensified only when the parents submit to his demands because they prefer "peace at any price." Cutting sarcasm is reinforced when laughed at. In order to eliminate or reduce the frequency of these responses, we must discover what the reinforcements are and then withhold them. Temper tantrums in the child eventually die out if ignored for a long enough time. Sometimes eliminating an undesirable act may involve the cooperation of a number of individuals who have operated to reinforce it. The fraternity house "show off" can be extinguished only by the cooperative attempts of the other members involved.

The consequences of extinction are well known to the clinical psychologist. The discouraged student is exhibiting behavior which is in the process of being extinguished. Where studying was earlier reinforced by good grades or perhaps by the material itself, the student now finds his courses, teachers, or textbooks dull. He finds it increasingly more difficult to remain at his tasks. Eventually he may quit school or flunk out.

The fact that a student does well in the courses he "likes" or has an interest in or does poorly in those he "dislikes" is evidence for reinforcement or absence of it. The more games a team loses, the more difficult they may find it to win, for losing a game has no reinforcement value. To counteract this, we manipulate all kinds of contingencies in order to encourage the play, by presenting pep talks, rallies, or getting a good turnout at the game. Apathy and disinterest in another's activity are effective means of extinguishing his responses.

Depression involves weakening of behavior to a degree greater than discouragement. Depressed people found inside and outside mental hospitals have little behavior being reinforced. It may be that the depression is partly caused by the loss of a member of his family who in the past had been one of the main furnishers of reinforcement. The depressed person is in such an advanced stage of extinction that little of his behavior is left. Many of the earlier reinforcing contingencies have been withdrawn. The depression may be related to the loss of a job which operated earlier as a reinforcer both monetary and otherwise. This person tries with continued failure to find another job (these attempts and failures constitute the early part of extinction). Eventually he may enter a severe depression if his failure continues long enough.

The state of complete extinction is sometimes described as "abulia," or lack of will. This suggests that all his voluntary behavior is gone. Of course the problem of "will" or lack of it is not involved in an operational analysis. What has happened is simply that the vast majority of reinforcers which operated previously have been withdrawn and all behavior has reached a stage of almost absolute extinction, so that little or no operant responses are left.

The job of the therapist in treating those discouraged and depressed people who have lost all interest in life is to supply some form of reinforcement to whatever behavior is left in order to get the response rate going again (see Chapter 17).

Sometimes this can be done through some form of verbal therapy whereby the person's verbal utterances are strongly rewarded (encouraged) by the therapist. In the beginning, the therapist, may reinforce anything he says. Therapy may involve the change in living conditions, presenting events which operate to reinforce in favor of those which have lost any reinforcing function. By "encouragement" we mean just that. Encouragement refers to the application of reinforcement, under conditions where a person is in a state of extinction, so that the weakened behavior can be returned to a level where it can be maintained. Occupational therapy, likewise, allows the person to engage in relatively simple tasks which have a reinforcing function in their accomplishment.

*The Use of Extinction Procedures in Behavior Therapy.*   Williams[27] reports the case of a 21-month-old boy who had been seriously ill during the first 18 months of his life, resulting in a physical weakness that necessitated a great deal of special care. At the time the experiment began his health was much improved, but he was still demanding excessive attention and care and enforced his wishes by tyrantlike tantrum behavior, especially at night. Ordinarily, when his parents put him to bed he would throw tantrums if they left the room before he was asleep. His parents felt that he enjoyed his control over them and would put off going to sleep as long as he could. Following medical reassurances that his health was good, it was decided to eliminate the tantrum behavior by withholding their reinforcement of attention and remaining with him. The child was put to bed in a leisurely and relaxed fashion. The parent left the room and closed the door, whereupon the child would begin to scream and rage. The first night this behavior lasted 45 minutes (see Figure 3–8). On the second night he did not cry at all. This was attributed to his extreme fatigue following the first occasion. By the tenth occasion (afternoon naps were also included) the tantrums were eliminated, and the child smiled when the parents left the room.

About a week later the child again exhibited the tantrum behavior when put to bed by his aunt in his parents' absence (possible sponta-

[27] C. D. Williams, The elimination of tantrum behavior by extinction procedures, *Jour. Abn. Soc. Psychol.*, **59** (1959), 260.

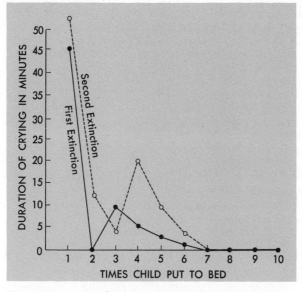

**Figure 3–8.** Length of crying in two extinction series as a function of successive occasions of being put to bed. (From C. D. Williams, The elimination of tantrum behavior by extinction procedures, *Journal of Abnormal and Social Psychology,* **59** [1959], 260.)

neous recovery). She reinforced the tantrum behavior by remaining in the room until he was asleep. It then became necessary to extinguish the behavior all over again. The results of the second period of extinction are shown in Figure 3–8. The second extinction period reached zero (tantrums) by the ninth session. According to the author, no further tantrum behavior has been reported in the succeeding two years.

*Extinction Procedures in a Psychiatric Hospital.* Ayllon and Michael[28] report the case of Lucile whose frequent visits to the nurses' office interrupted and interfered with their work. Although she had been told to stop, this annoying behavior went on for two years. Sometimes she was led by the hand out of the office. At other times she was pushed bodily back into the psychiatric ward. These procedures had had no effect in reducing the undesirable behavior. Since she had been considered mentally deficient, the nurses had resigned themselves to her behavior because she was considered "too dumb" to understand that she was not welcome. Consequently, the nurse in charge was instructed not to give Lucile any kind of reinforcement for entering the offices. Each response

[28] T. Ayllon and J. Michael, The psychiatric nurse as a behavioral engineer, *J. Exp. Analy. Behav.,* **2** (1959), 323–334.

was recorded. Prior to the study, the pretreatment rate of entering had been on the average of 16 times a day. But the end of the seventh week of extinction, the average rate had been reduced to two (see Figure 3–9).

A second case reported by Ayllon and Michael[29] concerned Helen, whose delusional talk had become so annoying that the other patients had resorted to beating her in an effort to keep her quiet. Her delusional conversations centered around her false belief that she had an illegitimate child and the man she claimed was responsible was pursuing her. It was the nurses' impression that she had "nothing else to talk about." Prior to the application of extinction, 30-minute intervals were observed to determine the relative frequencies of the delusional and rational (sensible) content of her conversations. It was felt that the nurses' attention to her had been maintaining this psychotic kind of speech. The nurses were instructed not to pay any attention to her psychotic talk but to reinforce sensible conversation. If another patient started to fight with the patient, the nurses were instructed to stop the fight but not to make an issue of it. By the ninth week the frequency of Helen's delusional talk was drastically reduced. Then, the rate drastically increased because, it is

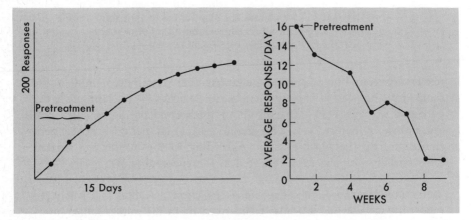

**Figure 3–9.** Extinction of response of "entering the nurses' office." Graph at left is a cumulative record of the extinction process of the psychotic patient. Graph at right shows the average number of "office entering" responses per day as plotted in terms of weeks. Note the gradual decline so that by the end of the seventh week, the number of responses per day was reduced to two. (From T. Ayllon, and J. Michael, The psychiatric nurse as a behavioral engineer, *Journal of the Experimental Analysis of Behavior*, 2 [1959] 323–334, Fig. 1, p. 327. Copyright 1959 by the Society for the Experimental Analysis of Behavior, Inc. Reproduced by permission of the authors and the publisher.)

[29] Ibid.

supposed, a social worker entered the situation. The patient later told the nurses, "Well, you're not listening to me. I'll have to go and see Miss —————— [the social worker] again, 'cause she told me that if she could listen to my past she could help me." [30]

*Extinction of "Soiling."*   Conger[31] used simple extinction techniques to eliminate encopresis ("soiling") in a nine-year-old boy, a problem which had been of four years' duration and had not responded to medical treatment. The technique involved a rearrangement of the social consequences when the boy soiled. Extinction consisted of the withdrawal of attention via verbal behavior and physical contact. After twelve weeks not a single case of soiling occurred.

*Use of Extinction to Eliminiate a Skin Rash.*   A final example will complete our discussion of the use of extinction in behavior therapy. Walton[32] describes the case of a woman who had developed a serious skin condition because of compulsive scratching. The subject had apparently received a good bit of positive reinforcement in the form of attention from her parents and fiancé. In order to accomplish extinction the family was instructed never to discuss her skin condition, and her fiancé was instructed to stop rubbing ointment on the afflicted area (the back of her neck). Following these conditions the scratching stopped within two months, and the rash completely disappeared a month later.

### EXTINCTION AND FORGETTING

The processes of extinction and forgetting must be clearly distinguished. Often they appear to be the same if one observes only the results and not the antecedent conditions. Extinction refers to the weakening of behavior through withholding the reinforcement. Forgetting *appears* to be the weakening of a response which results from the lapse of time between the learning and some later test of it. It should be realized that in both extinction and forgetting, behavior does *not* simply die out because of disuse. The idea that forgetting is merely a passive decay of what has previously been learned is quite incorrect, as we shall see. Actually, the processes operating in forgetting are similar to those mentioned earlier in our reference to *counterconditioning*, in which the new response conditioned is incompatible with one already existing in the behavioral repertoire of the individual.

[30] Ibid., p. 128.

[31] J. C. Conger, The treatment of encopresis by the management of social consequences, *Behav. Ther.*, 1 (1970), 386–390.

[32] D. Walton, The application of learning theory to the treatment of a case of neurodermititis. In H. J. Eysenck, ed., *Behavior therapy and the neuroses* (London: Pergamon Press, 1960), pp. 272–277.

Evidence available supports the notion that forgetting is due to activities which intervene between the conditioning of some response and a later test of it. The important fact in what appears to be forgetting is that a new response interferes with the emission of one learned earlier. The new conditioning reacts on the earlier conditioning. This interference is called *retroactive inhibition.* An earlier experiment performed by Jenkins and Dallenbach[33] illustrates the point fairly well. Their subjects were two college students who served over a period of two months in order to provide the necessary data. The materials they were asked to learn were lists of nonsense syllables. The syllables were presented one at a time for a brief period, and each subject spoke the syllables as he saw it. The lists were considered to have been learned when the subject could reproduce them in the correct order. Some of the lists were learned in the morning; other lists in the evening, just before retiring. Tests for recall were made 1, 2, 4, and 8 hours after learning. In some cases the test was made at the period of "forgetting" that was filled with sleep. In others it came when the subjects were occupied with everyday activities. The results appear in Figure 3–10. It is quite clear that the recall during sleep was far superior to that after a comparable period of waking

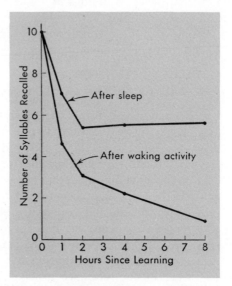

**Figure 3–10.** Forgetting curves for nonsense syllables after sleep and waking. (Adapted from J. G. Jenkins and K. M. Dallenbach, Odivescence during sleep and waking, *American Journal of Psychology* **35** [1942], 605–612, Fig. 1, p. 610.)

[33] J. G. Jenkins and K. M. Dallenbach, Oblivescence during sleep and waking, *Amer. Jour. Psychol.*, **35** (1924), 605–612.

activity. The experiment illustrates that the intervening activity had a lot to do with how much the person was able to remember.

We have said earlier that forgetting does not occur through disuse. One may ask: "But some forgetting did occur during sleep, although much less than during waking." The answer in all probability is that even during sleep we do not go into a psychological vacuum. Interfering activity is still going on in the form of dreaming and movements. Furthermore the students were awakened in order to test recall. Here, more activity interferes. It would be difficult to contrive a situation where some kind of active behavior would not interfere with one's remembering.

If we define "forgetting" simply as the disappearance of an act through disuse, in all probability no such thing occurs. If in the interval of time, other things are learned and maintained which conflict with a test of the original response, a process of what we commonly refer to as "forgetting" is the result.

All the studies illustrate the lawfulness of the learning process. Whether one is using rats, pigeons, children, or mature adults, many characteristics of the behavior are the same. Our discussion has emphasized the importance of reinforcement in developing and maintaining behavior, as well as the opposite principle of withholding the reinforcement in the process of extinction. In this latter way behavior can be weakened or eliminated. These two principles are perhaps the most basic to our understanding of how personality is acquired and changed. We have seen how, through the manipulation of reinforcement by presenting or withholding it, a great degree of control can be exercised over behavior.

# 4 Schedules of Reinforcement

IN OUR DISCUSSIONS OF CONDITIONING and extinction, we referred primarily to those procedures in which a reinforcement was given every time the organism responded. This procedure is called *conditioning* with *regular* or *continuous reinforcement*. If we stop to think for a moment, we realize that a vast amount of our behavior is maintained not through regular reinforcement but by means of some *intermittent* or *partial reinforcement*. Sometimes the reinforcement comes at given intervals in time, regular or irregular, or it may depend on how many responses the organism makes. Requests are not always granted; phone calls are not always answered; automobiles do not always start the first time we turn on the ignition; and we do not always win at sports or cards. Every effort in our work does not meet with the approval of our superiors, and each entertainment is not always worth our time. Lectures in class are sometimes dull, and dining hall food is occasionally tasteless.

Nevertheless, by skillful manipulations of the *schedules* used in applying reinforcement, it is possible to "get a good deal more out of a person" than one puts in by way of reinforcements. When reinforcement is applied on some basis other than a continuous one, it is referred to as an *intermittent* or *partial schedule*. Intermittent reinforcement has been carefully studied by psychologists, using both humans and animals as subjects under experimental conditions, so at this point some rather well-established principles are available, both with regard to the characteristics of the behavior maintained by the schedule and the extinction following it. We shall examine some of the general characteristics of a variety of the most common schedules and then see how they apply to the operation and development of our individual behavior.

## Fixed-Interval Schedules

This kind of schedule has been one of the most widely studied. The general characteristics of behavior emitted under it were carefully examined in one of Skinner's earlier works.[1] More recently, Ferster and Skinner[2] in their monumental volume, *Schedules of Reinforcement*, devote a little under 200 pages to the study of this schedule alone.

In a *fixed-interval* schedule (abbreviated FI) the reinforcement is presented for the first response that occurs after a prescribed interval of time. For example, if we were conditioning a rat under a FI schedule of 1 minute, we would reward him for the first response he made *after* 1 minute had passed, then reset our timer and reinforce for the first responses after the next minute, and so on. Intervals can vary from a few seconds to hours, days, weeks, or months, depending on the conditions and subjects used. An organism can respond often or infrequently during the interval and still get the maximum payoff if he responds only immediately after the interval has passed.

By using animals as subjects, a number of principles have been developed which characterize this schedule. In the beginning of conditioning on an FI scedule, the organism exhibits a series of small extinction curves between reinforcements, beginning with rapid response immediately after the reinforcement and followed by a slowdown prior to the next reinforcement. As a greater resistance to extinction develops, the rate becomes higher and more regular until a third stage is reached in which the organism begins to develop a *time discrimination*. This is based on the fact that a response which closely follows the one reinforced is never paid off. As the discrimination is built up, the behavior is characterized by a period of little or no response after reinforcement, followed by an acceleration of rate until the time for the next reinforcement is reached.[3] This can be illustrated by reference to Figure 4–1. Of course, if the interval between reinforcements happens to be a very long one, it may not be possible for such a discrimination to develop. In this

---

[1] B. F. Skinner, *The behavior of organisms* (New York: Appleton-Century, 1938).

[2] C. B. Ferster and B. F. Skinner, *Schedules of reinforcement* (New York: Appleton-Century-Crofts, 1957).

[3] B. F. Skinner, op. cit., chapter 5.

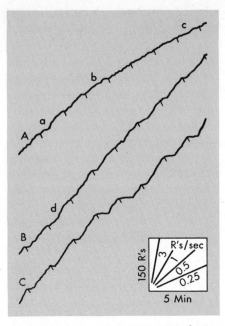

**Figure 4–1.** Cumulative response curves showing the
development of a temporal discrimination under a fixed-
interval schedule of reinforcement (FI 2). These are taken
from the second, fourth, and sixth sessions of conditioning.
(From C. B. Ferster and B. F. Skinner, *Schedules of
Reinforcement*, Fig. 128, p. 144. Copyright © 1957,
Appleton-Century-Crofts, Inc. Reproduced by permission.)

type of responding, it appears that the organism is being made to "tell
time." To facilitate this time-telling behavior, Skinner[4] has added the use
of an external stimulus called a *clock* (see Figure 4–2). In his experiments,
when pigeons pecked a key on an FI schedule, a small spot of light was
shown in front of the animal. As the spot became larger, the time for the
next reinforcement approached. At the point when the spot had reached
its maximum size, the reinforcement was presented. Through this device
the gradients of responding were made extremely sharp. Eventually the
pigeon's behavior could be controlled to the degree that no pecking
occurred in the first 7 or 8 minutes of a 10-minute fixed-interval period.
The clocks could be made to run fast or slow or even backwards. In the
latter case, reinforcement was given in initial training when the "clock"
was at maximal size. Then the experimental conditions were reversed and
reinforcement presented when the dot was smallest. In this case the
original discrimination broke down, and the rate became more regular
until the new discrimination was formed.

[4] B. F. Skinner, Some contributions to an experimental analysis of behavior and
to psychology as a whole, *Amer. Psychol.*, **8** (1953), 69–78.

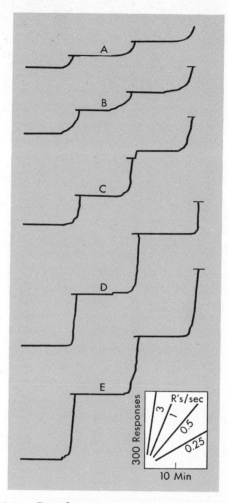

**Figure 4–2.** Cumulative response curves showing the development of a temporal discrimination with "clock." Pigeons were reinforced on a fixed-interval schedule of 10 minutes (FI 10). Segments were taken from the second and third sessions. (From C. B. Ferster and B. F. Skinner, *Schedules of Reinforcement*, Fig. 311, p. 268. Copyright © 1957, Appleton-Century-Crofts, Inc. Reproduced by permission.)

The application of fixed-interval schedules in human affairs are numerous. We attend classes at certain hours, eat at regular periods, and go to work at a given time. Behavior that is described as regular or habitual is often operating on fixed-interval reinforcement for which an accurate time discrimination has been developed. The payment of wages for work done by the hour, day, or week operates on this kind of schedule. However, because other operations and controlling stimuli appear in the process of human conditioning, the behavior may not always approximate that found in the lower animals. In working for pay, we do not perform our duties only just before pay time. Were this the case we should soon be replaced. A certain amount of output is expected throughout the week. Other reinforcements also operate to maintain at a steady rate, including the approval of our supervisors, verbal reinforcement from our co-workers, and less obvious reinforcements from the job itself. Add to these the aversive stimuli of supervisors or foremen who see to it that we do not loaf on the job. If no other variables were involved, it is quite likely that only a small amount of behavior might be generated in the intervals between reinforcements. Even so, we find the principle of increasing rate, prior to reinforcement, to have its application. We are more willing to work harder on pay day; absenteeism is less common; the student who has dawdled along all semester suddenly accelerates his study as examination time approaches in order to secure some slight reinforcement at the end of the term; the businessman makes a strong effort to "clean up his desk" in time for vacation; most people increase their efforts to make a reinforcing appointment on time.

Like the rat or pigeon that slows down its response rate just following a reinforcement, we, too, find this condition operating. Recall the difficulty of getting started on "blue Monday" after a weekend of play? The student often has a hard time resuming his study at the beginning of the term following vacation. It could be a long time before the next reinforcement comes along.

If the interval between reinforcements is too long, it is difficult to maintain behavior under some conditions. Some people do not like to work for a monthly wage but prefer to be paid by the day or week. Students are often unable to work consistently in courses where the term mark is the only reinforcement given; they would prefer weekly quizzes to "keep them on the ball." It should be remembered that at the human level, a variety of reinforcements may be working to maintain behavior. It is not only the money or marks which keep us at our jobs. When the only reinforcements operating occur at the end of the interval, the difficulty described above is evident. Hopefully, though, other reinforcements (such as interest or enjoyment in one's work and the approval of one's colleagues) should be present. In working with lower forms, we are controlling all variables except those to be studied, so that the principle may be demonstrated "in pure form."

Weisberg and Waldrop[5] have analyzed the rate at which Congress passes bills during its legislative sessions on a fixed-interval basis (third phase). The rate of the passage of bills is extremely low during the first

---

[5] P. Weisberg and P. B. Waldrop, Fixed-interval work habits of Congress, *Jour. appl. Behav. Anal.*, 5 (1972), 93–97.

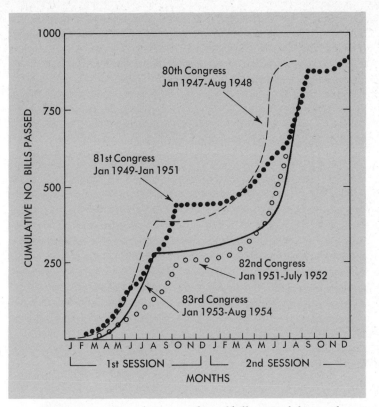

**Figure 4–3.** Cumulative number of bills passed during the legislative sessions of Congress from January 1947 to August 1954. (From P. Weisberg and P. B. Waldrop, Fixed-interval work habits of Congress, *Journal of Applied Behavior Analysis,* **5** [1972], 93–97. Copyright 1972 by the Society for the Experimental Analysis of Behavior, Inc.)

three or four months after convening. This is followed by a positively accelerated rate (see Figure 4–3 and 4–4) which continues to the time of adjournment. This scalloping is quite uniform during the sessions studied, which were sampled from 1947 to 1968, and holds for both houses. The possible reasons for these characteristic effects besides pressure of adjournment may be found in demands from organized lobbies, special interest groups, and influential constituents.

EXTINCTION UNDER FIXED-INTERVAL REINFORCEMENT

From the experimental literature, two general principles may be summarized: (1) In general the extinction follows a smoother and more regular rate of responding in contrast to that found during extinction in

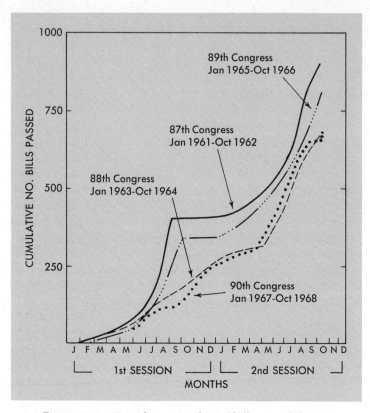

**Figure 4–4.**   Cumulative number of bills passed during the legislative sessions of Congress from January 1961 to October 1968.

regular reinforcement, and (2) other things being equal, the behavior is more resistant to extinction.[6] When equal numbers of reinforcements are given in regular or continuous and fixed-interval schedules, the extinction after fixed interval will give more responses. This has been demonstrated in animals and in humans, both adult and children (see p. 100).

Both these principles have interesting implications for human conduct, as demonstrated from our clinical observations in what is often referred to as *frustration tolerance,* or *stress tolerance.* This means that an individual is able to persist in his efforts despite the lack of reward or failure without developing the characteristic aggressive and emotional outbursts noted in extinction following regular reinforcement (see p. 76). We are very much aware of the individual differences in reactions to frustration. Some adults break down easily, whereas others seem to be like the rock of Gibraltar and can persist despite repeated failures, which in effect are extinction responses.

[6] C. B. Ferster and B. F. Skinner, op. cit., chapter 5.

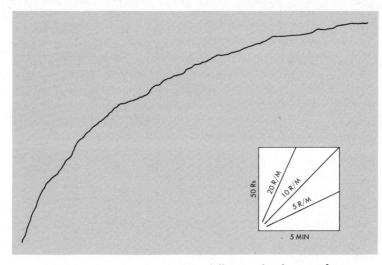

**Figure 4–5.** Extinction curve following fixed-interval one minute.

Some athletes blow up when the crowd jeers, their response becoming highly hostile and disorganized. Other people become angry and irritable when they are turned down for a job or fail an examination. During World War II the OSS (Office of Strategic Services) used a series of tests to evaluate the frustration tolerance of men who applied for these positions. For example, the men were asked to perform impossible tasks with the assistance of "helpers" who interfered more than they helped. Under stress of this sort some of the applicants became upset and anxious while others were able to continue in a calm manner. In the process of personality development, intermittent reinforcement is intrinsic to the training process and essential to stable behavior in adulthood. Such partial reinforcement gives stability to behavior and allows for persistence of effort when the reinforcement is withheld.

The application of the principle in training for adult maturity is clear. "Spoiled" or overindulged children are poor risks for later life.[7] In looking into their past histories of reinforcement, we find that those who break down easily or are readily set to aggression were as children too often *regularly* reinforced. Every demand was granted by their acquiescent parents. In youth they may have been so sheltered that failure was unknown to them. As a result these children have never built up a stability of response which would enable them to undergo periods of extinction and still maintain stable activity. The poor resistance to extinction is exemplified in their low frustration tolerance. As adults they are still operating like the rat who was reinforced on a regular schedule. Not

[7] D. M. Levy, *Maternal overprotection* (New York: Columbia University Press, 1943).

only do they exhibit the irregularities of response, but they are easily extinguished or discouraged.

Proper training requires the withholding of reinforcement from time to time. Fortunately for most of us, the contingencies of life allow for this as a part of our natural development. We did not always win the game as a child, nor did we get every candy bar we asked for. We were not given every attractive toy we saw in the store window. The emotionally healthy adult was not so overprotected in his childhood that he did not have to endure failure from time to time.

The resistance to extinction in FI schedule is also a function of the number of previous reinforcements. An experiment by Wilson,[8] using an FI of 2 minutes, found that more reinforcements given in conditioning yielded greater resistance to extinction. Exactly the same principle has been demonstrated with children (see pp. 103–104). The implications of these findings are clear and need not be belabored. A strong training of intermittent reinforcement will produce a personality that can persist for long periods of time without giving up, even in the face of adversity. Fortunately for most of us, this is the rule rather than the exception.


## Fixed-Ratio Schedules

In a fixed-ratio schedule (abbreviated FR) a response is reinforced only after it has been emitted a certain number of times. The ratio refers to the number of unreinforced to reinforced responses. For example, a FR of 6:1 means that the organism gives out six responses and is reinforced on the seventh. It can also be written FI 7, which means the same thing.

Experimental studies with animals yield a number of principles which may be summarized as follows.[9]

1. Higher rates of response tend to be developed under this kind of schedule than do those under fixed-interval or regular schedules.
2. By starting with a low ratio (say, 3:1) and gradually increasing the ratio in graded steps, very high ratios can be established, such as 500:1 or 1,000:1.
3. As in a fixed-interval conditioning, a discrimination is built up. There is a break after the reinforcement, followed by a rapid rate until the next reinforcement. This is based on the fact that the organism is

[8] M. P. Wilson, Periodic reinforcement interval and number of periodic reinforcements as parameters of response strength, *Jour. Comp. Physiol. Psychol.*, 47 (1954), 51–56.
[9] C. B. Ferster and B. F. Skinner, op. cit., chapter 4.

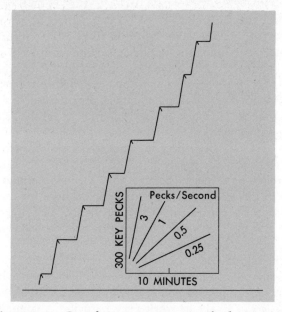

**Figure 4–6.** Cumulative response curve for key pressing of a pigeon reinforced after each 120th response. (From C. B. Ferster and B. F. Skinner, *Schedules of Reinforcement*, Fig. 24B, p. 162. Copyright © 1957 by Appleton-Century-Crofts, Inc. Reproduced by permission of Appleton-Century-Crofts, Division of Meredith Corporation.)

never reinforced for a response immediately following the last reinforcement.

4. The length of the break or a pause is a function of the size of the ratio. Once the response begins, following the break, it assumes a rapid rate until the next reinforcement.

All these general characteristics of fixed-ratio responding are found in human conduct even though conditions under which they occur cannot be subjected to the same precise experimental controls. FR schedules are frequently found in business or industry when a man is paid for the amount of work he puts out. Sometimes we call this *being paid on commission*, or piecework. Because of the possibility of high rates that this schedule can generate, it has frequently been opposed by organized labor.

There is an essential difference between the fixed-interval and fixed-ratio schedules which helps account for this opposition. In interval schedules the reinforcement is contingent upon some external agent. As long as the response comes at the right time, the organism will get the reinforcement. One can respond at a low or high rate and still get the same reinforcement, since the *rate* of his behavior in no way determines the reinforcement. On the other hand, in fixed-ratio reinforcement, the payoff is contingent upon the organism's responding. He may receive many or few reinforcements, depending on how much he cares to put out. A certain number of responses has to be made before the reinforcement will follow. This kind of schedule, of course, discourages "gold bricking," or loafing on the job. No work, no pay. In order to get the reinforcement, one must put out the work.

In selling, not only to protect the employer from unsuccessful salesmen as well as to provide greater "incentive" to the job, a fixed ratio is commonly applied by using the commission. A good salesman is rewarded by more pay in the amount of percentage he receives for the number of units sold. When the contractor is paid by the job, he is working on the FR schedule. In many crafts and arts one gets paid for a given product; if he produces nothing, he starves.

Such a schedule can be extremely effective if the ratio is not too high; that is, if the amount of work necessary for a given pay is within reasonable limits. Also, the reinforcement must not be too weak for the work done. A man is not likely to work very hard if the commission is too small. In all probability he will switch to a job that may pay off on some interval schedule instead. However, by supplying adequate commissions, the boss can induce his salesman to put out a high rate. He is likewise reinforced by success and prosperity.

Because of the great effectiveness in generating high rates, the use of ratio schedules is often opposed as being unfair or too dangerous to the individual's health. In laboratory animals it is possible to generate such high rates that the organism loses weight because the frequency of his reinforcement does not sustain him. Likewise, in human affairs, the salesman may suffer physical relapse because of working too long hours. Or, if heavy physical work is involved, the strain may be more than he can endure for a long period of time. As precautions, labor organizations may limit the number of units of work a man can put out in a given day. In the past, before labor organizations put a stop to abusive practices, some "Simon Legree's" took advantage of this principle by gradually increasing the ratios necessary for a reinforcement. In the old "sweat shop" days, when *piecework* pay was a more common practice than it is today, these men would require a given number of units for certain amount of pay. When this rate was established, they would increase the ratio for the same pay so that the workers had to work harder and harder in order to subsist. Fortunately this practice has been abolished today and is of only historical interest.

Just how high a fixed ratio can one develop? Findley and Brady[10] have

---

[10] J. D. Findley and J. V. Brady, Facilitation of large ratio performance by use of a conditioned reinforcement, *Jour. Exp. Anal. Behav.*, 8 (1965), 125–129.

demonstrated an FR of 120,000. In their procedure they used a chimpanzee as subject and developed this high stable ratio with the aid of a green light as a conditioned reinforcer (see Chapter 6). After each 4,000th response, the light, which had previously been associated with food, was presented alone. After 120,000 responses an almost unlimited supply of food became available as the primary reinforcer. The ratio break following the green light was about 15 minutes long before the animal began to respond again.

The characteristic break in responding following a reinforcement is also found in human behavior. This is especially true when the ratio is a high one. In education the student frequently has trouble getting back to work after completing a long assignment or term report. After putting out a big job of work, getting the newspaper out or the like, we take a rest. Of course, when the ratio is high and the reinforcement slim (as in mediocre grades), the possibility of early extinction is common. The student simply cannot get back to work. He may engage in a variety of excuses and alternate forms of activity, but studying he cannot do. Likewise, the aspiring young writer wonders why he can no longer take up his pen. It may be that his manuscripts (written under a FR schedule) are so infrequently accepted that the reinforcements are not sufficient to maintain behavior.

The characteristic break or pause in behavior following reinforcement under FR schedules has other applications in our everyday conduct. Consider the coffee break so common in business or industry today. The individuals who engage most frequently in this activity or spend their time hanging around the water cooler are, in all probability, finding little reinforcement from their jobs. Or the laborer who takes frequent breaks from his job may not be doing so simply to recover from fatigue. Often the reinforcements in the break activities—coffee, conversation, and so forth—are more reinforcing than the activity which is supposed to be maintained.

EXTINCTION FOLLOWING FIXED-RATIO CONDITIONING

Extinction following fixed-ratio reinforcement is characterized by a continuation of the responding rate at a high level, followed by a rather sudden cessation of behavior. This is sudden as compared to the gradual extinction under fixed-interval extinction. A long break may be followed by another run after which the organism suddenly stops responding. When extinction occurs, it is sudden and rather complete. The reason for this characteristic of the extinction behavior can be found in the organism's previous history of conditioning on this schedule. Reinforcement had been given following rapid responding. The reinforcement has been associated with the rapid rate. In extinction the organism reaches the end of his ratio, but no reinforcement is presented. Nevertheless the situation is the normal one for reinforcement, and therefore he continues to respond at the same rate because in his previous history it has been the occasion under which the reinforcement was presented. However, this cannot go on indefinitely because the behavior is becoming weakened. Finally the organism gives out all the behavior he has "in reserve." When this occurs, he is through, and extinction is complete (see Figure 4–7).

We often meet people whose behavior follows this same pattern. The musician who was trained for many years at the conservatory finds jobs hard to get. At some point in his history he quits, lays down his instrument, and never plays again. The author who cannot write another word "gives up" and may enter an entirely different occupation, never to write again.

Many professional and artistic behaviors are reinforced on ratio schedules, and when extinction occurs, this same kind of quitting or complete giving up of their occupations is the result. The college student quits to join the army and does not return to college. Much college work operates on ratio schedules, and if extinction occurs because of inadequate reinforcement, one can be certain the student will never return to his studies. This kind of extinction may be contrasted with that in which a person quits but tries again, gives up for a while and then resumes his activity, perhaps at a lower rate because the prior behavior was originally conditioned on another kind of schedule.

The present rate of college dropouts *could* be a function of this pat-

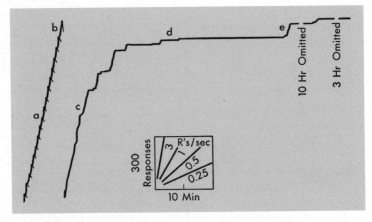

**Figure 4–7.** Cumulative response curve of a pigeon pecking a key under a fixed-ratio schedule of 60:1. The first part of the curve (ab at left) illustrates the conditioning and the second (cde) the extinction. Note how rather abruptly extinction comes to an end. (From C. B. Ferster and B. F. Skinner, *Schedules of Reinforcement.* Fig. 35, p. 60. Copyright © 1957, Appleton-Century-Crofts, Inc. Reproduced by permission.)

tern. With the present explosion of knowledge, perhaps too much was demanded of him in high school or college, and the reinforcements are simply not coming. Of course, in the current situation it is obvious that other variables are involved.

## Variable-Interval Schedules

In this type of schedule (abbreviated VI) the interval is randomly varied about some given time value, say, 5 minutes. The mean or average time at which reinforcement is given falls every 5 minutes, although any individual time for reinforcement may not fall at that point.

Experimental evidence indicates that after prolonged training on this type of schedule, the organism develops a steady rate of responding, the rate being a function of the size and range of the intervals employed (see Figure 4–5). The characteristic time discrimination found in the fixed-interval schedules is lacking because of the variability with which the reinforcement is applied. The rate will be high or low, depending on the size of the interval employed.[11]

A steadiness of rate is most characteristic of this schedule. In one of Ferster and Skinner's many experiments, pigeons were reinforced for pecking a key on a 3-minute VI schedule. The range of the intervals employed was from a few seconds to 6 minutes. The bird gave over 30,000 responses over a 15-hour period, and except for one pause, it never stopped between responses for more than 15 seconds during the entire experimental period.[12]

Actually, a large amount of our personal and social behavior operates on this type of schedule. Since the reinforcements are a function of some time interval, one must remember that the controlling agency that administers the reinforcement is in the environment. The responding organism does not know precisely when the reinforcement will occur. If he did, then the schedules would be fixed interval; and if the reinforcement is dependent on his rate of response, the schedule is some kind of ratio.

The dating behavior of the college coed often operates on this kind of schedule. Unless she is going steady, when her social engagements are guaranteed (regular reinforcement or fixed interval), she does not know precisely when the invitations are going to be forthcoming. If she operates as a strong reinforcer for the behavior of the men in her life, the variable interval may be a low one, and she may be called *popular*. On the other hand if her VI schedule is a long one (only occasional dates),

[11] C. B. Ferster and B. F. Skinner, op. cit., chapter 6.
[12] Ibid., 12, pp. 332–338.

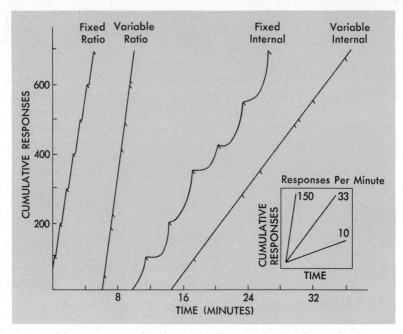

**Figure 4–8.** Stylized records of responding under each of the four basic schedules of reinforcement. Diagonal marks indicate the reinforcement. When the total number of reinforcements is about the same, the ratio schedules generate the most rapid rates. (From E. Reese, An analysis of human operant behavior. In J. Vernon, (ed.), *Introduction to Psychology: A Self-selection Text*, Fig. 10, p. 16. Copyright © 1966 by Wm. C. Brown Company. Reproduced by permission.)

she waits a long time between invitations, and we may say she is *not* so popular.

Some kinds of sports activities operate on this schedule, such as hunting and fishing. A fisherman drops in his line, and then he must wait. He does not know precisely when the fish will bite (maybe not at all), nor does he know when the game will fly, even though through past conditioning history he has found certain areas to be situations in which the reinforcements occur. Although these reinforcements of catching the fish or shooting the game are a function of his skill, the aspects of the availability of the reinforcements to him is a function of some undetermined schedule. The enthusiastic sportsman has a regularity of behavior which has had a past history of reinforcement, even though variable.

We attend social gatherings at irregular intervals. Some people, considered highly social, operate on low variable-interval schedules, while others considered antisocial may have long VI schedules. In any event we do not attend a party every day of every week nor do we always have a good time when we do. As long as reinforcements are sometimes forth-coming, we maintain our social behavior. If none turn up, we withdraw in favor of some kind of behavior in which reinforcements are not administered by other people.

We have noted that industry usually pays on a fixed-interval sched-ule. The Christmas bonus, to the degree that it comes regularly every year at a certain time, is still the fixed interval. If industry were to employ an unpredictable bonus, given at irregular intervals throughout the year, the rate of behavior of its employees might be increased. Since it has been demonstrated that variable-interval schedules generate higher rates than the fixed interval (number of reinforcements being constant), one wonders why this kind of procedure is not more frequently em-ployed as a means of economic control.[13]

EXTINCTION OF VARIABLE-INTERVAL SCHEDULES

The characteristic of extinction under variable-interval conditioning is similar to that found under fixed-interval extinction. It shows itself in a continuation of the behavior developed under conditioning. In the early part of extinction the behavior will be maintained at about the same rate as during conditioning. The rate will continue for a long time before showing signs of decreasing. In general, extinction is slow to take place. Behavior established under some kind of variable schedule shows con-siderable resistance to extinction. This characteristic is adequately sum-marized by Jenkins and Stanley in their review of experimental studies that use partial intermittent reinforcement.

> The most striking effects of partial reinforcement are apparent in response strength as measured by resistance to extinction. In almost every experi-ment, large and significant differences in extinction favoring the groups partially reinforced in conditioning over 100% (regular reinforcement) were found. The practical implications of this principle for maintaining behavior is obvious. Administer the reinforcing stimulus in conditioning according to a partial schedule, and behavior will be maintained for long periods in the absence of external support from primary reward.[14]

This principle seems to explain why most of us "keep going" in the face of failure. Often, despite infrequent reinforcements, we maintain our behavior at constant rates. As a matter of fact this is a good thing, for if our behavior were not reinforced irregularly, then when extinction did set in, we would act like the rats extinguished under regular rein-forcement, with bursts of activity accompanied by aggressive and other

---

[13] B. F. Skinner, *Science and human behavior* (New York: Macmillan, 1953).
[14] W. O. Jenkins and J. C. Stanley, Partial reinforcement: A review and critique, *Psychol. Bull.*, **47** (1950), 193–234 (p. 231).

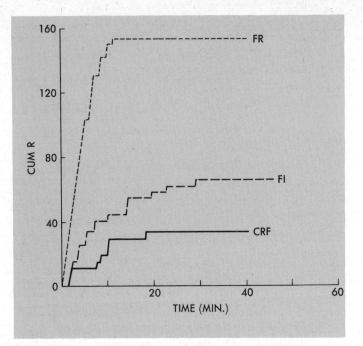

**Figure 4–9.** Extinction curves following 35 reinforcements on 3 schedules: CRF, FI, and FR. Subject: Silver
King pigeon; response: pecking. (From E. P. Reese,
*Experiments in Operant Behavior*, p. 84. Copyright ©
1964, Appleton-Century-Crofts, Inc. Reproduced by
permission.)

emotional responses. The fact that most of us maintain an even keel or
"steady pace" despite the adversities of life is evidence for the great
resistance to extinction that characterizes much of our behavior.


## Variable-Ratio Schedules

In this arrangement the number of responses required for a reinforcement varies around some average ratio. The behavior under VR reinforcement is characterized by:

1. A steady rate of responding without breaks, since there is no basis
   for the information of a discrimination like that under regular schedules.
2. Extremely high rates, which may be built up very quickly if the
   beginning ratio is small.[15] (See Figure 4–7.)

[15] C. B. Ferster and B. F. Skinner, op. cit., chapter 7.

One difference between response rates established under variable-interval and variable ratio is that ratio schedules ordinarily lead to higher rates than do interval schedules. The reason for this lies in the fact that a response following a break in interval schedules has a greater likelihood of being reinforced. A pause in the ratio schedule in no way increases the probability of the reinforcement, since such reinforcement is dependent on the organism's responding.

In one of Ferster and Skinner's pigeons, conditioning was established under a final VR of 110:1 with a range of zero (the very next response) to 500. This bird pecked the key at a rate of 12,000 per hour, which averages about 200 responses per minute or almost 4 per second.[16]

Perhaps the most striking illustration of the operation of VR schedules in human affairs is to be found in the multitude of gambling devices and games of chance that man engages in. Even in card games where skill is involved, the VR schedule operates, for if one does not have the right cards, victory is impossible. In these gambling operations the payoff is unpredictable and therefore a steady rate is maintained. Such schedules differ from the interval schedules because winning is contingent upon playing, and the more one plays, the greater the probability of winning even though the reinforcements distribute themselves in a very irregular manner. What is considered as a "winning streak" refers to a section of the schedule in which the payoff is coming after responses that occur closer together; the "losing streak" is the long stretch in the schedule between reinforcements.

In contrived devices like slot machines, the rate of payoff may be varied according to a number of several systems. Some slot machines pay off quite frequently (not enough to come out ahead, however) while others situated in a bus stop where a single visitor might never return will probably never give any returns.

The extremely high rates that can be generated by these schedules is ilustrated in the behavior of the compulsive gambler. Even though the returns are very slim, he never gives up. Families are ruined and fortunes lost; still the high rates of behavior are maintained, often to the exclusion of all alternate forms of activity. Witness the "all night" crap games in which a single person will remain until all his funds and resources are gone. His behavior is terminated only by his inability to perform operations necessary to stay in the game. And even on these occasions, if he can muster more funds by borrowing or stealing, he will return to the game. Although gambling may involve other auxiliary reinforcements, social and personal, the basic rate of behavior is maintained by the schedule itself. The degree of control exercised by such a schedule is tremendous. In these cases almost absolute control has been achieved, so that the behavior becomes as certain as that found in respondent conditioning. The degree of control is often unfortunate and

[16] Ibid., pp. 398–399.

dangerous to the individual and his family, and the paradoxical thing about it is that the controlling agency (unless the gambling devices are "fixed") is the simple factor of chance. For this reason one begins to understand why legalized gambling is prohibited in most states. Like Skinner's pigeons, the compulsive gambler is a victim of an unpredictable contingency of reinforcements.

Gambling is not the only area of conduct that operates on variable-ratio schedules. In any activity where a rate is necessary to secure reinforcement and that reinforcement is variable, such a schedule is operating. "If at first you don't succeed, try, try again." The trying is not always rewarded, but the more one tries, other things being equal, the more often he will succeed. Although one cannot always be certain of success, we see in "try, try again" the behavior of the constant plugger who finds achievements few and far apart.

Variable-ratio schedules operate similarly in education. A student is not always reinforced each time he raises his hand to answer a question, but the more often he raises his hand, the more likely he is to be called upon. Good marks and promotions may come at unpredictable times. Presumably, however, the greater effort put out, the more often the reinforcements should be forthcoming—unless, of course, one happens to be working for someone who has never heard of or understood the significance of reinforcement.

Yukl, Wexley, and Seymore[17] tested the effects of a VR schedule on human subjects in a simulated work situation. In this situation the task was scoring IBM answer cards. When a card was completed the subject took it to the experimenter, who then flipped a coin which the subject called. If he called it correct, he received 50 cents. If not, he got nothing. Thus, he worked on a VR 2 schedule in which he would be reinforced half of the time. Other subjects were paid for each card on a schedule of regular reinforcement, usually referred to as a crf schedule (continuous reinforcement). The results indicated that the VR 2 schedule was more effective as judged by performance rates. The experimenters point out, however, that this system would be doubtfully accepted as a substitute in a real-life work situation based on an hourly or a piece-rate basis. However, a VR schedule might be useful as a supplement to an organization's present pay system.

Sometimes it is difficult to determine whether a behavior is operating under a VI or VR schedule. A close examination and careful analysis of the contingencies is necessary. Take fishing, for example. If one is simply "still" fishing, the schedule is a variable interval at a given day. The time at which the fish will bite is the determining factor. The fisher-

[17] G. Yukl, K. N. Wexley, and J. Seymore, Effectiveness of pay incentives under variable ratio and continuous reinforcement schedules, *Jour. Appl. Psychol.*, **56** (1972), 10–13.

man may drop his line in and take it out of the water innumerable times, but if the fish are not biting, no reinforcement will be forthcoming. On the other hand, if he is casting, one could argue that the schedule is a variable ratio, for the more casts he makes, the more likely he will get a catch (assuming there are fish in the vicinity). Here the reinforcements are partly a function of the number of responses he makes.

Unwitting parents can often generate high rates of behavior which turn out to be inappropriate. Take, for example, a simple request which is turned down the first time it is made. Because the child has been reinforced in the past, the behavior persists until the parents break down and give in to the child's demands. Immediately a schedule is being established. On the next occasion of a request, a resistance to extinction is developing. The child persists again until the requests become annoying to the parents. This behavior we often call *teasing*, and it is established by the fact that the reinforcements come only when the request has been made numerous times on a variable ratio, depending on the circumstances involved and the immediate frustration tolerance of the parent.

### EXTINCTION UNDER VARIABLE-RATIO SCHEDULES

The behavior is somewhat characteristic of that found under fixed-ratio extinction.[18] There will be sustained runs of responses separated by pauses. As extinction becomes more complete, the pauses become longer and the overall rate is reduced. It contrasts with extinction under variable interval, where there is a fairly continuous decline from the original rate through to the point where the extinction is complete.

### SCHEDULES OF PARTIAL REINFORCEMENT WITH CHILDREN

In our discussion so far, we described the various effects of schedules of reinforcement on behavior as they are demonstrated in the laboratory, using animals as subjects. We then took these principles and applied them to human affairs, using our clinical observations as the source of data. Another approach is to study human subjects in experimental situations so as to demonstrate and compare the results with those already observed.

Children have often been subjects for this type of investigation in which, under controlled experimental conditions, they demonstrate behavior when exposed to experimental operations similar to those applied in other organisms. If the results turn out alike, the lawfulness of the principles is demonstrated.

Bijou has applied a variety of schedules in the conditioning of child-

[18] C. B. Ferster and B. F. Skinner, *Schedules of reinforcement* (New York: Appleton-Century-Crofts, 1957).

ren of preschool age. In one experiment[19] he took two groups of children, conditioned one under regular reinforcement (100 per cent) and the other on a variable-ratio schedule in which only 20 per cent of the responses were reinforced. The apparatus consisted of a wooden box with two holes in it, one above the other. In the lower hole a rubber ball was presented to the child which he was to put in the upper hole. The response, then, consisted of taking the ball from the lower hole and placing it in the upper one. Eighteen children were divided into the two groups matched for age and previous experience in the experimental situation. Prior to the experimental session each child was taken into the laboratory by a person familiar to him and asked to play with some toys. After this "warm-up" play activity, the child was taken to the table which contained the apparatus. He was told that he could get trinkets (reinforcing stimuli) to take home with him. The first group was given a trinket every time the appropriate response was made. In the second group the reinforcements were delivered after the 1, 6, 13, 17, 23, and 30 responses. In each group six reinforcements were delivered altogether. Resistance to extinction favored the group conditioned on the variable-ratio schedule. The regular reinforcement group gave 15.3 responses and the intermittent group gave 22 responses in the first 3½ minutes of extinction. These differences are found to be statistically significant and not due to chance.

In another group of studies, Bijou[20] compared regular reinforcement with intermittent schedules using a different kind of apparatus which resembled a top, being painted to resemble the head and face of a clown. A red lever, to be pressed downward (response), represented the nose of the clown; two colored signal lights were the eyes; and reinforcements were delivered through the mouth. In this case Bijou compared three fixed-interval schedules with the regular one. The intervals were 20, 30, and 60 seconds. Results indicated that the resistance to extinction is related to the size of the fixed interval, the larger interval yielding the greatest number of extinction responses. Bijou points out that differences may be accounted for by the greater variability among human subjects. The human may alter the extinction process, for example, by introducing stimuli not under the experimental control. If other "extra" responses have a reinforcing function, such as beating time or singing, the rate may be high. On the other hand, if the subject thinks the machine has broken down, the rate may decrease. Furthermore the response rate is also a function of the history of reinforcement and extinction under similar circumstances over which the experimenter has no control.[21]

[19] S. W. Bijou, Patterns of reinforcement and resistance to extinction in young children, *Child Dev.,* **28** (1957), 47–54.

[20] S. W. Bijou, Methodology for the experimental analysis of child behavior, *Psychol. Rep.,* **3** (1957), 243–250.

[21] S. W. Bijou, Operant extinction after fixed-interval reinforcement with young children, *Jour. Exp. Anal. Behav.,* **1** (1958), 25–30.

*Conditioning Mentally Deficient Children on Schedules.*　Orlando and Bijou[22] used 46 institutionalized mentally deficient children, ages 9 to 21, with IQs from 23 to 64. Reinforcements consisted of various candies. The characteristics of behavior generated by each of a variety of schedules were similar to those found using the same schedules with lower organisms. Rates were a function of the kind of schedule. Postreinforcement pauses were more likely in FR schedules than VR, and more likely in higher than lower ratios. These same relationships are also found with lower species. The amazing thing that all these studies have in common is the marked similarities of behavior under various schedules regardless of the species of organism used.

*Conditioning Infant Smiling Responses on Schedules.*　Brackbill[23] selected the smiling responses in infants to study. His subjects were eight normal infants between the ages of three and one-half and four and one-half months, about the age at which the smiling response first appears. In the conditioning procedure, as soon as the infant smiled the experimenter smiled in return, spoke softly, and picked up the infant. He was then held and patted and jostled about for 30 seconds. During extinction, all these reinforcements were eliminated. The infants were divided into two groups: one was reinforced on a crf schedule (continuous reinforcement), and the partial reinforcement group was put on a was increased to VR-4 and finally to VR-5 schedule. Results confirmed VR-3 schedule (on the average, every third response reinforced). This the general expectation that intermittent schedules are more powerful in maintaining response rate, particularly during extinction. Another interesting observation of the study was demonstration of the inverse relationship between infant protest responses (crying, etc.) and rate of smiling, both during conditioning and extinction. That is, the infants who protested the most smiled the least, and vice versa.

*A Study of Conditioning Responses with Normal College Students.*　A study of Verplanck,[24] using college students as subjects, will round out our analysis. His findings further support the point that humans act very much like experimental animals when subjected to the same kinds of experimental treatments. The technique described in his study demonstrates very dramatically how a variety of motor and verbal behaviors can be conditioned when practically no instructions are given. In trying this kind of experiment, he suggests telling the subject he is going to participate in

---

[22] R. Orlando and S. W. Bijou, Single and multiple schedules of reinforcement in developmentally retarded children, *Jour, Exp. Anal. Behav.*, **3** (1960), 339–348.

[23] Y. Brackbill, Extinction of the smiling response in infants as a function of reinforcement schedule, *Child Dev.*, **29** (1958), 115–124.

[24] W. S. Verplanck, The operant conditioning of human motor behavior, *Psychol. Bull.*, **53** (1956), 70–83.

a "game" or some other kind of test. Prior to the experiment proper, the experimenter should observe behavior of the individual and should select some response which he wants to condition by increasing its rate. Any number of responses can be selected without telling the subject; turning the head, smiling, putting the finger to the chin, scratching the ear, rubbing the eyebrow, ad infinitum. The only criterion is that the response should have some degree of frequency prior to experimentation. Verbal responses can also be conditioned. This matter will be discussed in greater detail in Chapter 6.

Reinforcements may simply consist of giving the subject "points" each time he makes the desired response. These the subject records for himself when the experimenter says, "point." They may or may not be exchanged for money later on, as the experimenter chooses. Often a response to be conditioned may be shaped out by a series of successive approximations (see Chapter 5).

In the beginning the response is usually reinforced regularly to ensure some resistance to extinction before the experimenter shifts to some other schedule. Verplanck has tried a variety of ratio and interval schedules. According to this experimenter:

> The behavior observed under these schedules corresponds closely with that observed in lower animals. As with lower animals, E will find it impossible to shift directly to a high ratio of reinforcement or to a long fixed interval without extinction. Fixed intervals of 15 seconds and fixed ratios of 6:1 may be established immediately without danger of extinction.[25]

Other results are characteristic of those found with other organisms. High rates of response occur under ratio schedules, and low but stable rates follow interval schedules with large, smooth extinction curves. Temporal discrimination, verbalized or not, may occur in the fixed-interval schedules. Extinction curves do not differ in any remarkable way from those with other organisms. The human may make statements to the effect that he is losing interest or is bored, or that he has a sudden pressing engagement. He may become angry and emit mildly insulting remarks in extinction such as "stupid game" or "silly experiment."

Since little or no instructions are necessary in this type of experiment, the question arises, "What about the subject's awareness of what is going on?" By awareness, Verplanck means simply the ability to make a verbal statement about one or more "rules" of the experiment. He found that in about half the cases, subjects had no awareness of the response being conditioned. They did not know precisely what they were doing to earn points until many responses had been conditioned and a stable rate established. Conditioning and extinction may take place without the

25 Ibid., pp. 77–78.

subject ever "figuring it out." When a particular schedule was being used, few subjects were aware of its particular characteristics, ratio or interval. Occasionally subjects would exhibit a sudden "aha." They stated that they knew *what* response gave them points. When more specific verbal instructions were given, the subject merely produced the rate of behavior characteristic of that schedule more quickly.

Since this technique involves such simple apparatus, any student can try it. All that is needed is paper and pencils and some timing device for the experimenter in order to determine what kind of rate is being established. Although, as Verplanck points out, the technique resembles a number of parlor games, one realizes that the procedure is much more than a parlor game. It establishes, under proper conditions, that a great many behaviors can be conditioned to certain rates, depending on the kind of schedule prescribed.

## Rate Conditioning

Rate schedules are variations of the ratio schedules already discussed. Reinforcement depends upon the attainment of responding, either *higher* or *lower* than some previous specified rate. In *differential high-rate* (drh) conditioning, reinforcement is given only when the rate of responding is *above* some specified standard, as when the responses come closer and closer together. It is through this technique of requiring higher and higher rates of responding that it is possible to get an organism to respond to the degree of his limits or, as we say, "as fast as he can." The reinforcement is selective and occurs only when the rate meets a specified standard. In the laboratory this is accomplished by using automatic timing devices that allow a reinforcement only when the organism exceeds a given rate. When this occurs, the minimal standard may be stepped up so that even a more rapid rate is necessary to secure the reinforcement.

When more and more work is required of an individual in a given unit of time in order to secure reinforcement, this type of schedule is in operation. Students sometimes complain that their instructors are guilty of this practice. They begin with relatively small assignments to be done the next day. As the semester progresses, more and more work is required to be done in the same specified time. Often in the learning of skills involved in acquiring a foreign language, this process is natural. As the student acquires a mastery of the language, he should be expected to read more and more in less time. The same is true in the apprenticeship of a job. The beginner is reinforced generously in the early part of his learning even though his rate is slow. As he improves, more and more is expected of him for the same reinforcement.

The use of differential high-rate reinforcement can have its damaging effects, as we have already mentioned, in the case of unscrupulous employers who demand more and more of their workers for the same pay, simply because these people have demonstrated that they can produce more. Through the operation of such a schedule, maximum rates can be achieved.

In *differential low-rate* (drl) conditioning, the reinforcement is contingent on the spacing of responses in time intervals which are designated farther apart from those prevailing under a previously specified schedule. Low and very steady rates of responding achieved in this way often are accompanied by a variety of auxiliary "marking time" devices which operate between the responses.[26] This procedure may be developed with considerably less effort than the high rates described above, simply by reinforcing a response only if it occurs after it is expected. Behavior is slowed down more and more as the schedule is readjusted to meet new standards of slowness.

An experiment by Wilson and Keller,[27] using rats as subjects, illustrates this process. The rats were given regular reinforcement for bar pressing in the first experimental session. Then reinforcement was given for responses which were at least 10 seconds apart. After that the time required was systematically increased in 5-second steps until 30 seconds had been reached. The results showed that the response rate dropped from an average of six responses per minute under a 10-second interval requirement to three per minute under the 30-second requirement. In all probability the rate could have been further reduced, but eventually, however, the demands would have been greater than that necessary to maintain behavior, and the response rate would have become extinguished.

Often people who apply their skimpy reinforcement too infrequently are actually applying this schedule. Such individuals are actually rather stingy people in supplying the reinforcements. Their personalities are such that to give a word of encouragement or praise seems to be aversive to themselves. As a result, instead of encouraging people under them to work harder, they actually generate lower rates of activity. Because they occasionally give a begrudging reinforcement, the behavior of those under their control is not completely extinguished but maintained at a minimum rate. Under these conditions one often speaks of a situation of low morale. The problem is that reinforcements are not given frequently enough to maintain a rate that is much above that required to prevent extinction.

One may wish to reduce the rate of behavior without extinguishing it completely; for example, in controlling the behavior of children. If one

---

26 Ibid.
27 M. P. Wilson and F. S. Keller, On the selective reinforcement of spaced responses, *Jour. Comp. Physiol., Psychol.*, 46 (1953), 190–193.

wished to reduce the frequent verbalizations of the child, he may offer a candy bar if the child keeps quiet for a long enough period of time.

## Combined Schedules

The preceding schedules may be combined in various ways: they may *alternate* (*multiple schedules*) or operate *simultaneously* (*concurrent*). Ratio and interval schedules will operate in such a way that the reinforcement depends on a time interval followed by a ratio schedule. The shift from one schedule to another may operate with or without the use of an external stimulus or cue. In the concurrent schedules two or more schedules may be independently arranged but may operate at the same time, the reinforcements being set up by both.

When a man starts out on a job selling some commodity such as insurance, let us say, he begins by being paid a weekly salary regardless of how many policies he is able to sell. As his sales ability increases, he is shifted to a commission basis arrangement in which he can make more money by selling more. This *mixed schedule* is advantageous both to the individual and his employer. In his initial efforts the sales may be slow, and therefore a weekly salary is necessary to enable him to meet his bills and to protect him from discouragement and quitting. Later on, as he learns more about the business, a greater rate can be generated by allowing him to work on a commission which allows him a certain percentage of the money taken in from his sales. This is more advantageous to the good worker and provides added incentive for doing a better job. In this case there has been a shift from a fixed-interval to a fixed-ratio schedule.

Sometimes two schedules are concurrent. In this case an automobile salesman is assured a weekly wage (FI) but is also given an extra commission (FR) for every car he sells above a given number. In this instance the incentive is added for extra work, but the man is still protected against extinction when the season for new cars is slack.

Actually, in the conduct of our daily affairs, we operate on a variety of schedules, both multiple and concurrent. We emit many different behaviors, each of which is reinforced on some schedule. The problem becomes extremely complex. Take, for example, the day-to-day activity of a college student. He eats, sleeps, takes his toilet on a variety of fixed-interval schedules, and does his assignments on ratio schedules. He takes weekly examinations in some courses (fixed interval) and is assigned only term papers in other seminar-type courses (ratio schedule). His social life operates by and large on variable-interval schedules, and much of his verbal behavior is on a regular schedule, since people ordinarily speak to him when he addresses them. If he happens to work in his spare time to help pay his way through school, he can earn extra money for typing papers for his fellow students, at so much per page (fixed ratio), or he may prefer to wait on tables in the cafeteria for an hourly wage (fixed interval). He engages in sports and games on some variable-ratio schedules; the more he plays, the more likely he is to win, although the winning is not regular or absolutely predictable. All these schedules and many more operate to maintain and increase or decrease his behavior. If he becomes more and more studious, the rate is obviously going up; if he gradually becomes discouraged, extinction is probably setting in, the reinforcements not being sufficient to maintain his behavior. One thing is certain—the operation of these various schedules maintains a considerable amount of control over his conduct.

# 5 Discrimination and Differentiation

THIS CHAPTER IS CONCERNED WITH TWO related principles of behavior which play a very important part in the development of our personalities: discrimination and differentiation. From the very beginning, the infant acquires simple *discriminations*; he learns to tell the difference between a bottle that has milk in it and one that does not. In learning to walk and talk, he *differentiates* more and more specific movements out of a mass of random activity. Discrimination is intimately involved in the so-called higher mental processes; it is the basis upon which we learn to think and solve problems. As our movements become more specialized and appropriate to specific situations, we learn highly differentiated skills and abilities. We shall discuss each process separately and then see how both operate together in the development of unique and organized personalities.

## Generalization

You will recall, in our earlier discussion in Chapter 3, Watson and Raynor's study of conditioned fear in Albert.[1] After Albert had been con-

[1] J. B. Watson and R. Raynor, Conditioned emotional reactions, *Jour. Exp. Psychol.*, 3 (1920), 1–14.

ditioned to elicit a fear response in the presence of the rat, without further training there was a spread of effect to other similar stimuli. Albert exhibited fear of rabbits, fur pieces, and a Santa Claus mask. This spread we call *generalization of the stimulus.* After initial conditioning to some stimulus, other stimuli can also operate in calling out the response. Pavlov's early work demonstrated the phenomenon in respondent behavior. If a dog is conditioned to salivate at the sound of a tone of a given frequency and intensity, other tones and sound stimuli also will bring out the salivary response. Stimuli can vary in frequency and even quality. If an organism is conditioned to respond to one stimulus, it also responds to a variety of other stimuli which bear some relationship to the initial conditioning stimulus.

Generalization is also characteristic of operant conditioning. Suppose a rat is conditioned to press the bar when a light of a certain intensity is presented prior to the response. An experiment of Frick[2] demonstrated this fact. When light of different degrees of intensity is presented, following the initial conditioning, a generalization curve or gradient appears. The closer the intensities are to the original one, the stronger the response is, measured in rate; the farther away in stimulus magnitude, the slower the rate.

Another example of generalization in the experimental laboratory is demonstrated by Gutman and Kalish.[3] They conditioned pigeons to peck at a lighted disc whose color was a yellow-green of a wavelength of 550 m$\mu$. (millimicrons). They used a VI schedule of partial reinforcement, which we have already learned yields a high resistance to extinction. It should also be pointed out that prior to the experiment the pigeons had not had any experience with other colors. Furthermore, it has already been demonstrated that birds in general have excellent color vision. After the pecking response to the yellow-green disc was stabilized, the effects of other colors were tested; sometimes the test light was yellow, other times blue, etc. The different colors were presented in random order. The number of responses made to other wavelengths (colors) are plotted in Figure 5-1. As can be seen, the closer the wavelength was to the original conditioning color, the greater was the response rate.

In a simple human situation we observe generalization in the process of a child learning to talk. Suppose a child learns the word "daddy" in the presence of a given stimulus, his father. Sometimes to the embarrassment of his parents he will also emit the same word to a variety of other stimuli, other men, old and young, tall and short, thin and fat. It takes further conditioning to narrow down the response of "daddy" to one

[2] F. C. Frick, An analysis of operant discriminations, *Jour. Psychol.*, **26** (1948), 93–123.

[3] N. Gutman and H. Kalish, Discriminability and stimulus generalization, *Jour. Exp. Psychol.*, **51** (1956), 79–88.

specific stimulus. Were it not for discrimination, the opposite process to generalization, life would be in a horrible chaos. We would constantly be calling people by the wrong names, eating improper kinds of food, and generally making a variety of inappropriate responses. In the process of our developmental history and out of responses to generalized stimuli, fine discriminations take place. In the development of a discrimination we take one aspect of the environment and reinforce selectively some response to it. When the behavior shows a specificity of response to one given stimulus to the exclusion of others, we may say that a discrimination has taken place.

## Development of Discriminations

In Chapter 3, in our reference to Skinner's conditioning of a bar-press response, you will recall that we did not know what the initial

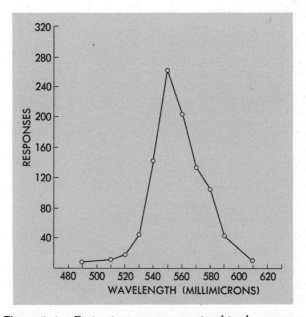

**Figure 5–1.** Extinction responses emitted in the presence of eleven different wavelengths projected one at a time on the bird's key. Training took place only at 550 mμ (greenish-yellow). (From N. Guttman and H. Kalish, Discriminability and generalization, *Journal of Experimental Psychology,* **51** [1956], 79–88, Fig. 3, p. 83. Reproduced by permission of the authors and the American Psychological Association.)

stimulus was that served to emit the bar press. When the rat was placed in the cage, it was necessary to wait until he pressed the bar for the first time. When this occurred, reinforcement was delivered and the rate of responding increased. It is entirely possible, as Skinner suggests, to describe the process of operant conditioning without making any reference to stimuli that operate in the organism's environment *before* the response is made. In Verplanck's study[4] of conditioning human motor behavior, he waited until some response occurred, such as pulling the ear, putting the finger to the chin, and so forth. Then the reinforcement was delivered. The initial stimulus that caused the ear pulling or movement to the chin was not specifically known.

However, if we add some "extra" external stimulus to the situation and present it prior to the response, then wait for the response to occur and reinforce that response in the presence of this stimulus, we are beginning to develop a discrimination. Something "extra" added to the environment adds to the control of the behavior. The process is quite simply demonstrated in the experimental laboratory in a manner like that suggested by Skinner[5] in one of his early experiments. The first step could be the conditioning of the animal to press the bar to receive food, although this is not necessary. The next step is to add a light to the situation. When the rat's bar pressing receives a food reinforcement, the light is immediately turned off. Because of generalization in the beginning, the rat will press the bar, with or without the light because in his previous history he has learned that pressing the bar gets reinforcement, under a variety of external stimuli not under the specific control of the experimenter. When the light is turned off, any response then made goes unreinforced; in other words, extinguished. When the rat has not responded during a given period, we again turn on the light and reinforce the first response to the bar, turn off the light again, and extinguish. Eventually a discrimination is built up through the combined operations of reinforcing when the light is on and extinguishing when the light is off. The rat learns a good discrimination, so that on future trials, he responds only when the light is on and almost never responds when the light is off. In this procedure an interesting phenomenon is taking place between the two opposite processes. As the rat receives food, because of generalization, the rate may increase when the light is off. On the other hand, since he is being extinguished when light is off, there may be a spread of extinction to the light-on period. In time these two processes become farther and farther apart as the discrimination develops.

[4] W. S. Verplanck, The operant conditioning of motor behavior, *Psychol. Bull.*, **53** (1956), 70–83.

[5] B. F. Skinner, The rate of establishment of a discrimination, *Jour. Gen. Psychol.*, **9** (1933), 302–350.

In this procedure we have added another stimulus to the event. This stimulus also operates to control the behavior of the organism. We designate $S^D$ as the discriminative stimulus in the presence of which the organism is reinforced. But there is another stimulus in the situation— the light off, in the presence of which the organism does not get reinforced. This is called the $S^\Delta$ (ess delta). Discrimination involves at least two stimuli. One cannot discriminate a single stimulus, but one can discriminate between stimuli. Of course most of our discrimination involves more than just two stimuli.

In this process we have demonstrated what Skinner[6] calls a *three-term contingency* by adding the discriminative stimulus. This may be diagrammed as

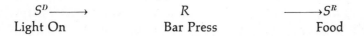

$$S^D \longrightarrow \qquad\qquad R \qquad\qquad \longrightarrow S^R$$
$$\text{Light On} \qquad\qquad \text{Bar Press} \qquad\qquad \text{Food}$$

Through this process a vast variety of new behavior comes into operation. We go picking wild strawberries and select the red ones ($S^D$) and ignore the green ones ($S^\Delta$). We stop at red traffic lights and keep going through green ones. The dinner bell signals "come to dinner," and the alarm clock serves to "get us up in the morning." While we are walking down the street, a familiar face is the $S^D$ for saying "hello," and a stranger is the $S^\Delta$ for saying nothing.

Occasionally our discriminations fail to operate, either because they have not been well established (still too much generalization) or because other stimuli interfere. We may call "Mary" by the name "Ethel." A child may call his mother "daddy." It is possible that generalization is still operating because of similar properties of both stimuli. Ethel is a girl and perhaps she looks like Mary, and "daddy" is also a parent, having many of the same stimulus functions as the child's mother.

The development of our verbal behavior follows the same process. Who knows what initial stimulus first caused the infant to say "da"; perhaps it was internal and was just one of a variety of vocalizations we refer to as babbling. But when the response was emitted, the occasion was just right; the father was present. He, in all likelihood, was anxious for his child to learn to talk and reinforced this response by strong affection or perhaps some primary reinforcement. Now the probability is greater that on similar occasions the presence of the father will bring out the response "da" or even "dada." This occurs more and more frequently. After a while we may become more selective in our reinforcement and will only reinforce "dada" so that eventually the response

[6] B. F. Skinner, *Science and human behavior* (New York: Macmillan, Inc., 1953), p. 100.

becomes "daddy." These external stimuli set the occasion for specific responses to occur in favor of others. The external stimuli operate as a further means of control over the behavior. The process comes about by manipulating the reinforcement in a special way through presenting it in the presence of the $S^D$ and withholding it in the presence of another stimulus $S^4$. Eventually the child learns that saying "daddy" is reinforced by only one stimulus—his father and not his mother, sister, or brother.

Discrimination is the basic process in learning a variety of other behaviors which go under the names of perception, thinking, problem solving, and imitation. In the process of perceiving our environment, for example, certain $S^D$'s serve as clues for our judgment of distance, like the *size* of the object. Large objects are judged to be closer (we get reinforced) and small objects are judged to be farther away. Interposition (one object placed in front of another) operates in the same way. The response of reaching is reinforced by receiving the closer object. Of course, since a number of $S^D$'s may operate in a given response, we may say that the discriminations are *compound*.

IMITATION, OR MODELING

What we call imitation operates on the same principle. Contrary to popular opinion, imitation is neither a natural nor an inherited capacity. *The behavior to be imitated* serves as the discriminative stimuli. We imitate a person looking up in the sky at an airplane because that behavior is somehow reinforced. Perhaps this was more common when airplanes were a novelty and not so frequently seen. Some form of excitement may have served as the reinforcing agent.

An interesting example that illustrates how the behavior of one organism serves as the $S^D$ for the responses of a second is described in a laboratory experiment by Miller and Dollard.[7] One rat, who acted as the leader, was taught to run down the stem of a T-maze and make a turn, either to the right or left, in the direction of a black card (see Figure 5–2). The positions of the black and white cards were reversed in a random order so that the $S^D$'s were these stimuli rather than some internal cues involved in making the turning response. Sometimes the black card was at the right, sometimes at the left. The black card operated as the $S^D$, since when the animal turned and ran toward that card, he was reinforced, whereas if he turned and ran to the white card $S\Delta$, he received nothing. After the first rat had learned this discrimination, another rat who had had no previous training was placed behind him. This follower was only reinforced if he turned in the direction of the

[7] N. E. Miller and J. Dollard, *Social learning and imitation* (New Haven: Yale University Press, 1941).

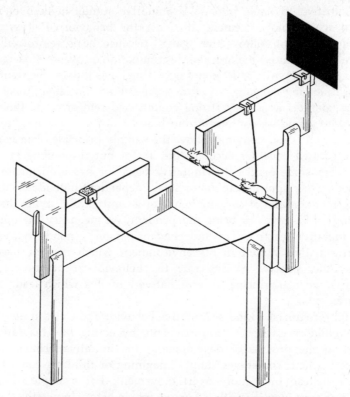

**Figure 5–2.** Apparatus for the study of imitative behavior in the rat. The food cup for the leader is located nearer the discriminative stimulus (black or white card). The food cup for the follower is located nearer the gap, which the rat is required to jump when he makes his choice. Each is covered by a hinged top that is removed at the time of reinforcement. (From N. E. Miller and J. Dollard, *Social Learning and Imitation*, New Haven: Yale University Press, 1949, p. 101.)

leader; if he turned in the opposite direction, he got no food. The follower was not dependent upon the cues received from the cards because his behavior persisted in the absence of any cards. The follower continued to respond to the leader as the $S^D$. Another interesting implication of this experiment is that the follower's behavior generalized to a variety of leaders. A well-trained follower would proceed after any number of leaders, all of whom had been trained in a manner described above.

This finding has implications for the variety of helpless followers among humans whose behavior has developed in such a way that the $S^D$'s operating in their lives become the behavior of others whom they imitate. Instead of using other discriminative stimuli in their environment to achieve reinforcement, they use the behavior of others. The juvenile delinquent follows the "gang" because he is reinforced with approval. Apparently, making the discrimination between what is right or wrong in his own conduct is not occurring, or if it does, the reinforcement of following the gang is a more powerful one. Social approval from a group operates as a very strong conditioned reinforcer. If this were not so, why would we conform as much as we do? Conformity, "following the crowd," and copying follow the sample principle. The gang or group or crowd behavior becomes the $S^D$ for our responding in a like manner. For some people this imitative behavior has unfortunate consequences. They appear helpless or solely dependent individuals. To get reinforcement, a kind of copying behavior is emitted. By saying that one is "acting on his own" or being independent, we mean just the opposite of this imitative reaction. This independent person responds to a variety of discriminative stimuli in his environment which may or may not involve other people. At any rate the behavior of others may not necessarily be the principal discriminative stimulus which leads to his reinforcements.

Freud recognized a kind of imitative behavior and called it *identification*. A child receives his reinforcements by acting like his father or mother. In the process of development, the imitative behavior often becomes implicit; sometimes simply imagining or thinking could be the response instead of a more overt movement. For example, the high school girl may identify with a famous movie actor. Implicitly she sees herself as his partner and confidante, sharing his success and prestige.

One of the variables affecting imitation is the consequence of the model's behavior. That is, if one sees another person positively reinforced for a given set of behavior, that behavior is then more likely to be imitated. Bandura et al.[8] have described some experiments with children in which the subjects were shown televised films where the models used for imitation exhibited both verbal and physical aggression. In one group the model's aggressive behavior is positively reinforced. In a second group it is punished, and in a third (control) group no particular consequences of the aggressive behavior are shown. Following these films the children were placed in a play situation and the degree of their aggression was rated (i.e., kicks Bobo doll, strikes it with a ball, shoots darts at plastic furry animals, etc.). Those children who had seen the model punished in the films showed significantly fewer imitative aggressive responses than those who had seen it positively reinforced, or the no-consequence condition. Later, when the children were offered incentives

[8] A. Bandura, D. Ross, and S. A. Ross, Vicarious reinforcement and imitative learning. In A. W. Statts, *Human learning* (Holt, Rinehart and Winston, 1964), 45–51.

for reproducing the model's behavior, all groups showed more imitative behavior than when no particular incentives were involved.

*Use of Modeling in Behavior Therapy.*   Bandura, Grusec, and Menlore[9] have applied modeling to reduce children's fears. They took a group of children who had extensive fears of dogs. After a jovial play-party session was well under way, a four-year-old boy entered the room leading a dog and performed prearranged interactions with the dog. The restraints of the dog in the play sessions were gradually lessened. As a result of this kind of modeling (watching another child play and interact with the dog without fear) the children's approach behavior toward both the experimental dog and another dog that was unfamiliar was greatly increased. Sixty-seven per cent of the children who were exposed to the modeling were eventually able to remain in the room with the dog without exhibiting fear.

O'Connor[10] used modeling to improve children's social behavior. In this study, teachers were asked to select a group of the most socially isolated children based on a variety of criteria that indicated a failure of interaction with other children. The children were shown a film which depicted other preschool children. The film depicted social interaction as being highly reinforcing, where the children smiled, played together, and gleefully tossed play equipment around the room. The children were then returned to their classroom, and their social interactions were again rated. A control group was also shown a film without social activity. This group had also previously been rated as being socially isolated. After the film the control group showed little change in their social behavior while the group that saw the social interaction film (referred to as symbolic modeling) increased their degree of social interaction to the level of those children who had previously been rated as nonsocially isolated.

## CONCEPTUALIZATION

Concept formation and problem solving are two processes involving generalization and discrimination. In the behavior of developing concepts (also called *thinking*), we are dealing with *classes* of objects as the stimuli. Take the class of objects called "tree"; this may include tall and short trees, oaks, maples, and elms as well as evergreens and deciduous trees. Since these objects share some properties in common, we discriminate them from other objects classed as "dogs," "houses," or

[9] A. Bandura, J. Grusec, and F. Menlore, Vicarious extinction of avoidance behavior, *Jour. Pers. and Soc. Psychol.*, **5** (1967), 16 ff.

[10] R. D. O'Connor, Modification of social withdrawal through symbolic modeling. *Jour. Appl. Behav. Anal.*, **2** (1969), 15–22.

"people." By conceptual behavior, or the forming of concepts, a class of objects brings out a discriminative response. We develop the concept by finding properties which these objects share. When classes of objects operate to bring out different responses, we distinguish between them. All this boils down to what we have already referred to as generalization and discrimination; "generalization within classes and discrimination between classes—this is the essence of concepts." [11] We generalize within the "dog" class of objects to include those of various shapes, sizes, colors, and so forth, but we discriminate them from the class of objects we call "horse," "tree," or "house." In the process of development, concept formation comes gradually. A child may call a cow by the name "horse." After all, they both have four legs and are frequently found in the pasture. As the discrimination becomes finer, the concepts are more clearly distinguished. Even as adults we make mistakes, just as the child did. Any experimental psychologist who is familiar with rats is amused when his friends who know little about the animal laboratory refer to his subjects as "mice." These people have generalized the two classes into one class, thus not having made the discrimination between classes that the psychologist makes. Throughout the process of education, new concepts are formed and sometimes the classes are rearranged in a variety of ways. How these principles are applied to the acquisition of concepts in humans, using operant techniques, is illustrated in an experiment by Green.[12] The development of a concept was controlled by fixed-ratio schedules of reinforcement and by the length of time the discriminative stimuli were presented to the subjects. The responses studied were those of tapping a telegraph key and verbalizing by the subject on what seemed to be the proper occasion for tapping the key. The proper occasions consisted of particular discriminative stimuli in the presence of which tapping the key resulted in reinforcement. The reinforcements consisted of crediting the subject with points on a counter for tapping in the presence of the appropriate stimulus patterns.

Subjects were reinforced for making the correct response according to three fixed-ratio schedules: 1:1, 15:1, and 30:1. The six discriminative stimuli patterns used could be made more or less alike by blacking in the same or different circles. The two stimulus classes, $S^D$ or $S^\Delta$ differed only in that the three top circles on the $S^D$ cards were always blocked in.

Response was characterized by very high rates under the fixed ratio, while extinction was characterized by rapid bursts, followed by intervals of no response. In the development of the concepts, responses in $S\Delta$ were more resistant to extinction in the higher ratios of reinforcement. This is generally true in extinction of the discrimination. Green concludes

[11] F. S. Keller and W. N. Schoenfeld, *Principles of psychology* (New York: Appleton-Century-Crofts, 1950), p. 155.

[12] E. J. Green, Concept formation: A problem in human operant conditioning, *Jour. Exp. Psychol.*, **49** (1955), 175–180.

that human operant behavior is controlled by the schedules of reinforcement in essentially the same ways as is the behavior of other species. The number of subjects who were able to verbalize the concept was related to the extent to which the key-tapping discrimination had been developed. The extent to which the discrimination was formed was inversely related to the ratio of the reinforcement used and was directly related to the time during which the discriminative stimuli were presented to the subjects (30 or 60 seconds).

Tests have been developed to measure the ability to make concepts. Although these can be used with normal people in examining the variety of possible concepts that can be developed, they are more frequently used as indicators of certain kinds of behavior disorders. It has been demonstrated that in certain classes of behavior disorder, the subjects either lack any ability to develop concepts or, having once possessed the behavior, it tends to break down. In one of the Goldstein-Sheerer tests[13] of concept formation, a variety of objects is presented to the subject. These consist of articles of tableware (spoons, knives, forks, saucer), food (crackers, sugar), children's toys, hand tools (hammer, nails), articles of msoking (pipes, cigars), and so forth. The articles are of various colors, sizes, shapes, and materials. The subject is given this mass of objects and asked to arrange them in groups. He may classify the objects by color, shape, use, or material. The more different kinds of classifications he can make, the greater his ability to form different concepts. This test is often used to discover behavior abnormalities. Often the test can discover mental deficiency, behavior disorganization, and some forms of brain damage. In these individuals the ability to develop concepts appears to be absent. In severe forms of mental deficiency the ability has never developed. Such subnormals are able only to deal with specific situations, and the capacity to generalize within a class is difficult or impossible. Likewise, in some behavior disorders the person loses this ability, a process previously acquired. The test does not tell us why the ability to form concepts is absent; it merely discovers the fact that the absence exists.

WHEN DISCRIMINATIONS BREAK DOWN

In the development of a discrimination through reinforcing when the $S^D$ is present, and extinguishing when the $S^\Delta$ appears, one reaches a point beyond which the discrimination cannot go. This occurs in both respondent and operant conditioning. In respondent conditioning, say, a dog is trained to salivate in the presence of a tone, whose frequency is 256 cps. After initial conditioning, the dog will salivate to a variety of

[13] K. Goldstein and M. Scheerer, Abstract and concrete behavior: An experimental study with special tests, *Psychol. Monogr.*, **53**, no. 2 (1941).

tones of different frequencies. By reinforcing only the response to the tone of 256 cps and never reinforcing responses to the other frequencies, a discrimination is built up. However, there are limits beyond which the discrimination cannot go; that is, when the $S^D$ and $S^\Delta$ are only a few cycles apart, the animal responds to both.

Pavlov discovered this in using a luminous circle as the $S^D$ and an ellipse as the $S^\Delta$.[14] The initial discrimination was easily formed. By a series of small steps he brought the ellipse nearer and nearer to the shape of the circle, reinforcing the presentation of the circle and never the elliptical shape. At one point the animal responded to the ellipse just as he did to the circle; that is, he salivated to both. At this point he had reached the *difference threshold*. Changes below this point could not be discriminated, but changes above it could. In these discrimination experiments, Pavlov went a step further. He had succeeded in developing a discrimination when the ratio of the axes of the two was 7:8. He then pressed the discrimination further and made the axes ratio 8:9, a point where the ellipse looked much like a circle. Here a peculiar thing happened in the behavior of the dog. The discrimination began to "break down." The animal salivated indiscriminately to either stimulus. Other responses were made; he salivated at the sight of the experimenter and the sight of the apparatus. He was no longer able to make the more gross discriminations he had made in the earlier part of the discriminative conditioning. A general disturbance in other behavior was noted. The dog whined, barked, tore at the harness, and tried to escape from the apparatus. Pavlov called this behavior "experimental neurosis," and we shall have a great deal more to say about it in Chapter 15, since the process has important implications for the development of human abnormalities. It is evident that when we are often pushed beyond our limits of ability, unfortunate behavior develops. A child, because of overaspiring parents, may be pushed too hard in his schoolwork and may become a behavior problem. At a given level in his development he is capable of making only a certain degree of discrimination. If pressed beyond that, trouble develops.

The same kind of discriminative conditioning can be demonstrated in operant behavior. A response is conditioned in the presence of some $S^D$. Generalization is eliminated through extinction in the presence of a series of other similar stimuli until a point is reached where the organism is no longer able to tell the difference between the $S^D$ and $S^\Delta$, as evidenced by his persistence in responding to both. If, besides reinforcing the $S^D$, the experimenter punishes the $S^\Delta$, the disruption is intensified. An experiment by Brown,[15] using rats as subjects, illustrates the point. Rats were

[14] I. P. Pavlov, *Conditioned reflexes*, trans. G. V. Anrep (London: Oxford University Press, 1927).

[15] J. S. Brown, Factors determining conflict reactions in different discriminations, *Jour. Exp. Psychol.*, **31** (1942), 272–292.

trained to discriminate between lights of two different degrees of brightness by approaching the brighter and retreating from the dimmer. When the difference in the intensities was very slight, the rats continued to be reinforced by food for the right response and punished by electric shock for the wrong response. The animals' behavior became extremely disruptive. They showed excitement, frequent urination and defecation, trembling, jumping, and even convulsive behavior. This kind of experimental investigation can give us a good deal of understanding about the precipitating causes of abnormal behavior in humans.

## Projective Tests and Discriminative Responding

In Chapter 1 we reviewed some of the widely used projective techniques. They purport to measure a variety of personality traits and in particular those personality variables which are not so outwardly apparent to the individual observer. A behavioral analysis of these devices tells us that the tests operate as discriminative stimuli for the emission of a large variety of verbal responses. They are devised in such a way as to act as occasions for the emission of certain verbal responses which would not otherwise be uttered. When stimuli such as ink blots, vague pictures, or words bring forth verbal responses which could not be identified beforehand, the process is called *probing*. (Skinner distinguishes the "probe" from a "prompt"; in the latter a called-for response is already known to the operator beforehand, as in theater prompting.) [16]

The process of probing is nicely demonstrated in Jung's *Word Association Test*.[17] A series of verbal stimuli is presented to the subject and he is asked to say "the first thing that comes to mind." Certain aspects of his verbal behavior are considered significant: the particular words emitted, whether they be common responses, unusual responses, or a repetition of the original word, and so forth. The test illustrates well the fact that verbal responses have multiple sources of strength which result from one's earlier verbal conditioning. If the subject "blocks" (cannot say anything quickly), it may be that conflicting responses are interfering with the emission; perhaps because that particular verbal behavior was punished in the past. The effects of this earlier punishment can also be seen in the flushing of the face and other respondents which are elicited when the verbal stimulus is presented. Jung interpreted these responses as "complex" indicators. Furthermore the response can be interpreted as typical or atypical of those in the verbal community of which the person is a member. (For example, most people respond with the word "black"

---

16 B. F. Skinner, *Verbal behavior* (New York: Appleton-Century-Crofts, 1957).
17 C. G. Jung, *Studies in word association* (London: Heinemann, 1918).

when the stimulus word "white" is presented.) However, since different subjects give different responses to the same verbal stimuli, these give indications of the differences in verbal-conditioning history or in the current circumstances. Again, unusual responses are considered indicative of possible personality problems.

Another example of the probe is found in Murray's *Thematic Apperception Test* (TAT).[18] A subject is asked to tell a story about a picture which is designed to be slightly "ambiguous," thus allowing for a wide variety of differences in individual responding. The test illustrates the probing of verbal responses through the presentation of inadequate discriminative stimuli. Along with the *Rorschach Technique* (ink blots), the *Thematic Apperception Test* also illustrates multiple causation in probing of verbal behavior. The effectiveness of the "ambiguous" $S^D$s in evoking verbal responses can be explained in terms of the numerous sources of strength of the verbal responses. A discovery of some of these sources is given as an indication of certain aspects (traits) of the personality. The problem of "need" as one source of strength of a discriminative response is illustrated in the next section.

### MOTIVATIONAL VARIABLES IN DISCRIMINATION

The projective tests often attempt to discover some of the "inner" variables in personality when the vague stimuli are presented and the subjects are asked to report what they "see." The *Thematic Apperception Test* attempts to analyze a subject's verbal responses to the pictures as discriminative stimuli in terms of his "needs," "conflicts," "emotions," and "presses" from the environment. If an independent variable such as deprivation and satiation (need) can be systematically manipulated and the effects on discriminative responding at the verbal level observed, some experimental verification of the rationale of such a projective technique can be made. In one study, Sanford[19] asked grade school children to make verbal associations to lists of words as well as to interpret 20 ambiguous pictures. When these stimuli were presented just before a meal, the children gave more food-related words than when tested just after eating. In a second experiment, Sanford[20] used college students as subjects. One group was tested after 24 hours of fasting and others were tested with lesser degrees of food deprivation. Again he found that the number of food-related words increased with the degree of food depriva-

---

[18] H. A. Murray, *Manual for thematic apperception test* (Cambridge, Mass.: Harvard University Press, 1943).

[19] R. N. Sanford, The effect of abstinence from food upon imaginal processes: A preliminary experiment, *Jour. Psychol.*, **2** (1936), 129–236.

[20] R. N. Sanford, The effect of abstinence from food upon imaginal processes: A further experiment, *Jour. Psychol.*, **3** (1937), 145–149.

tion. In a more recent study, McClelland and Atkinson[21] tested 130 candidates for submarine training, 1 to 2 hours, 4 to 5 hours, and 16 to 18 hours after eating. The subjects were asked to tell what "pictures" they saw being projected on a screen. Actually no pictures were shown at all, only a dim illumination. In three-quarters of the stimulus presentations, a choice among possible responses was required. In the remainder no "hints" were given. The frequency of the food-related responses was found to increase significantly with the number of hours of food deprivation. These results can be interpreted as a generalization of responding to stimuli which resembled the original $S^D$'s in the persons' early conditioning history under similar conditons of deprivation and satiation. Such a generalization is to be expected, since the present stimuli are not effective as immediate $S^D$'s in emitting conditioned verbal responses. Because of the ambiguity of the stimuli, the strength of the response becomes dependent on some other variable in the conditioning process; in this case, the degree of deprivation or satiation.

## Differentiation of Behavior (Shaping)

Out of a response to a variety of generalized stimuli, a discrimination to a specific stimulus is developed. In a discrimination the emphasis is placed on the stimulus side of the equation. In *differentiation* the emphasis for study is placed on the response side. In discrimination through selective reinforcement we eliminate the responses to other stimuli. In *differentiation*, through selective reinforcement of one of a number of related responses, we develop a very specific type of response in the presence of some stimulus. In order to understand the nature of differentiation of responses, we must first examine a very basic characteristic of behavior, its variability. Kantor observed many years ago that variability is one of the characteristics of psychological interactions which distinguishes them from other kinds of events.[22]

### VARIABILITY

When a response is repeated a number of times, it is not always made *in exactly the same manner*, even though the stimulus conditions between trials appear to be identical. In the simple bar-press response of the rat, a

[21] D. C. McClelland and J. W. Atkinson, The projective experience of needs: I. the effect of different intensities of hunger drive on perception, *Jour. Psychol.*, 25 (1948), 205–222.

[22] J. R. Kantor, *Principles of psychology*, vol. 1 (New York: Knopf, 1924).

variability from time to time is seen; this is particularly evident in the beginning of the conditioning process. The force exerted in order to press the bar varies, and ways in which the bar is approached are not always alike; sometimes the rat may approach it from above or from either side. Irrelevant movements occur, and the time taken to depress the bar differs on separate occasions. All these are variations of the basic bar-pressing response under our observation.

The same characteristic of variability exists also in human behavior. When a child learns to talk, he exhibits a variety of random vocalizations prior to the acquisition of *discrete* words. In learning specific motor tasks, we emit many excessive and unnecessary movements. Thorndike's cats showed a great deal of what he called "trial-and-error" activity in learning to open the door so that they could escape and get food. When we practice at a skill, variability is an obvious characteristic of the act. The golfer or tennis player is aware of this fact. Without variability the golf ball would always go straight as an arrow, assuming that weather conditions remained the same. The tennis ball would be placed precisely where it was intended. The shot for the basket or the kick for the extra point would never miss. Without variability the musician would never make a mistake, and the amateur carpenter never pound his thumb. Out of the mass of variability in a given kind of response, we apply the process of selective reinforcement, and differentiation then takes place.

### DIFFERENTIATION

Although complete stereotypy of behavior is never reached, differentiation reduces the variability of a given act, and consequently precise and more discrete responses are made. Were this not possible, skills could not be developed and organized modes of activity would fail to exist. Through differentiation, responses which did not ever exist in the initial behavioral repertoire of the organism studied can be made to come into existence and persist in great strength. Actually what is meant by teaching a skill, training a man for a job, or training an animal to do new tricks involves differentiation as the basic process.

The development of a differentiated response is easily illustrated in the basic experiment described by Ferster and Skinner for training a pigeon to peck a key placed on the side of its cage.[23] The pigeon is placed in the apparatus and allowed to move about and to become accustomed to it. In the beginning, the probability that the pigeon would peck at the key will be very small. The response of pecking at food, of course, is already in his behavioral repertoire. First of all, the experimenter will

---

[23] C. B. Ferster and B. F. Skinner, *Schedules of reinforcement* (New York: Appleton-Century-Crofts, 1957), pp. 31–32.

automatically control the presentation of food via a magazine. When feeding time is appropriate, a light flashes (and a buzzer sounds), the food tray is brought into view and is made accessible to the bird so that he may eat for a few seconds. This constitutes the training to receive reinforcement. Now, out of the variability of the movements around the cage, any responses made in the direction of the key and reinforcing food tray are reinforced. Soon the pigeon confines more and more of his activity to the tray side of the cage, thus reducing the initial variability. Later on, only the responses which bring the bird's head close to the key are reinforced. The next step reinforces only the response of moving the head toward the key. Eventually a peck occurs, and this, of course, is immediately reinforced. Soon only pecking action strong enough to record a response is reinforced. In this case the pigeon will have learned to respond in one section of the apparatus and will confine most of his activity to pecking. Through a series of *successive approximations* a response will have been shaped out or differentiated. Such a specific response will not have existed prior to experimentation but will have been made to occur and persist at a high rate through the appropriate manipulation of the reinforcements.

Many aspects of the response can become differentiated. In our example the *topography* of the response has been changed. A specific response to be conditioned is selected. Out of the variations in that response, changes are made in the direction toward which the experimenter is working. A new aspect of a new variation is then selected and reinforced until the final response is achieved.

This technique is basically the one used by animal trainers, whereby dogs can be taught to walk on their hind legs, jump through hoops, and shake hands. Pigeons can be taught to bowl and play ping-pong. Amazing results are achieved which never would have occurred without the application of the differentiation process. Suppose we want to train a pigeon to "play cards" or "play the piano." First of all, after the preliminary conditioning described above, we could place four cards of different suits—hearts, spades, diamonds, and clubs—on the side of the cage. Above them we would place a sample card, the same suit as one of the cards below. When the pigeon pecked at the sample, we would reinforce and uncover the other cards. When he pecked the right card, the one matching, we would reinforce and extinguish pecks to all other cards. Now we would change the sample card to another suit and progress in the same way. Eventually when the sample card appeared he would immediately peck below at the one that matched it. Pigeons can learn to play the piano by a similar method. Place a toy piano in front of him and reinforce any movements to the keys. Then build up a two-note sequence by failing to reinforce all sequences but the one desired. Other notes can be added until the pigeon is "playing a tune." Pigeons, dogs,

cats, and chickens have been taught four- or five-note melodies in this way. Difficulty beyond this point is both a function of the organism's capacity as well as the experimenter's.[24]
According to Keller and Schoenfeld:

> The technique is always the same. Some variant of an already conditioned response is selectively reinforced until it becomes more frequent than the others; when this is achieved, a variant of the new response is treated in the same way. Through a series of *successive approximations* to the desired reaction, the behavior is altered until it comes to bear little or no resemblance to the first conditioned form.[25]

The operation of differential reinforcement applies to all areas of human conduct. It accounts for how we acquire our most basic behavior of walking, talking, reading, and writing, as well as for the more complex skills in a man's job, his hobbies, and his sports activities. A few examples will suffice. Let us go back to the area of verbal behavior. An infant emits the word "ma" out of a variation in his babbling in the presence of his mother who reinforces him. The "ma" has variations that get differentially reinforced and may eventually become "mama." After a while we no longer tolerate this "baby talk" and only reinforce responses that resemble "mother." Other verbal behavior is acquired in a like manner. One of the reasons that "baby talk" frequently persists, long after the child has reached the developmental level where more mature vocal responses are possible, is because parents fail to reinforce differentially the "better" responses. Perhaps they can understand the child, even though few others are able to. When a child speaks in a manner that cannot be understood, these responses get extinguished in favor of the more easily perceived verbalizations. Baby talk may also persist because this form of vocalization is considered "cute" by some people, and hence the differential reinforcement is not applied.

Inadvertently, parents often differentially reinforce behavior which operates to the disadvantage of both parent and child. Suppose the child cries at night and the mother comes running. Because this crying behavior gets reinforced by the attention and affection of the parent, the initial cause of a "tummy ache" need not operate on later occasions. Soon the mother realizes the child is developing a "bad habit," so she resolves to let the child cry; but this response, having been reinforced in the past, is not going to die out immediately. In the variation, the child cries louder, and eventually the mother can no longer stand the screaming and she goes to comfort him. She is now differentially reinforcing

---

[24] B. F. Skinner, How to teach animals, *Scient. Amer.*, **185**, no. 6 (1951), 26–29.
[25] F. S. Keller and W. N. Schoenfeld, op. cit., p. 190.

the louder cries and screams. Child and clinical psychology case histories give ample evidence of the disastrous consequences of this kind of reinforcement. In one case known to the author, the crying became so intense that the neighbors threatened to call the police and have the family evicted from the neighborhood for disturbing the peace. Physicians examined the child and found nothing organically wrong. The simple solution was to extinguish the crying response. This was difficult in the beginning, but with perseverance the parents failed to "come running," and within two weeks the nightly disturbances had been eliminated.

Likewise, a child seeks parental attention by some irritating act. At first the parents fail to reinforce until they can no longer tolerate the "pesky" behavior. Eventually the child becomes more and more of a "pest," and the parents seek professional help, wondering why *their* child has developed such intolerable behavior.

Differentiation applies to the learning of many movements involved in industrial work, trade and professional skills, and artistic expression.[26] A successful coach or teacher applies the reinforcement at "just the right time," when the student or learner has made a particularly good response out of the variability of less successful efforts. Here, too, he uses the process of successive approximations, beginning by reinforcing only those movements that approach the desired end. As the student continues in his efforts, only those responses deemed superior are reinforced until finally a well-differentiated skilled movement is achieved. The process may be slow and may involve some backtracking. Sometimes the teacher or student is in too much of a hurry, and the right response occurs so infrequently that the whole process is extinguished. Then they must begin again to reinforce, using a more gradual set of approximations until the response is well established.

APPLICATION OF THE PRINCIPLES OF DIFFERENTIATION TO CORRECT
BEHAVIOR DISTURBANCES

Recently, psychologists have been concerned with the application of reinforcement principles in developing more appropriate behavior or altering inappropriate behavior. Research has been conducted with both children and adults. These are some applications to *behavior therapy,* which we shall discuss in more detail in Chapter 18. Through these techniques mute children have been made to speak, and people with very limited behavioral repertoires have become more useful citizens. Even mentally deficient children have been shaped into performing tasks never before thought possible of them. In this section we shall cite a few inter-

[26] B. F. Skinner, *Science and human behavior* (New York: Macmillan, Inc., 1953).

esting experimental examples to illustrate what can be done to alter or shape behavior. This is one area where the clinical and experimental psychologists are meeting on common ground.

*Shaping Cooperative Responses in Autistic Children.* Autistic children are frequently characterized by their inability to react appropriately to their environment. Sometimes they refuse to speak or communicate. Sometimes they are very aggressive and uncooperative. No one is really sure just how these inappropriate responses occur so early in life. Some would attribute the difficulty to hereditary factors, others prefer a more environmental explanation. Regardless of the cause, if shaping principles can be appropriately applied, something can be done to improve the child's condition.

Hingten et al.[27] used as their subjects six children with the diagnosis of childhood schizophrenia (often called autistic). These particular children were characterized as exhibiting little or no social interaction with each other or with others in their environment. They were trained to operate a lever on a schedule of FR 15 in order to receive tokens that later could be exchanged in a vending machine for candy, crackers, or cereal. They were then placed in a room in pairs, and the following sequence of responses was shaped out:

1. Both children in each pair were free to operate a coin lever at any time during the session.
2. In order to obtain coins, each child had to alternate with the other in using the coin lever.
3. In order to operate the coin lever, another lever had to be operated first. Again, each child was required to operate it alternately.
4. The first child was required to operate the new lever to enable the second child to operate the coin lever, and vice versa. The results indicated that it was possible to condition such cooperative (social) responses in these children within an average of 23 sessions. The subjects also appeared to make vocal and facial responses that appeared to be directed toward each other. By making a reinforcement, originally obtained in a nonsocial situation contingent on cooperative responses, the cooperative behavior was acquired.

In a second experiment Hingten and Frost[28] took four nonverbal schizophrenic children who had previously been observed to initiate little

[27] J. N. Hingten, B. J. Sanders, and M. K. DeMeyer, Shaping cooperative responses in early childhood schizophrenics, in L. P. Ullmann and L. Krasner, eds., *Case studies in behavior modification* (New York: Holt, Rinehart and Winston, 1965), 130–138.

[28] J. N. Hingten and F. C. Frost, Shaping cooperative responses in early childhood schizophrenics, II Reinforcement of mutual physical contact and vocal responses. In R. Ulrich, T. Stachnick, and J. Marby, eds., *Control of human behavior* (Glenview, Ill.: Scott, Foresman, 1966).

or no social interaction with other children. They were individually reinforced with M and M candies for making vocal responses in morning
sessions. In afternoon sessions they were paired and mutually reinforced
for making cooperative responses, defined as physical contact plus
vocalization. Because these responses had an operant level of nearly zero
at the beginning of the experiment, a good deal of shaping was necessary.
The procedure was as follows: First, reinforcement was contingent on a
physical contact, that is, the hand of either child touching the other child.
Then, reinforcement was only given when contact was accompanied by
some form of vocalization. In the next step reinforcement was given
when one subject touched the other with both hands accompanied by a
vocalization. Finally, both subjects were required to touch each other with
both hands and make vocal responses. The mutual physical contact was
shaped in 46 sessions, and vocal responses occurred in all but one subject.
The study demonstrates that schizophrenic children who previously
showed little or no physical interaction can be taught to cooperate if the
appropriate reinforcement contingencies are presented.

As we have already pointed out, autistic children have very limited
behavior repertoires, and appropriate responses to environmental stimuli
seldom occur. Ferster and DeMeyer[29] first selected a simple response to
study, such as pressing a key. They also designed an environment (see
Figure 5–3) for the children, which included a pinball machine, a picture
viewer, a pigeon and a monkey both trained only to perform when the
animal compartments were lighted, a television set, and an eight-column
vending machine that dispensed candy. Each of these devices could be
operated by a coin or a direct key. Each time the child pressed the key or
inserted a coin a reinforcing event followed. For example, the TV set
could turn on, or one of the animals would perform. The children were
deprived of all food between meals. During the first part of the study, the
experimenters observed the rate at which the children performed the
simple task which was followed by a reinforcement. Then further tasks
of a more complex nature were imposed. For example, (1) a child merely
had to press the key, then (2) coins were delivered only when the plastic
panel that delivered the coins was lighted (discrimination), and then (3)
coin insertions were reinforced only when the coin slot was lighted
(further discrimination). Coins were wasted if inserted when the panel
was unlighted. Consequently the children learned to save their coins
until the appropriate light was on. Still later a matching-to-sample device
was introduced (see Figure 5–3). This device operated in the following
way. If the child pressed the center panel, a figure matching it would
appear either to the right or left. When the child pressed that figure, a
coin was dispensed. Otherwise, the child received nothing. The study
demonstrates how complex behavior can be shaped of simple responses

[29] C. E. Ferster and M. K. DeMeyer, A method for the experimental analysis of
the behavior of autistic children, *Amer. Jour. Orthopsychiat.*, **32** (1962), 80–98.

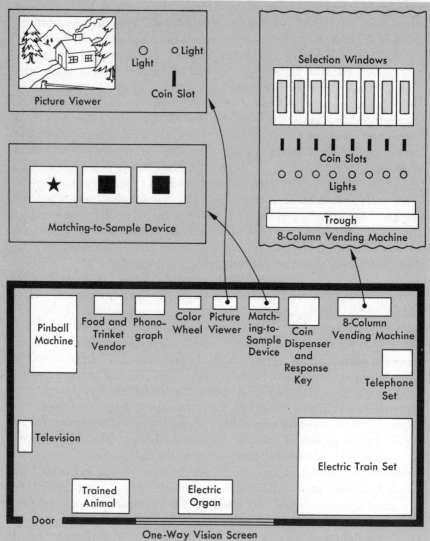

**Figure 5–3.** Schematic diagram of the experimental room. Each device had a coin slot, coin light, and light that was on whenever the device was operating. The detail of the picture viewer illustrates the typical arrangement. Also shown in detail are the matching-to-sample device and the coin slot, coin light arrangement on the 8-column vendor. (From C. E. Ferster and M. K. DeMeyer, A method for the experimental analysis of the behavior of autistic children, *American Journal of Orthopsychiatry*, **32** [1962], 89–98, p. 90. Copyright 1962, The American Orthopsychiatric Association, Inc. Reproduced by permission.)

in severely disturbed children. Consequently, if behavior can be so modified in the laboratory situation, why cannot the same occur in a real-life social situation?

*Shaping Response of "Wearing Glasses" in an Emotionally Disturbed Boy.* Wolf, Risley, and Mees[30] report an interesting case of shaping wearing glasses in a boy, Dicky, who manifested a variety of behavior problems early in life. Among other problems, he had developed cataracts in both eyes which necessitated operations and the subsequent wearing of glasses. At about this time severe temper tantrums appeared, along with sleeping problems. For about a year his parents had tried and failed in making him wear the glasses. The temper tantrums and sleeping problems were handled basically by extinction techniques, but the wearing of glasses was the most difficult problem to handle. At the beginning, several pairs of empty glass frames were placed around his room. When he picked one up, held it, or carried it about, he was reinforced with a bite of candy. By successive approximations he was reinforced for bringing the frames closer to his eyes. This gave way to considerable difficulty. Consequently a deprivation operation was introduced (see Chapter 8) by using bits of breakfast dependent on approximations to wearing glasses. Consequently, a "roll bar" was introduced on the back of the frames making them fit like a cap that would not slide off easily. Lenses were then introduced into the frames. Because eating was dependent on wearing glasses, Dicky was eventually wearing them during meals. Eventually more time was introduced, and at the time he was released from the hospital he was wearing the glasses approximately 12 hours a day.

One of the difficulties involved in this shaping behavior was that Dicky would take off the glasses and throw them on the floor. As this behavior worsened, the operation became moderately expensive because of breakage of the lenses. A technique to control this behavior was introduced. Following each glass throwing he was put in his room for 10 minutes. Throwing the glasses decreased to zero in five days.

*Shaping a Response in a Schizophrenic Woman with a Very Limited Behavior Repertoire.* Haughton and Ayllon[31] describe a 54-year-old schizophrenic woman who had been hospitalized for 23 years. Most of her time was spent either lying on a couch or in bed. She refused to do anything on the ward except smoke cigarettes. In order to develop some kind of behavior an arbitrary response was selected and cigarettes were

[30] M. Wolf, T. Risley, and H. Mees, Application of operant conditioning procedures to the behavior problems of an autistic child, *Behav. Res. Ther.*, **1** (1964), 305–312.

[31] E. Haughton and T. Ayllon, Production and elimination of symptomatic behavior. In L. P. Ullmann and L. Krasner, eds., *Case studies in behavior modification* (New York: Holt, Rinehart and Winston, 1965), pp. 94–98.

used as the reinforcement. The response selected for conditioning was holding a broom in an upright position. She was placed on her feet, given a broom by one of the staff attendants, while another approached and gave her a cigarette. Consequently, a conditioned reinforcer was given as a token if she responded properly by holding the broom in an upright position. The token could later be exchanged for a cigarette. At first when given the token she threw it away. Later she was asked if she had the token to exchange for a cigarette. As the response became conditioned, other patients tried to take the broom from her. The behavior of resisting was eventually maintained on a variable interval schedule of reinforcement. The length of the interval was gradually increased.

Her behavior was also observed by two psychiatrists who, not knowing the conditioning procedures, described the behavior in the following way:

> Her constant and compulsive pacing, holding a broom in the manner she does, could be seen as a ritualistic procedure, a magical action. Her broom would be then: (1) a child that gives her love and she gives him the return devotion, (2) a phallic symbol, (3) the sceptre of an omnipotent queen . . . this is a magical procedure in which the patient carries out her wishes, expressed in a way that is far beyond our solid rational and conventional way of thinking and acting. . . .[32]

What the psychiatrists did not know, of course, was that the symptoms had been developed through a simple conditioning procedure. The fact is, then, that many such abnormal symptoms are learned incidentally just as this was conditioned experimentally, and one does not need to appeal to magical or mystical principles in order to explain them.

*Shaping More Desirable Behavior in Delinquents.*   Schwitzgebel[33] had as his aim to get delinquent boys to put their feelings into words. The final goal or terminal behavior consisted in getting the boys to express their emotions verbally on a tape recorder. The following steps were taken:

1. Money and cigarettes were given as reinforcers for meeting the investigator at a street corner hangout.
2. Then he gave them money if they would take a trip with him on the subway.
3. Next, they had to meet him at a particular subway station acrosstown to get money.

---

[32] H. Ayllon, E. Haughton, and H. B. Hughes, Interpretation of symptoms: Fact or fiction, *Behav. Res. Ther.*, **3** (1965), 1–7 (p. 3).

[33] R. Schwitzgebel, *Street corner research* (Cambridge, Mass.: Harvard University Press, 1966).

4. Successively, he reinforced them for coming to his street corner office.
5. Saying anything into the tape recorder.
6. Talking about experiences and relationships, positive attachments and events emotionally important to them.

As a result of this street corner "research," the boys showed less delinquent behavior as contrasted to a control group that had not been so shaped.

IMPORTANCE OF IMMEDIACY IN REINFORCEMENT

The mark of the good coach or teacher lies in his ability to apply the reinforcement, often verbal, using such expressions as "good," "right," "fine," and so forth, at *just the right time.* By this we mean that the student is *immediately* reinforced after a better try occurs in the variability of efforts. The golf coach tells the learner, "good shot" on just that occasion when the ball has gone straight. In the beginning he may have had to reinforce even if the student barely hits the ball. After that, the poor shots are ignored and become extinguished while the better ones are strengthened. Of course other techniques may be involved in training the skill, but the one we are discussing is of greatest importance. The music teacher should say to his pupil "good" immediately after the passage has been played according to slightly better than usual standards. Then higher standards of performance can be set up until a finished and professional-type performance has been achieved.

Ferster[34] has demonstrated the importance of immediacy of reinforcement in conditioning birds. In his experiments pigeons were conditioned to peck a key on a VI schedule until a stable rate had been established as a base line for later comparisons. A 60-second delay was then introduced between the response and reinforcement. The effect was to reduce the previously acquired constant pecking rate to a value near zero in three out of his four birds.

At the human level, Greenspoon[35] has also demonstrated the importance of "immediacy" in conditioning behavior. He asked his subjects to draw a 3-inch straight line while they were blindfolded. The information (reinforcement) concerning their accuracy was delayed for 0 (immediate reinforcement), 10, 20, and 30 seconds after the response. Four different experimental groups were used and also a control group where no reinforcement was applied. His results showed that increasing the

[34] C. B. Ferster, Sustained behavior under delayed reinforcement, *Jour. Exp. Psychol.*, **45** (1953), 218–224.
[35] J. Greenspoon and S. Foreman, Effect of delay of knowledges of results on learning a motor task, *Jour. Exp. Psychol.*, **51** (1956), 226–228.

length of the delayed interval reduced the rate of proper learning. A delay of as long as 30 seconds, however, was found to be superior to no information (reinforcement) at all. As reinforcements he used verbal expressions of "long" if the line was too long, "short" if too short, or "right."

The following quotation made by the American patriot Benjamin Franklin many, many years ago illustrates very effectively the principle of immediate reinforcement:

> We had for our chaplain a zealous Presbyterian minister, Mr. Beatty, who complained to me that the men did not generally attend his prayers and exhortations. When they enlisted, they were promised besides pay and provisions, a gill of rum a day, which was punctually serv'd out to them, half in the morning, and the other half in the evening; and I observ'd that they were as punctual in attending to receive it; upon which I said to Mr. Beatty: "it is perhaps below the dignity of your profession to act as steward of the rum, but if you were to deal it out and only *just after prayers* [italics mine] you would have them all about you!" He liked the tho't, undertook the office, and, with the help of a few hands to measure out the liquor, executed it to satisfaction, and never were prayers more generally and more punctually attended: so that I thought this matter preferable to the punishment inflicted by some military laws for non-attendance on divine service.[36]

*Practical Applications of Shaping.*   We should realize that in the learning of skills in sports and the arts, it is not the mere act of practice which explains the improvement. Thorndike abandoned his earlier "law of frequency" long ago. So often, of course, we have the impression that "practice makes perfect." This impression is superficial and quite correct. All that practice does is to allow for variations to occur in an already existing response which can be differently reinforced. The fact that "something else" besides mere practice is operating in the learning process can be seen in the behavior of many performers and sportsmen who never get any better despite long hours of repeated effort. Some golfers play year after year without any noticeable improvement. The reinforcements they receive may come from the sunshine or fresh air, but these only reinforce "getting out on the links." If one does not improve, it is evident that he alone cannot apply the reinforcements appropriately to improve his game. He would, therefore, do well to engage some coach or teacher who can apply the proper principles.

Of course we often improve "with practice" by ourselves because the reinforcements are generated by some aspect of the activity itself or the external environment, exclusive of other persons. We "know" when the ball goes straight, and we can see the pins go down when we make a

---

[36] B. Franklin, Operant reinforcement of prayer, *Jour. Appl. Behav. Anal.*, **2** (1969), 247. (Quotation cited by B. F. Skinner.)

bowling strike. There is also a conditioned reinforcement in the "feel" of the shot. Good form can be reinforced by the feedback from one's own body movements. In music and art there is also the sensory feedback from seeing the painting or hearing the music. The significance of sensory feedback can easily be demonstrated by observing the behavior of the infant who reacts to the crumbling of newspapers, rattles, or tinklebells, all of which generate amusing and often violent behavior.

The effectiveness of the differential reinforcement is also a function of the discriminative capacity of the one who delivers the reinforcement, whether it be another person or the learner himself. A poor teacher or coach who cannot tell the difference between a good and bad performance can hardly be expected to apply the appropriate reinforcements to the student to such a degree that he will have discriminative capacity to "tell himself" when he plays well or badly. If one can "feel" the right shot or "hear" when the music is played correctly, he is in a position to improve by reinforcing himself. Part of the job of the teacher, of course, is to develop those discriminations in the student which he can apply in the teacher's absence.

Our discussion has been largely limited so far to examples where the differentiation has been applied to the *topography* or *shape* of the response. However, it can also be applied to changes in *rate, time,* or *force* of the response. We have already discussed the application of differentiation to the *rate* of responding in that exceptionally high rates can be established by applying a reinforcement at that point when the responding happens to be especially rapid. Once this new rate is established, a higher rate can be developed until the limits of the organism have been reached. In team sports the crowd yells loudest (most reinforcing) when the play is rapid and many points are scored.

The *force* or *magnitude* of the response also can be selectively reinforced. By gradually adding weights to the bar which the rat has been conditioned to press, a force equivalent to half his body weight can be achieved. Again when the football team fights harder, the crowd cheers louder and the touchdown is made.

Finally the *time* taken to make a response, called *response latency,* can be reduced (or lengthened) through selective reinforcement. If we do not catch the ball or if we duck when it comes our way, we miss or get hit. The improvement in "reaction time" is accountable by this process. A rat can be made to reduce the time from "light on" ($5''$) to response by gradually reducing the time period allowed, only reinforcing those responses which come faster and faster. We make a discrimination when we stop at a traffic light. Differentiation is also involved here; if we do not stop in time, we may be hit by the cars coming from the other direction. After a few accidents, perhaps the slow driver will find his reaction time reduced. In many sports like swimming or track a quick start gives the participant an added advantage. If he wins, this fast start has been selectively reinforced, for the slower starts get extinguished. In all activities involving the reduction of time through selective reinforcement, it should be understood that there is a limit in the organism's capacity. Furthermore, individual differences between people exist just as they do in the matter of reaching the discriminative capacity. Some people are considered "naturally" slower. However, this fact does not negate the principle that time for responding can be drastically reduced if the proper selective reinforcements are applied.

*Fading.* Fading is a procedure whereby behavior that occurs in one situation is made to occur in a second situation by gradually changing the stimuli in the first situation into the second.

In the first situation we may presume that the stimulus conditions that maintain the behavior are relatively strong. Gradually, desired stimulus changes are introduced. Old stimuli may be faded out and new stimuli faded in. Eventually the behavior specified will come under the control of a new or partially new set of discriminative stimuli.

Bentley[37] describes the case of a child who played with his toys at home in his playroom. The playing behavior was at high strength, since the toys acted as positive reinforcers. However, the child was afraid of bath water and showed strong avoidance reactions to it. In the fading procedure the toys were taken into the bathroom where he was allowed to play with them. Next, he was shown the empty bathtub, then a sink filled with water, and so forth, until the behavior of taking a bath was established and the toys gradually removed.

In one of the earliest studies on behavior modification, Jones[38] used basically a fading procedure. Her subject, a boy named Peter, had a strong fear of furry animals and similar furry objects. First the child was seated in a chair and fed a cookie, which was positively reinforcing. Then she introduced a rabbit at a considerable distance from the child and then gradually brought it closer and closer until the boy could touch it without evoking the fearful behavior, which included crying. The cookie was faded out and the furry animal faded in.

Thus in differentiation or shaping of behavior, successive approximations on the response side are developed and the behavior is modified. In fading, the successive approximations are applied on the stimulus side.

### DIFFERENTIATION AND DISCRIMINATION

The two processes of differentiation and discrimination operate simultaneously in our personality development. Very early in life a differentiated response becomes related to a discriminated stimulus. The

[37] P. M. Bentley, An infant's phobia treated with reciprocal inhibition therapy, *Jour. Child Psychol.*, **2** (1962), 185–189.

[38] M. C. Jones, A laboratory study of fear: The case of Peter, *Pedagogical Seminary*, **31** (1954), 308–315.

child says "daddy" in the presence of a specific person—his father, not his mother. And he makes the differentiated response of saying "daddy," not "gaga," because he has learned that this is the one that pays off. In driving an automobile, we differentiate pressing the brake, turning the wheel, or other coordinated activity. We have already made the discriminative responses to the traffic signals of red or green. The baseball player discriminates the actions of his team from those of his opponents. The actions of hitting, running, and catching involve highly differentiated responses. Sometimes one process may be more important in a given act or antecedent to the other. When playing cards, a variety of discriminations is made in distinguishing each card. Concepts are formed in generalizing the cards of one suit and discriminating between the suits, hearts, clubs, spades, and diamonds. When the cards are dealt "face down," this discrimination is intentionally made impossible. If the cards are marked, of course another kind of discrimination is made. A clever player may try to discriminate the facial expressions of his opponents (hence the "poker face" to prevent this). In the play of the cards, differentiation takes precedence. (We deal the cards face down, not up.) In athletic skills differentiation probably is more significant, although simpler discriminations are also involved in telling one player from another, finding where the ball is, and so forth.

In learning to read, discrimination has priority, and in learning to write, differentiation is preeminent. However, children are taught to discriminate words and letters before they can make the differentiated response of writing them. Thus the process of education involves the continuous operation of making differentiated and discriminative responses.

The uniqueness of each of our personalities is understood by looking into how each of these processes has operated in our life histories. The mental defect for reasons of either biological limitation or inadequate stimulation and reinforcement lacks the capacity to make very fine discriminations and finely differentiated responses. The juvenile delinquent, through a peculiar reinforcement history, makes discriminations regarding which acts to perform and which ones not to make; usually these discriminations are not in accordance with the ones commonly made by society. Children who are pressed beyond their discriminative ability, perhaps because of overly ambitious parents, develop "neurotic behavior" that is the outcome of too intensive attempts to teach discriminations. Of course, in so-called maladjusted people, other variables are likewise important. They may involve a variety of aversive stimuli, which will be discussed in Chapters 10 and 11. The person with "tact" has developed a highly discriminative ability in knowing just what to say at the right time to the appropriate people, whereas the person who continually puts his "foot in his mouth," simply cannot discriminate the proper occasions to make a particular differentiated response.

# 6  Conditioned Reinforcement

A NEUTRAL STIMULUS, BY REPEATED associations with one that is primarily reinforcing, can acquire a reinforcing function by itself. Such stimuli we call *conditioned* or *secondary* reinforcers, and we designate them by a symbol $S^r$ to distinguish it from the primary *reinforcer* $S^R$. Thus, the simplest paradigm to illustrate the secondary reinforcement and its relationship to the response it is conditioning would be:

$$R \xrightarrow{\hspace{4cm}} S^r$$

(Response)                    (Conditioned reinforcer)

Once established, these stimuli also possess the capacity to increase and maintain behavior in a manner like those of the primary reinforcers. However, unlike the primary reinforcers, which continue to operate as long as the organism is appropriately deprived, the conditioned reinforcing function *may* extinguish after a time if it is not further reinforced by association with the primary stimulus. Nevertheless the conditioned reinforcer is capable of operating to condition behavior in its own right. But in order for this neutral stimulus to acquire the function of a reinforcer, it must have had some previous history of association with the primary reinforcer.

Much of our human behavior is maintained in great strength by conditioned reinforcers. Consider the worker who is never given a word of praise or approval from his employer and hence extinguishes at his job; he has become discouraged and quits. Because of the absence of the necessary conditioned reinforcers, the behavior fails to be maintained. Of course one could argue that the man is being *paid for his work* (money is also a conditioned reinforcer). The intimate association of money to the primary reinforcer (money buys food) ought to be enough to maintain the behavior. The fact that the man has become extinguished at his work probably means that the pay either comes too infrequently or in too small amounts. Fortunately there are many important rewards in one's work besides the pay itself. A variety of conditioned reinforcers operate which may include encouragement and mutual verbal reinforcement from one's fellow workers, appreciation from those for whom we work, interest in our jobs, and the social reinforcement derived from being part of a working group. What this all boils down to is that there is a multitude of secondary or conditioned reinforcers that operate to maintain our behavior. To say that morale is good means that the behavior of the members of the group is being mutually reinforced by conditioned stimuli. Because of the powerful control that can be gained by applying these conditioned reinforcers, one often wonders why so many people in authority and in a position of control fail to use them to maintain good morale and efficient working behavior. Apparently, for some people, the presentation of conditioned reinforcers is aversive to themselves. They may be embarrassed to give compliments or hate to say "thank you" or find it difficult to recognize another's work.

To understand precisely how conditioned reinforcing functions are acquired and how they operate in our lives, we shall turn to the experimental laboratory and the studies with lower organisms. After we have examined the basic principles involved in conditioned reinforcers, we shall apply them to human personality.

The process whereby a neutral stimulus can take on the function of a secondary reinforcer ($S^r$) was simply demonstrated in an early experiment by Skinner.[1] The first step in developing an $S^r$ is for the stimulus to take on the function of a *discriminative stimulus*. Skinner trained his rats to approach a tray for a pellet of food when a sound was made from the discharging food magazine. Eventually, as soon as the click of the magazine was sounded, the rats approached the tray and ate the food. Once this rather simple discriminative behavior had been acquired, a bar was introduced into the cage as a novel stimulus. When the rat pressed the bar, a click was sounded, but no food was presented. As a result the rate of bar pressing *went up* and was maintained for a time, even though prior to the experiment no association had been made between

[1] B. F. Skinner, *The behavior of organisms* (New York: Appleton-Century, 1938), chapter vi.

the bar-press response and food. The click alone, which had previously served as a discriminative stimulus ($S^D$) to approach the tray and secure food, now became a conditioned reinforcer for a new response, the bar press. The experiment also demonstrated another characteristic of the $S^r$, that is, the capacity to generalize to other responses once it has been established. We note that in the original conditioning of tray approach, the "click" served as a discriminative stimulus for approaching and eating. In the later test, a new response was introduced, one that had had no previous association with the food. Once the response occurred, it became strengthened by the mere sound of the click following the pressing of the bar.

The first principle is clear: for a stimulus to operate a secondary reinforcer, it must have been first established as an $S^D$ for some response that had been primarily reinforced. Once this has been attained, the stimulus can then act as an $S^r$ to maintain other behavior having no previous history with the primary reinforcement.

The association of the neutral stimulus and the primary reinforcing stimulus must be of a particular sort; that is, it must *precede* the response as a discriminative stimulus. A study of Schoenfeld, Antonitis, and Bersh[2] illustrate the fact that other contingencies will not work. In their experiment, two groups of rats were conditioned to press a bar, using primary reinforcement of food. In their experimental group, a light was correlated with the reinforcement when the animal seized and ate the food; the light followed eating by approximately 1 second. The control group was conditioned in the same way except that the light was absent during conditioning. Following conditioning, both groups were extinguished 1 hour each day for four days. Results showed *no* significant differences in the extinction rates of either group. It is clear that the light did *not* act as a secondary reinforcer for the experimental group. If it had, the rate of bar pressing should have exceeded that of the control group conditioned without it. A mere correlation of the neutral stimulus and primary reinforcement is not enough to establish it as a conditioned reinforcer. For the neutral stimulus to operate as a secondary reinforcer, a temporal priority must be involved. It must precede the response and act as a discriminative stimulus in the initial conditioning.

We have established so far:

1. That a stimulus must acquire the status of a discriminative one first if it is to operate as a conditioned reinforcer later.
2. Once the $S^r$ function is established, it can act to reinforce other behaviors not previously associated with the primary reinforcement. It has a generality of function. This principle is of great importance in under-

[2] W. N. Shoenfeld, J. J. Antonitis, and P. J. Bersh, A preliminary study of learning conditions necessary for secondary reinforcement, *Jour. Exp. Psychol.*, **40** (1950), 40–45.

standing how conditioned reinforcers operate as they do in the development of human behaviors.

There are also a number of other variables of which the strength of the conditioned reinforcer is a function.

3. The strength of the conditioned reinforcer depends on the number of times it has been paired (as an $S^D$) with a primary reinforcer. Bersh[3] paired light with dropping of food into a tray, using different numbers of pairings with various groups of rats. He found that when the light was tested as an $S^r$, it served to maintain stronger behavior when the original conditioning had been greater. This finding has also been recently substantiated by Hall,[4] using a different type of apparatus. He placed a black-and-white goal box at each end of a T-maze as the secondary reinforcing stimulus. The animals had previously learned to receive food in either one of the boxes, white or black. He found that the strength of the secondary reinforcing stimuli, as measured by the number of times the rats would run to the white or black box in the absence of food, increased proportionately to the number of times it had been previously associated with the primary reinforcer of food.

4. The amount of primary reinforcement paired with the secondary reinforcers will determine the later strength of the $S^r$. D'Amato[5] used two conditions of primary reinforcement, called *high* and *low reward*. Rats were given 70 trials on a straight alley runway. Half the trials were reinforced with five pellets of food (high reward) when they reached the end of the runway and the goal box, while the other half of trials received one pellet (low reward) in a discriminatively different goal box. In the test sessions, a T-maze was used with no primary reinforcement. Only the goal boxes of the high and low reward were at either end of the maze. The preference for the high reward was extremely significant, even though no primary reinforcement was given at the time. He concludes that when one secondary reinforcer is pitted against another secondary reinforcer, the amount of previous association with primary reinforcement is important in determining the strength of the secondary reinforcer.

Butter and Thomas[6] measured the amount of primary reinforcement, using various concentrations of sucrose solution in water (8 and 24 per cent). Two groups of rats were trained to approach a dipper on presentation of a magazine click ($S^D$). Rats were tested by bar pressing

[3] P. J. Bersh, The influence of two variables upon the establishment of a secondary reinforcer of operant responses, *Jour. Exp. Psychol.*, **41** (1951), 62–73.

[4] J. F. Hall, Studies in secondary reinforcement, I. Secondary reinforcement as a function of the frequency of primary reinforcement, *Jour. Comp. Physiol. Psychol.*, **44** (1951), 246–251.

[5] M. R. D'Amato, Secondary reinforcement and magnitude of primary reinforcement, *Jour. Comp. Physiol. Psychol.*, **48** (1955), 378–380.

[6] C. M. Butter and D. R. Thomas, Secondary reinforcement as a function of the amount of primary reinforcement, *Jour. Comp. Physiol. Psychol.*, **51** (1958), 346–348.

to receive the click as an $S^r$, an experimental situation similar to that described at the beginning of this chapter. The 24 per cent group exceeded the 8 per cent group in speed of approach training and amount of later bar pressing. Both experimental groups pressed the bar significantly more often to get the click than did a control group which had received no sucrose solution in the training period.

5. We have already demonstrated that an $S^r$ will function to reinforce responses different from those operating during the original training. The same generality of function also operates under what are called *different drive* conditions (see Chapter 7). A neutral stimulus that becomes an $S^D$ correlated with one set of conditions (food reinforcement presented to food-deprived animals) will act as an $S^r$ when the deprivation is shifted to another drive (water deprivation and water reinforcement). Earlier studies have demonstrated that rats preferred the side of a T-maze in which food and water appeared, although they had been satiated with both at the time of testing, indicating that the sight of food or water has some $S^r$ function.[7] Furthermore, rats ran faster on a straightaway to an end box that contained food than they did to one that was empty, even though the animals had been satiated with food.[8]

More recently D'Amato[9] gave rats practice in running a straightaway, first depriving them of water and using water as the reinforcing stimulus. The goal box was painted dark gray, and a white card operated as the $S^D$. When tested in a T-maze after water deprivation, the subjects showed strong preference for the side of the T-maze in which the former goal box was located. In a second part of the experiment the reverse operations were presented, using only the secondary reinforcer. The secondary reinforcing functions of the goal boxes were equally effective in both situations.

Similar results have been described by Estes,[10] using the bar press as the response studied. He trained rats by water deprivation and an accompanying sound stimulus to press the bar. When reinforced by the stimulus under conditions of food deprivation, he concluded that the secondary reinforcer can be effective even though the original drive has been satiated, provided another one (in this case, water deprivation) was present in order to initiate activity.

6. A conditioned reinforcer will act as a more powerful reinforcer if it is applied on a schedule of partial reinforcement than if applied on a

[7] K. MacCorquodale and P. Meehl, "Cognitive" learning in the absence of competition of incentives, *Jour. Comp. Physiol. Psychol.*, 42 (1949), 383–390.

[8] P. Meehl and K. MacCorquodale, Drive conditioning as a function in latent learning, *Jour. Exp. Psychol.*, 45 (1953), 20–24.

[9] M. R. D'Amato, Training of secondary reinforcement across the hunger and thirst drives, *Jour. Exp. Psychol.*, 49 (1955), 352–355.

[10] W. K. Estes, A study of motivating conditions necessary for secondary reinforcement, *Jour. Exp. Psychol.*, 39 (1949), 306–310.

schedule of regular or continuous reinforcement. That is, its function will extinguish more slowly when applied on a schedule and consequently will maintain longer. Kelleher[11], working with pigeons, used the click of a food magazine as the $S^D$ for approaching the tray and eating grain. When the click was well established as an $S^D$ for approaching and eating, it was later used as an $S^r$ to reinforce key pecking on FI, FR, and drl schedules. He reports that the birds generated patterns of response similar to those of pigeons who were conditioned on the same schedules using primary reinforcement.

APPLICATION OF THE PRINCIPLES OF CONDITIONAL REINFORCEMENT

We have demonstrated through the use of laboratory experiments with animals how a stimulus can take on the function of a secondary reinforcer, as well as some of the variables of which the $S^r$ is a function. Since the vast amount of human behavior is developed and maintained through the operation of conditioned reinforcers, we shall devote the remainder of this chapter to them.

## Generalized Reinforcers

In our animal experiments we noted that when a particular stimulus is conditioned to one kind of response, it can also operate to reinforce other behaviors as well. Many of us have a certain similarity in our conditioning histories; we share a vast similarity of cultural stimuli, being brought up in a particular country where the inhabitants share certain codes of conduct, attitudes, and social customs. The reinforcers also have a commonness of function. They are generalized in two ways. Once established under one behavior, they reinforce other behaviors. They are also generalized in the sense that they are shared by many people. Knowing the exact number of these generalized reinforcers is of no great importance. Different terms are often used to describe them. As a point of departure, however, let us examine five kinds of generalized reinforcers suggested by Skinner.[12] They include: *attention, approval, affection, submission of others,* and *tokens.* For most people, these are positive reinforcers of behavior and in all probability account for a great deal of the reinforcement that keeps us going. In discussing them, we should keep in mind that as humans and primarily social individuals, the reinforcement function that comes from at least the first four involves

[11] R. Kelleher, Schedules of conditioned reinforcement during experimental extinction, *Jour. Exp. Anal. Behav.*, 4 (1961), 1–5.

[12] B. F. Skinner, *Science and human behavior* (New York: Macmillan, Inc., 1953), p. 78.

the behavior of other people. The reinforcing stimulus, then, *is* some aspect of the behavior of another person.

ATTENTION

The precise nature of attention differs both according to the response and the reinforcement. In reinforcing the behavior of someone else it can be applied by a mere glance, a wave of the hand, snap of the fingers, a verbal response such as "look here" or "hey you," or the calling of one by his name. At any rate the characteristics of the stimulus involve little more than setting the occasion for some activity. It may be difficult to state precisely where attention as a reinforcer ends off and approval begins. In earlier psychologies the "need for attention" was frequently understood as a basic drive in man, something no one could do without. In the framework of a more behavioristic psychology, attention simply refers to some response of a second person which acts as a reinforcing stimulus for the behavior of the first person.

Often attention is simply a condition prior to other reinforcements. For a person to receive a variety of other reinforcements, a recognition of his presence in a given place is necessary. Because it leads to the possibility of further and more powerful reinforcements, attention itself becomes powerful. Attention as a reinforcer involves little more than recognition, although in certain cases, such as "the attention-getting behaviors" of children and some adults, it can become a complex kind of reinforcement.

The operation of attention as a reinforcer begins early in life: the cry of the baby is reinforced by the mother's coming and picking him up. If this act is too strongly reinforced, the infant may grow up to become a "cry baby." Children often make noises, ask foolish questions, or interrupt as means of attracting attention. We are familiar with the child who "refuses to eat" simply to get attention. Here the secondary reinforcer is more powerful than the primary one of food. Sometimes deliberate disobedience is involved, and even though it will be punished, it persists. The child so deprived behaves in a way that will secure the reinforcement, despite its aversive consequences. The attention of the parents is more powerful than the aversive punishment.

The inventory of behaviors that are resorted to by the child in order to receive attention is a long one: complaining, crying, thumb-sucking, bed wetting. The problem in these situations is that the normal behavior of the child in his efforts at work and play may go unattended because of too busy or ignoring parents. The reinforcing function of attention has already been acquired in the child's early life, and consequently he may resort to a variety of unfortunate behaviors which will assure his receiving it. If he were given adequate attention reinforcements from his regular efforts in the course of his work and play, there should be no reason to resort to these devious techniques. Behavior that seeks this kind of attention reinforcement is often carried on into the years beyond childhood. The adolescent asks irrelevant questions, interrupts, or seeks a variety of ways to be unusual. He acts "cute," shows off, boasts, teases, talks roughly and obscenely, or becomes deliberately disobedient. Of course, if not excessive, all these can be considered part of normal growing up. When they become the dominant reactions in a personality to achieve reinforcement, difficulty arises. As a correction to these "attention-getting" reactions, other responses more socially acceptable must be reinforced. The person can be given special duties whose performance will achieve the sought-for reinforcement. So frequently, when children resort to the less acceptable and irritating behaviors that demand attention from others, it is because the more acceptable responses, normally rewarded, go unreinforced.

Behavior that requires attention as reinforcement sometimes becomes so excessive that we call it *abnormal*. It dominates the personality and becomes inappropriate to the situation. Frequently these exaggerated reactions develop in people who have been neglected or have received decidedly less attention than that they observe given to others. Because the usual responses to accomplishment which ordinarily call out attention are lacking, they resort to more distorted activities. The person whom we often call *egocentric*, or self-centered, is merely one whose every act demands a regular reinforcement. In their past histories such persons may have been strongly reinforced either wittingly or unwittingly by people about them. Maybe their parents thought they were terribly "cute," so "cute" behavior was strengthened.

In the most exaggerated forms, behaviors that require strong amounts of attention are found in behavior disorders. We have all encountered the complaining hypochondriac whose endless list of complaints and symptoms have been reinforced by the listening behavior of his friends and physicians. One of the most effective ways of eliminating these complaints is by extinction through failing to listen or through ignoring them. Of course, if one gives in or differentially reinforces their complaining, the symptoms become worse. One of the reasons much of the unfortunate behavior of this sort develops and persists is because the listener is required to hear and attend. Had these people received reinforcements of more appropriate behavior in their developmental years, these extreme behaviors might not have been resorted to. The failure to give proper attention as reinforcement is not meant to be given as an explanation for all behavior disorders, as indeed it is not. It is simply mentioned here as one kind of condition where the possibility exists.

What Alfred Adler[13] called the *character trait of vanity* is closely related to our description. In the development of a neurotic personality,

[13] A. Adler, *Understanding human nature* (New York: Greenberg, 1927).

he observed that the person exhibited excessive demands for recognition. He was intensely preoccupied with what other people were thinking of him and with the impression he was making on others. In athletics he "plays to the grandstand." In social gatherings, he must be the center of all conversation. For others to receive attention is an insult to his vain personality. Adler felt that this behavior had its origin in deep-seated feelings of weakness and inferiority. Although modern psychology no longer uses such terms as "inferiority complexes," as Adler did, an interpretation of Adler's ideas is possible. The "vanity syndrome" really means that an individual is resorting to numerous devices that will assure him attention as reinforcement. The reasons are to be found in his history of deprivation and failure to receive attention reinforcements for more appropriate behavior.

*The Use of Attention in Conditioning and Extinguishing Human Behavior.* Harris et al.[14] attempted to use attention as a reinforcer to develop walking behavior in a nursery school child three and one-half years old who had recently regressed to a more primitive crawling response. The child's typical pattern of behavior was to crawl to her locker area and leave her clothes. Then she would crawl to some out-of-the-way place and sit crouched. She would crawl to the bathroom, raise herself to the sink, rinse her hands, and crawl to groups of children gathered for small snacks. The usual friendly approaches of her teachers toward her resulted in strong withdrawal behavior. By the end of the second week in nursery school she was avoiding all contacts with children or adults and avoiding the use of playschool materials and equipment. It was estimated that 75 per cent of her time (exclusive of times when everyone was seated) was spent in an off-feet position. First it was decided to withhold any attention as reinforcement when she was in this position (except for normal sitting activities). Furthermore, teachers were not to show anger, disgust, or distaste for this activity. Concurrently, on-feet behavior was immediately and positively reinforced. She was to be given attention whenever she displayed standing behavior. During the initial days, behavior approximating standing had to be reinforced because she stood so infrequently. To be sure that the reinforcement was immediate, one teacher was always within range of her. Student observers kept a record of the time she was on and off her feet. One week from the beginning of the reinforcement procedures she was on her feet a large proportion of the time. By the end of the second week, her behavior was indistinguishable from the other children in the nursery school. She talked readily,

---

[14] F. R. Harris, M. K. Johnson, C. S. Kelley, and M. M. Wolf, Effects of positive social reinforcement on regressed crawling of a nursery school child, *Jour. Educ. Psychol.*, **55** (1964), 35–41.

smiled, used all the outdoor equipment. However, she was not making direct social responses to the other children. Much of her play was of the parallel nature (playing in proximity to other children without interaction).

In order to be sure the reinforcement was the significant variable, it was decided to reinstate the off-feet behavior and then once again establish the on-feet behavior. The procedure was to extinguish on-feet behavior by withholding reinforcement and then give continuous attention when she was off her feet. Accordingly, the off-feet behavior reached a frequency of about 80 per cent of the time spent in school. However, a reversal to on-feet activities was not difficult to recondition. By the end of the first week of reconditioning she was showing behavior that was normal of the group. In addition she was imitating other children and accepting social contacts with all the adult staff as well as several children in the group. The authors comment that within a five-week period the child's behavior showed a degree of progress that would have been expected within not less than five or six months under previous guidance techniques.

Allen et al.[15] report the case of a preschool child, Ann, who responded favorably to adult attention but seldom interacted with other children in her nursery school. She was spending increasing time just standing and looking. Frequently, she would make a "make-believe" bed out of a packing box and would retire to it in the play yard in order to "sleep." A plan was instituted which made adult attention contingent on play with another child. Teachers were physically present as usual, but the only change was the condition under which Ann might receive attention. Two independent observers recorded her behavior. For five days the baseline data were obtained (number of interactions with other children). In the beginning of conditioning, any behavior that approximated a social interaction was reinforced by adult attention—for example, standing near another child, playing beside another child, or in the sandbox or at a table. As soon as Ann interacted with another child, an adult immediately gave her attention.

The results indicated that at the time the baseline data were taken, Ann was spending about 10 per cent of her time interacting with other children, and 40 per cent with adults. During the rest of the time she was solitary. By the end of the sixth day of reinforcement, she was spending 60 per cent of her time in active play with other children, and the percentage of her adult interactions had dropped to 20 per cent. The experimental procedure was then reversed, and Ann quickly reverted to

[15] K. E. Allen, B. M. Hart, J. S. Buell, F. R. Harris, and M. M. Wolf, Effects of social reinforcement on isolate behavior of a nursery school child, *Child Dev.*, **35** (1964), 511–518.

her old ways. The procedure was again reversed and Ann's percentage of time spent with other children again rose to 60 per cent. Other improvements in her behavior occurred, which seemed to be the by-products of this conditioning procedure. For example, her speech improved and complaints about imaginary bumps on her head were eliminated entirely.

*Conditioning and Extinction of Crying Responses Using Attention as Reinforcement.* In all probability children who become "cry babies" do so out of the inadvertent attention given by overprotective parents or other adults. In order to understand how this may come about, a distinction between respondent and operant crying should be made. Hart et al.[16] have pointed out that respondent crying in children occurs in response to a sudden, unexpected, or painful stimulus—for example, being hit by a large child, falling and hurting, or being caught in playground equipment. Operant crying, on the other hand, is emitted and maintained by the reinforcement contingencies presented—for example, when an adult

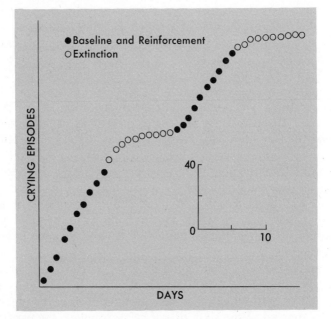

**Figure 6–1.** Conditioning and extinction records of operant crying in a preschool boy, named Bill. The conditioning periods are shown in dark circles, extinction in the open circles. (From B. M. Hart, E. K. Allen, J. S. Buell, F. R. Harris and M. M. Wolf, Effects of social reinforcement on operant crying, *Journal of Experimental Child Psychology* [1964], 145–153.

16 B. M. Hart, K. E. Allen, J. S. Buell, F. R. Harris, and M. M. Wolf, Effects of social reinforcement on operant crying, *Jour. Exp. Child Psychol.*, **1** (1964), 145–153.

fails to attend to a child's needs immediately, or when a child calls for help and mother fails to come right away. Crying that originated as respondent behavior can, of course, easily become operant.

To test whether or not operant crying could be made to come under the appropriate reinforcement contingencies such as attention, Hart et al.[17] selected two preschool boys from the Laboratory Preschool at the University of Washington because of their high rates of operant crying. In both cases the rate of crying was recorded by a teacher who kept a pocket counter. She depressed the lever for each crying episode. A cry was defined as one which could be heard for at least 50 feet and lasted five seconds or longer. For the first two days the rate of crying was recorded in order to get a baseline rate. Under this condition the crying usually lasted until the teacher came over and attended to the child. Extinction procedures were then introduced. Each time a child cried, the teachers ignored him. They were instructed not to approach the child, not to speak or look at him except for an initial glance in order to assess the situation. If he cried in proximity to the teacher, she was to turn her back and walk away. If, on the other hand, the child responded in a more appropriate way after a fall, scrape, or push, the teacher gave her attention and approved. At the beginning of the experiment (baseline rate) one child, Bill, was crying at the rate of 5 to 10 times every morning at school (see Figure 6–1). Within five days after the beginning of extinction procedures, his rate decreased to between zero and two episodes per morning. However, when the adult attention was again given to all operant cries, their approximation to the baseline rate was soon reinstated (second part of the graph). After four days, extinction was again reestablished. The study indicates that the rate of operant crying may be largely a function of adult attention procedures.

*Negative Attention as a Reinforcer.* Our everyday observations tell us that children (and adults) will behave in such a manner, particularly if they are generally ignored or socially isolated, to gain attention even though that attention may take the form of disapproval or sometimes even punishment. Sometimes children act as "brats" because that is the only way they can draw attention to themselves.

Experimentally Gallimore, Tharp and Kent[18] have demonstrated that children will respond to mild disapproval ("You're wrong") more frequently in a situation of social isolation than to no attention at all. The children participated in a game that involved matching in which face-to-face contact with the experimenter and mild disapproval were contingent on pressing a button that had little likelihood of "being right." The

---

[17] Ibid.

[18] R. Gallimore, R. Tharp, and B. Kemp, Positively reinforcing function of "negative attention," *Jour. Exp. Child Psychol.*, **8** (1969), 140–146.

children who had first been subjected to a period of social isolation prior to the experiment made more responses than the controls who had been "socially satiated" by warm attention from the experimenters. The positively reinforcing function was illustrated in one case where the experimenter neglected to open the panel and offer the negative comment, "You're wrong." The subject immediately asked, "Aren't you going to tell me I'm wrong?"

ACQUISITION OF ATTENTION AS AN S$^r$

We are all aware of the fact that no one has any inherent "need for attention." If our animal studies are correct, for attention to operate as a secondary reinforcer at the human level, it must have been previously conditioned as a $S^D$ under conditions where some behavior was primarily reinforced. This is exactly the case in the acquisition of attention. Take, for example, the crying of a baby which receives attention, to see how the process came about. Crying is about the earliest response to appear in our behavioral repertoires. The initial stimulus may be pain or discomfort from some internal or external condition such as the absence of food in the stomach, cramps in the bowels, or possibly the point of a diaper pin. As a result, vigorous activity is emitted, accompanied by the vocalizations. Crying brings the parent immediately, who attends the child, corrects the situation by removing the painful stimulus, gives the child the bottle, burps him, or removes the pin, thus providing some reinforcement. The adult's attentive behavior becomes the discriminative stimulus and the reinforcement is primary. The attentive behavior of the adult is the added stimulus to the occasion. Once acquired through early conditioning, attention on the part of our parents and other adults can later operate as a secondary reinforcer for a great variety of activities which may have no connection with the original conditioning situation.

APPROVAL

Often attention alone is not enough. To maintain behavior, approval is necessary. This takes the form of many gestures and verbal responses such as "good," "fine," "that's right," "good job," or any other form of commendation. Approval may involve some kind of public recognition, placing one's name on the honor roll or the "dean's list," indicating approval by the university of the work we have accomplished. Often what we call *praise* from our teachers, bosses, or elders amounts to simple approval.

In our American culture the approval of others is highly significant. Through differentiation we exhibit behavior that meets with approval by words, gestures, or facial expressions, rather than favor other kinds of activity that would go unapproved. The early behavior of the infant is "shaped out" through the selective application of approval. When the child drinks all his milk or walks across the room without falling on his face, approving smiles and words are presented by the adoring parents. Much behavior considered socially appropriate is strengthened and maintained by the approval of others. We frequently speak of "social acceptability," indicating that a person engages in behavior that meets with the approval of the group. In order to get the approval he must engage in this behavior to the exclusion of others. Because these reinforcers are often applied by a group instead of a single person, they are all the more powerful. The child learns to do the right thing because he is more likely to gain approval. Because the conditioned reinforcer may be weak in its early development, such approving reinforcements may have to be accompanied by more primary ones, such as a candy bar or a piece of chewing gum.

Our clinical observations give evidence that individuals who are not able to behave in ways that will meet with approval of others are often likely to find recourse to activity that will secure alternate reinforcements. They may become withdrawn or solitary because the reinforcements for "social behavior" have not been forthcoming, and therefore that behavior becomes extinguished.

Even though adult behavior is maintained by approval, sometimes we do not care to admit or verbalize it. The connections between the specific behaviors and the reinforcements given are often quite subtle and frequently operate without the person's being able to recognize such a connection. We attend church regularly if it is the approved thing to do. We accept social engagements because some form of approval is forthcoming. We dress in the prescribed manner because it is approved, and we drive those kinds of automobiles that are approved by our neighbors. Twenty years ago, a man's social status was somewhat determined by the kind of automobile he drove. Since the more expensive cars tended to gain more approval, they were bought exclusively by those who could afford them. Today an interesting cultural change has taken place; frequently the smaller foreign cars meet with more approval than the large expensive ones; in fact in some communities, to drive a big expensive car is considered ostentatious and meets with reactions quite in reverse of approval.

The college coed, or almost any female for that matter, may preen before the mirror for long periods, hoping to get the approving glance of her escort. Fads and fashions are subject to approval, and change as the functions of the reinforcement can change. They persist only as long as the approval is forthcoming and vanish as it is withdrawn. College men try out for sports or enter into extracurricular activities that meet with approval. To do what is the fashion, what is in vogue, and what the particular community thinks is "right" are all directed toward the same generalized reinforcer. Students study to the degree that such behavior is the approved thing to do; if they happen to belong to a group where studying is not too fashionable (a condition that unfortunately exists on some campuses), the students just manage to get by or do their work behind closed doors so as not to be discovered by their disapproving friends.

In the field of education, approval usually operates as a positive reinforcer. Through the selective administration of words like "good," "right," "correct," proper responses are learned and shaped out and irrelevant ones extinguished. The teacher reinforces the child when he does his arithmetic correctly. In this way the child learns much of his primary education. As he grows older, more complicated generalized reinforcers come into operation in the form of high marks, diplomas, high honors, and election to exclusive societies such as Phi Beta Kappa (see also the subsequent section, "Tokens").

*The Use of "Social Reinforcers" to Condition Behavior in Infants.*  The term *social reinforcer* is commonly applied to refer to any reinforcer that involves the behavior of another person. When our verbal behavior reinforces each other we can interpret the reinforcement as being social. Generally speaking, these social reinforcers fall into the group we are discussing as generalized reinforcers. They could involve attention, approval, affection, or the submission of others. We have already seen how attention can alter the behavior of preschool children either by presenting or withholding it.

An experiment by Rheingold, Gewitz, and Ross[19] shows how the social reinforcement, interpreted as the attention and possibly approval of an adult, can condition vocalization in young babies. Their subjects were 21 normal, healthy infants, 3 months of age, living in an institution. During the baseline days the experimenter leaned over the infants with an expressionless face and the number of vocalizations was counted. During the next two days, the experimenter responded to the infants' vocalization by smiling, clicking, or touching the infant's abdomen. In the following two days (extinction) the experimenters returned to the baseline conditions. Conditioning raised the number of vocalizations above the baseline rate. The average number at the start of the experiment was 13 to 14 vocalizations in a three-minute period. During conditioning the rate rose to an average of 18, indicating an increase of 39 per cent on the first day. On the second day of conditioning the average number rose to 25, a further increase of 34 per cent. Extinction reduced the number on the first day to 17 and to 15 on the second day, this latter figure approximating very closely the baseline rate. These results suggest that a social reinforcer can be effective as early as three months of age in

[19] H. L. Rheingold, J. L. Gewitz, and H. W. Ross, Social conditioning of vocalizations in the infant, *Jour. Comp. Physiol., Psychol.*, **52** (1959), 68–73.

modifying the responses of infants. Similar results also with three-month-old infants have been reported by Weisberg[20] when the social reinforcement consisted of leaning over, touching the infant's chin, smiling, and "talking" to him.

AFFECTION

Skinner suggests that of the three reinforcers mentioned so far, affection is the strongest. Here the connection with the primary rein-forcer is most obvious. In infancy the child received affection from his mother when some aversive stimulus was removed, a diaper changed, or an irritation relieved. In the early feeding stage, the child psychologists suggest we apply vast amounts of affection in the forms of cuddling, hugging, kissing, and embracing so as to "give the infant a feeling of security or of belonging." What they really mean is that such an affec-tionate response frequently facilitates the feeding process and becomes $S^D$'s for the responses of feeding and its primary reinforcement. Later on, such affectionate responses can operate as secondary reinforcers in their own right.

*Development of Affection as an $S^r$.* The secondary reinforcement of affection is derived from a variety of primary reinforcers in infancy and childhood other than those of feeding. The infant begins his postnatal life lacking any kind of social behavior. Because of his biological immaturity the few responses he exhibits are adequately reinforced. He is held, handled, carried, diapered, covered, and uncovered by his mother according to the particular primary reinforcement, either positive or negative, that happens to be operating. His mother becomes a dis-criminative stimulus, and her responses serve to relieve the uncomfort-able stimuli or terminate deprivation and become intimately related to the primary reinforcements. With maturation he develops more organized behaviors, and these patterns become more specifically related to the reinforcements. He is picked up and held when he falls down, is com-forted when he cries, is cleaned when he gets dirty, given food when hungry, all of which are behaviors developing in a close interaction between mother and child. As he gains control over his environment, the effective behavior of others begins to operate. The reinforcing func-tions of his mother's behavior becomes more generalized to include other people—father, brothers, sisters, relatives, friends, and teachers.

Likewise, other behaviors involved get reinforced. The friendships at childhood are mutually reinforced by supplementing each other. Close friendships of adolescence introduce new elements of affection reinforce-

[20] P. Weisberg, Social and nonsocial conditioning of infant vocalizations, *Child Dev.*, **34** (1963), 377–388.

ment between members of the same sex and pave the way for the operation of affection reinforcements exchanged between members of the
opposite sex. So intense a reinforcer is affection that the behavior we
call *crushes* often develops. The entire personality is directed toward the
giving and receiving affectionate reinforcements from a specific person.
By this time the reinforcements become intimately related to sexual
reinforcement, and the individual matures biologically to the point where
sexual stimulation has a stronger primary reinforcing function. Of course
the sexual reinforcements do not begin at adolescence. Erogenous zones
of the mouth and genitalia have been frequently stimulated through
affectionate contact in earlier years. Freud was aware of the significance
of these zones in infancy and childhood, and Kinsey[21] has demonstrated
that a variety of sexual outlets are operating long before a person reaches
puberty, masturbation being the most common one in the adolescent
years. In maturity, sexual outlets are preceded by a variety of affectionate
responses.

*Unfortunate Consequences in Affection as Reinforcement.*   When affection is withheld, alternate behaviors may be resorted to. We speak of the
unloved child, the lonely old maid, and the jilted lover. Like attention and
approval, when the common responses that have achieved the reinforcement of affection earlier are no longer capable of receiving it, behaviors
may be substituted that attempt to gain some other form of reinforcement. Levy[22] has carefully studied the problem of withholding affection
from children. In his study of abandoned and orphaned children and
children reared by indifferent nurses and governesses, he observed that
when children who previously had affection and were later denied it,
they would try to maneuver affection by pleading or exhibiting helpless
reactions. The "kissing bug" reaction exhibits such a demand for affection reinforcement. These children may also become whiners, naggers, or
complainers.

We have learned that the most stable behavior is maintained by some
form of intermittent reinforcement. Frequently parents overdo the
application of attention and affection to the extent that the children are
described as overprotected. Overprotection can take many forms. Levy[23]
describes the outstanding characteristics of this kind of behavior on the
part of the parents:

1. Excessive contact between mother and child, much fondling, kissing,
   hugging, holding of hands, keeping child in sight.

---

[21] A. C. Kinsey, W. B. Pomeroy and C. E. Martin, *Sexual behavior in the human
male* (Philadelphia: Blakiston, 1948).

[22] D. M. Levy, Primary affect hunger, *Amer. Jour. Psychiat.*, **94** (1937), 643–652.

[23] D. M. Levy, *Maternal overprotection* (New York: Columbia University Press,
1943).

2. Prolonged infantile care, weaning occurs long after the usual time, child is bathed, dressed, fed long after the average mother has given up these activities.

As a result of the excessive use of this kind of reinforcement, the child continues his infantile behavior (Why not? It is adequately reinforced!) He is described as dependent, selfish, and demanding. His frustration tolerance is low (because of too much regular reinforcement), so that when the affection is withheld, the child shows temper and regression. He has difficulty in adjusting to new situations, wants things his own way, and is restless under discipline.

SUBMISSION OF OTHERS

In older psychologies, one used to hear of the "need for power." As a matter of fact, psychoanalyst Alfred Adler postulated the need for power, later reduced it to the need for *superiority*, and still later translated it to *social interest* as the basic driving force in man. What Adler recognized, but put into rather mentalistic terms, was that the behavior of submission is a powerful reinforcer for the person to whom one submits. Sometimes we speak of the need to dominate, control, or overcome. The same operation is taking place here. Those individuals who apparently have strong "needs" to dominate or gain power have been brought up where the reinforcement contingencies were such that their behavior *achieved* submission from other people.

Giving in to the bully's demands serves to increase the probability of his bullying again. Through coercion of other people, the acquiescence of the subservient takes on a conditioned reinforcing function. Showing signs of defence to our superiors reinforces them. We are told that if we "give in," those to whom we have acquiesced will like us better. Behavior of cowardice implies acquiescence. To "butter up" somebody (your boss) involves submission as a secondary reinforcer because in telling him how great he is (also some approval maybe) or in expressing praise in more subtle phrasing, one implies that he, the giver of the reinforcer, is *not* so good and hence submissive. When we speak of prestige, we may mean nothing more than the application of attention and submission to a variety of behaviors emitted by those who "have the prestige." Those who rule or dominate require acquiescence as a reinforcement. The parent is reinforced often by the helplessness of his children. We learn that the "only way to get along with some people is to give in to them." We train our offsprings to be polite because politeness toward elders can serve as a powerful reinforcer.

By the proper and selective administration of submission, we in turn may be reinforced in other ways. The child who gives in to his parents' demands is saved the aversive stimuli of their punishment or is presented with the primary reinforcement of candy for "being good" and polite. We soon learn the value of submission in gaining the other reinforcements from those to whom we have acquiesced. In "being nice" to our boss, we may in turn be reinforced with a salary raise or at least relieved of the aversive effects of his tirades or nasty disposition. When the matter of control is not immediately within our reach, to acquiesce may be the most discreet move.

Some people whose behavior has been generously reinforced by submission find giving this reinforcement on their part very aversive. The person who dominates and is reinforced by submission, finds it hard to submit. The boss who is used to receiving deference from his workers does not like to be "told off." Those people who are commonly reinforced by submission find such behavior aversive and the antithesis of what they are used to receiving. "To eat crow" ordinarily implies that the individual "in the driver's seat" is put in the opposite position. He is used to being the boss, but suddenly the tables are turned, at least temporarily. There is the danger of retribution from the superior, but for the subservient, to have "the shoe on the other foot" is a mighty powerful reinforcer.

Much of the behavior of people in so-called "important positions" is maintained because of the reinforcement they receive from the submission of others. Were it not, they would soon leave their positions as president of the college, the company, chairman of the board, or head of the department because of the aversive aspects of these jobs.

Skinner suggests that the physical dimensions of acquiescence are not so subtle as those in attention, approval, and affection.

> It is difficult to define, observe, and measure attention, approval, and affection. They are not things but the aspect of the behavior of others. Their subtle physical dimensions present difficulties not only for the scientist who must study them, but also for the individual who is reinforced by them. If we do not easily see that someone is paying attention or that he approves or is affectionate, our behavior will not be consistently reinforced.[24]

However, in acquiescence the dictator may demand the specific signs of his power. The practices of respect and deference (that is, bowing, saluting, kneeling, and the like) are clear-cut. An apology is not easily misunderstood, and "buttering up" is only too clear to those who don't happen to be doing the buttering.

The kind of behavior described as submission was recognized earlier in Freud's concepts of the ego and superego. As the superego operated in its control, it demanded submission on the part of the ego. It was

---

[24] B. F. Skinner, *Science and human behavior* (New York: Macmillan, Inc., 1953) p. 79.

endowed with the power to destroy. The perfectionism demanded by the superego could only be achieved by the ego in the application of power. Karen Horney, a neo-Freudian, frequently found the "need for power" in neurotics and calls it a "neurotic need.[25] Such a need, she felt, had its genesis in the early insecurity of the child. It operated as a protective device against the basic anxiety felt by everyone because we are all born into a hostile world. The truth or falsity of such a hypothesis is difficult to test. We shall have more to say about these problems in Chapter 14. At this point a simpler and more empirical explanation is possible. Those who exhibit the so-called need for power are exhibiting behavior in great strength which achieves a degree of submission from some others. Because it has achieved reinforcement in the past, it is maintained. The contingencies are such that the behavior gets submission from others. So long as that behavior is reinforced, it will persist.

The effectiveness of submission as a reinforcer is seen in competition. If competitive behavior is successful in a society, it is reinforced accordingly by the submission of the loser. In sports the team or individual is reinforced for his winning by the submission of the other. Our economic system thrives on competition, and the behavior is maintained as long as the person who sells is reinforced by the submission of those who do not get the order. In societies where competition is less effective, the reinforcement of submission fails to operate as strongly as it does in our culture. Likewise in a competitive society, the importance of submission is seen in the behavior of those people who are considered ambitious. The more their behavior is reinforced, the more ambitious they become. We admire ambition to the degree that we accept submission as a reinforcing agent. When the behavior reaches such strength that we describe the individual as autocratic, overly dominant, or exploitative of others, the reinforcer has become too powerful, and the consequent behavior becomes exaggerated and approaches the abnormal.

## THE PREMACK PRINCIPLE

Premack[26] has outlined a procedure of reinforcement which involves behavior itself as a reinforcer. This has become known as the *Premack principle* and operates as follows: If the emission of one response is more probable than another response, the more probable response should reinforce it. Putting it another way, given two behaviors such as playing and eating spinach, the more probable one of playing can be used to reinforce the less probable one of eating spinach. Thus, the frequency of eating spinach can be increased if the opportunity to play is contingent

[25] K. Horney, *Self analysis* (New York: Norton, 1932).

[26] D. Premack, Reinforcement theory. In D. Levine, ed., *Nebraska symposium on motivation* (Lincoln: University of Nebraska Press, 1965).

on the eating. This principle has been applied to a number of different situations that require a person to emit some given behavior in order to have the opportunity to engage in another behavior.

Another example might involve a mental patient who does not carry out his work assignments but who frequently likes to converse with a nurse. The work assignments could be improved by making conversing with the nurse contingent on fulfilling the assignments.[27]

The application of the Premack principle allows one to select reinforcers that are appropriate for each individual. In a mental hospital not all patients are equally reinforced by candy, cigarettes, or an opportunity to watch TV. Others would prefer to mix with the opposite sex, and visit museums outside the institution. One way to find out what is reinforcing to a person is to observe the activities he prefers to engage in. Then these preferred activities can be linked to build up the less frequent behavior which still will be reinforcing to the individual.

The Premack principle has been applied to the control of classroom behavior of nursery school children. Highly probable behavior—such as running around the room, kicking a waste basket or screaming—has been made contingent on less probable behavior—such as sitting quietly in a chair. Applying the principle, Homme[28] found the less probable behavior to increase.

## TOKENS

A fifth class of conditioned reinforcers, which can be distinguished by their physical dimensions, is that of tokens. In Chapter 3 we mentioned money as a common conditioned reinforcer. Because it can be exchanged for so many primary reinforcers, its function seldom dies out. The connection between the behavior emitted and the reinforcing stimulus is quite evident. Ordinarily we can verbalize the relationship. For instance, certain work performed gets paid off by money; hard work receives its reward but loafing does not. The strength of the secondary reinforcer also has its dimensions. Five dollars has a stronger reinforcing function, ordinarily, than one dollar. In our feeding experiments with the lower forms, we noted that the strength of the behavior varies with the amount of reinforcement, either primary or secondary. Similarly, the worker becomes discouraged and quits if the pay is too small, since the amount of the reinforcement is not adequate to maintain it. On the other hand, a good salary is capable of maintaining behavior at a high rate.

Similar relationships between tokens as conditioned reinforcers and

[27] R. P. Liberman, A guide to behavior analysis and therapy (New York: Pergamon Press, 1972).

[28] L. E. Homme, Contingency theory and contingency management, *Psychol. Rec.*, **16** (1966), 233–241.

some form of primary reinforcement have been demonstrated in a number of experiments using apes as subjects. Perhaps two of the most relevant have been reported by Wolfe[29] and Cowles.[30] In one of these experiments chimpanzees were trained to insert discs into a vending machine that dispensed the primary reinforcement of grapes. The discs became the $S^D$'s for the response leading to the primary reinforcement of food. Later the animals learned to operate other machines like slot machines, merely to receive the tokens (discs) as their reinforcement. These could be saved up and at some later date exchanged for the primary reinforcement. The discs were given reinforcement values according to how many grapes they could be exchanged for. Blue chips could secure two grapes; white chips, one grape; and brass chips, nothing. They soon learned to cast aside the brass discs in favor of the others and to work best for the preferred blue chips.

In a later experiment, chimps were taught to operate a vending machine, called a *chimp-o-mat*, to secure a raisin. The fact that the chimps could save up their chips is illustrated by the observation that in later tests where the animals worked for chips alone, they would save up to 20 chips before exchanging them for the primary reinforcement. If the chimps were given the chips prior to the experiment, they would fail to work. For example, one subject who ordinarily would save up to 20 chips in a single work period was given 30 chips before beginning the experiment. In the experiment situation that followed, he would work for only 3 chips. This kind of behavior has its counterpart in humans. Some people quit work after they have saved up enough money to last for a while. The amount they will save depends on their previous conditioning history, or as is often said, depends on their personalities. The so-called shiftless may work for a short time only, perhaps until payday, and then quit to return to work only when their money is used up. Others work for many years until they have acquired savings large enough to allow them to "retire." Like the chimp who was given the tokens before working, we know of people who, through private endowments, quit work as soon as they receive their inheritance; others of inherited wealth never work at all.

Exactly how money acquires its conditioned reinforcing function is easily seen in the behavior of the preschool child. Ordinarily the child's first contact with money is as some "shiny stuff" which has only slight reinforcing powers in whatever sensory feedback the child gets from seeing and feeling it. At some point in his development he learns that this "stuff" can be exchanged for a candy bar, a piece of gum, or an all-day

[29] J. B. Wolfe, Effectiveness of token rewards for chimpanzees, *Comp. Psychol. Monogr.*, **12**, no. 5 (1936).
[30] J. T. Cowles, Food-tokens as incentives for learning in chimpanzees, *Comp. Psychol. Monogr.*, **14**, no. 5 (1937).

sucker. From this point it takes on the function of a discriminative stimulus, and the transition is simple to its later use as reinforcement for other activities. Also in his development the child learns the discriminations between penny, nickle, and dime. As secondary reinforcers these operate with different magnitudes for later behavior.

Although important, money is not the only token operating in our lives. The list is endless. Prizes, medals, blue ribbons, awards, and certificates of accomplishment, all act to reinforce specific behaviors. The field of education has appealed to the use of tokens in great variety to maintain behavior from the primary grades through college. Children receive gold stars for doing good work, older students work for marks, grades, and diplomas. Scholarship prizes in the form of medals, books, or money are also important. The granting of an advanced degree is a powerful secondary reinforcer. Doctors and professional people display certificates of their accomplishment in their offices for all to see.

*Use of Tokens to Condition More Appropriate Behavior in Disturbed Human Subjects.* One of the advantages of tokens as conditioned reinforcers is that they can be used to bridge the gap when there is a delay between the response being conditioned and the eventual, most desired reinforcer. In the previous chapter we cited a number of studies on shaping or differentiating more acceptable behavior using tokens that could later be exchanged for other reinforcers. Hingten, Bandura, and DeMeyer[31] taught autistic children to operate a lever for tokens that could later be exchanged for candy, crackers, or cereal. Ferster and DeMeyer[32] selected a simple response and gradually shaped more complex behavior that could be reinforced by tokens and exchanged for a great variety of reinforcers.

An interesting study reported by Ayllon and Azrin[33] involved nonresponding psychotic patients in which patients had to perform a variety of responses for tokens that could later be exchanged for privileges in the course of their everyday activities. Table 1 shows the different opportunities not ordinarily available to the patients and the number of tokens required for the patient to engage in these reinforcing activities. The first experiment consisted in having patients work in offward duties for tokens. In the extinction phase, the patients were told that working in these jobs could no longer pay tokens. Results showed that under the

[31] J. N. Hingten, B. J. Bandura, and M. K. DeMeyer, Shaping cooperative responses in early childhood schizophrenics. In L. P. Ullmann and L. Krasner, eds., *Case studies in behavior modification* (New York: Holt, Rinehart and Winston, 1965), 130–138.

[32] C. E. Ferster and M. K. DeMeyer, A method for the experimental analysis of the behavior of autistic children, *Amer. Jour. Orthopsychiat.,* **32** (1962), 80–98.

[33] T. Ayllon and N. H. Azrin, The measurement and reinforcement of behavior of psychotics, *Jour. Exp. Anal. Behav.,* **8** (1965), 357–383.

**TABLE 1.**  List of Reinforcers Available for Tokens

|  |  | No. of Tokens Daily |
|---|---|---|
| **I.** | Privacy | |
| | Selection of Room 1 | 1 |
| | Selection of Room 2 | 4 |
| | Selection of Room 3 | 8 |
| | Selection of Room 4 | 15 |
| | Selection of Room 5 | 30 |
| | Personal chair | 1 |
| | Choice of eating group | 1 |
| | Screen (room divider) | 1 |
| | Choice of bedspreads | 1 |
| | Coat rack | 1 |
| | Personal cabinet | 2 |
| | Placebo | 1–2 |
| **II.** | Leave from the ward | |
| | 20-min. walk on hospital grounds (with escort) | 2 |
| | 30-min. grounds pass (3 tokens for each additional 30 min.) | 10 |
| | Trip to town (with escort) | 100 |
| **III.** | Social interaction with staff | |
| | Private audience with chaplain, nurse | 5 min. free |
| | Private audience with ward staff, ward physician (for additional time—1 token per min.) | 5 min. free |
| | Private audience with ward psychologist | 20 |
| | Private audience with social worker | 100 |
| **IV.** | Devotional opportunities | |
| | Extra religious services on ward | 1 |
| | Extra religious services off ward | 10 |
| **V.** | Recreational opportunities | |
| | Movie on ward | 1 |
| | Opportunity to listen to live band | 1 |
| | Exclusive use of radio | 1 |
| | Television (choice of program) | 3 |
| **VI.** | Commisary Items | |
| | Consumable items such as candy, milk, cigarettes, coffee, and sandwiches | 1–5 |
| | Toilet articles such as Kleenex, toothpaste, comb, lipstick, and talcum powder | 1–10 |
| | Clothing and accessories such as gloves, headscarf, house slippers, handbag, and skirt | 12–400 |
| | Reading and writing materials such as stationery, pen, greeting card, newspaper, and magazine | 2–5 |
| | Miscellaneous items such as ashtray, throw rug, potted plant, picture holder, and stuffed animal | 1–50 |

SOURCE: T. Ayllon and N. H. Azrin. The measurement and reinforcement of behavior of psychotics, *Jour. exp. anal. Behav.*, **8** (1965), 357–383, Table, p. 360. Copyright 1965 by the Society for the Experimental Analysis of Behavior, Inc. Reproduced by permission of the authors and the publisher.

experimental circumstances provided, during conditioning patients performed consistently, and no additional reinforcers such as compliments from supervisors were used. The critical test of the conditioned reinforcing function of the tokens came when the patients were shifted from a preferred job to a nonpreferred one. This occurred when the patients were told that they would no longer receive tokens for working at the preferred job, but could continue to receive tokens for working at a nonpreferred job. Seven out of eight patients immediately shifted to the nonpreferred task. Thus, the token reinforcement was more enduring than any of the incidental or uncontrolled reinforcements a patient might get by performing a preferred task.

A second experiment was designed to test whether there was intrinsic reinforcement in the work itself. In Phase I of this second experiment

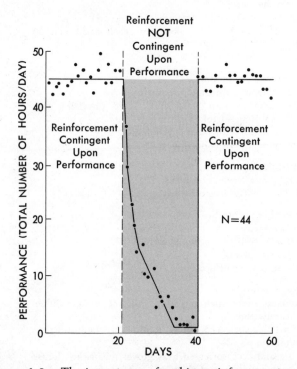

**Figure 6–2.** The importance of making reinforcement contingent on responding. Total number of hours worked by a group of psychotic patients when reinforcement was contingent on performance and when it was not. (From T. Ayllon and N. H. Azrin, The measurement and reinforcement of behavior of psychotics, *Journal of the Experimental Analysis of Behavior,* **8** [1965], 357–383, Fig. 4, p. 373. Copyright 1965 by the Society for the Experimental Analysis of Behavior, Inc. Reproduced by permission of the authors and the publisher.)

patients were reinforced with tokens at the end of the day's work (with reinforcement contingent upon responses). In Phase II the patients were paid in the morning before they started (vacation with pay?). Some patients inquired about whether they might get extra tokens if they worked. In this situation virtually no work was accomplished. In Phase III, the situation was the same as Phase I. Almost immediately, patients went back to work in order to get the tokens.

*The Token Economy.* Studies like the above have led Ayllon and Azrin[34] to outline a plan they refer to as the "token economy," which is currently in use in many institutions for retarded children and behaviorally disturbed people. Generally, the patients are given tokens for a variety of desirable behaviors such as working in the laundry, kitchen, waiting table, and so on. In return they can buy privacy, interact with the staff, eat at more attractive tables, in the dining room, have TVs in their rooms, recreational activities, or candy and cigarettes at the commissary. Through such a program patients can be led to perform more desirable activities and acquire more social behavior in favor of merely sitting on the ward and engaging in troublesome behavior. The ward assistants are trained to apply the token system. (For a further discussion see Chapter 18.)

## Effects of Individual Differences in the Function of Conditioned Reinforcers

Conditioned reinforcers do not share the universality of function that primary ones do. We have discussed at length the reinforcers of attention, affection, approval, and submission because they happen to operate quite effectively in our particular culture. Even though these have a generality of function as they are shared by most of us, individual differences do occur. The so-called cold fish apparently finds no value in affection as a reinforcer; it simply does not work for him. To understand this adequately, one would have to go back into the conditions in his development and early experience. In all probability he had been raised with a minimum of affection, so whatever operated in his early training has since been extinguished. Likewise, there are those who abhor the "limelight"—attention is just what they do not want. For it to operate as a reinforcer, the application must be quite subtle.

The individual differences in secondary reinforcements can also be understood by looking into comparative cultures. Take the Balinese, for

---

[34] T. Ayllon and N. Azrin, *The token economy* (New York: Appleton-Century-Crofts, 1968).

example. They are described as calm, gentle, relaxed. Dominant behavior is not reinforced by submission, nor is competition reinforced by approval. A look at the early developmental training of these people helps to account for the differences in comparison to our own culture. Small children are characteristically teased by their parents and elders. When emotional outbursts occur, they are ignored until these expressions become extinguished. If a little child wanders off, his parents do not chase him in a highly emotional manner (as ours may do). Some older child or adult who finds him will calmly lead him back home. Among the Balinese it is considered good manners to reach for things only with the right hand. If a child reaches with his left, the mother pulls back the wrong hand and gently extends the right. This is done not with emotion or scolding but regularly and peacefully. This kind of behavior gives us a little understanding of the differences between the Balinese and ourselves and why the reinforcements differ as they do. The Balinese child learns his conformity without ever being yelled at or threatened. His own childish emotional angers and tirades become extinguished early, and he acquires unaggressive and compliant behavior characteristics of his group.[35]

## EXTINCTION OF S$^{r}$'S

When the secondary reinforcer is withheld, ordinarily the organism's behavior becomes weakened. In human organisms, the extinction curve may not last so long as that of the rat because human beings are capable of complex discriminations which serve to tell us that this reinforcement no longer works, and thus they must seek alternate behavior that will be reinforced. The substitution of alternate forms of behavior is common when the conditioned reinforcement of a behavior in progress is withheld. The person accustomed to receiving attention or approval tries something else, often an unfortunate response when the ordinary behavior does not get reinforced.

When a secondary reinforcer is withheld and later presented, our efforts may be renewed. This is something similar to what happens when we report the response of "joy." The joy we experience from seeing old friends, old places, and the like illustrates this. Many of these things have operated as conditioned reinforcers in our earlier years. A secondary reinforcer, which has been withheld, is represented. Likewise, when familiar secondary reinforcers are withdrawn, we experience feelings of dejection. What we call sorrow or depression is just this. A friend, parent, or other relative dies or moves away, and we feel sad. The sudden withdrawal of this secondary reinforcer leads to this reaction. Often, we leave old familiar spots and move to a new environment. We feel home-

[35] J. Belo, The Balinese temper, *Char. and Pers.*, 4 (1935), 120–126.

sick, we long for the folks at home or the "good old days." The secondary reinforcers that have operated to maintain our behavior are absent.[36]

## VERBAL BEHAVIOR AS SECONDARY REINFORCEMENT

Sometimes the actual dimensions of the secondary reinforcers in approval, attention, and affection merely refer to a verbal response of another person: "look," "see" in attention, "good," "right" in approval, "darling" or "dear" or other expressions of endearment in affection, and "you win" or "I give up" in submission. Much of the reinforcement that maintains human behavior is purely verbal.

We have already discussed how verbal behavior is acquired. Once it exists it must be maintained. The reinforcing consequences of verbal behavior continue to be important. Whether or not a person will speak on a given occasion depends upon the overall frequency of reinforcement that response is given by the verbal community, the other speakers and listeners. If reinforcement fails, extinction takes place.

The verbal behavior is maintained in a number of ways. The response of listening in itself is reinforcing; it implies attention if nothing more. The teacher who finds his students sleeping or doing other homework or crossword puzzles in class finds it difficult to continue his lecture. Sometimes we ask the question, "Are you listening to me?" at a point when it is not apparent that our verbal behavior is being reinforced. Two speakers continue their conversations as long as they are able to reinforce each other mutually. Other discriminative stimuli come into the picture. Perhaps one speaker has another appointment or is interrupted by someone. Obviously the maintenance of verbal behavior is a function of a complex set of variables, and we are concerned only with a few of them at this time.[37]

The amount of reinforcement received by a verbal response varies from occasion to occasion and from group to group. A child reared in a situation where his verbal behavior has been generously reinforced is likely to possess such behavior in great strength and will speak on almost any occasion. On the other hand, the person reared in the absence of much verbal reinforcement is likely to be quiet and lacking much verbal facility. The speaker with an interested audience talks at great length, whereas the one with no listeners select alternate behaviors.

Verbal behavior may be deliberately strengthened or weakened by the proper application of some form of reinforcement, also verbal. Much of what we call *personality*, in the laymen's sense, involves the application of proper verbal reinforcements. The wise speaker draws the listener

[36] F. S. Keller and W. N. Schoenfeld, *Principles of psychology* (New York: Appleton-Century-Crofts, 1950).

[37] B. F. Skinner, *Verbal behavior* (New York: Appleton-Century-Crofts, 1957).

out, allowing him to emit verbal behavior that will be reinforced. Because lags in conversation tend to generate emotional behavior like embarrassment, the clever speaker is capable of maintaining the verbal interchange until some mutually reinforcing ground can be found.

The deliberate manipulation of verbal behavior is illustrated by experiments that use the kinds of reinforcement techniques we have already discussed. Greenspoon[38] used a situation designed to resemble an interview. Without giving specific instructions to subjects, he set out to manipulate through selective reinforcement the probability of certain verbal responses. His subjects were asked to say *any* words, singly, exclusive of sentences, phrases, or numbers—just any words they could think of. Two kinds of responses were defined; the first included any plural nouns and the second included verbal responses other than plural nouns. In the operation performed the investigator was to present one of two verbal stimuli, "mmm-hmm" or "huh-uh" after each of the two kinds of responses; accordingly he said "mmm-hmm" if a plural noun were spoken and "huh-uh" for any word not a plural noun. No information concerning the purpose of the experiment was given. During conditioning, the subjects showed a remarkable increase in the frequency of the plural noun responses which had been reinforced by "mmm-hmm" and a marked decrease in the frequency of other plural responses reinforced by "huh-uh." However, both stimuli had the effect of increasing nonplural responses (generalization).

In an experiment reported by Cohen et al.[39] a series of 80 cards, each containing a verb and six personal pronouns, was presented to subjects who were asked to make a sentence containing the verb and beginning with one of the personal pronouns on the cards. All responses beginning with "I" or "we" were reinforced by the investigator's saying "good." Results showed a successive increase in the responses reinforced. In another group no reinforcement was given and no change occurred in the frequency of either of the pronoun responses. In a second part of the experiment the "I" and "we" responses were extinguished and "he" and "they" responses were reinforced. The change operated according to the manipulation of the reinforcement given; the "I" and "we" responses decreased and the "he" and "they" responses increased.

Verplanck[40] applied the technique to shaping statements of opinion given in general conversations. This unique experiment was carried out as a series of ordinary conversations between people. Subjects were tested in a number of situations: student living quarters, private homes,

[38] J. Greenspoon, The reinforcing effects of two spoken sounds on the frequency of two responses, *Amer. Jour. Psychol.*, **68** (1955), 409—416.

[39] B. D. Cohen, H. I. Kalish, J. R. Thurston, and E. Cohen, Experimental manipulation of verbal behavior, *Jour. Exp. Psychol.*, **47** (1954), 106–110.

[40] W. S. Verplanck, The control of the content of conversation: Reinforcement of statements of opinion, *Jour. Abn. Soc. Psychol.*, **51** (1955), 668–676.

a public lounge, and even over the telephone. The experimenter would engage the subject in conversation for one-half hour. In the first 10 minutes no reinforcements were given for statements of opinion. This constituted what is called *operant level,* or a baseline, responding with which experimental operations could be compared. If we expect the application of positive reinforcement to statements of opinion to affect the rate of their emission, it is necessary to know what that rate is before reinforcement is applied. During the second 10-minute period, every response a subject made that indicated a statement of opinion was reinforced by the experimenter's saying, "Yes, you're right," or "That's so." Statements beginning with the words, "I think," "I believe," "It seems to me," or "I feel," were considered to be statements of opinion. In the final 10 minutes, these reinforcements were withheld, and this constituted the extinction period.

The topics of conversation ranged from the trivial to the "intellectual" and included a variety of subjects: college dates, vacations, Marxism, the need for religion, architecture, and Liberace. The experimenter made a record of the opinion responses by making some kind of mark or doodle in the margin of a magazine, book, or the like, in such a manner as to be unobtrusive to the subject. The rates of opinion statements showed a significant increase during the reinforcement period over the earlier "operant level" for all subjects. In the extinction period, 21 of 24 subjects showed a marked reduction in the frequency of opinion statements. In this last 10 minutes of the experiment, either the experimenter disagreed with the subject or said nothing. In some cases the subject became disturbed or angry during this period. In no case did the subject show any "awareness" of what was going on or that a contrived situation had been set up in which particular responses were being reinforced. It is quite evident, then, that the selective application of positive reinforcement to verbal behavior can increase certain classes of responding or decrease them according to the particular operations involved.

Verbal behavior can be reinforced on schedules. Another experiment by McNair[41] has applied schedules of reinforcement in a situation in which subjects were presented with slides of people in some kind of social situation as the discriminative stimuli (one slide showed a family seated before a fireplace, another a man and a woman embracing). Three groups of subjects were used: one was reinforced for statements, using a high rate; another, at a low rate; and the third group was not reinforced at all. The reinforcing stimulus was the sound of a bell tone that indicated to the subject that the experimenter approved of what he was saying. The rate of responding was measured in terms of the number of words

[41] D. M. McNair, Reinforcement of verbal behavior, *Jour. Exp. Psychol.,* **53** (1957), 40–46.

emitted in a 2-minute time interval. The number of responses (words) emitted was found to be a function of the schedule involved. When a variable interval of 15 seconds was used, the highest rate was generated. Next highest was for the VI of 60 seconds, and the lowest rates were emitted when no reinforcement was given. The rate was also a function of the particular picture: the picture of the man and woman embracing, for example, showed lower rates on the average than the one of the family before the fireplace. Here, again, the generous use of reinforcement will give rise to a higher rate of responding than when the reinforcements are rather stingily applied. With some people, we find it difficult to make a conversation. With others, it is easy to communicate. It all depends on how these people reinforce our own verbal responding.

Skinner[42] points out that a speaker can be induced to emphasize certain aspects of a subject and not others. In meeting a new acquaintance, one often confines his remarks to subjects that are mutually reinforced, other things being equal. If no common ground can be reached, the conversation is terminated. Thus, through the differential reinforcement of certain verbal responses or through some other kind of response such as a smile or a nod, behavior shaped by the speaker can reinforce the listener. Those people judged "bores" simply fail to emit much verbal behavior which listeners find reinforcing, while people considered scintillating or witty have developed verbal repertoires which are generally reinforcing to a vast number of people. The verbal behavior of the latter group may operate at a high rate because of their previous history of frequent reinforcement. You have heard the expression, "My, he's a talker, but it's usually interesting." The talker has had a strong history of reinforcement and continues to have, whereas the person who "doesn't have much to say" is operating at a lower rate according to his past reinforcement history.

One often wonders why some people, the bores, continue to verbalize at high rates when the apparent reinforcements from the verbal community do not seem to operate. A possible explanation for this fact is that the reinforcements for these people come from "within their own skins." As speakers they also hear themselves, just as a writer reads his own manuscript. In the absence of another person we often "talk to ourselves." Apparently, once verbal behavior has been established through the usual methods and the speaker has been conditioned as a self-listener, the speaker may continue to talk without further reinforcement from the community. Speakers described as egocentrics who love to hear themselves talk are an example of this.[43]

---

[42] B. F. Skinner, *Verbal behavior* (New York: Appleton-Century-Crofts, 1957), p. 149.

[43] Ibid., 153–154.

## VERBAL REINFORCEMENTS IN EDUCATION

Although education involves a variety of tokens as reinforcers, the process of learning is promoted through the presentation of a wide variety of verbal stimuli, whether oral or written. The responses of "good," "right," "correct," and so on are most commonly applied. Through the selective presentation of these reinforcing stimuli, the student learns progressively, year after year, the skills and tools which will enable him to get along in life after his formal education is finished.

The process is long and frequently inefficient. Children with different abilities are bunched together in the same classroom because of the accident of age and then the mass educational process is applied. Some get little reinforcement and show little progress, while others in a more advantageous position learn more rapidly. Good teachers apply the reinforcements appropriately and effectively. Others, either through a lack of proper discrimination on their own part or through ineffective use of reinforcements, serve as rather inappropriate stimuli in the advancement of the educational process.

## PROGRAMMED LEARNING AND THE TEACHING MACHINES

To remedy some of the problems current in education and to meet the greater demands for education in the light of teacher shortages, Skinner has proposed what is called the "teaching machine," which makes use of the principles of reinforcement in an effective and efficient manner. In the late 1950s and early 1960s when Skinner first developed the principles it was felt that the use of a "machine" (see Figure 6–3) was absolutely necessary because of greater controls it exerted and to keep the student from cheating himself (that is, looking for the answer before he writes it down). More subsequent research has indicated that the machine itself is not absolutely necessary, and that simple programmed learning in a book form is just as effective, and, in many cases, more so because books do not break down and machines frequently do. At any rate, the significance for learning lies in a good program that can be developed by careful research and testing. One of the basic principles of programmed learning is that of the immediacy of reinforcement. Ordinarily, when an examination is corrected and returned to the student, there is a delay of many hours or days. Who is not familiar with the instructor who took several months to return a paper? When the examination is corrected and returned to the student, there is a long delay. Under these conditions one can hardly expect the student's behavior to be appreciably modified. If an immediate report can be supplied by the program, allowing the correcting to follow the response at once, the educational process should be enhanced tremendously.

## THE PRINCIPLE OF REFLEX CONDITIONING (PAVLOVIAN CONDITIONING)

**1**

In a hungry dog, we can demonstrate the following reflex: *Food in mouth elicits salivation.*

In the paradigm below, FILL IN the parentheses with the names of the stimulus and the response for this reflex:

S————————►R

(——————) (——————————)

S————————►R

(food in            (salivation)
mouth)

- - - - - - - - - - - - - - - - - - - - - - - - - - -

**2**

*Light in eye elicits pupil contraction.*
COMPLETE the paradigm for the reflex above (two letters are required):

_____                          _____

(light                          (pupil
in eye)                         contraction)

S————————►R

(light              (pupil
in eye)             contraction)

- - - - - - - - - - - - - - - - - - - - - - - - - - -

**3**

*Electric shock applied to the hand elicits increased heart rate.*
DRAW and LABEL the complete paradigm for the reflex above:

S————————►R

(electric            (increased
shock                heart rate)
to hand)

- - - - - - - - - - - - - - - - - - - - - - - - - - -

**4**

Some stimuli elicit responses without previous learning. DRAW lines from the stimuli to the responses which they elicit:

| Stimuli | Responses |
|---|---|
| food | pupil contraction |
| light | increased heart rate |
| electric shock | salivation |

food ⟶ pupil contraction
light ⟶ increased heart rate
electric shock ⟶ salivation

---

**5**

A stimulus that elicits a response without previous training is called an *unconditioned stimulus*.

Which do you think is an unconditioned stimulus for the response of salivation?
☐ food in the mouth
☐ a menu

food in the mouth

---

**6**

Other stimuli acquire their power to elicit responses only through training or learning. These are called *conditioned stimuli*.

Which do you think might be a conditioned stimulus for increased heart rate?
☐ the sound of a nearby explosion (dynamite)
☐ the sight of the burning fuse

the sight of the burning fuse

---

**7**

A light in the eye is an unconditioned _____ for pupil contraction.

stimulus

---

**8**

The sound of a dentist's drill might be a(n) _____ stimulus for nausea and trembling.

conditioned

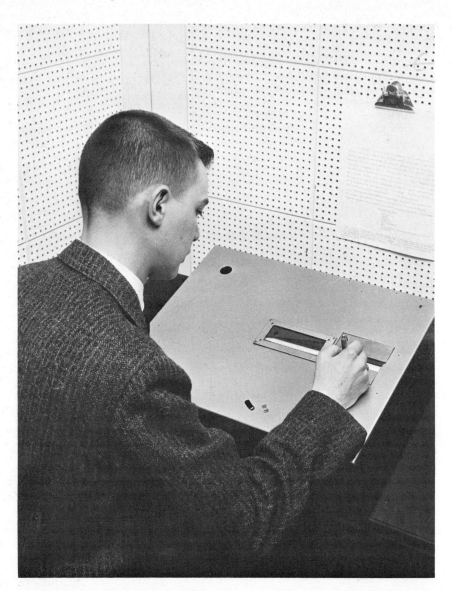

**Figure 6–3.** Student at work on teaching machine developed by B. F. Skinner. A frame of material is presented to the student in the lefthand window. He writes his response on the strip of paper at the right. By means of a lever on the left he advances the written response under a transparent window and exposes the right answer in the upper corner of the frame. If he is correct, he moves the lever to the right which alters the machine in such a way that the frame will not appear again on the second time around. A new frame appears when the lever is returned to the starting position. (Photograph courtesy of B. F. Skinner, Harvard University.)

Programmed learning takes into account a number of important behavior principles already referred to in our earlier discussion.[44]

1. The student is required to compose his own response to the question presented on a revolving disc, the $S^D$. The learning is facilitated by making a specific, differentiated response to the stimuli presented. When the question is presented, he is required to write out his answer. In contrast to some types of devices, which merely allow the student to select from among a variety of alternatives, no choice is given. The student writes a given response instead of selecting from among a variety of alternatives, in which acknowledged wrong answers are frequently included, so that an incorrect selection could be strengthened rather than the correct one.

2. In acquiring complex verbals skills in education, it is necessary for the learner to pass through a series of carefully designated steps. Each step is so small that it can be easily taken, but in so doing, the student moves closer and closer to the fully completed behavior to be mastered. The use of small steps has been found to be exceedingly important, for if they are too large, the student cannot master them and may become extinguished.

Programs are designed for all levels of the educational process. For children in the process of acquiring the early skills, the response to be made is that of moving a lever or figure. His setting is matched with a coded response. If the two correspond, the machine automatically presents the next frame. If they do not, the response is cleared from the machine and a similar problem is presented. Thus the child cannot proceed to the second step until the first has been mastered. Machines of this type have been used to study the skills of spelling, arithmetic, and similar subjects applicable to the lower grades.

For the more advanced students in high school and college, the subject compares his written response to that presented in the program. When a question is presented he writes his answer in the space provided by the program. In many programs, such as the one illustrated on pp. 172–173, the answer is provided alongside the question. A 3x5 card or other masking device is used by the student to cover up the answer until he is ready to check it. If a machine is used, when the question is presented (see Figure 6–3) he writes his answer on a paper slip exposed through an opening. By lifting a lever, he moves what he has written under a transparent cover and at the same time exposes the correct answer. If the two match he moves another lever which punches a hole in the paper opposite his response, thus recording the

[44] B. F. Skinner, Teaching machines, *Science*, **128** (1958), 969–977.

fact that he answered correctly. This alters the machine in such a way that the next frame or problem appears. The student proceeds in this way until he has answered all frames in a given series. He then works around the disc again, and does only those frames which he did not answer correctly the first time. When answering the frames he missed the first time, the machine tells him that a response is wrong and also tells him what ought to be the right answer, allowing him to make the right answer on the next time around.

Skinner suggests that the machine or program acts like a good tutor; it insists that a given point be thoroughly understood before the student is allowed to go on to the next; it presents the material for which the student is ready by allowing him to take very small steps in the learning process; it helps the student to come up with the right answer and, like a private tutor, it finally reinforces the student for every correct response he makes and reinforces him immediately after it has been made.[45]

The following sample[46] illustrates an early part of a program on respondent conditioning, a topic discussed in Chapter 3.

The example of programmed learning illustrates how the basic principles of reinforcement and learning can be more effectively applied to education. The use of teaching machines need not be limited to the classroom. In industry and business, where new procedures have to be learned, it can operate efficiently and effectively. Each year new automobiles come out with different kinds of motors, devices, and gadgets that have a peculiar capacity for getting out of order. Think how easy it would be for mechanics to fix our cars and understand them better if the principles explaining their operation could be put on the machine! Training periods would be shorter, and industry could operate on a higher level of efficiency.

[45] Ibid.

[46] From G. L. Geis, W. C. Stebbins, and R. W. Lundin, *Reflex and operant conditioning*, vol. I. In *A study of behavior* (New York, Appleton-Century-Crofts, 1965), pp. 42–43. Copyright Xerox Corporation.

# 7   Deprivation and Satiation

IN THEIR APPRAISAL OF CONTEMPORARY personality theories, Hall and Lindzey[1] stress, among other things, one characteristic common to almost all approaches to personality. They all place an emphasis on some kind of interpretation of the concept of motivation as necessary to their explanations. This importance of motivation is not limited to personality theories. Other learning theorists, including Hull[2] and Tolman,[3] make use of the concept in one way or another. Unfortunately the use of motivation in an explanation of behavior has been so badly handled by psychologists, both past and present, that its understanding has become a common stumbling block for both beginning and advanced students. Be that as it may, we start with one common premise, that some kind of explanation of motive or drive is necessary in the analysis of behavior.

This has not always been the case. Psychologists of the nineteenth century, such as Wundt[4] and Titchener,[5] stressed man as a conscious, rational being. They had little to say about desires,

[1] C. S. Hall and G. Lindzey, *Theories of personality*, 2nd ed. (New York: Wiley, 1970), chapter 1.

[2] C. L. Hull, *Principles of behavior* (New York: Appleton-Century-Crofts, 1943).

[3] E. C. Tolman, *Purposive behavior in animals and man* (New York: Century, 1932).

[4] W. Wundt, *Grundzuge der physiologischen Psychologie*, 2nd ed. (Leipzig: Englemans, 1880).

[5] E. B. Titchener, *Systematic psychology* (New York: Macmillan Inc., 1929).

motives, needs, or drives. Although they spoke of emotions, a related concept, it was treated as a subsidiary to sensation, which contained the main events of their study.

## Motivation Theories

INSTINCT THEORIES

Freud was one of the first to throw out the idea that man was basically a rational and conscious being, and he substituted a kind of irrational nature, based on the belief that inherent instincts resided in man's unconscious mind. Freud, in his early writings, stressed the sexual desires as being the source of all energy (libido) which directed human behavior.[6] In his discussion of how personality develops, the sex drive was of utmost importance (see pp. 20–22). He stressed the importance of infantile sexuality and blew up the notion that humans developed an interest in sex only after they had reached puberty. In his later writings, Freud realized that there were other instincts besides sex which motivated man, such as hunger and thirst, so he combined them all into what he called the *life instinct* as being those impulses which directed toward man's preservation.[7] The instincts residing in the unconscious id were the ultimate source of all the psychic energy that governed the personality. By a process of identification, the ego eventually developed as it siphoned off some of the energy from the id, and finally the superego developed as it was able to get energy from the ego. The instincts are repetitious in nature, going from a state of quiescence or satisfaction to one of tension, and back to quiescence at which time the instinct is satisfied. Later, after World War I, Freud realized that the life instincts and their energy did not provide a sufficient explanation for all of man's nature, and he added the death instinct.[8] Just as the life instinct provides for the preservation of life, the death instinct operates in the opposite way. In its simplest form it is the force that drives a man to death, and of course eventually wins out. However, because of the controls exerted by the ego over the unconscious id, the death instinct must manifest itself in diverse and subtle ways in the form of aggression, destructiveness, and hostility. Rather than be directed toward oneself, these feelings can be aimed at

[6] S. Freud, *Three essays on sexuality*. In the *Standard edition of the complete works of Sigmund Freud* (London: Hogarth Press, 1953, vol. VII; first German ed., 1905).

[7] S. Freud, *The ego and the id* (London: Hogarth Press, 1947; first German ed., 1923).

[8] S. Freud, *Beyond the pleasure principle* (Standard ed.; London: Hogarth Press, 1955, vol. XVIII, first German ed., 1920).

other people and things. In this way, the death instinct can gain its satisfaction. The job of the ego, as the mediator between the id in the unconscious and the world outside, was to find ways in which the instincts could be satisfied.

Later psychoanalysts took up the idea, differing from Freud as to just what the instincts were. Adler thought of the basic driving force as an inherent need for superiority, interpreted in his early writings as a drive for power and later as a more altruistic "social interest." [9] That is, the need to get ahead is not limited to oneself but is an inherent desire to improve the whole status of our society. Jung[10] also found a need for instinct and took Freud's libido, extracted the sex out of it, and made it merely a general life energy which originated in the metabolic processes of the body.

A more academic psychologist, William McDougall[11] in England and later in this country, set the psychological world on fire when he posited a rather elaborate set of instincts, later called *propensities*, because by 1930 the term *instinct* in human behavior had become rather unpopular. But call them what you like, the ideas were the same; instincts were inner springs of action that directed and controlled a variety of behavior for all of us, McDougall's list included instincts for escape, pugnacity, gregariousness, sex, hunger, curiosity, self-assertion, hoarding, and so on. This doctrine upset the social psychologists and sociologists of the day because they had been used to explaining social behavior in terms of some kind of group mind, social interaction, or cultural influence. For McDougall, people were social not so much because of the social influences resident in the culture but because they were all born the same way, sharing instincts to do certain things. If a particular behavior needed explaining, he simply posited some instinct for it. The bully fights because of a strong instinct for pugnacity. The very social or party-loving person has a strong gregarious instinct, and the miser's instinct for acquisitiveness accounts for his hoarding. According to this doctrine, man is predisposed to act in certain ways if the appropriate stimuli are presented to pull out the response. The individual is either pushed, pulled, or prodded into his activity by some aspect of these unseen forces.

The main difficulty with the instinct theories is that they account for the effect (resulting behavior) by resorting to some intervening variable as a hypothetical construct as the cause. The source was some place, either inside the body or in the psyche. Furthermore the instincts were used not only to account for the causes of behavior but also to prove

[9] A. Adler, *Social interest* (New York: Putnam, 1939).

[10] C. G. Jung, *Symbols of transformation, Collected works* (London: Routledge and Kegan Paul, 1956), vol. 5.

[11] W. McDougall, *Outline of abnormal psychology* (New York: Scribner, 1926).

that behavior itself was predetermined. Little evidence for this kind of explanation exists today at the human level, and except for the psycho-analysts the appeal to instincts as an explanation of behavior has nearly vanished from psychology. The psychoanalysts, still true to Freud, hold to some variation of his doctrine. Since their concepts are so ill-defined anyway, they do not seem to worry too much about the problem.

NEED THEORIES

More recent personality theories stress the idea that the cause of behavior is to be found in some *need* or *drive* in the organism. In general form the basic concept is this: In man's search for survival, there occur from time to time, certain deficiencies or needs. When these arise (lack of food, water, and the like), the organism is set into a state of disequi-librium; producing tension, either physiological or psychic, depending on the specific theory. This activity produced by the tension eventually leads the person to the satisfaction of his need, and hence the state of equi-librium is restored. Need implies a deficiency in something, either psy-chological or physiological. Some theorists stress physiological functions which set the chain of events going—hunger, sex, or thirst.[12] Others stress the fact that although need can be acquired, once it is set up, its origin may be either related to the physiological function or set in some brain state.[13]

A contemporary personality theorist, Henry A. Murray,[14] considers *need* as some kind of force set up in the brain region. This force can organize psychological activity in such a way as to direct the organism into a satisfying or out of an unsatisfying situation. The need is a kind of hypothetical construct that accounts for activity. But the existence of these needs can be measured. The list is rather elaborate, including needs for achievement, affiliation, aggression, abasement, autonomy, dom-inance, order, play, sex, and so on. By use of a technique called the *Thematic Apperception Test*, the strength and prominence of certain needs can be discovered. The subject is given a series of pictures, some quite vague, and asked to tell a story about each. It is assumed that the individual taking the test projects himself into the role of the hero of the story so that the needs expressed by the hero are his own. The stories are then analyzed for the list of dominant needs existing in the person-ality (see pp. 123–125).

The "field theorists," whose major proponent was Kurt Lewin,[15] also

---

[12] N. Cameron and A. Magaret, *Behavior pathology* (Boston: Houghton Mifflin, 1951).

[13] H. A. Murray et al., *Explorations in personality* (New York: Oxford University Press, 1938).

[14] H. A. Murray, *Manual for thematic apperception test* (Cambridge, Mass.: Har-vard University Press, 1943).

[15] K. Lewin, A dynamic theory of personality (New York: McGraw-Hill, 1935).

found necessary the concept of need to explain personality. They assume the personality to be a complex of energy systems. A need exists when one energy system within the personality is out of balance with the others and thus sets up a state of psychic tension. The needs could have their source in some physiological processes such as hunger or thirst, or they could arise out of a desire for some external object not intimately related to any biological function. Once the need exists, a corresponding valence is set up in the object desired, and in some mysterious way the person is pushed to the object and the need satisfied.

## STIMULUS THEORIES

Although the concept of equilibrium may also be implied in these theories, the idea of need, drive, or motive is more intimately related to some stimulus object.[16] The point stressed is that some stimulus arising inside the body (such as hunger pangs, dryness in the throat, or a surge of hormones from the sex glands) sets off the activity which eventually ends up in the satisfying state of the organism. On the other hand, the stimulus could arise in the environment. It could be an insult (stimulus for fighting) or a threat (stimulus for running away). This has sometimes been called an *itch theory*, since the response is set off by some kind of irritating stimulus. We noted, of course, in our discussion of respondent behavior that certain stimuli can naturally elicit responses. However, to suggest that more complex behavior is initiated and maintained in a similar way is at best an oversimplification of the facts. What this kind of theory does is to take some eliciting or discriminative stimulus and give it the status of a drive or need. Even though these stimuli operate to set the occasion for an activity, they alone are not sufficient to explain all "the variables of which behavior is a function."

In summary, we find that psychologists have handled the problem of motivation in a variety of ways. Some consider it as an internal condition that initiates the organism to activity. What the condition may be is often ill defined; it may be a physiological process or some hypothetical psychic state. Sometimes the reference is specific to rhythm changes in stomach activity, lowering of blood sugar, or a discharge of sex hormones into the bloodstream. The idea of a state of disequilibrium is often added. Resulting activity in one way or other operates to return the organism to the equilibrium most advantageous for survival. The idea of motive or need may be given the status of an intervening variable, an inferred state which is neither observable nor measurable but somehow exists. The states are inferred from the resulting behavior, such as: when the organism eats, drinks, or copulates, he must be hungry, thirsty, or sexy.

In an empirical psychology, references to "inferred states," "energy,"

[16] S. Diamond, *Personality and temperament* (New York: Harper & Brothers, 1957).

"instincts," and the like have no place. Yet we must account for the concept in motivation in some way. Although it is interesting to know what goes on inside the organism, such information is not necessary in an empirical analysis of behavior (see pp. 43–45). Instead of trying to give as the origin of behavior some intervening variable, inferred state, or psychic cause, we go back to the operational approach and consider what operations are performed and what changes take place in behavior.

### DEPRIVATION AND SATIATION

An interpretation of motivation in terms of the operations of depriving and satiating fits an empirical approach to the problem. These events are observable and measurable, and as clearly defined operations they can be varied and the resulting changes in behavior observed. Instead of saying that an organism has a strong *drive* or *need* for food, we merely say that, for so many hours or days, he has been deprived of food. If he has little or no drive for food, we are merely saying that at a given time he has eaten so much food that food does not operate as a reinforcer to strengthen his behavior.

A second kind of operation using deprivation involves keeping the organism on a diet so that only a certain percentage of his normal body weight is maintained. Ferster and Skinner[17] find that with this procedure, two organisms will differ less in their behavior than when a deprivation level is maintained by feeding the organism a given amount of food each day. A common practice is to maintain the animal on 80 per cent of his normal body weight. The percentage can be decreased or raised, depending on what characteristics of deprivation one wishes to study.

By the use of the operations of deprivation and satiation, we can ordinarily alter the probability of a given response occurring. By using them appropriately, we add another condition or variable under our control. The concept of motivation is reduced to simple operations, and we eliminate all the problems of inferences and unseen variables.

Kantor clarifies the problem quite simply in his definition of motivation by saying; "Factors of motivation in psychological events consist of setting conditions favoring or hindering performances." [18]

*Motivationlike Operations.*  Before we examine some of the experimental examples of deprivation and satiation, let us consider for a moment certain operations or conditions that alter behavior but would not come strictly under this heading. These certainly are conditions

---

[17] C. B. Ferster and B. F. Skinner, *Schedules of reinforcement* (New York: Appleton-Century-Crofts, 1957), p. 29.

[18] J. R. Kantor, *Interbehavioral psychology* (Bloomington, Ind.: Principia Press, 1958), p. 75.

worthy of psychological study and are closely related to what we are to consider. We refer to events such as drug taking, illness, pregnancy, fatigue, and even brain stimulation or removal of its parts. Most college students are familiar with the effects of alcohol on behavior. This, of course, can be studied experimentally, and we shall consider in more detail some of these experiments in Chapter 15. Tranquilizers are another example of how drugs can affect behavior. In many mental institutions, severely disturbed patients are brought under better control with these drugs. Narcotics are of special interest to the psychologist because of the dependence they cause and how they more indirectly alter a person's moral conduct, in that as he becomes addicted he may have to steal to get enough money to maintain his supply or "habit."

Pregnancy alters a female's behavior in many ways; not only may it incapacitate her, but she may report certain cravings or hungers. The same is true for illness. It is difficult to perform at one's maximum efficiency if one is stricken with the flu or even a common cold.

EXPERIMENTAL STUDIES OF FOOD DEPRIVATION

In animal experimentation where primary reinforcements are ordinarily applied, some condition of deprivation is necessary. For food to operate as a reinforcer, the animal must be deprived of it for a given period of time prior to the beginning of experimentation. Under these conditions food operates to strengthen the behavior under study when applied following the response, provided that the organism has been deprived. If food is presented frequently enough in a long experimental session, there comes a time when the response rate drops off because satiation is beginning to take place. Figure 7–1 from Ferster and Skinner,[19] illustrates the satiation effects of a pigeon conditioned under a fixed-interval schedule of 2 minutes. For the first 9 hours the rate appears fairly constant (about 0.35 responses per minute). As satiation proceeds, the effect on behavior is to increase the pause following the reinforcement. Toward the end of the period, few responses occur except at the end of the interval, and most reinforcements are received as soon as scheduled.

Another way to study the satiation effects is to give the animal access to food before he is placed in the experimental chamber. If he is well fed prior to experimentation, the food fails to operate as a reinforcer to any great extent. Skinner[20] fed rats various amounts of food immediately before conditioning them to respond. The prefeeding consisted of 0, 2, 4,

---

[19] C. B. Ferster and B. F. Skinner, op. cit.

[20] B. F. Skinner, Conditioning and extinction and their relation to the state of drive, *Jour. Gen. Psychol.*, **14** (1936), 295–317.

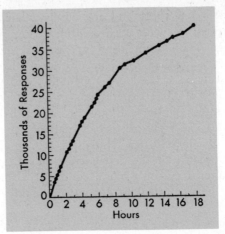

**Figure 7–1.** Satiation curve using fixed-interval reinforcement for a pigeon conditioned to peck a key on a schedule of FI 2. The conditioning session lasted 18 hours and the bird received over 500 reinforcements. Note the reduction in response rate during the last 9 hours when the bird begins to become satiated. However, satiation is not complete even at the end of the session. (From C. B. Ferster and B. F. Skinner, *Schedules of Reinforcement*, Fig. 380, p. 321. Copyright © 1957, Appleton-Century-Crofts, Inc. Reproduced by permission.)

and 6 grams. After eating, the rats were conditioned on an intermittent schedule. The average rates of responding for the different groups are indicated in Figure 7–2. It is clear that the amount of prefeeding, the lower the rate of response.

The opposite operation to satiation, that of deprivation, is commonly used to study its effects on responses of the organism. A number of experimental studies demonstrates the fact that the amount of deprivation (as measured in terms of length of time since last feeding) is positively related to the magnitude of the response, other things being equal; that is, deprivation has a strengthening effect on the response rate. One way to study this effect is under the extinction process. Perin[21] conditioned four groups of rats all under the same conditions of deprivation and using the same amount of reinforcement for each group. He then extinguished them under *different* degrees of deprivation; namely after 1, 3, 16, and 32 hours of deprivation. His results indicated that the rats extinguished under the highest deprivation (32 hours) gave out the most responses, while those extinguished under only slight deprivation emitted the fewest responses.

[21] C. T. Perin, Behavior potentiality as a joint function of the amount of training and the degree of hunger at the time of extinction, *Jour. Exp. Psychol.*, **30** (1942), 93–113.

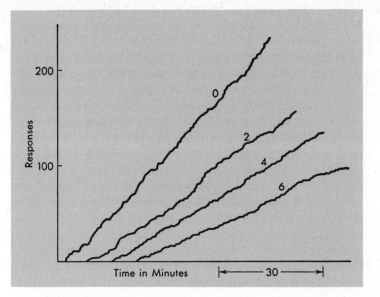

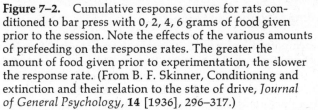

**Figure 7–2.** Cumulative response curves for rats conditioned to bar press with 0, 2, 4, 6 grams of food given prior to the session. Note the effects of the various amounts of prefeeding on the response rates. The greater the amount of food given prior to experimentation, the slower the response rate. (From B. F. Skinner, Conditioning and extinction and their relation to the state of drive, *Journal of General Psychology,* **14** [1936], 296–317.)

One question may arise concerning the effects of deprivation on response rate. Just how far does the relationship between the two variables extend? Our results so far indicate that deprivation and satiation directly affect response rate: the greater the deprivation, the stronger the response under either conditioning or extinction; and the greater the satiation, the slower the response rate. However, in the deprivation process there comes a time when the organism, if deprived long enough, will starve to death. An experiment by Heron and Skinner[22] illustrates this relationship (see Figure 7–3). The animals were conditioned under intermittent reinforcement. They were then tested on different succeeding days until death by starvation. In general the response rate increased with the period of starvation (deprivation) until a maximal rate was reached. After that point, there was a rapid decline in rate and death. In the group studied, the average maximum rate was reached on the fifth day of deprivation, although it should be realized that individual differences among the rats existed.

[22] W. T. Heron and B. F. Skinner, Changes in hunger during starvation, *Psychol. Rec.,* **1** (1937), 51–60.

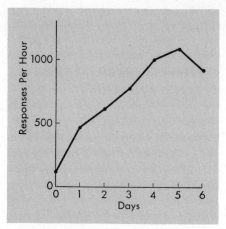

**Figure 7–3.**   Response rates as a function of days of food deprivation. (From W. T. Heron and B. F. Skinner, Changes in hunger during starvation, *Psychological Record,* **1** [1937], 51–60.)

According to Heron and Skinner:

After each animal had passed its peak, it was obvious that it was in an extremely impoverished condition. It was cold to the touch (bodily temperatures were not taken), its hair was erect and shaggy, and in many cases a normal posture could not be maintained. From these observations and from the early death of the animal after its peak was reached, it may be concluded that the decline in rate was due to physical weakness rather than to any independent decrease in the state of the drive.[23]

A few studies of the effects of food deprivation at the human level are also available. In general, moderate amounts of food deprivation facilitate behavior. Tests indicate that steadiness, muscular coordination, and speed of reaction are increased when one is in a deprived state. Although food deprivation experiments running over a long period of time are rare, one study during World War II, using conscientious objectors as subjects, illustrates the possible changes in behavior which occur when men were placed on semistarvation diets for six months.[24] During this time the men were placed on such restricted diets that their average weights dropped from 155 to 120 pounds. Their daily existence became preoccupied with discussions about food. They talked constantly about food, and their favorite reading material was cookbooks. Activities other than those connected with food were of little interest. As starvation increased, the men talked and moved about less. They never indulged in

[23] Ibid.
[24] A. B. Keys, J. Brozek, A. Henshel, O. Mickelson and H. L. Taylor, *The biology of human starvation* (Minneapolis: University of Minnesota Press, 1950).

unnecessary movements, lost interest in sex, showed poor sense of humor, and regarded outsiders with suspicion.

*Controlling Psychotic Behavior Through Food Deprivation.* Refusal to eat is a frequent problem in many mental patients. Frequently, the patients will refuse because they claim the food is poisoned, or God has forbidden them to eat. In such cases traditional treatments have been coaxing by the nurses, leading patients by the hand to the dining room, spoon feeding, tube feeding, intravenous feeding, etc. In other words, refusal to eat becomes socially reinforced in a variety of ways by a hospital staff. If one craves attention, refusal to eat may be a way of achieving that attention. In an experiment with 32 female psychiatric patients, Ayllon and Haughton[25] first discontinued these traditional methods. Patients were no longer coaxed, reminded, led, or escorted to eat. All social reinforcements in the form of sympathy and attention were discontinued. When mealtime came, a time interval of 30 minutes was allowed for the patients to go on their own volition to the dining room. At the end of that time, the dining room was locked. Gradually, during the experiment this time interval, during which the patients could enter following the call to meals, was reduced to 25 minutes, then 20 minutes, and finally to 5 minutes. At the beginning of the experiment the patients with eating problems showed a low percentage of meals eaten upon the removal of all the assistance previously used. Gradually, the eating problems began to disappear. When the end of the time to enter the dining room approached, a patient might say to a nurse, "I haven't eaten yet today, should I go eat now?" The nurses were instructed to ignore all such statements. The results show dramatically that when the proper controls are taken, almost all patients will eat without coaxing. Contrary to common psychiatric attitudes, the authors point out that patients will eat and without assistance. In fact, the previous assistance procedures seem to have produced whatever problems existed. Earlier, fears had been expressed that if patients were not coaxed to eat they might eventually starve. This obviously was not found to be the case. Most of the patients ate 90 per cent of the meals available to them. Of course, there were individual variations in the amount of time taken for their behavior to come under the control of food alone. One patient who had a 17-year problem of eating fasted for the first 15 days of the experiment. Previously, she had refused to eat unless the head nurse personally escorted her to eat. However, finally after her fast, she submitted and went to the dining room on her own accord. This experiment demonstrates that problem eaters are actually encouraged (shaped) by their social environment into refusing to eat, and that food alone can be a sufficient reinforcer to control normal eating in mental patients.

[25] T. Ayllon and E. Haughton, Control of behavior of schizophrenic patients by food, *Jour. Exp. Anal. Behav.*, **5** (1962), 343–352.

In succeeding experiments, these authors conditioned their patients to seek a penny from the nurse, which was dropped into a slot before they could gain admittance to the dining room, and finally to condition a social response of cooperation in a game in order to obtain a penny. Because these patients were considered chronic schizophrenics and seemed very much unaware of each other, the results were quite surprising to the hospital staff.

Ayllon[26] describes a patient who suffered from a variety of undesirable behaviors. The modification of some of these was made possible through the use of food deprivation. Her symptoms involved stealing food, hoarding towels, and wearing excessive clothing (i.e., half a dozen dresses, several pairs of stockings, sweaters, and so forth). For appropriate behavioral modification each of these symptoms had to be treated

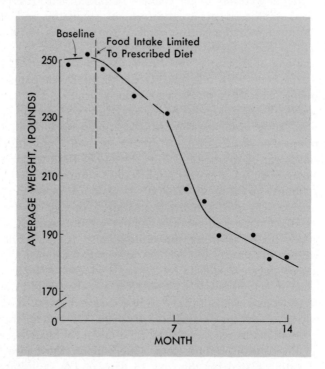

**Figure 7–4.**   Control of food-stealing behavior resulting in reduction in body weight when patient's eating was limited to her prescribed diet. (From T. Ayllon, Intensive treatment of psychotic behavior by stimulus satiation and food reinforcement, *Behavior Research and Therapy,* **1** [1963], 53–61, Fig. 2, p. 55. Copyright © 1963, Pergamon Press, Inc. Reproduced by permission.)

[26] T. Ayllon, Intensive treatment of psychotic behavior by stimulus satiation and food reinforcement, *Behav. Res. Ther.,* **1** (1963), 53–61.

separately. We will describe the techniques involving food in this section; the problem of towel hoarding will be discussed later. At the time the experiment was begun the patient weighed 250 pounds and had for several years. She was in the habit of not only eating the food from her own tray but stealing additional food from the counter as well as from other patients. First, she was assigned to a table in the patients' dining room all by herself. Whenever she approached the tables of other patients, the nurses immediately removed her from the dining room, or when she picked up unauthorized food from the counter, she was likewise discharged from the dining room. When the withdrawal of positive reinforcement (food) was dependent on her "stealing," the undesirable responses were eliminated in two weeks. Figure 7–4 shows the rather drastic reduction in her body weight over several months when she was restricted to a diet consisting of her own food. Treatment of the symptoms of wearing excessive clothing was also made contingent upon food reinforcement. To determine how much extra clothing she was wearing, the patient was weighed before each meal. In this situation her meal was made contingent on the removal of the superfluous clothing. This was gradually reduced until she met the requirement of wearing a normal amount of clothing (3 pounds) compared to the 25 pounds she had been wearing previously. At the start of the experiment the patient missed a few meals because she failed to meet the specified minimum weight requirement for that day. When the requirement was met, she was reinforced by being given access to her meals. There was also emotional behavior expressed in the forms of shouting, crying, and throwing chairs. The nurses were instructed to ignore this behavior, and the withholding of such "social" reinforcements led to the extinction of the emotional behavior.

STUDIES OF SEXUAL BEHAVIOR

Sexual behavior and its relation to satiation and deprivation has been studied experimentally with lower animals, and at the human level, is at least the subject of considerable discussion. One way of measuring the relationship between deprivation and strength of the responses is suggested by Warden.[27] The animal is placed at one end of an obstruction box. It is necessary for him to pass over an electrically charged grid in order to receive the reinforcement from which he has been deprived. The strength of the response can then be measured in terms of the number of crossings a male animal will make to receive a receptive female at the other end. He observed that a short period of deprivation is sufficient to bring the strength of the response to a maximum (less than one day,

[27] C. J. Warden, *Animal motivation studies: The albino rat* (New York: Columbia University Press, 1931).

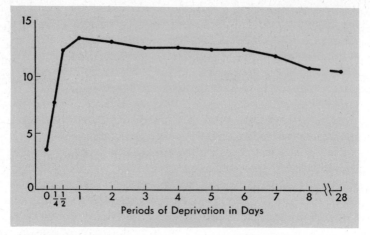

**Figure 7–5.** Strength of the sex drive as measured by
number of crossings of an electric grid on successive days
following sex deprivation. (From C. J. Warden, *Animal
Motivation Studies, The Albino Rat,* New York: Columbia
University Press, 1931, p. 154.)

Figure 7–5). Longer periods of deprivation did not strengthen the response beyond that point. The situation is quite different in the female,
since the strength of her behavior depends on that part of the menstrual
cycle she happens to be in.

At the human level the operation of deprivation and satiation are impossible to study experimentally. The strength of sexual behavior is a
function of so many variables that it is difficult to isolate these deprivation and satiation operations. Often, all we can do is to infer from the
behavior reported by the person in question. For one thing, in the American male the degree of sexual behavior measured in terms of number of
orgasms declines steadily with age, reaching its peak between fifteen and
twenty years of age and then gradually declining from then on.

Kinsey[28] has pointed out that the rate of sexual outlet is a function of
one's educational status, being most frequent among men who never
studied beyond the grades and least frequent among men who had attended college. Furthermore, masturbation was least frequent among the
poorly educated and most frequent among college men.[29] Here, the findings in all probability can be accounted for in terms of deprivation,
since college men marry later and have stronger attitudes against pre-
marital intercourse. The findings illustrate that the strength of the
response is a function of many discriminative stimuli other than con-

[28] A. C. Kinsey, W. B. Pomeroy and C. E. Martin, *Sexual behavior in the human
male* (Philadelphia: Saunders, 1948).
[29] Ibid.

ditions of deprivation. Undoubtedly, at the human level, the operation of secondary reinforcements plays a strong role in human sexual behavior. Much of the preparatory behavior for heterosexual relations is of this sort. According to Keller and Schoenfeld,[30] cases of men castrated after puberty or injured accidentally show that the frequency of intercourse and pleasure reported is reduced only little by these operations.

When deprived of heterosexual outlets, almost all species (including man) resort to alternate forms of sexual behavior. Included among these are homosexuality, masturbation, and intercourse with other species.[31] Although these also exist among lower animals, their frequency at the human level is most easily enforced by the deprivation of the hetero-sexual reinforcements prescribed by society. The adolescent is as func-tional as he will ever be, but society defers the reinforcements of intercourse until sometime in his twenties, when he is capable of assum-ing the responsibilities of marriage. Kinsey estimates that some 30 per cent of the male population has had some kind of homosexual contact and about 4 per cent are confirmed homosexuals. In the female, the percent-age of homosexual contacts is considerably less, being only 10 per cent at one time or other.[32]

Likewise, masturbation is almost universal among men prior to mar-riage. Kinsey estimated about 92 per cent have masturbated at some time during their lives. It is probable that it is the first sex outlet experienced by most American boys and serves as the chief source of sexual reinforce-ment during adolescence.[33]

Approximately 8 per cent of American males, according to Kinsey, have had intercourse with animals at one time or another. The figure is lower for the city-bred males, who would have little opportunity for animal contacts, but is as high as 40 to 50 per cent among boys reared on farms and who participate in some kind of sex activity with other species. About 17 per cent of this group actually achieve orgasm during the rela-tionship.[34]

## DEPRIVATION OF SENSORY STIMULI

In our discussion in Chapter 3 on the general characteristics of rein-forcement, we spoke of the possibility of sensory "feedback" operating as primary reinforcement. Visual, auditory, taste, smell, and touch stimuli seem to have reinforcement functions. Evidence of this comes from

---

[30] F. S. Keller and W. N. Schoenfeld, *Principles of psychology* (New York: Apple-ton-Century-Crofts, 1950), p. 301.

[31] C. S. Ford and F. A. Beach, *Patterns of sexual behavior* (New York: Hoeber, 1952).

[32] A. C. Kinsey, W. B. Pomeroy, C. E. Martin, and P. H. Gebhard, *Sexual be-havior in the human female* (Philadelphia: Saunders, 1953).

[33] A. C. Kinsey, W. B. Pomeroy, and C. E. Martin, op. cit.

[34] Ibid.

studies in which the organism is deprived of these reinforcements. It is clear that individuals raised in restricted environments fail to behave like normal persons. It is extremely difficult to keep a man quiet for any extended period of time. Clinical evidence tells us that when people are deprived of ordinary verbal contacts, they substitute "talking to themselves." The controlling effect of such deprivation was discovered long ago when prisons placed men in solitary confinement for long periods in order to get them to talk.

Likewise, when persons have to work at the same tasks where there is little *change in stimulation,* they become bored and dissatisfied with their jobs. In fact, people accustomed to frequent change in stimulation find working at monotonous tasks impossible. During World War II it was observed that radar operators on antisubmarine patrol often failed to detect U-boats. Furthermore the longer the men remained at their tasks, the more their efficiency declined. Holland[35] has found that the detection of a signal can operate as a reinforcer in observing responses. His subjects, Navy enlisted men working in the dark, were required to report deflections of a pointer on a dial when they pressed a key which provided a brief flash of light that illuminated the dial. When the subject observed the dial deflection, he pressed another key to reset the dial. In this way the deflections could be studied, using various schedules of reinforcement. He found that the percentage of signals detected increased with the number of signals presented. Not only does this study demonstrate that the detection of signals can serve as a reinforcer but it also shows that observing response rates vary with the particlar schedule employed, in a manner characteristic of the schedule. Although this study does not get at the deprivation operation directly, it illustrates the function of some sensory reinforcing agent in the absence of other stimuli.

Another way to study the effects of sensory deprivation has been undertaken by Heron.[36] He designed an experiment using college students as subjects, paying them $20 a day for their participation. They were required to lie on a bed in a cubicle for 24 hours a day, with time out only for meals (which they ate sitting on the edge of the bed) and going to the toilet. They wore translucent plastic visors which transmitted only diffused light and prevented any pattern vision. Cotton gloves, which extended beyond the fingers, prevented any perception of touch. The only sound they heard was the monotonous hum of the air conditioning, which masked any small changes in sound stimulation.

After being placed in the experimental booths at the beginning of the study, the subjects usually went to sleep shortly. When they awakened, they showed signs of restlessness which appeared from time to time; they talked to themselves, whistled, and sang. When going to the toilet, they

---

[35] J. C. Holland, Human vigilance, *Science,* **128** (1958), 61–67.
[36] W. Heron, The pathology of boredom, *Scient. Amer.,* **196**, no. 1 (1957), 52–69.

appeared dazed and confused and had increasing difficulty in finding their way about the bathroom. In the beginning, they thought about various things such as their studies or movies they had seen. As the experiment continued, the students began to hallucinate, seeing dots and other geometrical forms before their eyes. These were often described as looking like animated cartoons. The pictures became increasingly disturbing and would interfere with the subjects' sleep. The hallucinations were not confined to the visual sense alone. Some heard music or people talking to them; others had tactile hallucinations of feeling electric shocks or of being hit.

After the subjects emerged from several days of isolation, they reported that the whole room seemed to be in motion. Surfaces appeared curved, and objects seemed to change in size and shape. These findings confirm the less controlled reports that come to us from truck drivers; for example, those who "see" nonexistent objects on the road after driving many hours, or find "giant red spiders" on their windshields. In his autobiography, Charles Lindbergh describes similar phenomenon on his trans-Atlantic flight in 1927.

The experiment demonstrates the effects of prolonged sensory deprivation. When reinforcements from sensory stimulation are not forthcoming, the subject will manufacture them in the form of hallucinations or will try to generate them from his own behavior.

A number of subsequent studies have corroborated the work of Heron and his colleagues. Vernon[37] studied the effects of sensory deprivation upon various perceptual and motor skills. The subjects were isolated from one to three days and then tested. The performances were most markedly impaired following two days of deprivation, which may be explained by some compensation and adjustment that the subjects developed after two days of isolation. They found that deprivation had a damaging effect upon such motor skills as the pursuit rotor (following a target that rotates), mirror tracing, general motor coordination, and color perception. Depth perception did not seem to be affected. Their subjects also lost weight, although food was readily available. Other studies reported by Kubzansky and Leidermann[38] show a general decrease in learning ability during isolation as well as fatigue, drowsiness, and feelings of being dazed, confused, and disoriented following the period of deprivation.

*The Effects of Extended Visual Deprivation.* One of the suppositions of Gestalt psychology has been that the ability to see certain relationships in

[37] J. A. Vernon, T. W. McGill, W. L. Gulick, and D. Candland, The effect of human isolation upon some perceptual and motor skills. In P. Solomon, ed., *Sensory deprivation* (Cambridge, Mass.: Harvard University Press, 1961).

[38] P. E. Kubzansky and F. H. Leidermann, Sensory deprivation: An overview. In P. Solomon, ed., *Sensory deprivation*, op. cit.

the environment is not the result of learning but is due to native endow-
ment.[39] This school does not deny altogether the effects of learning but
maintains that there is a certain "primitive organization of behavior."
The implication is that we see a number of visual configurations naturally
and these perceptions do not need past experience to shape them. Because
of the difficulties in experimenting with newborn infants, the Gestalt
hypothesis has been difficult to prove or disprove. Ordinarily, because of
the importance of vision in our lives, it is not possible to prevent a person
from seeing for the first part of his life and then suddenly remove the
blindfold and observe what happens. However, if people who are born
blind and at some later time in either their childhood or adulthood have
their vision restored, the observations can test the Gestalt hypothesis of
"innate perceptions" as well as demonstrate the effects of long-term
deprivation on their seeing behavior. Some individuals develop cataracts
in both eyes at, or shortly after, birth. In this disease the lens of the eye
is semiopaque, so that the person may distinguish light from dark; but
apart from that discrimination, for all practical purposes he is blind. One
investigator, von Senden,[40] collected 66 cases in which cataracts were
removed in people who had had them for all or the major portion of their
lives. He made certain observations and tests to find out how these people
reacted after many years of visual deprivation. When the bandages were
removed after the operation, the patients were asked to answer questions
about how the world looked to them. One of the most significant observations was that they reported being bewildered and confused by the new
visual stimuli. Although all had the use of language as well as the muscle
and touch senses, they found it difficult to describe what they saw. The
acquisition of new visual discriminations did not come easily. It took
weeks or months or even longer. The subjects felt that too much was
being expected of them by their relatives and friends, who did not understand why these people could not see like normal human beings. Some of
the patients became discouraged and even quit trying to see. Only simple
visual responses such as fixating on an object or scanning the environment were easily acquired.

Tests indicated that a person could not tell whether there were two or
three black dots on a white piece of paper. Two strips of cardboard (10
cm and 20 cm long) could be reported as being different, after a little
training, but the subjects could not *say* which one was longer. Familiar
objects like a key, pencil, or knife could not be described when placed in
front of the subjects, but as soon as they were placed in the patients'
hands, they were immediately identified. Even though the patients were
thoroughly acquainted with tactual differences between curved and

[39] K. Koffka, *Principles of Gestalt psychology* (New York: Harcourt, Brace, 1935).
[40] M. von Senden, *Raum und Gestaltauffassung bei operierten Blindgeborenen vor
und nach Operation* (Leipzig: Barth, 1932).

straight, square and round, thick and thin, they could not apply these words to the same objects when looked at.

As time passed following the operation, the patients learned to identify colors, large and small objects, visual movement, and so forth. However, it took many weeks, even months, to identify common objects and people, and still longer to learn symbols. Distinguishing a square from a triangle was no easy task. They first learned that the two shapes were different, and then by painstakingly counting the corners, the task of identifying one from the other was accomplished, but only after some weeks of practice.

Another interesting observation was that once a discrimination had been learned, it was difficult to form any generalization of it. For example, when the name for an object was learned, the response would not occur if that object were slightly changed or placed in a new setting. A white square was identified but could not be successfully named as a square when it was turned over on its yellow side.

This study is significant in that it illustrates the importance of early learning for visual discriminations as well as the tremendous effect a long period of sensory deprivation has on the responses that will be emitted. The observations also illustrate the statement made several centuries ago by the British philosopher John Locke.[41] Locke wrote that the man born blind and suddenly made to see would not know the world as we do until he had associated his new knowledge with that already acquired from the other senses. Locke was one of the founders of the empirical movement in psychology and never accepted the notion that ideas could be inherited.

## APPLICATION OF SATIATION AND DEPRIVATION
### IN THE CONTROL OF BEHAVIOR

In order for a particular reinforcer to operate in strengthening behavior, it must be applied under a given state of deprivation. The function of the reinforcing stimulus, therefore, is to bring the behavior under the control of the appropriate deprivation. As we go about our daily affairs, we see the operation of these principles all about us. Take the control of children's behavior, for example. We deprive a child of food between meals so that the appropriate behavior of eating will be forthcoming when mealtime arrives. We refrain from giving him sweets or crackers. just prior to dinner so as not to satiate him and prevent his eating of the more nourishing food. When a child fails to eat his meal, instead of coaxing, bribing, and applying some aversive stimuli, a more appropriate means would be to excuse him from the table, thus increasing the degree of deprivation and increasing also the probability of eating at the next

[41] J. Locke, *An essay concerning human understanding* (London: A. and J. Churchel, 1694).

meal. In an attempt to increase children's study activity, one teacher known to the author deprived them of "drinks of water" until their work was done. Their rate was greatly increased. However, since this kind of operation was not acceptable to the parents or authorities, she was severely criticized for it, effective as it was. It is interesting to note, however, that those parents who found this method of control aversive had no objection to the use of food deprivation when children were naughty. Frequently we use deprivation as "punishment" as a means of controlling behavior (see Chapter 11). When a child is naughty, he is deprived of candy or other reinforcements or sent to bed without dinner in an attempt to generate alternate forms of behavior.

In adult behavior appropriate deprivation and satiation may be equally effective forms of control. Setting the time for a dinner party long enough after the guests' accustomed eating hour ordinarily generates a good rate of eating behavior. The hostess is also reinforced because the guests eat so heartily. The most bland food may be quite reinforcing if the individual is in a high enough state of deprivation. If the hostess has miscalculated the quantity of food adequate to serve her guests, she can satiate them before the meal with crackers and other tidbits. Restaurants that cater to preparing food "to order" sometimes supply hors d'oeuvres, bread, and the like to prevent complaints from the guests during the necessary delay in preparing the desired food. Frequently restaurants and bars supply "free" salty pretzels or potato chips to generate drinking behavior.

If you want a meeting to be short, schedule it at a time prior to the hour for eating so that adjournment will be imminent as mealtime approaches. If one wishes to make a man susceptible to bribery, encourage him to live beyond his means. The church has used the technique of deprivation for centuries as a means of controlling the moral conduct of its members. It may deny the sacraments to those who have erred in their ways, until penance has been achieved. The encouragement of fasting is likewise aimed at achieving greater recognition of behavior that is considered good.

Business and industry manipulate satiation and deprivation in controlling the price of goods. When the supply is short (deprivation), people are willing to pay high prices if no alternates are available. When the market is flooded (satiation), low prices are demanded because people will do little to achieve the goods. The salesman buys his customer a good meal in order to reinforce him for later favors. Advertisers appeal to deprivation and satiation as in the following: "The supply is limited, to buy now," or "Get them while they last."

*Use of Satiation to Alter Cigarette Smoking.*　　Various attempts to alter the behavior of cigarette smoking using operant conditioning techniques have not met with overwhelming success (see Chapter 18). The following

experiment by Marrone et al.[42] illustrates the attempt to achieve abstinence from smoking using a satiation technique. Thirty-two subjects
whose ages ranged from 23 to 56 were employed, all of whom had
smoked cigarettes regularly in varying amounts from one-half a pack per
day to over two packs. They were divided into three groups. The first
group was instructed to chain-smoke cigarettes for twenty hours, the
second for ten hours, and the third to smoke as they so desired. The aim
for the first two groups was to obtain total abstinence from further
smoking. After four months a follow-up study was made which revealed
the following results. Of the first group 6 (out of 10) subjects were still
not smoking. In the second group only 2 (out of 11) remained abstainers,
while in the third group 9 (out of 10) were continuing to smoke. These
results are interpreted by the investigators that the satiation technique
was at least partially successful probably because the continuous smoking
became extremely aversive. The subjects reported dizziness, dulled sensi-
tivity, burning of the eyes, sore throat, and nausea during the chain-
smoking period.

*Controlling Psychotic Behavior Through Deprivation and Satiation.* We
have already cited the work of Ayllon and Haughton[43] in controlling the
behavior of psychotic patients going to the dining room by deprivation
when they failed to go within a specified period of time, and the work by
Ayllon[44] in controlling food "stealing" through deprivation.

Satiation is also an effective means of controlling behavior. Ayllon[45]
also mentions the case of a psychotic patient who insisted on hoarding as
many of the institution's towels as she could. Previous means of removing
excess towels from the patient's room had been ineffective. Consequently,
a satiation procedure was implemented. Periodically, nurses would bring
more and more towels to her room. They would simply hand them to her
without comment. During the first week she was given an average of
seven towels a day. By the third week the number had increased to 60.
When the number of towels in the room totaled 625, she started taking
a few of them out. During the next year, the average number was reduced
until she kept only 1.5 towels at a time (see Figure 7–6).

Ayllon and Michael[46] report the cases of several psychotic patients
who hoarded rubbish. For five years these two mentally defective boys

---

[42] R. I. Marrone, M. A. Merksomer, and P. M. Salzberg, A short duration group
treatment for smoking behavior by stimulus satisfaction, *Behav. Res. and Ther.*, **8**
(1970), 347–352.

[43] T. Ayllon and E. Haughton, Control of behavior of schizophrenic patients by
food, *Jour. Exp. Anal. Behav.*, **5** (1962), 343–352.

[44] Ibid.

[45] T. Ayllon, Intensive treatment of psychotic behavior by stimulus satiation and
food reinforcement, *Behav. Res. Ther.*, **1** (1963), 53–61.

[46] T. Ayllon and J. Michael, The psychiatric nurse as a behavioral engineer, *Jour.
Exp. Anal. Behav.*, **2** (1959), 323–334.

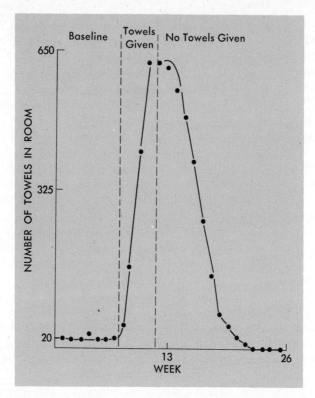

**Figure 7–6.**    Elimination of towel-hoarding behavior in a
psychiatric patient by satiation procedures. After establishing a base-line of about 20 towels, nurses continued to give
patient towels every day until the total had reached 625
towels. At this point patient began returning them until an
average of only 1.5 were kept in her room. (From T.
Ayllon, Intensive treatment of psychotic behavior by
stimulus satiation and food reinforcement, *Behavior Research and Therapy,* **1** [1963], 53–61, Fig. 3, p. 57. Copyright © 1963, Pergamon Press, Inc. Reproduced by
permission.)

had been carrying around papers, rubbish, and magazines inside their
clothes next to their skin. Because of skin rashes they periodically had to
be "dejunked" regularly by the attending nurses. It was believed that the
hoarding behavior was being maintained by the attention derived from it.
Two procedures were applied to alter their behavior. Because newspapers
and magazines are not common articles on the ward, it was suspected that
flooding the ward with newspapers might tend to satiate this behavior.
In addition, any attention to the patients was withheld (extinction). The
results of these patients are shown in Figure 7–7. The findings were the
same in all patients, namely a gradual decrease in the hoarding behavior.

## Deprivation and Satiation with Conditioned Reinforcers

The question now arises as to whether or not the same operation of deprivation and satiation can apply to the use of conditioned reinforcers once they have acquired their function as conditioned reinforcers. An experiment by Gewitz and Baer[47] indicates that the same operations are possible. They used the verbal approval of a female experimenter contingent on the response in a two-response game with normal children from a laboratory nursery school. In this game the child was to place a marble in either of two holes of a toy while the experimenter sat beside him. Such verbal approval consisted of statements of "good," "fine," and "Hm-hmmm." The change in the relative response frequencies from a baseline level following the introduction of the reinforcement indicated the degree to which the reinforcement was operating for a child.

Before playing the game, the children were subjected to one of three experimental conditions. Group 1 (34 children) was placed in 20-minute

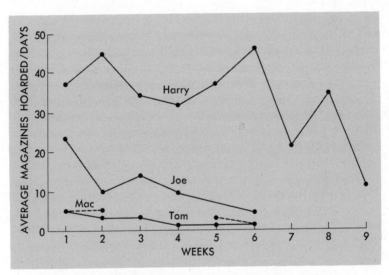

**Figure 7–7.** Satiation and extinction of two forms of magazine hoarding. Two patients, Harry and Joe, are the ones referred to in the text. The others showed it to a much lesser extent. (From T. Ayllon and J. Michael, The psychiatric nurse as a behavioral engineer, *Journal of the Experimental Analysis of Behavior*, **2** [1959], 323–334, Fig. 5, p. 333. Copyright 1959 by the Society for the Experimental Analysis of Behavior, Inc. Reproduced by permission of the authors and the publisher.)

[47] J. L. Gewitz and D. M. Baer, Deprivation and satiation of social reinforcers as drive conditions, *Jour. Abn. Soc. Psychol.*, **57** (1958), 165–172.

isolation (deprivation of social reinforcement). In this situation each child was led into the room that had a table and chair and was left to wait. The second group immediately played the game upon being led from the classroom (conceived of as an intermediate condition between deprivation and satiation). In the third group, children devoted 20 minutes to drawing and cutting out designs, in which the experimenter maintained a stream of friendly conversation and approved and admired their art efforts (satiation group). The results showed that the reinforcing power of approval was most obvious in the deprivation group (placed for 20 minutes in social isolation). Thus, a reinforcer that is typical in children's social interactions appears to be affected by deprivation and satiation in a similar manner to that found for the more primary reinforcers.

# 8　The Influence of Biological and Early Environmental Conditions on Personality Development

EACH TIME AN ORGANISM LEARNS A NEW response, personality is developing. In the preceding chapters, we considered the basic principles governing the acquisition of behavior. In subsequent chapters we shall consider supplemental principles. An approach to personality that stresses the processes in learning *is* a study of psychological development. We share with Freud the conviction that the best understanding of personality is to be had by taking the longitudinal approach. In the use of the case history, he asked his patients to recall the events of their past, including the significant experiences of their infancy, childhood, and adolescence. The reverse procedure is also possible by observing a young organism and noting the modifications of behavior which take place under many changing stimulus conditions. Any currently observable response or chain of responses is a function of the many variables that have affected the individual in his history of conditioning.

The viewpoint of this book has stressed and will continue to emphasize behavioral changes that take place as an organism interacts with the stimuli in his environment. In this chapter we shall limit ourselves to two special problems in personality development: (1) the biological limitations and potentialities for specific learning and (2) the effects of early environmental stimulation on later personality development.

HEREDITY

In Chapter 2 we made clear that heredity is *not* the cause of behavior. We do not inherit intelligence, special abilities, or personality characteristics. Heredity merely sets the limits within which an organism can respond. Between species and within species a great variation exists in the kinds of structures that have been inherited. In all species where reproduction is bisexual, the organism starts life as a uniting of two cells, one from each parent. Within this new cell unit are chromosomes (colored bodies) which occur in pairs, the two members of each pair having certain likenesses in appearance and function. In the union of the two original cells, one chromosome in each pair comes from both parents. The number of chromosomes in each cell differs from one species to another, but they are ordinarily the same in number within any one species. Within these chromosomes are the *genes*, the basic carriers of the hereditary traits.

Heredity, then, consists of the specific genes an individual receives from each parent at the moment of conception. Ordinarily, the genes are so minute that they are not visible even under a high-powered microscope. After the union of the two parent cells, a process of cell division takes place and continues until billions of cells, which make up the mature organism, have developed. All cells in the body thus possess the same heredity. The fact that some develop into eye cells, others into skin cells, and others into hair cells, and so forth depends on the special environment of the cells. This includes gravity, pressure, availability of oxygen, other chemicals that act differentially upon the cells, and the influence of each cell upon other cells.

At sexual maturity, a different kind of cell division occurs in which special cells for reproduction are formed. There is a reduction in the amount of division, since the chromosomes in each division have been reduced to half the original number. In this kind of division each reproductive cell can receive a different combination of chromosomes. When conception takes place by the uniting of the mother and father reproductive cells (ova and spermatozoon), the full number of chromosomes is restored and continues through subsequent cell division.

Even a simple biological characteristic depends on a number of genes. These interact in determining a particular structure that the parents transmit to the offspring. The traits that are passed on are only those that the parents themselves have received. The cells that eventually determine the mature structures, through a complex interaction, may represent a vast assortment of genes derived from the entire ancestry of the individual. It is possible to have a characteristic quite unlike one's parents but one that is still due to heredity. Brown-eyed parents usually produce brown-eyed children, but an occasional blue-eyed one is possible. The Mendelian laws explain quite clearly how this is possible. Some traits are dominant and others recessive, so that the presence of brown or blue eyes depends on the combination of genes inherited from both parents, which eventually determines the color.

The genes operate only in determining the structure of an individual. The growth of the structure progresses through an interaction with the environment. Early theorists supposed the possibility of the exclusive influence of heredity in determining a specific characteristic. However, in every developing structure there is both the influence of heredity and environment. An illustration of this interaction effect in determining a specific structure is seen in the fruit fly *Drosophila*, which has been extensively studied by geneticists. The number of facets in the eyes of the fruit fly differ in various types, depending on the particular gene constitution of each. However, the temperature at which the larvae are kept also influences the number of facets that will develop.

### ENVIRONMENT

Environment has been used to refer to many things. We speak of the *prenatal environment* consisting of the diet, nutrition, glandular secretions, and other conditions of the mother which affect the growing fetus. The lasting influence of this environment is shown in the experimentally produced "monsters." Siamese-type twin fish can be developed by artificially subjecting the eggs to slower development, low temperatures, insufficient oxygen, or ultraviolet rays.[1] Likewise, by the application of various chemicals, "two-headed" tadpoles can be produced. We are also familiar with the studies conducted to show the effects of radiation on prenatal development. Such exposure during the embryonic stage of growth results in a number of abnormalities, including changes in size and shape of the head and other parts of the body.[2]

Biologists also speak of *intercellular environment*, which consists of the surrounding cells in which each individual cell develops. These surrounding cells can influence the special way a designated cell grows. There is also *intracellular environment*. The genes within a cell are surrounded by a substance known as *cytoplasm*. Geneticists have suggested that these genes act as enzymes, inducing chemical changes in the cytoplasm. The action of a particular gene has different effects, depending on the specific chemical composition of a certain cell. Each gene also operates in an environment of other genes within any one cell.

Psychologists speak of the *behavioral environment*, a rather inclusive concept referring to current stimuli with which an organism interacts and

[1] C. R. Stockard, *The physical basis of personality* (New York: Norton, 1931).

[2] L. B. Russell, The effects of radiation on mammalian prenatal development. In A. Hollaender *Radiation biology*, vol. I (New York: McGraw-Hill, 1954).

to his earlier history of stimulation. Kantor[3] suggests environment to be the sum total of stimulation a person has received from conception until death. Since the stimuli in an organism's environment (discriminative, reinforcing, and so forth) and the responses he makes to these stimuli are difficult to separate in his developmental history, Kantor proposes the concept of *reactional biography*, which constitutes the sum total of responses an organism has made to stimuli up to any particular stage in his development. It is his total life history of interacting with stimuli. This conception of environment not only includes the ordinary notion of present environment as stimuli but the past environment as well, since at any point in the development of an organism, the present responding is going to be a function of both. The concept of behavioral environment is not merely limited to objects in one's physical surroundings, for unless they act as stimuli, they will not exert any influence on his behavior.

Stimuli have different kinds of functions, depending on the relationships that exist between them and the responses an organism makes. There are *eliciting stimuli* found in respondent behavior. These can, if appropriate, "pull out" a response with or without prior conditioning, depending on their properties. (Salivation can occur on presentation of meat or the ringing of a bell if the appropriate stimulus association has developed.) We have frequently mentioned *reinforcing stimuli* which strengthen or weaken a response when they are presented or withdrawn. *Discriminative stimuli* set the occasion for an organism to respond or not to respond, according to the contingencies of reinforcement presented or withheld. Furthermore the *secondary or conditioned reinforcing stimuli* take on the function of a primary reinforcer through prior association with it. In the next section we shall discuss *aversive stimuli*, which are really not classified as special stimuli because their functions are also involved in primary and secondary reinforcement and discrimination. However, their effects on the responses tend to be the opposite of positive reinforcement. Those stimuli, then, both present and in the past history of the organism, that exert and have exerted an influence on its behavior (whether they be primary or conditioned, internal or external) constitute what we call the organism's psychological or behavioral environment.

### BIOLOGICAL LIMITATIONS AND POTENTIALITIES

In speaking of limitations or potentialities, we are referring to opposite sides of the same coin. Certain structures can act as an advantage in learning some behavior or a disadvantage in acquiring other kinds of behavior. For example, inheriting two hands with four fingers and the opposed thumb on each is an advantage or structural potentiality for

---

[3] J. R. Kantor, *Principles of psychology*, vol. I (New York: Knopf, 1924).

acquiring many kinds of manipulatory behavior. An absence or a defect in structure acts as a disadvantage and limits the possibilities of acquiring certain behaviors. Birds, lacking hand structures, cannot acquire many manipulatory behaviors, but having wings, can locomote in a manner unavailable to most mammals.

**1.** *Hereditary Structures.*   The nature and development of bodily structures limit in some cases the possibility of behavior acquisition. The cat cannot learn to fly nor can the dog learn to climb a tree. The fact that humans have hands, vocal mechanisms, an upright posture, and a nervous system more complex than lower forms acts as a potentiality for the development of behavior not found among some other species. On the other hand, birds can see better, dogs can smell better, and monkeys can climb better than man because of structural advantages. The presence of a structure is a necessary but not a sufficient condition for behavioral acquisition. It does not assure a response. If no bars ever existed in the rat's environment, he would not learn to press them, although he has the structure that allows the possibility of this response. At the human level, the structural equipment of most persons allows a tremendous and almost limitless variety of behavioral possibilities. These structures are inherited, but the behavior is not. The structure merely acts as a limitation or potentiality within which behavior can or cannot be acquired, depending on the environmental contingencies.

**2.** *Structural Defects.*   An individual may possess structural limitations that can be due either to heredity, accident, or disease. These last two conditions are, in the strict sense, environmental. The child with cerebral palsy is limited because of brain damage before birth in the acquisition of certain coordinated and skilled movements. He has been the victim of an environmental accident in the same sense that a man is blinded by fire. Often, following epidemic encephalitis (sleeping sickness), a child (or adult) is left mentally deficient after recovery from the immediate effects of the virus. Because of cerebral inflammation, his brain has been left damaged, thus limiting to some degree the kinds of behavior he can emit or will be able to learn in the future. Many forms of structural abnormalities leading to peculiar development and deficiency are the result of environmental accident, disease, insufficient nutrition, drugs, and poisons to which the fetus was subjected in its prenatal development.

Structural defects can also be inherited. Thyroid deficiency has been fairly well established as operating in a disorder known as *cretinism*. The child's condition is readily diagnosed by his stunted growth, coarse, thick skin, underdeveloped genitalia, and protruding abdomen. If defective genes were contributing to the inadequate thyroid development, the disorder would be, in this sense, inherited. From a point of view of behavior,

the physical weaknesses have limited the possibility of the cretin's learning many responses, some intellectual in character, which are typical of
the normal child. Another clearly identifiable disorder which acts as a
limiter in behavior acquisition is a condition known as *phenylpyruvic
oligophrenia*. The disorder is typified by the presence of phenylpyruvic
acid in the urine because of the inability of the liver to manufacture an
enzyme to utilize it. Geneticists believe that the condition depends on the
presence of a simple recessive gene. The individual has very limited
ability and is severely retarded mentally as a result. He often cannot
learn to talk or to control his bladder or bowel movements. The heredity
condition in this unusual case has placed a severe limitation on the
amount and kinds of behavior that can be acquired.

Heredity does not cause behavior or lack of it. Neither do accidents
or disease cause mental deficiency. In both cases the biological limitations
and disadvantages have limited the acquisition of behavior through
structures of the body. By structure we mean any organic, somatic, or
psysiognomic condition. Included are anatomical, psysiological, and biochemical conditions that might indirectly influence behavioral development and acquisition.[4]

**3.** *Maturation.*   The particular species to which an organism belongs
determines his final level of biological development. Rats, dogs, monkeys,
and men develop at different rates and reach maturity at different times.
The ultimate level achieved will differ widely in each. There is a wide
variation from species to species in the ultimate limits that each can
achieve.

Frequently, in any one species it is difficult to distinguish between
the effects of maturation and learning. With continued growth, new
biological potentialities become available, enabling the more mature
organism to acquire more complex responses. There is an interdependence
of biological maturation (growth of structures) and learning (acquisition
of new behavior). It is clear that the child cannot stand until his muscles
and bones are strong enough to support his weight. He can only learn to
walk after the mechanisms of equilibrium are sufficiently matured. The
same is true of manipulatory movements and speech. Forcing a child to
make discriminations beyond those which his biological mechanisms have
set at any stage in development only leads to frustration and conflict.

As the organs of speech grow and change in shape, it becomes pos-
sible for greater variety of sounds to occur in the infant's vocal repertoire.
At any stage in the development, maturation sets the limits for learning.
Just as species differ in the rate and final limits of biological growth, so

---

[4] A. Anastasi, *Differential psychology*, 3rd ed. (New York: Macmillan, Inc.,
1958).

also do individuals within a species. Other things being equal, some children walk at 11 months, others not until 17 months. Two children, both 3 years old, may speak quite differently; one is difficult to comprehend, the other is quite articulate in his talking. Although variations in learning opportunity may quite obviously account in part for these differences, it is also possible that the better speaker is more mature in his vocal development.

On occasion, one meets a child who is exceedingly slow in his development, with his final limit of growth lower than most. We call this child *developmentally retarded*. Because of his slow and limited maturation, he is slower to acquire new responses required at any level of development. He may show marked deficiency in acquisition of intellectual, interpersonal and emotional behaviors typified by any stage in development.

From a biological standpoint, maturation refers to the process of structural growth determined by heredity, but it is also obviously affected by environmental influences. We can also speak of maturation from a psychological standpoint. In this sense it means the progression from lesser to more mature forms of behavior.[5] The criterion for maturity would ordinarily be set by the norm for any age group. The changes in behavioral development are both a function of the learning process and the limitations set by biological maturation at any stage of development. A simple example is seen in the changes that take place in feeding behavior. To begin with, an infant gets his nourishment from sucking from the bottle or his mother's nipple. From birth through the first few months this process becomes more efficient. Then weaning begins. It may be introduced gradually by giving small amounts of mashed food from a spoon and occasionally milk from a cup. Eventually the process is complete and the nipple is abandoned. Another shift soon occurs from eating with mother's help to eating alone. As the child becomes stronger and more coordinated, the efficiency of the process improves. He spills less and begins to use adult utensils. Eventually he is able to make use of the knife for cutting. The change is gradual, over many years, and depends on the potentialities if maturation and the availability of learning.

The sequences of many kinds of behavior development at the human level have been extensively studied. Halverson,[6] for example, observed the development of the grasping response in the infant. Young infants, 20 weeks old, use a sweeping motion of the whole arm and hand in order to secure an object. At about 28 weeks the arm moves more directly outward beyond the object and then back to grasp it. At 36 weeks the grasp

---

[5] N. Cameron and A. Magaret, *Behavior pathology* (Boston: Houghton Mifflin, 1951).

[6] H. M. Halverson, The acquisition of skill in infancy, *Jour. Genet. Psychol.*, **43** (1933), 3–48.

is more differentiated, and by a year it is quite direct. Psychologists have also studied the schedules of motor development[7] from lifting the head to creeping to standing to walking, as well as language, affectional and intellectual development.[8]

Without a particular degree of development or growth, learning is impossible. Maturation thus provides the foundations on which learning is built. For example, a child learns to walk at that stage when he is maturatively ready, and his developing vocabulary depends to a degree on the maturation of the vocal apparatus and its neural control. For instance, it is ordinarily foolish to try to begin toilet training before a child can control his sphincter muscles. A study of the developmental schedules that indicate the average time at which behavior can be acquired is helpful for anyone interested in the proper training of the child. However, it should be made clear that individuals differ in the rate and often in the progression of development, so that the schedules can act only as guides and not as absolute standards.

An interesting experiment that shows both the significance of species limitations on behavioral acquisition as well as the limits set by maturation was performed over 30 years ago by Kellogg and Kellogg.[9] It is considered a classical experiment today, and it is familiar to many students. We mention it here because it demonstrates most adequately the principles we have been stressing concerning the limits of heredity on behavior development.

These investigators brought an infant chimpanzee, Gua, into their home and raised it with their son, Donald, for a period of about nine months. Every effort was made to treat Gua as a child rather than a pet, as an attempt to ensure identical opportunity to learn for both organisms. The ape was dressed in child's clothes, toilet trained, taught to eat from a spoon, drink from a cup, and was given the same affectional treatment, and so on. During the study, the Kelloggs made a series of comparative tests of the behavior of the two species at different stages of their development. Both liked looking at picture books, scribbling with a pencil, and playing "go hide." In tests where physical maturation was important, the ape succeeded earlier. Gua learned to climb a ladder and swing down, open a door, and operate a light switch more quickly than Donald. She drank from a glass, ate with a spoon, and was toilet trained earlier. On the other hand, Donald was superior in social games (pat-a-cake) and more dexterous with his hands (the ape's hand is not so well adapted to handling small objects). At the end of the experiment Donald was begin-

[7] M. M. Shirley, *The first two years*, vol. I: *Postural and locomotor development;* vol. II: *Intellectual development* (Minneapolis: University of Minnesota Press, 1931, 1933).

[8] A. Gesell, et al., *The first five years* (New York: Harper & Brothers, 1940).

[9] W. N. Kellogg and L. A. Kellogg, *The ape and the child* (New York: Whittlesey House, McGraw-Hill, 1933).

ning to exceed Gua in many of the performances, even though she was 2½ months older. It is clear that at certain points in the maturational process. Gua exceeded Donald, but her early advantage was overcome by Donald's preferred evolutionary status.

Compared with lower organisms, man's maturation is slower. However, his longer maturative history gives him the greater advantage of behavior modification by external stimulus control, whereas in lower forms it is possible to effect almost complete enslavement by the immediately present stimuli. Man's behavior, on the other hand, is more frequently a function of more remote stimulus conditions in his past. There is no reason to believe, however, that man acts free from stimulus control (free will). His behavior is just as determinable as the rat's. By the complexity of man's biological potentiality, it is more likely that stimuli in his past history will operate on his present behavior. This, of course, makes the study of human personality development all the more difficult. It accounts, however, for our resorting to animal investigation, where variables can be better handled and are not so numerous, as a means of understanding the developmental process.

Studies using the method of co-twin control, by Gesell and Thompson,[10] likewise illustrate the limiting as well as the maturative potentialities for behavior development. In their studies of stair climbing and cube behavior (reaching, manipulating, and playing with the cubes), they took identical twins who were 46 weeks old at the start of the experiment. Twin *T* (trained) underwent a 20-minute training period each day in these two behaviors. At the end of the training period, twin *C* (control) had had no specific training in either of these two behaviors. She proved equal to the trained twin in the cube behavior but did not come up to the trained twin in the stair climbing. Twin *T* readily climbed a five-tread staircase, while twin *C* was not able to do so even with the assistance of the experimenter. However, two weeks later, without any intervening training, the control twin was able to climb. Then, at age 53 weeks, the control twin was given two weeks of extensive practice at the end of which she approximated the trained twin in his skill. Because of greater maturative development, a two-week training at age 53 weeks was as effective as a six-week training at 46 weeks old. In interpreting these results, it should be kept in mind that the problem is not one of heredity (maturation) versus environment (learning). A comparison is made between a specific period of controlled learning at one time and the combined efforts of maturation and uncontrolled learning (exercise of related behavior which the subjects underwent outside the laboratory) on the other.[11]

---

[10] A. Gesell and H. Thompson, Twins *T* and *C* from infancy to adolescence: A biogenic study of individual differences by the method of co-twin control, *Genet. Psychol. Monogr.*, **24** (1941), 3–122.

[11] A. Anastasi, op. cit.

THE PROBLEM OF UNLEARNED BEHAVIOR

In Chapter 3 we spoke of two classes of behavior, learned and un-learned. At the human level the amount of behavior in the latter class is rather small, being limited to simple reflexes. This is not the case in many lower species. In a comparative approach to psychology, where species differences are obvious, the problem of unlearned behavior is necessarily important. Unlearned behavior usually refers to behavior that is exhibited upon presentation of certain stimuli in the absence of any possible prior conditioning. The criteria proposed from time to time that a behavior must meet in order to qualify as unlearned have included (1) universality within the species, (2) uniformity among members of the species, (3) sudden appearance, (4) absence of opportunity for previous learning, and (5) possession of survival value. Of all these, the only really dependable criterion is the absence of any prior opportunity to learn.[12]

It is not correct to call unlearned behavior simply *inherited* behavior, since only structural characteristics are directly influenced by the genes. In unlearned behavior the response automatically occurs in the presence of certain stimuli which are sufficient in themselves to call out the re-sponse. However, without these stimuli, the response does not appear. Unlearned behavior has traditionally be classed into (1) tropisms, (2) reflexes, and (3) instincts. These divisions are not sharply differentiated. A tropism usually means an orienting of the entire organism toward a stimulus. The response is forced by the properties of the stimulus and the responding organism. We note the turning of plants toward the sun, flying of moths to the light, withdrawal of the cockroach from a light, and movement of the loggerhead turtle toward the sea.

Reflex generally implies a specific response of some part of the organ-ism to a particular kind of stimulus: the contraction of the pupil to light, "knee jerk" to a tap on the patellar tendon, or the lacrimal secretion (tears) in the eye when some foreign matter enters it.

Instinct is less clearly defined. Some writers refer merely to internal functions; contractions of the stomach and dryness of the throat are called instincts and used interchangeably with the nebulous concept of drive. More properly, instinct implies a chain of reflexes as a complex stereotyped sequence of responses. The behavior of many insects as well as higher organisms fits this definition. The pollinating behavior of the yucca moth is a favorite example. After emerging from its chrysalis, it travels to the yucca flower, obtains pollen, then goes to another yucca flower and deposits its eggs as well as the newly found pollen.[13] Nest building, copulating behavior, and migration in many species have been considered to be instinctive.

At the human level, some have implied the concepts of "native

---

[12] Ibid.
[13] C. P. Stone, Maturation and "instinctive" functions. In C. P. Stone, ed., *Comparative psychology*, 3rd ed. (Englewood Cliffs, N.J.: Prentice-Hall, 1951).

capacity" or "innate ability" to mean that the expression of some behavior or proficiency has its roots in an inherited potential. Inherited intelligence, musical talent, and predisposition to personality traits frequently suggest that the behavior somehow is inborn. Nothing could be further from the truth. All that we can say is that structures are inherited. Behavior is not. Because of a given structural advantage, a person may be able to learn some kinds of behavior better than others. Only in this way is heredity operating. Tall men are more disposed to basketball playing than short men, a large physique is an advantage for the football player, and two hands with five fingers on each hand are necessary for piano playing. These are the biological potentialities and serve only to give one a structure that can be used in some behavioral acquisition. Organisms and species differ in the structural advantages and limitations that they inherit. Behavior operates within these limits whether it is a direct function of that structure in unlearned behavior or expression by the principles of behavior acquisition discussed in previous chapters.

*Species Differences in Learned and Unlearned Behavior.*   At the level of the jelly fish it is possible to predict just about the entire repertoire of responses if one knows the stimuli affecting it. The behavior consists of almost completely unlearned responses. If we know about the environmental stimuli and their properties to elicit the responses, our knowledge of the behavior of this organism is almost complete. In the comparison of the jelly fish with the bee, for example, the repertoire of the latter is more complex. Although the bee's behavior is partially unlearned, its other activity can be acquired and modified. The rat, a familiar animal by now, also exhibits a variety of unlearned responses. These have not previously been stressed because our discussion has been concerned with the principles of behavior acquisition. However, many of the responses concerned with reproduction, exploration, foraging, nest building, care of the young, and defense appear to be in the unlearned class. When we get to man, we see the unlearned portion playing a less important role than in the rat. With much greater biological potential than any other species, man's repertoire of unlearned behavior is limited to simple reflexes, although these also can be modified, as we have seen, through conditioning.

## Effects of Early Experience on Behavior

A vast amount of research has become available on the effects of early experience, particularly at the animal level. Space does not permit the enumeration of many of these studies. The interested student, however, can look into reviews by Orlansky[14] at the human level and Beach

[14] H. Orlansky, Infant care and personality, *Psychol. Bull.*, **46** (1949), 1–48.

and Jaynes[15] at the animal level. We shall attempt to mention a few representative examples in various areas of study.

## EARLY DEPRIVATION AND RESTRICTION OF ENVIRONMENT

Riesen[16] kept chimpanzees in darkness for the first 16 months of life. When removed from the restricted environment, they showed typical reflexive pupillary responses to light but a great deficiency in depth perception. In one of his subjects, 50 hours of visual experience elapsed before the simple discriminative response of reaching and grasping a nursing bottle could be acquired.

Restriction has been studied in a number of species of birds. Padilla[17] kept chicks from pecking by rearing them in darkness, later tested them for accuracy. They tended to be inferior to normals at first but ordinarily improved rapidly when taken out of the restricted environment. However, when the chicks were fed in the dark artificially from a spoon after hatching and later placed in the light, they never developed the pecking responses when placed in a pen with grain and grit. It would appear, according to the author, that these birds were starving to death in the midst of plenty. The evidence seems to point in the direction that when organisms are deprived of normal visual stimulation during the developmental period, they may be unable to respond properly to visual stimuli when these later become available.

Numerous investigations have been conducted on the hoarding behavior of the rat. Hunt[18] deprived one group of rats of food for 15 days, beginning at the age of 24 days. A second group was subjected to a similar period of deprivation except that the experiment started at the age of 32 days. Both groups were then given regular feeding for the next five months, after which they were again starved along with a control group that had not been deprived during infancy. The rats in the 24-day deprived group responded to the second period of deprivation by hoarding more than two and a half times as many food pellets as did the control rats who had not been starved in infancy. The 32-day group did not show any excess hoarding. Hunt interprets these findings as indicating that the early infantile feeding frustration had a greater effect upon adult hoarding behavior than did later frustration.

A study by McKelvey and Marx[19] used partial water deprivation for

[15] F. A. Beach and J. Jaynes, Effects of early experience on behavior, *Psychol. Bull.*, **51** (1954), 239–263.

[16] A. H. Riessen, The development of visual perception in man and chimpanzee, *Science*, **106** (1949), 107–108.

[17] S. G. Padilla, Further studies on delayed pecking in chicks, *Jour. Comp. Psychol.*, **20** (1935), 413–443.

[18] J. McV. Hunt, The effects of infant feeding frustration upon adult hoarding in the albino rat, *Jour. Abn. Soc. Psychol.*, **36** (1941), 338–360.

[19] R. K. McKelvey and M. H. Marx, Effects of infantile food and water deprivation on adult hoarding in the rat, *Jour. Comp. Physiol. Psychol.*, **44** (1951), 423–430.

one group of rats for 15 days after weaning. A second group was partially deprived of food. A control group had both food and water accessible at all times. After 130 days, hoarding tests were conducted both before and after a period of complete deprivation. The food deprivation in the male rats showed significantly more hoarding than the controls, but no significant differences were found in the hoarding of the water-deprived rats.

*Effects of Environmental Restriction in Scotties.*    A series of experiments by Thompson and Melzack and their associates with dogs illustrates the effects of severe restriction of opportunities for development in early life on later behavioral acquisition.[20] They have studied the effects of a barren environment on later behavior in a number of areas of development: social, emotional, and general learning ability.

Shortly after weaning (4 weeks) Scotties were divided into two groups. One group (control) was raised as pets by families outside the laboratory; the other group (experimental) was confined to cages, one to a cage. The cage was opaque so that the dog could not see outside. Furthermore, although food was delivered to him, he never saw his keepers. The dogs were raised in this isolated environment for seven to ten months, at which time the two groups were first tested. The first test was for activity. The normal group was placed in a small room. After exploring the room a bit, they soon lay down and relaxed. The experimental group continued active, exploring for a longer time. Measurements of time were taken during activity and nonactivity. Similar results occurred when each group was placed in a maze. When the same animals were tested in these situations several years later, the earlier restricted dogs still showed considerable more activity than the normal ones, even though both groups were then of the same age.[21]

In another experiment, the effects of early restriction of activity was studied on the emotional behavior of the Scotties.[22] Three weeks after restriction, the experimental animals were exposed to a series of objects with which they had had no previous contact such as a human skull, a slowly inflating balloon, an opened umbrella. The normal dogs usually ran from these strange objects without showing much excitement, while the restricted dogs became very agitated, jumped back and forth, whirled around, or "stalked" the objects. A year later the restricted and normal dogs were again compared in the same situation. The normal dogs were by now more aggressive, growling, barking, and snapping at the objects, while the restricted dogs still showed their earlier diffuse emotional excitement. However, they had by this time developed an avoidant re-

[20] W. R. Thompson and R. Melzack, Early environment, *Scient. Amer.*, **194**, no. 1 (1956), 38–42.

[21] W. R. Thompson and W. Heron, The effects of early restriction of activity in dogs, *Jour. Comp. Physiol. Psychol.*, **47** (1954), 77–82.

[22] R. Melzack, The genesis of emotional behavior: An experimental study of the dog, *Jour. Comp. Physiol. Psychol.*, **47** (1954), 166–168.

sponse, typical of the normal dogs a year earlier. Melzack concluded that the environmental experience with objects that apparently are emotionally provoking is necessary for the development of adaptive responses such as avoidance and aggression.

In a third experiment, attempts were made to discover the effects of early restriction on the responses to such primary aversive stimuli as an electric shock or a burning object.[23] Scotties were first pursued by a toy car that gave them an electric shock when they touched it. The normal dogs quickly learned to avoid being hit by the car. They would jump out of its way or flick a leg or tail to prevent being hit. The restricted dogs behaved in a much less organized manner. They jumped about, galloped in circles, and actually ran into the car. It took about 25 shocks for them to learn the avoidance response, as compared with the average of six shocks for the normals. Even then the restricted dogs became agitated and excited when they saw the car. Two years later, the restricted dogs still showed their earlier agitation when tested. In tests using nose burning with a safety match, the normal dogs quickly learned to turn their noses when the match was struck, while seven out of ten restricted dogs made no attempt to avoid the noxious stimulus. They "appeared unaware" of the source of the aversive stimulus. These dogs often "toyed" with the painful stimulus and even walked into it. The authors conclude that responses to noxious stimuli are at least in part learned. If an organism does not learn them in infancy, he may never achieve the proper avoidance behavior characteristic of a normal adult.[24]

In studies of learning where chicken wire was placed between the dog and a positive reinforcement of food, the normal dogs quickly learned to go around the barrier to receive food, while the restricted animals dashed up to the barrier and pushed at it, trying to get their noses through the wire mesh. In delayed-reaction tests, both groups observed the experimenter put food in one of the pair of boxes. They were then released at various times later, to test whether or not they could still select the correct box. The normal dogs were able to make the correct selection of going to the box with the food in it even after a delay of 4 minutes, while the restricted dogs usually could not select the right box even after being released without any delay at all.

In a final study, tests of dominance were attempted. A restricted dog and a normally reared one were allowed to compete for a bone. Almost without exception the normal dogs dominated the restricted ones. Furthermore the normal dogs still dominated the restricted dogs even in cases where the latter were several years older.[25]

---

[23] R. Melzack and T. H. Scott, The effect of early experience on the response to pain, *Jour. Comp. Physiol. Psychol.*, **50** (1957), 155–161.
[24] Ibid.
[25] W. R. Thompson and R. Melzack, op. cit.

It is dangerous, of course, to extrapolate these results too far and imply that a direct comparison between dogs and humans is possible. At the level of the Scottie it is clear that an environment of many stimuli to which he can acquire a variety of discriminative responses early in life is an important condition for normal development. Restriction results in behavioral impoverishment and often permanent retardation.

Similar observations are found at the human level, although it is impossible to conduct controlled experiments by placing an organism in such a restricted environment shortly after birth and keeping him there for several years before testing the effects on behavior. Some studies have been done on early restriction of movement, but they have not been carried on over a very long period of time, and the results, in general, have been negative.[26] Surveys of children reared in institutions like orphanages have some bearing on the problem. It has been fairly well established that orphanage children do not perform as well on tests of intelligence as those reared in their own homes. There may be a number of variables operating which account for these differences, and it is difficult to isolate them all. However, institutional environments are relatively lacking in stimuli for the developing child. There are problems of overcrowding, lack of personnel, and little necessary equipment for appropriate discriminative learning. There is also evidence indicating that the development of verbal behavior is slower among children reared in institutions.[27] The degree and variety of stimuli in the environment are obviously important conditions for acquiring a verbal response. Another interesting observation of institutionalized children is that their relative performances on intelligence tests tend to decline with age and time spent in the institution, whereas (ordinarily) that of children reared outside the environment tends to stay relatively constant.[28]

Further light is shed on the problem of restricted environment in studies of the so-called wild children. Although lacking any experimental control, they do show the effects of a kind of restriction in that the environment in which they grow up is dissimilar to that of a civilized one. An early report by the French physician Itard[29] describes the case of Victor, the wild boy of Aveyron. In September 1799, three sportsmen came upon a boy of about eleven or twelve years old wandering about in one of the forests of France. The boy was naked, dirty, unable to speak, and seemed frightened. It appeared that he had led a wild animal-like ex-

---

[26] W. Dennis, Infant reaction to restriction, *Trans. N. Y. Acad. Sci.*, **2** (1940), 202–218.

[27] A. Anastasi, op. cit., chapter xii.

[28] W. Sloan and H. H. Harman, The constancy of the I.Q. in mental defectives, *Jour. Genet. Psychol.*, **71** (1947), 177–185.

[29] J. M. G. Itard, *The wild boy of Aveyron*, trans. G. and M. Humphrey (New York: Appleton-Century-Crofts, 1932).

istence. He was seized by the men and brought to the attention of Itard. The characteristics of this case are similar to others in the literature and have been summarized by Zingg.[30] These children are usually mute and walk on all fours. Their sensory responses are typically quite acute; sight (particularly at night), smell, and hearing appear to show better discriminations than those found in civilized groups. They show no need to cover their bodies with clothing and seem to develop a resistance to heat and cold. In particular, in the case of the wild boy of Aveyron, a marked deficiency in perception of depth and distance was observed. He could not discriminate solid objects from pictures of them. When such children are placed in a more civilized environment, they ordinarily show rapid improvement in learning, although they *seldom* come up to the level of the normal children of the same age.

However, this should not be expected and is no evidence for any kind of "inherited" feeblemindedness. The long periods of isolation, where opportunities for normal behavioral acquisition in a civilized environment are lacking, certainly is not going to facilitate the learning process in dogs or man. Furthermore, in these human cases there is the possibility of interference from earlier acquired responses, well established, which were acquired in the "wild" and must be extinguished, depressed, or interfered with before other activities can be adequately learned. Although the studies of the "wild children" are uncontrolled and somewhat anecdotical, the findings are similar to those developed in the more controlled animal studies. In early restriction and lack of environmental stimuli, there appears to be a profound and lasting effect, to the disadvantage of the behaving organism, on the learning of later behavior.

Harlow and Zimmermann[31] have tested the effects of raising young monkeys on "surrogate" mothers. These mothers were made of wire mesh and terry cloth, the latter being soft to the touch. Some of the monkeys were nursed with the milk bottle attached to the wire mesh and others were similarly fed with the bottle attached to the breast of the terry-cloth mother. When the monkeys were given the choice of going to either mother, they typically chose the terry-cloth mother regardless of which "surrogate" mother had previously fed them. This preference continued for many months.

When fearsome stimuli were presented to the monkeys in the form of a large wooden spider or other strange and unfamiliar objects, they would typically run to the terry-cloth mother. In her presence, however, the monkeys were more likely to explore the unfamiliar objects. Harlow and Zimmermann concluded that the contact with the terry cloth is

---

[30] R. M. Zingg, Feral man and extreme cases of isolation, *Amer. Jour. Psychol.*, 53 (1940), 487–515.

[31] H. F. Harlow and R. R. Zimmermann, Affectional responses in infant monkeys, *Science*, 130 (1959), 421–432.

primarily reinforcing to the infant monkeys. Since both of the "surrogate" mothers gave adequate nourishment, it is not the food alone that is reinforcing, but touching the soft mother is equally important.

There also appear to be other stimuli that real mothers provide that are important for normal development. Even the monkeys raised on the terry-cloth mothers developed peculiar behaviors as they grew up. They tended to be more aggressive and unsocial and had great difficulty in having sexual intercourse with other normally raised monkeys of the opposite sex. These findings would seem to have some implication for the significance of early contact stimulation for normal development.[32]

*Environmental Restriction of Institutionally Raised Children.*    Spitz[33] has observed the behavior of human infants raised in an institutional environment. He found that children who spent the first year in such a deprived environment showed marked retardation in their behavioral development. When he returned to the institution two years later, he noticed that the general development of those children who had remained was definitely retarded. Some could not walk without help, and others had not learned enough speech to enable them to communicate in a fashion characteristic of their chronological age.

One possible explanation for the retardation could be a lack of sensory stimulation. Spitz had observed that the sides of the infants' cribs were covered, few or no toys were provided, and visual stimulation was restricted to staring at the blank ceiling. The wards were usually quiet so that the babies received little auditory stimulation. Children were rarely handled, so kinesthetic and tactile stimulation was at a minimum. In institutions that are understaffed, it is possible that sources of emotional, intellectual, and social stimuli were absent.

Goldfarb[34] has compared children raised in an institution with another group reared in foster homes; the groups were matched for age and sex. In many respects he found the institutionally raised children inferior. On tests of intelligence, there was a greater weakness in concept formation and abstract thinking. Some of the institutional children were later adopted into foster homes that were intellectually and socially more stimulating. Further tests showed that the early deficit remained. He concludes that the early deprivations exert a lasting influence on a child's development that is not easily overcome even by subsequent periods of normal school, family, and community environment.

---

[32] H. F. Harlow, The heterosexual affectional response in monkeys, *Amer. Psychologist,* **17** (1962), 1–9.

[33] R. A. Spitz. Hospitalism: An inquiry into the genesis of psychiatric conditions in early childhood, *Psychoanal. Stud. Child,* **1** (1945), 53–74; **2** (1945), 113–117.

[34] W. Goldfarb, Effects of psychological deprivation in infancy and subsequent stimulation, *Amer. Jour. Psychiat.,* **102** (1945), 18–33.

STUDIES OF IMPRINTING

Recently psychologists have been particularly concerned with the effects of stimuli that are presented very early in the organism's postnatal existence. The results of such experiments is that the first stimulus to elicit a response in the very young organism becomes the only stimulus that will henceforth arouse that response. Usually the experimental operation in this procedure is to prevent some visual stimulus (along with an auditory one sometimes) of a moving object (exclusive of members of his own species) during the first hours after birth. The imprinting is said to occur if the organism subsequently exhibits behavior toward that object (and others like it) which usually is exhibited only toward members of its own species.

The operation has been studied in a variety of species under controlled and uncontrolled conditions. Birds, fish, and some mammals (goats, sheep, deer, and guinea pigs) have served as subjects, although birds have been the most popular subjects so far. The problem was first investigated by an Austrian zoologist, Konrad Lorenz,[35] with geese as his subjects. He divided a clutch of eggs laid by a graylag goose into two groups; one group was hatched by the mother and the other in an incubator. The goslings hatched by the mother immediately followed her. However, those hatched in the incubator, never saw their mother, only the experimenter. They continued to follow Lorenz. He then marked the incubator-hatched birds and placed both groups together in a large box. When first let out, each member of the two groups went immediately to its respective "parent." The experience that determined the behavior was referred to as "imprinting."

Hess[36] has studied the phenomenon under laboratory conditions, using mallard ducklings as subjects. His apparatus consisted of a circular runway. The imprinting object was a model of a male mallard duck, the kind used by hunters as a decoy. The model could be moved around the runway at various speeds and distances from the birds. Inside the model, a tape-recorded sound was played. After being hatched in the laboratory incubator, the birds were isolated in individual boxes without visual stimulation until the time came for them to be placed in the apparatus. They were exposed to the model one at a time and then returned to their boxes by means of a trap door. Imprinting was accomplished by placing the ducklings on the runway about a foot away from the decoy. A noise "gock, gock, gock" was played from inside the decoy as it moved along the runway. Testing for the effects of imprinting were made by placing the duckling between two decoy ducks, one the original and the other a

[35] K. Z. Lorenz, *King Solomon's ring: A new light on animal ways* (New York: Crowell, 1952).

[36] E. H. Hess, "Imprinting" in animals, *Scient. Amer.*, **198**, no. 3 (1958), 81–90.

female model differing in color and "call." Tests indicated that imprinting occurs soon after the hatching but is most successful between 13 and 16 hours after birth.

Another series of tests varied the distance between the model and the subject at the time of imprinting, from 12½ to 100 feet. As the distance increased up to 50 feet between subject and object, the strength of the imprinting increased. The amount of time in the imprinting sessions was also varied. The strength of the imprinting appeared to be dependent not so much on the duration of the imprinting period as on the effort the bird exerted in following the object. When the ducklings had to follow a decoy up an incline or over a hurdle, the imprinting results were better than on the plane. Furthermore the effect of the imprinting became progressively weaker when the birds were given meprobamate (Miltown), which is a muscle relaxant.[37]

Jaynes[38] investigated imprinting with young chicks by exposing new-born chicks to a 7-inch, moving green cube which traveled irregularly along a 10-foot alley. In testing for the effects, he found the degree of strength of imprinting *was* a function of practice or time spent in the initial imprinting sessions. The birds exposed to the moving object in longer daily periods were more likely to become imprinted; they followed the object more vigorously than those exposed for a shorter time. The degree of retention of the imprinting in later life was also related to the amount of early practice.

The implications of these findings have been subject to considerable theorizing. Some psychologists liken imprinting to a seal which with one swift blow stamps an ineradicable impression on the mind or brain.[39] However, these studies certainly imply that learning is operating in the development of the response. Much of the behavior that is modified by imprinting is of the respondent sort. We have already seen that unlearned responses can be modified through the process of conditioning.

Child and comparative psychologists have also demonstrated that a certain amount of visual stimulation and handling is important in early life. Ribble[40] has stressed consistently the significance of "mothering" for proper personality development. By "mothering" she means handling, cuddling, loving, embracing, and similar affectionate responses. Clinical evidence indicates that this kind of treatment facilitates eating and sleeping, and leads to less crying and frustrated responses. Many feel that

[37] E. H. Hess, Effects of meprobamate on imprinting in waterfowl, *Ann. N. Y. Acad. Sci.*, **67** (1957), 724–733.

[38] J. Jaynes, Imprinting: The interaction of learned and innate behavior, III. Practice effects on performance, retention and fear, *Jour. Comp. Psysiol. Psychol.*, **51** (1958), 234–237.

[39] D. O. Hebb, *The organization of behavior* (New York: Wiley, 1949).

[40] M. H. Ribble, *The rights of infants* (New York: Columbia University Press, 1943).

under these conditions, the infant develops greater frustration tolerance and is better able to adjust to his environment as he grows older.[41]

It has been suggested that the early responses of smiling on the part of the human infant, which ordinarily occur at about the third month of life, are of a respondent sort and related to the problem of imprinting. Experimental investigations have shown that a young infant will smile at the human face as well as a variety of objects resembling it, whether they be artificial or real.[42] If such imprinting exists at the human level, it probably extends over a period of several months (probably the first six) instead of the few hours found in animal or bird experiments.

### EFFECTS OF EARLY TRAUMA

Freud[43] stressed the effects of early traumatizing experiences in infancy and childhood on later behavior. Certain intense, shocking, or frightening stimuli made strong impressions on the personality which were never lost to the behavior of the organism, even though they might occur so early in life that they could not be consciously recalled. Freud's associate, Otto Rank,[44] stressed in particular the trauma of birth as the cause of the basic anxiety. Birth was a sudden shock or change from a sublime uterine existence into a hostile world where a continuous fight for survival existed. Although there is little evidence for Rank's hypothesis of the birth trauma, it is possible to consider some effects on later development of strong aversive stimuli delivered early in life.

As an experimental analogue to Freud's emphasis on the traumatizing experience, we mention an experiment by Baron and his associates.[45] Three groups of rats were subjected to severe electric shock, each at the age of 20 days, 36 days, and adulthood (90 to 120) days. A fourth group of adult rats acted as a control. All adult subjects were then subsequently trained to escape or avoid one of the two shock intensities by pressing a bar. They were placed on a grid floor and shock was delivered to their feet. By pressing a bar in one operation, they could terminate the shock (escape), or in another operation, prevent its onset (avoidance). One-half of each group served under each of the two shock intensity conditions. The animals who had been subjected to any kind of earlier shocking were more successful in acquiring the escape or avoidance responses. All groups, regardless of age at first shocking, learned the tasks better than the control group that had never been subjected to prior shocking. Like-

[41] H. Orlansky, op. cit.

[42] E. H. Hess, "Imprinting" in animals, *Scient. Amer.*, **198**, no. 3 (1958), 81–90.

[43] S. Freud, *The problem of anxiety* (New York: Psychoanalytic Quarterly Press 1936).

[44] O. Rank, *The trauma of birth* (New York: Harcourt, Brace, 1929).

[45] O. Baron, K. H. Brookshire, and R. H. Littman, Effects of infantile and adult shock-trauma upon learning in the adult white rat, *Jour. Comp. Physiol. Psychol.*, **40** (1957), 530–534.

wise, those animals that had received the more intense shock in their early life, extinguished their escape and avoidance responding more slowly than did either the less intense shocking group or the controls. These results emphasize the importance of the early traumatizing experience on later learning where aversive stimuli are involved, as well as the permanence of effect of the experience.

After reviewing the studies of early experience (or lack of it) on later development, what conclusions may we suggest? Early experience, whether it be in the form of a kind of restriction, deprivation, frustration, or special stimulation, does have an important effect on subsequent behavior. This being the case, the next question is, how or in what ways do these early experiences influence the behavior later on? Three generalizations may be made:

1. Behavior learned in infancy is among the first to be acquired and persists into adult life. Such persistence without extinction is, of course, a basic principle of behavior. When a young organism learns a response, the repetition of that response (if reinforced) is likely to prevent the acquisition of other types of behavior that might interfere. This explains the chicks who acquired the unnatural eating by spoon, which prevented the development of their normal pecking responses.
2. Deprivation in infancy is relatively stronger than the same amount in adult life. When an organism is deprived shortly after weaning, the operation has a greater effect on behavior than when it occurs later in life. Since the young organism is lighter in weight and less strong, equal amounts of deprivation in the young and mature organism will produce greater effects on the younger organism. Hunt found that the early deprivation of food affected hoarding behavior significantly more than when the animals were deprived later in life.
3. There appear to be certain periods that are *critical* in the developmental process. During these, certain types of behavior are normally shaped. The observation is true in experimental embryology. Studies of imprinting strongly suggest that there are specific and restricted periods during which stimuli can elicit responses which later would not succeed.[46]

## Summary

The developmental approach to personality from an experimental point of view is plagued with methodological problems. At the human level, to study the same organism over a period of years and control every

[46] F. A. Beach and J. Jaynes, op. cit.

possible variable is impossible. Likewise, to investigate the effects of early restriction of environment is not allowable under the present cultural tradition. The best sources of study are in uncontrolled case histories. For these reasons we often depend on the animal investigations to give us some understanding of how the developmental process operates in molding the mature personality of the individual. Even at the animal level, a truly longitudinal approach is difficult. Some organisms have limited life spans. It takes a dedicated researcher to devote many, many years to the investigation of one single problem of growth. Finally, the longer the period of experimentation, the more difficult it is to control the necessary variables for a study to be experimentally sound. Despite these handicaps, both at the animal and human levels, investigations have given us a considerable knowledge about the relations between heredity and environment and the effects of early environmental stimulation or lack of it on the later development of the organism.

# 9 Escape

ANYBODY WHO HAS LIVED VERY LONG IS quite aware of the fact that life is no "bed of roses." Although there are many positive reinforcements which maintain our activities, another class of stimuli called *aversive*, exerts powerful control over our behavior. Life is full of annoyances, harassments, and threats. We put up with disagreeable people or try to get away from them. Sometimes dangers are unavoidable; at other times proper conduct keeps us out of trouble. Oftentimes we behave prudently, not because of any positive reinforcements derived from our proper actions but to avoid punishment that might ensue if we did not.

The class of stimuli that operates to control behavior in ways described above is called *aversive*. Since there are a number of ways that these stimuli work, the particular arrangement of relations between the stimuli and responses defines the kind of aversive operations: *escape*, *avoidance*, *punishment*, or *anxiety*. Although in any chain of activity, they may be interrelated, it is possible to distinguish them for purposes of behavioral analysis.

We are already familiar with *escape*, for it is merely the conditioning of a response through negative reinforcement. A *response is strengthened by the removal of some stimulus.* When it rains outside, we step indoors. By our action of going inside, the stimulus (rain) is removed. The behavior is therefore strength-ened so that in the future when it rains, we quickly seek shelter.

In the aversive condition called *avoidance, a response is made in order to prevent the onset of some stimulus.* As long as that response is maintained, the stimulus will not impinge upon the organism. As long as we stay on the straight and narrow path, we keep out of trouble. The response of being "good" avoids the consequences of troublesome condi-tions. A source of confusion frequently arises between escape and avoidance, since avoidance is commonly the consequence of escape behavior. Once we have learned to escape from an aversive situation, it is possible to maintain that same behavior in order to avoid its recurrence. We *escape* indoors out of the rain and consequently remain indoors in order to *avoid* effects of getting wet.

A third operation is *punishment.* In this contingency *a response is followed by a stimulus. The effect of that stimulus is to depress that behavior on future occasions.* Unlike escape, where a response terminates an aversive stimulus and is therefore strengthened, in punishment the response is followed by the aversive stimulus and is depressed. You will note that the arrangement of stimuli and responses in punishment is the same as that in positive reinforcement. However, the consequences are different. In positive reinforcement, the response is strengthened when *followed by stimulus. The effect of that stimulus is to depress that* is naughty (behavior) and he gets spanked (stimulus). The spanking is intended to weaken the behavior of being naughty on future occasions. We shall see in Chapter II just how effective this operation really is.

A final aversive condition is called *anxiety.* Here *a neutral stimulus is followed by one that is aversive.* The contingency is such that the or-ganism can do nothing to avoid or escape from the stimulus. The inter-mittent behavior on the part of the organism is described as anxiety. We perceive a threat (originally a neutral stimulus) but are in no position to combat it. The threat tells us that there is trouble ahead. All we can do is wait for the axe to fall and suffer the consequences. On future occasions the presentation of such a neutral stimulus is sufficient in itself to put us in a state of anxiety.

## Aversive Stimuli

The four conditions we have described—escape, avoidance, punish-ment and anxiety—all involve the use of aversive stimuli that operate to control behavior in one way or another. The specific operations differ, but they share one thing in common, a stimulus that has particular noxious qualities.

Our task in the subsequent four chapters will be to examine each of these operations in order to discover their specific characteristics and consequences. A first job is to examine the general qualities of those stimuli we class as aversive. Ordinarily we think of these stimuli as being unpleasant, annoying, or painful. At the level of common parlance there is nothing wrong with such descriptions, but in the experimental analysis of behavior, a more precise definition is necessary. Aversive stimuli may be *primary*, in that a response is related to their natural properties; we withdraw from an electric shock or turn away from a bright light. They may also be *conditioned* or *secondary*, their properties having been derived from some previous association with primary ones. Verbal threats, the sight of unpleasant people, or a frightening experience may act as conditioned aversive stimuli. To be operational in our definition, we say that *a stimulus is aversive if a response is strengthened by its removal or depressed by its presentation.* In general, the effects are the opposite of what we found in stimuli which were *positively reinforcing.*

## ESCAPE EXPERIMENTS

The behavioral operation of escape refers to *the strengthening of a response by the removal of a stimulus.* This is what we referred to as *negative reinforcement* in Chapter 3. You will recall that in positive reinforcement, behavior is strengthened by presenting a stimulus following a response. In negative reinforcement or escape, behavior is likewise strengthened, but by the removal of a stimulus. In positive reinforcement, conditioning *can* take place without any prior knowledge of stimuli which preceded the response. Such is not the case in negative reinforcement, for quite obviously, if a response is to be strengthened by taking away a stimulus, that stimulus must have been present before the response occurred. The operation may be illustrated by the following paradigm:

$$S^{-R} \longrightarrow R_t$$

The $S^{-R}$ refers to a primary aversive stimulus, such as shock, loud noise, or bright light. The $R_t$ refers to the response that terminates the stimulus; thus one escapes the shock by pressing a lever, or shuts the door to escape the noise of the neighbors next door. It is also possible for one to escape conditioned negative reinforcers. Then the paradigm would read:

$$S^{-r} \longrightarrow R_t$$

One can leave the room to escape an annoying person.

*Studies of Escape with Animals.* One of the earliest experiments on escape by Mowrer[1] illustrates clearly how the response is developed. A rat was placed in an experimental box wired with an electric grid on the floor of the chamber. The animal, never before subjected to shock, was allowed to receive it at gradually increasing intensities, beginning at zero, until a maximum was reached at the end of 2¼ minutes. During the first minute, the shock apparently was subliminal, since no particular changes in the behavior of the animal were noted. Eventually, there appeared minor periods of agitation as the current became stronger. As the intensity increased even more, the agitation grew more violent, culminating in jumping, squealing, biting the grill, climbing the walls of the apparatus and running about the experimental chamber.

The response selected for reinforcement was the pressing of a pedal at one end of the box. This response terminated the shock until the next trial. On the first trial Mowrer observed that it took his rats from 3 to 6 minutes to make the required response. On the second trial the time was considerably reduced, averaging from 2 to 4 minutes before the appropriate response was made. The animals characteristically "froze" in the position that they happened to be in at the instant the shock was terminated. By the tenth trial, the random behavior, characteristic of the earlier trials, was practically eliminated, and the pedal pushing responses became prompt and specific.

Dinsmoor and Hughes[2] have examined the effects of electric shock on escape responding by varying both the strength of the shock stimulus and the time of the reinforcement; that is, the length of the shock-free period following the bar-press response and before the next trial. When a high current was used as the aversive stimulus, the rats responded much more promptly to terminate the shock during the first 100 trials, as compared with a low current. To test the second variable, the length of time that the shock was turned off after each response, the high and low currents were used for two different groups, and the periods free from shock varied by 5, 10, 20, and 40 seconds. The latency of the response declined as a function of the interval up to 20 seconds for the high-current group and up to 40 seconds for the low-current group. That is, as the time free from shock increased (as reinforcement), the animals responded more quickly by turning off the shock with the bar press. At the various intervals free from shock, the high-current group always showed shorter latencies than the low-current group. It is evident that in this kind of escape conditioning, the strength of the response is related both the intensity of the aversive stimulus (stronger shocks, quicker responses) as well as to the amount of reinforcement measured by the

---

[1] O. H. Mowrer, An experimental analogue of "regression" with incidental observations on "reaction-formation," *Jour. Abn. Soc. Psychol.*, **35** (1940), 56–87.

[2] J. A. Dinsmoor and L. H. Hughes, Training rats to press a bar to turn off shock, *Jour. Comp. Physiol. Psychol.*, **49** (1956), 235–238.

length of the period free from shock (longer shock-free periods, faster responses).

The use of light as an aversive stimulus has also been experimentally studied in escape. Since the white rat is primarily a nocturnal animal, it was demonstrated some years ago by Keller[3] that the removal of light can operate as a reinforcer. In Keller's study the response that terminated the light was the bar press. However, one of the difficulties in this technique as an experimental procedure in studying escape is that alternate behaviors may be selected by the rat which escape the stimulus but give no measure of responding and not under the control of the experimenter. The rat may crouch in the corner with his head between his paws, cover his eyes with his tail, or roll up in a ball. Although these actions are apparently adequate escape responses in themselves, they are of little value to the experimenter if they are not under his control for measurement.

To avoid these difficulties, Kaplan[4] devised a technique whereby a rat was placed in the experimental chamber on a perch, too high for him to jump down. This eliminated the possibility of the rat's using alternate forms of escape behavior described above, for there was not that much room for him to move around. However, he still was allowed the selected response of pressing a bar, which was about the only possible one that could help him escape the aversive light. Kaplan's study was aimed at investigating both the effects of various intensities of light as aversive stimuli as well as a number of fixed-interval schedules of negative reinforcement. The rats were first trained to stand on the perch in which each bar press terminated the light for 1.1 minutes (regular reinforcement). His fixed intervals ranged from 0.2 to 5 minutes, indicating that the light could be terminated only by the first response after that time had elapsed. As the intervals increased, the actual response rate declined, a result similar to that found by Skinner and others in using fixed intervals of positive reinforcement.

When the rate of responding was studied as a function of the intensity of the light, Kaplan found that as intensity increased, there was a corresponding increase in the rate up to a point, followed by a gradual decline. Apparently the response-depressing effect of the aversive stimulus eventually became increasingly more powerful over the reinforcing influence exerted by the termination of the noxious light stimulus.

When we compare these findings in negative reinforcement with those already examined under positive reinforcement, we are overwhelmed by the universality of the findings. Even though entirely different organisms may be used (rats, pigeons, humans) and the kinds

---

[3] F. S. Keller, Light-aversion in the white rat, *Psychol. Rec.*, **4** (1941), 235–250.

[4] M. Kaplan, The effect of noxious stimulus intensity and duration during intermittent reinforcement of escape behavior, *Jour. Comp. Psychol.*, **45** (1952), 538–549.

of reinforcement changed (positive or negative), the basic characteristics of the behaviors are the same!

*Escape and Conditioned Reinforcement.* Previously neutral stimuli, when paired with the primary aversive ones, can take on a conditioned reinforcement function in a manner similar to positive reinforcement. By using conditioned negative reinforcers, our paradigm becomes:

$$S^n \longrightarrow S^{-R} \longrightarrow R_t$$

in which the $S^n$ is a neutral stimulus, the $S^{-R}$ a primary aversive stimulus or negative reinforcer, and $R_t$ the response that terminates the stimulus. When the neutral stimulus and primary aversive stimulus are paired together, the neutral stimulus takes on the function of the conditioned negative reinforcer $S^{-r}$ and our paradigm then reads:

$$S^{-r} \longrightarrow R_t$$

Miller[5] has illustrated experimentally how this function may be acquired. Rats were placed in an apparatus containing two compartments (Figure 9–1). The left compartment was painted white and the right compartment black. In the white compartment the rat received an electric shock administered from the grid on the floor. To begin with, the door between the two compartments was locked so that rats had to take the unavoidable shocks without any possibility of escaping. Next the rats were allowed to escape into a black compartment where no shock was applied. After ten trials, the rats were again placed in the white box, but no shock was applied. They readily ran to the black compartment. On subsequent trials the rats could escape from the white box only by turning a small wheel above the door. The speed with which they made this new escape response is seen in the graph in Figure 9–2. Remembering that no shock was ever applied in this test period, it is clear how the white box became the conditioned negative reinforcer and operated to condition escape behavior. In still a later test session, the wheel was rendered nonfunctional and the rats had to press a lever to open the door in order to escape. Again the rats learned this new response without use of the shock. The experiment not only demonstrates how the removal of a conditioned negative reinforcer can operate to strengthen behavior but also shows the generality of the function that the $S^{-r}$ acquires, a characteristic also of the conditioned positive reinforcer. In subsequent chapters

[5] N. E. Miller, Studies of fear as an acquirable drive. Fear as motivation and fear reduction as reinforcement in the learning of new responses, *Jour. Exp. Psychol.*, **38** (1948), 89–101.

we shall learn how these conditioned negative reinforcers can operate in avoidance, punishment, and anxiety responses.

### ESCAPE BEHAVIOR IN HUMANS

Precisely the same kinds of operations described in the preceding section are involved in our daily activities as part of our learning escape. We move into the shade when the sun gets too hot or put on our dark glasses to escape from its penetrating rays. We dress in warm clothes when the temperature outdoors drops to an uncomfortably low level and take them off when we are inside where it is warmer. Shoes are removed when our feet hurt, and painful slivers are taken from our

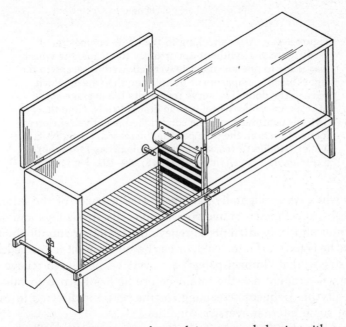

**Figure 9–1.** Apparatus for studying escape behavior with a conditioned negative reinforcer. The left compartment is painted white and contains a floor grid from which an electric shock is delivered. The right compartment is painted black. The rat escapes from left to right by operating the door mechanism on the wall in between the two compartments. (From N. E. Miller, Studies of fear as an acquirable drive, 1. Fear as motivation and fear reduction as reinforcement in the learning of a new response, *Journal of Experimental Psychology*, **38** [1948], 80–101, Fig. 1, p. 90.)

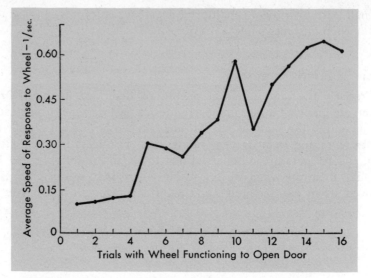

**Figure 9–2.** After shocking in the white compartment (see Figure 9–1) without opportunity to escape, the wheel was made to operate and rats were allowed to escape to the right (black) compartment by rotating the wheel, which opened the door. The curve represents the average speed of response to the wheel for the first 16 trials. Note that as trials continued and the conditioned negative reinforcer lost its function, the time per trial increased. (From N. E. Miller, Studies of fear as an acquirable drive, *Journal of Experimental Psychology,* **38** [1948], 89–101, Fig. 2, p. 94.)

fingers when we accidentally get stuck. The behavior of the infant like-wise seeks to escape from aversive stimuli. His stretchings and squirm-ings represent feeble attempts to relieve the irritating stimuli about him. Perhaps he is too warm, too cold, or has become caught in his bedclothes. To the degree that "hunger pangs" are aversive, he eats to relieve them.[6] Although we cannot ask the infant before he has learned to talk, in all probability his frequent screaming for the bottle is directed toward the relief of some internal aversive condition.

Conditioned stimuli operate in the same way. We walk away from people who are annoying or rude, and we turn off the TV when the program bores us. The sight of a vicious animal becomes the $S^{-r}$ for getting out of its way, and the tirades of our elders and superiors serve to bring on behavior that will enable us to escape them. A date on the calendar tells us that summer is approaching, and we should make plans to go to the mountains or seashore. Verbal stimuli can operate similarly as conditioned $S^{-r}$'s for escape behavior. The threat of a spanking

[6] B. F. Skinner, *Science and human behavior* (New York: Macmillan, Inc., 1953).

induces the child to obey. We shame people into doing our commands by calling them cowards. They comply to escape the embarrassing consequences of our harassments.

*Escape Conditioning in Human Stuttering.*  Flanagan, Goldiamond, and Azrin[7] have applied escape conditioning as a means of treating stuttering as well as producing it. In one experiment they asked three male stutterers to read from loose printed pages. In the beginning of the experiment when a subject stuttered, a microswitch was pressed to make a record. After a rate of stuttering had been determined, each stutter caused a loud tone to sound in the subject's earphones. During this period a subsequent stutter could turn off the tone for five seconds, that is, escape from it. Consequently, the rate of stuttering *increased* when escape from the loud tone was contingent on stuttering. In a subsequent period a punishment operation was established (see Chapter 11). In this instance a stutter produced the loud tone. Consequently, the rate of stuttering decreased. In another experiment these same authors[8] induced stuttering in normally fluent subjects by using the escape conditioning procedures. In this instance each stutter removed an aversive electric shock for ten seconds.

In a later study,[9] Goldiamond used as the aversive stimulus a delayed auditory feedback. In this procedure a person talks into a microphone and instead of hearing his voice simultaneously as he speaks, there is a slight delay between what he says and what he hears. The experience is very aversive to most people. In this instance the technique was used as a therapeutic method to develop normal speech. As subjects read, proper speech escaped the aversive feedback while stuttering produced it. In the beginning of treatment the reading rate was reduced and so was the stuttering. The subject was speaking slowly in order to avoid the feedback, but as he continued, the rate of reading went up and the rate of stuttering went down.

*The Use of Escape Conditioning in Treating Homosexuals.*  Mandel[10] applied escape conditioning to the treatment of a male homosexual in the following way. First, the subject was asked to concentrate on a colored slide of a naked male. The experimenter then transposed over

[7] B. Flanagan, I. Goldiamond, and N. Azrin, Operant stuttering in the control of stuttering behavior through response contingent consequences, *Jour. Exp. Anal. Behav.*, **1** (1958), 173–178.

[8] B. Flanagan, I. Goldiamond, and N. Azrin, Instatement of stuttering in normally fluent individuals through operant procedures, *Science* (1959), 978–981.

[9] I. Goldiamond, Stuttering and fluency as manipulatable operant response classes. In L. Krasner and L. P. Ullman, eds., *Research in behavior modification* (New York: Holt, Rinehart and Winston, 1965).

[10] K. N. Mandel, Preliminary report on a new aversion therapy for homosexuals, *Behav. Res. Ther.*, **8** (1970), 93–95.

the original slide another slide of hideous running sores. The subject was then asked to concentrate on the parts of the body covered with the sores. Five seconds after the subject reported a feeling of disgust, the slides were simultaneously turned off. Thus, the subject escaped from seeing the noxious stimuli. Following this procedure, the subject was shown a slide of an attractive female. This was intended to function as a relief from the aversive stimulus, much in the same way one is relieved following the presentation and termination of an electric shock. As time went by, the subject began to express a feeling of sexual arousal in response to the female slide. Thus the treatment actually involved two procedures: it not only eliminated the homosexual feelings through escape from the noxious slides but also provided a counterconditioning of more appropriate sexual activity.

Feldman and MacCulloch[11] used a variation of the same technique to treat a group of homosexual men. Prior to conditioning, they asked the men to rank a series of slides of men both nude and with clothes on in order of their sexual attractiveness, in ascending order from the least exciting to the most exciting. They then asked the same subjects to rank a series of slides of females in descending order, from the most attractive to the least attractive. A subject was then presented with the slide of the male along with an electric shock. He was asked to look at the slide as long as he could stand the shock and the picture remained sexually exciting. The shock could then be terminated by his pressing a button in order to escape the shock. Thus, when the subjects felt indifferent to the male slides, the picture of a female was presented. The presentation of the female as in the previous study was intended to operate as a relief from the shock. In a follow-up study 52 per cent of the homosexuals reported they were completely heterosexual a year later.

*Respondent Escape.*   Respondent behavior likewise can be conditioned by aversive stimuli, at both the human and subhuman leved. Pavlov's early associate, Bechterev,[12] conditioned dogs to withdraw their foot to the sound of a buzzer, previously associated with shock. At the human level, the hand or finger withdrawal to an electric shock can be conditioned to a bell, buzzer, or other visual stimuli. An interesting application of a kind of conditioned withdrawal (escape) involving some respondent behavior is described by Mowrer.[13] His technique involved conditioning as a means of curing enuresis (bed wetting). In enuresis the problem is not so much one of getting the child to "control his elimination" as it is to awaken him to the internal stimuli provided by bladder

[11] M. P. Feldman and M. J. MacCulloch, Aversive therapy and the management of homosexuals, *Brit. Med. Jour.*, 1 (1967), 594.

[12] V. M. Bechterev, *General principles of human reflexology*, trans. W. H. Gantt (New York: International Universities Press, 1932).

[13] O. H. Mowrer, Enuresis: A method for its study and treatment, *Amer. Jour. Orthopsychiat.*, 8 (1938), 436–459.

tension. Since these stimuli are relatively weak during sleep, the common occurrence of bed wetting results. Mowrer had the child sleep on a special pad containing two pieces of bronze screening between heavy cotton fabric. When the urine struck the pad, it seeped through the fabric and penetrated the metal conductor, causing an electric switch to turn on a doorbell, thus awakening the child and permitting him to take himself to the bathroom. After considerable training, the child learned to awaken before wetting the bed, in response to smaller amounts of bladder tension. In this experiment the stimuli from the bladder served as the conditioned stimuli which, paired with the bell, elicited the waking behavior.

Likewise the cures for alcoholism mentioned in our earlier discussions of respondent behavior (Chapter 3) operate to condition escape behavior. The "addict" withdraws from the sight of a drink because of its previous association with some nauseating consequences of drinking.

### ESCAPE AND PERSONALITY DEVELOPMENT

Escape behavior examples given thus far at the human level have involved rather simple acts. As we examine the cumulation of many different aversive stimuli in our lives, we realize the problem of escaping can become complex. The behavior of the organism shows a great generalization of responses which can remove him from these stimuli. Some psychologists have used the term *escape mechanisms* to describe the operations of escape and avoidance as they work in human personality development. All they really mean by these "mechanisms" is that much of the organism's behavior is oriented toward escaping and avoiding aversive stimuli, conditioned or primary. An examination of the characteristics of this generalized escape behavior and its antecedents enables us to apply the knowledge we have achieved so far from our animal studies to an understanding of human personality and how it develops.

We are all aware of the asocial, withdrawn, seclusive, or shy personalities about us. In them we see the two processes of escape and avoidance continually operating. Since avoidance is the subject of the next chapter, we will attempt to limit our discussion primarily to escape at this point. In these shy and seclusive personalities, what frequently happens is that a response begins as an escape reaction. Because of its reinforcement in the reduction of the aversive stimuli, the reaction soon becomes a continuous avoidance act. As a child, this person may have escaped the tirades of overly demanding parents by hiding in the closet. Other escape responses soon developed. As he grew older, the earlier escape responses were maintained, and others added, all of which kept him pretty much out of contact with the aversive stimuli about him. As these attempts were reinforced, he arranged his behavior in such a manner that any contact with people would be avoided.

We find a similar shift from escape to avoidance in the animal laboratory. Mowrer[14] observed that the rats frequently remained "frozen" to the bar they had pressed to escape shock, even after the shock was no longer operating. Likewise, when we condition an animal to escape an aversive light, we note frequently a "holding" response which not only has terminated the stimulus but continues to operate long afterward. In this sense the response is no longer simply terminating the stimulus; it is attempting to keep it off.

One of the most common characteristics of escape behavior in a human is that, by his responding, he renders himself inaccessible to other people.[15] The reason is obvious. Other people, and in particular their behavior, have become conditioned aversive stimuli that can be terminated only by rendering oneself inaccessible to them. To the degree that his behavior is continued, of course, it becomes avoidance, since avoidance behavior prevents the onset of the aversive stimulus.

The actions of the adult who escapes from his enemies or retreats from human contacts is merely an extension of the shrinking and hiding reactions found frequently in children and animals. As far as the clinical psychologist is concerned, occasional reactions of this sort occur in most children from time to time and are not serious. When they become chronic, we can consider them more insidious than the aggressive response that appears to be more annoying to others around them. There are two reasons for the greater dangers in excessive escape behavior. First of all, escape is more difficult to treat when it becomes chronic. Secondly, the exaggeration of escape, especially from human contact, is more likely to lead to behavior disorders.[16]

*Origins of Escape Behavior.* The seclusive child in his daily contacts with other children escapes their company whenever possible. As daily recess time approaches, he goes off by himself until the period is over. In the classroom he speaks only when called upon; he may frequently say, "I don't know," in order to terminate the aversive questioning of his teacher. As these methods persist, they pave the way for the avoidance reactions of adult life, where behavior is maintained for long periods of time in the insulated and withdrawn personality or in the behavior of the hermit who geographically separates himself from human contacts. The child who used escape persistently should be expected to maintain the same kind of behavior as he develops, since the withdrawal of the aversive stimuli is reinforcing.

[14] O. H. Mowrer, An experimental analogue of "regression" with incidental observations on "reaction-formation," *Jour. Abn. Soc. Psychol.*, **35** (1940), 56–87.

[15] N. Cameron, *The psychology of behavior disorders* (Boston: Houghton Mifflin, 1948).

[16] L. F. Schaffer and E. J. Shoben, Jr., *The psychology of adjustment*, 2nd ed. (Boston: Houghton Mifflin, 1956).

The causes of escape are to be found in the multitude of aversive stimuli presented to a person in the history of his conditioning. For one thing, a child reared with few contacts with other children may not develop social behavior which enables him to overcome aversive stimuli when they are presented to him later on. Lacking the early experience in overcoming the aversive stimuli in his environment, he becomes ill equipped to handle them later on. Aversive stimuli in the form of other children, parents, teachers, and the like are most easily met by running away from them. Likewise, the adolescent leaves home for good at that point when he can no longer tolerate his environment.

Physical weakness, although not the direct cause of escape, can be a contributing factor in the same way that any physical limitation reduces the variety of behavior possible. A child unable to overcome the bully must submit to his demands. Later on, the occasion of seeing the bully leads him to run and hide. Not only is this escape reinforcing to the child in its relief from the aversive bully, but by his submission he has strengthened the behavior of bullying. Frequently the child who lacks the stamina to overcome aversive elements in his environment may substitute alternate behaviors which allow him to escape. Fantasy or daydreaming commonly operate in this way.

Case studies of children exhibiting chronic escape show frequently the origin of their behavior to be in overly demanding and abusive parents whose punishments, threats, and scoldings act as stimuli from which to escape. The demanding, aggressive, and punitive father becomes the conditioned stimulus for these responses. As behavior generalizes, other people (strangers as well as friends, other children as well as adults) become the conditioned aversive stimuli.

As compared to behavior that is aggressive and more likely to meet with direct punishment, escape has its immediate advantages. It is less likely to arouse hostility or invite retaliation from others. It saves the person from a myriad of futile responses against an adversity which cannot be conquered. It also prevents humiliating defeat. These negative reinforcers rapidly strengthen the behavior. Unfortunately, as we have already pointed out, chronic escape reactions ordinary lead to more serious consequences for the individual.

There are also positive reinforcements to be found in the consequent activities of escape. Solitary activities get reinforced in their own right. A child is happy playing with his toys by himself, where there is no rivalry of sharing or competition. In doing a job by oneself, not only does a person escape the possible criticism of others, but he can also accomplish it in a manner he finds most reinforcing. Many individuals, the "lone wolves" who work by themselves, seldom asking advice or counsel from others, have had in their past too many aversive stimuli in the presence and activities of other people.

The child as well as the adult can manufacture reinforcements from the feedback in his own fantasy. Here the reinforcements are so contrived that the imagined behavior cannot go unreinforced. He succeeds, is famous, receives all the positive reinforcements of attention, affection, and approval from his own imagined relationships with other people.

The solitary activity that gets reinforced from one's own self-reactions to the exclusion of others cannot go on indefinitely without leading the person into difficulty. For public interaction he has substituted private preoccupation.[17] When the behavior gets exaggerated, it becomes so pathological that ordinary responses necessary to maintain the organism's health become impaired. Persistent escape and avoidance are found in schizophrenia, a condition where the reinforcements come almost exclusively from one's own self-reactions. As this behavior persists, it prevents an individual from carrying out his personal, social, and business affairs with any degree of required efficiency. Consequently, the condition frequency results in the institutionalization of a person, where long periods of therapy may be necessary in order that other behaviors which achieve reinforcement from people must be substituted for the reinforcements coming from his own fantasy.

## Summary

The effects of aversive stimuli upon the organism tend to be the opposite of those stimuli that are positively reinforcing. They strengthen a response when removed and depress a response when presented. The operation of escape or conditioning with negative reinforcement involves strengthening a response by removing an aversive stimulus. The characteristics of the response rates are similar to those found in positive reinforcement using regular, interval, and ratio schedules.

Once an escape response has developed, it frequently leads to a continuous avoidance reaction if the contingencies are appropriate for an avoidance response to be maintained. In lower species and man, the escape reaction attempts to remove the organism from aversive stimuli, either primary or conditioned. When the escape reactions become well conditioned, particularly at the human level, chronic withdrawal from human contacts is the result, since people become conditioned negative reinforcers. A look into the occasions for escape in the developmental history of the organism enables us to understand how many pathological escape reactions are conditioned and maintained.

[17] N. Cameron and A. Magaret, *Behavior pathology* (Boston: Houghton Mifflin, 1951).

# 10 Avoidance

IN ESCAPING FROM NOXIOUS STIMULUS, IT is clear that the reinforcement of the organism comes from the removal of that stimulus. On subsequent occasions, when the aversive stimulus is presented, the organism quickly withdraws if possible. Perhaps even more common than escape is avoidance responding. As we profit from past experiences, it is not necessary on each new occasion to have the aversive stimulus presented before we do something about it. We learn to anticipate trouble when we see signs of it coming. The prudent person does something to stay out of its way. We shun people who annoy us, evade situations that may be dangerous, and take steps to avoid those who would molest us. If the reinforcement in escape comes from the removal of a noxious stimulus, what is the reinforcement in avoidance where no noxious stimulus is presented? Why are we able to maintain avoidance behavior as we do? The experimental analysis of this problem enables us to answer these questions and has important implications for understanding normal as well as pathological personalities.

In the most common avoidance situation, *the organism learns to make a response that prevents the onset of an aversive stimulus.* It may be described by the following paradigm:

$$S^n \xrightarrow{\phantom{aaa}} / \xrightarrow{\phantom{aaa}} S^{-R}$$
$$\uparrow R_t$$

The $S^n$ is initially a neutral stimulus that functions neither positively nor negatively. The $S^{-R}$ is a primary aversive one. The $R_t$ stands for a response that can terminate the original stimulus. The ———/——— indicates the point of occurrence of the $R_t$ which breaks the connection between $S^n$ *and* $S^{-R}$. To begin, let us suppose that I am given some warning signal, which at this point I do not understand—consequently the $S^n$. Because I do not heed the warning I am punished ($S^{-R}$). Through the pairing of the two $S$'s, the $S^n$ takes on the function of a *conditioned negative reinforcer* and becomes $S^{-r}$. If I heed the warning now and respond appropriately ($R_t$) I avoid the punishment—that is, ———/——— means *is not followed by*. By responding properly my response is not followed by the punishment. After conditioning, the paradigm will read:

$$ S^{-r} \;\underline{\quad\quad}/\underline{\quad\quad}\longrightarrow S^{-R} $$
$$ \uparrow R_t $$

I heed the warning signal, respond, and the warning signal is not followed by the punishment or aversive stimulus. An examination of the paradigm shows a resemblance to escape conditioning in a situation where the response terminates a conditioned negative reinforcer. It is also related to anxiety where a neutral stimulus is inevitably followed by a primary aversive one. In avoidance, if the organism does not make the appropriate response, the aversive stimulus will follow. In avoidance conditioning, the reinforcement is the termination of the conditioned negative reinforcer (see below).

## Experiments Demonstrating Avoidance Conditioning

Recently, avoidance has been the subject of considerable experimental investigation. A study by Warner[1] will illustrate the basic experimental operations. He used a warning buzzer as the $S_1$ and an electric shock as the $S_2$. Rats were trained to avoid the shock by jumping over a hurdle in the experimental box. The length of time between the warning signal and the actual shock was varied by 1, 10, 20, and 30 seconds. Four different groups of animals were used in each of the delay periods. He found that the shortest period of 1 second enabled all the animals to learn the task of jumping to avoid the shock. As the time intervals between the warning signal and shock increased, it took longer for the animals to learn the jumping response. In the 20-second group, three animals failed to learn the response, and in the 30-second group, none of the animals was successful.

[1] L. H. Warner, The association span of the white rat, *Jour. Genet. Psychol.*, **41** (1932), 51–90.

An experiment by Solomon and Wynne[2] using dogs as subjects illustrates the basic technique for avoidance learning very clearly. They placed a dog in a compartment that was divided down the middle by a low fence which the dog could easily jump over. The floor had an electric grid through which shock could be administered. In each trial a buzzer was sounded, followed in 10 seconds by the shock on the side of the compartment where the dog happened to be standing. The dog was supposed to jump over into the other compartment within the 10-second warning period; otherwise he would receive the shock. If he jumped within the 10-second period, the buzzer was turned off. If not, the shock was presented until he did jump. Results showed that within 10 trials, the dog had learned the avoidance response. On the eighteenth trial he missed and received the shock again. From then on, until trial 60, a correct response was made every time in which he usually jumped within one or two seconds from the time the buzzer was initially sounded.

AVOIDANCE EXPERIMENTS WITH HUMAN SUBJECTS

In an experiment undertaken by Ericksen and Kuethe[3] subjects were presented with a 15-item word association list and given the impression that they were in an experiment to determine the limit of speed of their associations to these words. They were instructed to respond as quickly as possible with the first word that came to mind when the stimulus word was presented to them. For example, to the word "black," the subject was to respond with the first word he could think of. During the first run-through of the list the experimenter administered a strong electric shock immediately after five arbitrarily selected response words were given. Subjects were then given further trials on the 15-word list. Each time a subject was presented with one of the five first trial shocked words, he received another electric shock. At the conclusion of this phase of the experiment subjects were informed that there would be no further shocks. They were then asked to make a chain association to each of the original words, that is, continue to give associations, one word leading to another. On the basis of verbal questioning the subjects were classified into "insight" and "noninsight" groups. The "insight" group indicated a high degree of awareness of the basis for receiving the electric shocks and what they could do to avoid receiving the shock, that is, avoid repeating the response word that had led to being shocked. The "noninsight" group had little awareness of the reasons for the shocks or how to avoid receiving them. Both groups, however, showed rapid learning of the avoidance response, that is, they did not repeat the response words that had resulted in shocks. There were no significant differences be-

[2] R. L. Solomon and L. C. Wynne, Traumatic avoidance learning acquisition in normal dogs, *Psychol. Monogr.*, **67**, no. 4 (1953).

[3] C. W. Ericksen and J. L. Kuethe, Avoidance conditioning of verbal behavior without awareness, *Jour. Abn. Soc. Psychol.*, **53** (1956), 203–209.

tween the groups in terms of the avoidance learning—namely the number of trials necessary to achieve the criterion of two successive trials without the occurrence of the punished (shocked) response. However, there were clear differences in the reaction times to the stimulus words in the two groups. The "insight" group showed a clear increase in their reaction times. Because those in this group knew what word to avoid saying when the stimulus word was presented, they had to grope for another word that would not bring on the shock.

An interesting application of avoidance conditioning to the treatment of psychotic behavior is described by Ayllon and Michael.[4] They noted two psychotic patients who manifested eating problems. In one case, Janet had to be forcefully taken to the dining room where she would permit nurses to spoon-feed her. The other, Nancy, had to be spoon-fed in a room adjacent to the dining room. Both patients were relatively unsocial and seemed to react indifferently to attention by the nurses. However, both were very much concerned with being neat and clean in their appearance and clothing. The treatment involved a combination of escape and avoidance conditioning with *food spilling* as the aversive stimulus. The spoon-feeding was accompanied by some food spilling, which the patient could avoid by feeding herself for the entire meal. In both cases complete self-feeding was achieved, which at the time of the report had been maintained for over ten months. In the process, nurses were advised to spoon-feed with only slight spilling, not to overdo the process. The record of one of the patients is shown in Figure 10–1. Notice the beginning of a relapse on the fifth week. No reasonable explanation is given, except for a rumor that someone had informed the patient that food spilling on the nurses' part was not accidental. In any event, the self-feeding responses returned.

Before describing some of the variations on this basic avoidance procedure, let us pause for a moment to examine this kind of conditioning in our everyday lives and to explain precisely how avoidance conditioning works. A lot more of our behavior is under the control of conditioned aversive stimuli than we are likely to realize. Many of our laws, rules, and regulations for proper conduct and even customs operate as discriminative stimuli for avoiding unpleasant consequences. A failure to comply brings on some kind of punishment (aversive stimulus). Some students attend class to avoid flunking out or receiving failing grades. The discriminative stimulus may be the teacher, classroom, or ringing of a bell to indicate the beginning of the hour of class. Some people attend church to save themselves from going to hell. A worker remains at his job to keep clear of the consequent punishment of the aversive foreman. Stimuli like policemen, supervisors, guards, college deans, teachers, and

---

[4] T. Ayllon and J. Michael, The psychiatric nurse as a behavioral engineer, *Jour. Exp. Anal. Behav.*, **2** (1959), 223–234.

parents are discriminative stimuli for staying out of trouble. As long as the child is good, he avoids his parent's punishments. And as long as we obey the law, we evade the consequences of its punishments.

For an avoidance response to take place, there is always some kind of an $S^D$ that has come into operation as a result of prior conditioning. This stimulus acts as a warning signal. Because of its previous association with the aversive stimulus, it acquires a discriminative function. *The same stimulus also becomes a conditioned negative reinforcer.* We have already learned that as a stimulus acquires its function to discriminate, it can also operate to reinforce in either a positive or negative manner. The temporal arrangement for this development is appropriate, since the neutral stimulus has preceded the aversive one at some point in time. The conditioned stimulus can be terminated only by making the proper

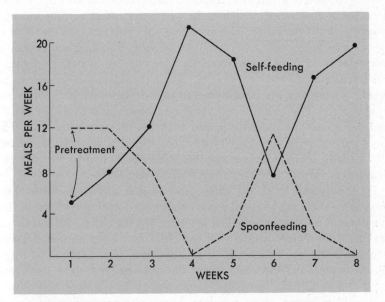

**Figure 10–1.** Escape and avoidance conditioning of self-feeding in a psychotic patient. The aversive stimulus was the spilling of a little food by the nurse. Note as the weeks progressed the rate of self-feeding went up and that of being spoon-fed by the nurse went down. Between weeks five and seven, the process was reversed. A possible explanation is that the patient heard the rumor that the nurses were intentionally doing a little spilling. In any event, by the eighth week self-feeding was literally complete. (From T. Ayllon and J. Michael, The psychiatric nurse as a behavioral engineer, *Journal of the Experimental Analysis of Behavior,* **2** [1959], 223–234, Fig. 4, p. 331. Copyright 1959 by the Society for the Experimental Analysis of Behavior, Inc. Reproduced by permission of the authors and the publisher.)

avoidance response. As in escape training, any response that removes the negative reinforcer is strengthened.

*We cannot say,* however, that the conditioning occurs or is successful because the aversive stimulus is avoided, for how can the absence or non-occurrence of a primary stimulus be reinforcing? This is an important point and a source of confusion for some. For a stimulus to operate as a reinforcer, it must either be added (as in a positive reinforcer) or taken away (as in a negative reinforcer). Its nonoccurrence cannot reinforce. Therefore the reinforcement operating in an avoidance response *has to be the removal of the conditioned negative reinforcer which has also operated as the discriminative stimulus for making the avoidance response.* The function of the primary aversive stimulus which follows if the avoidance response fails is merely to recondition that response.

Why does the avoidance response sometimes fail to occur? We are all aware of the many occasions in which we failed to respond appropriately and got punished. The experimental evidence indicates that even after an avoidance response is well established, the organism occasionally misses (fails to avoid) and receives the aversive shock or light. The question is not difficult to answer. As an avoidance response is maintained by removing the conditioned negative reinforcer, extinction begins to take place. The conditioned reinforcer eventually loses its ability to condition if not occasionally paired with the primary reinforcer. Therefore a pairing with the primary aversive stimulus is occasionally necessary. Usually a single instance of this will be sufficient to recondition the organism in further avoidance behavior for some time.

At the human level, the same process operates. A threat is the discriminative stimulus to avoid some annoying condition such as an injury, punishment, or deprivation. The statement to the child, "I'll spank you if you don't obey me," means that the child had been punished by some spanking in the past. Later the threat operates as a conditioned negative reinforcer to make the child obey. By obeying, the child removes the threat and avoids the spanking. However, as time passes and more and more threats ensue, their function becomes weakened until the child fails to obey and gets another spanking. If on later occasions the parent fails to follow through with the primary negative reinforcer, the avoidance response will be further extinguished, and the threat will eventually become meaningless. However, many parents fail to realize this and wonder why their children never obey, even though they give out numerous threats.

We also must understand why it is necessary to carry through on our threats if we want them to operate in controlling avoidance behavior. One of the reasons avoidance responding persists as well as it does with many responses and only an occasional failure which has to be reinforced by the aversive stimulus is that the *behavior is actually operating on* some kind of intermittent schedule of negative reinforcement. It has been shown clearly that intermittent schedules apply to negative as well as positive reinforcement.[5] The basic principle is the same; responses can be maintained at a higher rate with fewer reinforcements when they are given intermittently than they can under conditions of regular reinforcement.

Further analysis of the nature of avoidance responding indicates that the *behavior is also anxiety reducing*. We shall consider this matter of anxiety in more detail in Chapter 12, but because of its implications for avoidance it should be mentioned here. Strong aversive stimuli have the quality of generating highly emotional behavior in lower organisms as well as man. Through conditioning, neutral stimuli can also acquire the properties of generating the emotional activity. The child who has waited in the dentist's office and subsequently experiences the painful drill will on future occasions exhibit highly emotional behavior of crying, agitation, clinging to the parent, simply by visiting the waiting room. If the avoidance response can terminate the conditioned negative reinforcer, it will also reduce the intermediate anxiety that has been generated. Just as long as the conditioned stimulus is capable of generating that anxiety, the avoidance response that terminates it will reduce the anxiety and consequently will be reinforcing. As the anxiety becomes extinguished along with the function of the conditioned reinforcer, the avoidance behavior also becomes extinguished and fails to operate at some future time. It will therefore require another presentation of the primary stimulus. Avoidance involves a continuous process of negative conditioning and extinction. When the response fails to operate and forestall the aversive stimulus, extinction is beginning to occur. When the aversive stimulus is presented, reconditioning begins and the avoidance behavior is strengthened.

## AVOIDANCE WITHOUT WARNING SIGNAL (SIDMAN AVOIDANCE)

Our discussion thus far has considered avoidance as a response to some discriminative stimulus which has also acted as a negative conditioned reinforcer when removed. In other words, a warning signal is presented to the organism, which tells him to "get out of the way or the axe will fall." What happens when no warning signal is presented? Is it possible to condition avoidance behavior in the absence of some external cue? If so, how do we explain it?

These questions have been extensively studied by Sidman and his

[5] M. Kaplan, The effects of noxious stimulus intensity and duration during intermittent reinforcement of escape behavior, *Jour. Comp. Physiol. Psychol.*, **45** (1952), 538–549.

associates over several years. Although some of their experiments extend beyond the scope of this book, a number of relevant findings are worth our careful consideration. Sidman[6] first examined avoidance behavior without any external warning signal in the following way: White rats were trained to press a lever as the avoidance response. A shock was delivered to the animal through the grid floor of the cage at regular intervals *unless* the bar was pressed. Each time the animal pressed the lever, a timer that controlled the shock was reset, delaying its onset for 20 seconds. In other words, following a lever press, a 20-second period free from shock was assured. Each intervening press always put off the shock for another 20 seconds. It was possible, therefore, for the animal to avoid the shock indefinitely, as long as he pressed the bar before his time was up.

As conditioning progressed, Sidman observed an abrupt increase in the rate of bar pressing from it initial level of near zero. At first the responding occurred in cyclic bursts, but soon a stable rate was maintained as high as 17 responses per minute over a 20-hour period. This rate was far in excess of that necessary to avoid the shock. It is clear that with such a high rate, hardly any shocks were actually received by the animals over this period of time. He observed further that the animals tended to eliminate all other forms of behavior except that of bar pressing; that is, walking around the cage, standing on their hind legs, grooming, sniffing about, and so forth. Alternate behaviors seemed to be eliminated, to the exclusion of the one, single response of pressing the bar. By this technique Sidman demonstrated how powerful an aversive stimulus can be in controlling the behavior of an organism.

Under these conditions avoidance behavior becomes very persistent and resistant to extinction.[7] In another study Sidman[8] used a slight variation of the foregoing technique. As before, each time the animals pressed the bar, the shock was forestalled for 20 seconds. However, if the animal did not press it within the specified time, he received a shock every 5 seconds until the bar press was made. As might have been expected, this technique produced rapid conditioning and showed a strong resistance to extinction, even when no shock was applied. The persistence of responding in extinction was, of course, positively related to the strength of the original conditioning. During extinction, even when there were pauses in responding longer than the response-shock interval of 20 seconds, the avoidance behavior continued and did not extinguish at that point, even though no shocks were applied.

[6] M. Sidman, Avoidance conditioning with brief shock and no exteroceptive warning signal, *Science*, **118** (1953), 157–158.

[7] M. Sidman, On the persistence of avoidance behavior, *Jour. Abn. Soc. Psychol.*, **50** (1955), 217–220.

[8] M. Sidman, The temporal distribution of avoidance responses, *Jour. Comp. Physiol. Psychol.*, **47** (1954), 199–402.

We must ask ourselves, *how* was it possible for the animals to learn so effectively the avoidance behavior *in the absence of any external warning or cue?* We have learned that for the avoidance response to work, it should be preceded by some discriminative stimulus. Furthermore, if before the response no stimulus is present to act as a negative reinforcer when removed, what is the reinforcement that maintains the behavior? Simply avoiding something that does not occur is not a reinforcement. A first hunch might be that the animal was making a time discrimination because a 20-second interval elapsed between shocks. Certainly time discriminations are possible, as we have discovered in our analysis of fixed-interval schedules. However, Sidman's data do not support such an explanation, for the responses were distributed over a period of time. Only if the rat pressed the bar just prior to each shock would the 20-second interval between shocks be constant. However, you will recall that each time the rat pressed a bar, the interval was forestalled for another 20 seconds, so that any response within the interval (whether it came at the beginning or end) would put off the shock for another 20 seconds. Since animals went for hours without receiving shocks, it would be impossible to make such a discrimination.

Another suggestion was made by Dinsmoor.[9] Since any response the animal happened to be making, other than pressing the bar, might receive the shock, practically all other stimuli in the environment that happened to accompany the behavior might eventually be followed by shock. They could therefore acquire the aversive character of a conditioned reinforcer in their own right through pairing with the shock stimulus. As the experiment continues, more and more behavior gets followed by shock, and more and more negative reinforcers begin to operate to initiate avoidance behavior. Further experimental evidence is needed to support this notion.[10]

In the light of most recent findings, the best answer to the question of why this kind of avoidance conditioning works so well in the absence of a warning signal is to be found in what we know about the effects of punishment on responses. A *response that is followed by an aversive stimulus tends to be depressed.* A child who gets spanked for being naughty is less likely in the immediate future to be naughty again. For the moment, at least, the spanking serves to depress the behavior it has punished. The more the response is punished, the greater the depression will be; therefore a longer time will elapse before the response recurs. As the rat continues to be conditioned without a warning signal, literally *every* response he makes gets punished—except one—pressing the bar. Sidman noted in his original experiment that more and more of the

[9] J. H. Dinsmoor, Punishment: I. the avoidance hypothesis, *Psychol. Rev.*, **61** (1954), 34–46.

[10] M. Sidman, A comparison of two types of warning stimulus in an avoidance situation, *Jour. Comp. Physiol. Psychol.*, **50** (1957), 282–287.

animal's behavior was confined to bar pressing. This was to be expected, for when he was not pressing the bar, he would be "doing something else" when the shock came. The next time he was "doing something else," the shock again came. Since the animal's repertoire of behavior in this situation is somewhat limited, it does not take long before "doing everything else" gets punished. Consequently the only behavior that is not punished is pressing the bar.

This situation has its parallel in human conditions where a person gets punished for everything except the desired behavior.[11] If you want the child to obey your every command, punish everything else but compliance with your commands. The results of this kind of training are occasionally seen in the so-called perfect children. An extreme and fictional example of this type of control is described in Orwell's novel, *1984*. Were it not for the unfortunate consequences this kind of control has on the organism, the control would appear to be extremely useful. But as we shall see in the next chapter, the results of excessive punishment can be disastrous to the organism, particularly at the human level, if carried too far.

*Human Experiments Employing the Sidman Avoidance Technique.* Using the shock avoidance technique with human adults (medical and graduate students), Ader and Tatum[12] found similar findings to those Sidman had discovered using rats as subjects. In this instance, a button had to be pressed to avoid electric shock. Again, no warning signal was given, nor were instructions presented as to what to do. They found that about half their subjects (17 out of 36) achieved the predetermined criterion of acquisition and maintained their responding at a stable rate. The rates co-varied with the amount of time the response was able to delay the shock. Rapid rates occurred if the period between shocks was short and a slower rate if the delay period was long. However, there were qualitative and quantitative differences among the subjects. Some of them failed to acquire the response, while others simply "walked out" of the experimental situation despite the fact that they were being paid to act as subjects.

Baer[13] has tried the technique on children. In this instance he used the withdrawal of positive reinforcement as the aversive condition instead of shock or other primarily aversive stimuli. A child was seated at a table facing a movie screen with a bar to press, which was located at his right hand. This could be operated while he watched cartoons

---

[11] The compulsive neurotic (see my Chapter 15) persists in his ritualistic and repetitive behavior because it "prevents him from doing something else" which may be punishing.

[12] R. Ader and R. Tatum, Free operant avoidance conditioning in humans, *Jour. Exp. Anal. Behav.*, 4 (1961), 275–276.

[13] D. M. Baer, Escape and avoidance responses of pre-school children on two schedules of reinforcement withdrawal, *Jour. Exp. Anal. Behav.*, 3 (1960), 155–159.

(Woody Woodpecker) projected on the screen in front of him. During the first session the children were allowed to see two or three cartoons completely through. On the next session the cartoons were interrupted after one minute (withdrawal of positive reinforcement). The cartoons did not appear until the child responded by depressing the bar. The schedule of the response was programmed on the Sidman avoidance technique; each response postponed the withdrawal of the cartoon for a given number of seconds. Typically, the children operated at a minimum rate of avoidance, just keeping ahead of the next interruption, thus allowing for a continuous showing of the film.

*Conditioning the "Unconscious."* Hefferline[14] has applied avoidance conditioning techniques to the minute thumb twitch response in the following way. A subject was seated in a comfortable reclining chair, and recording electrodes were attached to the left thumb. The small thumb twitches were recorded electromyographically so that these tiny muscle action potentials could be amplified to a factor of one million. Subjects then listened to tape-recorded music presented through earphones. After an operant level of "twitching" had been established, conditioning was begun by superimposing a loud "noise" (60-cycle hum) over the music. Whenever a thumb twitch occurred of a specific magnitude, the hum was turned off for 15 seconds. (At this stage of the investigation the conditioning would be considered as an escape.) However, if the twitch occurred again within the 15-second period, the hum remained off for another 15 seconds (Sidman avoidance technique). After an hour of conditioning, extinction was begun during which time the subject's response (twitch) failed to turn off the aversive noise. The subjects responded appropriately with a marked increase in rate of twitching during conditioning and reduction during extinction. Subjects who had simply been instructed to relax and listen to music gave no indication that they understood what had been going on. Hefferline[15] has suggested that there may be a continuity between the thumb twitch, which evoked no awareness in the subjects but still constituted a measurable event, and the notion of the "unconscious" proposed by the psychoanalysts. Here is an objective study previously considered inescapably private. Furthermore, Hefferline suggests that the region "under the skin" is the psychologists' new frontier.

*Consequences of Avoidance Conditioning.* At the level of the rat, the only apparent consequence of the avoidance conditioning is to continue

[14] R. F. Hefferline, B. Keenan, and R. A. Harford, Escape and avoidance conditioning in human subjects without their observation of the response, *Science,* **130** (1959), 1338—1339.

[15] R. F. Hefferline, Learning theory and clinical psychology—An eventual symbiosis? In A. J. Bachrach, ed., *Experimental foundations of clinical psychology* (New York: Basic Books, 1962).

to avoid. However, as we consider the possibility of such a situation in our own lives, it does not appear very pleasant. Certainly our clinical evidence tells us that people held under such aversive control frequently end up with mental disorders. The multitude of anxiety disorders, psychosomatic illness as well as more severe psychotic behavior, suggest an inability of the organism to react indefinitely under stressful situations.

To test the effects of avoidance conditioning on primates Brady, Porter, Conrad, and Mason[16] placed monkeys in restraining chairs (Figure 10–2), divided them into pairs, and conditioned them according to a "yoked chair" avoidance procedure. Each pair of the monkeys received brief electric shocks to the feet unless one of the animals (the experimental one) pressed a lever and delayed the shock for 20 seconds. (Sidman's technique.) Both monkeys received the same number and temporal distribution of schocks if the experimental or "executive" monkey missed. The only difference was that the executive monkey could put off the shock, whereas the control monkey could do nothing but take the shock. Under these conditions both animals were subjected to the same physical stress, but only the executive monkey was under the psychological stress of having to press the lever. Each pair of monkeys received 6-hour sessions of this procedure, alternating with 6-hour "off periods" of rest and no shocks for 24-hours a day for as long as 6 or 7 weeks. When the 6-hour "avoidance" session was on, a red light was illuminated in plain view of both monkeys, and during the rest sessions, the light was off. Within a few hours after the initial conditioning, the experimental animals in each pair developed a stable avoidance lever-pressing rate which showed little change throughout the experiment. The rates averaged from 15 to 20 times per minute. At first the control animal, in plain sight of the experimental one, also pressed his bar (nonfunctional) periodically, but this behavior soon extinguished in a few days.

After 23 days of the continuous schedule of 6 hours' avoidance conditioning and 6 hours' rest, one of the experimental animals died during an avoidance session. Prior to this event, no evidence was observed that this was about to occur except that on the previous day the monkey had not eaten. His response rate in the avoiding shock had been steady up to the very end, when he had to be sacrificed (term used to indicate "killing" for proper experimental reasons). A postmortem examination showed a large perforation in the upper wall of the small intestine near its junction with the stomach (the duodenum). This is also a common location of ulcers in man. The control monkey showed no abnormalities upon autopsy. A second pair produced precisely the same results, only in this case the executive monkey collapsed in 25 days and developed ulcers in both the stomach and duodenum. The control animal was again

[16] J. V. Brady, R. W. Porter, D. G. Conrad, and J. W. Mason, Avoidance behavior and the development of gastro-duodenal ulcers, *Jour. Exp. Analys. Behav.*, **1** (1958), 69–72.

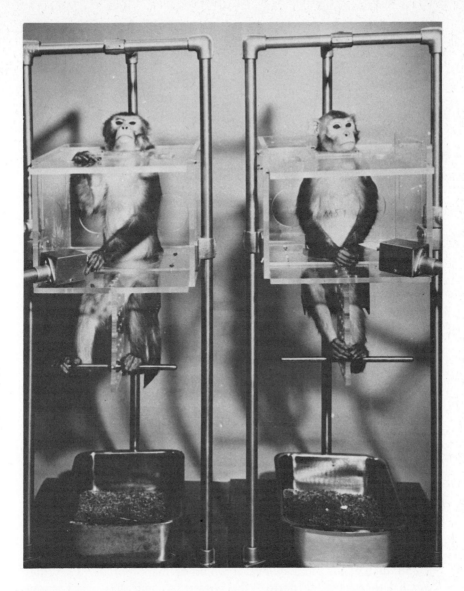

**Figure 10–2.** Monkeys in restraining chairs. Each pair of monkeys received electric shock to the foot unless one of the animals (the "executive monkey") pressed the lever with his hand to forestall the shock for 20 seconds. (Photograph courtesy J. V. Brady, Walter Reed Army Institute for Research, Washington, D.C.)

perfectly normal. In a third pair, the experimental monkey expired after only 9 days of experimentation. In eight pairs, the experimental monkey developed some sort of lesion with ulceration, and none of the control animals (also sacrificed for comparison) indicated any gastrointestinal disorders.

A follow-up study[17] isolated the executive monkey from the control one in soundproofed "telephone booths," with the idea that some form of communication between the animals might account for the results. At the human level we often think that talking to some people is enough to give us ulcers—in fact, even looking at them. However, the effect of isolation in no way changed the results. The executive monkeys continued to develop ulcers. To investigate the problem further as an attempt to "guarantee" the ulcers, Brady attempted to increase the stress by putting animals on 18-hour avoidance conditioning and only 6 hours' rest in a 24-hour period. After a few weeks one of the monkeys died of tuberculosis, not ulcers. The rest of the animals continued to press their levers week after week with no apparent ill effects. Finally, when it seemed that the subjects (and experimenters) would die of old age before any results were forthcoming, the animals were sacrificed, but no abnormalities were discovered. Another group was put on an even more strenuous schedule of 30 minutes on and 30 minutes off, with the shocks programmed every 2 seconds instead of the traditional 20. Again nothing happened.

On the basis of these extensive studies, Brady concludes that the crucial factor was not the degree of stress but the time relationship between stress and no stress. Apparently the 6 hours on and 6 hours off was the one completely effective in producing the ulcers. Investigations of the monkeys' stomachs, using a fistula injected into the stomach wall so that secretions could be analyzed, showed that a considerable amount of acid was secreted in the stomachs of the executive monkeys, not during the "avoidance conditioning" periods but during the rest periods! Apparently this kind of stress, in order to be effective, must be intermittent.

Although at the monkey level it would be inappropriate to say they "worried themselves to death," the phrase is commonly heard among humans. In the light of what we do know about psychosomatic disorders, it is clear that anxiety plays a predominant role in the development of these disorders (see Chapter 12). We also know from our clinical evidence that when a man is busy or occupied, even under stress, he is able to maintain stable behavior. It is not until the stress is over, that he often suffers its consequences. Like Brady's monkeys the significant variable in human anxiety is the period when one knows that the aversive stimuli are coming but can do nothing about them.

[17] J. V. Brady, Ulcers in "executive" monkeys, *Scient. Amer.*, **199**, no. 4 (1958), 95–103.

## Implications of Avoidance Behavior in Humans

The experimental analysis of avoidance behavior gives us considerable understanding of how the same behavior operates at the human level. Previous associations with aversive stimuli serve to condition a vast amount of neutral stimuli. Take verbal behavior, for example. Telling a child, "Don't do that," is sufficient to exhibit the avoidance response if on previous occasions it has been followed by a slap or spanking. The verbal apology also serves to avoid the continuation of aversive threats, "If you don't apologize, you will regret it." The exact nature of the "aversive consequences may not always be known to the apologizer, but his previous conditioning has generalized sufficiently to tell him that if the apology is not forthcoming, he will suffer some kind of damage.

We have seen with the animal studies how a vast degree of control can be achieved in avoidance conditioning. However, the persistent use of aversive stimuli (see Chapters 11 and 12) often generates anxiety which may have disastrous effects on the organism. Many of the effects of excessive avoidance conditioning in early life are seen in the behavior of the adult who chooses a vocation that avoids human contacts as much as possible. We are all familiar with the reserved and "distant" individual who becomes tense at the approach of a friend and shuns people like a frightened dog. The effects of early conditioning are still operating. The stimuli of other people function as conditioned negative reinforcers for the avoidance response.

### INSULATION AND SECLUSION

The hazards of chronic avoidance are seen in the child who, excessively conditioned in avoidance, becomes asocial and seclusive. Like Sidman's rats, he has learned well the effectiveness of persistent avoidance behavior, since everything else he does is punished. The person faced with overwhelming odds finds withdrawal an appropriate reaction. In his seclusion he avoids the difficulties of his environment. In all probability the condition began as simple escape behavior, but with repeated conditioning, the avoidance reaction developed.

A common example of conditioned avoidance in adults is found in *invalidism*. The person acts like a sick or disabled individual but differs from a real invalid in that his behavior of being "sick" is not justified by the biological conditions alone. It includes, of course, some who are disabled or chronically ill but whose avoidance of human contacts and other threatening stimuli is not warranted by the severity of the sickness or disability. The condition includes a variety of hypochondriacs and chronically fatigued persons whose exhaustion is not due to physical exercise. Their manifested symptoms have little or no basis in biological malfunction or disease. The behavior operates effectively in avoiding the aversive consequences of people, for psychological invalids have never developed adequate ways of social interaction. Their behavior enables them to decline any active social participation, for sickness is usually excusable. In so doing, what social facility they may have developed earlier in their lives gets extinguished or depressed. Although living in a world surrounded by human stimuli they *insulate* themselves from their environment in the same way a hermit withdraws from society. The two behaviors are similar; the difference lies only in the geographical relationships.

## FANTASY

Excessive avoidance like escape frequently takes the form of fantasy or daydreaming in which implicit (not so observable) responses get reinforced and substituted for overt activity. In general, there is nothing wrong with fantasy as a source of reinforcement. We tell ourselves amusing stories when we are bored, recall the past, foretell the future, solve problems immediately instead of at a later time. Solutions of problems in fantasy are frequently unrealistic and indeed are fantastic! When this kind of avoidance responding gets chronically substituted for realistic and more overt activity which could do something to overcome the aversive stimuli, it becomes dangerous to the person. Clinical evidence supports as causes of this kind of excessive avoidance behavior the following conditions: (1) long subjection to restrictive and excessive discipline in childhood, (2) excessive criticism of one's acts by other people, (3) deprivation and neglect, and (4) inadequate occasions for social stimuli to operate as conditioned positive reinforcers.[18]

## SCHIZOPHRENIA

In their most extreme form the exaggerated avoidance responses are seen in one of the most common of mental disorders called *schizophrenia* (see also Chapter 16). The disorder is characterized by a multitude of symptoms whose interrelationship is far from obvious. It is not possible to enumerate them all here. One of the most common characteristics of the disorder, however, which is relevant to this discussion, is described as *desocialization*.[19] The person becomes detached from other people, loses social articulation, avoids all activities involving other

---

[18] N. Cameron, *The psychology of behavior disorders* (Boston: Houghton Mifflin, 1947).

[19] N. Cameron and A. Magaret, *Behavior pathology* (Boston: Houghton Mifflin, 1951).

people. He becomes preoccupied with his own fantasies, thoughts, and imaginings. He is able to exclude the effects of external stimuli that ordinarily operate to control the behavior of most normal people. As he becomes more and more detached and loses his social facility, the final step in the development of the disorder is achieved. Cameron and Magaret suggest that this avoidance is the product of anxiety and fear of rejection or ridicule.[20] You will recall our earlier discussion of how avoidance behavior can be reinforced by the reduction of anxiety that had been generated by conditioned aversive stimuli.

Schizophrenia is also characterized by highly disorganized activity (the person misspeaks, fumbles, forgets, randomizes verbally) in which hallucinations and delusions are also predominant. The disorder is far from understood even today, and its origins are difficult to identify. However, a number of environmental conditions (independent variables) are suggested which may be significant in the development of the disorder.[21] For one thing, childhood training is one of the most common participating factors. The individual may never have learned proper behavior necessary to deal with other people. Adequate social skills were never acquired. When aversive stimuli were presented, in lacking the means of controlling them, he resorted to fantasy or a pseudoworld, not inhabited by real individuals but by the products of his own daydreams. Too frequently, the child's training was too rigid. Demands were made which he could not properly handle. To run away and hide became the result, either by physical removal from the aversive stimuli or by substituting other behavior (whose reinforcements are ensured) for those not forthcoming from his environment. Eventually the person so insulates himself from the environmental stimuli through his avoidance behavior that he is deprived of all sources of social reinforcement and opportunities to behave in a manner involving other persons.

The result at this stage is often institutionalization, where it may take a long time to recondition behavior that has either been suppressed or extinguished. Reinforcement from other people has to be substituted for the reinforcements he has been receiving from his own hallucinations and delusions. He has to be taught, through psychotherapy (see Chapters 17 and 18), how to handle the aversive stimuli that in the past have led to his chronic avoidance. As he becomes able to overcome these conditions, the avoidance responses are no longer necessary and can be substituted for by social activities that ordinarily involve positive reinforcements themselves.

The commonness of this disorder as well as the lesser degrees of avoidance behavior which become chronic are ample evidence for the

20 Ibid.
21 Ibid.

preponderance of aversive stimuli which exist in the world in which we live. Although the control exerted by aversive stimuli can be tremendous, effects are often disastrous.

## FREEDOM

It is clear by now that a good bit of our behavior operates under aversive controls. Everything in our lives is not positively reinforcing. The government and the law operate primarily to control our behavior by the use of aversive stimuli. I am not paid a bonus at the end of the year for being a safe driver, but obey the traffic and speed signals to avoid getting a ticket and being find. Do I pay taxes because the government is so good to me? More likely for some of us, at least, we file our income statements as accurately as possible to avoid fines or even imprisonment.

In Skinner's latest book. *Beyond Freedom and Dignity*,[22] he poses the question, What does it mean to be free? Many authors, particularly literary ones, give rather nebulous answers that cannot be reduced to behavioral terms. What Skinner suggests is that to be free is to be in a situation where one is able to escape or avoid the aversive stimuli in our environments. Freedom means, then, that we can be under the control of the more desirable positive reinforcers, rather than the aversive ones that surround us.

## Summary

In avoidance conditioning, the organism learns to make a response that prevents the onset of an aversive stimulus. The avoidance occurs because the presentation of a discriminative stimulus (warning signal) also acts as a conditioned negative reinforcer when removed. As long as its removal is reinforcing, the avoidance is maintained. When the function of the conditioned negative reinforcer gets extinguished, the organism will fail to make the avoidance response and the aversive stimulus will follow, thus reconditioning the avoidance response for future occasions. Avoidance responding operates as a continuous process of extinction and reconditioning of the conditioned negative reinforcer, which also serves as a warning signal to make the avoidance response.

It is possible to condition avoidance behavior without any discriminative warning signal. This is done by punishing the organism for everything he does except the desired avoidance response. Powerful control

---

[22] B. F. Skinner, *Beyond freedom and dignity* (New York: Knopf, 1971).

can be exercised over the organism in this way, but the consequences are often disastrous, particularly for the human. At this level chronic avoidance reactions result in insulated and secluded personalities who seek reinforcements in illness and fantasy. In severe cases like schizophrenia, the avoidance responses have so protected the organism from other people and stimuli in the environment that these stimuli fail to exercise any degree of control over the person. Instead he substitutes reinforcements from his own hallucinatory and delusional reactions, where manufactured reinforcements may be assured.

Thus, in this chapter we have mentioned two types of avoidance: (1) the classical avoidance in which a warning signal is terminated by the avoidance response, and (2) the avoidance without warning signal in which all responses are punished except the one that avoids that punishment. It might be that the term *avoidance* is really a superficial term, for actually, classical avoidance is functionally *escape*, since the organism escapes the $S^{-r}$, and in the avoidance without warning signal is functionally *punishment*.

# 11 Punishment

THE OPERATION OF PUNISHMENT SHOULD
not be confused with those for escape or avoidance.
In these last two conditions an aversive stimulus
reinforces behavior through its removal. In *punishment the effect of the aversive stimulus is to
depress the behavior* when it is presented, rather
than *strengthen* it. The stimulus is contingent upon
the response in the same way that a positive reinforcer follows a response. However, its effect is
not to increase the rate of responding but to
weaken it or temporarily depress it. The relationship can be shown in the following paradigm:

$$R \longrightarrow S^{-R}$$

A response, $R$, is already in operation at some
degree of strength through prior positive reinforcement. It is then followed by an aversive stimulus
$S^{-R}$. In the typical bar-pressing situation, a rat
receives a shock whenever he presses the bar. The
operation can occur while the organism is still
being positively reinforced, either regularly or on
some intermittent schedule or during extinction.

The aversive stimulus could also be a conditioned one, such as a "verbal spanking," ridicule,
or a threatening gesture. In this case the paradigm
reads:

$$R \longrightarrow S^{-r}$$

Other conditioned aversive stimuli that could depress behavior may include: the sight of a dangerous object, an annoying person, a gesture (shaking of the finger), a variety of verbal statements such as "wrong," "naughty," "bad," as well as threats, curses, shaming, and so forth.

Certainly, punishment is an operation with which we are all familiar. We are criticized for inappropriate actions, blamed for our mistakes, or penalized for an infraction of the rule. The child is spanked for his misbehavior or spoken to harshly. One of the favorite techniques of the law in controlling people is the use of punishment. We receive traffic tickets, are fined, have our licenses taken away, or are even sent to jail. Business and industry punish a worker by firing him, docking his pay, or demoting him to a lower-paying job, because for one reason or another, the superiors do not feel his work is meeting the standards they require. Colleges punish a student by sending him "cut" warnings, placing him on social probation, or even dismissing him.

Punishment is one of the oldest forms of control known to man. Enemies were punished by torture or confinement. Early educators and child-rearing practices fostered it in great abundance. Some states today still allow corporeal punishment of children who misbehave in school. When a student fails to tend to his business, "box his ears." "Spare the rod and spoil the child" is still adhered to by many authoritarian disciplinarians. In the early days of the Christian church, punishment was used as a customary means of controlling the conduct of its members. Many of these practices still exist today. The violator of proper moral conduct could be excommunicated, banished, or even physically chastised.

Early psychologists who dared to suggest that punishment really was not very effective were branded as crackpots. Authorities who supposedly "knew better" considered such theories inane, with no substantiation in actual fact. In Thorndike's early formulation of the *Law of Effect*, he suggested as the second part that responses which led to unsatisfying consequences could be "stamped out." However, he later realized that this was not really the case and abandoned this second part of the principle in favor of the first part, which stated that responses followed by satisfying consequences were "stamped in." Since Thorndike's time, much experimental evidence has accumulated to support his abandonment of the notion, for responses that lead to "unpleasant consequences" are not necessarily *eliminated* from the organism's repertoire, once they have been conditioned.

We should, therefore, not think of punishment as having necessarily the opposite effect of positive reinforcement. Although punishment can depress a response, it does not permanently eliminate it from the behavior of the individual. Unfortunately many people still feel that punishment *has* the opposite effects of positive reinforcement and consequently is an effective means of control. A child reaches for a piece of candy, is spanked, and does not reach again in the immediate future, particularly if the parent is still present. However, what happens later when the adult is not in the room is another story, which many adults fail to realize.

## Experimental Studies of Punishment

One way to study punishment is to condition an organism by using positive reinforcement, and after a stable rate of responding has been established, apply punishment, still keeping the reinforcer operating. After a period of time, cease the punishment, continue the reinforcement, and observe the results. (See pp. 261–264.) Another method is to condition an organism, again with positive reinforcement, and then study the effects of punishment during the extinction process.

Skinner[1] did just this. He divided rats into two groups, conditioning both with positive reinforcement on an intermittent schedule until a stable rate had been established. Extinction was then carried out in both groups. However, there was one important difference: The experimental group received a period of punishment in the first 10 minutes of extinction, which consisted of a slap to the animal's paws from the bar itself. After the bar was pressed, there was a quick "snap back" to the animal's front paws. The control group was extinguished continuously without punishment. Following the cessation of punishment, the experimental group was extinguished further. The results are shown in Figure 11–1.

The effects of the punishment are clear and demonstrate two important characteristics of the behavior. First, punishment had the effect of depressing the response rate, which is what one would expect from common observations. The second effect is more remarkable, however, and not what might have been anticipated. After punishment was terminated, the experimental group *recovered* from the effect and ended up with as many extinction responses as did the unpunished group. The result of the punishment, then, was only a temporary depression of responding. Punishment did *not* reduce the overall strength of the response. If extinction is continued long enough, one ought to expect an eventual recovery.

A series of experiments by Estes[2] followed up Skinner's original observations and pointed to a number of other variables of which punishment may be a function. His first experiment was, in effect, a repetition of the original Skinner study. Animals were conditioned on an FI schedule of positive reinforcement, and then punished for a short period

[1] B. F. Skinner, *The behavior of organisms* (New York: Appleton-Century, 1938).
[2] W. K. Estes, An experimental study of punishment, *Psychol. Monogr.*, **57**, no. 263 (1944), iii and 1–40.

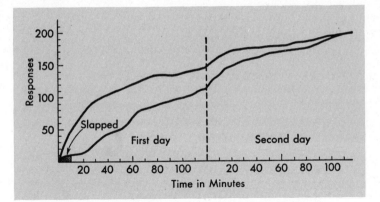

**Figure 11–1.** Curve of response rates in recovery from
punishment. The two curves are from groups of four rats
each with the same experimental history. Both curves
show response rates during examination. All responses
made by one group (lower curve) were slapped during the
first 10 minutes of extinction. Note that for the punished
group, the rate is depressed, but eventually recovers to the
same total number of extinguished responses as the unpunished group. (From B. F. Skinner, *The Behavior of
Organisms*, p. 68. Copyright 1938, D. Appleton-Century
Co., Inc. Reproduced by permission of Appleton-Century-
Crofts, Inc.)

of time during extinction. For the punishing stimulus, he used an electric
shock administered to the bar when the rat pressed it. Like Skinner, he
'found that the final number of extinction responses was not reduced by
the punishment stimulus. The rate of extinction recovered after its
original depression.

Estes then tried long periods of conditioning prior to extinction, after
which punishment was given. The results of this procedure showed that
when a response is well established, it is less susceptible to the effects of
punishment. The better a task is learned through positive reinforcement,
the more difficult it will be to depress through punishment.

In a third experiment Estes varied the number of punished responses
(many or few responses punished in extinction) as well as the intensity
of the punishment (strong or weak shock). A long period of mild punishment or a short or long period of severe punishment had the greatest
effects in depressing the response rate and subsequent recovery. Under
these conditions the number of subsequent (recovery) responses in extinction after punishment had ceased was reduced, but the time required
to complete the extinction remained the same for the punished and
nonpunished groups.

Estes also compared the effects of punishment after each bar press
with intermittent punishment. The shock was thus delivered on a regular

schedule or some intermittent schedule during the extinction process. These results are particularly significant. With continuous punishment of the response, there is a greater *initial* depression of the bar-pressing rate, but with the periodic punishment, the results showed a more persistent inhibitory effect during the subsequent extinction.

### THE WORK OF AZRIN

In the earlier studies of Skinner and Estes the operation of punishment during the process of extinction was applied. Azrin and his colleagues have studied many aspects of punishment while the organism is being conditioned using positive reinforcement. That is, the punishment is superimposed while the organism is being conditioned rather than extinguished. This procedure would appear to be more comparable to a human situation because one may presume that the behavior, prior to punishment, has a positively reinforcing function; otherwise, it would not continue to be maintained.

In one study Azrin[3] observed the effects of various degrees of severity of punishment on response rate (see Figure 11–2). Here we can see the effects of various intensities of punishment as measured in terms of the strength of electric shock. In this study the response measured was the key peck of a pigeon. In two birds, the figure shows the very lawful relationship between the severity of the shock and the rate of response. The greater the shock intensity, the lower the rate of pecking.

Another variable studied by Azrin[4] is the schedule on which the punishment is given. In this experiment the pigeons were first conditioned on a VI 3 for food reinforcement. Superimposed on this were the various schedules in which punishment could be presented. The intensity of the shock was constant, fixed at 240 volts, and the schedule of intermittent reinforcement was altered (see Figure 11–3). When every response is punished (FR 1) (lower line on graph) the response rate is very low—only about 20 per cent of the unpunished rate. Even when only one out of every 100 responses is punished (FR 100), the rate is still only 40 per cent of the unpunished rate. The same kind of suppression is seen as in earlier studies. Again, we note a very lawful relationship: the higher the ratio of punishment (fewer punished responses) the higher the response rate will be.

Another variable relating to the rate of response during punishment is the degree of food deprivation that is operating. In this respect the degree of deprivation is indicated as a percentage of normal body weight

[3] N. H. Azrin, Effects of punishment intensity during variable interval reinforcement, *Jour. Exp. Anal. Behav.*, **3** (1960), 123–142.

[4] N. H. Azrin, W. C. Holz, and D. F. Hake, Fixed ratio punishment, *Jour. Exp. Anal. Behav.*, **6** (1963), 141–148.

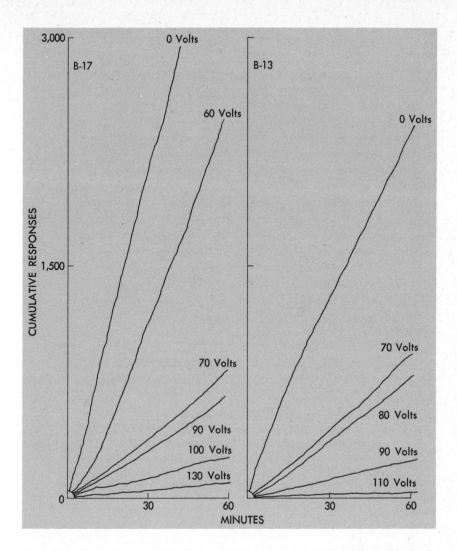

**Figure 11–2.** Effect of punishment intensity on response suppression. Response rate during punishment of various intensities for two different pigeons responding on a variable interval schedule for food reinforcement. Each curve was obtained after a minimum of 10 sessions of stable performance under the particular intensity of punishment. (From N. H. Azrin, Effects of punishment intensity during variable-interval reinforcement, *Journal of the Experimental Analysis of Behavior*, **3** [1960], 123–142, Fig. 12, p. 138. Copyright 1960 by the Society for the Experimental Analysis of Behavior, Inc. Reproduced by permission of the author and the publisher.)

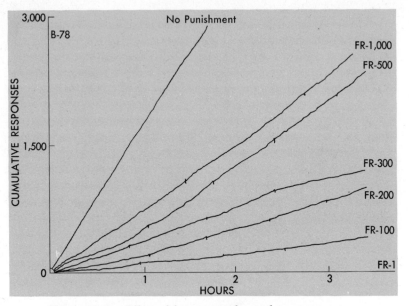

**Figure 11–3.** Effect of frequency of punishment on response suppression. Response rate during FR punishment
of 240 volts shock presented at various fixed ratios from
1 to 1,000. The diagonal lines indicate shock. The pigeons
are also reinforced with food on a VI 3 schedule. (From
N. H. Azrin, W. C. Holz, and D. F. Hake, Fixed ratio
punishment, *Journal of the Experimental Analysis of
Behavior*, **6** [1963], 141–148, Fig. 5, p. 146. Copyright 1963
by the Society for the Experimental Analysis of Behavior,
Inc. Reproduced by permission of the authors and the
publisher.)

when the bird has free access to food.[5] The usual percentage of body
weight for most experiments is 80 per cent normal weight. Figure 11–4
shows that the relationships are very clear; the greater the deprivation,
the more resistant the organism is to the effects of the punishment.
Although these studies were done with pigeons, the implications for
human response should be equally clear. For example, in the last
instance, if the motivation to make the punished response is great
enough, the organism will continue to respond despite the fact that he is
punished for so doing.

SUMMARY OF PRINCIPLES

The experimental literature is fairly clear in pointing out a set of
principles about punishment when different variables are manipulated.

[5] Ibid.

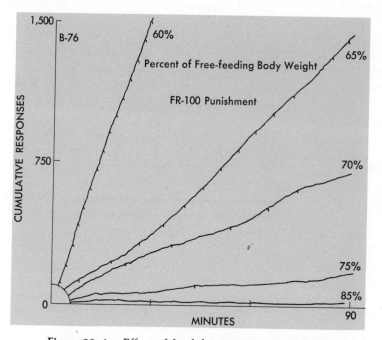

**Figure 11–4.** Effect of food deprivation on responding during fixed-ratio punishment. Pigeon is responding under a V 13 schedule of positive reinforcement and punished (100 v) on a schedule of FR-100 (diagonal lines). The percentages indicated at each lines indicates the degree of deprivation as indicated in percentage of prior free-feeding body weight. (From N. H. Azrin, W. C. Holz and D. F. Hake, Fixed-ratio punishment, *Journal of the Experimental Analysis of Behavior*, 6 [1963], 141–148, Fig. 3, p. 138. Copyright 1963 by the Society for the Experimental Analysis of Behavior, Inc. Reproduced by permission of the authors and the publisher.)

Let us summarize these and point out a few examples of their application.

1. Punishment has, in general, the effect of depressing a response that has been previously conditioned through some kind of positive reinforcement. This immediate effect is easily observed. A child grabs a cookie, is slapped, and does not reach again. A man freely speaks his opinion, is criticized, and subsequently keeps his mouth shut.
2. The depressing effects of punishment are, however, often only temporary for a response that has been positively reinforced. After the traffic ticket, the driver reduces his speed but in a few days resumes his rate, particularly on those occasions when no policemen are

around. A criminal, institutionalized for theft, more than likely resumes his old ways. Without further rehabilitation, efforts to "go straight" seldom last very long after release from confinement. The child who finds positive reinforcement in pinching his younger brother may desist only temporarily after he has been spanked.

3. Strong punishment is more effective in depressing responses than weak punishment. A harsh lashing will control the misbehaved more effectively than a weak slap. A long, intense verbal tirade ordinarily will "set the other straight" for a longer time than a mere "caustic word"—other things being equal. A good, sound spanking keeps the child in line better than a mild, "No, no!" More severe punishment may permanently suppress behavior.

4. To be most effective, punishment should be delivered immediately following the act. To tell a child at noon that he will be punished for his misbehavior when his father comes home that night is, in effect, telling him he will be spanked *for* his parent's return that evening. Criticism delivered a week or so after the act is done, loses its "punch" as compared to a reprimand given immediately following the occurrence.

5. Regular punishment for an act will depress the response much more effectively than occasional punishment. If the child is spanked each time he is naughty, he is more likely to be "good," knowing that the spanking is certain if he is "bad." However, once the punishing control is lifted, the prior behavior returns, often in full strength.

6. Punishment has the effect of generalizing its depressing characteristic. A verbal chastisement given for a single inappropriate remark, often renders the speaker silent on all subjects. A severe spanking will reduce a previously active child to one of considerable homage and restraint. A fine for speeding may render the driver generally cautious in all his relations with the law.

7. The effectiveness of the punishment will depend on the degree of *motivation to perform the punished act.* If one is highly motivated to perform the punished response (degree of deprivation), the depressing effects of the punishment are much less than if the motivation is not so great.

## Forms of Punishment

Punishment can involve basically one of two kinds of operations. The first, which we have discussed giving experimental examples using animals, involves the *presentation* of some aversive stimulus following a response. The aversive stimulus can be either a primary or conditioned negative reinforcer. The second operation suggested by Skinner is the *withholding* of response contingent positive reinforcement.[6] Some experimental examples of this will be presented in the next section.

In the first class we can include primary aversive stimuli such as electric shock, bright lights, loud noise, physical beating, slapping, burning, and torturing. Likewise, conditioned negative stimuli can depress behavior. Verbal responses of "No," "Bad," "Naughty" ordinarily operate as mild punishers. Criticisms, verbal accusations, damning, cursing, ridicule, and caustic remarks likewise have their punishing effects. All these stimuli have their effects when administered following a response.

Examples in the second class of withholding positive reinforcement can operate in the same way. Disapproval (withholding approval), ignoring (withholding attention), legal fines (taking away money), and denial can operate as punishments. Refusing to give to a cause and withholding the supply of food (as in prison camps) operate likewise. This writer recalls one charitable organization that nearly folded up because one of its wealthiest benefactors disapproved of the moral conduct of its leader. Consequently he withheld his very substantial contributions on which the organization depended for its survival. When we wish to punish a child and cringe at physical means, we may deny or deprive him of privileges or reinforcements he is accustomed to. Governmental techniques of control are often of this sort. Fining a man, disposing of his belongings, or depriving him of the ordinary social contacts by confinement within the walls of an institution can operate as punishments.

Self-punishment is also possible. In budgeting our money, we restrict ourselves by withholding money and denying ourselves the reinforcements we enjoy. Dieting is a similar case. Withholding sufficient nourishment depresses eating. However, the conflicts that result from this self-imposed treatment are obvious in one's inability to remain on a restricted schedule of eating for any length of time. The recovery rate is equally clear. After sufficient weight is lost and the diet over, one compensates by overeating so that the lost weight is soon recovered. Of course such a punishment can have its positive reinforcements in the relief of guilt which one felt from being too fat. Furthermore the social approval received when a few pounds are taken off can be equally reinforcing.

## STUDIES OF PUNISHMENT AS THE PRESENTATION
## OF AN AVERSIVE STIMULUS IN HUMANS

The studies of Azrin cited in an earlier section employed pigeons as experimental subjects. In the present study[7] he used as a punishing

---

[6] B. F. Skinner, *Science and human behavior* (New York: Macmillan, Inc., 1953).

[7] N. H. Azrin, Some effects of noise on human behavior, *Jour. Exp. Anal. Behav.*, **1** (1958), 183–200.

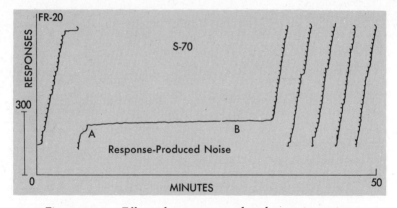

**Figure 11–5.** Effect of response-produced, aversive noise
on responding in a human subject performing an observing
task. The observing responses were reinforced on a FR-20
schedule (diagonal lines) by presentation of a target. The
response recovers when the noise as punishment is removed. (From N. H. Azrin, Some effects of noise on human
behavior, *Journal of the Experimental Analysis of Behavior,* **1** [1958], 183–200, Fig. 11, p. 197. Copyright 1958
by the Society for the Experimental Analysis of Behavior,
Inc. Reproduced by permission of the author and the
publisher.)

stimulus a loud noise of 110 decibels (100 decibels is about the noise
level of a twin-engine airplane). (See Figure 11–5.) In this instance the
response of looking for a target was reinforced on an FR-20 schedule by
the presentation of the target. When the punishing noise was introduced,
the rate of response was reduced to zero. When the noise was eliminated,
the rate returned to normal. This finding is similar to the results obtained
by Estes and Skinner cited earlier using animals as subjects.

*The Use of Punishment in Behavior Therapy.* Lovaas et al.[8] used a pair
of five-year-old twins who had been diagnosed as schizophrenic. These
children showed no social responsiveness; they refused to talk and
seemed not to even recognize each other or adults. They were not toilet
trained and handled blocks and other objects in a very stereotyped
manner by either "fiddling with" or spinning them. The children spent
most of their time in rocking motions or fondling themselves. They exhibited tantrums from time to time by screaming, throwing objects, or
biting themselves. Conventional methods of psychotherapy had failed
utterly. In light of the hopelessness of their condition it did not seem
improper (or immoral) to attempt the use of electric shock. Prior to
shock, a baseline performance was taken of the frequency of the follow-

---

[8] O. I. Lovaas, B. Schaeffer, and J. Q. Simmons, Building social behavior in
autistic children by use of electric shock, *Jour. Exp. Res. Personal.,* **1** (1965), 99–109.

ing behaviors: physical contact with experimenters, self-stimulation, tantrums, and responses to the experimenter's command to "Come here." During the baseline, the children had failed to make physical contact with the experimenter or respond to the call, "Come here."

During the experimental session, the shock was turned on (delivered from the floor) whenever they engaged in self-stimulation or tantrum behavior and was turned off when they responded to the experimenter's commands. In other words, the approach to the experimenter was conditioned by a shock avoidance. Results showed a moderate increase in contact with the experimenter and a marked increase in responding to the experimenter's commands. This was coupled by a suppression of the more undesirable behaviors of self-stimulation and tantrums. These improvements continued for a period of 10 months, at which time they began to extinguish and had to be reconditioned.

Then, the verbal command, "No," was paired with the shock when they engaged in self-stimulation. Before the word "No" had been paired with the shock, it had no effect on their behavior. However, when "No" was paired with the shock, it took on the function of a conditioned negative reinforcer. Later, adults were associated with the avoidance of shock, and there was an increase in social behavior toward adults. The authors suggest that the major benefits derived were not the use of shock to suppress the undesirable behavior but the conditioning of the more social behavior through escape and avoidance procedures.

Flanagan, Goldiamond, and Azrin[9] have applied punishing procedures in the control of chronic stuttering. They were able to increase the frequency of stuttering by allowing the subject to turn off a loud sound (19 decibels) for each instance of nonfluency; conversely, they decreased the frequency of stuttering by punishing each nonfluency with the same loud sound. They suggest that the control of stuttering can be more directly treated by these techniques than by treating the disorder as a by-product of anxiety.

Lang and Malamed[10] reported treating a nine-month-old male infant whose life was seriously endangered by persistent vomiting. They applied electric shock each time the child vomited. This maladaptive behavior was eliminated in a few conditioning sessions. As a result the child showed marked weight increases and a greater responsiveness to people.

Meyer and Crisp[11] report treating a case of compulsive eating in a

[9] B. Flanagan, I. Goldiamond, and N. Azrin, Operant stuttering: The control of stuttering behavior through response contingent consequences, *Jour. Exp. Anal. Behav.*, **1** (1958), 173–177.

[10] P. J. Lang and B. G. Malemed, Case report: Avoidance conditioning therapy in an infant with chronic ruminative vomiting, *Jour. Abn. Psychol.*, **74** (1969), 1–8.

[11] A. Meyer and V. Crisp, Aversion therapy in two cases of obesity, *Behav. Res. and Ther.*, **2** (1964), 143–147.

female subject, using punishment procedures. When she reached for "temptation food" she received an electric shock. However, she received no shock when she reached for "prescribed foods." During her first treatment session she received five shocks, but then only five more during the subsequent thirty sessions. Her weight fell from 91 kg to 82 kg. A six-month follow-up showed she had persisted in avoiding "temptation foods." Her weight dropped and settled between 55 and 59 kg. A year later she still maintained her reduced weight. It might also be pointed out that the punishment operated in the development of a discrimination between eating appropriate foods and "temptation foods."

Powell and Azrin[12] have used electric shock as punishment to reduce cigarette smoking. The shock was delivered by means of a special cigarette case when opened. The rate of smoking was reduced as a function of the intensity of the shock. However, the rate of smoking returned to its previous unpunished level after the shock stimulus was discontinued. As indicated earlier various behavior therapy techniques have not been overly successful in treating cigarette-smoking behavior. (See also Chapter 18.)

Mausner[13] suggests several reasons for the rather mediocre results of behavior therapy to eliminate cigarette smoking when punishment procedures are used. After the person is removed from the punishing situation, his behavior returns because cigarette smoking is positively reinforcing (pleasure reported verbally, relief of tension, social affiliation with other smokers, etc.). Further, alternative positive reinforcers are hard to find.

PUNISHMENT AS "TIME OUT"

Another kind of punishment involves arranging the circumstances so that a previously reinforced response is made impossible. This is known as "time out." It was first described by Ferster and Skinner as "any period of time during which the organism is prevented from emitting the behavior under observation." This can be arranged in a number of ways:

1. Removing the subject from the reinforcing situation such as sending a child to his room.
2. Removing the opportunity to respond, such as removing the bar from the cage for a rat or the response key for a pigeon.
3. Turning out the lights as in a "blackout"; this is often done with pigeons because they are extremely dependent upon their vision.

---

[12] J. Powell and N. Azrin, The effects of shock as a punisher for cigarette smoking, *Jour. Appl. Behav. Anal.*, **1** (1968), 63–71.

[13] B. Mausner, Some comments on the failure of behavior therapy as a technique for modifying cigarette smoking, *Jour. Couns. and Clin. Psychol.*, **36** (1971), 167–170.

4. By presenting a stimulus which has not been correlated with a reinforcement.

In all instances the "time out" can be interpreted as a response contingent $S\Delta$.

Baer[14] has used this procedure to control thumb-sucking in a five-year-old boy. During preliminary sessions, the boy was shown cartoons, which played for 21 minutes. During this period the boy was observed to suck his thumb nearly 100 per cent of the time. During the experimental sessions, Baer attempted to control the thumb-sucking by means of withdrawing the cartoons, both picture and sound. Each time the thumb was placed in the mouth, the cartoon was cut off. It remained terminated as soon and as long as the thumb remained in the mouth. Under these conditions, the thumb-sucking was virtually eliminated, but when placing the thumb in the mouth did not remove the picture, the previous rate of thumb-sucking returned.

In another experiment Baer[15] trained young children to press a bar for peanuts as positive reinforcement. He then showed a cartoon to the children, but each time they pressed the bar for a peanut, the cartoon was turned off for two seconds. Compared with control subjects, the bar-pressing responses were markedly reduced.

We employ "time out" in a number of our everyday activities. We may send a child to his room when he is naughty or otherwise confine him. A hockey player is penalized for a given number of minutes in the penalty box for an infraction of the rules of the game. In severe cases we place a man in jail.

*Use of "Time Out" in Behavior Therapy.* Barton et al.[16] were able to modify undesirable mealtime behaviors in a group of severe retardates whose ages ranged from 9 to 23 and who resided in a hospital cottage. Undesirable behaviors were identified as stealing food from another's plate, using fingers inappropriately, messy use of utensils, and "pigging" (eating directly with the mouth or eating spilled food). In the first two instances, time out was put into operation by removing a subject from the table and putting him in an isolation booth until the meal was finished. In other cases, depending on the health of the individual, time out consisted of a 15-second removal of the meal tray. Time-out procedures led to a marked reduction of undesirable eating procedures and an increase in proper eating habits. In most cases the undesirable behavior

[14] D. M. Baer, Laboratory control of thumbsucking by withdrawal and re-presentation of reinforcements, *Jour. Exp. Anal. Behav.*, 5 (1962), 525–528.

[15] D. M. Baer, Effect of withdrawal of positive reinforcement on the extinguishing response in young children, *Child Dev.*, 32 (1962), 67–74.

[16] E. S. Barton, D. Guess, E. Garcia, and D. M. Baer, Improvement of retardates mealtime behavior by time out procedures using multiple baseline techniques, *Jour. Appl. Behav. Anal.*, 3 (1970), 77–84.

was reduced to zero. An interesting sidelight was that there was no weight loss at the end of the experimental period, which lasted for 120 meals (lunches and suppers).

Martin and Haroldson[17] placed two stutterers in a conversational situation. When either of the subjects emitted a nonfluency (stutter) the experimenter immediately depressed a hand switch which turned on a "time-out" light, which lasted for ten seconds, indicating that neither subject could speak to each other. During this procedure the rate of stuttering was reduced to zero, but when the "time-out" procedure was discontinued the rate of stuttering partially increased, but not to its previous level.

Brown and Tyler[18] report the use of time out in controlling extremely aggressive behavior in an institutionalized delinquent boy of sixteen. In the institution, which consisted of a cottage of delinquent boys, it was apparent that the subject was being strongly reinforced for his aggression and bullying and behavior described as acting like a "duke." Accordingly, he was told that aggression or inappropriate behavior on his part or those of his peers would result in his being put in social isolation. By being dethroned as the "duke" of the group the reinforcing behavior of the submission of the group to his demands could be eliminated. The constant application of the time-out procedure, or being put in the "pokey" as he called it, had a marked effect not only on reducing his own aggressive behavior but also on improving his relations with his peers and staff, since he was able to discourage disruptive behavior of the group. If not, he would be punished by the time out. In addition, however, positive reinforcers were also offered from the staff in the form of approval for his more appropriate behavior.

## How Punishment Works

To say that the effects of punishment are merely to depress behavior is not a sufficient explanation for the proper analysis of behavior. In Chapter 2 we dispensed with the notion that self-will could act as an explanatory principle. Purposeful inhibition, deliberate intentions of inhibition, tell us nothing about behavioral prediction and control. If inhibition operates, there must be stimuli in the situation that exercise some kind of control over the organism's behavior. The answer to the

---

[17] R. R. Martin and S. K. Haroldson, Time out as punishment for stuttering during conversation, *Jour. Commun. Dis.*, 4 (1971), 15–19.

[18] G. D. Brown and V. O. Tyler, Time out from reinforcement: A technique for dethroning the "duke" of an institutionalized delinquent group, *Jour. Child. Psychol. and Psychiat.*, 9 (1969), 203–211.

question of how punishment works is to be found in what we already have learned about aversive stimuli and their effects.

ANXIETY

You will recall that the effects of strong aversive stimuli can be made to generate certain respondent behavior which is often interpreted as emotional in character. We see this in the animal laboratory as well as in human activity. Following an electric shock, an animal may jump, cower in the corner of his cage, defecate, or urinate. After a spanking, a child cries, whimpers, cringes, and behaves in a temporarily disorganized manner. At the adult level, an intense shock or burn causes changes in respondent and operant behaviors. These are at least temporarily disrupting and disorganizing. Neutral stimuli that precede or accompany a primary aversive stimulus take on the function of that stimulus. An example at the level of verbal behavior will illustrate the point.

Consider for a moment an occasion where one has expressed an inadvertent insult and consequently has brought down the wrath of others upon himself. An inappropriate remark has been severely criticized by a superior or by those whose opinion we respect. As a result we feel embarrassed, are upset, and rendered speechless. We may perspire, have flushed cheeks, or have difficulty in swallowing. If nothing happens further, the situation may be only temporary, and eventually these responses subside. However, other stimuli present at the time take on the function of operating on later occasions to generate the same emotional responses. We may find it difficult to talk to those people who caused our embarrassment. The function of these emotional responses has been *to interfere with the expression of the behavior that was punished.*

A similar situation occurs when we feel shame or guilt. Aversive stimuli have aroused responses in the muscles and glands that participate in these emotions. The heart beats faster, blood pressure goes up, and one may feel sick to his stomach. Other stimuli get conditioned easily. In a child punished by a strong spanking, the emotion is obvious. He cries and struggles and a variety of respondent behaviors are elicited. At least on a few later occasions the accompanying stimuli (his parents) can generate the same emotional behavior. The result is that either the punished behavior itself or other stimuli present in the environment become the source of incompatible emotional reactions. As time passes, the emotion subsides and the interference no longer functions to inhibit the punished behavior.

Estes[19] interpreted the effects of punishment in just this way. He considered that the stimuli from the animal's environment (the bar, etc),

---

[19] W. K. Estes, op. cit.

as well as from his own movements of initiating and approaching the lever, which occurred prior to the shock could acquire the power to evoke emotional conditions that would disrupt the previously conditioned bar pressing. In support of this interpretation, he observed that a substantial part of the depressant effect of the punishment disappeared when the animal was placed in his experimental box without the shocks or lever present. The anxiety, therefore, had been incompatible with the previously acquired behavior of bar pressing.

## AVOIDANCE

Although incompatible emotional responses can interfere with the expression of behavior that is punished, they usually function only for a short time following the punishment. Probably more significance in explaining the longer effects of punishment is to be found in avoidance activities. When a response is punished, there are other stimuli in the environment as well as in the behavior itself which become conditioned negative reinforcers. Therefore there is reinforcement of any response following the punished response which reduces the effect of these conditioned negative stimuli. In other words, avoidance conditioning operates.

In Estes' experiments a rat was shocked when he pressed the bar. On future occasions the lever as well as the responses of approaching the lever operated as conditioned negative reinforcers. Any responses which reduced these stimuli (turning around, etc.) were reinforced. The conditioned aversive stimuli can be eliminated by the organism's doing something else. The behavior that *avoids* the punishment continues to operate until the conditioned reinforcer gets extinguished. When this happens, the interference no longer holds. The punished response returns, since it was never extinguished but only interfered with by the incompatible avoidance reactions. As the punished behavior emerges, it may get reconditioned by another aversive stimulus so that the alternate avoiding behavior again is reinforced. The effects of the punishment depend largely on the conditioning of specific aversive stimuli in the environment and from the punished response itself.

## COMPARISON OF SEVERAL PROCEDURES FOR REDUCING RESPONSE RATE

Holz and Azrin[20] have compared the relative effectiveness of various methods employed to weaken behavior; such as (1) stimulus change, (2) extinction, (3) satiation, (4) physical restraint, and (5) punishment.

---

[20] W. C. Holz and N. H. Azrin, A comparison of several procedures for eliminating behavior, *Jour. Exp. Anal. Behav.*, 6 (1963), 399–406.

**1.** *Stimulus Change.* It has often been observed that altering various aspects of the environment will also alter behavior. For example, the removal of $S^D$'s and the introduction of neutral stimuli leave an organism in a situation where he is unable to respond. Often, taking a vacation has the advantageous effect of weakening a subject's undesirable behavior such as worrying, insomnia, etc. Sometimes, in the cases of severely disturbed persons who are in institutions, their disturbed behavior is weakened and more desirable behavior strengthened by a simple change in the environment. In the experiment by Holz and Azrin[21] the change in the stimuli consisted in changing the color of the response key on which pigeons had been pecking. The birds had been conditioned for 60 hours to peck on a white key. When the color was changed to green, the birds ceased pecking for 20 minutes, but then their rate gradually resumed. They concluded that this operation had only an immediate effect in reducing the rate. In human affairs, if after a vacation one returns to his previous anxiety-arousing environment, his worrying, insomnia, etc. will return to their prior intensity.

**2.** *Extinction.* We have already learned that eventual extinction will completely eliminate behavior, but it may take a long time. Holz and Azrin point out, however, that the length of time necessary to eliminate the behavior and effect frequent spontaneous recovery, plus the fact that animals (and people) readily recondition when reinforcement is made available again, make extinction a technique that should not always be the final answer to our problem of eliminating behavior.

**3.** *Satiation.* Some psychologists have suggested that one way to get rid of a bad habit is to satiate it. For example, drink yourself under the table, or smoke until you are blue in the face, or eat until your belly bursts. Holz and Azrin[22] found that satiation led to complete suppression of behavior when their birds exceeded their normal body weight. Furthermore, when they were kept at more than 80 per cent of their normal body weight (partial deprivation), the rate of responding was reduced. However, like stimulus change, the effect is only temporary, because with the return of deprivation the response rate recovers rapidly and completely.

**4.** *Restraint.* Placing a man in prison certainly leads to an immediate cessation of his criminal behavior. Holz and Azrin[23] simply removed the bird from the experimental chamber. In his home cage he could not peck

[21] Ibid.
[22] Ibid.
[23] Ibid.

at the response key. However, when the bird was returned to the apparatus, the previous behavior was resumed. As long as the organism is restrained, there is no return of certain behaviors. However, when criminals are returned to society it is likely that they will return to their old ways unless during confinement, therapeutic procedures are introduced that will help alter the old behavior and recondition more socially desirable activities. One of the difficulties of treating drug addiction is that after the patient is "cured"—that is, has been withdrawn from drugs—he frequently then returns to the old area where drug peddling and addiction are rampant and consequently quickly resumes his habit. The only way that restraint and confinement can be effective is to keep the organism confined.[24]

**5.** *Punishment.* Finally, we have seen that weak or moderate punishment only temporarily suppressed behavior. As long as the punishment is in effect the behavior will remain weakened. However, usually after its cessation, the behavior will return to its regular rate, particularly if that behavior was positively reinforcing. However, when strong punishment is applied (for example, experimentally in the form of strong electric shock), there is evidence that the response fails to recover completely. For example, if an animal has never been shocked before, one severe shock may be enough to suppress behavior permanently and completely. We can take a naive laboratory rat and so shock him (with an intensity short of causing death) that he will be useless in any further experimentation.

In a sense, the question of what is the most effective method of weakening behavior is still unanswered. Stimulus change, restraint, and satiation are only effective as long as the conditions are in operation. Extinction will eliminate behavior, but the process may be long and tedious, and further conditioning will quickly restore it. Punishment in mild or moderate forms only works temporarily, while strong punishment may be very effective, but it generates many unfortunate consequences in the forms of anxiety and aggression.

## The Popularity of Punishment

Since the effects of punishment are ordinarily only temporary in depressing an act, how is it that this form of control is so popular and almost universally used? A number of reasons can be suggested as answers to the question.

[24] Ibid.

1. First of all, the immediate effects of suppressing a response are obvious. The objectionable behavior is depressed for the moment. A person untrained in the analysis of behavior might not look further. He would observe that the consequences were just what were desired, "elimination" of the act that was punished. He might not take into account the future occasions where the response recovered in full strength. Furthermore, the punishment was simple, easy, and quick to administer.

2. A second reason is suggested by Keller and Schoenfeld.[25] In depressing the wrong responses, it is possible to pave the way for the right response. We have already seen that one reason punishment works is that it *does* lead to incompatible avoidance behavior. However, since the avoidance behavior is maintained only by the conditioned negative reinforcers, when they extinguish, the punished response returns.

   But, is it not possible to condition the alternate responses through positive reinforcement? The answer is, indeed yes. The experimental literature is full of examples where animals were rewarded for right responses and shocked for wrong ones, to facilitate learning. Skinner[26] suggests that the acquisition of a discrimination in pigeons could use these principles. Positive reinforcement of food can be presented when the proper discrimination is made and a "blackout" punishment applied when the inappropriate response occurs. In the blackout following the incorrect response, the house lights go out and the bird is left in darkness for a minute or so. Skinner has found this procedure to have a facilitating effect on the formation of a discrimination in favor of the simple use of extinction without it. Actually, when the pigeon makes a wrong response, he not only gets mildly punished by the blackout but extinguished as well, since the response is not reinforced.

   At the human level it is also evident that the verbal terms "right" or "wrong" are used; one is positively reinforcing and the other is mildly punishing. Skinner's teaching machine makes use of this technique. When a student writes his response to a given question, he finds out immediately whether his answer is correct (see Chapter 6). The additive result of both is more effective than either alone.

3. A third possible reason for the popularity of punishment is that it is positively reinforcing to the user.[27] The stronger man is reinforced by the submission of the weaker one who got punished. The authoritarian boss is reinforced by putting his subservient employee in his place. The parent is reinforced by making the child submit to pain in

---

[25] F. S. Keller and W. N. Schoenfeld, *Principles of psychology* (New York: Appleton-Century-Crofts, 1950).

[26] B. F. Skinner, How to teach animals, *Scient. Amer.*, **185** (1951), 26–29.

[27] F. S. Keller and W. N. Schoenfeld, op. cit.

return for his annoying conduct. To have the upper hand means that we can deal out the punishments as we choose, thus making submission on the part of others inevitable. It is not surprising, then, that punishment is so widely used. Perhaps, there is a little bit of the sadist in all of us to the degree that we are reinforced by submission. However, in its more exaggerated form, sadism implies that the punisher receives a positive reinforcement far in excess of that which one should expect from such action (see next section).

## Punishment and Personality Development

### REPRESSION

The Freudian concept of repression has received a great deal of attention by psychologists ever since Freud first "discovered" it. He gave it considerable importance, even in his early works. It was used as a major concept in interpreting dreams,[28] accounting for the little slips and mistakes we make in our everyday life,[29] as well as explaining why we forget unpleasant things and develop many behavior abnormalities. In Freud's interpretation, repression constituted some kind of restraining force within the personality, an anticathexis in which the ego's energy was expended against the opposing forces of the id. Things repressed could be ideas, thoughts, memories, as well as actions. Inborn ideas could be kept down in the id by the forces of the ego and might never reach consciousness. He considered this kind of repression as *primal*, or *archaic*. For example, the desire to have intercourse with one's mother as part of the Oedipus complex was never consciously understood by the child. The acceptance of such an idea by the ego would be too threatening and painful.

A more common type of repression (called *repression proper*) involved an experience that came from the outside world, but because of its unpleasant nature, was quickly forced down into the id, along with ideas associated with it. However, the ideas were not forgotten in the sense that they were lost from the personality; they were merely suppressed until some later time when they could be allowed back into consciousness. The repressions could distort perceptions of the outside world, as when a person fails to perceive actual dangers or denies seeing annoying people. They could also be involved in the loss of motor functions found in hysterical paralyses and mutism. Because the recollection of events or ones associated with them were painful, the ego

[28] S. Freud, *The interpretation of dreams*. In Standard ed., vols. IV and V (London: Hogarth Press, 1953; first German ed., 1900).

[29] S. Freud, *The psychopathology of everyday life*. In The basic writings of Sigmund Freud (New York: Random House; first German ed., 1904).

kept them in the unconscious id through the anticathetic psychic energy. As long as the ego exercised its forces, the repressed ideas remained in the unconscious. If it relaxed its efforts, the idea could pop back into consciousness to cause pain. These might take the form of a slip of the tongue, a mistake, an accident, or an impulsive act. Frequently, the repression could invade the consciousness in some disguised form, a symbolic act or a dream, for during sleep the anticathexis of the ego was partly relaxed. When the cause of the danger was removed, the repression could be lifted, since it was no longer necessary for the ego to exert its energy.

The function of the repression was primarily to save the ego from damaging threats and anxiety that the conscious ideas would evoke. However, even in unconsciousness the idea was not dormant; it could cause tension. When the repressions mounted up so that the majority of the ego's energy became involved in keeping them submerged, the rest of the personality was bound to suffer. As the ego had little energy left over for useful activities, abnormal conditions resulted. Frequently some form of therapy aimed at relieving the repressions through free association and dream analysis was necessary. In free association the troubles were eventually unearthed and the ego left free to invest its energy in more constructive work. The analysis of dreams enabled the therapist to gain some understanding of the repressions and so direct the patient's free associations toward unearthing them. Freud considered repression to be one of the most primary of the ego defenses. We shall have more to say about that in Chapter 14.

## An Objective Interpretation of Repression

Perhaps as you have read the preceding discussion of Freud's theory of repression, a striking similarity between this concept and what we have been saying about punishment has occurred to you. This is no accident. In fact, the experimental studies of punishment give validity to one of Freud's most important concepts. Of course some reinterpretation is necessary. We must dispense with such hypothetical constructs as cathexis versus anticathexis, psychic energies and forces, submergence into the unconscious, and the like. When stripped of these fictional concepts, the facts become quite evident.

Just as Freud realized that a repressed memory was not forgotten but only inhibited from reaching consciousness, so we observed that the effects of punishment are to depress behavior as long as the punishment is operating. The punished behavior is not lost to the organism any more than Freud's repressions were. At some later time when the punishment ceases, the response ordinarily recurs to its earlier strength. In the

Freudian analysis the repression was lifted. We have already noted that punishment generates stimuli that can be aversive to the individual. To reduce these stimuli, avoidance responses result which interfere with the punished response and continue to operate as long as the conditioned aversive stimuli maintain their function. As the function is extinguished without further association with the punished stimulus, the avoidance behavior extinguishes and the original response returns. Freud felt that the recollection of these repressed memories would cause anxiety that was painful. He even mentioned the possibilities of alternate behaviors that would allow the repressed energies to be released. The function of the repression was to save the ego from the anxiety of unpleasant memories.

Likewise, we have noted how strong aversive stimuli can be the source of emotional behavior that interferes with the behavior being punished, and this behavior *is* anxiety. We are harshly criticized, become embarrassed, and "forget" what we are saying. Behaviorally, the same principles operate in the rat's lever pressing or the human's response of observing. If we perceive an unpleasant event, it may be followed by merely "thinking about it," a more implicit response. Soon we do not even like to "think about it" and eventually deny it. The act of denying something is nothing more than the avoiding response that reduced the conditioned aversive stimulus for the rat.

The failure to recall an event does not necessarily mean that the response has been forgotten or extinguished. To say that a repressed memory goes somewhere (into the unconscious), tells us nothing. The response, be it either verbal or bar pressing, does not "go anywhere"; it is merely interfered with by some alternate avoidance behavior.

GUILT

The emotional response commonly generated by the punishing stimulus at the human level is sometimes referred to as "feelings of guilt" or "shame" or a "sense of sin"; the situation becomes one in which punishment is anticipated. Using the word "guilt" merely refers to the fact that the behavior punished was of a moral or ethical nature. We can be punished for many things, some of which, quite naturally in our cultural tradition, have to do with what is good or bad. The child who is excessively punished for being naughty exhibits on future occasions a preponderance of this kind of emotional behavior.

The consequent responses that are exhibited to avoid the punishing situation come to be accepted as "good" and free the person of his guilt. If being "bad" is punished, the purpose of the punishment is to generate avoidance responses of being good. However, for being good to continue, it must have some other positive reinforcements to maintain it. If sinful behavior is punished, righteous behavior must also be positively reinforced. If being good is nothing more than an avoidance response because being bad was punished and anxiety generated, the behavior will eventually become extinguished in favor of the bad behavior.

## AGGRESSION

We have considered in some detail the consequences of punishment in terms of anxiety and guilt. We should not ignore another aspect of punishment—namely that when a person is punished, either by another organism or some accidental aspect of his environment, he frequently gets downright angry. Unless we have been conditioned otherwise, we are not likely just to sit or take our punishment lying down. This aggression, which punishment may generate, can be either of an *operant* or *respondent* sort. In operant aggression one might, if possible, destroy or immobilize the person who is delivering the punishment. Successful aggression of this sort will presumably eliminate the source of the punishing stimulus. In respondent aggression the painful stimulus is delivered to a person who is in the company of another organism. For example, two rats are placed in a cage without shock; they do not aggress. But when shock is applied by the experimenter, the rats will turn and attack each other.[30] Unlike operant aggression, the respondent kind cannot serve the function of reducing the aversive stimulus because neither of the combatants is in any way responsible for the aversive stimulation. Instead, when the intense pain is induced, the attack is directed toward any nearby organism.[31] Under these circumstances, Azrin[32] suggests three further disadvantages of punishment:

1. The punished individual is driven away from the punishing agent, thereby destroying their social relationship.
2. The punished individual may engage in operant aggression by immobilizing or destroying the punishing agent.
3. If the punishment is employed by physical means rather than by another organism, respondent aggression may be expected to be directed toward nearby individuals who were not responsible for the punishment.

## SADISM AND MASOCHISM

Deriving positive reinforcement through punishing others is commonly referred to as *sadism*. The term, of course, is not usually applied

[30] R. E. Ulrich and N. H. Azrin, Reflexive fighting in response to aversive stimulation, *Jour. Exp. Anal. Behav.*, **5** (1962), 511–520.

[31] N. H. Azrin and W. C. Holz, Punishment. In W. Honig, ed., *Operant behavior: Areas of research and applications* (New York: Appleton-Century-Crofts, 1966).

[32] N. H. Azrin, Suggested effects of punishment. In T. Verhave, ed., *The experimental analysis of behavior* (New York: Appleton-Century-Crofts, 1966).

unless the behavior seems to be extreme and the apparent reinforcement derived in excess of what most people would expect. The opposite response of deriving positive reinforcement through punishing oneself or receiving punishment is called *masochism*.

We have already mentioned reinforcements gained through punishment by the submission of those we punish. In the literature of abnormal psychology, one frequently discovers that the reinforcements characteristically received in sadistic behavior are of a sexual nature. There is a basis for this in the ordinary courting and mating behavior found in most animals and man, where the male of the species is the aggressor and the female is the more passive recipient. Often a disproportionate emphasis is placed in our society on the preliminaries in courting and mating.[33] Consequently the relationship implied by the domination, restraint, and the pain becomes familiar aspects of romantic love. Either wittingly or unwittingly we revolve much of our verbal discussions of sin and punishment around matters and attitudes of sex. Aggression, including sex aggression, results in the submission of the opposite party. The punishing responses also achieve sexual reinforcements. Through simple generalization, it is not difficult to see how much sadistic behavior of inflicting punishment on others can in itself achieve sexual reinforcement.

There are also individuals in society who do not receive the reinforcement from giving the punishment so much as from receiving it. These are the *masochists*. Everybody is acquainted with people who seem to "enjoy poor health," the hypochondriacs, the invalids, the chronically ill, who would just as soon die as give up their symptoms. We also know people who seem to thrive on suffering, either their own or that of others. For them, stimuli that are aversive to most people seem to be positively reinforcing. Although their responses seem to seek pain and punishment, they become maintained at high rates because of some positive reinforcement derived from it.

The development of such masochistic behavior is neatly illustrated in an experiment suggested by Keller and Schoenfeld.[34] Rats are conditioned to press a bar, with food as positive reinforcement. Each reinforcement is also accompanied by an electric shock (mild enough so as not to disorganize the animal). Extinction is then begun, with neither shock nor food presented. After the extinction is well along and the response rate has appreciably slowed down, the shock is reintroduced following each response. The result is characteristically a marked acceleration of the rate, indicating that the shock is operating as a conditioned reinforcer. It would appear that the rats were "deliberately" punishing themselves by pressing the bar to receive the shock.

A similar relation was observed some years earlier by Pavlov[35] in his experiments with respondent conditioning. When a dog was presented with a "painful" stimulus to the skin, such as an electric shock, he noted withdrawal responses which included struggling. When feeding the dog was combined with the injurious shocking, Pavlov found that the defensive struggling against the shock stimulus ceased, even though the skin might be subsequently cut or burned. The dog would turn toward the experimenter, make licking motions, and the salivation persisted.

In human affairs, aversive stimuli are often paired with positive reinforcements and can acquire the same reinforcing function. If a sexual act gets paired with painful stimuli, the recipient gets reinforced from it. The individuals who thrive on misery and trouble are undoubtedly receiving positive reinforcement from their difficulties, perhaps in the form of sympathy, attention, and affection from others.

## Summary

From earliest times, punishment has been one of the most common means of controlling the behaviors of others. Early psychologists and educators assumed it to have the opposite effects of positive reinforcement. However, more recently this notion has been abandoned by psychologists in the light of experimental analysis of punishment operations where simple responses can be observed and the effects carefully examined. Instead of eliminating a response from the behavioral repertoire, the effects of punishment tend to interfere with it by the generation of anxiety and avoidance behaviors that are incompatible with the response being punished. As the avoidance and anxiety responses become extinguished, the punished behavior returns until some future occasion when it will again be depressed and the avoidance and anxiety reconditioned.

Despite the temporary effects of punishment, it is still commonly applied in controlling behavior because its initial results are the obvious depression of behavior. Furthermore it does make way for the possibility of alternate behavior that can be positively reinforced. The act of punishing is frequently reinforcing to the giver in the submission of those who are punished.

What Freud interpreted as repression is closely related to punishment

[35] H. P. Pavlov, *Lectures on conditioned reflexes*, trans. W. H. Gantt (New York: International Universities Press, 1928).

and its effects. Freud believed ideas and memories were suppressed into the unconscious because their presence was painful to the ego. There they remained until some future time when the ego could lift its anti-cathectic forces and allow the person to recall the repressed idea. Punished responses are likewise depressed. When the punishment is no longer in operation, the behavior returns because the anxiety and avoidance behavior that has interfered with the punished response has become extinguished.

# 12 Anxiety

POETS AND SCIENTISTS ALIKE HAVE SAID we live in an age of anxiety. The problem has been attacked from every conceivable angle: interviews, ratings, paper-and-pencil tests, physiological measurements, and experimental analysis. Factor analysts (as, for example, Cattell)[1] have examined the problem extensively and believe anxiety to consist of some unitary factor. That is, in all the measures Cattell could find—tests of steadiness, analysis of blood chemistry and the variety of verbal reports given—there was something in common in all, anxiety. The approach of this chapter is somewhat different for we shall consider anxiety as the group of responses an organism makes under certain stimulus operations.

## EMOTIONAL RESPONSES

Before we delve into the study of anxiety, which many personality theorists agree is a most important aspect of personality study, we would do well to consider for a moment the meaning of a class of behavior that is ordinarily referred to as *emotional*. Many of the problems encountered in the study of emotion are similar to those in motivation, or drive. If you were to pick at random a group of psycho-

[1] R. B. Cattell, The principal replicated factors discovered in objective personality test, *Jour. Abn. Soc. Psychol.*, **50** (1955), 291–314.

logists and ask each to define "emotion," you might come out with as
many different definitions as you had psychologists. Some might say
that emotion was a disturbed state of the organism, an acquired drive,
changes in physiological functioning resulting from intense stimulation,
an instinct or predisposition, or a psychological "freezing." Emotion
might be defined as the cause of behavior (a man runs because he is
afraid) or an intervening variable (fear as an inferred state which leads
to escape from painful stimuli), or behavior itself, resulting from certain
operations. Although most might agree on a verbal enumeration of what
*the* emotions were (fear, hate, rage, jealousy, sorrow, and so forth), they
would have difficulty in finding much common ground which could
characterize all emotional activity. In fact some beginning texts in psychology no longer include emotion as a special topic for discussion. Instead, the various emotions are included in discussion of other topics
(motivation, adjustment, conflict, etc.).[2] The reason for the difficulty
is quite obvious, for in the various emotions, the antecedents as well as
the responses are very different. Is anger the same as joy or sorrow?
What about the differences in physiological functioning that accompany
these behaviors? The fact that some psysiological changes do occur during emotional activity is very true, but it is equally true that many of the
same changes also take place during hard work or excessive exercise.

In the final analysis of emotional responses, we come down to two
events: the emotional behavior and the manipulable conditions of which
that behavior is a function.[3] We must look into the specific operations
performed and note the resulting changes that take place. Something
happens: A stimulus is presented or taken away, a reinforcement is presented or withheld.[4]

In our earlier discussions we have had occasion to refer to emotional
operations and their results. In describing the typical extinction curve
resulting from conditioning with regular reinforcement (Chapter 3), we
noted the bursts and depressions in activity that followed, and interpreted them as emotional, perhaps aggression. Likewise, when an intense
aversion stimulus is presented, the organism will crouch, climb, jump
around the cage, and squeal, if he happens to be a rat. When a conditioned negative reinforcer is presented, we often interpret the resulting
behavior of escape or avoidance as fear. And when we withold a conditioned positive reinforcer, the behavior is sometimes identified as sorrow or depression. The actual labels or terms applied to the results of
these operations are not important. What counts is that we know how to
manipulate the stimuli and how to find out what happens in the be-

---

[2] G. A. Kimble, *Principles of general psychology* (New York: Ronald Press, 1956).
  [3] B. F. Skinner, *Science and human behavior* (New York: Macmillan, Inc., 1953),
chapter x.
  [4] F. S. Keller and W. N. Schoenfeld, *Principles of psychology* (New York:
Appleton-Century-Crofts, 1950).

havioral consequences. One operation of particular interest to us in the study of personality is that of *anxiety*.

## The Operation of Anxiety

The operation for producing anxiety is for *a neutral stimulus to be followed by a primary aversive stimulus.*[5] The paradigm reads:

$$S^n \longrightarrow S^{-R}$$

The $S^n$ would be the neutral stimulus that is followed at some point in time by a primary aversive one, $S^{-R}$. When the operation is repeated the $S^n$ takes on the function of an $S^{-r}$, a conditioned aversive stimulus, because of its pairing with the primary one. After conditioning, the paradigm reads:

$$S^{-r} \longrightarrow S^{-R}$$

The behavioral consequences of this operation are termed *anxiety*. The $S^{-r}$ has taken on the function of a conditioned negative reinforcer and that some of the consequences of that pairing will involve respondent behavior. At this level of analysis, the paradigm resembles that for the classical, or Pavlovian, conditioned withdrawal to an aversive stimulus:

$$S_2 \longrightarrow R$$
$$\text{(Shock)} \nearrow \quad \text{(Foot withdrawal)}$$
$$S_1 \nearrow$$
$$\text{(Tone)}$$

However, for the operation to be properly identified as anxiety, the temporal separation between the two stimuli must be of sufficient duration to allow the behavioral changes to occur. Second, there is the matter of the inevitability of the aversive stimulus that follows the neutral one. If the organism can do something to terminate it, the condition then becomes avoidance and not anxiety. From our earlier discussion of avoidance, the close relationship that exists between the two operations is obvious.

Examples of anxiety are common enough in our everyday life. The sight of the whip in the hands of the approaching father is meaningful enough to the terrorized child. The air-raid warnings signalize the onset

[5] W. K. Estes and B. F. Skinner, Some quantitative properties of anxiety, *Jour. Exp. Psychol.*, **29** (1941), 390–400.

of a bombing raid in which some may perish. The student called to the dean's office shows signs of agitation and apprehension because this call has in the past been followed by some kind of aversive stimulation. The impossibility of escape is characteristic of the anxiety operation and helps us distinguish anxiety from other operations.

## Experimental Studies of Anxiety

In recent years considerable experimental evidence has accumulated which enables us to understand fairly clearly the effects of a number of variations on the basic anxiety paradigm. A systematic investigation by Estes and Skinner[6] will illustrate the basic operation and its effects on behavior. They conditioned rats to press a bar for food reinforcement on an FI schedule of four minutes. After this response was established, the $S^{-r} \longrightarrow S^{-R}$ sequence was introduced. $S^{-r}$ became a tone presented for five minutes and sounded continuously before the $S^{-R}$, a momentary electric shock, was presented through a grid on the floor of the experimental chamber. They noted several effects on the behavior of the animals. First, there was a general depression in the rate of bar pressing during the interval between $S^{-r}$ and $S^{-R}$, although specific care was taken so that the bar pressing response was not immediately followed by shock (otherwise it would be punishment).

As the experiment progressed through successive pairings of these two stimuli, the depression became more and more marked. Interestingly, following $S^{-R}$ (shock), there was an increase in the rate as a *compensation* for the depression. Estes and Skinner then tested the effects of the $S^{-r} \longrightarrow S^{-R}$ sequence during the extinction of the bar press. The effects were typically the same as during the conditioning period with positive reinforcement. A depression in rate was evident following the $S^{-r}$ and an increase in the extinction rate following $S^{-R}$, so that the final height of the extinction curve was probably not modified (see Figure 12–1). They then attempted to extinguish the anxiety reaction by presenting the tone for a prolonged period of time without any shock following. The rate of response was delayed when the tone was first introduced but eventually increased when no shock was forthcoming. Thus, the previously acquired response rate was resumed. However, this extinction of anxiety was only temporary, for on successive occasions the depression in rate occurred, indicating that the effects of the anxiety had not completely worn off. In this experiment the anxiety was measured only indirectly in terms of the effects on the response rate that had been positively reinforced. However, the anxiety was more than an inference,

[6] Ibid.

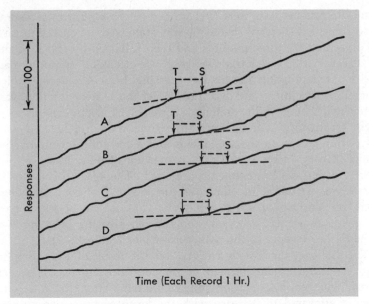

**Figure 12–1.** The effects of conditioned anxiety on response rate. The letter *T* on the cumulative response curves denotes the onset of a tone; *S* indicates the recurrence of electric shock. The response curves (A, B, C, D) represent the responses on four successive days. Note the reduction of the response rates to almost no responding during the period of conditioned anxiety. Each curve is the average for a group of six rats. (From W. K. Estes and B. F. Skinner, Some quantitative properties of anxiety, *Journal of Experimental Psychology*, **29** [1941], 390–400, Fig. 2, p. 393.)

as evidenced by the fact that the depression in response rate that followed the tone was considerably more apparent than when the animals received "unanticipated shocks" without any warning signal.

### EFFECTS OF ELECTROCONVULSIVE SHOCK ON ANXIETY

In an extensive series of experiments, Hunt and Brady and their associates attempted to study the effects of electroconvulsive shock (ECS) on a previously conditioned anxiety reaction. These experiments have considerable implication for human personality, and in particular for therapy, since the use of shock in treating human behavior disorders has been extremely popular in recent years.

In the first experiment, Hunt and Brady[7] modified the Estes and

[7] H. F. Hunt and J. V. Brady, Some effects of electro-convulsive shock on a conditioned emotional response ("anxiety"), *Jour. Comp. Physiol. Psychol.*, **44** (1951), 88–98.

Skinner technique. Rats were first trained to press a bar to receive water reinforcement. When this behavior was stabilized, a "clicker noise" ($S_1$) was presented for three minutes and then followed by shock to the animal's feet. Within a few trials the response of anxiety began to manifest itself by a depression in the bar-pressing behavior, accompanied by crouching, immobility, and defecation. After the anxiety reaction was well established, they gave the animals a series of 21 electroconvulsive shock (ECS) "treatments," administered three times a day for seven days. Electrodes were placed on the rats' heads and a current momentarily passed through, strong enough to produce convulsions similar to those found in humans when shock treatments are used. The result of these "treatments" was virtually to eliminate the anxiety *without* showing any effects on the bar-pressing behavior. That is the shock apparently weakened the anxiety reaction, and the bar-pressing behavior was resumed in the presence of the clicker noise (see Figure 12–2).

The fact that the loss of anxiety was the result of the shock "treatments" and not an impairment of the rats' hearing was later demonstrated.[8] Further investigation showed that the strength of the anxiety response appeared to increase with the lapse of time, without further exercise and without further conditioning[9] (often called *incubation*). As a matter of fact, within 30 days after the shock treatments that had reduced the anxiety, the response appeared stronger than ever. This was demonstrated in the following way: Four days after the completion of the intial shock treatments, rats were first tested and it was found that the emotional reaction (anxiety) had virtually disappeared. Then, subsequent tests were conducted 30, 60, and 90 days later. In these tests the anxiety response reappeared as though it had never been depressed by shock. However, if the shock treatments were delayed for as long as 30 days after the original anxiety conditioning, instead of occurring shortly after its development, the effect produced no change in the reduction of the anxiety. That is, anxiety was not depressed following the delayed shock treatments.[10] This may have some implications in understanding why shock treatments in humans do not always work in relieving the behavioral symptoms.

Numerous implications can be drawn from these studies. In treating people who suffer from behavior disorders where anxiety has been a part of the pattern, it is not uncommon for the effects of the shock treatments to be temporary. This reason is, apparently, that the effects of the shock

[8] J. V. Brady and H. F. Hunt, The effect of electro-convulsive shock on a conditioned emotional response: A control for impaired hearing, *Jour. Comp. Physiol.* **45** (1952), 180–182.

[9] J. V. Brady, The effect of electro-convulsive shock on a conditioned emotional response: The permanency of effect, *Jour. Comp. Physiol. Psychol.*, **44** (1951), 507–511.

[10] J. V. Brady, The effect of electro-convulsive shock on a conditioned emotional response: The significance of the interval between the emotional conditioning and the electro-convulsive shock, *Jour. Comp. Physiol. Psychol.*, **45** (1952), 9–13.

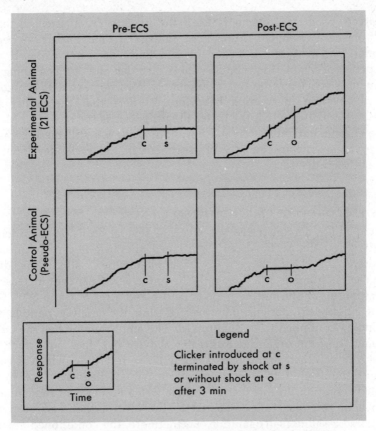

**Figure 12–2.** The effect of electroconvulsive shock (ECS) on the conditioned anxiety response. The response curves for both the control and experimental animals show the characteristic depression in response rate during the conditioned anxiety period. Observe the absence of anxiety in the experimental animal following the electric shock. (From H. F. Hunt and J. V. Brady, Some effects of electro-convulsive shock on a conditioned emotional response ("anxiety"), *Journal of Comparative and Physiological Psychology,* **44** [1951], 988–998, Fig. 2, p. 992.

do not eliminate the behavioral symptoms but only suppress them. We observed that the rat's anxiety was depressed following treatments but that the condition was only temporary. However, when the anxiety was extinguished following the shock treatments, it failed to reappear. This is a fundamental principle of behavior therapy. About the best way to eliminate a response is to extinguish it. Many other methods may only depress it. Likewise, the fact that additional shock treatments facilitated the elimination of anxiety has its human applications.

Ordinarily, treatments are given over a period of time. When their effect is only temporary, another series is frequently applied. Presumably the effects of these treatments keep the anxiety from strengthening, which ordinarily happens through the passage of time. Finally we begin to understand why shock treatment sometimes does not work. If the time between original development of a disorder and the beginning of treatment is too long, the treatment simply does not work. It is a common observation in treating behavior disorders that the earlier the symptoms are discovered, the better the prognosis is for recovery. Many of the chronic patients in mental hospitals today are still there because nothing was done in the way of treatment in the early development stages of their disorder.

### THE EFFECT OF DRUGS ON CONDITIONED ANXIETY

Brady[11] has demonstrated the effects of several drugs on conditioned anxiety. After the rat has been conditioned, the drug is usually injected into the animal. Using large doses of amphetamine, a stimulating drug often used in humans as a "pep pill," he found a 100 per cent increase in the response rate during the periods before and after $S^{-r}$ and $S^{-R}$, that is, the no-anxiety periods. However, during the anxiety periods the responding continued to be suppressed. The amphetamine has the effect of stimulating the organism to greater activity but does not affect the anxiety. In contrast, Brady used a tranquilizer, reserpine, which is commonly administered to psychotics, particularly when they are in an agitated condition. In this instance, there was a 50 per cent reduction in the overall response rate compared to the control that had been administered a saline (salt) solution. Furthermore, the conditioned anxiety periods were virtually eliminated. The animal continued to respond during the three-minute clicker periods at the same rate, although reduced, as during the seven-minute non-clicker periods, even though the shock continued to be presented at the end of each clicker period. It should be realized that at the time of this experiment (1956) the use of tranquilizers was a relatively new technique in treating psychologically disturbed persons. Thus, the technique described is significant in testing the effects of new drugs as they are being developed and often before they are tried out on humans. Many drug companies employ psychologists who use various conditioning techniques to test new drugs.

### SURGICAL LESIONS

Sidman[12] has demonstrated that when surgical lesions are made in the septal area of the brain, the previously conditioned anxiety seems to

---

[11] J. V. Brady, Assessment of drug effects on emotional behavior, *Science*, **123** (1956), 1033–1034.

[12] M. Sidman, Normal sources of pathological behavior, *Science*, **132** (1960), 61–68.

disappear; that is, when the clicker is sounded, the animal does not reduce his response rate.

## Anxiety in Humans

As we shall see in the following section, the occasions for arousing anxiety in humans fit the general paradigm that we used for conditioning the operation at the animal level. The behavioral manifestations at the human level are bound to be more complex. However, we are justified in identifying both conditions as anxiety if the behavior expressed on such occasions occurs in a situation where a neutral stimulus is inevitably followed by an aversive one. That neutral stimulus takes on the conditioning function. Once this happens, the behavior resulting from the $S^{-r}$ before the onset of $S^{-R}$ is properly interpreted as anxiety by definition of our operation. Too frequently, psychologists err (the factor analysts in particular) in defining a concept merely on the basis of results obtained from a series of tests, rating, or interviews, without ever bothering to consider the antecedent conditions.

In humans the behavior has many manifestations, including both respondent and operant reactions. Included among these are changes in physiological functioning as well as overt actions. Furthermore, when the internal changes occur, they can operate as stimuli for verbal responses that add to the description of anxiety. The responses may be implicit and become verbalized as "feelings."

Under the stimulus operations we have defined, many changes in activity, especially of a respondent sort, are a function of the autonomic nervous system: increases in blood pressure and pulse rate, cessation of digestion, frequency of urination and defecation (also noted in the rat). Breathing often becomes shallow and rapid, pupils dilate, excessive perspiration appears, with cessation of normal salivary secretion. More overtly, anxiety is expressed in an increase in motor activity, sometimes described as restlessness or heightened muscular rigidity. If one wishes exact measures of these changes, many tests are available for steadiness, body sway, and the like. Reaction time is reduced; jumpiness is evident at even the presentation of mild stimuli. Increased muscular rigidity operates to interfere with sleep, and if intense enough, disturbs coordinated movements.

When asked to verbalize his responses, the anxious person reports a "feeling of dread, impending doom or disaster." He is apprehensive about the future. The exact nature of these verbal responses is often ill defined and hard to measure. However, the overall changes in behavior are obvious enough, and this complex of response patterns constitutes the anxiety reaction.

OCCASIONS FOR ANXIETY

Cameron and Magaret[13] suggest several conditions that occur frequently in our everyday existence and fit our operational definition.

1. *Impossibility of Overt Escape.* One of the differences between escape and anxiety is that in the former the organism can terminate the aversive stimulus; in anxiety he cannot. $S^{-r}$ is presented and $S_2$ will follow at some future time. The $S^{-R}$ has been an inevitable consequence in the past conditioning history of the organism. One of the most clearcut examples of this condition is to be found under conditions of combat. A soldier is frequently placed in a situation where his life is in danger; escape is impossible. The pilot brings his plane to its target in the face of enemy attack. Civilians under similar conditions of war are frequently placed under bombardment without defense. To a lesser degree we are all placed "under combat" when we face the dentist's drill or the surgeon's knife. The child waiting to take his bitter medicine or the criminal awaiting his sentence exhibit similar reactions.

2. *Anticipation of Punishment.* This situation is really very similar to that in (1). A punishment is threatened ($S^{-r}$) and later carried out ($S^{-R}$). The child, waiting for his spanking, whines and cries frequently more during the interval than after the aversive stimulus is presented. The worker, waiting to be called down by his foreman, exhibits the nervousness of a frightened child. A forbidden act has been performed; the individual awaits the aversive disapproval. Frequently, when the actual punishment is not known, the person may confess his crime in order to receive the punishment and be rid of the anxiety. When anxiety manifests itself on occasions where moral misconduct will be punished, it is ordinarily described as guilt. The behavioral manifestations are the same as in other forms of anxiety. The difference lies only in the precise character of the $S_1$ and the previous conduct that has been positively reinforced.

3. *Separation from Support.* If we interpret the withdrawing of a positive reinforcer as punishment, and consequently aversive, this situation also fits our operation.[14] A child accustomed to receiving reinforcement from his parents and familiar surroundings is suddenly separated from them. This typifies the anxiety of the lost child, the infant separated from his parents through adoption, or the homesickness of the girl who goes off to school and leaves her parents for the first time. As a matter of fact, Freud recognized this condition and

---

[13] N. Cameron and A. Magaret, *Behavior pathology* (Boston: Houghton Mifflin, 1951).

[14] B. F. Skinner, op. cit.

referred to it as *separation anxiety*.[15] On the occasion of its separation, the child may first call for his mother. When she does not come, he cries, trembles, or may remain unable to move (like the crouching behavior of Brady's rats). During World War II evidence of separation anxiety was common in Great Britain where children were taken from their parents and evacuated from the cities to safer rural areas. Anna Freud and D. T. Burlingham[16] describe the anxiety of these children in the following way: After separation some refused to eat; they would cling for days to some parting gift from their mothers; an occasional child repeated over and over again the name of his mother. These authors interpreted the separation as abandonment and the abandonment as punishment.

### INDIVIDUAL DIFFERENCES IN ANXIETY REACTIONS

It is evident that everybody does not act in exactly the same way when placed in the $S^{-r} \longrightarrow S^{-R}$ situation. Not only may the topography of the responses differ but their frequency and intensity may differ as well. As with Brady's rats, the severity of the response is positively related both to the intensity of the aversive stimulus and the previous conditioning history of the organism.[17] An examination of the events in the developmental history of the personality gives us some understanding of why some people exhibit severe anxiety reactions and others react only mildly when placed in the same situation.

1. *Conditioning History.* A child ordinarily receives his first conditioning in anxiety from his parents. They, as objects, represent the $S_1$ in his life, and their punishments the $S_2$'s. An overly restrictive mother interprets a new situation in which her child finds himself as one for punishment. The occasion for this is like the rat's pressing the bar to get positive reinforcement. He *was* having a good time until this behavior was suddenly interrupted, mother came running, cried, screamed, and lifted him bodily from the scene. She may have relieved her own anxiety or fear of his danger by punishing him physically and removing him from the situation that had previously positively reinforced him. The stage is then set for future anxiety.

Punishment that is inevitable, unavoidable, intense, and preceded

[15] S. Freud, *New introductory lectures on psychoanalysis* (New York: Norton, 1933; first German ed., 1933).

[16] A. Freud and D. T. Burlingham, *War and children* (New York: Ernst Willard, 1943).

[17] J. V. Brady and H. F. Hunt, An experimental approach to the analysis of emotional behavior, *Jour. Psychol.*, **40** (1955), 313–324. See also R. W. Goy, The effect of electro-convulsive shock on a conditioned emotional response: The relation between the amount of attenuation and the strength of the conditioned emotional response. Unpublished Ph.D. dissertation, University of Chicago, 1953.

by some form of threat is literally *training a child in anxiety*. He is punished by cross-examination for every move he makes, or rejected because his behavior does not meet with the approval of his parents; he is being well conditioned for the future. Perfectionistic training, likewise, has its anxiety consequences. Demanding parents who insist on better and better performance, higher and higher achievements from their children set the occasion for aversive conditioning when their demands are not fulfilled by their offsprings. The verbal demands became conditioning stimuli and the aversive consequences the resulting punishment, when the child fails to succeed. As we know, aversive stimuli of this sort can take many forms: parental disapproval, disappointment, rejection, or even physical injury. The youngster is left as helpless in these situations as the rat who cannot avoid the shock. Since he lacks the maturity to meet the parental expectations and receive the positive reinforcements that may be forthcoming for his success, the child can only fail and take the consequent punishment.

2. *Imitation.* We have learned (Chapter 5) that the behavior of other organisms can set the stage for responses that lead to reinforcement. These responses of others act as discriminative stimuli for us. In following them, we are reinforced; in not following, we are extinguished or punished. If a person is brought up in a home where anxiety is the prevailing pattern, it is quite likely for him to acquire that same pattern.[18] Without prior conditioning, the parents' own anxiety reactions are ordinarily met with indifference. But the child learns that following the patterns of his parents, anxious though they may be, is met with some kind of approval or attention. Clinical evidence is inexorably clear that anxious parents are likely to raise anxious offsprings.[19] These parents are apt to utilize other sources of reinforcement in reducing their own anxiety. An adult faced with a threat attempts to avoid the ensuing punishment by clutching to the arm of a friend or, like the child, by running to the arms of another for comfort. Although seemingly paradoxical, the anxious mother may seek relief of her own fright through comforting her child.

3. *Persistence of Anxiety.* In the animal laboratory, once anxiety is conditioned, it functions to increase and spread its effect.[20] There appears to be an intensification of the response through the passage of time if nothing is done to counteract it. This same kind of observation is well known to the clinical psychologist and helps to account for the

[18] N. Cameron and A. Magaret, op. cit.

[19] Ibid.

[20] J. V. Brady, The effect of electro-convulsive shock on a conditioned emotional response: The permanency of effect, *Jour. Comp. Physiol. Psychol.*, **44** (1951), 507–511.

individual differences in reactions to a current anxiety situation. This persistence is called *incubation,* and spread of effect is known as the *generalization of anxiety.* These have been reported by various investigators, regardless of their theoretical orientation.[21] As the generalization proceeds, the person is often unable to identify the stimulus that originally initiated the response. Under these conditions, not knowing the occasions which bring forth his anxiety, he is rendered helpless to control them.

An example of how the process of generalization develops at the human level is illustrated in an experiment by Diven.[22] In this study, subjects were asked to verbalize a chain of words to a stimulus presented by the experimenter for a period of 12 seconds. Then the next word was presented for association. To most stimuli, the subject merely associated for 12 seconds. However, whenever in his list the word *red* was followed by the word *barn* an unexpected electric shock was presented 12 seconds later at the end of the association. This variation occurred six times in the list for each subject. Although anxiety was defined by the changes in galvanic skin resistance (GSR), which at best is a rather limited measure, the results were taken as evidence of the generalization effects. (GSR refers to the resistance of the skin, usually the palm of the hand, to the passage of an imperceptible electric current.) The amount of GSR was taken as an indication of the subject's anxiety. Although GSR is not restricted to an indication of anxiety alone, it is commonly correlated, in the opinion of many psychologists, with some degree of emotional response. For Diven's subjects the strongest "anxiety" reaction occurred when the word *barn* was presented because it had always been followed by shock. However, significant reactions also occurred to the word *red*, which always preceded *barn* on the list, and also to whatever words had followed barn in the list. Other words that had a rural connotation, such as sheep, plow, and pasture, also showed marked changes, although to a lesser extent than the ones most closely associated with the shocked stimulus. The anxiety reaction had generalized from the original word that was always shocked, to words close to it in time as well as related in meaning. Also of special significance to our analysis was the fact that half the subjects were *unable to recall* the word that had been followed by the shock. It was impossible to identify the stimuli that had operated as the $S^{-r}$. This finding has important implications for our understanding of some more severe manifestations of anxiety.

Diven also demonstrated the effects of incubation. For subjects who

[21] J. Dollard and N. E. Miller, *Personality and psychotherapy* (New York: McGraw-Hill, 1950).

[22] K. Diven, Certain determinants in the conditioning of anxiety reactions, *Jour. Psychol.*, 3 (1937), 291–308.

received the second series of words without shock almost immediately after the first, the GSR as an index of general anxiety was less on the second session, but in subjects who were forced to wait 24 to 48 hours before the presentation of the list, the GSR index was greater in the second series even though no shock was presented.

A further attempt to verify incubation effects was attempted by Bindra and Cameron,[23] since Diven's experiment had made no attempt to control the activity of the subjects during the rest period. Accordingly, these investigators set up an experiment that was somewhat similar to Diven's. As stimuli they presented visually a series of letters and numbers both before and after a 10-minute rest period. Out of 12 trials, half of the stimuli began with the letter *B*; the other half began with *V* and were followed by shock when each letter was presented. Subjects were asked to make a verbal response to the stimuli by counting by two's. Results indicated that anxiety increased significantly even after as short a period as a 10-minute rest. This is all the more significant if we realize that there is a typical adaptation effect of the GSR following the repetition of the same stimuli.

### PATHOLOGICAL ANXIETY

Pathological anxiety reactions are merely direct exaggerations of the normal anxiety we have discussed so far. The observations from experiments help us understand these characteristics of the behavior. (1) Once anxiety is developed through the usual conditioning technique, it becomes intensified without further trials through the passage of time. (2) When the anxiety response is developed, it has the capacity to generalize to other stimuli besides the ones used in the initial conditioning. This incubation and generalization often make it impossible to identify the stimuli that initiated the anxiety response.

Pathological anxiety is identified by three behavioral patterns: *chronic anxiety*, the *anxiety attack* or *panic*, and the *phobia*. *Chronic anxiety* means simply that the individual is persistently, day in and day out, exhibiting the responses. He is continuously living under the influence of conditioned negative stimuli. The results are manifested in his tense posture, strained facial expression, frequent undirected movements (nervousness), and in the many respondents that operate in the smooth muscles or glands of internal secretion. He verbally complains of pains, headaches, upset stomach, clammy hands. He may describe his responses as "shaky" or "jittery." He often reports a feeling of danger, of impending doom. He says he is afraid but does not know what he fears. The condition was recognized by Freud who called it *free floating anxiety*; that is, anxiety without a known cause.

---

[23] D. Bindra and L. Cameron, Changes in experimentally produced anxiety with the passage of time: Incubation effect, *Jour. Exp. Psychol.*, **45** (1953), 197–203.

The *anxiety attack* is merely a more acute episode of the reactions described above. There appears a sudden emotional outburst, resembling terror or intense fright. The subject trembles, is agitated. Vomiting and uncontrolled voiding are not uncommon. Heart rate suddenly increases; he may gasp for breath; and he interprets these events often as signs of approaching death. Frequently the stimuli that initiate his pattern are not known. In other cases, he can forestall the anxiety attack by persisting in some avoidance response. In most cases the attack subsides in a few minutes or half an hour.

The *phobia* involves an intense anxiety reaction in which specific stimuli that arouse the reaction can be identified, but the original conditioning event cannot be explained. Usually the object or event that is so intensely feared actually lacks the dangerous qualities the subject expects. Thus the intensity of the response is out of proportion with the nature of the danger.

*Generalization of Anxiety.*   In the process of chronic anxiety conditioning, a variety of emotional responses often develops. Each response is conditioned to a specific stimulus which could arouse the anxiety if presented. Through further conditioning, other stimuli act to evoke anxiety. Each of these original stimuli has the capacity to generalize, so that by the time the stage of chronic anxiety is reached, there are so many stimuli which can bring on the anxiety reaction plus the generalization that the person is no longer able to discriminate between them. Many stimuli operate to initiate the anxiety, and the person fails to identify them. They can be quite irrelevant and incidental. Consequently, the person literally lives in a state of anxiety. If the responses do not extinguish, they grow in intensity and persist; hence the term *chronic anxiety*. In the anxiety attack (again), the stimuli often cannot be identified. The attack can occur at any time, in any place, day or night. Now, it is not that specific stimuli do not bring on the reaction; they are merely so varied and manifold that the sufferer is unable to identify them all.

The explanation of phobias involves no new principles. Typically, the person reports intense fears but cannot explain why he has them. They may be of high places, closed places, open places, animals, dirt, germs, or even people. If one shows anxiety over dogs because he recalls being bitten by a dog, or fears horses because he was thrown from one, we do not consider these reactions as phobic. Frequently the list of phobias a person may have would fill a large-sized notebook. Take the case of a man who had a phobia for red skies,[24] although he could not explain why. After psychotherapy, which attempted to extinguish the phobia, he eventually recalled that as a boy he had been terrified by the red flames from a tenement fire in which he and his mother were caught and in which they could have been burned to death. The red skies became an

[24] N. Cameron and A. Margaret, op. cit.

equivalent stimulus for the original aversive stimulus of fire. Through
the generalization of the red fire, the phobia was retained.

Because of the aversive nature of a frightening event, avoidance behavior characteristically develops in the phobia. This helps distinguish it
from chronic anxiety or the anxiety attack. As long as the phobic person
stays away from the stimulus that arouses his anxiety, he is safe enough.
Unfortunately, phobias often serve to limit or disturb the lives of those
who exhibit them. Their lives seem an endless chain of avoidance reactions. Consider a person with a phobia for closed places; he cannot go
to the movies, enter small rooms, elevators, or telephone booths. Like
punishment, the primary aversive stimulus in the phobia operates to depress the response. The initially exciting event has been replaced by other
activity. The person realizes the stimuli that can evoke his phobia but
cannot tell their origin. In the Freudian sense, the repression is incomplete.

CONSEQUENCES OF ANXIETY

When anxiety persists and is generated by a multitude of stimuli, its
consequences are many and often unfortunate. In the behavioral manifestations of the anxiety which are many, the person is left in a miserable
condition. His sleep is interfered with, his relations with other people are
jeopardized. Positive reinforcements available to most people are deprived because of the restrictions placed on his activity by the anxiety
reaction. In the case of the man with a phobia for closed places, he is
denied the positive reinforcement of entertainment; he cannot greet
people in small rooms and has to walk ten flights of stairs because he
cannot take the elevator.

Because part of the anxiety is commonly manifested in respondent
behavior which persists and increases, the organs and tissues that participate in these reactions may undergo excessive strain which leads to
organ pathology. Disorders that develop in this way are called *psychosomatic*. The gastric ulcers in monkeys, described by Brady[25] give clear
evidence of the consequences of such behavior. Although the monkeys
were successful in avoiding the shocks, the anticipation of the shocking
situation was sufficient to generate a considerable amount of anxiety.
When the avoidance reactions were not operating and the animals were
placed on "off" or rest periods, examination of their stomachs indicated
an increase in acidity, a common accompaniment of anxiety. In other
words, the monkeys were anxious about the next troublesome session.

At the human level, an experiment by Wolf and Wolff[26] illustrates the
effects of anxiety on internal functions. Their patient had suffered from a

---

[25] J. V. Brady, Ulcers in "executive monkeys," *Scient. Amer.*, **199**, no. 4 (1958),
95–104.

[26] S. Wolf and H. Wolff, Evidence on the genesis of peptic ulcer in man, *Jour.
Amer. Med. Assn.*, **120** (1942), 670–675.

childhood injury which involved placing a fistula in the stomach's wall. At the age of nine, the boy had drunk some scalding soup which burned the esophagus, and the resulting scar tissue had closed the opening, making normal eating impossible. As a result, it was necessary to feed him directly through the stomach. This opening permitted the experimenters to make direct observations of what activity went on inside their patient. They found that when the subject manifested anxiety or resentment, the gastric mucosa became engorged with blood and he complained of an upset stomach. If the tissue was scraped slightly, the consequence was a small mucosal lesion which tended to persist. In this way the experimenters created a small gastric ulcer that persisted as long as the man remained upset. The gastric reactions in anxiety, which persist for long times in the chronically anxious person, can readily render him susceptible to the formulation of such an ulcer. Other pathological conditions of organs and tissues can also result from persistent respondents; they can result in heart disease, high blood pressure, disorders of the skin, and respiratory disorders such as hay fever and asthma. These afflictions have frequently been interpreted as the consequences of the bodily changes that participated in a number of anxiety responses. As the anxiety generalizes, they, too, become chronic.

Chronic anxiety is believed by many behavior pathologists to be an antecedent of more serious behavior disorders. In later chapters we shall see how anxiety operates in obsessions and compulsions, alcoholism, and the even more severe psychotic episodes of the manic-depressive and schizophrenic.

## Freud's Theory of Anxiety

Having examined a behavioristic interpretation of anxiety, let us compare this explanation with that formulated earlier but which is still exceedingly popular in psychology today. Freud[27] placed great emphasis on the importance of anxiety in problems of personality. In his theory anxiety was one of the most important concepts as a condition determining the process of personality development and in understanding how personality functioned and how neuroses developed. His whole theory of the defense mechanisms of the ego (see Chapter 14) is built around anxiety, for the defenses operated in ways of protecting the ego from painful anxiety.

Freud considered anxiety as a consciously painful experience which arose from excitations of the internal organs of the body. In a conscious

[27] S. Freud, *Inhibitions, symptoms and anxiety* (London: Hogarth Press, 1936; first German, ed., 1926). See also *New introductory lectures on psychoanalysis* (New York: Norton, 1933), chapter iv.

state, the person was able to distinguish anxiety from other experiences of pain. Precisely how this was possible was never made clear. It might depend on a specific kind or quality of the internal functions. However, the feeling of anxiety was never unconscious, although its origins could be.

Freud distinguished three kinds of anxiety: *reality anxiety*, *neurotic anxiety*, and *moral anxiety*. All had the quality of being unpleasant and differed only in their sources. They all shared the main function of acting as a warning signal to the person. It was a signal to his ego (who felt the anxiety) to do something about it by evading, escaping, overcoming, or building up defenses. If the ego could do nothing about the anxiety, it would pile up and eventually overwhelm the personality. The result would be some sort of nervous breakdown or psychosis. *Reality anxiety* was merely anxiety felt from the threats of the outside world. Although heredity might make one susceptible to threat, the danger had to be perceived for the anxiety to become entirely manifest. This kind of anxiety we commonly interpret as fear. A child sees a dog, is afraid, and runs. Sudden and intense experiences, called traumatic, childhood dangers, threats of punishment, all have their origin in external reality.

In *neurotic anxiety* the threat came from the id. It could take the form of free floating anxiety, since the person could not identify its source (in the unconscious). The phobia or panic reaction (anxiety attack) were also manifestations of what Freud called the *neurotic* anxiety. In the free floating kind, the person appeared afraid of his own id. The phobia was more specific and its intensity out of proportion to the danger. According to Freud, the person actually wanted the feared object. In the panic reactions the anxiety was sudden and unexplainable. These reactions were attempts to discharge threats from the id by doing what the id demanded, despite the restrictions placed by the ego. Neurotic anxiety exercised more of a strain on the ego than did the reality anxiety, for the person in the former case did not know what he feared. Because the source lay within the self, it would be more difficult to deal with and literally impossible to flee from. The expression, "all we have to fear is fear itself," characterized Freud's neurotic anxiety. However, Freud did not consider neurotic anxiety limited only to his neurotic patients. Normal people could experience it as well; the difference was one of degree, not kind.

*Moral anxiety* was experienced by the ego as a sense of shame or guilt and had its origin in the superego, or more specifically, the conscience. The conscience often used this moral anxiety to punish the ego when it had done wrong. The original source of the moral anxiety might have been in the world of reality, in the form of parental threats of punishment. As the conscience developed out of the perception of parental demands regarding right and wrong, it was able to punish in its own right. Like neurotic anxiety the threat lay within the personality, and therefore the person could not escape his own conscience. One of the paradoxes of life, Freud pointed out, is that the extremely moral person experiences more guilt (moral anxiety) than does the less virtuous one. The moral man is constantly threatened with anxiety as a means of control which begins in his own conscience.

### REANALYSIS OF FREUD'S THEORY OF ANXIETY

Freud's theory is not difficult to account for in more objective terms, but again we must strip it of the fictional concepts. Instead of defining anxiety as a feeling of pain known to the ego, we describe the behavior resulting from certain operations. Freud's reality anxiety can be reduced to our basic paradigm: $S^{-r} \longrightarrow S^{-R}$. The threat comes from association of a neutral stimulus with an aversive one. We may fear snakes because we have been bitten by one. To account for his theory of neurotic anxiety, we need to make use of the concept of *generalization*. The origin of the anxiety is not in any fictional id but in some external stimulus object. Because of the multiplicity of conditionings and generalizations, one is not able to identify the specific stimuli that are operating to evoke the anxiety reaction. This inability to identify the specific stimuli is merely what Freud called *free floating*. Since the origins of the fears were not known, he placed them in the unconscious. The notion that a phobic person really wants the object he fears is nothing more than prior conditioning through positive reinforcement and then having the anxiety situation imposed upon it. The rat presses the bar to receive food and then finds later that a clicker and shock have been added. The effects of the shock operate to depress the response and then other anxiety responses occur. Moral anxiety is merely a limitation of the anxiety reaction to specific kinds of stimuli which operate in the realm of conduct designated as moral or ethical, right or wrong. Some responses to discriminative stimuli get punished. The feelings of guilt or shame arise from the conditioned moral stimuli which on past occasions have been followed by the aversive conditions. These aversive stimuli can be avoided by doing something that is right or good.

Freud, as well as most objective psychologists, recognized the importance of anxiety, its antecedents, and consequences. His explanations were unduly involved, making use of mentalistic concepts, unnecessary to an empirical behavior analysis. But we have noted the similarity between the two interpretations. Unfortunately, Freud never bothered to examine very carefully the behavioral manifestations of anxiety or its sources. Of course he did not have available to him the technique of the modern experimental laboratory and the knowledge and means of control available to us today.

There is still a great deal to be learned about anxiety and its consequences in psychosomatic and behavioral disorders and about its precise relationship to escape, avoidance, and punishment.

# 13 Frustration and Conflict I

PSYCHOLOGISTS, REGARDLESS OF THEIR theoretical orientations, are fairly well agreed that frustration in some form or other has important implications for personality development and behavior pathology. A day hardly goes by which is not filled with numerous frustrations and conflicts —some severe, others trivial. We learn to cope with them by various techniques: by overcoming the difficulty, avoiding it, attacking it indirectly, or developing some kind of defensive reaction against it. Earlier in our discussion (Chapter 4) we mentioned one kind of frustrating situation in which an organism is extinguished after regular reinforcement. We noted that when an organism is reinforced on some kind of intermittent schedule, a degree of *frustration tolerance* is built up which enables him to continue behaving at a fairly regular rate despite the cessation of reinforcement.

Child psychologists, particularly those more psychoanalytically minded, have stressed the implications of early frustrations in the processes of feeding, eliminating, and sex training. When too much frustration occurs because the infant gets insufficient nourishment, or suffers from too long a delay between feedings, or is fed forcibly, the consequences are not happy ones. In the process of weaning, there is a sudden shift from one type of feeding to another. Often the change is made too rapidly and without adequate preparation. Likewise, toilet training involves a variety of frustrations for both the parents and child. The demands of the training system may not take into account individual differences in readiness to acquire the proper responses. Soon afterwards taboos prescribed by society set the occasion for frustration in early sex behavior and its education. Long before the appropriate sexual reinforcements are available, the human organism is biologically capable of performing appropriate sex behavior, but a period of delay is almost inevitable in Western civilization.

Nor are the frustrations limited to blocking primary reinforcers. A list of secondary reinforcers may be withheld, or the organism somehow kept from attaining them. The child does not always win his game; competition, inherent in a democratic society, leads to frustration for the loser. Children have to compete with older or younger siblings for parental affection and approval. Activity is blocked from time to time by customs, laws, principles of training and manners, all of which can make reinforcements frequently inaccessible.

Every day in our lives is filled with frustration. We get up in the morning, perhaps with insufficient rest. The coffee is cold. Because of interruptions, we are late for an appointment. The book we ordered is out of print. Other people interrupt our conversations. Our car fails to start or some part gets out of order. The clerk in the store is too busy to wait on us. We are forced to make difficult decisions. An engagement we were planning is canceled. We have more things to accomplish than time will permit. We have to deal with unreasonable people and, at least in our opinion, we are not always treated fairly.

The frustrating conditions we have described are an integral part of development and are inevitable in our daily lives. However, we have not defined specifically what frustration is. Let us, therefore, examine the operations, see how they may apply to experimentally contrived conditions, and then examine the findings in everyday living.

## The Operations of Frustration

In a general way the operation of frustration involves *preventing the organism from making some response.*[1] There is more than one way in which this can be accomplished. A careful behavioral analysis will discover that the operations of frustration tend to fall into three classes. It should be pointed out, however, that the consequences of these operations are not always the same. Verplanck[2] has suggested as a matter of fact, that perhaps some other terms could better be applied.

[1] W. S. Verplanck, A glossary of some terms used in the objective science of behavior, *Psychol. Rev.* (supp.), **44**, no. 6, pt. 2 (1957), viii, 1–42.
[2] Ibid.

1. The first operation refers to the *withholding of the reinforcement that ordinarily occurs from an organism that has already been conditioned in a particular way*. We have already observed this operation in *extinction*. When a response has been regularly reinforced, and then extinguished, there are often characteristic emotional consequences. This operation has also been referred to as *frustration by delay*.[3]
2. A second operation involves *mechanically preventing a response from occurring*.[4] In a typical bar-pressing situation, one could place a glass barrier between the animal and the bar, make the bar inoperable, or even physically restrain the organism so that movement becomes impossible. We also refer to this as *frustration by thwarting*.
3. The third operation involves *placing the organism in a conflict situation, by making reinforcing stimuli simultaneously available for two incompatible responses*. If either stimulus were presented alone, a response would be forthcoming. The conflict operation can be further broken down into *approach–approach* conflict, *approach–avoidance* conflict, and *avoidance–avoidance* conflict.

## FRUSTRATION BY DELAY

The delay in reinforcement may vary from only a slight instant to an indefinite period of time. On occasions of only a slight delay, an $S^D$ is presented that has customarily been the occasion for a response to be reinforced. The chain of responding is broken at some point by the withholding of a reinforcer, either primary or conditioned.[5] The break can occur anywhere in the chain or just before the final reinforcement. Although not inevitable, the consequences of this kind of operation are frequently emotional, described as anger or aggression. A child is impatient while waiting for his candy, or one becomes annoyed when people are late for their appointments. If they fail to appear altogether, we express our anger in no uncertain terms. Schedules of feeding and toilet training often impose this kind of frustration on the child. If he is fed by the "clock," he must wait until the required time has passed before the reinforcement is presented. Before children become sensitive to the discriminative stimuli from their bladders or bowels, they will ordinarily wait until the last minute before signaling their parents, who take them to the bathroom, etc. The period of delay before the proper elimination can take place may be extremely frustrating, and the consequent punishment equally aversive if they "miss."

[3] N. Cameron and A. Magaret, *Behavior pathology* (Boston: Houghton Mifflin, 1951).

[4] W. S. Verplanck, op. cit.

[5] F. S. Keller and W. N. Schoenfeld, *Principles of psychology* (New York: Appleton-Century-Crofts, 1950).

Delay in achieving sexual reinforcement is one of the commonest sources of frustration for the developing adolescent. Alternate responses of masturbation or homosexuality ordinarily lead to aversive consequences, imposed either by the family or the group. The adolescent is placed in a situation where appropriate reinforcements are delayed and alternate behavior is punished. It is no wonder that clinical evidence is strong in placing much emphasis on sexual frustration as a source of later personality problems in adulthood.

At the adult level, frustration by delay is common enough. Recall the occasion when everybody was ready to go on an outing and one person was late. The picnic may have been spoiled because of the consequent behavior of those who were left waiting. Or recall the occasion when you were in the process of repairing some object and an essential tool was mislaid. Even though the events are trivial enough, the resulting anger is not uncommon.

The same operations can be easily demonstrated in the experimental laboratory. Let us consider examples from the animal and human laboratory. An experiment by Mowrer[6] illustrates the operations and consequent behavior at the animal level. A situation was presented in which rats were required to press a bar with various degrees of force in order to receive reinforcement. In the conditioning process, they were first required to press with a minimum of 5 grams force to receive the food reinforcement. After this behavior was well established, a force of 30 grams was required; then 80 grams, alternating on subsequent experimental days with the 5-gram force. In extinction, the animals were divided into three groups. One group pressed a bar requiring a 5-gram force; another, 42.5-gram force; and the third, 80-gram force. Of particular interest for our analysis were the groups that had to press with 42.5 grams force and 80 grams force for the bar to be depressed. They showed "considerable frustration and aggression." They attacked the bar more vigorously, gnawed at the bar and other parts of the apparatus, jumped about and showed general signs of agitated behavior. The operations were simple, and the consequent behavior illustrates the common characteristics of what we call *anger* or *aggression*.

At the human level, an experiment by Sears, Hovland, and Miller[7] shows the typical reactions to frustration by withholding reinforcement. These experimenters kept a group of college students awake all night (withholding sleep as reinforcement), using as their "reason" the fact that they were attempting to study the effects of fatigue. During this period, the men were also subjected to a series of further frustrations.

[6] O. H. Mowrer and H. Jones, Extinction and behavior variability as a function of the effortfulness of task, *Jour. Exp. Psychol.*, 33 (1943), 369–386.

[7] R. R. Sears, C. I. Hovland, and N. E. Miller, Minor studies of aggression, I. Measurement of aggressive behavior, *Jour. Psychol.*, 9 (1940), 275–295.

They were forbidden to smoke, conversations were broken up, and food and entertainment which had been promised were withheld. The students showed aggressive behavior, directed mainly toward the experimenters. They made derogatory remarks, calling the psychologists crazy, and belittled the experiment in general. One of the men made sketches of a mutilated and bleeding body. When asked the significance of the picture, he suggested "psychologists."

### FRUSTRATION BY THWARTING

Perhaps even more common than frustration by delay is that of thwarting an ongoing chain of behavior. At some point in an organism's activity, a barrier is introduced and behavior is prevented. Like delay, the chain is also broken, but instead of reinforcement merely being withheld, an obstacle is introduced that prevents the response from occurring. Watson[8] observed some years ago that the emotion of "rage" was a characteristic consequence when an infant's movements were restrained. Other restrictions are common enough for the infant in his binding clothes and placement in a pen or crib. As he develops, the child has other restrictions and inhibitions placed on his activity. He is prevented from reaching because the objects may be dangerous. Rules, regulations, and manners are imposed which, at the level of his intellectual development, have little meaning. The only consolation he may get is that "Mama knows best" or "wait until you grow up." If no other behaviors are available which may secure the reinforcement, the child remains in the frustrated condition.

As we grow older and are allowed more freedom of activity, other restrictions are placed upon us. The obstacles that thwart us are many. They may be *physical*, similar to the glass placed in front of the rat, preventing his bar-pressing activity. A door is locked blocking our entry; guards or doormen inhibit access to an entertainment or seeing a friend. A student is prevented from visiting his girl because of the geographical distance between them, or a researcher cannot complete his work because of inadequate equipment.

Frequently the objects that thwart us are *social* or *legal*. Propriety prevents a man from telling his neighbor what he really thinks of him. Rules prescribing proper conduct prevent more reinforcing activities from taking place. Family background, level of income, occupation in some circumstances do not allow one to secure the many rewards placed before him. Marriages are prevented because of religious, educational, or social barriers. Group membership places certain restrictions on

---

[8] J. B. Watson, Experimental studies on the growth of the emotions. In *Psychologies of 1925* (Worcester, Mass.: Clark University Press, 1926).

behavior, and some persons may be excluded because of their religion, race, or the national origin of their parents. In the eyes of the college student, many regulations of his education, social life, and moral conduct may seem unreasonable.

The source of the thwarting can come from the *person himself.* Limitations in knowledge, ability, or training serve to block activity. Characteristics of physique, handicaps, features, or facial complexion may interfere with a student's social interactions. We speak, furthermore, of a person with undesirable personality traits as being frustrated, to whom social reinforcements become unattainable.

Finally, the *behavior of other people* operates as a constant source of frustration for most of us. In a rather extreme form we occasionally encounter a person whose behavior appears to us as arbitrary and unreasonable. The child often feels this about his parents. As adults we encounter unreasonable people in our social, educational, and business affairs. If possible, we try to avoid them. But there are occasions, perhaps because of their authority, when we are forced to deal with them. Here frustration begins. After exhausting the techniques available to us in reasoning, we end up with the attitude that they seem to be frustrating us intentionally. It is not, of course, that these individuals are acting out of stimulus control; it is merely that in their peculiar reinforcement histories, they have never acquired the adequate behavior equipment necessary to get along with other people in a way generally acceptable. On our part, we lack both adequate knowledge for predicting their unreasonable moves and methods for controlling their arbitrary behavior. In positions of authority they become the autocrats, the tyrants, the unfair and unreasonable, and get their own reinforcements from the submissions of others—indeed, in frustrating others. They are the "personality killers" and, in general, make those about them miserable.

*Age* itself acts as a common enough source of thwarting. A child is aware of this. He may be capable intellectually of perceiving the reinforcements in his environment but lack the physique, maturity or behavior necessary to get them. Different age levels carry with them special demands and expectations to which he is supposed to conform. The little boy of four is supposed to act "cute," but the same behavior exhibited three years later is considered infantile and foolish. When adolescence arrives, it brings new demands to which one is supposed to conform. The adolescent wants to become an adult but is not ready for the responsibilities of adulthood. Furthermore the parents may be unwilling to "give him up" and insist he continue to be their "little boy."

Like frustration by delay, one of the common consequences of thwarting is anger and aggression. A common hypothesis has been that the strength of the frustrated behavior is a function of the degree of thwarting. An illustration of this idea is found and studied by Sears and

Sears,[9] using infants as their subjects. Over a period of three weeks the babies were observed at their bottle feeding. At various intervals following the presentation of the bottle, it was removed before the feeding had been completed. The chief measure of aggression was the latency of crying. That is, the time it took the child to begin to cry after his bottle had been taken away. When the bottle was removed after the babies had consumed only ½ an ounce of milk, the latency was only 5 seconds. After 2½ ounces, the latency was 9.9 seconds, and after 4½ ounces had been consumed, it took the average infant 11.5 seconds to begin to cry. For the baby thwarted early in his feeding period, the aggression was stronger than toward the end of the period when there was a lower degree of deprivation.

At the adult level a number of contrived laboratory situations illustrate the process of thwarting. Typically, the experimenter sets a difficult or impossible task for the subject and insists on a solution with speed and accuracy. He is then interrupted and told that he has failed. Behavior never gets reinforced, since the task goes uncompleted. Under these conditions, subjects exhibit reactions, often less severe but characteristic of those found in similar situations outside the laboratory.

An experiment by McClelland and Apicella[10] illustrates the typical procedure. The frustration was produced in a group of male college students who were persuaded to participate in a card-sorting task in which they were required to reach a final goal of efficiency. False scores were reported, so that a failure to reach their prescribed goal was experienced on every two out of three trials. The frustration was increased by the experimenter's remarks, which were hostile and derogatory to one-half of the subjects and moderate for the other half. The experimenter was an undergraduate who set the stage for unrestraint by swearing at the subjects freely. The verbal responses of the subjects were recorded and later classified. The more severely frustrated subjects gave more overt responses than the moderately frustrated group. As the experimenter's hostility toward the subjects increased, the proportion of verbal responses shifted in the direction of anger and aggression.

Experiments by Masserman[11] illustrate the reactions of animals toward thwarting. Cats were placed in a glass cage and trained to open a food box and eat at the presentation of a light and buzzer signal. They were then frustrated by having the food box locked after the animals had learned to eat from it. In another frustrating situation, they were confined behind a glass partition in full view of the food box when the

[9] R. R. Sears and P. S. Sears, Minor studies of aggression, V. Strength of function of the attack and attacker, *Jour. Abnorm. Soc. Psychol.*, **46** (1951), 297–300.

[10] D. McClelland and F. Apicella, A functional classification of verbal reactions to experimentally induced failure, *Jour. Abn. Soc. Psychol.*, **40** (1945), 376–390.

[11] J. H. Masserman, *Behavior and neurosis* (Chicago: University of Chicago Press, 1943).

feeding signals were given. The reactions were characteristic of what we have already described. Vigorous activity was evidenced, accompanied by loud mewing. These responses were eventually extinguished as the animals failed to respond to the signals in the absence of primary reinforcement.

CONSEQUENCES OF FRUSTRATION

The evidence from our experiments as well as from our incidental observations indicates that organisms react to thwarting or delay in more than one way. Some of these reactions will be discussed in more detail in the subsequent chapters. However, one response pattern that appears commonly, following the operations we have described, is aggression. We find it at both the human and animal level. The aggression may be directed toward the object involved in the frustration (attacking the bar or person), or it may generalize to other stimuli in the environment (see Chapter 14). Rosenzweig[12] has suggested that the directions of aggression, particularly at the human level, fall into three classes: (1) *extrapunitive*, in which the aggression is directed outwardly toward the objects involved in the thwarting or toward other objects in the environment; (2) *intropunitive*, where the organism directs aggressive behavior toward himself as a stimulus; and (3) *impunitive*, in which some type of avoidance response is utilized. The avoidance may merely interfere with the aggressive activity (repression) or seek some alternate form of reinforcement following the frustration.

*The Frustration–Aggression Hypothesis.* In 1939 a group of psychologists at Yale University collaborated in a series of studies published under the title, *Frustration and Aggression*.[13] Their basic premise was that aggression was *always* a consequence of frustration. Sometimes the aggression was directed at the frustrating agent, at other times it was aimed at innocent bystanders (displacement). The forms the aggression could take might be vigorous and undisguised, while at other times it might be subtle and roundabout.

These psychologists stated further that the strength of the frustrated response varied systematically with a number of conditions. (1) The strength of instigation to aggression will vary directly with the strength of instigation to the frustrated response. Sears and Sears[14] (cited earlier)

---

[12] S. Rosenzweig, An outline of frustration theory. In J. McV. Hunt, ed., *Personality and the behavior disorders* (New York: Ronald Press, 1944), chap. xi.

[13] J. Dollard, L. W. Doob, N. E. Miller, O. H. Mowrer, and R. R. Sears, *Frustration and aggression* (New Haven: Yale University Press, 1939).

[14] R. R. Sears and P. S. Sears, Minor studies in aggression, V. Strength of frustration reaction as a function of strength of drive, *Jour. Psychol.*, **9** (1940), 297–300.

produced frustration in infants by withdrawing the bottle before the infants were satiated. The strength of instigation of feeding was varied by withdrawing the bottle after various amounts of milk had been consumed (½, 2½, and 4½ ounces). The strength of instigation to aggression was measured by the latency (in seconds) of crying. For the ½ ounce the latency was 5.0 seconds; for 2½ ounces latency was 9.9 seconds; and for 4½ ounces the latency was 11.5 seconds. The experiment clearly supported this part of the hypothesis.

(2) The strength of instigation to aggression will vary directly with the degree of interference with the frustrated response. Hovland and Sears[15] have argued that aggression should increase during the depression years, since necessary reinforcements (often of a primary sort) would be frustrated during these years. They showed a positive correlation between the number of lynchings per year and changes in acre value of cotton in 14 southern states. In a study by Graham et al.[16] adolescent boys and girls were required to complete sentences, and their completions were rated for degrees of aggression (*He hit me, so I . . .*). They then discovered that the degree of frustration indicated by the aggression ratings of the incomplete sentences themselves was partially related to the degree of aggression showed in the actual aggressive responses.

(3) The strength of instigation to aggression will vary directly with the number of response sequences. In other words, the frustrated responses will add up. Palmer[17] has found that convicted murderers had been subjected to significantly more physical and psychological frustrations during their childhood than their control brothers. Thus a number of frustrated responses can be added together to produce aggression responses of greater strength than might have been expected to occur from merely the currently frustrating event.

Some of the experiments cited to support the frustration-aggression hypothesis are of questionable value. Furthermore psychologists in general have been reluctant to accept the universality of many of the statements, since the evidence is not strong enough to support them or, indeed, is often lacking. For example, one can think of numerous exceptions to the statement that aggression *always* follows frustration. If we are to accept this premise at face value, then it will be necessary for us to broaden our definition of aggression to include anything an organism does following the operation of frustration.

The fact that *aggression is not always the result of frustration* has

[15] C. L. Hovland and R. R. Sears, Minor studies of aggression, VI. Correlation of lynchings with economic indices, *Jour. Psychol.*, **9** (1940), 301–310.

[16] F. K. Graham, W. A. Charwat, A. S. Honig, and P. C. Weltz, Aggression as a function of the attack and attacker, *Jour. Abnorm. Soc. Psychol.*, **46** (1951), 512–520.

[17] S. Palmer, Frustration, aggression, and murder, *Jour. Abnorm. Soc. Psychol.*, **60** (1960), 430–432.

been adequately demonstrated by Bandura and Walters.[18] They have demonstrated that aggression can occur in the absence of frustration. In one study they selected a group of preschool children and had them observe an adult model physically aggress against a Bobo doll. Later on these same children imitated the model's aggressive behavior and attacked the Bobo doll after the model had left the room. Furthermore, these same investigators have observed that when children watched models being reinforced for their aggressive behavior, the children became more aggressive than those who had watched the model being punished for his aggressive behavior.

## FRUSTRATION AND DISPLACEMENT

Another common consequence of frustration is displacement (generalization) (see next chapter). The person frustrated may not be able to take out his frustrations (whatever they may be) directly on the frustrating object or person, and so directs his reactions (often aggressive) against some other person or object. There is much experimental evidence available to support this hypothesis. Some of it is reviewed in the following chapter under the topic of *displacement* as a defensive reaction. Our discussion here will be limited to one aspect of displacement, namely the *scapegoat theory of prejudice*, wherein aggression is displaced on minority groups. In one study Mussen[19] found that the degree of aggression as expressed in responses to pictures on the *Thematic Apperception Test* (TAT) correlated with more overt attitudes towards black boys on two attitude tests before and after black and white boys had spent time together at an integrated camp. He found that aggression and prejudice correlated .39 before the camps and .59 after the camping experience. Furthermore, the boys high in prejudice before the camp showed more hostility toward their parents and more frustration from their environment than the boys with low prejudice.

For further discussion and experimental evidence concerning this scapegoat theory the reader is referred to Yates' book, *Frustration and Conflict*.[20]

## FRUSTRATION AND REGRESSION

Regression is interpreted in this context as a reversion to modes of behavior more typical of an earlier period in one's development. In both

---

[18] A. Bandura and R. Walters *Social learning and personality development* (New York: Holt, Rinehart and Winston, 1963).

[19] P. H. Mussen, Some personality and social factors related to changes in children's attitudes towards Negroes, *Jour. Abnorm. Soc. Psychol.*, **45** (1950), 150–157.

[20] A. J. Yates, *Frustration and conflict* (London: Methuen, 1962).

our psychological and physical development we pass through various phases of behavioral change. Patterns typified by each period—infancy, childhood, preadolescence, adolescence, and maturity—each suggests special modes of behavior. These are partly a function of physical growth and biological capacity, as well as the effects of social and cultural demands in any given society. Barker, Dembo, and Lewin[21] have referred to this backward movement, or return to forms of behavior more appropriate of an early age, as a *primitivation of behavior*. The standards of any age can be determined by that characteristic of a group, so that a five-year-old may have regressed if his behavior under frustration is more like the average behavior of a three-year-old.

In an experiment now considered a classic, Barker, Dembo, and Lewin[22] first studied a group of 30 preschool children in a free-play situation. Attractive toys were available—crayons, dolls, teddy bear, toy telephone, etc. Following this session, the children were presented with even more attractive toys, including a large dollhouse in which the children could enter, amply furnished with various devices and electrically lighted. Outside the house was a miniature lake with real water, an island, a wharf, and toy boats that could be sailed. After playing with the attractive toys, a screen was lowered so the children were no longer allowed in this play situation. They were given the simpler toys, and their behavior was rated by the experimenters. The constructive nature was significantly reduced. For example, prior to frustration a child would talk into the toy telephone and engage in make-believe conversations. Later, he simply pounded the telephone on the floor in the manner of a baby. Using an index of constructiveness and relating it to the typical behavior of that age, these experimenters found that the children regressed an average of 17.2 months.

Further analysis and experimental evidence of regression will be presented in the following chapter.


## Conflict

Conflict has been the subject of considerable experimental investigation at both the human and animal levels. We shall consider the basic operations in this chapter and leave to our discussion in the next chapter some further implications of the problem. The basic operation of conflict involves the *presentation of simultaneous stimuli for two incompatible*

---

[21] R. G. Barker, T. Dembo, and K. Lewin, Frustration and regression. In R. G. Barker, J. S. Kounin, and H. F. Wright, eds., *Child development* (New York: McGraw-Hill, 1943).
[22] Ibid.

*responses in a situation where, if presented alone, each would yield a response.*[23] From the early days of psychoanalysis, conflicts have been considered of great significance in understanding personality. Freud[24] referred to the continuous conflict between the systems of personality, the ego, id, and superego. He believed conflict to be intrapsychic, within the self, and distinguished it from frustration, which originated in barriers from external reality. Karen Horney[25] a neo-Freudian, also interpreted conflicts as being "inner" but believed they consisted of opposing tendencies to move, either toward, away from, or against people. Other writers have spoken of the conflict of drives or motives, tendencies or dispositions. We shall have occasion later to consider in more detail Freud's interpretations of conflict and its consequences.

The best way to begin, however, is to define conflicts in terms of the responses and operations involved. Depending on the number or complexity of the competing responses, a variety of conflict operations can be described. We shall limit ourselves mainly to the three basic ones involving approach—approach conflict, avoidance–avoidance conflict, and approach–avoidance conflict. Other operations involving more complicated arrangements are simply variations of these basic operations.

APPROACH—APPROACH CONFLICT

Two reinforcing stimuli toward either of which the organism would move if given alone are presented simultaneously but in different locations so that approaching one takes the organism away from the other. In other words, alternate stimuli are presented to the organism, both of which are positively reinforcing. A simple example may involve depriving a rat of water and then placing him in the middle of an alley with water reinforcement at either end.

Hovland and Sears[26] sat subjects at a table on which was exposed a piece of paper 6 inches square, framed by brass strips. At the two corners away from each subject were two green lights. Subjects were simply instructed to place a pencil at the bottom of the paper and draw a diagonal line as quickly as possible directly to whatever light was flashed on. After about 20 practice trials of this sort, the conflict was produced without any prior instruction by flashing on both lights at the same time. Only 9 per cent of those instructed to go directly to one light or the other was unable to react to the conflict test. The remainder made some

[23] W. S. Verplanck, op. cit.

[24] S. Freud, *New introductory lectures on psychoanalysis* (New York: Norton, 1933).

[25] K. Horney, *Our inner conflicts* (New York: Norton, 1945).

[26] C. I. Hovland and R. R. Sears, Experiments on motor conflict, I. Types of conflict and their modes of resolution, *Jour. Psychol.*, **23** (1938), 477–493.

kind of response. Breaking down the results further, the experimenters found differences in the group that did respond: 58 per cent drew a line to one or the other of the lights; 12 per cent drew a line halfway between the two, down the center of the page; and 21 per cent drew a line to one light and then across to the other. These findings illustrate some of the major ways in which we go about solving such a conflict problem. When forced to make a choice between two incompatible, positively reinforcing stimuli, some subjects may (1) *make a decision* (go to one or other of the lights); or (2) try to "have their cake and eat it" (go to both lights); or (3) *make a compromise* (go between the two lights). The remaining 9 per cent that "blocked" represent those people who simply cannot make up their minds, like the woman trying to choose between two or more hats. It would be a matter of conjecture as to who was more frustrated, the buyer or the saleslady!

Of the three basic conflicts, this is probably the least serious, and when it occurs, our experimental evidence indicates it is the easiest to solve. As a matter of fact, a perfect conflict of this sort seldom occurs outside the experimental laboratory, according to Miller.[27] *The closer we get to one goal object, the stronger the behavior toward that goal becomes, and the weaker the behavior toward the other becomes.* This is called the *approach gradient*. Furthermore, in most cases outside the laboratory, we shall ordinarily be closer to one goal than the other, and therefore a real conflict-type situation will not occur. It is extremely unlikely that two alternatives are going to be absolutely the same.

Although situations resembling this kind of conflict seldom lead to serious consequences, a degree of it does exist in our everyday affairs. A child cannot simultaneously retrieve two attractive toys. We cannot see two movies playing at opposite sides of town. One man cannot take two young ladies to the same party without incurring their collective wrath upon him. Some students would like to elect more courses of study than their programs will allow. (Unfortunately the opposite situation also occurs, where a student cannot find any course he would like to take. Here the conflict becomes avoidance–avoidance.)

AVOIDANCE–AVOIDANCE CONFLICT

This operation is the opposite of that described in (1) and has considerably more implications for consequent behavior. *Two stimuli, either of which the organism moves away from, are presented simultaneously so that escape from one places him in the presence of the other.* In other words, both stimuli are negatively reinforcing, or aversive. An

---

[27] N. E. Miller, Experimental studies of conflict. In J. McV. Hunt, ed., *Personality and the behavior disorders* (New York: Ronald Press, 1944).

animal confined to an alley moves in one direction and receives an electric shock, while moving in the other direction also gives him a shock. If he were not confined to the alley, he could escape, but in the avoidance–avoidance conflict this is impossible.

An experimental example is illustrated by the same technique described by Hovland and Sears.[28] In the avoidance situation, subjects were required to draw a line diagonally to the corner *opposite* that of the flashing light. After several practice trials, conflict was induced by flashing both lights on at the same time. In contrast to the 9 per cent of subjects who "blocked" in the approach–approach conflict, 46 per cent of the subjects in this conflict failed to make a response.

Barker[29] required 10-year-old boys to choose between two liquids which they were going to drink; for example, vinegar versus a saturated salt solution. Each boy indicated his choice by moving a lever in the direction of the glass he would have to drink from. Movements were timed by a device attached to the lever and concealed from the subjects. When confronted with these aversive alternatives, the boys took much longer and shifted the lever back and forth more times than when they were to choose between two alternatives that were positively reinforcing, like orange versus pineapple juice. The gradient of avoidance is opposite that of approach. *The nearer one gets to an aversive stimulus, the stronger the avoidance behavior becomes.*

Hovland and Sears found that not only a greater percentage of their subjects "blocked" in the double avoidance conflict (46 percent) but also that many of those who did respond drew a straight line up the center of the page. They attempted to escape from the aversive stimuli. In effect, in the avoidance conflict, the organism is in a "box." He is damned if he does and damned if he doesn't. Hypothetically, he finds himself surrounded by aversive stimuli. Decision is more difficult and vacillation more common. As we saw in our earlier discussions, a human placed in an aversive situation often attempts to escape to unrealistic behavior. Behavior pathologists believe that many of the common disorders of acute depression and withdrawal have their genesis in avoidance–avoidance conflict.[30]

Avoidance–avoidance conflicts are common enough. In childhood, aversive regulations set by one's parents are punished if not conformed to. A boy is forced to go to a party that he abhors or stay at home and receive a spanking. A student has to take undesirable courses that are

[28] C. I. Hovland and R. R. Sears, op. cit.

[29] R. G. Barker, An experimental study of the resolution of conflict in children; Time elapsing and amount of vicarious trial-and-error behavior occurring. In Q. McNemar and M. A. Merrill, eds., *Studies of personality* (New York: McGraw-Hill, 1942).

[30] N. Cameron and A. Magaret, op. cit.

boring or leave school and join the army. We must face our aversive superiors or be fired from our jobs. In whatever direction we move, we face pain, reproach and punishment.

*Animal Studies Comparing Approach and Avoidance Conflicts.*  Klebanoff[31] trained rats by depriving them of food, which to secure, they had to approach either end of an alley, each designated by a flashing light and buzzer. He then placed them in an approach–approach conflict by turning on the lights and sounding the buzzers simultaneously. If the animals were started at some distance from the center of the alley, they went directly to the nearest reinforcement. If they were started directly in the center, they went to one or the other with little vacillation. Another group of rats was trained to escape an electric shock by running away from either end of an alley when a light and buzzer were presented. He then set up an avoidance–avoidance conflict by turning on the buzzers and lights at the same time. When released in an off-center position, the animals typically ran in the direction opposite the nearest light, but when released in the center of the alley, they started more slowly than in the approach–approach conflict situation. After running in one direction, they would stop, turn back, and run in the other, eventually ending up between the two lights near the center point. Furthermore, in this conflict they showed attempts to escape by trying to climb out of the alley.

The findings comparing the approach and avoidance conflicts at the human and animal level are remarkably similar. In both cases, approach conflicts are more easily solved. Likewise, the organism placed in the avoidance conflict shows more "blocking" and vacillation and attempts to "escape" from the conflicts.

APPROACH–AVOIDANCE CONFLICT

Perhaps the most common of all conflicts is the *approach–avoidance* type and its variation, the *double approach–avoidance* conflict. In the first operation *two stimuli (one of which is positively reinforcing and toward which the organism moves, and the other which is negatively reinforcing and away from which he actively moves) are presented together at the same or approximately the same location.* The alley apparatus can be used to illustrate this conflict. Reinforcements, both positive and negative, are located at one end. Conflict arises when the rat has on some occasions been positively reinforced for approaching

[31] S. G. Klebanoff (dissertation), An experimental analysis of approach–approach and avoidance–avoidance conflict (New Haven: Reported by N. E. Miller; see note 27 in this chapter).

and on other occasions shocked for the same response. There is, then, an approach and an avoidance gradient operating at the same time. To best understand this kind of conflict, we must consider another principle: *The gradient of avoidance is ordinarily steeper than the gradient for approach.* The rate at which avoidance behavior operates is stronger than the rate at which approach behavior operates under the same conditions.

To study the approach gradient, Brown[32] measured the strength of the response by the amount of effort expended against a temporary restraint. He trained a group of food-deprived rats to run down an alley to an $S^D$ light that signaled food. The animals wore little harnesses attached to a cord which did not serve as a hindrance to movement. Some animals were restrained at a point near the food; others, at a point of greater distance. During a period of 1-second restraint, they pulled against a calibrated string attached to a marker so the average force of their pull could be computed. The animals restrained near the food pulled considerably harder than those restrained farther away.

To test the avoidance gradient, Brown[33] gave shocks to another group of rats at one end of the alley. After two shocks they were then placed at the same end without shock. He then restrained them as before, half at a point near where they had been shocked and half at a point more distant. Rats pulled harder when restrained near the previous shock point than when placed farther away. These experiments are given as evidence verifying the approach and avoidance gradients.

Furthermore a comparison of the measurements of the approach and avoidance pulls indicated that the strength of the avoidance increases more rapidly with nearness than does that of approach. Therefore the avoidance gradient is steeper than the approach (see Figure 13–1). Finally Brown[34] demonstrated that a reduction in the food deprivation or a lessening of the shock intensity produced a reduction in the strength of the pull. The heights of the gradients varied with the particular operations involved: Greater or less food deprivation produced corresponding changes in the gradients of approach, and stronger or weaker shocks produced corresponding changes in the strength of the avoidance gradient.

*Experimental Evidence of Approach–Avoidance Conflicts.* A considerable amount of evidence is available in verifying this kind of conflict, both at the human and subhuman levels. A few representative examples

[32] J. S. Brown, (dissertation) Generalized approach and avoidance responses in relation to conflict behavior (New Haven: Reported by N. E. Miller (see note 27 in this chapter).

[33] Ibid.

[34] Ibid.

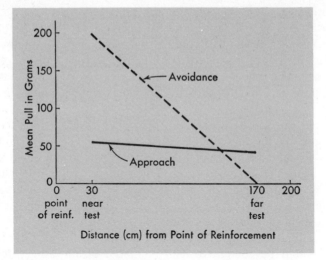

**Figure 13–1.** Gradients of approach and avoidance. The approach gradient represents the force with which rats under 48-hour food deprivation pulled against a restraining harness at various distances from the point at which they had been fed. The avoidance gradient represents the force with which they pulled away from the point where they had been shocked. (From N. E. Miller, Experimental studies of conflict. In J. McV. Hunt, ed., *Personality and the Behavior Disorders,* Vol. I, p. 434. Copyright 1944 The Ronald Press Company. Reproduced by permission.)

will suffice for our discussion. Miller, Brown, and Lipofsky[35] utilized the techniques described earlier. Rats were first trained to run the length of an alley to secure food, indicated by a small $S^D$ light. They were then given brief shocks while they were eating. A test without shock was then presented by placing the animals at the end of the alley opposite that where they had received food and shock. As before, the animals wore a light harness with a cord attached so that the strength of the pull toward and away from the goal could be measured. To test different degrees of avoidance, animals were further divided into groups and given different degrees of shock intensity while eating. The strength of the approach was also tested by classifying the animal further into varying degrees of food deprivation. The characteristic behavior exhibited by the animals when started at the far end of the alley was to start, approach partway, and then stop.

[35] N. E. Miller, J. S. Brown, and H. Lipofsky, A theoretical and experimental analysis of conflict, III. Approach-avoidance conflict as a function of the strength of drive (New Haven: Reported in N. E. Miller; see note 27 in this chapter).

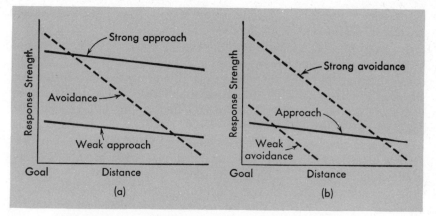

**Figure 13–2.** Changes in strength of approach and avoidance gradients. Diagram (a) indicates that an increase in the strength of the approach gradient moves the intersection nearer to the goal and also occurs on a higher point on the avoidance gradient. Diagram (b) shows that within the limits in which the two gradients cross, a decrease in the strength of the avoidance brings the point of interaction nearer the goal. (From N. E. Miller, Experimental studies of conflict. In J. McV. Hunt, ed., *Personality and the Behavior Disorders*, Vol. I, p. 440. Copyright 1944 The Ronald Press Company. Reproduced by permission.)

The point at which the animals stopped was a function of the two conflicting operations, the strength of shock and degree of food deprivation. Greater food deprivation and weaker shock led the animals to come nearer the goal before stopping (see Figure 13–2). Lesser food deprivation and stronger shock led the animals to stop at a greater distance from the end of the alley. We observe from the figure that there is a point where two gradients cross. The subjects would be expected to stop and oscillate around this point. This is precisely what happened. An increasingly hesitant approach was followed by an abrupt retreat. With greater food deprivation and stronger shock, the vacillation in response was greater than with little food deprivation and weak shock, thus substantiating the hypothesis that the degree of conflict is related to the strength of the two competing responses.

An experiment by Tolcott,[36] using a different type of apparatus, seems to confirm Miller's findings. In this experiment the avoidance response consists of pressing a pedal that turned off a bright light over the center of the experimental cage. The approach response was made

[36] M. A. Tolcott, Conflict: A study of some interactions between appetite and aversion in the white rat, *Genet. Psychol. Monog.*, **38** (1948), 83–142.

by pressing a bar to secure food reinforcement. Rats were first trained in separate sessions to secure food by pressing the bar at one end of the cage and to turn off the light by pressing the pedal at the opposite end of the cage. The responses were incompatible in that the animal could not do both at the same time because of the distance between the two response mechanisms. The conflict situation was introduced by having both stimuli present at the same time. As long as the rat kept the pedal down, the light stayed off, but in so doing he received no food. If he went to press the bar to secure food, the light was flashed on.

The behavior of the animals is similar to that found in Miller's study. In the conflict there was a rapid alteration between the two responses—short periods of pedal holding which alternated with brief periods of rapid bar pressing. It is further interesting to note that over half of the experimental sessions was spent on the pedal, indicating the greater steepness of the avoidance gradient. Even more significant, although not measured in the Miller study, was the fact that in the conflict situation, there was the same number of bar presses to secure food as there was when the food alone had been presented. This was possible because, during conflict, the rate of bar pressing at times when the animal received food was more rapid than before.

In an extension of Tolcott's work, Winnick[37] studied in greater detail the characteristics of the avoidance response of the rat in pressing his nose against a panel to turn off a light, under (1) conditions of simple avoidance by the light removal and (2) when it was in conflict with the bar-pressing response for food. The varying force of panel pushing was continuously recorded graphically in order to study fluctuations in amplitude under the different experimental conditions.

As might have been expected, the light removal operated as an effective reinforcement for the panel-pushing response. When placed in conflict with the bar-pressing response, the time spent in avoiding was significantly reduced. In the conflict situation Winnick observed that the rats made a series of slight incipient movements in releasing the pressure on the panel during avoidance. These fluctuations in the avoidance response were present during the simple avoidance conditioning but were more obvious under conflict. In the extinction of the avoidance response, the panel push was reduced either to the same or a kind of responding similar to that found prior to conditioning. The incipient movements in withdrawing from the panel are interpreted as tactile and proprioceptive $S^D$'s which serve as conditioned negative reinforcers. They lead to the reversal of movement and an avoidance of the aversive light. This occurs because the cues become conditioned to the anxiety produced by the light onset and in themselves are capable of setting up anxiety. The anxiety is reduced when these danger signals are removed.

[37] W. A. Winnick, Anxiety indicators in an avoidance response during conflict and nonconflict, *Jour. Comp. Physiol. Psychol.*, **49** (1956), 52–59.

Masserman has performed a series of experiments involving approach–avoidance conflict in cats.[38] In contrast to the more quantitative descriptions of most laboratory experiments, his results have been reported in a more qualitative fashion, since his procedures often varied from one animal to another, and the results therefore have a more "clinical" connotation. Although not the most desirable way to report experimental data, this criticism is perhaps partly offset by the direct applicability of the data to human conflict situations. His general procedure was to place a cat in a glass cage with food at one end. Cats learned to lift the lid of the box and eat the food inside when an $S^D$ signal of light and buzzer were presented (in a manner like the experiments described under frustration). Some of the cats were trained to step on a pedal that activated the signals and made food accessible. Conflict was then introduced by subjecting the animals to an air blast at the instant they started to eat or by an electric shock delivered from the grid floor of the cage.

In this approach–avoidance situation the typical reactions of the cats could be described as emotional. Their posture became erect; a pilomotor reaction occurred (extending of the hair); pupils became dilated, and the animals made frantic movements. As the conflicts continued, they crouched, hid in the corner, and tried to escape from the apparatus when the light was presented. Some of the cats showed adaptive movements of licking and cleaning their fur and sought attention and petting from the experimenters. It is most likely that the avoidance gradients were stronger than those of approach. If it were not for a control experiment, one might have considered this to be basically an escape or avoidance type of procedure. However, Masserman did subject some of the cats to the air blast without any prior association with feeding. In this situation, after the first few emotional reactions, the animals adapted quickly to the blast by avoiding it. This behavior was in marked contrast to the *persistence of responding* in the conflict situation where the air blast was paired with food.

You will recall the earlier reference to Masserman's study of frustration where cats were thwarted from attaining food when signals were given. It is interesting to compare these results. In no case did the frustration or simple avoidance procedures cause the intense behavioral disorganization that resulted in the conflict described in these experiments. It would appear that the consequences of conflict tend to be more severe for the organism.

*Approach–Avoidance Conflicts in Humans.*   Not only are approach–avoidance conflicts the most common in human affairs, but it is possible for them to be the most disrupting as well. The adolescent boy both welcomes and fears his first date with a pretty girl. A promotion brings

[38] J. H. Masserman, op. cit.

with it more money, but the added responsibilities accompanying it may be just what one would like to avoid. The bride-to-be looks forward to and dreads the first night with her new husband. The child wants to pet the dog but fears him too. A student would like to elect certain courses because of the interesting material but is hesitant because of the aversive assignments involved. The seeker of donations for charity must be pleasant to people who give to his cause, but he finds this difficult because he does not approve of their moral conduct.

The characteristic reactions of vacillation we observed in the animal experiments are also seen in the conflict of the child at the seashore getting ready to jump into the water. The ocean is attractive and rewarding in the fun he has playing and splashing about, but it is also cold upon first entering. He runs to the water's edge, stops, and turns in the opposite direction. He continues back and forth until one reaction wins out. Similar vacillation is seen in the behavior of the young man deciding whether or not to call a girl for a date. He anticipates the pleasant consequences of their meeting but also considers the humiliation of a rebuff. His hand may approach the telephone and then be drawn back. He may merely stand beside the phone for a number of minutes "trying to work up enough courage" to call. Cameron[39] reports the case of a young man who sat in a telephone booth for one hour in such a conflict situation. He finally left the telephone booth, feeling he had missed the chance of a lifetime for gaining happiness and security.

### DOUBLE APPROACH—AVOIDANCE CONFLICT

A variation of approach–avoidance conflict will complete our discussion of the different conflict operations. In this situation two stimuli are available, each of which is both positively reinforcing and aversive. For example, a rat is placed in the center of an alley with both food and shock at either end. The conflict is multiplied. There is an approach–approach conflict in the choice of one object; by attaining one, he relinquishes the other. There is also the avoidance property of each stimulus. The organism both approaches and avoids two stimuli at the same time.

An experiment with children by Godbeer[40] illustrates this kind of conflict situation. A child was seated in front of two glass windows, each covered with a shutter. The experimenter could lift either of the shutters and reveal a piece of candy behind the glass window. Prior to experimentation, the children had learned to secure candy by pushing a handle forward. In the first part of the experiment, only one window was exposed at a time. In the second part, both windows were left unexposed,

[39] N. Cameron, *The psychology of behavior disorders* (Boston: Houghton Mifflin, 1947).

[40] E. Godbeer (dissertation), Factors introducing conflict in the choice behavior of children (New Haven: Yale University, 1940).

but the child could still secure the candy by pressing the lever. In neither of these procedures did the children show any particular conflict behavior. In the third part, both windows were uncovered simultaneously, and the child was told that when he selected one candy the other window would be closed. Each approach reaction (securing candy) was accompanied by an avoidance reaction (relinquishing the other). Miller[41] interprets this as a double approach–avoidance conflict, although some authors may consider it simply an approach–approach conflict. The children responded by moving the lever first toward one window, then toward the other and away from the first. Furthermore, photographs taken of the subjects' eye movements indicated considerable vacillation back and forth from one window to the other. More time was taken in making the choice than in either of the first two procedures.

As is sometimes the case, one may receive two invitations to different parties on the same day. He cannot decide which to accept, since he does not know whether he will have a good time at either. Yet, on the other hand, he may enjoy himself at both. The factor of uncertainty (typified by much behavioral vacillation) is also characteristic of this kind of conflict. Godbeer,[42] in another experiment with children, exposed two small boxes before them, either of which might or might not contain candy. Under these conflict conditions there was also much vacillation of hand and eye movements back and forth from one box to the other.

The conflict is also illustrated in an offer of two job possibilities: one may be in a pleasant climate but with lower pay, while the other may require more traveling but involve a kind of work one prefers doing. Human conflicts in which a decision has to be made by weighing the merits and demerits of each possibility characterize some form of double approach–avoidance conflict.

CONSEQUENCES OF CONFLICT

On the basis of the evidence so far presented in our experimental studies, let us try to summarize some of the relationships between the kinds of conflict and their consequences.

1. Behavior most often observed in conflict can be described as *impoverished* and *distorted*. Impoverishment is seen in the blocking of a response and the slowing down of responding. Previously acquired behavior fails to operate. Distortion is indicated by agitation, aggression, and vacillation.
2. The degree of behavioral change (blocking, vacillation, etc.) is a function of the type of conflict situation; approach–approach conflicts

[41] N. E. Miller, op. cit.
[42] E. Godbeer, op. cit.

show less change than avoidance–avoidance or approach–avoidance conflicts.

3. Simple frustration or avoidance situations provide less evidence of behavioral disturbance than do conflict situations. In the two former conditions the organism can frequently make some adaptive response that will either achieve positive reinforcement or escape or avoid a negative reinforcer.

4. Reactions to conflict, particularly where avoidance reactions are involved, are commonly characterized by anxiety, since aversive stimuli are employed. In double avoidance, escape is impossible; and in approach–avoidance, if one escapes, positive reinforcement is denied. In the anxiety operations as we have described them, avoidance of aversive stimuli is not possible (see Estes and Skinner[43] and Brady[44]). Masserman's observations[45] with cats also illustrate vividly the emotional disturbances in conflict situations in which crouching, pupil dilation, and pilomotor reactions appear.

By tolerance we mean the persistence of responding that ordinarily has achieved reinforcement in the face of delay, thwarting, or conflict. Simple observations of humans and animals in frustrating situations give clear evidence of the vast individual differences in the capacity to tolerate the situation.[46] Animal studies by Miller,[47] Masserman,[48] and Mowrer[49] have shown differences in the organisms' reactivity to the same conditions. At the human level, the same is also true. Some people show marked behavioral disorganization, while others appear to carry on for long times under similar frustrating circumstances. Clinical observations of men under conditions similar to combat gives us further evidence. If absolute prediction of possible breakdown could be made, those men who could not endure the frustration and conflict of war might be eliminated from the draft or prevented from enlisting.

Much is yet to be learned about the causes that explain these individual differences in frustration tolerance. On the basis of experimental evidence that we do have, however, it is possible to give some indications. This is far from the whole story, but it is a beginning.

---

[43] W. K. Estes and B. F. Skinner, Some quantitative properties of anxiety, *Jour. Exp. Psychol.*, **29** (1941), 390–400.

[44] J. V. Brady, A comparative approach to the experimental analysis of emotional behavior. In P. H. Hoch and J. Zubin, eds., *Experimental psychopathology* (New York: Grune & Stratton, 1957).

[45] J. H. Masserman, op. cit.

[46] Ibid.

[47] N. E. Miller, op. cit.

[48] J. H. Masserman, op. cit.

[49] O. H. Mowrer, op. cit.

1. Conditioning an organism on some intermittent schedule of reinforcement appears to increase his tolerance for frustration. Relevant here is evidence that regular reinforcement seems to "spoil" an individual so that later he is unable to withstand frustration adequately.[50] Rosenzweig[51] and Levy[52] have pointed out that the "spoiled child" (too regularly reinforced) who has had little experience with frustration is poorly equipped for the later problems and conflicts of life.

2. In the same vein, tolerance is a function of an individual's previous conditioning history. Too much frustration in the early developmental years does not allow an organism to acquire adequate reactions to it.[53] On the other hand an early exposure to frustration and conflict in gradual stages enables a person to handle it better. An experiment by Keister and Updegraff[54] illustrates this point. They trained children over a six-week period on problems of gradually increasing difficulty. Under these conditions the children were able to tolerate increasingly more difficult tasks and demands without resorting to aggressive and destructive behavior, as compared with children who had not had this experience. Furthermore, the effects of early experience on later behavior (see Chapter 8) are relevant here.

3. Assuming that aging brings with it more experience with frustration, enabling one to develop more and better techniques of handling it, there is evidence that the ability to endure frustration increases with age. Older children as compared with younger ones persist longer and repeat more often those tasks they have previously been made to fail in.[55]

## Summary

Our discussion in this chapter has been confined mainly to the basic operations of frustration and conflict and the immediate consequences of these operations to the behavior of the organism. Aggression is the most common response to frustration by delay or thwarting. Conflict com-

[50] F. S. Keller and W. N. Schoenfeld, op. cit.

[51] S. Rosenzweig, op cit.

[52] D. Levy, *Maternal overprotection* (New York: Columbia University Press, 1943).

[53] S. Rosenzweig, op. cit.

[54] M. E. Keister and R. Updegraff, A study of children's reactions to failure and an experimental attempt to modify them, *Child Develop.*, 8 (1937), 241–248.

[55] S. Rosenzweig, Preferences in the repetition of successful and unsuccessful activities as a function of age and personality, *Jour. Genet. Psychol.*, 42 (1933), 423–441.

monly leads to an impoverishment and distortion of previously acquired responses. In the next chapter we shall look into some of the other possible consequences of frustration and conflict as exemplified in the many behavioral techniques an organism resorts to. These have been classified as repression, displacement, regression, projection, and reaction formation—the so-called defense mechanisms.

# 14 Frustration and Conflict II

IN THE OPERATIONS OF FRUSTRATION, conflict, and anxiety, there is ordinarily a disruption of earlier established relationships between the organism and the various stimuli in his environment. The operations are such that responses that were reinforced, either positively or negatively, no longer secure these reinforcements. Another occasion, implied in our earlier discussion, arises when the organism is overwhelmed by some intensely aversive stimulus. This event we call *traumatic* or traumatizing to the organism. In this chapter we shall discuss further some of the different behaviors that result from the above-mentioned operations of frustration, conflict, anxiety, and trauma.

## Freud's Theory of Frustration and Defense[1]

Freud considered frustration to be anything that prevented a painful or uncomfortable excitation *within* the personality from being relieved. The satisfaction of the pleasure principle, the goal of the id, was denied. The goal could be withheld

---

[1] S. Freud, *An outline of psychoanalysis* (New York: Norton, 1949; first German ed., 1940). See also, A. Freud, *The ego and the mechanisms of defense* (New York: International Universities Press, 1946).

(privation) or removed (deprivation). In both cases the origin of the difficulty lay in external reality. Frustration could also occur within the personality itself. Opposing forces, cathexis versus anticathexis, abounded within the three systems. When these forces opposed each other, conflict resulted. It was always *intrapsychic,* between the forces of the ego and the id or between the superego and ego. Freud made it clear that there were no superego–id conflicts because the opposition of these two systems always involved the ego. Both systems tried to use the ego for their own advantage. In fact some authors have interpreted this conflict as a war between the superego and id, with the ego as the battlefield.

The ego could try many things in order to deal with its frustrations and conflicts; it could attempt some realistic solution by overcoming, circumventing, escaping, or avoiding the frustration. When reasonable means of achieving the goals of the instincts were impossible, it resorted to other methods. The ego could deny, falsify, or distort the relationships between itself and the environment, making the frustrations and conflicts less painful. These latter techniques were called the *defense mechanisms of the ego.* Among them were included displacement, repression, regression, projection, fixation, and reaction formation. Although these were inadequate solutions to the problems forced upon the ego, they did serve to protect it from the opposing forces inflicted upon it. Freud considered them as sort of an armor which protected the conscious ego from further disrupting circumstances. Frustration, conflict, and anxiety caused pain for the ego, and the defenses served to protect it, at least in part, from this painful experience.

Although we do not follow Freud's theoretical reasoning, the defense mechanisms were not mere products of his imagination. He was an astute observer. In his casual observations of people, the free associations reported to him by patients as they lay on his couch, and the dreams they reported, led him to feel that the ego did some remarkable things when the pain of anxiety was felt. A careful analysis and reinterpretation of Freud's defense mechanisms will discover that most of them can be experimentally verified with animals and humans alike. The defenses must be put to an operational test.

We have already dealt with an objective examination of frustration, conflict, and anxiety. Our next problem is to consider the so-called defense mechanisms as responses an organism makes when accustomed reinforcements are unavailable. We shall take each mechanism as Freud explained it and then consider an alternate interpretation based on observable operations and observations from the experimental laboratory.

## An Objective Analysis of Defense Mechanisms

REPRESSION

Freud's interpretation of repression, noted in Chapter 11, was relative to our observations of the effects of punishment. He considered it the most basic of the ego defenses. By exerting its anticathectic forces, the ego was able to keep from consciousness those dangerous object choices, memories, and ideas that would be painful if allowed out of the unconscious. A reinterpretation is not difficult. The effect of punishment is to set up behavior that competes with or replaces the behavior that is being punished. We described this condition earlier by saying that the punished response, previously reinforced, is depressed (or repressed). The repressing force is not an anticathecting psychic energy but merely some incompatible avoidance reaction. Just as Freud believed that a repressed memory was not lost from the self, but only submerged, experimental evidence indicates that the punished response recovers after the punishing stimulus has ceased. Following the end of punishment, the behavior ordinarily recovers in full strength. In the Freudian sense the repression is lifted, since its recall is no longer painful to the ego (see Estes' study,[2] pp. 258–259).

At the human level much of the repressed behavior is verbal. We make an inappropriate remark, are criticized for it, and "forget" (repress) what we have said, at least for the moment. In the process of verbal recall, psychologists have emphasized the selectivity of forgetting. We are more likely to remember those events that were positively reinforced than those associated with punishment. We verbalize them as being pleasant or unpleasant. A vast amount of experimentation has been tried, using verbal behavior as the data in order to verify the existence of repression. Some call it *selective* forgetting, *motivated* forgetting, or just plain suppression. The interested student can look further into reviews by Zeller[3] and Blum[4] which concern themselves with the experimental verification of the phenomenon.

One representative study by Meltzer[5] will illustrate the point. Following Christmas vacation, students were asked to list and briefly describe all the experiences they could remember during that period. If the experience was recalled as pleasant (positively reinforced), they

[2] W. K. Estes, An experimental study of punishment, *Psycholog. Monogr.*, **57**, no. 263 (1944), iii–40.

[3] A. F. Zeller, An experimental analogue of repression, I. Historical summary, *Psychol. Bull.*, **47** (1950), 39–51.

[4] G. S. Blum, *Psychoanalytic theories of personality* (New York: McGraw-Hill, 1953).

[5] H. Meltzer, Individual differences in forgetting pleasant and unpleasant experiences, *Jour. Educ. Psychol.*, **21** (1930), 399–409.

marked it with a *P*; unpleasant (punishing) recollections were marked with a *U*. Students reported 68 per cent of their experiences as pleasant and 38 per cent as unpleasant. This in itself gives no evidence for repression because in all likelihood more of their vacation activities had been positively reinforcing. Six weeks later, without warning, the same students were again asked to recall their vacation experiences. Any "new" recalls not previously listed were eliminated from the data analysis. After the six-week period, 53 per cent of the original pleasant experiences were again recalled, but only 40 per cent of the original unpleasant experiences were remembered. The fact that the differences were statistically significant, as being due to other variables than chance, is given as proof of the existence of repression of verbal behavior. Some other condition besides normal forgetting was operating to account for the poorer recall of the unpleasant experiences.

In a more recent study, D'Zurilla[6] selected two groups of college students (experimental and control) who were first shown 20 words and then tested for recall to establish that there were no preexperimental group differences. Then the subjects were shown 10 Holtzman ink blot slides (a modification of the Rorschach ink blots), along with two words for each slide. These words had been shown in the initial 20-word list. For each slide the subjects were asked to indicate the word that best described the ink blot. The experimental group was told that this was a test to detect latent homosexual tendencies. Thus, one of the words was the response that homosexuals were likely to make. The other word would more likely be selected by normal people. After responding to all the cards, both groups were given another recall test. No group differences appeared. Then the experimental group was told that they had picked nine out of the ten "typical" homosexual responses, whereas the control group was simply told it had responded very well. Five minutes later all subjects again took the recall test. The control group improved over their previously recall test, whereas the experimental subjects did more poorly than they had done before. This was interpreted as due to repression. In an attempt to "lift" the repression, the experimental group was told of the deception, and it was explained to them that the ink blot test and words had nothing to do with homosexuality. A final recall test was administered to both groups, and there were no significant differences in recall for both groups.

IDENTIFICATION

Freud considered identification as a rather basic process in personality development. It was through a simple process of identification that the

---

[6] T. D'Zurilla, Recall efficiency and mediating cognitive events in "experimental repression," *Jour. Pers. and Soc. Psychol.*, **1** (1965), 253–257.

ego obtained energy from the id for its own purposes, and the superego, later in development, sapped some energy from the ego to use for its own purposes of controlling it. Later, other forms of identification appeared. *Narcissistic* identification amounted to a form in which we identify with people who share the same qualities we ourselves already possess; for example, the sports car set or the country club set. We tend to involve ourselves with people who share the same interests as our own or are from the same socioeconomic background, and so on. In *object-loss* identification we identify with people who have things we no longer possess. A boy may assume the role of his father as head of the family after the father dies. Some southerners still like to believe that the Old South still exists with its culture, elegance, and gracious way of living, when in fact that way of life went with the Civil War (remember *Gone With the Wind?*). In *goal-oriented* identification, one tries to identify with that which he at the moment does not yet have. Children often like to "play" as if they were adults. Little girls have tea parties, and boys ride around in play automobiles. If one is not particularly popular, he may seek as his friend someone who is. Often in spectator sports we identify with the team that is playing because we may not have the skills to actually participate.

If we think of identification in a more objective manner, we realize that all it amounts to is a matter of *imitation* or *modeling*. In this instance we are reinforced by copying the behavior of another person whom we observe receiving these reinforcements. You will recall the experiment of Miller and Dollard, mentioned in Chapter 5, in which the first rat learned a simple discrimination in an elevated T-maze.[7] A second rat was then placed to follow the first, and if he made the correct turn he also was reinforced. It turned out that the discriminative stimulus in the situation was the behavior of another organism. Also, the studies of modeling cited in the same chapter illustrate the same point. Much of our behavior, particularly in our early lives, is acquired by this process. The expressions "chip off the old block," or "like father like son" illustrate this basic process of learning. There is no reason to believe that we actually "take on the qualities of the other person." If our behavior matches the behavior of the other one, and we are reinforced, the behavior is strengthened and we ordinarily call it imitation.

DISPLACEMENT

In its attempt to cathect its energy, Freud believed the ego to be blocked from time to time. If one object was not available, there could be a shift of energy to another object. (If no bread, eat cake.) This

[7] N. E. Miller and J. Dollard, *Social learning and imitation* (New Haven, Conn.: Yale University Press, 1941).

process, whereby the energy could be rechanneled from one object to another, was called *displacement*—personality developed by a series of energy displacements and object substitutions. The process was normal in all people, and in the strict sense of the word, it was not merely a defense against anxiety. Because frustration and conflict are so much a part of personality development, displacements were occurring all the time. Smoking, drinking from beer cans, drinking from a Coke bottle instead of a cup, pencil sucking, gum chewing, etc., were all displacements at the adult level of the still-unfulfilled infantile desire to suck from mother's nipples. These displacements of energy to an object could be closely related to the instinctual choice or they could be quite diverse. The direction of the displacement would depend either on the availability of the object or the dictates of society. Since the normal infantile satisfactions of the oral period are lacking (sucking), the adults' must choose some alternate form. They may smoke cigarettes but cannot suck their thumbs.

When the displacements were directed to a higher cultural goal, the mechanism was called *sublimation*. The dynamics were the same as in displacement. A frustrated old maid might become a kindergarten teacher. Maternal instincts were redirected toward other people's children. Wagner's frustrated sex life was sublimated into some of his most ecstatic love music. Da Vinci's strong interest in painting Madonnas was a sublimation for his longing for his mother, from whom he had been separated as a child.[8]

A careful look into this "technique" reveals that it is really nothing more than *generalization*. Pavlov[9] was the first to recognize the condition experimentally when he conditioned a dog to salivate when the conditioned stimulus of a tone was presented. Without further trials, the dog also salivated to a numbr of other auditory stimuli. Albert's fear, originally conditioned to a rat, generalized to many other "furry" stimuli. Generalization is also characteristic of operant conditioning as well. A rat, conditioned to press a bar using a light as an $S^D$ of a certain intensity, will also press that bar when different illuminations are present. When the original conditioning stimulus is not presented (in the Freudian terms, deprived or unavailable), the organism will respond to stimuli that resemble the original one.

To test more specifically the experimental operations in displacement, Miller and his colleagues have reported a series of studies which seem to demonstrate quite dramatically the existence of this psychoanalytic phenomenon. In an early study,[10] rats were trained to strike each other

[8] S. Freud, *Leonardo da Vinci: A study in psychosexuality* (New York: Random House, 1947; first German ed., 1910).

[9] I. P. Pavlov, *Conditioned reflexes*, trans. G. V. Anrep (London: Oxford University Press, 1927).

[10] N. E. Miller, Theory and experiment relating psychoanalytic displacement to stimulus-response generalization, *Jour. Abn. Soc. Psychol.*, **43** (1948), 155–178.

when they were placed, two at a time, in an experimental chamber with an electric grid floor. A shock was applied to their feet, strong enough to keep the animals active. As soon as the animals struck each other, the shock was immediately turned off. After a minute of no shock, the second trial began. Soon they quickly struck each other and tended to remain in the "sparring" position assumed at the time of reinforcement. Up to this point the experiment is one of simple escape, with removal of shock as the negative reinforcement. To test the displacement (generalization) of the response, a celluloid doll was placed in the cage in the presence of both rats. They continued to strike each other. (In the Freudian sense, a person will seek the object that best satisfies his instinct if a choice is available.) However, when one of the animals was placed alone in the cage with the doll, he readily struck at the doll. Miller suggests that if the original striking can be called *aggression,* then the aggression was displaced to the doll which served as a scapegoat. Freud felt that in the absence of the inherent object of the instinct, the person will choose one that is next best.

Freud also stressed the belief that there was a considerable amount of energy exchange among the instincts: they could fuse, alternate, or compensate for each other. For example, if one instinct was blocked (like hunger), another might operate to achieve a substitute satisfaction: Overeating might be a substitute for lack of sexual satisfaction. To test this aspects of Freud's theory, Miller[11] trained rats to receive water at the end of an alley. He then divided the rats into two groups, both of whom were satiated with water but one of which was deprived of food, the other satiated with it. The food-deprived rats ran down the alley faster than the satiated rats, although neither group had had any previous conditioning with food as a reinforcement. The response of running for water had been displaced by running for food.

Miller and Bugelski[12] studied the possibility of displacement of aggression in humans. A group of boys at a summer camp were asked to fill out questionnaires regarding their attitudes toward two minority groups, Mexicans and Japanese. They were then told, during the time spent filling out the questionnaires, that they were missing a prized social event. A comparison was made between the answers to the questionnaires before and after the frustration. There was a marked increase in negative attitudes expressed toward the minority groups after the frustration. The increase in hostility was interpreted as a displacement of the hostility aroused by the experimenters. Hostility felt toward the adults was displaced onto minority groups, or the responses were generalized from one stimulus to another.

---

[11] Ibid.

[12] N. E. Miller and B. Bugelski, Minor studies in aggression: II. The influence of frustrations imposed by the in-group on attitudes expressed toward out-groups, *Jour. Psychol.,* **25** (1948), 437–442.

Miller and his colleagues have attempted to apply the concept of displacement to the approach and avoidance gradients discussed in the preceding chapter. One experiment by Murray and Miller[13] used food as a reinforcer for approach behavior and escape from shock as the avoidance response. Two groups of animals were trained to approach and avoid, respectively, with the same schedule of training trials. Two alleys were used, one 6 inches wide and white, the other 3 inches wide and black. As in the earlier studies, subjects were given test trials to measure the strength of pull in the absence of reinforcement. These were given in the same alley in which the animals had learned the responses and also in a different alley. The difference between the strength of pull in the same alley and in the different ally was greater for the avoidance response than for the approach response.

A familiar example of displacement in our everyday living is the man who is called down by his boss. Unable to retaliate, he goes home and makes life miserable for his wife and children. The hostility against the superior generalizes to members of his immediate family. The statement, "He has a mad on," illustrates the development of aggression in one situation which is generalized to many other stimuli in the environment, other people as well as inanimate objects. Miller[14] reports a typical example of a boy, considered a problem child because of his school behavior; he would bite, pinch, and scratch his little playmates. Investigation revealed that the fault lay not in the school situation but at home. He hated his foster parents; he had begun by pinching, biting, and scratching these adults but was forced to cease. Later the behavior appeared in the school environment. When the home situation was cleared up, the trouble at school was also brought to an end. The displacement (generalization) of aggression has been given as the cause of many social problems. Adolescents, frustrated by their immediate environments, parents, or poor economic conditions, generalize their hostility to society in general in the form of delinquent behavior. Innocent people other than their own age-mates become the victims of their displacements.

More than likely the delinquents who roam the streets of our large cities and attack innocent people exhibit the displacement of aggression fostered by poor living conditions and other social and cultural disadvantages. The general rioting at political rallies and on college campuses today illustrates the same point.

Other behaviors as well as aggression are capable of generalization. Anxiety characteristically generalizes to stimuli besides the primary aver-

[13] E. J. Murray and N. E. Miller, Displacement: Steeper gradient of generalization of avoidance than of approach with age of habit controlled, *Jour. Exp. Psychol.*, 43 (1952), 222–226.
[14] N. E. Miller, op. cit.

sive one. The phobia is a case in point. Likewise, a piece of good news makes us joyful, and our happiness so generalizes that we love everybody, even our enemies.

REGRESSION

In order to relieve the tensions of frustration, Freud believed that people frequently reverted to modes of adjustment typical of an earlier period in their lives or even in the development of the race. When more primitive ways were set aside in favor of mature activities, the ego developed. One of the ego's main functions was to allow the id's satisfactions to be achieved in ways acceptable to the superego as well as to society in general. Often, in development, acceptable modes of satisfaction were not available. As a result the ego frequently reverted to earlier and more childlike ways of behaving. A young married woman might return to her parents following a quarrel with her husband. A preschool child, anxious about the forthcoming birth of a new sibling, would revert to wetting his pants again, even though he had been trained for over a year. Instincts were characteristically regressive, since the earliest and more primitive attachments were the most satisfying. In the process of normal development, these energies were properly displaced in keeping with the external and internal demands on the person. When these relatively satisfactory displacements could no longer operate, regression could be expected to occur.

In observing regression in the experimental laboratory, we note that it most commonly occurs as a reaction in either of two different kinds of operations: (1) extinction and (2) punishment. In extinction the organism frequently makes responses that have been conditioned (and extinguished) prior to the extinction of the response being studied. In punishment the organism frequently emits behavior that has been conditioned prior to the punishment operation.

*Regression in Extinction.* We have observed that during extinction, a kind of frustration is operating. Previously conditioned responses become weakened by withholding of the reinforcement. Consequently the organism regresses to behaviors that were effective earlier in achieving reinforcement. The process is simply illustrated in a laboratory demonstration. A rat is trained to press a bar and receive positive reinforcement. If we observe carefully the acquisition of the operant response, we note that a considerable amount of differentiation takes place. In the early trials the rat may be quite inefficient in his approach to the bar, pressing it, and going to the tray to secure the food pellet. He may approach it from various angles, from above or either side; he may nose the bar, chew it, or make numerous irrelevant movements. After the bar is pressed, he may look about until he finally discovers the food in the tray below. Between bar presses, he will move about the cage, groom himself, and climb on the sides. As conditioning continues, these earlier and relatively ineffective responses drop out in favor of a direct approach and quick seizing of the food. When extinction is then begun, many of the earlier responses reappear.

In one of Masserman's[15] many experiments, cats were conditioned to press a pedal three times, then go to a food box for reinforcement. The cats next learned that they could receive the food with only one press of the pedal. When this response was extinguished (food withheld) the cats typically regressed to pressing three times before looking for food.

A similar result was described by Hull[16] some years ago. Rats were trained to run down an alley 40 feet long to get food. The speed of running through successive 5-foot sections was measured, and a clearly defined speed gradient in the early trials was noted. The closer the rat came to the goal, the faster he ran. After several days of this conditioning, the gradient tended to disappear but reappeared at once when no food was made available in the goal box. To investigate further, Hull trained another group of rats in an alley 20 feet long. Extinction produced the same effect. These rats were then retrained in the 40-foot alley. At first there was a considerable slowing down after 20 feet had been run, at the point where the gradient had ended in their earlier training. However, with further training, the rats achieved time scores similar to those of the rats originally conditioned in the 40-foot alley. The slowing-down behavior disappeared, and the rats ran straight for the food. When these rats were punished, they resumed the earlier "hump" pattern. They had regressed to a behavior learned in the original series of trials when the alley was only 20 feet long.

*Regression after Punishment.*    An experimental demonstration of this operation is found in the study by Mowrer[17] cited later (p. 343). One group of rats was conditioned to push a panel to turn off an electric shock coming from the cage floor. Shock was begun at a mild intensity and gradually increased to and maintained at a maximum until they made the required escape response. A second group of rats was given shock for approximately the same amount of time but with no panel press available for relieving it. These animals learned to sit up on their hind legs to escape the major effects of the shock. After this behavior had been

[15] J. H. Masserman, *Principles of dynamic psychiatry* (Philadelphia: Saunders, 1946).

[16] C. L. Hull, The rat's speed of locomotion gradient in the approach to food, *Jour. Comp. Psychol.*, **17** (1934), 398–422.

[17] O. H. Mowrer, An experimental analogue of "regression" with incidental observations on "reaction-formation," *Jour. Abn. Soc. Psychol.*, **35** (1940), 56–87.

well conditioned, the panel was made available for the first time, and they were trained to press it to turn off the shock. Both groups were then punished by having the shock administered to the panel when they pressed it, as well as to the floor. The second group, which had learned a previous response of sitting on their hind legs, almost immediately regressed to this escape, while the other rats, who had not learned the earlier response, continued to press the panel.

Further light on the relationships between regression and other variables is found in a study by Martin,[18] who demonstrated that the mode of regression is dependent on the organism's previous conditioning history. Three groups of rats were trained in a T-maze to make a choice of going to the right or left to receive positive reinforcement. The amount of training differed in each group. The problem was then reversed, and rats who had learned to go to the right to get food were required to turn to the left. In the course of learning the second task, an electrical shock was introduced at the choice point. Many of the rats regressed to the originally learned response. The number regressing depended on the degree of previous learning of the first response. The rats that had received the most practice in the original task were most likely to regress, whereas those with the least training showed the fewest regressive responses.

FIXATION

The mechanism of fixation and regression were closely related in Freud's theory.[19] In his discussion of the *Instincts and Their Vicissitudes* he stated that an instinct had a source (in the id), an object (goal which satisfied it), an aim (direction of the energy), and an impetus (strength of the drive). The developmental periods themselves (oral, anal, genital, etc.) represented different sources whereby an instinct could be satisfied. Regression to these periods depended on two things: fixation and frustration. By "fixation" Freud meant a close attachment by an instinct to its object. Frustration, as we have noted, referred to prevention of satisfaction of an instinct. If a person had a strong attachment to an object and later abandoned it, the frustration would ordinarily cause him to go back to the earlier object choice. Such fixations were prior conditions to regression. They operated to relieve the personality of anxiety when dangers impinged. The attachments served as a means of security and protection for the individual, even though they might be typical of an earlier stage of the developmental process. In fixation the person

---

[18] R. F. Martin, "Native" traits and regression in rats, *Jour. Comp. Psychol.*, **30** (1940), 1–16.

[19] S. Freud, Instincts and their vicissitudes. In *Collected papers*, vol. IV, 60–85 (London: Hogarth Press, 1925; first German ed., 1915).

usually failed to give up some early mode of activity, even though other people no longer stayed with it. In regression he gave up the earlier pattern but reverted back to it.

Fixation can be interpreted in two ways. Mowrer[20] simply considers it a well-conditioned response. In our discussion of the schedules of reinforcement (Chapter 4) we observed that extremely high rates of responding which become exceedingly resistant to extinction can be developed (see differential high-rate conditioning on p. 107). In this sense the high rates of responding or extreme resistance to extinction can be interpreted as *fixated*. The response persists for long periods of time, even though one operation of frustration has been introduced, namely that of extinction.

A second interpretation of fixation infers the persistence of a response in the face of conflict. A previously acquired response persists in favor of one that at a later time may be more reinforcing. A child continues to suck at his bottle long after other children have abandoned the habit in favor of getting more nourishing food in a more accessible way. A young man who masturbated frequently in his earlier years persists at this form of sexual outlet in favor of heterosexual opportunities available to him. The bachelor becomes fixated in his selfish ways in favor of the more reinforcing activities of family living. The unwillingness to give up older, well-established ways in favor of more recent and more reinforcing activity is the key to fixation.

PROJECTION

Freud interpreted projection as an externalizing of conflicts or other internal conditions that had given rise to conscious pain and anxiety. If one were afraid of his id, it would be far easier to attribute the causation to some external object than to an internal threat. The ego could more effectively cope with an external danger than an internal one. The defense ordinarily developed against neurotic or moral anxiety. Consequently the ego tried to defend itself by transferring the source of the pain to a realistic condition. Let us say a man is afraid of his own aggressiveness or sexual impulses. He attributes them to other people, blaming them rather than himself. The hostile man calls others hostile, and the fearful person attributes his anxiety to his friends. The boy who calls his chums "fraidy cats" may more likely be afraid himself.

Two automobiles collide in an accident due to the carelessness of each driver. For either one to admit to himself that he was not paying attention to his driving would be too threatening to his ego, so each blames the other fellow. In the same way a man feeling guilty because of his own

[20] H. Mowrer, op. cit.

infidelity, accuses his wife of faithlessness. The threat from his own superego is too difficult for the ego to endure and so it attributes the guilt to his wife.

An inept college instructor who cannot get his points across calls his students "stupid." On the other hand, the student who has prepared insufficiently for a test and fails it may say the teacher gives impossible tests that nobody could pass. "Passing the buck" or blaming others for our own inadequacies are common examples of projection.

An objective interpretation of projection reveals that the one doing the "projecting" is simply *making a rather poor discrimination*, which is either ineffective or inaccurate. In the example of the men in the automobile accident, it is clear that more accurate discriminations could have prevented the collision. But more important, once the accident took place, instead of each discriminating the error as the result of his own carelessness, each falsely responds by attributing it to the other driver. Skinner[21] points out, furthermore, that the origin of these incorrect discriminations typically comes out of an avoidance response. The projected response acts to avoid (for the individual) certain stimuli that are aversive and that generate anxiety. To admit one's own mistake or fault is to face up to an aversive situation. In projecting by blaming the other person, he avoids at least momentarily the aversive stimuli and their consequences.

The experimental literature is rather meager on objective verifications of projection, probably because it is primarily a verbal defense. However, one study by O'Kelley and Steckle[22] gives us at least what may be called an experimental analogue of projection. They placed six rats at one time in a shock cage and gave them 1 hour of intermittent shocks delivered from the floor of the cage at about once every 105 seconds. There was no way that the animals could avoid or escape the shocks. Under these conditions the characteristic response on the part of the animals was highly aggressive; they attacked each other in a vicious and violent manner, even for a considerable time after the shocks had ceased. Under the same shocking conditions, when each animal was placed alone in the cage, he would attack the grid or some other part of the cage in an indiscriminate manner. However, when more than one animal was shocked at the same time, the behavior narrowed down into a definite aggressive relationship among the animals. Apparently a false connection was made between the cage mates and the shock. In the limited behavior of the rat, the responses could be called *projection*. They had all the qualities we find in projection at the human level. They were indiscriminate (attacking each other instead of the source of the aversive

---

[21] B. F. Skinner, *Science and human behavior* (New York: Macmillan, Inc., 1953).
[22] L. I. O'Kelley and L. C. Steckle, A note on long-enduring emotional responses in the rat, *Jour. Psychol.*, 8 (1939), 125–131.

stimuli), and their responses developed as an attempt at avoiding the aversive stimuli.

One kind of projection at the human level where improper discriminations are typical is in *suspicious behavior*. The suspicious person falsely accuses others, blames them for taking things he himself has lost. He accuses them of saying things that are incorrect. In some behavior disorders like *paranoia* the suspicion takes the form of delusions of persecution. In his distorted discriminations he attempts to avoid punishment. He blames others for his troubles, his frailities, and hostilities. He may think people are talking about him, or even that there may be an organized plot involving himself as the center of the collusion. People are poisoning his food or setting traps to destroy him. This kind of reaction develops in the false connections he makes between himself and the stimuli about him. When he sees people talking, he infers they are laying a plot to destroy him. Never bothering to validate his false inferences, he goes on believing them as an attempt to avoid the anxiety generated from his own responses.

SUPERSTITION

Although Freud did not include superstitious behavior among the defenses of the ego, he did attempt to explain it. Like projection, it was an externalizing of an unknown cause. When a person did not know the origin of some event, this could be a threatening experience. To falsely attribute it to some external source relieved that threat.

An objective analysis tells us that superstitious behavior arises from time to time because of accidental contingencies that happen to occur in our environments. Ordinarily we observe a functional relationship between two events in space and time. A rat is shocked; he jumps. A child is hit; he cries. Several repetitions of this contingency allow us to infer some cause-effect relation between the two. However, in superstitious behavior the relationship between the two events is quite accidental. A student wears a particular sweater while taking an examination and receives an "A" on his paper. We spit on the dice and the roll is favorable. In both cases a false connection between the two events has led to a belief that a true functional relationship exists.

In circumstances where chance contingencies are common, superstitions abound. Gambling is a typical example. Gamblers wear certain clothes, carry special articles, and indulge in a variety of rituals which "will bring them luck." Superstitions can be positive or negative. We walk around the bridge table and start to get better cards. On later occasions when the cards are running badly for us, we perform the same ritual, inferring that some relationship exists between the two events. Certain acts can also lead to punishing consequences. "Step on a crack, break your mother's back." "Break a mirror, seven years' bad luck." We fail to carry the rabbit's foot, and bad luck follows. No good will come of seeing a black cat cross our path. In all cases some accidental contingency has developed. A response was followed by positive reinforcement or punishment.

Superstitious behavior can be demonstrated in the laboratory where reinforcements can be delivered without reference to the behavior that is going on at the time they are delivered. Skinner[23] gave pigeons small amounts of food at regular intervals regardless of what they happened to be doing at the time the reinforcement was delivered. A food hopper attached to the cage swung into position so that the pigeons could eat from it once every 15 seconds. At the end of the experimental period Skinner found that six out of eight birds had developed some kind of superstitious response which was fairly well defined. One pigeon was walking around the cage in a counterclockwise position; two were thrusting their heads in an upper corner of the cage; two made pendulum movements of the head and body; one gave a "tossing" response as though he were lifting an invisible bar; and another gave incomplete pecking and brushing movements. The response that *happened* to occur at the time the reinforcement came got conditioned. The birds "acted" as though there were some causal connection between their behavior and the reinforcement presented, although such a relationship was lacking.

In a later experiment Skinner and Morse[24] made use of a "discriminative" stimulus in conditioning the superstitious behavior. Pigeons were each placed in a cage and conditioned to peck at an orange disc, illuminated from behind. They were reinforced on a VI schedule of 30 minutes (range of reinforcement from 1 minute to 39 minutes). The result was a low rate of responding with some local irregularity. Against this baseline of responding, a blue disc (incidental stimulus) was presented instead of the orange one for 4 minutes, once per hour. However, the schedule of presentation of the blue disc was independent of the programming of the variable-interval reinforcement.

Two kinds of superstitious behavior developed. In one case (negative superstition) the rates *dropped* during the period of the "incidental" stimulus. In the positive superstition the rates showed a marked increase during the periods of the blue disc. The direction of the superstition was not necessarily stable, since it would change during successive experimental periods. The changes in response rate can be easily explained in terms of presence or absence of the reinforcement that *happened* to be operating during the period of the incidental stimulus. Had the incidental stimulus been present for a shorter time, the negative superstition might have been more likely to occur because it would be present during more

[23] B. F. Skinner, "Superstition" in the pigeon, *Jour. Exp. Psychol.*, **38** (1948), 168–172.

[24] B. F. Skinner and W. H. Morse, A second type of superstition in the pigeon, *Amer. Jour. Psychol.*, **70** (1957), 308–311.

of the nonreinforced periods. On the other hand, if the time of the incidental stimulus were increased to one-half of each experimental period, there would probably have been no appreciable change in rates because the periods of reinforcement during their presence and absence would have been the same.

These two experimental demonstrations have their analogues in many of our human superstitious behaviors. Superstitions that attempt to "bring us luck" are common enough. Some "discriminative" stimulus happened to bring us luck. The lucky penny or trinket, finding the four-leaf clover—all have been followed on some occasion by positive reinforcement. A few connections between the response and the reinforcement in the presence or absence of some "discriminative" stimulus are all that is needed to maintain the behavior. Undoubtedly many of the "cures" of the medicine men and pseudopractitioners developed in the same way. Some "mumbo jumbo" was performed and the patient got well. If he was "cursed" and happened to die, another relationship was set up. Frequently, only one occasion is sufficient to develop a superstition and maintain it for some time.

Often, of course, superstitious behavior is not the result of a single person's own conditioning history. Much of it is passed down in the form of verbal stimuli from one generation to another. Its origin occurred in the past, however, but on this occasion in antiquity the contingency was just right. Other people tried the same formula and it happened to work. Consequently it became a part of some person's response equipment and continued to operate until the time when it got extinguished. Like Skinner's pigeons, once the superstitious response got established, further accidental contingencies could keep the behavior operating.


REACTION FORMATION

A final example of Freud's mechanisms of defense has had experimental verification. When one of the instincts pressured the ego and caused threat either directly or indirectly, the ego could avert the danger by substituting the opposite instinct. You will recall the two basic instincts, life and death, were at opposite poles. Since each of these had many derivatives, a variety of alternatives was possible. One substitutes love for hate, desirable objects for those he fears. High ideas of virtue may be reaction formations against more primitive sexual impulses. The maiden lady who is extremely fearful about the devices of men, may actually wish some man would attack her. Since the superego would not allow such a desire to come to consciousness, she substitutes the opposite fear reaction. We are cautioned to beware of the arden attempts of vice crusaders, the efforts of antidrinking groups, and those people who tirade against sin and set themselves up as perfectionists and "holier than thou." These efforts may be reaction formations against the more basic impulses which are suppressed. The highly virtuous people really "want" to sin, drink, and indulge in the lowly pleasures of the common man.

The reformed cigarette smoker who has given up his habit out of fear of its eventual consequences in endangering his health often gives us a good example of reaction formation. He still remembers the pleasures of smoking but tells others at great length of the dangers of smoking and they ought to quit, or he may say, "I know so few people who smoke anymore that I don't even keep ashtrays around anymore."

If we examine reaction formation more objectively, we find it to be a case of *excessive conditioning in avoidance behavior*. This conditioning involves the opposite of what may be followed by an aversive stimulus. Sometimes the response might have been positively reinforcing in the early conditioning history. In an experiment quoted earlier, Mowrer[25] placed rats in an experimental chamber in which they received gradually increasing shocks that could be terminated by pressing a panel at one end of the cage. For some of the animals the panel was also charged with electricity, so that when they pressed it, further shocks were received. He observed that as the shock from the grid floor increased in intensity, some of the rats moved to the *end of the cage opposite* the panel. These rats behaved as though they "wanted" to press the panel and relieve the shock but retreated from it to protect themselves from the further shock which would have to be taken if they pressed it. They were like people who express the response opposite from that which might be reinforcing —and punishing too. The adult who "avoids temptation" by being virtuous is both reinforced and punished. One enjoys a drink but feels guilty; he avoids the anxiety by developing the reaction formation of crusading against drink. Anxiety generated by aversive stimuli is relieved by the avoidance response of being "good." [26]

## Summary

Freud believed the ego was capable of developing defenses against the painful anxiety generated by frustration and conflict. Although they were not adequate solutions that enabled the instincts to achieve their goals, the defenses did protect the ego, at least partially. It is possible to

[25] O. H. Mowrer, An experimental analogue of "regression" with incidental observations on "reaction-formation," *Jour. Abn. Soc. Psychol.*, 35 (1940), 56–87.

[26] For another discussion of the "defense mechanisms" demonstrated in laboratory experiments with animals, see J. A. Dinsmoor, Studies of abnormal behavior in animals. In R. H. Waters, D. A. Rethlingshafer, and W. E. Caldwell, eds., *Principles of comparative psychology* (New York: McGraw-Hill, 1960), pp. 289–334.

interpret these defenses in the light of objective psychology and give experimental evidence to support their validity.

In *repression* a response is depressed because it is followed by some punishing stimulus. The effect of the aversive stimulus is to generate avoidance behavior that interfers with the emission of the response being punished. After the punishment ceases, the avoidance response is extinguished and the punished response returns. The repression is lifted.

*Identification,* as Freud considered it, involved taking on the qualities of another person or object. Objectively, it amounts to nothing more than imitation or modeling, as we consider it as a process of learning in which one is reinforced by copying the behavior of another organism.

*Displacement* is merely the generalization of a conditioned response to a variety of other similar stimuli, characteristically in the absence of the original conditioning stimulus.

*Regression* involves making a response, previously conditioned but not currently operating because of either of two operations, extinction or punishment. As the more recent response is being either weakened or depressed, the organism reverts to an earlier response which had on prior occasions been reinforced.

*Fixation* involves a response so strongly conditioned that operations which attempt to weaken it or depress it show little effect. Because of the previous conditioning history, the response persists in favor of subsequent responses which may be more reinforcing.

*Projection* refers to making a poor discrimination that had its origin in some avoidance response.

*Superstition* originates in accidental contingencies that occur between the organism's response and stimuli in the environment, both reinforcing and discriminative. Responses that occur are reinforced or not reinforced, but the connections between the responses and the reinforcements are quite accidental.

*Reaction formation* may be interpreted as excessive conditioning in avoidance behavior. A response to an aversive stimulus had been positively reinforced on earlier occasions.

Clinical psychologists and personality theorists have placed great emphasis on the importance of the defense mechanisms as reactions an organism makes to events involving aversive stimuli, frustration, and conflict. A proper understanding is necessary for interpreting the nature of personality development. A reinterpretation on the basis of experimental evidence ought to be an important advance in the scientific study of personality.

# 15  Neurotic Behavior

"NEUROTIC" IS A TERM TRADITIONALLY applied to a class of behaviors that have been described as deviating from conventional ways of responding. When the deviations become extremely severe, the term *psychotic* has been applied. In the original concept, the former term implied that something was wrong either with the functioning of a person's nervous system or with his psyche. The early interpretation of one neurotic condition, *neurasthenia*, was that the sufferer's nerves were exhausted. His nerves were weak and worn out, and the most appropriate treatment that could be prescribed was complete rest in order to allow the person to recover from the effects of his strain. The symptoms of the neurasthenic had not been caused by the more common muscular strain and fatigue due to excessive exercise or physical work but from a nervous strain resulting from psychological strain and trauma.[1]

Another disorder, which was also called neurotic, was *psychasthenia*. This was supposed to have resulted from a weak mind or psyche. The disorder was characterized by phobias, obsessions, and compulsions. A lack of self-control or "will" was the most predominant characteristic. The sufferer might exhibit uncontrollable fears (phobias), persistent and recurrent ideas (obsessions), or irresis-

[1] S. Weir-Mitchell, *Fat and blood*, 8th ed. (Philadelphia: Lippincott, 1900).

tible tendencies to take things, repeat acts, or perform complicated rituals (compulsions). The person had simply lost his self-control. He could no longer resist the temptations emanating from his ideas and thoughts. Having a weak mind, he lacked any normal degree of will. The two disorders, neurasthenia and psychasthenia, along with hysteria and a variety of anxiety disorders, constituted the various kinds of neurotic behavior viewed by the practitioners of the early twentieth century.

Different authorities on the problem of neurosis as Freud,[2] the French physicians Charcot[3] and Janet,[4] and other students of abnormal behavior differed among themselves as to the interpretations of these neurotic disorders, their causes, and treatments. For example, Charcot believed the source of the trouble in hysteria was to be found in an inherited weakness, while Freud believed it to be a weakness of the ego overpowered by a stronger superego. Janet, on the other hand, believed hysteria to be a splitting of the psyche or mind.

Some of these earlier notions about behavior disorders often implied a qualitative difference between the neurotic and the normal. The former was different from his fellowmen, either by the inherited weakness of his nervous system or the kind of development his psychic structure had. Today the majority of theorists and practitioners are no longer of this old opinion. They believe rather that the neurotic behavior is learned according to the same basic principles of learning by which other kinds of activity are acquired. In the treatment of these unfortunate behaviors, the responses must be modified in the same way that normal responses are changed or extinguished.

If we do not hold to these earlier interpretations of neurotic behavior, how can we explain the symptoms that psychiatrists call typically neurotic? Before any objective analysis of neurotic behavior can be made, however, we must first ask the question, how does neurotic behavior differ from the so-called normal? We label a compulsive handwasher as neurotic because he washes his hands 40 times a day. By most standards of cleanliness this appears an exaggeration of normal handwashing. However, an examining physician may perform the same act, but we do not call his behavior abnormal. Another man may spend considerable time trying to wash grease and tar from his hands. On the basis of mere exaggeration alone, his behavior would appear to be neurotic because he washes for so long a time.

One common neurotic disorder is called the *anxiety neurosis* (see Chapter 12). As we have seen, the sufferer is chronically fearful. He

---

[2] S. Freud, *A general introduction to psychoanalysis* (New York: Garden City Publishing Co., 1943; first German ed., 1917).

[3] J. M. Charcot, *Lectures on the diseases of the nervous system* (London: New Sydenham Society, 1877).

[4] P. Janet, *L'état mentale des hystériques* (Paris: Reuff, 1893–1894).

exhibits emotional reactions that include many of the same intense respondent and operant activities found in the frightened child. Still, there
is nothing necessarily neurotic about fear or even a man terrorized under
the stress of combat. A phobic person, considered neurotic, frequently
avoids a variety of anxiety-inducing situations for him by remaining
inside his home, never venturing out. But to remain at home, even for
long periods of time, is not necessarily neurotic if the conditions are appropriate; illness, bad weather, and the like.

Sometimes, besides exaggeration, the distinction between neurotic and
normal is made on the basis of behavioral *distortion*. When the discriminative response of a lower organism is pressed too far, certain previously
acquired discriminations break down (see next section). Furthermore,
you will recall that in the anxiety operation, an organism ceases responding in the way that he has in the past, even though the reinforcements
are still available to him at the time the anxiety operation is superimposed. The anxiety responses in the rat in the cessation of bar pressing,
crouching, and defecating will be considered distortions of the earlier
conditioned behavior. Still, anxiety is not necessarily neurotic nor is
defecation necessarily abnormal. Under the operations of conflict, we are
described as behaving inappropriately. Yet we all react to conflict, often
violently, almost every day and are not considered neurotic.

How then can we describe neurotic behavior so as to distinguish it
from its normal counterpart? We cannot distinguish the neurotic from
normal behavior on the basis of the responses alone, although it is true
that an anxiety neurotic, for example, is anxious most of the time, and the
compulsive handwasher accomplishes little more than chapped and sore
hands. In order to distinguish these two forms of behavior we must look
to the stimulus conditions surrounding the expression of the neurotic
behavior and compare these with those surrounding a similar response in
the normal. These conditions refer both to the *discriminative* and *reinforcing stimuli*. This may not tell us the whole story, since an individual's
neurotic behavior is going to be a function of many variables in his past
conditioning history. However, it will give us some knowledge of the
occasions under which neurotic behavior is emitted and the peculiar reinforcement contingencies that happen to be operating.

It is perfectly appropriate for a physician to wash his hands 40 times
in an afternoon if he happens to have examined 40 different patients at
that time. The compulsive handwasher, on the other hand, is acting under
a different set of circumstances. The discriminative stimuli ($S^D$'s) are quite
unique. He has done so, perhaps, because of a complicated history of
avoidance conditioning in which a variety of neutral stimuli that signify
dirt, germs, and disease are constantly surrounding him. The only way to
remove these conditioned negative reinforcers is to wash regularly and
frequently. A soldier under battle combat may be traumatized by the
many really dangerous stimuli surrounding him. He may attempt to

escape to safer ground. The anxiety neurotic is exhibiting the same kind of terror from a response point of view, but he is not under combat. He may be sitting in a quiet living room or preparing for bed when he is overwhelmed with an anxiety attack. The terrorized soldier can verbalize the stimulus conditions that have given rise to his intense fear. The anxiety neurotic, in all likelihood, will not be able to. For him, the stimulus conditions are very different.

As with the discriminative stimuli that set the occasion for a response in the normal and neurotic, so also the reinforcing contingencies will be different for the two cases. The physician's handwashing response is reinforced in the protection he gives himself and his patients from the spreading of communicable diseases. What can be the reinforcement for the compulsive handwasher? It could be the avoidance or escape from a variety of conditioned negative reinforcers which would be neutral stimuli for most people. Furthermore the neurotic may have to go through a series of punishing events before he can receive his reinforcement. As he washes his hands with strong soap, sores begin to appear on his hands, which are extremely painful when irritated. Yet he persists because the reduction of his anxiety is a more powerful reinforcer than avoiding the painful stimulation resulting from washing. Frequently the neurotic appears to be reinforced by stimuli which to most people are aversive.

In the past, psychologists and psychiatrists have usually distinguished between the neurotic and normal on the basis of either qualitative or quantitative differences in the behavior itself without regard to the stimulus conditions surrounding the events. We realize that much is still to be learned about the nature of neurotic behavior as well as the many variables that have led to its development. However, one step in the direction of understanding the differences between the two is to look at the particular discriminative stimuli which have set the occasion for the behavior, as well as the special reinforcements obtained.

In Chapter 1 we defined personality in terms of uniqueness. Every one of us has had his own special conditioning history. We do not all adapt to every situation in the same way, and still we adapt. As Kantor[5] suggests, what might be abnormal for one person in a given situation might be perfectly normal for another. The kinds of adaptive behavior necessary for one person to get along in society might not be the same for someone else. Accordingly, because each person exhibits a variation in his conduct it would be a difficult task to separate one person from another in order to call him neurotic or normal without taking into account the present reinforcing and discriminative stimuli in his environment as well as his own unique conditioning history. Bearing this in mind, let us first examine some of the experimental studies leading to the development of neurotic symptoms in animals. We shall then direct our

---

[5] J. R. Kantor, *Principles of psychology*, vol. II (New York: Knopf, 1926).

attention to some of the neurotic symptoms commonly found at the human level, along with experimental evidence in order to discover what the operations are in these behaviors and how the responses might have been developed.

## Development of Experimental Neurosis

One approach to the problem of understanding neurotic behavior is to attempt artificially under laboratory conditions and with lower organisms to set up situations of stress and/or conflict which may be analogous to human situations. The technique has its limitations, since ordinarily we are dealing with simpler organisms whose past conditioning has not been subjected to the many variables that people encounter. The behavior of the laboratory animal is quite limited as compared to the human; therefore, to extrapolate too far would be a dangerous assertion when dealing with such a complex problem as human neurosis.

In 1927 Pavlov[6] reported an experimental technique whereby marked changes could be made to occur by forcing the development of a discrimination beyond the limits of an organism's capacity. After he had conditioned a dog's salivary response to a luminous circle, he presented an elliptical figure as the $S\Delta$. He continued to reinforce in the presence of the circle and extinguish in the presence of the ellipse. By gradually reducing the ratio of the semi-axes of the two figures, the ellipse came to resemble the shape of the circle. When the ratio of the semi-axes reached 9:8, the dog's discrimination failed to improve. Instead, it became considerably worse and finally disappeared altogether. The behavior of the dog showed some abrupt changes. He began to squeal (previously quiet), tore at his harness with his teeth, and struggled in an attempt to escape from the apparatus. When removed from the harness, he barked violently. None of these behaviors had been part of his customary pattern in the early stages of conditioning. When Pavlov later tested the earlier discriminations, which had been established without such difficulty (when the semi-axes, for example, were at a ratio of 2:1), he found that these also had completely broken down. He designated the condition of behavioral change as *experimental neurosis*.

Following Pavlov's early experiments, Liddell[7] and his associates studied the problem extensively in a number of farm animals such as sheep, goats, and pigs. As the response to be conditioned, they selected

[6] I. P. Pavlov, *Conditioned reflexes*, trans., G. V. Anrep (London: Oxford University Press, 1927).

[7] H. S. Liddell and T. L. Bayne, The development of "experimental neurasthenia" in sheep during the formation of a difficult conditioned reflex, *Amer. Jour. Physiol.*, **81** (1927). 494.

the foot withdrawal from an electric shock, using a sound as the conditioning stimulus. In the establishment of this type of conditioning there is a considerable amount of generalized activity in the beginning when the shock is applied. As the conditioning progresses, many of the undifferentiated movements of struggling (such as lifting other limbs other than the one shocked) extinguish until the response of lifting one leg is well established. In goats and sheep they found that with long continuation of the procedures, the animals became agitated and were increasingly unable to make the proper withdrawal response. The leg that had previously responded to the presentation of the conditioned stimulus became increasingly incapacitated by remaining stiff and rigid. Liddell has interpreted this leg stiffening and inability to make a previously acquired appropriate response as a kind of inhibitory experimental neurosis.

In another study Anderson and Liddell[8] determined the limits of a discrimination in sheep by using metronome beats as conditioned stimuli. The withdrawal of the foreleg from an electric shock was the unconditioned response, with the sound of the metronome at one beat per second as the conditioned stimulus. (See Fig. 3–1) The animals soon learned to lift their legs at regular intervals, remaining quiet when no stimulus was presented. As the shock was paired with the metronome beat, an animal would flex its leg once a second to the beat of the metronome alone. Animals could also be conditioned when the shock was paired with the beat every 5, 10, 15, or 25 seconds. But if the interval between beats was advanced to 30 seconds, a profound behavioral disturbance occurred. The animal would wait too long and shock would come, or it would not wait long enough. It became restless even when the metronome was not beating and would flex other limbs.

In the early stages of experimentation, the sheep would go to the laboratory without resistance. Later on it resisted vigorously and had to be placed by force on the experimental table. It became restless in its pen even outside the experimental room and at times would crouch in a corner. Measurement of the sheep's pulse indicated a sharp increase, with marked irregularity in beating. When one animal was kept away from the laboratory for over a year, its condition was reported improved, but with further testing the "nervous symptoms" recurred. In one of the animals these symptoms persisted until its death at the age of 13 years.

The neurotic behavior developed in the laboratory, as we have seen, generalizes to situations outside. When animals were placed in their normal living quarters following experimentation, both Pavlov and Liddell reported that the neurotic responses persisted. However, Liddell[9]

---

[8] O. D. Anderson and H. S. Liddell, Observations on experimental neurosis in sheep, *Arch. Neurol. Psychiat.*, **34** (1935), 330–354.

[9] H. S. Liddell, Experimental neurosis. In J. McV. Hunt, ed., *Personality and the behavior disorders* (New York: Ronald Press, 1944), chapter xii.

found that if given greater freedom of activity during the conditioning process, the generalization of the disturbance was less severe. For example, when a sheep was placed in a pen 5 feet square where it could move about freely, the conditioning did not produce such generalized disturbances. Freedom, he felt, could give an animal opportunity to develop alternate avoidance behaviors when attempts to induce "experimental neurosis" were made. On the basis of evidence accumulated, Liddell has stressed the significance of the following experimental conditions for the development of neurosis:

1. A considerable degree of restraint is necessary so that when an animal is placed in an experimental situation any possibilities of escape or avoidance are eliminated.
2. A situation is presented which the animal cannot master so that achievement of positive or escape from negative reiforcement is impossible. By placing an animal in a situation in which it is forced beyond its discriminative capacity, for example, a degree of conflict is induced.

The development of experimental neurosis applies also to operant conditioning. You will recall our earlier discussions of Masserman's[10] studies with cats. When cats were trained to lift the lid of a box to receive food, with a sound or a light as $S^D$'s, without warning a strong aversive air blast was blown across the box at the moment they began to eat. If the aversive stimulus was strong enough, a disruption in behavior took place despite deprivation, which Masserman has interpreted as "experimental neurosis." He likened the cats' behavior to human (1) anxiety, (2) phobias, and (3) regression. Anxiety reactions were manifested by restlessness and trembling, crouching, hiding, and startled reactions when incidental stimuli were given. Among the phobic responses the animals exhibited were tendencies to avoid the food box despite their food deprivation. Some of the cats would starve themselves, whereas others would eat only small amounts of food given from the hand of the experimenter. Among the regressive responses, the cats would give kittenish reactions of mewing, excessive licking, and cleaning themselves; often they reacted aggressively toward other cats.

Bijou[11] developed a conditioning technique with rats in which the experimental procedures and results are similar to those of Pavlov and Liddell. The animal's head was placed in a stock, which was locked in

---

[10] J. H. Masserman, Behavior and neurosis (Chicago: University of Chicago Press, 1943).

[11] S. Bijou, The development of a conditioning methodology for studying experimental neurosis in the rat, *Jour. Comp. Psychol.*, **34** (1942), 91–106. See also S. Bijou, A study of "experimental neurosis" in the rat by conditioned response techniques, *Jour. Comp. Psychol.*, **36** (1943), 1–20.

place. A wire cage was then placed over its body while it remained in a natural sitting position. In some of his experiments Bijou placed a further restraint by tying the rat's hind legs. A food cup available directly below the animal's head provided the reinforcement when the rat made the appropriate response of pushing a bar upward. As conditioning stimuli, lights of different intensities were presented.

When the difference between the two light intensities was great, appropriate discriminations were easily made, but when the discriminations were made much more difficult so that the difference between the $S^D$ and $S\Delta$ was less marked, behavioral changes occurred analogous to those reported earlier by Pavlov and Liddell. There was an increase in the number of erroneous responses, a loss of a previously acquired differential reaction to striking the bar and eating the food, and an increase in excitable behavior of struggling, squealing, cup biting, attacking the response bar, and excessive urination and defecation. When shock was introduced for erroneous responses, the degree of excitement increased. As training was prolonged at the difficult discrimination levels, not only did the discriminations break down, but the animals also failed to relearn the simpler discriminations that they had developed earlier.

## Neurotic Behavior in Humans

Our experiments with animals under contrived laboratory conditions tell us a great deal about the development of neurotic behavior and the conditions favoring it. They do not, of course, give us the whole story. First of all we realize that the development of neurotic symptoms sometimes involves some kind of conflict. However, conflict alone may not be enough, for we have observed in both animals and humans that they may be subjected to conflict from time to time without suffering any disastrous results. Ordinarily the conflict must *persist*. The organism must be continuously forced into conflict situations without any opportunity to escape or avoid. At the human level, clinical evidence supports the notion that neurotic behavior does not develop in a person overnight. It may be the result of a long history of subjection to excessive conflict often beginning in childhood. Furthermore the responses that result are the best attempt the organism has to adapt to an impossible situation.

To best understand the ways in which neurotic behavior in humans develops, we must propose two questions. First, what are the circumstances that set the occasion for learning of neurotic behavior? Most people are not neurotic. If the basic principles of learning apply to neurotic as well as normal behavior, what variables in a person's present situation as well as his past life history of conditioning seem to lead to the acquisition of this maladaptive responding? Second, in observing the

behavior of the neurotic, we see that he is usually miserable and un-
happy. His behavior is inappropriate and ineffectual. Nevertheless it
persists. Freud[12] recognized this condition in the resistance and unwillingness of his patients to give up their symptoms. Mowrer[13] has
referred to the condition as the *neurotic paradox;* that is, behavior that
appears to be self-perpetuating is at the same time self-defeating.

Our second question is, then, why does behavior persist which
apparently is not only unreinforcing but punishing as well? In our earlier
discussions of escape, avoidance, punishment, and anxiety, we have
given a partial answer to the first question. These operations set the
occasion for behavior that, on some occasions at least, leads the person
into difficulty in his interactions with other individuals. We have already
mentioned many of the consequences of excessive conditioning with
aversive stimuli. Conditioning in escape and avoidance can often lead to
excessive withdrawal behaviors which inhibit the procurement of more
positive reinforcements ordinarily achieved in human contacts. Further-
excessive punishment generates anxiety that can disrupt normal human
relations and lead the person to shun human contacts. Anxiety itself is
disruptive. Typically in this operation an individual fails to attain positive reinforcements which his previous conditioning history has developed. In later sections we shall discuss more specific neurotic patterns
of behavior in which escape, avoidance, punishment, and anxiety participate.

Our experimental evidence also demonstrates the strong influence of
conflict for the development of maladaptive behaviors. This is observed
in the impoverishment and distortion of behavior in experimental studies
of approach–avoidance and avoidance–avoidance conflicts. Finally we
saw the development of "experimental neurosis" in the studies of Pavlov
and Liddell, where an organism was forced into a conflict in which appropriate discriminations could not be made.

The importance of conflict for the development of behavioral disorders is no new observation to psychology. Freud[14] noted that society
frequently induced in infancy and childhood certain conflicts that could
serve as the seeds of later neurotic behavior. For example, he observed
that a child is supposed to be meek and obedient to his parents but
strong and aggressive outside the home. There is no doubt that the kinds
of behavior learned in childhood are basic and important for later behavioral development. We have already seen the lasting effects of early
infantile experiences on later development (see Chapter 8). The studies
on infantile frustration and deprivation give sufficient evidence for the

---

[12] S. Freud, op. cit.

[13] O. H. Mowrer, Learning theory and the neurotic paradox, *Amer. Jour. Orthopsychiat.,* **18** (1948), 571–610.

[14] S. Freud, *Civilization and its discontents* (London: Hogarth Press, 1930; first
German ed., 1930).

significance of early life conditions on later behavioral development. Conflict begins early for the infant in feeding that is forced, insufficient nourishment, or inappropriate weaning. Early conflicts involve problems of cleanliness and elimination. The first years of life involve inconsistent application of reinforcements and punishing stimuli, depending on the particular circumstances and the mood of the parents. Sometimes accomplishments in toilet training are strongly reinforced. At other times they are ignored. A "mistake" may be forgiven at one moment and punished at another. One parent may be permissive in his training procedures, the other overly strict.

As a result of these incompatible desciplines, numerous conflicts are imposed on the child. Early sex training becomes the next source of conflict. A child masturbates, is caught and punished—for doing something he finds reinforcing. Taboos and restrictions are placed upon him which have no meaning. Dirty words are laughed at in school but punished at home. At this stage of his development, discriminations often forced upon a child by parents and teachers may be beyond his capacity to acquire. Strong attachments often develop between members of the same sex which are mutually reinforcing but receive punishment from the outsiders. A boy develops a liking for his teacher but is ridiculed by his classmates for being "teacher's pet." Heterosexual conflicts of adolescence need not be belabored. A more precocious boy finds reinforcement in the company of girls, but is jeered at by his less developed age-mates. Custom allows sexual excitement without its culmination.

Another common area of conflict is found in what Dollard and Miller[15] call anger-anxiety conflicts. Anger is a common enough response to the frustrating events in a child's life when appropriate solutions to his problems are not available. The child's expressions of anger and aggression are inappropriate and often get punished. A polite and well-behaved boy is supposed to "inhibit" these expressions. Such chastisements are apparently inherent in a culture that demands proper subservience to elders. It is a rare family in which sibling rivalry does not exist. Still, aggression toward a brother or sister may get punished. Punishment of these aggressive responses does not weaken them but merely leads to displacement. A child observes the outlets for anger permitted in adulthood but which are punished in childhood.

There is an inevitability of conflict at every age level in the development of the human organism. Conflicts differ in number and strength. When alternate solutions are impossible, the conflicts persist. The inaccessibility of proper solutions that achieve positive reinforcement or avoid aversive stimuli lead to the persistence of maladaptive behavior.

[15] J. Dollard and N. E. Miller, *Personality and psychotherapy* (New York: McGraw-Hill, 1950).

With continued maturation, alternative behaviors are possible, but even in adulthood, conflict persists. We are reinforced for telling the truth, but the blunt or frank person is criticized. It is considered socially appropriate to have ambition to get ahead, but we punish if one gets too "pushy."

What, then, accounts for the difference between the neurotics and the normals? Both are frequently subjected to punishment, anxiety, and conflict. As far as our clinical evidence can tell us, the difference is to be found in the number and kinds of situations encountered, as well as the possibility of appropriate reinforcement. When alternate behaviors that are positively reinforcing can be substituted for those punished, a solution is generally considered adequate. If avoidance or escape from anxiety situations is possible, the anxiety is relieved. A normal person may have less conflict because the conditions for the resolution of his conflicts in ways condoned by his family and society may be more numerous.

The maladaptive consequences of these operations for the normals have been less persistent. Thus the conditions of development are not the same for the normal and the neurotic. Some individuals have had more intense and frequent conflicts than others. Others have been less able to solve their difficulties, either because of the inaccessibility of solutions or of the lack of behavior equipment already learned, which may not allow more appropriate responses. A child, for example, is obviously less well equipped behaviorally to handle a tyrannical adult than is a more mature adolescent. We have already mentioned conditions such as overly strict discipline, excessive punishment, and overprotection which limit for the child the learning of adequate alternative behaviors. Finally, when the neurotic symtoms become more manifest in adulthood, it is likely that the circumstances that initiated the major symptoms were more severe.

Much of the available data that suggest the circumstances for neurotic development comes from case histories. It is possible, of course, that when more controlled evidence is developed, our inferences may be altered. However, on the basis of available knowledge, including experimental studies, it seems clear that the conditions so far discussed (excessive conditioning in escape and avoidance, punishment, anxiety, and conflict) are some of the circumstances that are more likely to lead to maladaptive behavior. The greater the restrictions, the more difficult the behavior problems become.

## Neurotic Symptoms

### ANXIETY DISORDERS

In Chapter 12 we discussed the operations of anxiety and how its behavioral manifestations can generalize. When an organism is placed in a situation where an aversive stimulus can be neither avoided nor escaped, anxiety results. The manifestations are found in the impoverishments and distortions of operant responding as well as in the multitude of respondents that accompany the responses. None of these seems to facilitate adaptive responding. Although not defined as a conflict operation, anxiety has many of its ingredients. The fact that conflict situations are often likely to lead to the same behavioral consequences as anxiety operations is clear evidence. As the number of conditions that give rise to anxiety multiply in a person's conditioning history, the behavior becomes more and more impoverished and disruptive. Conditioned stimuli that previously served as warning signals for oncoming aversive stimuli can no longer be identified by the person. As these conditions multiply, the anxiety becomes chronic. It interferes with the achievement of positive reinforcement or more appropriate avoidance behavior. There comes a point somewhere in the development of anxiety when a person's behavior has become so impoverished that he becomes ineffective in dealing with other people and in carrying out the affairs that lead to positive reinforcements for himself and his family. At that point we label him an anxiety neurotic.

The point at which this happens is quite arbitrary. The important fact is that the behavior of the anxiety neurotic differs in a most impressive manner from that of the occasional anxiety responses we exhibit from time to time in our everyday living. The chronically anxious person is merely exhibiting anxiety that is more intense and more frequent than the occasional ones we all manifest as we endure the adversities of life. Anxiety neurosis has developed through excessive conditioning in anxiety, avoidance, and punishment. The responding has become so *generalized* that the person can no longer identify the incidental discriminative stimuli which incite the responses.

As a person responds to the many internal respondents that constitute part of his anxiety reaction (increased pulse rate, elevated blood pressure, more frequent urination, heightened muscular tension, stiffness, aching, etc.), he tends to verbalize another set of responses. He says he feels tense or nervous, cannot concentrate, has difficulty sleeping. Often he reports a feeling of apprehension or impending doom, but *he cannot tell why.* Because there have been so many occasions that have generated anxiety in his past, and because these occasions as stimuli have generalized, he can no longer make the *discriminations* that he could in the past or that the normal person can. Neither can he tell precisely what he is afraid of or why.

We cannot ignore the part that *incubation* plays in the development of neurotic anxiety. Perhaps there were many occasions in this person's earlier life that generated anxiety. If these were not extinguished, they may have continued to grow, as was experimentally demonstrated in Chapter 12. Incubation is an experimentally demonstrated phenomenon, and not merely a hypothetical construct. The conditions of generalization and incubation plus a situation of excessive conditioning in anxiety-arousing circumstances, both in the individual's past history and present environment, affords some understanding of the nature of neurotic anxiety.

The phobia is merely a special case of anxiety. Some fear-producing situation has developed in the usual way. The anxiety responses have generalized to a number of $S^D$'s but not to the degree that they have in chronic anxiety. Consider a man who had a phobia for closed places. At one time he suffered an automobile accident in which he was caught for several hours underneath his car with no possibility for escape. He assumed death was inevitable. However, in the course of time he was discovered and freed. Because of the intensity of the event, he developed avoidance behaviors that operated to reduce the anxiety which a recall of the incident would provoke. As time passed, the anxiety intensified and generalized to include any enclosed place. Unlike the chronically anxious person, the phobic one finds it possible to develop specific avoidance behaviors that reduce his anxiety. However, the avoidance may become extremely restrictive. He must stay out of all enclosed places. The phobic avoidance behavior serves to reduce the anxiety generated by the conditioned aversive stimuli. Although there has been some generalization from the initial anxiety-arousing situation, the behavior has not sufficiently generalized so as to make some kind of avoidance responding impossible. Because of the aversive nature of the initial event, complete recall is often not possible. The avoidance behavior has interfered with that. Thus a degree of incomplete repression is operating.

## OBSESSIONS AND COMPULSIONS

Avoidance responding is also operating in obsessive and compulsive behavior. Since the avoidance is reinforced, it continues. Compulsions and obsessions differ from each other only in the observable characteristics of the response. Obsessions are more implicit acts, whereas compulsions involve a degree of overt activity. Both involve the continuous repetition of some response that often appears to be unnecessary and absurd. A compulsion may be merely a persistent repetition of some simple act or a series of ritualistic movements. Obsessions are often described in common parlance as "persistent ideas running through one's head" or a constant recurrence of "evil thoughts which one cannot get out of his mind."

As an example of a compulsion, take the case of compulsive hand-washing. The person washes his hands over and over again beyond the limits that normal cleanliness demands. The act is repeated so frequently that his hands become sore and raw. The persistent use of strong soap and vigorous rubbing results in a painful condition. The response continues to the point where more and more aversive consequences result.

For this response to persist as it does, there must be some kind of reinforcement forthcoming. Such reinforcements have traditionally been interpreted as involving the reduction of anxiety (Fenichel,[16] White,[17] Cameron,[18] and Dollard and Miller[19]). Undoubtedly the compulsion as an avoidance response is reinforced by the reduction of anxiety. As long as a person washes his hands, performs some ritualistic acts, exhibits seemingly magical acts, or becomes excessively orderly, *he reports that he feels better.* Like other kinds of avoidance responding, the reinforcement comes from the elimination of aversive stimuli as well as from the reduction of anxiety generated by the circumstances surrounding the act.

The avoidance responses in compulsions and phobias are often intimately related. A person may have a phobia for dirt and germs. He does all he can to evade them because their presence initiates intense anxiety. To reduce this anxiety, one possible kind of avoidance is to indulge in excessive cleanliness, orderliness, or handwashing to eliminate the stimuli. Psychologists have frequently found that the anxiety in compulsive behavior is of a moral sort which we commonly call *guilt.* Perhaps the compulsively clean person has been trained by excessive punishment for dirtiness, punishment for masturbation, or training in the dreads of venereal disease. The response itself operates to inhibit the stimuli that would arouse anxiety.

Sometimes an avoidance response of a compulsive nature serves as a substitute for some other act that would arouse anxiety. One woman developed a compulsive knitting response. She had to keep her hands busy at all times during her waking hours. In this case the act of knitting kept her hands so occupied that she was free from taking her pulse regularly, since she had feared heart disease.

Because the compulsive act only temporarily avoids the conditioned aversive stimuli, its effects are very short. As soon as the act is terminated, the aversive stimulus returns. Like the holding response of the rat that keeps the bar down to avoid a light or presses the bar to forestall the onset of shock, the only way that a person can avoid the aversive stimuli and the anxiety they generate is constantly to engage in the compulsive act. The conditions that generate his anxiety may be so numerous that the effects of the conditioned aversive stimuli do not easily extinguish. As soon as the avoidance response is terminated, he is back among the many conditioned stimuli which will generate more

---

[16] O. Fenichel, *The psychoanalytic theory of neurosis* (New York: Norton, 1943).

[17] R. S. White, *The abnormal personality,* 2nd ed. (New York: Ronald Press, 1956).

[18] N. Cameron, *The psychology of behavior disorders* (Boston: Houghton Mifflin 1947).

[19] J. Dollard and N. E. Miller, op. cit.

anxiety. Only as long as he continually performs his compulsive act can he keep from the aversive stimuli and their consequences.

Many sexual aberrations or peculiarities are basically compulsive reactions. These include fetishes (see Chapter 18), homosexuality, sadism, or exhibitionism. Sometimes these may have been developed by a simple process of respondent conditioning, as we saw in the case of the men who were conditioned to develop fetish (sexually attractive) responses toward women's boots (Chapter 3). At other times they may have developed as avoidance reactions to normal sexual contacts. Many homosexuals, for example, have acquired avoidance reactions to normal heterosexual contacts because of unfortunate conditioning (training that sex is sin, for example), so that they substitute other sexual contacts that have at least a partial sexual reinforcing function. Many inspectionists ("peeping Toms") are too anxious about normal sexual contacts and substitute a "looking" response instead. These avoidance responses of normal sexual contacts reduce anxiety over normal contacts and do have some partial sexual reinforcing functions in themselves. Examples of attempts to treat a variety of sexual deviations by means of behavior therapy will be discussed in Chapter 18.

## HYSTERICAL SYMPTOMS

Like compulsions, obsessions, and phobias, hysterical symptoms develop in people who are exhibiting strong anxiety responses. Sometimes the origin of the anxiety has been in some intense traumatic situation like that commonly observed under conditions of war and combat.[20] At other times the progress of the anxiety has developed over a longer period of time, dating back to childhood.

Hysteria is derived from the Greek word *hystera*, meaning uterus. It was believed by the ancient Greek physicians that the uterus wandered about the female body. When it happened to land someplace, the symptom appeared. Since it was believed to be most responsive to odors, a common practice was to apply foul or fragrant oils to the female genitalia in order to lure the wandering uterus back to place. The French physician Pierre Janet[21] studied the problem extensively, as did his predecessors Charcot and Liebeault. Janet considered that hysterical symptoms resulted from a splitting of behavior or mental acts (dissociation). The split could be some little fragment of mental functioning from the whole organization of personality or it could involve large segments of action such as those found in the double or multiple personality. Freud[22] considered the hysterical symptoms to be a conversion of repressed

---

[20] R. R. Grinker and J. P. Spiegel, *War neuroses* (Philadelphia: Blakiston, 1945).

[21] P. Janet, op. cit.

[22] S. Freud, Fragment of an analysis of a case of hysteria. In *Collected papers*, vol. III (London: Hogarth Press, 1933; first published in Germany, 1905).

psychic energy. The symptom operated as a symbolic disguise, allowing repressed ideas a chance to relieve the tension of being repressed and still be admissible to the ego.

Hysterical symptoms tend to fall into two groups. In the first class a fragment or a combination of responses operate apart from the normal organization of behavior (a tic, tremor, cramp, seizure, somnambulism, or even a double personality). In the second group there is an apparent loss of behavioral function as found in hysterical amnesias, blindness, deafness, paralyses, anesthesias, or mutism. These two kinds of hysterical symptoms superficially resemble either some response change or functional loss that would ordinarily result from an organ or tissue pathology. Tics, tremors, amnesias, paralyses, and anesthesias are often found in conditions where some damage or disease has occurred in the central nervous system. Such organic conditions should not be confused with the hysterical, although on the surface they may appear the same. Some proof that an hysterical symptom is not organic can be found in their reduction or complete elimination under conditions of psychotherapy or drug administration. It is not uncommon for a person suffering from a hysterical paralysis, for example, to be unable to walk during his waking hours but be able to move his limbs about quite normally during sleep.

The development of hysterical symptoms can be illustrated by taking the example of a young violinist who had studied for many years with the intention of being a concert artist. Unfortunately his performance was not equal to his own opinion of his ability. As he continued to have difficulty in finding engagements or played to empty houses, his available funds became completely exhausted. He began to develop cramps in his fingers and arms, particularly his bowing arm. When he took up his violin, he had difficulty in drawing the bow aross the strings. When he placed the instrument down, the cramps soon disappeared and he was able to use the same muscles in other movements.

Like the other symptoms we have discussed, the hysterical response develops as an avoidance reaction. In the case of the violinist, his symptoms enabled him to stay clear of situations that would generate the anxiety induced by his failure and humiliation. It is relatively common for the hysterical symptoms to be related to the specific event which initially aroused the anxiety. Grinker and Spiegel[23] report in their studies of hysterical symptoms among men under combat during World War II that aviators, for example, suffered from disturbances in depth perception and night vision, whereas paratroopers were more likely to develop paralyzed legs. Writer's cramp, similarly, is commonly found among authors who fail to find sources for publication of their efforts.

As the conditions necessary for avoidance behavior to operate disappear, the symptoms also vanish. A college student developed an intense pain in his back which interfered with his walking between

23 R. R. Grinker and J. P. Spiegel, op. cit.

classes. Since the pain was quite incapacitating, it made locomotion extremely difficult. When he failed in his courses and left school, his condition rapidly improved. In this case his intellectual ability was not up to the demands placed upon him by academic work. Under war conditions, when soldiers are hospitalized, and they are convinced that their return to battle is not imminent, the conditions of a hysterical nature frequently improve rapidly.

It is clear that the reinforcement in hysteria comes from an avoidance of an aversive situation and a reduction of anxiety that that situation has precipitated. This kind of negative reinforcement facilitates learning. When occasions are appropriate and where the conditioned aversive stimuli no longer function, the responses become extinguished. The symptoms disappear, and we say the condition has improved. In the case of the violinist, the cramps appeared only when he took up his bow to play. This was sufficient to protect him from a situation of failure in which anxiety had previously been generated.

As an avoidance reaction, the hysterical symptoms operate very effectively. Janet[24] as early as 1893 observed what he called *"la belle indifférence,"* the indifference that the patient had for his trouble. Unlike the hypochondriac who constantly worries about his aches and pains, his supposed brain tumors, or imagined heart ailments, the hysteric is quite stoic about his difficulty. His symptoms enable him to free himself from an aversive situation and the painful anxiety produced by it.

A distinction ought to be made between hysterical disorders and *malingering*. In malingering anxiety may also be aroused from combat, taking a test for which one is unprepared, or some unpleasant social affair. However, the hysteric does not verbalize the relationship between his difficulty and the situation which set the occasion for it. The malingerer can. In fact the avoidance behavior of the malingerer is strictly at the verbal level. He feigns illness to get out of trouble. A student *says* he is sick to avoid taking an aversive test, or the housewife *says* she has a terrible headache in order to avoid meeting some people she dislikes. There are some people who lie, say they have a pain or some other disability which is nonexistent. Of course there is probably no clear-cut dichotomy between the two kinds of responding. Both are avoidant. Perhaps at one end of the continuum is the deliberate liar, in the middle are those cases in which a person can be temporarily talked out of his ailment (the hypochondriacs, for example), and at the other end are the true hysterics who are convinced of the reality of their symptoms. For this last group, the disorder is as real as if it had its basis in some organic pathology.

*Some Cases of Hysterical Symptoms and Their Treatment Through Modern Behavior Principles (behavior therapy) (see also Chapter 18).*

---

[24] P. Janet, op. cit.

Brady and Lind[25] report the case of a man who developed total hysterical blindness, which had not improved with traditional psychiatric treatment of various sorts over a period of two years. The new behavioral treatment consisted of leading the patient into a small rectangular room and seating him at a desk with his hand placed on a small button mounted in a box. He was told to try and space his responses of button-pressing between 18 and 21 seconds apart. A correctly spaced response (between 18 and 21 seconds) allowed a buzzer to ring (conditioned reinforcement of correctness), while an incorrect response (below 18 seconds or over 21 seconds) merely reset the apparatus for another interval. After practice trials, visual stimuli of varying intensities were introduced into the room. In the first phase the light bulb in back of the patient came on after 18 seconds and went off after 21 seconds. In other words, the correct interval during which the patient was to respond was indicated by the illumination of the bulb—but remember, he was hysterically blind and reported that he could not see. Thus, the patient could greatly improve his score if he could respond to the visual cues presented. In the next set, the light was presented off and on at full intensity. During succeeding sets of trials the illumination was reduced. It was then decided to introduce more difficult visual cues; for example, changing the pattern of flashing lights on a stimulus panel in front of the subject signaled the onset of the proper interval. After this, a panel of various geometrical patterns was placed in front of him. Figure 15–1 shows the range of inter-response times. The bar in black indicates the correct interval. It can be seen that over a period of trials the patient's performance gradually improved, even though greater demands were placed on him to use visual cues. Following this experimental procedure, the patient was reported to be able to read small-case print and to identify geometrical patterns and small objects.

Barrett[26] reports the case of a 38-year-old hospitalized veteran who had developed multiple tics (twitchings) fourteen years ago. He had recently developed spasmodic movements in much of his body. At the time of the experiment, the man's major movements included contractions of the neck, shoulder, chest, with head nodding, bilateral eye blinking, and other facial movements. In the experimental room, the patient sat in a chair that had a large U-shaped magnet attached to the outside of the back. An induction coil rested in a nest of electrical tape strung between the poles of the magnet. When the patient was seated in the chair, the spasmodic movements created a slight movement of the coil in the magnetic field. The current in the moving coil was amplified to

[25] J. P. Brady and D. L. Lind, Experimental analysis of hysterical blindness. In L. P. Ullmann and L. Krasner, op. cit.

[26] B. H. Barrett, Reduction of multiple tics by free operant conditioning methods, *Jour. Nerv. Ment. Dis.*, **135** (1962), 187–195.

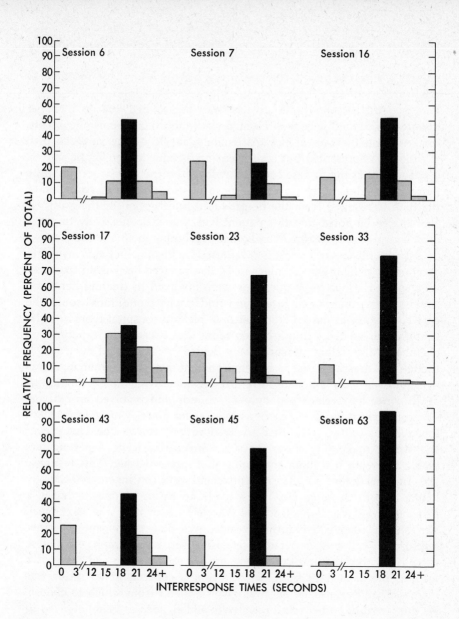

**Figure 15–1.** Relative frequency distributions of interresponse times (IRT) grouped into class intervals of 3 seconds each. Responses falling into 18–21 second interval (black) are reinforced. IRT's between 3- and 12-second intervals (occurring only rarely) have been omitted. (From J. P. Brady, and D. L. Lind, Relative frequency distributions of interresponse times (IRT), *Archives of General Psychiatry,* **4** [1961], 331–339.

operate a sensitive relay. The operations of this relay were recorded as the tics.

Once the baseline rate of tics was determined (64 to 116 per minute), white noise was presented (shhhhhhh) as punishment contingent upon the rate of tics. Alternately, music of the subject's own selection was presented but contingent on a reduction of his tic rate. It was found that the tic rate could be reduced by the production of white noise as punishment. However, the most drastic and reliable reduction of the tic rate resulted from the tic-produced interruption of the music. It should also be noted that this patient had reacted ineffectively to pharmacological (drug) treatment and other psychotherapeutic techniques.

Finally, the last of our cases is reported by Bachrach et al.[27] involving an anorexic patient whose failure to eat had reduced her weight from 120 to 47 pounds. Two basic questions were involved in treating her: how could she be conditioned to eat and under what conditions would she eat? First, she was moved from her own pleasant hospital room with its hospital conveniences into a barren room that became the experimental chamber. All possible pleasures were denied her if she did not eat. Although this drastic change in her environment may seem inhuman, it was thought even more inhuman to return her home with the expectation of death, since her weight was only 47 pounds and involved an extreme state of emaciation. The experimenters set up a series of reinforcement schedules as follows. The first involved verbal reinforcement whenever she would make any movements toward eating. The experimenters would talk with her about something that interested her. This response was further shaped so that reinforcement was contingent on actually lifting a fork, chewing, etc. If she made no eating responses during a meal, nothing was done, and she was left alone until the next meal. Amount of food eaten during a meal was also contingent on other reinforcers: bringing in a radio, television set, phonograph, etc. These extra reinforcers became contingent on her eating more and more of a meal as the days went by. Later, the caloric content of her meals was increased, and eventually she was given a menu from which to choose. As time went on, other reinforcers were added, such as being allowed to eat with other patients of her own choice, being taken on walks around the grounds, etc. Eventually, only actual weight gain could bring about further reinforcement. When she was discharged from the hospital other controls had to be devised because she was still grossly underweight. The cooperation of the family had to be enlisted; they were cautioned not to make an issue out of eating, not to reinforce invalid behavior, never to

[27] A. J. Bachrach, W. J. Erwin, and J. P. Mohr, The control of eating behavior in an anorexic by operant conditioning techniques. In L. P. Ullmann and L. Krasner, eds., *Case studies in behavior modification* (New York: Holt, Rinehart, and Winston, 1965), pp. 152–163.

let her eat alone or discuss any unpleasant subject at mealtime. Three years later she was reported to be maintaining her weight at 78 to 80 pounds and working happily at a university hospital nursery.

## THE EFFECTS OF ALCOHOL AND ALCOHOLISM

The effects of alcohol on human behavior are a function of many variables surrounding the drinking process: the time at which the alcohol is taken, how rapidly it is consumed, the organism's previous history of drinking, the amount consumed at any given time and so forth. Some light can be shed on these effects on behavior from experimental studies with lower animals.

In one study, Sidman[28] investigated the effects of alcohol on timing behavior. Initially, he trained rats to press a lever to receive a drop of water as reinforcement. After the initial conditioning, the rats were required to wait a period of 21 seconds before responding in order to get their reinforcement. If the response was not made within a critical period (it was too short or too long), the reinforcement was withheld. After training in this technique, the animals were able to make fairly accurate temporal discriminations, with the peak of their responding falling between 18 to 21 seconds from the previous response. When the rats were given injections of 3 ml of a 20 per cent ethyl alcohol solution, he found a decline of about 50 per cent in the response rate. However, the alcohol had little effect on the timing behavior. As is commonly observed in humans, alcohol appeared to have a depressing effect on the response rate.

Stebbins, Lundin, and Lyon[29] have studied the effects of alcohol on reaction time in the white rat. After their animals had acquired a simple light-dark discrimination, reaction time training was begun. In this procedure the rats were required to press a lever for food reinforcement within 3 seconds after the onset of a light. Any response that the animals made after that time went unreinforced, and the light was turned off for 30 seconds. After the reaction times had become stabilized at about 1½ seconds following the onset of the light, the animals were injected with a saline solution as a control, alternating with injections of from 2 to 3 ml of a 20 per cent ethyl alcohol solution. The experimenters found that the effect of the alcohol injections was to cause a significant increase in the reaction time from all the animals. However, it had only a slight effect in decreasing the rate of responding. These results have their corollary in human responding. In a situation where an individual after several

[28] H. Sidman, Technique for assessing the effects of drugs on timing behavior, *Science*, **122** (1955), 925.

[29] W. C. Stebbins, R. W. Lundin, and D. Lyon, The effect of alcohol upon reaction time in the white rat, *Psychol. Rec.*, **10** (1960), 15–19.

drinks shows little observable change in his activity (he does not appear tight) before getting into his automobile, the reduction in his reflexes becomes marked when he takes the wheel.

Relative to the effects of alcohol and in particular to alcoholism are the experiments by Masserman and Yum.[30] They found that when cats were placed in a conflict situation (see p. 321), they preferred milk containing alcohol to milk without it. However, when the same cats were removed from the conflict, their preference changed to milk without the alcohol. We have already observed the behavioral disturbances manifested by cats under conflict. They become highly emotional, would crouch in the corner, and displayed a variety of maladaptive behaviors. Under these conditions when the cats were given milk with alcohol in it, the symptoms disappeared, despite the fact that they remained in the conflict situation. As with humans, the person under stress finds relief from his symptoms by means of alcohol.

In another series of experiments, Conger[31] attempted to determine the effects of alcohol on a rat's behavior when placed in a simple approach–avoidance conflict situation. The approach behavior was established by training the rats to run a straight alley for food, with a light as the $S^D$. The rats were then shocked when they started to eat food. This procedure is the same as that described on pages 316–319. After the approach conflict was established, alcohol was administered. All the animals injected with alcohol went to the food and ate it immediately, while none of the controls injected with water would eat. Alcohol had a marked effect of reducing the strength of the avoidance gradient away from the reinforcement.

In a second experiment, Conger[32] trained one group of animals to approach the lighted end of the alley for food; a second group was trained to avoid the lighted end as they were shocked. Half the approach animals were given alcohol. It was found that their behavior differed little from the control "sober" animals in their approach toward the food. When the avoidance animals were divided into "drunk" and "sober" groups, the animals given the alcohol markedly decreased their efforts to avoid the shock. (See Figure 15–2.)

Casey[33] studied the relative intake of an alcohol solution and plain water in rats who were placed in an aversive situation of stress where intermittent electric shocks were programmed on a variable interval

[30] H. Masserman and K. S. Yum, An analysis of the influence of alcohol in experimental neurosis in cats, *Psychosomat. Med.*, **8** (1946), 36–52.

[31] J. J. Conger, The effects of alcohol on conflict behavior in the albino rat, *Quart. Jour. Stud. Alcohol.*, **12** (1951), 1–29.

[32] Ibid.

[33] H. Casey, The effects of stress on the consumption of alcohol, *Quart, Jour, Stud. Alcohol.*, **21** (1960), 208–216.

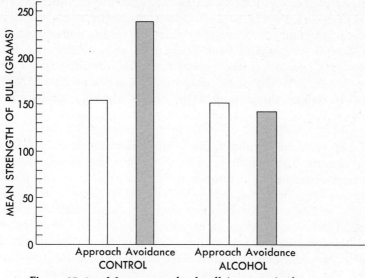

**Figure 15–2.** Mean strength of pull (in grams) of approach and avoidance groups. In typical experiments of this sort, the avoidance gradients appear stronger (control group), but under the influence of alcohol, the avoidance gradient is reduced. The experimental group received injections of alcohol while the control group received injections of water. (From J. J. Conger, The effects of alcohol on conflict behavior in the albino rat, *Quarterly Journal of Studies on Alcohol,* **12** [1951], 1–29, Fig. 2, p. 13. Copyright 1951 by Journal of Studies on Alcohol, Inc., New Brunswick, N.J. Reproduced by permission of the publisher.)

schedule (regardless of what the rats were doing). Under these conditions the rats drank considerably more from the alcohol solution than did the controls. Furthermore, the rats consumed even more alcohol during the following month after the shock situation had been terminated.

### ALCOHOLISM IN HUMANS

The chronic and excessive consumption of alcohol becomes a behavioral disturbance when the drinker can no longer carry on his personal affairs effectively, when drinking interferes with his work and upsets his family relationships. The ordinary reinforcements to be found in business, family, and social activities are abandoned for the reinforcements to be found in alcohol.

Excessive drinking has been interpreted by some as basically an anxiety disorder in which the chronic consumption of alcohol is merely an auxiliary characteristic. Often by accident the chronically anxious person discovers alcohol to be a powerful reinforcer in reducing his anxiety, a condition which he has been unable to accomplish in any other way. Alcoholism has also been interpreted as a compulsive disorder (dipsomania) because of the powerful control the drug has over the imbiber's behavior. The drinking is frequent and repetitive. Anxiety is reduced by taking the drug, but the effects are only temporary. The actual label one cares to attach to the disorder is quite arbitrary.

*The Reinforcers in Alcohol.* From our observations it is clear that alcohol operates as a reinforcer in its own right. First of all, when taken under normal conditions in solution with some other beverage, it satiates a deprived organism. Secondly, its effects, at least with moderate amounts, facilitate verbal behavior and act as an effective social reinforcer. Furthermore, when an organism is placed in a situation where anxiety is aroused, the reinforcing effects appear to be all the more powerful. Not only does it act to reduce the behavioral manifestations of anxiety, but if taken in large enough amounts, it can allow a complete escape from aversive circumstances when the degree of intoxication reaches a state of delirium or even stupor.

For an already disturbed person, then, alcohol acts as a temporary escape in the relief of his symptoms, as well as an avoidance of the events that incite his symptoms. As the alcoholic discovers these reinforcements, a kind of "vicious circle" develops. Following an excessive bout of drinking, the person awakens, feeling miserable. Perhaps he is upset about the overconfidence and irresponsibility manifested the day or night before. Along with his "hangover" these reactions have a punishing effect upon him. As Skinner[34] suggests, if punishment had the opposite effect of positive reinforcement, we might expect as a result of the combination of the two processes (reinforcement and punishment) a moderate or intermediate form of drinking. But such is not the case. Punishment does not extinguish behavior but only suppresses it. Thus the effect of the self-punishment in the form of guilt and shame following the most recent drinking bout is only temporary. The drinker learns that one of the best ways to relieve these aversive consequences is to drink some more. Often a morning "quickie" will reduce much of the misery caused by the events of the night before.

Finally, like other drugs that are used with regularity and then withheld, certain "withdrawal" symptoms result. These symptoms are far more common and pronounced in morphine or heroin but operate at least to a slight degree in alcohol. Similar withdrawal symptoms, although relatively mild, are also seen in the behavior of the chronic coffee drinker or cigarette smoker who suddenly finds himself without a

[34] B. F. Skinner, *Science and human behavior* (New York: Macmillan, Inc., 1953).

source of supply. As a habit-forming drug, alcohol acts much like the others in its increasing power of reinforcement when deprivation arises. As the alcoholic tries to stay away from his drink, he reaches a point in the deprivation process when he can abstain no longer. If the drink is accessible, he takes to his bottle just as surely as a dog will withdraw his leg when it is shocked. Under these circumstances the degree of control the reinforcing drug gains over the organism's behavior is as great as that found in any respondent activity.

The many variables that have contributed to the resulting behavior of chronic and excessive drinking are far from simple. We have enumerated some of the reinforcements to be found in alcoholic consumption and in particular for the individual who is living under conditions of conflict and anxiety. Since alcohol operates so effectively in the relief of anxiety, allowing escape from the aversive conditions of life, it is no wonder that its use is so widespread today.

Can the reformed alcoholic ever return to be a social drinker? Most methods of treating alcoholism such as Alcoholics Anonymous or aversion therapy, mentioned in Chapters 3 and 18, require complete abstinence as the goal of treatment. Yet in our culture there are strong social pressures for social drinking. For many complete abstainers matters become quite difficult for a particular individual. It may require, for example, an immense restriction of one's friends and an elimination of much social activity. Mills et al.[35] have described a technique whereby alcoholics may be conditioned to return to become social drinkers. In their study 13 hospitalized male alcoholics volunteered as subjects for a study to explore whether drinking habits typical of the alcoholic (drinking liquor straight, in large gulps and large amounts) could be changed to drinking typical of social drinkers (drinking mixed drinks, in small sips and in small amounts over a longer period of time). A specially simulated bar was set up at which the subjects sat. During the experimental drinking sessions the subjects could avoid electric shock by drinking in the typical social way, but received painful electric shocks to their fingers which was 30 per cent above their individual pain threshold if they drank in the typical alcoholic way. These contingencies were explained to the subjects beforehand. Four of the subjects emitted the desired behavior from the first day. They never ordered more than three drinks during an experimental session and consumed these in exceedingly small sips. The remaining subects learned the desired behavior over a period of from 12 to 14 sessions.

The question arose of how effective these social drinking patterns would generalize outside the experimental hospital setting. Follow-up studies six weeks later reported that at least five of the subjects had

---

[35] K. C. Mills, M. B. Sobell, and H. H. Schaffer, Training social drinking as an alternate to abstinence in alcoholics, *Behav. Ther.*, **2** (1971), 18–27.

retained the social drinking habits. Others were reported as "improved." The authors also suggest the advisability of additional training sessions or "booster" treatments (like those used in aversion therapy) to maintain the effect achieved in the original experimental sessions.

DRUG ADDICTION

Much has been written about the nature of addiction to opium and its derivatives (morphine, heroin, codeine, etc.). We know that when used medically for nonaddicted persons its effects are to relieve pain and induce sleep if given in large enough amounts. In smaller doses, it may, like alcohol, relieve anxiety and induce a feeling of well-being, without the possible intoxicating effects of alcohol. If used with regularity, as by addicts, it leads to an increased tolerance; consequently, the typical addict uses larger and larger doses in order to achieve the positive reinforcing effects (generally called the "kick"). Furthermore, a genuine physical dependence occurs, which means that when an addict is deprived of his drug, marked symptoms of withdrawal occur, also called the abstinence syndrome. The severity of these symptoms depends on the dosage level one is using, as well as the length of his addiction. Lindesmith[36] points out that there comes a time in the life of the addict when he realizes that he must have the drug to relieve these withdrawal symptoms, and at this point in the process of addiction he is "hooked." At this point the behavioral process is no longer one of taking the drugs for their positive reinforcing effects, but as either escape or avoidance behavior, to relieve the aversive symptoms once they have occurred (escape) or to avoid their onset. The withdrawal symptoms include yawning, tearing at the eyes, nasal discharge, vomiting, tremors, cramps, gooseflesh, muscle twitching, diarrhea, elevated body temperature. The more operant kinds of responses are largely centered around the addict's behavior toward obtaining the drug. These can be expressed verbally in terms of demands and craving. Other responses may include threatening suicide, violence, or an exaggeration of the distress pattern. The addict frequently curls up in a corner with a blanket wrapped around him.

*Experimental Studies.* Spragg[37] observed withdrawal symptoms in chimpanzees after they had developed a tolerance for morphine following frequent and regular injections. Prior to being given the drug, these animals had been trained to solve a series of stick-and-box problems with food as the reinforcement. When given access to a syringe with morphine (prior to addiction), the animals did poorly. However, when

[36] A. R. Lindesmith, *Opiate addiction* (Bloomington, Ind.: Principia Press, 1947).
[37] S. D. S. Spragg, Morphine addiction in chimpanzees, *Comp. Psychol. Monogr.*, **15** (1940), 1–132.

the chimps had developed a tolerance for the drug from regular injections and when the drug was withdrawn, the performance in the two situations was reversed. They did poorly for the food, but solved the problems successfully to receive an injection of the drug. These animals also displayed other withdrawal symptoms similar to those observed in human addicts. Furthermore, they assumed postures similar to those associated with morphine injections (holding out the arm, pointing to the arm where the needle was to be injected). Following recovery from the withdrawal symptoms, the animals again reversed their behavior patterns to the preaddiction level.

In a more recent experiment by Weeks,[38] which somewhat resembled the human situation of addiction, rats and monkeys developed a degree of tolerance and physical dependence on morphine. A tube, placed in the vein of each animal, was connected to an injection machine. Each animal had free access of movement in his experimental chamber. Whenever he pressed a pedal at the side of the cage, he automatically received an injection of the drug as reinforcement. Prior to actual experimentation, for the drug to take on reinforcing properties a tolerance first had to be developed. This was done by injecting him with morphine at specified regular intervals with gradually increasing doses. Then the automatic injections were stopped, and the animal had to press the pedal in order to receive an injection. Soon the animals were observed to press the pedal at regular intervals, once every hour or so. When the dose was reduced with each succeeding press, the rate of responding increased in order that the animals could get enough of the drug to "maintain their habit." When the supply of drugs was cut off completely, the rate increased at first and then gradually tapered off (extinction) until the withdrawal symptoms began to appear. The behavior changes resembled in many ways those found in human addicts. They became agitated, breathing was more rapid, and they tried to escape from their cages. By the end of 12 hours, they were very "sick" animals, but a single injection of morphine completely eliminated their symptoms.

In a second experiment Weeks[39] set up a ratio schedule of reinforcement so that the rats had to press the pedal a designated number of times in order to receive the injection. FR schedules started at FR 10 and then increased to FR 20, FR 50, FR 75, FR 150, etc. As the ratios were increased so did the response rate. In a variation of this experiment, the same ratio was maintained, but the amount of drug was gradually decreased. As the dosage was cut each day, the rate increased so that the actual number of injections was also increased over a period of time. Finally, very small doses failed to have a sufficient reinforcing effect, and

---

[38] J. R. Weeks, Experimental narcotic addiction, *Scient. Amer.*, **210**, no. 3 (1964), 46–52.
[39] Ibid.

the rate dropped off. It seems clear from these studies that for both animals and man, opiates such as morphine or heroin have a strong reinforcing function once a dependence has been developed.

In drugs like the opiates, when taken over a period of time, a physical or psysiological dependence occurs which is evidenced by the withdrawal distress the person exhibits when his drugs are suddenly withdrawn, as when a source of supply is cut off or he decides to "kick the habit" because it is becoming too expensive. On the other hand, there are a number of drugs frequently used in the population today by high school and college students that do not develop in the user any physical dependence—drugs like cocaine or marijuana. Yet in these latter cases one may develop a psychological or "behavioral" dependence. Obviously, in these cases some kinds of reinforcements are involved.

Cahoon and Crosby[40] have suggested the following possible reinforcements that operate to strengthen the behavior of drug taking and usage. In other words, the behavior of taking drugs obviously involves learning. The reinforcements, will, of course, depend to some degree on the particular drugs involved.

The following possibilities are suggested:

1. Positive reinforcement in which the reinforcements are primarily social. By this is meant the reinforcement of approval of the community of drug users.
2. Positive reinforcement as a direct effect of the drug. The reinforcement is usually a private one and may be only described verbally as a "feeling of euphoria," "good," "high." Although this kind of reinforcement appears in the opiates, it obviously holds true for such drugs as marijuana, alcohol, amphetamines, and cocaine, which do not develop physiological dependence.
3. Negative reinforcement involving aversive external stimuli. In this sense the drug user removes himself, either allowing him to escape or avoid noxious stimuli in his environment. Typical examples here would be the excessive use of alcohol which removes one from the aversive conditions of his environment, as in solitary drinking. Most often an addict to heroin or morphine takes his drugs in privacy.
4. Negative reinforcement involving "internal" aversive stimuli. The best example here is the use of the opiates which are often taken, as we suggested before, by the addict to ward off the aversive characteristics of the withdrawal symptoms. These can be described by any addict as extremely painful. Other possibilities involving nonphysiologically dependent drugs might involve relief of anxiety or fatigue. A tired businessman comes home and takes several drinks to get a "lift," or a person who has gone through an intensely anxiety-arous-

[40] D. D. Cahoon and C. Crosby, A learning approach to chronic drug use: Sources of reinforcement, *Behav. Ther.*, **2** (1972), 64–71.

ing experience finds that many drugs will relax his muscle tensions, which are part of the anxiety response.

## THE NEUROTIC PARADOX

In the light of our knowledge of reinforcement, the question of the "neurotic paradox" is not difficult to answer. You will recall Mowrer's[41] statement of the neurotic paradox as behavior that is self-perpetuating and at the same time self-defeating. We have restated the question as follows: Why does the neurotic continue to manifest his symptoms which appear to us on the outside to be punishing rather than reinforcing?

The neurotic paradox implies that behavior is operating at a high rate which not only goes unreinforced but is also punishing. From our experimental observations we have learned that withholding a reinforcement leads to the extinction of the response. Furthermore, if we add a punishment to the extinction process, the response should not only continue to weaken but be depressed as well. The behavior of the neurotic does neither. Either we must find out what reinforcements keep the neurotic's behavior operating at a high rate or abandon the principle at least in part and say that the neurotic is not operating under the same principles of learning that apply to normal people. In his interpretation of the fixated behavior of rats, Maier[42] has suggested the latter interpretation, but this explanation has been subject to considerable criticism. Before we abandon the principle of reinforcement in explaining the learning of neurotic symptoms and accept Maier's suggestion, let us pursue the problem and see how reinforcement could operate in maintaining neurotic behavior.

The first step in explaining the persistence of a behavior that is apparently unreinforcing and punishing as well (neurotic paradox) is to realize that the neurotic is somewhat limited in the behaviors that can achieve reinforcement. When placed in a situation of frustration where reinforcements are blocked or withheld, a normal person with an adequate behavior repertoire will find some alternate solution by making use of some previously acquired responses. Similarly, when placed in a conflict, the normal person attempts to resolve his conflict or escape from it. Neither of these alternatives seems to be available for the neurotic. In his behavioral development, somewhere along the line he "got stuck." Mowrer[43] suggests that the neurotic can go neither forward nor backward. He suffers from a learning deficit, one which he is unable to correct. In other words, the neurotic lacks adequate behavior which would allow him to resolve his conflicts and overcome his frustrations.

However, this is only the first step. It explains why the neurotic does

---

[41] O. H. Mowrer, op. cit.

[42] N. R. F. Maier, *Frustration: A study of behavior without a goal* (New York: McGraw-Hill, 1949).

[43] O. H. Mowrer, op. cit.

not select alternative reinforcements. He lacks the appropriate behavior to attain them. It does not tell us why the neurotic continues to respond sometimes at a high rate when no appropriate reinforcement seems to be forthcoming but, rather, only punishment. The answer is, of course, that the behavior of the neurotic *is reinforced*. What the reinforcements happen to be in an interesting question. What, for example, is the reinforcement for a compulsive handwasher who continues to scrub his hands, even though they are painfully cracked and bleeding? Why does the hysteric perpetuate his paralysis or seizures when they limit his social activities and keep him a dependent invalid? What is the reinforcement for the alcoholic who is so sick the next morning after a drinking bout that he wants to die? The answer to these questions is that the neurotic is reinforced because his symptoms allow him to escape or avoid an aversive stimulus, either primary or secondary. By the elimination of these aversive stimuli and the reduction of anxiety that they generate (as well as that generated from his own behavior), the reinforcing effects are far more powerful than the punishing consequences of his acts. The phobic person avoids all generalized stimuli that would initiate anxiety, despite the limitations this avoidance behavior places on him. In his actions he is "safe" from the threats of the stimuli he fears. Through the compulsive's acts and rituals, he is able to reduce, albeit temporarily, the anxiety generated by the surrounding stimuli. He can avoid them only through his repetitious acts. Similarly, the hysteric's paralysis enables him to keep safe from the punishing effects of the trauma that may have threatened him. As long as the conditioned aversive stimuli remain and set the occasion for the avoidance behavior, the reinforced behavior is not extinguished. As long as the threat of combat remains, the paralysis protects the hysteric from it. The many reinforcements for the alcoholic in his escape and avoidance behavior are sufficient to perpetuate a drinking response besides the positive reinforcements ordinarily found in alcohol.

## Summary

Finding negative reinforcement in his symptoms, the neurotic persists in his behavior. His previous history of conflict, frustration, and conditioning in anxiety and punishment have limited the development of behavior that would be more positively reinforcing for people with different developmental histories.

In this chapter we have seen how neurotic behavior is developed and maintained. The principles of learning that apply to the acquisition of neurotic symptoms also apply to learning of the many other operant and respondent activities shared by a majority of people. The differences between neurotic and normal responses lie in the stimulus conditions precipitating them, as well as the reinforcement contingencies perpetuating them. In some cases the neurotic's reactions are merely an exaggeration of what we would consider normal. The point at which one can draw a line between these maladaptive responses and the normal is quite arbitrary. In his symptomatic behavior the neurotic often fails to find what most people would judge to be the more appropriate reinforcements. The adoptive responses that are effectively reinforced in normal behaving do not appear available for the neurotic. Because of the many difficulties arising in the developmental process of the neurotic, he has failed to learn the most efficient and effective ways of responding, at least according to the standards set by the majority of the population. The neurotic's responses are judged inadequate, largely because most people behave otherwise. That is to say, he responds to a different set of discriminative stimuli and is reinforced by what is normally believed to be less appropriate rewards.

# 16 Psychotic Behavior

IN THE PRECEDING CHAPTER WE DISCUSSED a series of behavioral changes that have traditionally been classified as neurotic. These behaviors are considered abnormal because they usually lead to difficulties for the person manifesting them or for others around him. When the changes appear to be more marked and become increasingly more troublesome and dangerous, the behavior has customarily been called *psychotic*, although there is no clear line of demarcation between the two classes. As a matter of fact, Redlich[1] suggests that the distinction between neurotic and psychotic behavior is not based on any scientific differentiation of the disorders themselves but on a differentiation of the social responses people make to them. For example, psychiatrists have usually asserted that the psychotic patient should be hospitalized but the neurotic need not be. A survey of the kinds of disorders manifested by patients residing in most mental hospitals, excluding those for mental retardation, finds that the vast majority of institutionalized patients are classified as psychotic.

For legal convenience a psychotic is considered (1) not socially responsive to others, (2) not morally responsible for his actions, and (3) in need of help.[2] The first two criteria ordinarily do not

---

[1] F. C. Redlich, Some sociological aspects of the psychoses. In *Theory and treatment of the psychoses: Some newer aspects* (St. Louis: Washington University, 1956).
[2] Ibid.

apply to neurotics. As a result of such legal distinctions a person is judged either sane or insane. If he is judged insane, he becomes a charge of society because he is no longer responsible or capable of carrying on his affairs.

## DIFFERENCES AS TO THE NATURE AND CAUSES OF PSYCHOTIC BEHAVIOR

In the last half of the nineteenth century, when serious attempts were first being made to understand behavioral disorders, a "mental disease'" approach predominated. This was an advance over earlier notions which had considered the mentally ill to be morally degraded or "possessed" by some unseen force. A "mental disease" theory arose naturally as a parallel to the notion of physical disease. Like the common cold, one had a mental disorder or he did not have it. When infection was present, symptoms were obviously manifested. As one recovered, the symptoms subsided and he was judged well. The basic difference between the two was that the mind was diseased instead of the body.

Like some physical disorders in which an inherited weakness may pre-dispose one to disease, psychotic behavior could result from a variety of different inherited dispositions, differing according to the disorder. Today such a viewpoint is strongly fostered by men like Kallmann.[3] The disorders run in families and appear to follow the same Mendelian laws that influence the inheritance of other traits like eye color or bodily build. Precisely what is inherited is not identified. The fact that a disposition to some disorder *is* inherited seems to be satisfactory enough. The manic-depressive would inherit a disposition different from that of the schizophrenic.

Among behavior pathologists, Kallmann takes probably the most extreme hereditary point of view. However, many researchers in this field raise serious objections to his interpretations. For example, the validity of his diagnoses is often questionable, since he has included many so-called doubtful cases. Furthermore he has depended too often on anecdotal evidence, and environmental variables have been almost completely ignored. It is a common clinical observation, for example, that the mental illness of a parent, whether it be mild or severe, can have a marked effect on the offspring raised in the unhealthy environment.[4]

A related view fostered by Cobb[5] attempts to be more specific. The cause of a disorder lies in some hidden lesion of the brain or in some hereditary defect that will be (or should be) manifested in a structural abnormality, a metabolic disturbance, or a pathological biochemical con-

---

[3] F. J. Kallmann, *The genetics of schizophrenia* (New York: Augustin, 1938).

[4] N. Cameron and A. Magaret, *Behavior pathology* (Boston: Houghton Mifflin, 1951), 31.

[5] S. Cobb, Contemporary problems in psychiatry. In *Theory and treatment of the psychoses: Some newer aspects* (St. Louis: Washington University, 1956).

dition. Different diseases are supposed to arise from the particular location of a lesion or special chemical condition of the blood. Even if the
general viewpoint is simple and intriguing in attempting to show close
cause-effect relationships between physiological and behavioral conditions, the evidence is not very conclusive. Although it is quite evident in
many organic psychotic conditions that brain disturbances and physiological deficiencies participate, no such evidence is available for the
functional psychoses or neuroses. Cobb has suggested that brain disturbances are the causes of neurotic behavior, lesions not yet having been
discovered. Furthermore, Kantor[6] has surveyed much clinical evidence in
which marked brain damage and extirpation has occurred without any
appreciable changes in behavior.

Such approaches pay little attention to the environmental variables
involved. Among those to stress a more "psychogenic" view of behavior
disorders were Sigmund Freud and Adolph Meyer. Although they both
stressed the importance of events in a person's past, their explanations
were very different. Freud,[7] of course, gave a mentalistic explanation of
the problem; the causes of a person's difficulty originated in a disordered
psyche. For example, as early as 1896 he reported a case of "chronic
paranoia" which he believed to be a defense against childhood sexual
memories and homosexual fantasies. Adolph Meyer,[8] although a brain
pathologist, believed that behavioral disturbances were disorders of the
entire personality of an individual and had their origin in his social
environment.

Following Meyer's initial lead, Cameron[9] has more recently stressed
the many possible independent variables in a person's life history that
can account for the marked and deviant behavioral changes. These include early family relationships, excessive conflict and frustration, punishment, and training in anxiety. As a result of these various conditions,
a person frequently fails to acquire adequate "social roles." One may interpret this as a failure to react to other people as conditioned reinforcers.
Some verification of this notion can be found in the studies of Lindsley.[10]
By using operant conditioning techniques in which mental patients pulled
a plunger to receive candy, nickels, pictures of nudes, seeing a kitten fed,
and other conditioned reinforcers, he found that many of the patients
failed to respond to these stimuli in the same way as his normal controls.

[6] J. R. Kantor, *Problems in physiological psychology* (Bloomington, Ind.: Principia
Press, 1947), chapters xv and xvi.

[7] S. Freud, Further remarks on the defense neuropsychoses. In *Collected Papers*,
vol. I (International Psychoanalytic Press, 1924; first published in Germany, 1896).

[8] A. Meyer, The psychobiological point of view. In M. Bentley and E. Cowdry,
eds., *The problem of mental disorders* (New York: McGraw-Hill, 1934).

[9] N. Cameron, *The psychology of behavior disorders* (Boston: Houghton Mifflin
1947).

[10] O. R. Lindsley, Operant conditioning methods applied to research in chronic
schizophrenia, *Psychiat. Res. Rep.*, 5 (1956), 104–153.

Viewpoints that stress the study of entire behavioral development of an individual along with those conditions in his past and present environment which participate in particular behavioral manifestations, are bound to find the differences between neurotic and psychotic or between normal and disordered behavior to be more quantitative than qualitative. According to Skinner:

> Modes of behavior characteristic of mental disease may be simply the result of a history of reinforcement, an unusual condition of deprivation or satiation, or an emotionally exciting circumstance. Except for the fact that they are troublesome or dangerous, they may not be distinguishable from the rest of the behavior of an individual.[11]

What, then, is psychotic behavior? Although medical classifications of behavioral disturbances are helpful for practical purposes in preserving society from the excessive aggressions of a manic or in helping the schizophrenic by caring for and treating him, they have not gone far enough in the basic analysis of the behavior itself. What we do end up with is a number of behavioral manifestations that appear to be at variance with the normal. The answer is to be found in the experimental analysis of psychotic behavior and the discovery of the conditions which have led up to it. We then should understand, for example, why some psychotics do not respond to the same reinforcements that most normal people do, or why one disturbed person responds to stimuli generally considered aversive as though they were positively reinforcing. If the psychotic is "out of stimulus control," which means that he is no longer reacting to the usual controlling stimuli from his environment, how did this change come about?

At the present time, steps are being taken to analyze under controlled experimental conditions the behavior of those individuals called psychotic (see subsequent text). As Skinner suggests:

> At least we can say: this is what the psychotic subject did under these (experimental) circumstances, and this is what he failed to do under circumstances which would have had a different effect had he not been psychotic.[12]

The remainder of this chapter will be devoted to two approaches to the analysis of psychotic behavior. The first is the traditional one, based on the commonly accepted categories of medical classification. It has resulted from the accumulation over the years of many diverse theories

[11] B. F. Skinner, Psychology in the understanding of mental disease. In *Integrating the approaches to mental disease* (New York: Hoeber, 1957).

[12] B. F. Skinner, What is psychotic behavior? In *Theory and treatment of the psychoses: Some newer aspects* (St. Louis: Washington University, 1956), 98.

and observations. Although unsatisfactory to many, the analysis has remained through lack of a better one to replace it. The second approach is based on the controlled observation of psychotic individuals under experimental conditions. This research is based on operant conditioning techniques. The results so far are significant in contributing to a more valid analysis of psychotic behavior.

TRADITIONAL INTERPRETATIONS OF PSYCHOTIC BEHAVIOR

Psychiatric classifications ordinarily distinguish between two main groups of psychotic disorders, *functional* and *organic*. The organic can be most readily identified as involving (usually) some damage or change in functioning of the central nervous system. Accompanying these are numerous behavioral disturbances such as loss of reflexive function, muscle paralyses, anesthesias, seizures, or impairment in sense organ functioning. In addition to these, one often observes impairment in learning, difficulty in remembering recent events, and a general inefficiency in interacting with one's environment. These symptoms are commonly found in disorders of aging, cerebrosyphilis, or chronic alcoholic deterioration. Many theorists assume a direct cause-effect relationship between the amount of the organic damage and the behavioral change.[13]

Others suggest that although the central nervous system obviously is involved, the inability of the brain to operate efficiently is simply one of a number of participating conditions.[14] For example, if we consider acute alcoholic intoxication to be a behavioral disturbance, we shall observe that the person becomes increasingly less coordinated, with marked disorganization of his verbal responding as the amount of alcohol taken increases. If the alcoholic content of the blood becomes high enough, a stuporous condition may result. However, there are happy drunks, sad drunks, funny drunks, and hostile drunks. The special behavioral characteristics are presumably related in some way to the previous conditioning history of the organism before he started taking the drug. The specific manifestations of behavioral change in other organic disturbances would also be related to earlier conditions. Some senile psychotics are extremely suspicious and paranoid; others are more disorganized; still others may be elated or depressed. The specific organic involvements themselves can hardly account for the marked individual differences in behavior which result. Although there are marked variations in the behavioral manifestations among people classified as to the *same* organic psychosis, the system of classification only includes some readily identifiable changes in organic

[13] S. Cobb, *Foundations of neuropsychiatry* (Baltimore: Williams & Wilkins, 1952).
[14] N. Cameron, The functional psychoses. In J. McV. Hunt, ed., *Personality and the behavior disorders* (New York: Ronald Press, 1944).

functioning in which behavior may occur to the disadvantage of the person.

The functional disorders are even less easily identified. They are called *functional* because organic involvements are not so apparent, although some insist that changes in some kind of internal functioning, whether it be the brain or central nervous system or blood chemistry,[15] must be implied. The official classification of the American Psychiatric Association seems to be based on convenience, little more. One will seldom find in the wards of a mental hospital any case in which the patient typifies the general descriptions of symptoms. For example, the manic is supposed to be elated, but there are manics in which episodes of sadness and helplessness are evident. Schizophrenia is characterized by withdrawal and disorganization, but some schizophrenics are highly aggressive at times as well as lucid at other times.

If one takes the position that these psychotic behaviors arise out of an extremely complex history of unusual conditioning, each person will exhibit symptoms very different from those of the next person. The specific manifestations constitute his own special behavior equipment. Symptoms are shared between patients (consequently classified alike) to the degree that they must have shared something in common in their earlier conditioning histories. Precisely what these events are is often not known. If, however, we are ever going to understand the exact nature of mental disorders, the variables that have participated in the behavioral changes must be identified.

> Causal factors important in understanding mental disease are, however, to be found among the independent variables to which the psychologist characteristically turns. An excessive emotional condition, a dangerous mode of escape from anxiety, a troublesome preoccupation with sex, or an excessive enthusiasm for gambling may be nothing more than extreme cases of the effects of environmental conditions.[16]

### SCHIZOPHRENIA

As the most common of all behavioral disorders, schizophrenia (formerly called *dementia praecox*) has been typified by its early onset, usually in late adolescence or early adulthood. The main expressions of the behavioral disturbances have included excessive withdrawal (escape and avoidance) and marked disorganizations of behavior, including hallucinations and delusions. Emil Kraepelin, in his encyclopedic *Psychiatrie:*

---

[15] S. Cobb, Personality as affected by lesions in the brain. In J. McV. Hunt, ed., *Personality and the behavior disorders* (New York: Ronald Press, 1944).

[16] B. F. Skinner, Psychology in the understanding of mental disease. In *Integrating the approaches to mental disease* (New York: Hoeber, 1957).

*ein Lehrbuch fur Studierende und Arate* (4 vols.)[17] classified the disorder into four subtypes, a division which holds today in most psychiatric circles: (1) dementia simplex, (2) hebephrenia, (3) catatonia, and (4) paranoia. Ever since its identification as a behavioral disorder, psychologists and psychiatrists have theorized as to the causes of schizophrenia. Kraepelin[18] favored an organic interpretation, as did Bleuler.[19] However, being strongly influenced by Freud and his psychological interpretations, Bleuler placed additional emphasis on the importance of disordered associations. At least from a descriptive point, the verbalizations and other motor behavior of the schizophrenic are frequently fragmentary, without apparent connection. Consequently, his speech is often incomprehensible.

We have already mentioned Kallmann, who has stressed a strong hereditary origin of the disorder. This opinion has had strong support in the medical profession. As early as 1911 Freud[20] interpreted schizophrenia as a regression to an infantile period of libidinal attachments. The regression was a strong defense against external and internal threats on the personality. This approach has led to the "regression hypothesis" which is still popular[21] in some psychiatric circles. It has been commonly observed, for example, that the hebephrenic type exhibits considerable childishness and silliness in his giggling and facial mannerisms. The catatonic type, in his stuporous withdrawal, assumes prenatal postures. Other behavioral interpretations like those of Meyer,[22] Cameron,[23] and Lundin[24] have placed importance on the particular life history of conditioning a person has had as the basis for the behavioral difficulties. The fact that so many diverse opinions and theories as to the origin of the disorder exist today is clear evidence that the variables that have participated in the development of the trouble are poorly identified, if at all.

*Types of Schizophrenia.*   There are four types of schizophrenia:

1. Dementia simplex or the simple type. The simple type was not in Kraepelin's original group but was added by Bleuler and later accepted by Kraepelin. It is called "simple" because of its absence of gross

[17] E. Kraepelin, *Psychiatrie: ein Lehrbuch fur Studierende und Arate*, 4 vols. (Leipzig: Barth, 1909–1913).

[18] Ibid.

[19] E. Bleuler, *Dementia praecox oder Gruppe der Schizophrenen* (Leipzig: Deuticke, 1911).

[20] S. Freud, Psychoanalytic notes upon an autobiographical account of a case of paranoia (dementia praecox). In *Collected papers*, vol. III. (London: Hogarth, 1928; first published in Germany, 1911.)

[21] N. Cameron, op. cit.

[22] A. Meyer, The nature and conception of dementia praecox, *Jour. Abn. Soc. Psychol.*, **21** (1910), 385–403.

[23] N. Cameron, *The psychology of behavior disorders* (Boston: Houghton Mifflin, 1947).

[24] R. W. Lundin, *Principles of psychopathology* (Columbus: Merrill Books, 1965).

behavioral manifestations. As is characteristic of many schizophrenics, the simple type is quite withdrawn. He will speak when spoken to but seldom adds anything more. He may sit and stare into space for hours. A second characteristic is extreme emotional apathy. He is generally emotionally unresponsive to his environment. Unlike the other types, the simple schizophrenic does not exhibit delusions (false beliefs) or hallucinations (false sensory perceptions).

2. The hebephrenic type is often referred to as the "dump basket" of schizophrenics. Often, if a person does not seem to fit into any of the other types, he may be classified as hebephrenic. The textbooks typically describe the hebephrenic as regressive and silly, indeed, childlike. Often he is extremely disorganized in his behavior. This becomes particularly apparent in chronic cases.

3. The catatonic type manifests itself in either (or both) of two ways: catatonic excitement and catatonic stupor. In the stuporous type he appears completely unresponsive to his environment, is mute, and will simply curl up in a chair (or on the floor), assuming a fetal posture. He also often expresses other bizarre postures. In catatonic excitement there is gross hyperactivity and strong disorganization in overt behavior and speech. However, with the current tranquilizing drugs, the aggressive, hard-to-manage behavior is reduced, so the patient can usually be easily handled.

4. The paranoid type is most typified by strong delusions, although they may be found in the other types, except for the simple type. The delusions are usually of persecution and grandeur. In the early stages, the delusions may be quite systematized; that is, even though they are false beliefs, they follow some order. Plots may be laid against the person; people are spying on him or stealing his property. In the cases of delusions of grandeur he may consider himself a person with tremendous talents, or a great inventor, or a personage of royal blood.

## MANIC AND DEPRESSIVE DISORDERS

In his *Lehrbuch*, Kraepelin[25] identified 20 varieties of the "manic-depressive insanity." The two main phases, mania and depression, could appear separately within an individual or follow each other in various cycles. Manic excitement and depression as behavioral disorders follow the principle of exaggeration quite clearly. As we observe the behavior, we are impressed with the fact that milder or less extreme reactions normally follow certain operations of presenting or withholding conditioned reinforcers. When a conditioned reinforcer, after being absent, is presented following a response, behavior that is excitable, joyful, and elated is expressed. Likewise, in the process of extinction when certain

[25] E. Kraepelin, op. cit.

conditioned reinforcers are withheld, we express sorrow, sadness, or dejection.[26]

Often, however, in exaggerated manic excitement the episode of elation follows a piece of bad news, the loss of a job, or some other event that ordinarily would lead to despondency. Cameron[27] suggests that the behavior may actually be a *compensation*, or what Freud called a *reaction formation*. The person behaves in a manner opposite to what he feels as an attempt to reduce his anxiety. In his excitement the maniac is described as highly excited, distractable, overactive, with a high level of verbal behavior. At times he may become irritable and aggressive, particularly when his behavior is thwarted or blocked.

Extreme forms of depression have been observed since the time of Hippocrates (see Chapter 1), who called it *melancholia* and included it among the four temperaments. More recently, Farrar[28] described it as a "lowness of spirits without fever." In severe forms the patient is described as deeply dejected, inactive, with delusions of worthlessness, although others express more agitation and anxiety.

The kinds of hypotheses offered to account for the causes of the disorder are similar to those found for schizophrenia. Kraepelin[29] suggested a disturbance in metabolic functioning. Kallmann[30] reports the best evidence of hereditary mechanisms working in all behavioral disorders. Those more psychologically minded look for the origins in conditions giving rise to chronic anxiety.[31] Events such as financial loss, sudden death of a loved one, or even physical trauma often precipitate the onset of an episode. This interpretation is not out of line with our discussion of extinction in Chapter 3.

An interesting phenomenon is occurring on the American scene today with regard to manic and depressive disorders. They are less commonly found in mental hospitals today than they were 20 or 30 years ago. In fact many psychiatrists report that a "good" manic is hard to find any more. If this is the case, how are we to account for the gradual disappearance of the manic-depressive psychosis (particularly the manic form)? Although no strong evidence is available, some interesting hypotheses are possible. Perhaps many individuals classified as manics in earlier years are now being categorized into other disorders such as schizophrenia. Such an interpretation gives weight to the inadequacy of our present classification system. It is also possible that many maniacs and depressives are no longer hospitalized. With more recent advances in drug therapy (tranquilizers, for example), patients are treated at home.

[26] F. S. Keller and W. N. Schoenfeld, *Principles of psychology* (New York: Appleton-Century-Crofts, 1950).

[27] N. Cameron, op. cit.

[28] C. Farrar, Some origins in psychiatry, *Amer. Jour. Insan.*, **64** (1908), 523–552.

[29] E. Kraepelin, op. cit.

[30] F. Kallmann, *Heredity in health and medicine* (New York: Norton, 1953).

[31] N. Cameron, op. cit.

Finally, it is possible that the disorder is a cultural phenomenon, being somehow affected by the conditions that exist in a society during any particular era. For example, one no longer sees or hears of the "dancing mania" or tarantism common in Italy and Spain during the seventeenth century.[32] Nor do ladies of good breeding so commonly faint as they did during the Victorian era.

In a similar vein, we no longer find cases of *lycanthropy* in our mental hospitals today. This disorder, in which an individual believed himself turned into a wolf, was reportedly common during the Middle Ages. Since the threats of wolves are no longer with us, the disorder has vanished. There is no question that the delusional behavior of psychotics reflects the events of the times. Today, deluded psychotics are more likely to believe themselves affected by atomic fall-out, television waves, or X-rays.

Further evidence of the broad influence of environmental factors in behavior disorders comes from a study by Opler[33] who investigated two groups of males who had been hospitalized and all diagnosed as schizophrenic. Half the men (30) were directly of Irish descent, more particularly, the south of Ireland; the other half were of direct Italian descent. Both groups were matched for mean age, education, general intellectual level, and time spent in the hospital. The patterning of symptoms in each group showed a relationship to the family cultural patterning. In the majority of the Irish group their homosexuality was latent and repressed, expressed mostly in fantasy. The Italians' homosexuality was much more overtly expressed. They expressed considerable hostility toward their fathers and brothers. In the Irishmen, sexuality in general was more inhibited. Furthermore, they were tormented with feelings of guilt over sex, whereas the Italians were not. The Italians showed far more temper tantrums and emotional outbursts, attempts to destroy property, assault with suicidal tendencies; they were more difficult to manage. In contrast, the Irish were more passive, compliant, and withdrawn; they were quiet, anxious, and fearful. Two-thirds of the Irish group had also been considered alcoholic before hospitalization. Although the Italians drank, only one member of their group had been considered alcoholic.

Although it was not an experimental investigation in the strict sense, this study does illustrate the effects of cultural background as reflected in the family conditioning, and how behavioral disorders are influenced by discriminative stimuli in the environment.

Until recently, no systematic experimental analysis of psychotic behavior has been attempted. The present system of classification suffers from the same resistance to change as do many of our attitudes and

[32] R. W. Lundin, *An objective psychology of music*, rev. ed. (New York: Ronald Press, 1967).

[33] M. K. Opler, Schizophrenia and culture, *Scient. Amer.*, **157**, no. 2 (1957).

prejudices. Few experimental controls have ever been exercised in attempts to analyze precisely how psychotic behavior has developed. As the techniques of operant conditioning have proved themselves to be valid tools for analysis, it has become apparent that these techniques can also be applied to the study of psychotic behavior.

## Operant Conditioning and the Study of Psychotic Behavior

Prior to 1954 the application of careful experimental analysis to the study of abnormal behavior had largely been limited to animals. Although useful in contributing to our understanding of behavioral difficulties, animal studies have their limitations in this area, as we have already noted. In 1954 Skinner, Solomon, and Lindsley[34] described a technique whereby the analysis of behavioral abnormalities in the human could be made under controlled experimental conditions so that the changes in behavior which might occur following the experimental operations could be carefully measured and observed. These results with patients diagnosed as psychotic could then be compared to those individuals considered to be normal.

The technique is an adaptation of that first described by Skinner.[35] In applying this experimental procedure to human psychotics, who often manifest behavioral disturbances at the time of experimentation, a number of changes had to be made from Skinner's basic bar press for the rat's receiving reinforcement of food.

In Lindsley's procedure,[36] subjects are placed in soundproofed experimental rooms which can be easily cleaned and are not likely to be destroyed by the more aggressive patients. Opportunity for one-way observation from the outside is necessary so that the experimenter can note qualitative changes in behavior which may not be directly measured by the recording devices at hand. Each room is furnished with a chair, plastic ash tray, and a response mechanism (called a manipulandum) as well as a dispenser for whatever reinforcement may be delivered (see Figures 16–1 and 16–2). Instead of the traditional lever used with lower organisms for responding, an apparatus resembling a candy dispensing machine is in front of the subject. This consists of a plunger made of iron and brass that can be pulled at rates up to 10,000 times per hour. Reinforcements are delivered according to whatever schedule happens to

---

[34] B. F. Skinner, H. C. Solomon, and O. R. Lindsley, A new method for the experimental analysis of the behavior of psychotic patients, *Jour. Nerv. Ment. Dis.*, **120** (1954), 403–406.

[35] B. F. Skinner, On the rate of formation of a conditioned reflex, *Jour. Gen. Psychol.*, **7** (1932), 274–285.

[36] O. R. Lindsley, Operant conditioning methods applied to research in chronic schizophrenia, *Psychiat. Res. Rep.*, **5** (1956), 140–153.

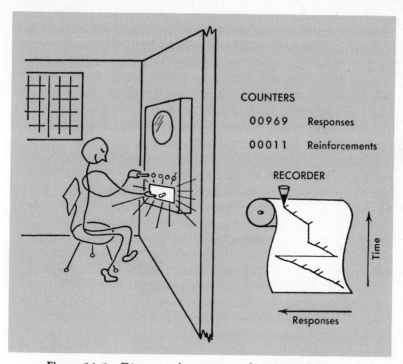

COUNTERS

00969   Responses

00011   Reinforcements

RECORDER

Time

Responses

**Figure 16–1.** Diagram of experimental room used for operant conditioning in human psychotic patients. Various kinds of reinforcements can be delivered (candy, cigarettes, nickels, etc.) when subject pulls plunger (called a manipulandum). (From O. R. Lindsley, Operant conditioning methods applied to research in chronic schizophrenia, *Psychiatric Research Reports,* No. 5, American Psychiatric Assn., June 1956.)

be in operation during a given experimental session. Ordinarily, subjects are placed in the experimental rooms for one hour per day, five days a week. Since the laboratory is operated in conjunction with a state mental hospital, the subjects are readily accessible.

The procedure is to ask a patient on the ward if he would like to come with the experimenter or his assistant to get some candy or cigarettes. If he refuses, he is not forced. (Only 10 per cent of patients refuse to leave the ward, even though many are highly disturbed.) The subject is led into the experimental room and given the following instructions, or some variation, depending on the particular experiment. "This is a candy machine. If you pull the knob, you will get candy that you can eat or keep, but you will not get candy every time you pull the knob." [37] The subject is then left alone in the room. If no response is made within

[37] Ibid.

**Figure 16–2.** Booths used by subjects in operant conditioning of human psychotics. The plexiglass windows between the rooms can be made transparent for visual communication as possible social reinforcers. No. 2 represents the manipulandum, 3 the reinforcement magazine, 4 the stimulus panel, 5 the automatic controlling and recording mechanisms. (From O. R. Lindsley, Operant conditioning methods applied to research in chronic schizophrenia, *Psychiatric Research Reports*, No. 5, American Psychiatric Assn., June 1956.)

15 minutes after the initial instructions, the experimenter enters the room again, places the subject's hand on the knob, and helps him pull it. A reinforcement is then presented, following the initial response.

On the other side of the cinder-block walls of the rooms are the counters and recording devices that measure the rate of responding, time between responses, and the like (see Figures 16–3 and 16–4).

SOME EXPERIMENTAL FINDINGS

The primary purpose of these investigations to date has been the analysis of psychotic behavior. Skinner[38] has pointed out that the

[38] B. F. Skinner, What is psychotic behavior? In *Theory and treatment of the psychoses: Some newer aspects* (St. Louis: Washington University, 1956).

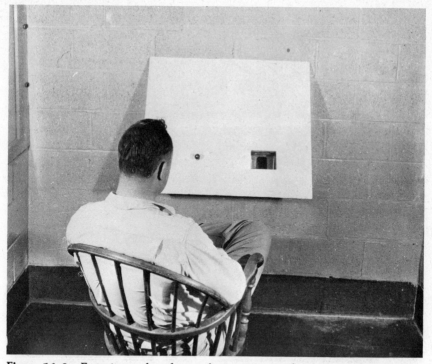

**Figure 16–3.** Experimental enclosure for operant conditioning of chronic psychotics. Reinforcements are presented automatically through the aperture at right by pulling the plunger at left. (Photograph courtesy O. R. Lindsley.)

method has the great advantage of objectivity when compared to other attempts to study psychotic behavior. The reports that follow are based on a series of experimental investigations in progress since 1954. Because the project is a long-term one, our summary is of necessity incomplete. However, the studies have been going on long enough to indicate that many significant findings are beginning to emerge. The cases used in the investigation do not fall into any clinical "type," although many have been diagnosed as schizophrenic. Other kinds of disorders, functional as well as organic, are included. They all share one characteristic in common: the subjects are all chronic patients, having been institutionalized for a considerable period of time.

### CHARACTERISTICS OF PSYCHOTIC RESPONDING

In the analysis of some 50 records of chronic psychotic patients, one of the most dramatic results typified in the records is the *irregularity of responding.* This is most typical of the more disturbed patients. Unlike normal controls, the psychotic records are typified by pauses (often

**Figure 16–4.** Apparatus used for measuring the operant responses of chronic psychotics. Automatic timers and recorders are at the right, while patients can be viewed through the "one way periscope" at the left. (Photograph courtesy O. R. Lindsley.)

long) between more regular rates. During these pauses, the patient usually engages in his particular psychotic symptoms. Lindsley[39] has found that this irregularity is one of the most valid indices of the presence of psychosis and increases with the severity of the disorder. When patients are most severely disordered, the pauses will be longest. During periods of better adjustment to their environment outside the experimental room, the pauses are shorter.

Qualitative observations as well as the more quantitative response rate can be made. When viewed through a one-way screen from outside, patients are found to be pacing the floor, gesturing, talking to themselves, hallucinating, or engaging in more violent activity (breaking chairs and the like) during these pauses. These psychotic episodes naturally interfere with the rate of operant responding. The topography of these responses has been found to correlate with the particular psychiatric

[39] O. R. Lindsley, Progress report I (an experimental analysis of psychotic behavior) Research Grant MH-977. National Institute of Mental Health, June 1956.

diagnosis. Each patient typically has his own pattern of "psychotic distraction"; some are short, others long. When the same patient's record is kept for a period of time, these pauses assume daily and monthly rhythms.

The frequency of the pauses or their duration is not specifically related to a particular psychiatric diagnosis (schizophrenia, manic-depressive). It is interpreted, rather, as a measure of the *degree* of the disturbance; that is, the amount of disorganization or deterioration of behavior typified by the psychotic symptom. When a measure of interresponse time (time taken between responses) is made, few normal subjects ever pause longer than 10 seconds. This is about the length of time it would take to look at one's watch, light a cigarette, or engage in a variety of normal "distractions."

## SCHEDULES OF REINFORCEMENT

For most of the experiments a schedule that ought to give a regularity of rate is used. As we have learned, a variable-interval schedule will produce such regularity. Lindsley[40] has found that a VI 1 (variable interval, 1 minute) produces an even rate of responding with at least one response every 10 seconds from normals. When fixed-ratio schedules are used, there is a typical pause following reinforcements in normal people. When these two kinds of schedules are tried with psychotics, the patients exhibit frequent pauses on the VI schedule. When put on a fixed-ratio schedule, the pauses that normally follow the reinforcement tend to be longer than those of normals. One interesting application of the FR schedule is that in some patients, it is possible to alter the pause by bringing it after the reinforcement. In this sense the psychotic episodes can be "forced" into a temporal position (after the reinforcement).

## PSYCHOTIC RESPONDING AND OTHER CLINICAL MEASURES

In the early stages of his research, Lindsley[41] observed that patients whose response rates were low and erratic on the variable-interval schedule came from the most disturbed wards of the hospital. They were unable to work at any of the hospital industries or workshops and were untidy and less able to care for themselves.

In an attempt to compare the characteristics of the psychotic response rate with other measures of behavior, those patients who were testable were given a number of different independent measures, including an intelligence test (Wechsler–Bellevue) and the Rorschach test. Besides

[40] Ibid.

[41] O. R. Lindsley, New techniques of analysis of psychotic behavior and final technical report for contract N5-ori-07662, Annual Tech. Rep. 3, Behavior Research Laboratory, Metropolitan State Hospital, Waltham, Mass., November 1956.

these, the patients were rated on the *L-M Ferges-Falls Behavior Rating Sheet*.[42] Lindsley has found this particular scale to be most adaptable, since it (1) can be easily filled out by ward attendants; (2) is restricted to observable behavior; that is what the patient is actually doing on the ward; and (3) it is an indication of gross disturbance independent of any specific psychiatric diagnosis.

When the ratings on the ward behavior were compared with the rates of operant responding, a correlation of .81 was found. This indicates a fairly close relationship between the two measures (1.00 would be perfect, but this is hypothetical). The patients rated as most disturbed showed lowest rates in the operant conditioning, with many pauses and long interresponse times, while those rated as least disturbed showed higher rates of responding and fewer pauses. Since all patients were chronically ill, Lindsley and Mednick[43] interpret these findings as an indication that the patients who respond at higher rates are more sensitive to the reinforcements in their social environment and capable of learning to manipulate the environment to obtain reinforcements.

About half of the patients studied who would respond to the experimental situation were either so disturbed or deteriorated that they could not be tested by other measures. Ordinarily those people in this class from the more regressed wards of the hospital showed greater disturbances as measured by the ward-rating scale and the operant response rate. Those patients who could be tested by the *Wechsler Adult Intelligence Scale* showed subnormal scores, and the results of the Rorschach test indicated the typical patterns found in psychotic patients. The advantages of operant measures of behavior over other clinical indices are (1) that it gives an indication of the degree or severity of the psychosis; and (2) that it is able to reach 80 per cent of the hospital population, whereas more conventional clinical measures (Rorschach test and the like) can reach only 40 per cent of such a group.

KINDS OF REINFORCEMENT

When an organism fails to respond with any degree of frequency even though a reinforcement is forthcoming, it is possible that the reinforcement is ineffective; that is, it fails to reinforce. The fact that Lindsley's subjects responded with low and erratic rates when compared with normals in the same task and with the same reinforcements indicates either a lack or loss of reinforcement function.

In order to discover whether these low response rates were typical of

[42] R. J. Lucero and B. F. Meyer, A behavior rating scale suitable for use in mental hospitals, *Jour. Clin. Psychol.*, 7 (1951), 250–254.

[43] M. T. Mednick and O. R. Lindsley, Some clinical correlates of operant behavior, *Jour. Abn. Soc. Psychol.*, 57 (1958), 13–16.

psychotic behavior or merely a function of a poor reinforcer, Lindsley[44] attempted to explore a number of reinforcing stimuli with both psychotic patients and normal subjects, using the usual VI schedule of 1 minute. The following reinforcers were compared: (1) candy, (2) female nude picture shown on the wall, (3) male nude picture, (4) five-cent pieces, (5) seeing a kitten fed milk. These response rates were compared with the rates for normals working for nickels and dogs working for food.

The reinforcer found *most* effective with the *average* psychotic was candy. Although slightly slower, in general, these compared most favorably of all the reinforcers tried with normals working for nickels. When the psychotic patients pulled the knob to receive a picture of a male or female nude flashed on the screen in front of them, no preference was found. This suggests that among psychotics, the motivation for homosexual pictures (all patients were male) was as strong as for the heterosexual ones. The marked interest in homosexuality may be accounted for by the long period of isolation in a homosexual environment (sexes are segregated in mental hospitals), or the homosexual pattern may be characteristic of some psychotic behaviors. This latter possibility has long been suggested by a number of theorists, perhaps first by Freud.

When the rates of responding for different reinforcers are compared with the ratings on ward behavior (see above), the best-adjusted patients show good rates for male nude pictures as reinforcers. The reason for this is not yet clear. Reinforcement by female nude pictures is the next best predictor of adjustment, with candy and nickels tied for third. However, for all psychotics taken as a group, the candy is the best reinforcer, and it compares most favorably (although slower) with normals working for nickels and dogs working for food.

When extinction rates are compared for psychotics and normals, some amazing results are found. Normals extinguish easily, usually by the end of the third experimental session (third hour). After that they refuse to come to the experimental rooms. However, when psychotics are extinguished by withholding candy reinforcement, many patients continue to respond, hour after hour, day after day. Many extinguish so slowly that it would appear that they are *not extinguishing at all.*

*Feeding a Kitten as a Social Reinforcer.*    Of special interest in the study of psychotic behavior is the use of a "social" reinforcer. Keller and Schoenfeld have defined social behavior as "behavior for which the reinforcing or discriminative stimuli are, or have been, mediated by the behavior of another organism." [45] In this situation a kitten has been well trained to drink milk from a dipper when it is automatically presented to

[44] O. R. Lindsley, New techniques of analysis of psychotic behavior.
[45] F. S. Keller and W. N. Schoenfeld, op. cit., p. 238.

him (see Figure 16–5). At the time of experiment the kitten was placed in a cage with a plexiglass front and was visible to the patient at all times. The subject would respond by pulling the knob in front of him and a reinforcement (the dipper with milk in it) would become accessible to the kitten for 5 seconds; at this time the lights in the room would go out, but the kitten's cage would remain lighted. At times when no reinforcement was given, the kitten was still visible to the patient, and the animal soon learned to scratch the window with its paw and "beg for milk." The only way that the kitten could get fed was for the patient to respond by pulling the knob in front of him.

One of the patients responded at his highest rate for this "social reinforcement." This same patient had refused to respond for any other reinforcer. Two patients in the experimental group also responded at a rate higher than for other reinforcers. Other patients responded at low rates, and half the group (13 patients) responded at a rate equal or lower than their extinction rates for other reinforcers, thus indicating that "seeing a kitten fed" was either not reinforcing or aversive to them. Those who did respond to the kitten as a reinforcer refused to do so when the kitten was

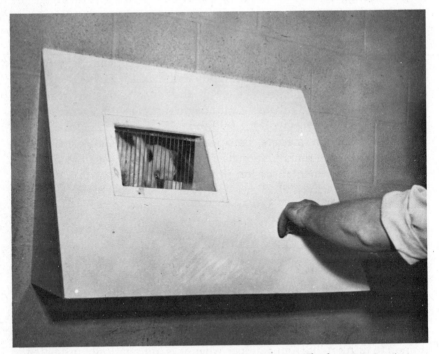

**Figure 16–5.** "Seeing a kitten fed" as a reinforcement. The kitten is in view through the plexiglass window by the patient at all times. By pulling the plunger, the patient can deliver a dipper of milk to the kitten. Otherwise, the kitten goes unfed. The situation is designed to act as a social reinforcement for the patient. (Photograph courtesy O. R. Lindsley.)

satiated. Apparently, the seeing response itself was the reinforcement and not some other aspect of the experimental situation. Lindsley feels that this kind of reinforcement may have some kind of implication for so-called altruistic behavior. Some patients on the wards will refuse to eat but will bring food to other patients. Furthermore the reinforcer may operate as a relief from anxiety (guilt feelings possibly) by helping another. Certainly guilt, anxiety, and many of the "defenses" are commonly found in behaviorally disturbed people.

### LONG-TERM STUDY WITH PATIENTS

In a longitudinal study of this kind, it is possible to observe the behavior of some patients for many experimental sessions extending over many months, even years.[46] The analysis of individual records yields some interesting results and allows for a regular comparison with behavioral observations outside the laboratory. Several patients have shown overall rate increases over months of responding, indicating a possible therapeutic effect of the experiment, although this has not been the basic aim of the study. Since Lindsley has found that the rate of responding is related to the degree of severity of a disorder, these increasing rates are encouraging signs. Another patient responded regularly for 230 hours without showing any signs of extinction. This kind of behavior has not been found to date in normal subjects. Since extinction is a kind of learning *not* to respond, a failure to extinguish may give some understanding of the behavioral deficit. In general, psychotics are slower to extinguish than normal people.

*Psychotic Incidents, Episodes, and Phases.* By studying the behavior of the same patients over long periods of time, it is possible to observe "seasonal fluctuations" in the response rate. Unlike normal individuals, the psychotic is found to exhibit periods of apparent "no responding"; that is, as far as the measurable operant response is concerned. On a variable interval schedule of 1 minute, a normal person seldom stops responding for a period of over 10 seconds. The psychotic frequently ceases his responding for periods much longer than that. If the period of no responding is relatively short (1 minute), it is designated as a *psychotic incident*. When the very low, erratic responding lasts as long as 20 to 30 minutes (of each hour), Lindsley designates this as a *psychotic episode*. And when the rate remains very low for several weeks or months, the period is designated as a *psychotic phase*.

During the psychotic episodes, the patients can be seen displaying their hallucinations and other disturbed and destructive symptoms. It is this typically psychotic behavior that keeps the patient hospitalized. If

[46] O. R. Lindsley (see note 39 in this chapter).

the patient is observed over weeks or months the psychotic phases often occur. A patient may have been responding consistently on a VI schedule, for example. Then for a period of weeks or even months his rate becomes exceedingly low. This kind of rhythm frequently will repeat itself. Figure 16–6 shows such a pattern in a patient who had been hospitalized for 20 of his 52 years. He was admitted at the age of 18, being diagnosed as manic-depressive. The diagnosis has since changed to schizophrenia, hebephrenic type.

During these episodes and phases, patients frequently express their hallucinations verbally (talk to themselves). Lindsley has been able to introduce a "voice key" that automatically records the vocal stresses the

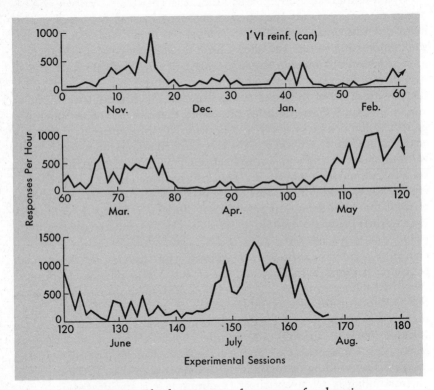

**Figure 16–6.** Rhythms in rate of response of a chronic psychotic patient working on a 1-minute variable interval schedule of reinforcement for candy as reinforcement. Each experimental session lasted 1 hour and was conducted on successive week days. The months of the year are plotted below the experimental sessions closer to the first of each month to indicate calendar time. (From O. R. Lindsley, Report for the third and fourth years, *An Experimental Analysis of Psychotic Behavior*. Detailed progress report II, p. 28. Reproduced by permission of the author.)

patient makes while in the experimental room.[47] The pauses in the operant responding are due to the competition from the patient's hallucinations. These compete strongly with the nonsymptomatic response of pulling the plunger for candy reinforcement. Lindsley feels that this kind of behavior typically distinguishes the psychotic from the nonpsychotic individual.

Another technique used to study the hallucinatory behavior of the patients in the operant responding situation is to present a "hidden" auditory stimulus while the patient is working for his reinforcement. A wide variety of "hidden" auditory stimuli can be presented which serve to bring on a patient's hallucinations or verbalizations. When these same stimuli are presented to patients with no previous history of hallucinations on the ward, they often can bring on hallucinations when the appropriate stimuli are employed.

### EFFECTS OF DRUGS

The techniques of operant conditioning lend themselves well to the study of drug effects on behavior. Many studies currently in progress illustrate how the behavior of lower animals can be changed by using a variety of behavioral situations, including visual discrimination, time discrimination, escape, avoidance, and anxiety. Although the use of animals is an efficient means of screening drugs and is a common practice in pharmacological laboratories all over the country, even more effective should be an experimental analysis of human subjects on whom the drugs are to be administered. Lindsley's technique allows just this.

One of the most popular of the tranquilizing drugs used with behaviorally disturbed people has been chlorpromazine. This has been tried on a variety of psychotic patients with reports ranging from "no change" to remarkable "improvement."[48] Lindsley[49] has also found great individual differences among the patients he has studied. When patients are given the drug and then placed in the experimental situation, some show increases in rate, others do not. The evidence thus far accumulated suggests that although marked individual differences exist, the operant technique appears to be a very sensitive measure of changes in behavior produced by the drug.

For example, one patient placed on 150 mg increased from 20 responses to a median of 170 responses per hour during the last ten sessions of

[47] O. R. Lindsley, Detailed progress report II, Report for the third and fourth years on an experimental analysis of psychotic behavior, Behavior Research Laboratory, Metropolitan State Hospital, Waltham, Mass. (June 1956–November, 1958).

[48] A. Wikler, *The relation of pharmacology to psychiatry* (Baltimore: Williams & Wilkins, 1957).

[49] O. R. Lindsley, see note 42 in this chapter.

experimentation. However, no change was observed in the same patient's ward behavior. When the drug dosage was gradually increased to 900 mg, the rate of responding was reduced to 75 per hour. At this point he was reported as being less abusive and talked more softly, but his actual adjustment on the ward did not improve. Another patient was given 150 mg with a rate increase for both candy and nickels as reinforcers from about zero to 15 responses per hour. The dosage was increased to 300 mg, with further increases for response rate to 165 responses per hour. Ratings of ward behavior showed no significant changes, however. When taken off the medication, the same patient's rate dropped to zero again. The patient had been considered very regressed, and although the drug did not alter his ward behavior, it showed marked changes in the rate of operant responding. This observation would suggest that the method is a sensitive measure of individual changes in behavior resulting from the drug. Because of the individual differences in rate changes (up or down), Lindsley suggests that the study of drug effects would be more adequately applied by using individual cases.

THE WORK OF AYLLON AND HIS COLLEAGUES

Much of the work reported by Ayllon has been in the form of the application of behavioral principles to modify the behavior of psychotics through conditioning, extinction, deprivation, satiation, and shaping. There is further discussion of this work in Chapter 18, "Behavior Therapy."

Frequently psychiatric diagnosis of personality disorders is determined, at least in part, by the kinds of verbal behavior a patient emits. For example, if one were to say that there was a plot in progress to do him in, or that he was being influenced by television radiation, he might likely be classified as paranoid. Likewise, the rate of his verbal utterances might be taken into account. Contrast the person who talks constantly from morning to night with the person who never talks at all, that is, one who is mute—both might be equally abnormal. The aim of many therapies is to get the person to talk about things that would rarely be said outside the therapist's office—for example, the patient's sexual difficulties.

MODIFICATION OF PSYCHOTIC VERBAL BEHAVIOR

In two experiments described by Ayllon and Haughton,[50] using the procedures of positive reinforcement and extinction, an attempt was made to modify the patients' verbal utterances. The first patient, Kathy,

---

[50] T. Ayllon and E. Haughton, Modification of symptomatic verbal behavior of mental patients, *Behav. Res. Ther.*, **2** (1964), 87–97.

had been classified as a chronic schizophrenic. An analysis of her verbal behavior prior to the experiment indicated that much of her content centered around delusions. She made frequent references to Queen Elizabeth, King George, and the royal family ("I'm the Queen. The Queen wants to smoke." "How is King George, have you seen him?") Two classes of verbal behavior were distinguished: (1) the verbal responses defined as psychotic (delusional), which included references to the King, Queen, royal family; (2) those responses consisting of neutral verbal responses ("It's a nice day," or "What time is it?"). To explore the possibilities of the control of the distinct classes, for the first 75 days (at three-minute intervals) throughout the day, the class of verbal responses designated as psychotic was reinforced. The reinforcements consisted in the experimenter's listening, attention, offering or lighting the patient's cigarette, etc. Extinction of the neutral class consisted of withdrawal of cigarettes and social attention. The frequency of the psychotic responses rose to twice their original baseline frequency. Despite the patient's severe psychosis, the authors noted that the modification of the content of what they said was possible through the presentation or withholding of reinforcement.

A second experiment concerned two patients who were generally classified as depressed, and the two classes of behavior were designated as somatic and neutral. Examples of somatic verbalizations were "My shoulder is bothering me," "I got gas on my stomach," "My nerves are shot," "I feel I'm going to die." Basically, the same procedure was followed as in the earlier experiment. Somatic responses were reinforced by listening, paying attention, showing interest, and the neutral responses were ignored. Results also showed that a class of verbal responses can be strengthened or weakened by the application or withholding of reinforcement. During the somatic conditioning there frequently occurred other emotional responses associated with depression, such as crying, sobbing, sniffing; these were also reinforced adventitiously. During the extinction of the somatic responses the patients complained that they had not eaten, when in fact they had. They complained they had been up all night unable to sleep; the ward record showed that not only had they slept, but they had snored. At the end of the experiment (extinction of somatic responses) one of the patients was released from the hospital. She has remained in the community for three years at the time of the report. The other patient's relatives refused to take her back, but made arrangements for her to visit from time to time. The experiments show that social reinforcements can be arranged to modify either normal or abnormal verbal behavior.

Ayllon and Michael[51] have applied extinction procedures to modify

[51] T. Ayllon and J. Michael, The psychiatric nurse as a behavioral engineer, *Jour. Exp. Anal. Behav.*, **2** (1959), 323–334.

other kinds of psychotic behavior. One patient made so many visits to nurses' offices that she interrupted and interfered with their work. The nurses had resigned themselves to the idea that the patient was "too dumb" to know she was not welcome because the patient had mental deficiency. Prior to the experiment the rate of entering had been on the average of 16 times a day. By the end of the seventh week of extinction, the average had been reduced to two. (See p. 79–80.)

Another patient's delusional talk[52] had become so annoying for the past four months that other patients had sometimes resorted to beating her up in an effort to keep her quiet. Her delusions centered around having an illegitimate child and being chased and pursued by men. Nurses were instructed to ignore her delusional talk but to reinforce sensible talk. By the ninth week the frequency of her delusional talk had drastically reduced. The rate increased when a social worker entered the situation and started listening to her.

Another patient described by Ayllon and Michael was treated by a combination of extinction and satiation. For five years two mental defectives had been carrying around papers, rubbish, and magazines inside their clothing next to their skin. Skin rashes had developed, and the patients regularly had to be "dejunked." It was believed that the hoarding behavior was being sustained by the attention the patients received. Because newspapers and magazines were not common articles in the ward, it was suspected that flooding the ward with these articles might tend to satiate the behavior. In addition, any reinforcement of this behavior was withheld. Results in both patients were the same—a gradual decrease in the hoarding behavior (p. 199).

Ayllon[53] describes a patient who had a number of undesirable symptoms that included food stealing, hoarding of the ward's towels, and the wearing of excessive clothing. Each response was treated separately. The first attempt was to modify the food stealing. First, the patient was assigned to a table in the patients' dining room all by herself. When she approached the tables of other patients or when she picked up unauthorized food, she was removed from the dining room. When the withdrawal of the positive reinforcement of food was dependent on "stealing," the response was eliminated in two weeks. (See p. 188.)

The second symptom, which involved hoarding of towels, was treated by satiation. Periodically nurses simply brought her more and more towels, bringing them to her without comment. By the end of the third week the average number of towels had increased to 60. When the number of towels reached 625, she started taking a few of them out of

---

[52] Ibid.
[53] T. Ayllon, Intensive treatment of psychotic behavior by stimulus satiation and food reinforcement, *Behav. Res. Ther.*, **1** (1963), 53–61.

her room. During the next year the average number of towels hoarded dropped to between 1 and 5 towels at any one time.

The treatment of the third symptom of wearing excessive clothing had to be handled in the following way. To determine how much extra clothing she was wearing, the patient was weighed before each meal. In this situation the food as reinforcement was made contingent on the removal of superfluous clothing. Clothing was gradually reduced until she met the requirement of a normal amount of 3 pounds compared to the earlier 25 pounds of clothing. At the beginning of the experiment the patient missed a few meals because she failed to meet the specific requirements for that day. When the requirement was met she was given access to meals. Much emotional behavior was displayed in the form of crying and throwing of chairs. Nurses were instructed to ignore this behavior, and withholding of any "social" reinforcement led to the rapid extinction of this emotional behavior.

Other references to the work of Ayllon and his colleagues may be found in Chapters 3, 5, 7, and 18.

## Summary

The current system of classifying psychotic behavior is based on a long tradition beginning with Emil Kraepelin. Many have recognized its inadequacy, and minor attempts at change have been made from time to time. Even though it lacks practical utility, it persists because none better has been offered in substitution. The system is based on tradition and convenience. Qualitative differences are frequently recognized between symptomatic behaviors of patients exhibiting diverse changes, but there is so much overlap between classes that even the most qualified diagnosticians will often disagree intensely on a particular diagnosis. By means of this traditional system an attempt is made to "pigeonhole" individuals on the basis of some behavioral manifestations, even when such categorizing is not warranted by the behavior expressed. Yet, a disordered person must be labeled as something. He is recognized as being severely disordered, and as such he must fit somewhere into the classification system even though his symptoms may show signs of a number of different categories or do not fit into any category at all.

A different approach to the analysis of psychotic behavior is presently being attempted by Lindsley, using operant conditioning techniques. Patients are studied by taking recordings of their rate of responding under specified and controlled stimulus conditions. This technique cuts across the traditional classification boundaries, enabling the student of behavior pathology to examine and analyze from a quantitative point of view the degree of behavioral disturbance and allowing him to examine other relationships that exist between the discriminative and reinforcing stimuli and the behavior itself. It tells us how the psychotic differs from the normal when each is placed in the same experimental situation. Although it is too early to tell, it may be that this approach will unlock the door for many of the hidden mysteries of psychotic behavior.

# 17 Conventional Psychotherapies

IN CHAPTERS 15 AND 16 WE DISCUSSED how behavior that appears to be troublesome and disturbed developed through the process of learning. The inadequate responses a person makes to his friends, parents, siblings, and other aspects of his environment *are acquired.* Although apparently ineffectual in achieving the reinforcements provided in the environment and community of people about him, the troubled individual persists in his reactions because of the unique reinforcing contingencies that have already developed. It is also through the process of learning that the disturbed individual must acquire more adequate, useful, and appropriate behavior enabling him to interact in a more effective way with other people and stimuli in his environment. One means whereby behavioral changes are attempted in the direction of an individual's improvement is psychotherapy.

Although the field of psychotherapy does not lend itself readily to experimental analysis, a number of recent researches have attempted to analyze precisely what is happening in the process. Their basic aim has been to demonstrate, usually through the analysis of the verbal behavior emitted, that *change does occur.* And if the psychotherapy is effective, the change is in the direction of improvement. In this chapter our goal is not to devise a "new" technique or method of psychotherapy but to describe in terms of some of the principles of learning already discussed just what, if anything, happens in the processes involved in conventional therapies. Chapter 18 is devoted to the newer and more behavioristically oriented techniques, which are known as *behavior therapy*. In order to understand precisely what is happening in the traditional therapies, we shall do well first to review briefly a few of these conventional methods. All claim success, but in certain cases the positive evidence is somewhat open to question, at least in terms of any empirical standards of success.

## Varieties of Conventional Therapy

The principles of learning that may be applied in explaining the treatment of behavior disorders differ according to the techniques employed by any particular therapy. Some procedures involve the establishment of a close "interpersonal relationship" between the therapist and patient, or client, as he is sometimes called. These are considered analogous to the relationships that existed in the patient's earlier life history between himself and his parents. Other "schools" of therapy also stress a "friendly" relationship but place more emphasis on unearthing "unconscious processes." We can interpret this to mean a verbalizing of relationships that exist between an individual and the controlling stimuli in his environment, stressing in particular an understanding of the past history of development. Still other methods stress the significance of social stimuli in the forms of groups of people (group therapy), which may act to shape more adequately those responses which at the beginning of therapy are almost extinguished or are interfered with by incompatible behavior.

### EARLY FORMS OF THERAPY

At a time when the psychoanalytic theory of Freud was in its infancy and the client-centered therapy of Carl Rogers had not yet become a realization, the practices at the beginning of this century were to suggest, advise, try to reason with, persuade, demand, or use some other means (usually verbal) to bring about a change in a person's behavior. The discussions between therapist and patient usually involved a high degree of moralizing. The patient was told the nature of his symptoms as the therapist saw them, given direct advice on what he could and *ought* to do to change his miserable ways.[1] These techniques usually assumed that the individual, being born of a free will, was master of his own fate. He and he alone had the power to do something about it, if the way were

---

[1] N. Cameron and A. Magaret, *Behavior pathology* (Boston: Houghton Mifflin, 1951), p. 561.

pointed out to him. No consideration was given to the significance of the controlling environment that had determined his condition, nor did the therapist make any concentrated effort to manipulate the variables that might allow for new learning to occur.

### PSYCHOANALYTIC THERAPY

In many of the previous chapters we have discussed Freud's interpretation of a number of personality variables. We have said little, however, about his methods of treatment. As we have already noted, Freud stressed the significance of unconscious conflict, frustrated impulses from the id, and the resulting anxiety as the basic determiners of a person's difficulties. He believed further that early infantile and childhood conflicts and trauma, long since repressed, must be made accessible to the person's conscious mind. Because many manifestations of the patient's trouble were fixations at earlier periods of development, for improvement to occur, he had to relinquish these attachments in favor of ones that would be more acceptable to society and to his superego. The process of therapy in which the individual could grow from his infantile attachments to more mature ways involved learning, although Freud did not state that fact explicitly. Nevertheless childish ways had to be abandoned in favor of more adult activities.

Freud, along with his colleague Joseph Breuer,[2] first tried hypnosis as a means of unearthing unconscious conflicts. This attempt was first reported in a case of a woman suffering from hysteria. They found that the significant cause of her trouble was to be found in a repressed trauma which she had suffered from childhood. The release of this suppressed emotion was designated as the "abreaction," or a reliving of the experience under hypnosis. As a result of this discovery, when taken out of the hypnotic "state," the patient showed improvement. In terms of more modern learning principles, the patient was actually extinguishing the response that had been suppressed by the painful punishment of the event. The actual recall of the childhood experience, which had occurred in relation to her father's illness and eventual death, was "relived" through the verbal expression. Prior to the hypnotic event, the condition had been too painful to remember.

However, Freud found that all people could not be hypnotized, and furthermore the method did not always work. He therefore abandoned hypnosis and substituted a technique whereby the patient could verbalize at random whatever happened to occur to him while he lay on a couch in the therapist's office. This method Freud called *free association*. He felt that the technique could make accessible to both the therapist and patient reactions that had previously been unavailable. In this method

[2] J. Breuer and S. Freud, *Studies in hysteria* (New York: Nervous and Mental Disease Publishing Co., 1936).

the patient was trained to say anything and everything that would be provoked by the numerous exteroceptive and proprioceptive stimuli, no matter how trivial, ridiculous, embarrassing, or anxiety arousing they happened to be. The responses that resulted were often fragmentary, disorganized, and apparently unrelated.

The function of the therapist, once the patient had learned how to free-associate, was to interpret the meaning of what he said. The therapist pointed out that the patient might be trying to avoid something, for example, or was employing some defense, or was repressing part of what he was attempting to say. The therapist verbalized his interpretation to the patient by explaining its significance in terms of psychoanalytic principles. During the many therapeutic sessions the patient responded in a variety of ways. At times he expressed strong affectionate responses toward the therapist (positive transference), at other times he was extremely hostile (negative transference). Freud believed this *transference* was important for successful treatment. In his responses the patient was expressing toward the therapist the earlier reactions he had exhibited toward his parents, brothers and sisters, friends, or spouse.

There were times in the therapeutic interviews when the patient would have difficulty in saying anything. Often this occurred when some previous association had served as stimuli for strong anxiety reactions. These responses served to inhibit a further flow of the associative responses. The behavior was blocked and disrupted. Often signs of disorganization occurred. Such blockings in a patient who had learned the method of free associations had served as stimuli for strong anxiety reactions. These came at times when the verbal associations were leading to responses that were highly painful. The patient might be close to revealing some important repressed conflict or trauma which was directly related to his problem.

The methods of psychoanalysis are of necessity extremely long and tedious. The patient may have to come several times a week, even daily, to the therapist's office for a year and often longer. Because of the highly personal nature of the reactions and the confidences involved, it has been impossible to subject the method to any real experimental test. Analysts report complete cures or marked improvement. Tests have been devised to measure changes in behavior. But this is as far as any experimental analysis has gone. Antagonists (and there are many) feel it is futile and expensive and ought to be abandoned in favor of a more direct approach.[3]

Thus, the successes or failures of conventional psychoanalysis are impossible to assess. Wolpe et al.[4] point out that no psychoanalyst has

---

[3] A. Salter, *The case against psychoanalysis* (New York: Holt, 1957).

[4] J. Wolpe, A. Salter, and L. J. Reyna, *The conditioning therapies* (New York: Holt, Rinehart and Winston, 1964).

ever published a statistical study of his successes or failures, and Mowrer[5] (see Chapter 18) suggests that psychoanalysis may be a way of life, but as far as therapy is concerned it is notable for its lack of success. It should be pointed out, however, that both these psychologists favor the newer behavior therapy (see Chapter 18).

CLIENT–CENTERED THERAPY

A more recent development in the field of psychotherapy, and one that has had considerable impact on clinical psychology in America, is a method developed by Carl Rogers. It had its first complete and formal statement in 1942 with the publication of Rogers' *Counseling and Psychotherapy*.[6] Like psychoanalysis, client-centered therapy, or *nondirective* therapy as it is also called, stresses what is referred to as the "growth process," which proponents interpret as a development toward maturity if the environmental conditions are proper. Behavioral deviations are interpreted as a blocking of this process. Unlike the orthodox procedures of psychoanalysis in which the patient rests on a couch in a position where he cannot see the therapist, the nondirective approach uses a face-to-face interview situation. One of the most essential features of the technique is the permissive and accepting attitude of the therapist regarding anything the patient may say. The therapist does not judge, advise, or suggest. He accepts completely whatever the patient says or does, and in particular the emotional responses the patient (client) happens to make, whether they be friendly or hostile. Stress is placed on the significance of these emotional vocalizations. In his reply to the patient, the therapist restates (but does not interpret) the verbal responses in an attempt to clarify them for him. Sometimes he merely says "mmm-hmm" to keep the patient's talk going. For example, consider the following two excerpts:

1. PATIENT: Some days I just feel sick and tired all over. I can hardly drag myself around. Everything I try to do seems to be an effort. I really feel miserable.
   THERAPIST: You feel that a great many symptoms are bothering you. . . .

2. PATIENT: I wish you would give me some idea of what I can do when this awful feeling comes over me. I feel so helpless. I want to run but I can't. I just feel tense and nervous all over.
   THERAPIST: You would like me to tell you what to do when these feelings come over you. . . .

[5] O. H. Mowrer, *The crisis in psychiatry and religion* (New York: Van Nostrand, 1959).
[6] C. R. Rogers, *Counseling and psychotherapy* (Boston: Houghton Mifflin, 1942).

In each instance you will notice that no advice is given, nor are the complaints interpreted. The therapist merely restates for the person, often in similar words, the feelings that he had reported. Those who follow these procedures report that quite regular and predictable progress occurs in the course of therapeutic interviewing. The permissiveness of the situation allows the patient to express freely his fears as well as his hostilities. As the more implicit reactions become overtly verbalized, the patient becomes better able to recognize them and proceed toward a more mature and positive approach to his troubles. The reorganization of behavior, which occurs in the process of growth, is called *therapeutic insight*. As the therapy progresses toward its goal, the patient becomes able to verbalize the possible courses of action open to him. He was unable to do this in the beginning. The growth that has developed within the confines of the therapeutic session can generalize (transfer) to the patient's life situations ouside the therapist's office.

The method has been subjected to a number of experimental analyses to demonstrate its validity. Some of these have depended on the analysis of statements made by a number of patients over a period of several interviews.[7] Others have employed psychological tests of "adjustment" before and after therapy, to measure the improvements.[8] Still others make use of highly complicated statistical techniques to measure the change.[9]

In one typical study, Seeman[10] attempted a quantitative measurement of behavioral change that took place during a number of interviews. The therapeutic sessions were recorded verbatim and later transcribed. The analysis consisted of taking 16 interviews involving 10 patients at various stages of therapy. The verbal statements of patients were categorized into the following four groups: (1) expression of problems or symptoms, (2) acceptance of therapist's responses, (3) understanding or insight, (4) discussion of plans for future. The kinds of statements were counted to reveal the differences between early, middle, and late therapeutic sessions. He found that as therapy progressed, the patients made fewer statements of their troubles and problems, and signs of acceptance rose in the first sessions and then declined. In later interviews patients showed greater understanding of their difficulties, gave more statements expressing plans for the future (see Figure 17–1). This study is given as validation of the basic theory of growth as outlined by Rogers.

[7] J. Seeman, A study of the process of nondirective therapy, *Jour. Consult. Psychol.*, **13** (1949), 157–168.

[8] J. Seeman, Research perspectives in psychotherapy, in O. H. Mowrer, ed., *Psychotherapy, theory and research* (New York: Ronald Press, 1953).

[9] O. H. Mowrer, "Q-technique," description, history and critique, in O. H. Mowrer, ed., *Psychotherapy, theory and research* (New York: Ronald Press, 1953).

[10] J. Seeman (see note 7 in this chapter).

In another study, Raimy[11] followed a similar procedure but used different categories for classification. The transcribed records of 14 cases were itemized and sorted into the following kinds of statements: (1) positive, (2) negative self-reference, (3) ambivalent self-reference, (4) ambiguous self-reference, (5) reference to other persons and objects, and (6) questions. At the start of therapy he found that patients gave a preponderance of statements of either negative or ambivalent self-reference. As the counseling progressed, the number of positive self-reference increased. At the conclusion of therapy with those patients who were judged "improved," the number of positive or self-approving

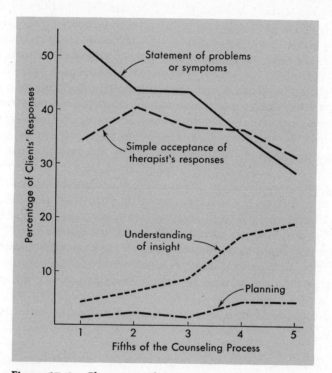

**Figure 17–1.** Changes in clients' statements during psychotherapy. The statements of the clients undergoing nondirective psychotherapy were classified into four main categories and counted for each fifth of the series of interviews. Statements of problems or symptoms declined while statements of insights and plans emerged in later interviews. (From J. Seeman, A study of the process of non-directive therapy, *Journal of Consulting Psychology,* **13** [1949] 157–168, p. 162, Fig. 1.)

[11] V. C. Raimy, Self-reference in counseling interviews, *Jour. Consult. Psychol.,* **12** (1948), 153–163.

statements was dominant, while those patients not judged improved were still making a majority of ambivalent and disapproving statements about themselves.

#### DIRECTIVE THERAPY

Directive therapy developed somewhat as a reaction against client-centered therapy. The main proponent has been Frederick Thorne,[12] who suggested a straightforward plan of behavioral change. The causes of a particular maladjustment must be directly identified and a plan introduced for appropriate behavioral modification. The healthy personality has less need for such a direction. In fact, the troubled person needs the help of a properly trained therapist. In contrast to the psychoanalytical methods, which attempt to discover latent causes, symbolism, unconscious conflicts, etc., the directive approach considers the obvious behavior of a patient in terms of scientific psychology, including the laws of learning as they are currently understood. However, directive therapy is eclectic and does not attempt to follow any particular learning theory. Thorne believes that a considerable amount of time can be saved by directing the course of treatment along lines that the therapist believes will be the most pragmatic. A developmental history is taken and the therapist tries to discover the causes of the maladaptive responding. Early childhood conditions are analyzed, especially for the possibilities of their traumatic emotional nature. Therapeutic insights must be translated into action. It is not only necessary to *know* what the trouble is with oneself and what one ought to do about it, but to work actively toward a new style of life. These personality readjustments can be regarded as an exercise in problem solving in which new learning is the principle technique.

According to Thorne, directive therapy is based on the following premises:[13]

1. The therapist plays the role of the master educator who takes over when other conditions (family, society, education) have failed.
2. The first phase of therapy consists in establishing suitable conditions for learning a new style of life.
3. Directive therapy means that someone (the therapist) must discover what the difficulty is, what is to be done, and see that it is done.
4. The therapist must be trained as a scientist and act accordingly as a scientist, to go about solving the problem in a scientific manner.

[12] F. Thorne, Directive and eclectic personality counseling. In J. L. McCary, ed., *Six approaches to psychotherapy* (New York: Dryden Press, 1955).
[13] Ibid.

## Psychotherapy and Learning

The basic function of psychotherapy is to provide a situation in which learning can take place; that is, learning of responses that are more appropriate than those existing in a person's repertoire at the time he entered the therapeutic relationship. The patient comes to the therapist with a set behavior that is ineffective and inadequate in dealing with his environment. The job of the therapist is to do something about it.

The progress of therapy involves a number of learning principles. These include: (1) providing conditioned positive reinforcements for behavior that may be weak and in need of strengthening; (2) extinguishing many anxiety reactions that are interfering with the more adequate responses that have already been conditioned in the person's earlier life history (to facilitate this the therapist acts as a nonpunishing audience); (3) application of selective reinforcements to develop new discriminations that are going to be more effective than those currently operating; and (4) through possible counterconditioning a substitution of new responses that may be more reinforcing to the patient and others about him.

### THE THERAPIST AS A SOURCE OF POSITIVE REINFORCEMENT

One of the initial tasks in most forms of therapy is *to get the patient to talk*. In both psychoanalysis and client-centered therapy, a situation is presented which allows the person an opportunity to express himself. He is never in competition with the therapist to get "a word in edgewise." This condition may have commonly occurred outside the therapist's office. In this sense he has the upper hand and is reinforced by the therapist's submission. (The therapeutic situation is permissive.) Furthermore the therapist expresses an understanding and friendly attitude. This may be quite novel to the patient. Maybe the patient's escape and avoidance behavior has developed because most people have become highly aversive to him. Instead of providing positive reinforcements, other individuals have become conditioned negative stimuli.

There are other reinforcements the therapist provides. For one thing he gives the patient his undivided *attention*, simply in being a good listener. To a patient who has found most people in his environment unwilling to listen to his troubles, this comes as a striking change. The function of the therapist is not, of course, merely to reinforce these verbal complaints, but this may be necessary in the beginning to get the patient's verbal behavior going.

In the beginning the therapist may not actually approve of everything the patient says, but neither does he disapprove. This lack of disapproval, at least, does not generate more anxiety, which already is conditioned by previous punishment. The therapist accepts what the patient has to say about his past and what has happened. This acceptance has been interpreted by Dollard and Miller as a kind of "forgiveness," [14] and operates to extinguish some of the anxiety already present. The *acquiescence* of the therapist is evidence that he understands what the patient is saying and he replies in a calm and sympathetic manner. As the interviews progress and the patient presumably improves, the therapist may begin to *approve* of what the patient is saying, particularly if it happens to be a statement that shows considerable understanding of problems and plans for the future.

*An experiment with psychotics.* In the preceding chapter we discussed in some detail the techniques used by Lindsley for studying the behavior of psychotics in an operant conditioning situation. In a preliminary investigation (see Figure 17–2) Lindsley has examined the

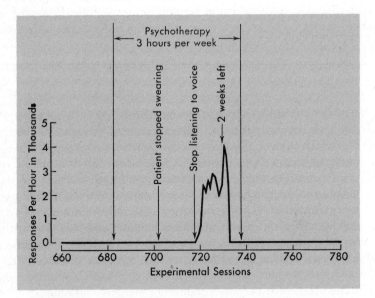

**Figure 17–2.** Effects of psychotherapy sessions on operant responding in a chronic psychotic. A student nurse conducted the one-hour therapy sessions three times a week. Details of the graph are explained in the text. (From O. R. Lindsley, Characteristics of the behavior of chronic psychotics by free-operant conditioning methods, *Diseases of the Nervous System* [Monograph supplement], **21** [1960], 1–15, p. 12, Fig. 12.)

[14] J. Dollard and N. E. Miller, *Personality and psychotherapy* (New York: McGraw-Hill, 1950).

effects of psychotherapy by a student nurse on the response rate of pulling a plunger for candy reinforcement by the psychotic patient. Therapeutic 1-hour sessions were conducted three days a week over several weeks. These were correlated with the daily 1-hour sessions of the patient in the operant conditioning situation. The results appear in Figure 17–2. The first arrow shows where therapy was begun. At the second arrow the patient stopped swearing. At the third arrow the patient was told to stop listening to his voices because they were part of his illness and he should not be bothered by them. By the sixth experimental (conditioning) session, the patient's response rate had climbed to over 2,000 responses per hour. The response rate continued steady even on days when the nurse did not see the patient.

At the fourth arrow the nurse told the patient that there were only two more weeks left for therapy. The rate jumped again and then abruptly fell to zero. At the fifth arrow the therapy was terminated. We see a marked change in rate, both following the onset of therapy and following its termination. Apparently the effects of therapy were not permanent and may be interpreted as being only "supportive" in character. We do see here, however, an objective measure of the effects of a single therapist's interviews in a case of chronic psychosis. Lindsley plans to continue this line of investigation, using more highly trained therapists.

### ANXIETY AND ITS EXTINCTION

Very often a patient comes to the therapist manifesting many expressions of anxiety, both operant and respondent. Anxiety has generalized to the therapeutic situation from the many circumstances in the patient's environment. The therapist is a stranger at first. The situation, being unfamiliar, bears a certain similarity to other novel situations which have earlier set the occasions for anxiety. The patient may regard the therapist as he has many others in his social environment; that is, as a conditioned stimulus to be feared. The therapist may function as an object to be escaped from or avoided.

*The therapist as a Nonpunishing Audience.* When a person comes for therapy, he is often suffering from conditions that are highly aversive to him. The causes of his condition are not readily known to him or the therapist. Earlier attempts on his part have been generally unsuccessful in overcoming his troubles. The advice and suggestions from his friends and family have failed in bringing about any change in his behavior. As Skinner suggests, the therapeutic situation is similar to other controlling agencies like government, religion, or education, although it is less formally organized. If therapy is to be successful, the therapist must gain some measure of control.

The steps which must be taken to correct a given condition of behavior follow directly from an analysis of that condition. Whether they can be taken will depend, of course, upon whether the therapist has control over the relevant variables.[15]

We have already mentioned the use of various positive reinforcements that the therapist can employ. Another kind of situation, not unrelated to the above, is for the therapist to constitute himself as a nonpunishing audience. This sets the occasion for the release of a variety of emotional behaviors. An aggressive remark is not met with counterattack from the therapist. Verbalizations of sin and guilt are not frowned upon. The patient is left free to do and say anything at all about the aversive control. At the beginning of therapy, often much of the person's behavior has been suppressed because of frequent punishments. Therefore the therapist must avoid any verbal comments that may further act as punishment stimuli. To criticize or ridicule could only intensify a situation that is already troublesome. He avoids references to moral judgments which in the patient's past have operated in arousing anxiety. A therapist who moralizes and passes judgment, who attempts to sermonize, is going to be quite ineffectual in changing a condition that has had a long history of development. By avoiding criticism, the therapist sets the occasion for the patient's verbalizations of anxiety, along with other manifestations of it. Although painful they can only be extinguished by their expression. In Estes' study of punishment, you will recall, the functions of punishment were only to suppress responses by setting up alternative stimuli that had the properties of generating anxiety and avoidance behavior. These responses were eliminated most rapidly by providing conditions favorable for extinction. According to Estes:

> . . . a response cannot be eliminated from an organism's repertoire more readily with the aid of punishment than without it. In fact, severe punishment may have precisely the opposite effect . . . the punished response continues to exist in the organism's repertoire with most of its original latent strength. While it is suppressed, the response is not only protected from extinction, but it also may become a source of conflict. An emotional state, such as "anxiety" or "dread" which has become conditioned to the incipient movements of making the response will be aroused by other stimuli which formerly acted as occasions for the occurrence of the response.[16]

The common anxiety manifested by the patient is interfering with expressions of behavior which in the past have achieved some kind of

[15] B. F. Skinner, *Science and human behavior* (New York: Macmillan, Inc., 1953), p. 368.
[16] W. K. Estes, An experimental study of punishment, *Psychol. Monogr.*, **57**, no. 263 (1944), 37–38.

positive reinforcement. If eliminated in the future, the conditions are appropriate for responses to occur that would again achieve that reinforcement. Therefore an important task in therapy is the extinction of the anxiety and the restoration of behavior which previously has led to more effective responding for the patient.

The extinction of anxiety also plays a very major role in Wolpe's behavior therapy[17] by reciprocal inhibition (see first section of Chapter 18). Wolpe believes that not only can anxiety be extinguished, but perhaps more important from his point of view is the conditioning of muscle relaxation, which is the antithesis of anxiety and consequently will inhibit it.

*Lifting the Repressions.* As the therapist acts as a nonpunishing audience, he permits the expressions of anxiety and hostility from the patient. Since the anxiety has been generated by aversive stimuli, such a situation allows for the free expression of anxiety and its extinction in the absence of aversive stimuli that have generated it.

In Freud's conception of therapy, the lifting of repressions allowed the unobservable conflicts and memories to be let out of the unconscious into the open where the person could face them. The ego's energy, then, was not wasted in keeping ideas and memories repressed but could be engaged in cathecting it in more useful directions. When the ego was strong enough to face up to the repressed impulses, it would again have the controlling hand. Therapy was concerned with discovering the "repressions" and rooting them out.

Although the aim of all therapies is not merely the lifting of repressions, what we have learned about disordered personalities tells us that punishment and other aversive conditions are so commonly operating in contributing to the development of the disturbance, the creation of a situation that is no longer punishing is one that will allow anxiety to extinguish and earlier behavior to be reinstated. If a therapeutic situation allows for the extinction of anxiety, it will then permit the expression of earlier behaviors which have been supplanted by the anxiety. As the therapist acts as a nonpunishing audience, he allow this to occur. This is precisely what Freud meant when he said the "repression was lifted."

The process is a gradual one, since the extinction of anxiety, well conditioned earlier, does not come about immediately. However, through the communication between therapist and patient, the latter begins to recall episodes in his life that had been "forgotten." He may recall some earlier events in which he had been punished, as well as their aversive consequences. He may remember the hostility felt toward his father or mother. Gradually the punishing experiences of his earlier life become revealed.

[17] J. Wolpe, *Psychotherapy by reciprocal inhibition* (Stanford, Calif.: Stanford University Press, 1958).

The patient may also begin to describe current tendencies to behave in punishable ways—for example, aggressively. He may also begin to behave in punishable ways: he may speak ungrammatically, illogically or in obscene and blasphemous terms, or he may criticize or insult the therapist. Nonverbal behavior which has previously been punished may also begin to appear; he may become socially aggressive or may indulge himself selfishly. If such behavior has been wholly repressed, it may first reach only the covert level. . . . The behavior later may be brought to the overt level. The patient may also begin to exhibit strong emotions; he may have a good cry, make a violent display of temper, or be "hysterically silly." [18]

As time goes by, more and more of the earlier punished behavior gets expressed. The manifestations of anxiety become less and less severe as the person gets these reactions "out of his system." As the extinction process continues, the stimuli that have so commonly set the occasion for these responses become less and less effective in arousing future emotional behavior. The person reports he "feels better," is less anxious, or guilty, or sinful. The earlier acquired escape and avoidance behavior loses its effectiveness and is also extinguished.

The detrimental effect of the therapist as a punishing audience has been experimentally demonstrated. Erickson and Kuethe[19] presented subjects with a 15-word free association test and asked them to respond to each stimulus word with the first word that came to mind. The subjects were told that they were taking part in an experiment to determine the limit of speed upon associations. During the first presentations of the list, a shock was given immediately after five arbitrarily selected words. On further trials, each time the subject responded by a word that had been one of the earlier shocked responses, another shock was given. Subjects were then told there would be no more shocks and that they could chain-associate each of the stimulus words previously given. Some subjects were able to verbalize the conditions that had given rise to shock; others could not. However, both kinds of subjects showed a rapid conditioning of the avoidance behavior. That is, *they avoided saying words that had been shocked.* When no shock was given, and all subjects asked to associate, whether or not they were aware of the experimental contingencies, they showed a significant decline in the number of earlier punished (shocked) responses.

GENERALIZATION, DISCRIMINATION, AND DIFFERENTIATION IN THERAPY

In the therapeutic situation, the processes of generalization, discrimination, and differentiation go hand in hand as the patient shows

---

[18] B. F. Skinner, op. cit., pp. 370–371.
[19] C. W. Erickson and J. L. Kuethe, Avoidance conditioning of verbal behavior without awareness, a paradigm for repression, *Jour. Abn. Soc. Psychol.*, 53 (1956), 203–209.

improvement. First of all, as he learns to react to the therapist as a nonpunishing audience and is reinforced for increasingly more appropriate verbal discriminations, his anxiety becomes gradually extinguished, repressions are lifted, more appropriate responses become recovered, and new responses are shaped out. The patient learns to react to the therapist as a friendly individual. Appropriate responses learned in the therapeutic interview can be carried over to his activities outside the therapist's office. The process is one of simple generalization. If no generalization occurred, the patient might always be expected to respond effectively in the presence of the therapist but maintain his earlier ineffective behavior outside. The fact that generalization does occur is one of the reasons for the success of therapy. In a sense the therapist does not act as a single individual but as many persons. As the patient learns more adequate social responses to the therapist, he can generalize the same responses to the many social stimuli in his environment.[20]

But in order for the more appropriate responses to be generalized to life situations, a new set of discriminations must be learned. Not only must the patient learn about conditions in his past that have participated in the development of his trouble, but he must also acquire the more adequate responses that are going to achieve positive reinforcements in the future. The job of the therapist is to facilitate these discriminations through selective reinforcement. Likewise, the therapist must shape out, through differentiation, responses that may have a low probability in the beginning. In this situation the function of the therapist is much like that of a good coach or teacher. He must shape out the little effective behavior that may be left in the patient's behavioral repertoire. In the beginning, the therapist may have to reinforce generously any verbal behavior that the patient may emit. He may begin by reinforcing anything the patient says, including his complaints and miseries. If therapy is successful, the reinforcements become more selective when responses that show some understanding and indicate a more positive approach to life are emitted. When significant statements concerning the patient's past or relations with his present environment are made, reinforcements are given. The therapist gradually tries to extinguish those responses which seem to be expressions of avoidance and anxiety, including verbalizations of hopelessness and despair.

The therapist may first concentrate on expression of events in the patient's past. These may include statements referring to his brothers and sisters, parents, illnesses, conflict, and so forth. When past relations are adequately clarified, they can be contrasted with the present to show how things have changed. Objects of childhood fear are no longer in existence. Sibling rivalries have disappeared, and childhood dependencies are no longer available. It is a generally valid clinical fact that it is

[20] A. Magaret, Generalization in successful psychotherapy, *Jour. Consult. Psychol.*, **14** (1950), 64–69.

helpful to recall events of the past. Knowledge of the past helps to explain present conditions, since it was under earlier circumstances that the present difficulties have arisen.[21]

Differentiation and discrimination go hand in hand. On the discriminative side, responses related to the present are distinguished from those in his past. The patient must learn to react to neutral stimuli without fear or despair, and he must discriminate real dangers from artificial ones. He must learn that most people are neither hostile nor dangerous and can be the source of much positive reinforcement. By recalling events in the past, which may have been traumatic or in some other way the source of anxiety, he learns to discriminate them from present events. The objects of childhood fears are no longer dangers for adults. The conditions of adulthood, the threats as well as the reinforcements, are different in many ways from those of childhood.

Differentiation or shaping is also a tremendously important principle in many forms of behavior therapy, particularly reinforcement therapy (see pp. 433–438). In this latter instance, the therapist works more directly with specific forms of behavior, which may or may not be verbal. His job may be to shape new responses or reestablish responses that have been lost to the person's behavioral repertoire.

## Summary

We have described three kinds of conventional therapy: psychoanalytic, client-centered, and directive. Of the three, psychoanalysis is the oldest, having had its beginnings with Sigmund Freud about the turn of the century. Carl Rogers' client-centered therapy began in the early forties, and directive therapy of Thorne shortly thereafter. Whether or not psychoanalysis works or is worth the time and expense is open to question. Its opponents certainly do not think so. Regrettably, psychoanalysis has not presented any objective proof of its successes or failures.

There is some quasi-experimental evidence to indicate that client-centered therapy is successful, at least in some instances. The same is true for directive therapy. There are, of course, other forms of conventional therapy not mentioned in this chapter, such as psychodrama, hypnosis, and hypnoanalysis, as well as various forms of group therapy. If these therapies are successful, it is because appropriate learning has taken place. In the second part of the chapter we presented some of the principles of learning, including positive reinforcement, extinction, differentiation, and discriminaton, which could operate in the development of more adaptive forms of behavior.

21 J. Dollard and N. E. Miller, op. cit.

In the following chapter we shall discuss some forms of the newer behavior therapy. In these instances an experimental approach to the modification of behavior is attempted, and in many of the studies as well as individual case reports the evidence seems to favor a definite improvement. Behavior therapy does not claim 100 per cent improvement or cures, but at least statistical data are readily available and the behavior therapist is not afraid to present his results. If behavior therapy is successful, it is because the proper learning principles have been applied. These are explicitly stated, and the successes are less open to question than in the more conventional forms of therapy.

# 18 Behavior Therapy

THE TERM *BEHAVIOR THERAPY* REFERS TO those techniques of therapy which make obvious use of learning theory or the principles of behavioral analysis developed from learning theory. The techniques make use of many kinds of behavior control involving both operant and respondent conditioning. These include conditioning with positive reinforcement, extinction, shaping, deprivation, and satiation, as well as aversive conditioning in avoidance and punishment. In many of our chapters we have cited examples of different kinds of behavior therapy dealing with children and adult disorders either of a neurotic or psychotic nature. The basic premise in behavior therapy is that maladaptive behavior, like adaptive behavior, *is learned*. The problem for the therapist is either to get rid of the maladaptive forms of responding or to condition and shape more appropriate forms of conduct that will be incompatible with the maladaptive behavior already developed.

## Systematic Desensitization or Reciprocal Inhibition

Dissatisfied with the results of the more conventional therapies of psychoanalysis and client-centered therapy, Wolpe attempted a more experimental approach.[1] In the 1920s Watson and Jones had described the conditioning and elimination of children's fears, and from these studies Wolpe took his lead. He started by conditioning experimental neuroses in cats. He then came to the conclusion that the most successful methods of treating these conditions was a process of gradual desensitization. He began by feeding his neurotic cats in an environment that was vastly dissimilar to the one in which they had been originally conditioned. He proceeded through a carefully worked out series of environments that approximated more and more the one in which the neuroses had been originally conditioned. He found that this process gradually reduced the cats' neurotic activity and eventually returned them to more normal activity. At this stage of his experimentation, he found the majority of his human subjects suffering from anxiety. In 1924, Mary Cover Jones[2] had successfully eliminated a boy's fear for all sorts of furry animals by bringing the animal closer and closer to the boy (desensitization) and also by feeding him at the same time. However, it did not appear too feasible to use the feeding response and neurotically anxious human adults. Wolpe desired to find a response that could be conditioned to be the antithesis of anxiety and came upon Jacobson's technique of progressive relaxation.[3]

In his initial attempts, Wolpe[4] tried to teach relaxation in the actual presence of his feared objects. This became somewhat impractical because it involved the actual collection of feared objects in the treatment of each person. He then substituted the imagining of the anxiety-arousing situations and objects. For example, if a patient had a phobia for snakes, instead of presenting the actual snakes (sometimes difficult to acquire) Wolpe simply asked the patient to imagine looking at a snake. This method not only produced positive results but made the matter much easier to handle in a therapeutic situation taking place in his office.

The relaxation procedure as described by Wolpe in 1969[5] involves tensing various muscles and asking the subject to concentrate on the tension, then relaxing the muscles and concentrating likewise. The therapist then instructs the subject to follow the same procedure through various muscle groups (face, neck, shoulders, chest, arms, stomach, hips, thighs, calves, etc.). After several sessions plus practice on his own the subject should be able to engage in deep relaxation whenever he wishes

---

[1] J. Wolpe, *Psychotherapy by reciprocal inhibition* (Stanford, Calif.: Stanford University Press, 1958).

[2] M. C. Jones, A laboratory study of fear: The case of Peter, *Pedagog. Sem.*, **31** (1924), 308–315.

[3] E. Jacobson, *Progressive relaxation* (Chicago: University of Chicago Press, 1938).

[4] J. Wolpe, op. cit.

[5] J. Wolpe, *The practice of behavior therapy* (Elmsford, N.Y.: Pergamon Press, 1969).

or is instructed to do so when given a particular cue by the therapist. Other procedures also suggested by Wolpe include imagining pleasant events, hypnosis, and the use of drugs.

After relaxation is well trained, the subject is asked to establish a hierarchy of a group of things which trouble him. These are often anxiety-arousing events related to a particular problem such as a snake phobia. Later on, these events will be presented to him while he attempts to maintain a state of relaxation. Thus, a conditioned inhibition is built up in which the patient can imagine the most troublesome event and still remain relaxed.

Of course, before the actual desensitization process takes place the person gives a complete history of his problem (as he can recall it) as well as a general life history.

*Establishing a Hierarchy.*   Rank orders of hierarchies are established for each category or situation that a person is usually anxious about in terms of the degree of anxiety the person reports he feels. After the hierarchy is established the subjct is asked to imagine the least anxiety-arousing situation and then work through the group to the most severe. In some cases, such of fear of snakes or test anxiety, it may involve only a single hierarchy while in other cases there may be several hierarchies for a given subject.

The following is a sample hierarchy regarding fear of death. In this particular subject the most anxious situation is listed first, but in going through the desensitization procedure the subject would begin at the bottom and work up.

> *Hierarchy of a Fear of Death*
> 1. You are at your father's funeral viewing him in the coffin.
> 2. Phone call from your aunt saying your mother is dead.
> 3. Picturing self in coffin.
> 4. Thought occurs to you. "Someday I will die, my folks will die."
> 5. Wife in coffin.
> 6. Hearing that grandfather on your mother's side has died.
> 7. Listening to the Indianapolis 400-mile race on radio; announcer describes the deaths of Ed Sachs and Ed McDonald.
> 8. Hear on radio that President Kennedy is dead.
> 9. You read in the newspaper that Clark Gable is dead.
> 10. You read in the paper that Fred Harvey, age 24 . . . died of a heart attack.
> 11. You read in the paper that Fred Anderson, age 58, died of a heart attack.
> 12. Mentioned in family discussion that great-great grandfather starved to death in the potato famine.[6]

[6] J. N. Marquis, W. G. Masgan, and G. W. Piaget, *A guidebook for systematic desensitization*, 2nd ed. (Palo Alto, Calif.: Veterans Administration Workshop, Veterans Administration Hospital, 1971), p. 45.

When all this has been completed, the actual process of desensitization begins. As Wolpe suggests, if a response that is antagonistic to anxiety can be developed in the presence of the anxiety-arousing stimulus, the result must be a suppression of the anxiety, and the bond between the stimuli and anxiety responses will be weakened.

Usually the establishment of the anxiety hierarchy takes from one to three interviews. In an individual session, the patient is presented with the anxiety-arousing stimulus to imagine. He is also told to signal the therapist with his hand if the stimulus disturbs him excessively. This is a necessary part of the procedure because the arousal of excessive anxiety during the therapeutic session would disrupt the whole therapeutic process. With most patients the therapist can also tell if the anxiety is excessive by observing facial expressions, muscular tensions, respiration, etc. After relaxation the therapist asks the patient to visualize the object of his fear. Each of these visualizations is called a *presentation*. Each image is presented two or three times in any one therapeutic session. The items lowest on the hierarchy are presented first. The therapist then proceeds gradually up the list on succeeding sessions depending on how rapidly the patient is able to visualize it. The aim of the therapy is to enable the patient to visualize the most traumatic stimuli without arousing any anxiety. For inhibition to work properly, it is necessary for the patient to experience some anxiety during the session, but the success of the treatment depends on the inhibition of small signs of anxiety in a gradual manner. Rachman[7] has pointed out that understanding the origins of the neurotic symptoms are helpful, but therapeutic sessions can still be successful without such knowledge.

In our discussion we have implied that anxieties are particularly susceptible to treatment by systematic desensitization. The treatment of anxiety disorders has been a most common application of the technique. However, other disorders can also be treated. Shortly we will describe a case of treatment of exhibitionism by this method.

*Group Desensitization.* The process of desensitization can also be applied to groups. However, it is necessary to construct a hierarchy common for all members. This can be done if the fear, for example, is a relatively common one such as a fear of snakes, test anxiety in students, or fear of speaking in public. One limiting factor tends to operate when the therapy is done with groups—namely the rate of progress through the hierarchy has to be geared to the slowest person.

A common criticism of the technique is that it merely treats symptoms and does not get at the root of a person's disorder. According to

---

[7] S. Rachman, Objective psychotherapy: Some theoretical considerations, *S. Afri. Med. J.*, **33** (1958), 19–21.

Wolpe[8] this criticism is not valid, because anxiety that is conditioned can be permanently removed by deconditioning. The aim of the therapy is the lasting elimination of the neurotic symptoms.

Freud's theory of neurosis states that neurotic symptoms are outward manifestations of emotional forces that have been repressed and constitute a compromise between the partial discharge of these forces and the various defences that resist this discharge. According to Freud, the therapeutic benefits of psychoanalysis are the result of making the repressed impulses conscious by overcoming the resistances that are aroused to thwart them. Wolpe[9] contends that the elimination of neurotic symptoms can be obtained *without the use of psychoanalytic procedures*, which are lasting and expensive; that is, he believes that what psychoanalysis maintains is necessary for permanent recovery is *not* indeed necessary. Wolpe says:

> We need to consider to what extent the therapeutic procedures based on psychoanalytic theory have been effective in bringing about recovery from neurosis. It must be said at once that the evidence available is remarkable for its paucity, considering that psychoanalysis has been practiced for sixty years. It is also remarkable that, as far as I have been able to discover, not a single individual psychoanalyst has ever published a statistical survey of his own practice. Is it unreasonable to ask if this may be at least partly because they have not been very happy with their results.[10]

And according to Mowrer,

> From testimony now available from both friends and foes of analysis, it is clear that, at best, analysis casts a spell but does not cure.
>
> .    .    .
>
> There is not a shred of evidence that psychoanalyzed individuals permanently benefit from the experience and there are equally clear indications that psychoanalysis, as a common philosophy of life, is not only nontherapeutic but actively pernicious.[11]

### RESULTS OF THERAPY BY SYSTEMATIC DESENSITIZATION

Lazarus[12] has reported on the treatment of 408 patients treated by Wolpe's method. He reports significant improvement in 321 patients (78

[8] J. Wolpe, The prognosis in unpsychoanalyzed recovery from neurosis, *Amer. J. Psychiat.*, **117** (1961), 35–39.

[9] J. Wolpe, *Psychotherapy by reciprocal inhibition* (Stanford, Calif.: Stanford University Press, 1958).

[10] J. Wolpe, A. Salter, and L. J. Reyna, eds., *The conditioning therapies* (New York: Holt, Rinehart and Winston, 1964), pp. 7–8.

[11] O. H. Mowrer, *The crisis in psychiatry and religion* (New York: Van Nostrand, 1959), pp. 121–161.

[12] A. Lazarus, The results of behavior therapy in 126 cases of severe neurosis, *Behav. Res. Ther.*, **1** (1963), 63–78.

per cent). He made a further analysis of 126 patients who were described as suffering from "widespread, diffuse, and pervasive neurotic disorders" because there was criticism on the part of the more traditional therapists that this form of behavior therapy dealt with simple neurotic conditions in which there were one or two easily identified symptoms. Of these severe cases, 62 per cent were cured or much improved. The average number of therapeutic sessions was only 15—quite a difference from the hundreds usually required by the traditional psychotherapies. In a follow-up study of all 126 cases, only one had shown a severe relapse. The average time of follow-up was 2.15 years.

In another study by Lang and Lazovik,[13] a carefully controlled experimental procedure was followed. They chose as subjects individuals all of whom had snake phobias, chosen because of the prevalence of this kind of phobia.

Following training in relaxation, an experimental group was given eleven sessions of systematic desensitization. Furthermore, half of the experimental subjects were exposed to a live snake prior to treatment. The controls did not receive treatment in desensitization. All available subjects were evaluated six months after the completion of therapy. As measures of behavioral change they used a subjective rating scale for the fear and overt avoidance behavior in the presence of the snake. Both measures supported the improvement. The control group's responses on both tests were much higher, indicating the positive effects of the therapy.

Wolpe[14] has reported positive results with a variety of different kinds of phobias. In 30 cases, all of whom responded favorably, he found that claustrophobia (fear of closed places) requires more visualizations in working up the anxiety hierarchy. Agoraphobia (fear of open places) requires more visualizations at the lower end of the hierarchy but relatively few as one goes up.

Tooley and Pratt[15] have applied a variation of systematic desensitization in the elimination of smoking behavior. Two subjects, husband and wife, were reported to be heavy smokers. Ray was smoking 50 cigarettes a day and Marty, his wife, 35. After training in relaxation they were asked to imagine sitting before their television set, picking up a cigarette, and lighting it. They were then told that as soon as they tasted the cigarette they would feel sick to their stomachs and nauseated. The more they smoked, the more nauseated they would become. In further sessions they were told to imagine smoking in a variety of situations in which

---

[13] P. J. Lang and A. D. Lazovik, The experimental desensitization of a phobia, *Jour. Abn. Soc. Psychol.*, **66** (1963), 319–325.

[14] J. Wolpe, Quantitative relationships in the systematic desensitization of a phobia, *Amer. J. Psychiat.*, **119** (1963), 1062–1068.

[15] J. T. Tooley and S. Pratt, An experimental procedure for the extinction of smoking behavior, *Psychol. Rec.*, **17** (1967), 209–218.

smoking is likely to occur—with friends, while drinking coffee, after a meal, etc. In each instance the feeling of nausea was suggested. By the end of the third session, the subjects had reduced their cigarettes to about half a pack a day.

The second phase of this treatment was called *contingency management*. Each subject was asked to think of all the aversive effects of smoking, such as bad influences on their children, bad taste in the mouth, waste of money, etc. Then a highly probable behavior was suggested as a positive reinforcer—for Ray, drinking coffee, and for Marty, drinking water. After five sessions of this treatment Ray was down to five cigarettes a day and Marty to one.

At this point a *contractual commitment* was added. Both parties agreed to give up the first cigarette of the day and never smoke in the presence of the other. Ray dropped to two cigarettes a day and Marty to none. By the ninth session, Ray had agreed to join his wife and become "clean" of smoking. After four "clean" days, Ray was called to San Francisco and away from his nonsmoking contracts. He had a relapse of two days. One relapse occurred on the plane when he was offered free cigarettes by the stewardess. The other was at a social gathering when his associates insisted that he have a cigarette. Upon his return, he recommitted himself to abstinence, even to the extent of expressing publicly, "No, thank you. I've given up smoking" (see Fig. 18–1).

*Treating Exhibitionism Through Desensitization.* Bond and Hutchison[16] report a case of the elimination of exhibitionism by systematic desensitization. In this case a 25-year-old man had a practice of hiding completely in the nude in a small wooded area in the center of the town where he lived. He would then spring out and expose himself to the first woman who passed by. Another practice of his was to hide in the cloakroom of a girls' school and expose himself when a girl went to the lavatory. If the door was locked, he would lie on the floor and thrust his erect penis under the door for the occupant to view. In treatment a hierarchy of exposure-producing stimuli was established in terms of the type of femal physical attributes and places of exposure. After the twentieth session the treatment was terminated, although he continued to practice relaxation at home. However, subsequently he felt compelled to follow women around a department store. At this point he passed the lingerie counter and exposed his penis in the presence of ladies, but he did not achieve erection. He was subsequently arrested; but the court was lenient and he returned for thirteen more sessions, after which he appeared to be completely free of his symptoms. He found

[16] I. K. Bond and H. C. Hutchison, Application of reciprocal inhibition therapy to exhibitionism, *Canadian Med. Assn. Jour.*, **83** (1960).

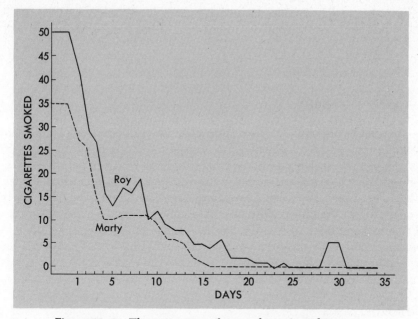

**Figure 18–1.** The extinction of two subjects' smoking behavior over time. (From J. T. Tooley and S. Pratt, An experimental procedure for the extinction of smoking behavior, *Psychological Record,* **17** [1967], 209–218, p. 214. Copyright 1967, *The Psychological Records.* Reproduced by permission of the author and the publisher.)

a job involving manual labor and reported that lewd jokes, which previously would have "set him on a rampage," now had no effect on him.

Considering its brief history, it would seem that behavior therapy by reciprocal inhibition has been quite successful. Eysenck and Rachman[17] report that this kind of treatment has several advantages. First, it is based on established psychological principles that have a large body of experimental evidence in their support. Further, the therapeutic process is open to quantification. It permits a systematic planning of treatment. These authors report an estimate based on a number of large-scale studies, which indicates that about 80 per cent of patients treated were either apparently cured or markedly improved.

Finally, the length of time required to effect these recoveries is significantly smaller than that required by conventional types of therapy, in particular, psychoanalysis. Although systematic desensitization tech-

[17] H. J. Eysenck and S. Rachman, *The causes and cures of neurosis* (San Diego, Calif.: Robert R. Knapp, 1965).

niques are widely applied to anxiety states (especially phobias), it has been demonstrated to apply to other forms of neurotic conditions as well.

## Aversion Therapy

Aversion therapy is based primarily on principles of respondent conditioning and punishment. Ordinarily the Conditioned Stimulus (CS) is paired with an Unconditional Stimulus (US) which is naturally aversive to the organism; a stimulus inducing nausea or pain, such as electric shock, are commonly used. Aversion therapy has found to be particularly successful in treating conditions of alcoholism and sexual disorders. Prior to conditioning, the CS has had some reinforcing function, but when paired with the primary aversive one (US) it also takes on the function of becoming aversive.

### ALCOHOLISM

In treating alcoholism by the method described by Voeglin and Lemere,[18] the patient is given a hypodermic injection of emetine, a nausea-producing substance, plus an oral dose of the same substance to bring him to the verge of nausea and vomiting. Under these conditions nausea is produced in about 30 to 60 seconds, and vomiting is delayed for another two minutes. They suggest that the treatment be given in a small darkened room with a spotlight on a row of bottles in front of the patient to act as the conditioning stimuli. Soft drinks are given freely during the sessions. Over 4,000 patients have been followed up after a year or more with the following percentages reaching complete abstinence:

| Length of Abstinence | Percentage Remaining Cured |
|---|---|
| 1 to 2 years | 60% |
| 2 to 5 years | 51% |
| 5 to 10 years | 38% |
| 10 to 13 years | 23% |

These figures are taken from a follow-up study done in 1950 with an overall abstinence rate of 51 per cent for all patients studied.[19]

[18] W. L. Voeglin and F. Lemere, The treatment of alcohol addiction, *Quart. Jour. Stud. Alcohol.*, 2 (1942), 717–803.

[19] F. Lemere and W. Voeglin, An evaluation of aversion treatment of alcoholism, *Quart. Jour. Stud. Alcohol*, 11 (1950), 199–204.

Voeglin[20] also describes some variations on the above technique. He suggests that the conditioned stimuli may not only consist of the sight of alcoholic substances, but the taste as well as the smell of alcohol may be associated with nausea and vomiting.

Bandura[21] has reviewed the results of 15 studies using various kinds of aversion treatment with alcoholics (involving either induced nausea or electric shock). The studies involved from 15 to 4,000 subjects, and follow-ups ran from a few months to ten years. He found that the percentage of complete alcohol abstinence ranged from 23 per cent to 96 per cent.

Much of the early work involving treating alcoholics involved the use of some chemical which induced nausea as described above. More recent studies have tended to favor the use of electric shock according to Rachman and Teasdale.[22] They suggest the following reasons:

1. Drugs which produce nausea and vomiting are more difficult to work with for both subjects and staff.
2. There are often undesirable side effects with drugs, for example, depression.
3. Fewer trials per day can be run with drugs than with shock.
4. It is more difficult to control many of the variables involved in successful treatment with drugs, such as the onset of the unconditioned response, duration, and intensity of the nausea.

*Cigarette Smoking.* The use of aversion therapy for cigarette smoking has not generally met with great success. Usually electric shock is paired with smoking or some aspect of it such as opening a pack (see p. 268). However, Schmahl et al.[23] have reported some success in getting habitual smokers to quit by using warm, smokey air blown into the subjects' faces as they continued to smoke. They were asked to continue to smoke cigarettes until they could no longer tolerate the aversive stimuli. At the termination of the therapeutic sessions all 25 subjects were abstainers. The sessions averaged eight trials for each subject. A follow-up study six months later found 16 had not returned to their previous smoking habits.

In a comparative study Mastron and McFall[24] used four different methods in an attempt to reduce cigarette smoking. The procedures were

[20] W. L. Voeglin, The treatment of alcoholism by establishing a conditioned reflex, *Amer. Jour. Med. Sci.*, **119** (1940), 125–128.

[21] A. Bandura, *Principles of behavior modification* (New York: Holt, Rinehart and Winston, 1969).

[22] S. Rachman and J. Teasdale, *Aversion therapy and behavior disorders: An analysis* (Coral Gables, Fla.: University of Miami Press, 1969).

[23] D. P. Schmahl, E. Lichtenstein, and D. E. Harris, Successful treatment of habitual smokers with warm, smokey air and rapid smoking, *Jour. Cons. and Clin. Psychol.*, **38** (1972), 105–111.

[24] A. R. Mastron and R. M. McFall, Comparison of behavior modification approaches to smoking reduction, *Jour. Cons. and Clin. Psychol.*, **36** (1971), 153–162.

(1) use of a pill which coated the mouth and make smoking aversive (aversion therapy), (2) slight satiation in which subjects smoked three cigarettes in a row during each session, (3) development of a hierarchy in which subjects "cut down," smoking fewer cigarettes each day, and (4) quitting "cold turkey." Prior to the use of the various methods an average of 28 cigarettes per day was smoked by the subjects. At the end of the seventh day of treatment, the average number of cigarettes smoked had reduced to 14 per day, but a six months' follow-up indicated that subjects were smoking 20 cigarettes per day. The investigators also reported that the four methods were quite similar in their effectiveness and rate of relapse.

### FETISHISM

Raymond[25] reports the case of a man who had a fetish for ladies' handbags and perambulators, which brought him into frequent brushes with the law because he frequently smeared mucus on the ladies' handbags and destroyed the perambulators by running into them with his motorcycle. The treatment consisted of showing him a collection of handbags and perambulators along with colored pictures of them just before the onset of nausea produced by an injection of apomorphine. Not only was the fetish successfully eliminated, but the man showed a great improvement in his social and legal relationships. He was promoted to a more responsible position at his work and no longer required fetish fantasies to enable him to have sexual intercourse.

Kushner[26] reports the case of a 33-year-old man who had a fetish for women's panties, which presumably had its start when he recalled masturbating while wearing the panties he usually took from clotheslines. When none was available he stimulated himself by looking at pictures of scantily clad women or by fantasies of women wearing panties. The fetish not only led to impotency but to antisocial behavior which had led first to a confinement in a boys' reformatory and later in prison. Realizing that his fetish was at least indirectly related to his antisocial behavior, he sought treatment. The fetish was considered to be the product of maladaptive learning, and aversion therapy was instituted. He recalled that the first time he became sexually excited was when he watched girls sliding down a sliding board with their panties exposed. In this instance the unconditioned stimulus was electric shock, which was adjusted until it became so uncomfortable that he wanted it removed. Conditioning stimuli consisted of magazine-size pictures of

25 M. S. Raymond, Case of fetishism treated by aversion therapy, *Brit. Med. Jour.*, 21 (1956), 854–857.

26 M. Kushner, The reduction of a long-standing fetish by means of aversive conditioning. In L. P. Ullmann and L. Krasner, eds., *Case studies in behavior modification* (New York: Holt, Rinehart and Winston, 1965).

the rear view of a woman wearing panties as well as an actual pair of panties placed in his hand. He was also asked to imagine that he was wearing panties. Treatment consisted of 41 sessions spread over 14 weeks. Conditioning was stopped when the patient reported he no longer was troubled by the fetish. Approximately one month following the treatment, spontaneous recovery of the fetish appeared. Two more treatment sessions were prescribed. At the last report he was married and holding a job. He occasionally has fleeting recurrence of the fetish, but has no difficulty in thinking of other things and does not dwell on the fetish as in the past.

TRANSVESTISM

Lavin et al.[27] have applied aversive conditioning to treatment of a transvestite (one who gets sexual excitement out of dressing up in the clothes of the opposite sex). As the unconditioned stimulus, they used apomorphine as a nausea-producing substance. The conditioning stimuli consisted of a series of slides taken of the patient himself in various stages of dressing, with a tape recording of his voice describing his clothes. The recording was used to ensure the continued presence of the CS even when his eyes were closed during vomiting. The drug (US) was injected, and just before nausea set in, a slide was projected on the screen and the voice recording presented. Treatment consisted of the presentation of the paired stimuli every two hours both day and night. After six days of this procedure the patient was judged cured.

One of the questions that arises with regard to aversion therapy is the matter of generalization. For example, if a man is made rid of his fetish for women's clothing, as in transvestism, will the aversion generalize to women in general? Gelder and Marks[28] paired electric shock with various pieces of women's underclothing (panties, pajamas, a slip, etc.) After the completion of aversion therapy, they found that the man in question was still sexually responsive to heterosexual stimuli, for example, pictures of female nudes.

*Covert Sensitization in Aversion Therapy.* A variation in aversion therapy is called *covert sensitization,* or *aversion imagery.* In this instance imagined scenes are used. For example, Cautela[29] had a subject, an excessive drinker, close his eyes and imagine that he had a highball

[27] N. I. Lavin, J. G. Thorpe, J. C. Barker, C. B. Blakemore, and C. G. Conway, Behavior therapy in the case of transvestism, *Jour. Nerv. Ment. Dis.,* **133** (1961), 346–353.

[28] M. G. Gelder and I. M. Marks, Aversion treatment in transvestism and transexualism. In R. Green, ed., *Transvestism and sex management* (Baltimore: Johns Hopkins Press, 1969).

[29] J. R. Cautela, Treatment of compulsive behavior by covert sensitization, *Psychol. Rec.,* **16** (1966), 33–41.

glass with a drink obviously in it, then, bring it to his lips. Just as the glass was about to touch his lips, he imagined feeling sick and vomiting. He then put the glass down and relaxed. Gautela feels the same procedure can be applied to a variety of other behaviors that one might wish to eliminate including smoking, sexual deviations, and compulsive eating.

*Disadvantages of Aversion Therapy.* Rachman and Teasdale[30] have suggested some of the disadvantages of aversion therapy, particularly when electric shock is used.

1. Subjects do not like it.
2. Subjects often become more aggressive.
3. It may cause an increase in anxiety. If the problem, for example, in alcoholism is based on anxiety, the treatment may increase that anxiety.
4. It cannot be used with everyone, particularly cardiac patients.

IMPLOSIVE THERAPY

A recent innovation has been developed by Stampff and Lewin[31] called *implosive therapy*, or *flooding*. Usually, the subject is presented with stimuli that are highly anxiety arousing (sometimes imaginal). The technique basically involves the process of extinction. For example, if a person has a strong fear of snakes, he might be asked to close his eyes and imagine a series of scenes; watching a rattler coil ready to strike, having the snake crawl over him, and so on. After a number of such treatments it is presumed that the fear will die out.

The effectiveness of implosive therapy is still somewhat in question. According to Mikulas,[32] there are a number of confounding variables; for example, positive incentives are used to get the subject to approach the feared stimulus. Furthermore, many of the scenes used (images), are more revolting than those naturally occurring—for example, asking the subject who fears snakes to imagine a snake pulling out his eyes and then crawling into the socket. There is also the possibility suggested by Mikulas[33] that using implosive therapy may actually condition more anxiety instead of producing extinction. If it does work it is due to contrast; that is, after imagining the terrifying scenes, the real situation seems milder by contrast.

[30] S. Rachman and J. Teasdale, *Aversion therapy and behavior disorders: An analysis* (Coral Gables, Fla.: University of Miami Press, 1969).
[31] T. G. Stampff and D. J. Lewin, Essentials of implosive therapy: A learning theory based psychological therapy, *Jour. Abn. Psychol.,* 72 (1967), 496—503.
[32] W. L. Mikulas, *Behavior modification: An overview* (New York: Harper & Row, 1972).
[33] Ibid.

Wolpe[34] has reported his own experiences with implosive therapy. He has expressed a reluctance to the free use of the flooding technique except only as a final recourse after all other techniques have failed.

On the more positive side, Barrett[35] has compared systematic desensitization therapy with implosive therapy for their effectiveness in reducing snake phobias in otherwise normal adults. He found both techniques to be equally effective. The phobias remained reduced in a six-month follow-up study. Both overt avoidance (refusing to handle a harmless snake) and verbal reports of fear were reduced. He also found implosive therapy to be shorter, being completed in 45 per cent of the time required by systematic desensitization. However, the subjects in implosive therapy showed more inconsistencies; that is, some subjects relapsed after therapy.

## Reinforcement Therapy

Many examples of reinforcement therapy have already been presented (see Chapter 5, "Discrimination and Differentiation"; Chapter 15, Neurotic Behavior"; and Chapter 16, "Psychotic Behavior") to show how operant conditioning techniques, using positive reinforcement, can be applied to establish, maintain, or modify behavior. The basic principle is the establishment and conditioning of new behavior or, through the process of shaping, the reconditioning of more adaptive behavior in lieu of persistent maladaptive responding. In the examples that follow we shall present a variety of different conditions in which this technique is applied. With proper ingenuity on the part of the therapist, reinforcement therapy can be applied to a wide variety of conditions, including verbal behavior, stuttering, toilet training, and many kinds of neurotic and psychotic symptoms.

### CONDITIONING VERBAL BEHAVIOR IN MENTAL PATIENTS

Ayllon and Azrin[36] have observed that some psychiatric patients fail to pick up the proper eating utensils before receiving their food trays in a cafeteria line at mealtimes. Under these conditions the patients must either eat with what they have, eat with their hands, or not eat at all. It

---

[34] J. Wolpe, *The practice of behavior therapy* (Elmsford, N.Y.: Pergamon Press, 1969), 189.

[35] C. L. Barrett, Systematic desensitization vs. implosive therapy, *Jour. Abn. Psychol.*, **74** (1969), 587–592.

[36] T. Ayllon and N. H. Azrin, Reinforcement and instructions with mental patients, *Jour. Exp. Anal. Behav.*, **7** (1964), 327–331.

is also a common observation that many mental patients, particularly chronic or long-standing cases, are so withdrawn that they fail to react very effectively to verbal instructions. A group of patients who failed to pick up the knife, fork, and spoon before meals was chosen as subjects for treatment. If a patient made the appropriate response of picking up the three utensils, he was allowed immediate access to the food counter. If the appropriate response was not made, there was a delay in which the patient had to return to the end of the line, or if he was the last in line a delay of five minutes was introduced before he was allowed access to the serving counter. The first period of treatment or experimentation consisted of 10 meals during which no instructions or consequences were arranged. During the next 10 meals, instructions were given to each patient at each meal but no consequences occurred if he failed to follow them. During the third period of 10 meals, instructions were continued and consequences were added. If the patient responded appropriately to the instructions of picking up knife, fork, and spoon, he was given immediate access to food; if not, he went to the end of the line. In the initial period the appropriate response seldom occurred. When the instructions alone were added, about 40 per cent of the patients responded accordingly. However, on succeeding days the percentage of response on any day was quite erratic. During the third period when the correct response to the instructions led to immediate access to food and failure led to the delay, the percentage of correct responses to instructions jumped to 80 per cent on the first four meals. By the fifth meal, the percentage had jumped to 90 per cent of the patients responding correctly.

Ayllon and Azrin believe that the above results have many applications to verbal therapy. In most forms of therapy, the patient is offered either verbal advice, verbal interpretation, or verbal agreement. In this study it was necessary to provide or withhold consequences (reinforcement), in addition to giving verbal instructions. When verbal instructions led to immediate consequences (in this instance, food) their effectiveness was dramatically increased with regard to mental patients.

In some chronic schizophrenics, the verbal responses are entirely absent—that is, the patients are mute. Isaacs, Thomas, and Goldiamond[37] describe the case of shaping vocal responses in a chronic catatonic schizophrenic who had been mute for 19 years. For the first two weeks a piece of chewing gum was placed before the subject. The experimenter waited until the patient noticed it. He was then given the gum. During the next two weeks, the therapist waited until lip-moving responses were made before giving the patient the gum. By the end of this time, both lip and eye movements occurred prior to the presentation of the gum as reinforcement. During the succeeding three weeks the gum was held up

[37] W. Isaacs, J. Thomas, and I. Goldiamond, Shaping vocal responses in mute catatonic schizophrenics, *Jour. Speech and Hear. Dis.*, 25 (1960), 8–12.

and the subject was instructed to say "Gum." Obtaining the gum was contingent upon vocalizations that successively approximated the word *gum*. Thereafter, other vocal responses were shaped out, then vocal responses in the presence of other persons were demanded. Subsequently, it was possible to get the patient to speak in group therapy sessions.[38]

Using candy, peanuts, sips of soda, and praise as reinforcers, Salzinger et al.[39] were able to shape out verbal responses in a speech-deficient child. At the beginning of treatment the child's vocabulary was almost entirely limited to the word *no*, although used appropriately. The child occasionally said other words, such as *key*, but only infrequently. In the beginning the child was difficult to work with because of his extreme fear of participation—that is, fear of therapist (experimenter), fear of going to the test room, etc. By the end of 20 months, the boy was speaking almost entirely in sentences and employing a variety of grammatical constructions. Likewise, his social behavior was markedly improved, particularly in regard to his responses to strangers.

REINFORCEMENT THERAPY AND STUTTERING

It is generally agreed that stuttering is a maladaptive form of behavior acquired in the presence of certain discriminative stimuli and is maintained through some form of reinforcement. Precisely what the reinforcers are that maintain the behavior are not always identifiable. Many psychologists have presumed that stuttering is merely symptomatic of some much greater underlying personality problem, but this assumption has certainly not been definitely proven empirically.

Rickard and Mundy[40] have studied the case of a nine-year-old boy who was a chronic stutterer. The treatment procedure consisted of presenting points that led to a more extrinsic reinforcement following the emission of nonstuttering speech. All stuttering behavior was ignored. The boy was first presented with very small units, such as a phrase that he was to repeat. Phrases were followed by sentences and finally paragraphs to be read aloud. The final unit consisted of whole conversations with his parents. Figure 18–2 gives an example of the improvement gained over 25 sessions in which the percentage of errors

---

[38] For a comprehensive review of recent studies on operant conditioning with children, see S. W. Bijou and D. M. Baer, Operant methods in child behavior and development. In W. K. Honig, ed., *Operant behavior: Areas of research and application* (New York: Appleton-Century-Crofts, 1966).

[39] K. Salzinger, R. S. Feldman, J. E. Cowan, and S. Salzinger, Operant conditioning of verbal behavior in two speech deficient boys. In L. Krasner and L. P. Ullmann, eds., *Research in behavior modification* (New York: Holt, Rinehart and Winston, 1965), 82–105.

[40] H. C. Rickard and M. B. Mundy, District manipulation of stuttering behavior: An experimental–clinical approach. In L. P. Ullmann and L. Krasner, eds., *Case studies in behavior modification* (New York: Holt, Rinehart and Winston, 1965).

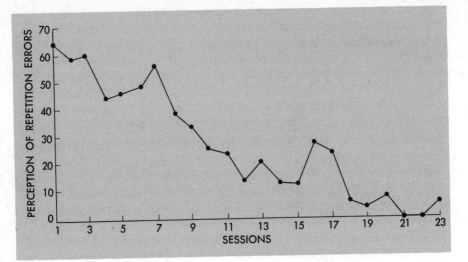

**Figure 18–2.** Per cent of phrase-reading trials in which repetition errors (stuttering) occurred. Note as the subject's fluency of reading was positively reinforced (non-stuttering), the rate of stuttering gradually decreased. (From an article entitled "Direct Manipulation of Stuttering Behavior: An Experimental-Clinical Approach" by Henry C. Rickard and Martha B. Mundy, from *Case Studies in Behavior Modification* edited by Leonard P. Ullmann and Leonard Krasner. Copyright © 1965 by Holt, Rinehart and Winston, Inc. Reproduced by permission of Holt, Rinehart and Winston, Inc.)

(stuttering) decreased to nearly zero. Similar improvement occurred in the more difficult tasks. A follow-up study was made six months after the termination of treatment, which indicated that initially the changes that occurred during conditioning applied generally to the home and school situations but that the gains were only partially maintained, and later testing showed a partial recurrence of the stuttering.

REINFORCEMENT THERAPY IN TOILET TRAINING

Madsen[41] reports a case in which a child was ready to be toilet trained, but the procedure of simply placing her on the toilet and waiting for her to eliminate was becoming unsuccessful because as soon as the child was placed on the stool she began to cry. It was decided to give the child a piece of candy as reinforcement whenever she was placed on

[41] C. H. Madsen, Positive reinforcement in training a normal child: A case report. In L. P. Ullmann and L. Krasner, eds., *Case studies in behavior modification* (New York: Holt, Rinehart and Winston, 1965).

the toilet, and successful elimination followed. Other techniques were also used. Following a "dry" nap, she was placed on the toilet while her mother read to her and otherwise entertained her. Candy was withheld following failures. The program was started when the child was almost 19 months old. By the fifth day of training the child began to ask to go to the toilet instead of merely being placed there and waiting for something to happen. By the twelfth day, the parents were satisfied that she was trained. By the fifteenth day candy was given only if the child requested it. Two months after the start of the program, the child's requests for candy had dropped to zero, and she was going to the bathroom on her own.

REINFORCEMENT THERAPY IN TRAINING THE MENTALLY DEFICIENT

In recent years there have been several studies using positive reinforcement to condition and shape useful behavior in mentally deficient and autistic children. It has been found that much useful behavior can be established if the appropriate reinforcers can be found, and, indeed, behavior developed which previously would have not been thought possible. A recent study by Ferster and Simmons[42] illustrates the point. They describe the shaping of puzzle-solving behavior in a retarded boy. In this case the therapist or experimenter held the boy in front of the puzzle, placed one piece in his hand, and held it over the appropriate place on the puzzle-board until it dropped. Because the puzzle was of a relatively simple sort, the piece was easily jarred into place. The therapist then reacted with enthusiasm, led him into an open area, and played roughhouse for one minute. On the second occasion the boy not only dropped the piece into place but nudged it into position by himself. Again, his behavior was reinforced by the roughhousing for one minute. In succeeding trials, the therapist required a little more of the patient each time until finally he (1) could pick up the piece, (2) could put it into place, (3) walked to where he had been taken to play, and (5) would lie down on the floor with his feet up waiting for the therapist to play with him. On successive days the reinforcement of roughhousing was contingent on more sustained and complicated performances with puzzles, which were much more difficult than the first.

*Contingency Contracting.* Contingency contracting involves explaining to a person what behavior he must emit before he can be reinforced. Thus, a contract is made with a person with regard to certain reinforcement contingencies. The reinforcement cannot be available outside the contract, and a balance between the desired behavior and the power of

[42] C. B. Ferster and J. Simmons, Behavior therapy with children, *Psychol. Rec.,* **16** (1966), 65–71.

the reinforcement must be made. If too much is asked of a subject for the amount of the reinforcement received, the person will not comply.

Homme[43] has described the application of contingency contracting to a classroom situation. He divided the classroom into two areas: one in which the students worked, the other in which they could engage in more reinforcing activities. In the reinforcing area the students could read material of their own choosing, play checkers, or listen to music. The procedure involved outlining for each student the required amounts of work for an appropriate time in the reinforcing area. For example, for ten minutes in the reinforcing area, a student might have to read five pages of history and correctly answer the first three questions at the end of the chapter. The author suggests that the advantages of this kind of program can allow for student individual differences and can give rise to a self-paced educational program.

*The Token Economy.*[44]  We have already made reference to the token economy in Chapter 6. It is another example of contingency contracting. One of the most important aspects of the token economy program (usually in some kind of hospital) is the appropriate involvement of staff members (ward attendants) who dispense the tokens. In most mental institutions these people take pretty much of a custodial attitude toward the patients. In the token economy the patients receive tokens for desirable behavior which can be exchanged for various privileges (see pp. 162–165). For proper application, the staff must be taught the basic principles of reinforcement, particularly the importance of specific behaviors for each patient. The tokens cannot be given out indiscriminately, but instead selectively, reinforcing desirable behavior in the areas of personal hygiene, social behavior, and work. The use of the technique of shaping and modeling are also important. The ward attendants involved are given direct responsibility for handling the patients instead of taking orders from above. Generally, each attendant is given a small group of people to work with personally.

Behavior therapy is not limited to the three basic techniques we have described in this chapter. Punishment is sometimes successfully applied. We refer specifically to the work of Flanagan, Goldiamond, and Azrin[45] who used punishment to suppress stuttering behavior (see Chapter 11).

Extinction is also a useful technique in eliminating undesirable be-

---

43 L. Homme, *How to use contingency contracting in the classroom* (Champaign, Ill.: Research Press, 1969).

44 T. Ayllon and N. Azrin, *The token economy* (New York: Appleton-Century-Crofts, 1968).

45 B. Flanagan, I. Goldiamond, and N. Azrin, Operant stuttering in the control of stuttering behavior through response contingent consequences, *Jour. Exp. Anal. Behav.* 7 (1958), 173–178.

havior. For example, Williams successfully used this procedure to eliminate temper tantrums[46] (see Chapter 3).

All in all, behavior therapy of various sorts seems to have a most promising future. The previously held notions that maladaptive behavior can be cured only by digging into its origins through long therapeutic sessions in which the original cause or causes of the difficulty are uprooted so that the patient eventually gains "therapeutic insight" do not hold. If, through various conditioning procedures, more adaptable behavior can be substituted and maintained, there may be little use in delving into the past. In some disorders that seem to display a multitude of symptoms, the behavior therapist must take each one separately in order to modify it. In other cases where the symptoms are relatively well defined, he can work specifically with them.

One of the criticisms leveled by the traditional therapists is that through behavior therapy a symptom may be eliminated but another one will be substituted because the behavior therapist did not seek the roots of the difficulty. Present evidence, however, does not tend to support this fear. Symptom substitution simply does not occur.

Other advantages of behavior therapy are the time and money saved compared with traditional therapies: behavior therapy usually requires relatively few therapeutic sessions as compared to the possible hundreds of hours involved in traditional therapies. Finally, the results of behavior therapy can be objectively determined as to success, partial success, or failure. The behavior to be modified is always specified so that accurate records can be made in regard to progress, as shown by several of the graphs illustrated in this chapter.

[46] C. D. Williams, The elimination of tantrum behavior by extinction procedures, *Jour. Abn. Soc. Psychol.*, **59** (1959), 260.

# 19 The Practical Control of Behavior

ALTHOUGH IT IS NOT ALWAYS FASHION-able to say so, it is nevertheless a fact that we are constantly engaged in controlling behavior, our own as well as that of other organisms. We hear much discourse today about freedom. The implication is that certain agencies in our society exercise too much control, or that their methods of control are undesirable and are not generally contributing to the best interests of those controlled. Freedom, however, does not mean that a response cannot be predicted or controlled. It means, rather, that the controlling agencies are employing methods of control by using positive reinforcement instead of those methods that involve threats and force and generate consequences that are aversive to the controlled individuals.[1] The techniques of control such as threats and force are not the most efficient methods known to man, when judged in terms of their lasting effects. Governments and social institutions, including the church, as well as single individuals have frequently applied punishment because the immediate effects can readily be observed and the methods are simple to apply. Without more appropriate knowledge of the effects of control by punishment, these ancient methods persist and are applied by the stubborn minded and those who get their reinforcements from witnessing the suffering of others.

[1] B. F. Skinner, *Beyond freedom and dignity* (New York: Knopf, 1971).

The problem of whether or not behavior *can* be controlled is likewise apparent. As more is learned about the problems involving control, the answers become clearer. Because we lack anything like adequate knowledge about the causes of an individual's behavior, we are inclined to think that behavior goes uncontrolled. Or since much human conduct is multi-caused, the effects do not seem so clearly related to what knowledge we have of the causes. As we are able to gain more adequate knowledge about the environmental variables affecting behavior, as well as the lawful changes in behavior which do occur when these variables are manipulated, the problems of control are more easily managed.

For many years Skinner has been intensely concerned with the matter of control. The following comments of his are worth noting:

> We are all controlled by the world in which we live, and part of that world has been and will be controlled by men. The question is this: Are we to be controlled by accident, by tyrants, or by ourselves in effective cultural design?
>
> .  .  .
>
> The danger of the misuse of power is probably greater than ever. It is not allayed by disguising the facts. We cannot make wise decisions if we continue to pretend that human behavior is not controlled, or if we refuse to engage in control when valuable results might be forthcoming. Such measures weaken only ourselves, leaving strength of science in others. The first step in a defense against tyranny is the fullest possible exposure of controlling techniques. . . .
>
> .  .  .
>
> It is no time for self-deception, emotional indulgence, or the assumption of attitudes which are no longer useful. Man is facing a difficult test. He must keep his head now, and he must start again—or look way back.[2]

Psychologists are sometimes misunderstood in regard to their aim of control. Indeed, there are some schools of psychology that would deny this primary aim. They may say that they are concerned with altering behavior but not controlling it. But in the final analysis, if they have altered it—for example, by means of therapy as discussed in the last chapter—have they not used themselves as agencies of control? Before a psychologist—or anyone else, for that matter—is going to engage in control, he must first learn what the basic laws of behavior are. This is best achieved through appropriate experimentation in the laboratory, which has been going on for a long time and is continuing through basic research. We hope we have discussed the most significant of these researches in the previous chapters. After research comes the application of the principles to human endeavors. In particular, the newer forms of psychotherapy, discussed in Chapter 18, are applying these principles

[2] B. F. Skinner, Freedom and the control of man, *Amer. Scholar*, **25** (1955), 55–57.

toward removing unfortunate symptoms that will enable a person to better cope with his environment.

The critics of this approach, of course, bring up the matter of ethics. Psychologists will be in control of what? Man's betterment or destruction? A practicing psychologist such as a therapist must operate under an appropriate code of ethics so that for the most part this use of control will be to man's advantage in not only creating a better person but a better society in which to live, as well as equipping the individual personality with a new set of behaviors that will enable him to live better in that society.

### SELF-CONTROL

If we are going to involve ourselves in the control of others in our environment, what about ourselves on our own behavior? The services of a good therapist are not always available to operate in changing our ways. What can we, ourselves do, if anything, to modify our own behavior? Goldiamond[3] has suggested two kinds of procedures for the development of self-control: (1) The first involves instructing the subject who wishes to engage in self-control in setting up procedures that change his environment and will bring his own behavior under appropriate controls. We must be ever mindful that even though we are engaging in self-control, it is *not* a matter of our own "free will" to do or not do certain things. Regardless of the kind of control, we are always under environmental control. In self-control we reorder the environmental stimuli. In other forms of control, either other people or the environment itself are the agencies of control. (2) The second procedure is to train the person in the functional analysis of behavior (which is what we have been attempting to do throughout most of this book). We then ask them to determine for themselves the procedures that should be applied—that is, knowing the principles for yourself and pick the ones you wish to use for self-control.

Goldiamond cities the case of a married couple who complained of inadequate sexual contacts. Both attributed the inadequacy to the husband. After some discussion it was learned that both were extremely neat and clean. The wife visited the beauty shop every week and the husband the barber every other week. It was decided to make these visits contingent on their own nightly "appointments" with each other. In the event that the appointments were not kept, the visits to the beauty parlor and barber were not allowed and could be resumed only

[3] I. Goldiamond, Self-control procedures in personal behavior problems, *Psychol. Rep.*, **17** (1965), 851–858.

when the appointments were kept. The results were effective, as both kept their appointments, at least for the time of the study.

Suppose one wishes to go on a diet—a real exercise in self-control. By arranging the stimuli properly, he can determine that eating can occur only at a specific time and place. One should determine the ultimate aversive consequences of overweight and spell them out: danger of heart disease, unattractive physique, tight clothes, etc. One might arrange the stimuli so that behavior incompatible to eating will occur, such as reading a newspaper or making a telephone call. Severe dieting is aversive; "crash diets" usually do not work. Therefore, a proper diet should be eaten with a regimented plan for slow weight loss (perhaps one pound a week). One should also determine the exact caloric content of all foods he eats and keep records to guarantee that he does not go over the caloric content of foods eaten in a given day.[4]

The crucial matter in self-control, as we have mentioned earlier, is to realize that we are under the control of the stimuli in our environment, whether they be people or things. We have already learned countless discriminations and we are under the control of these discriminative stimuli; we have already learned what to avoid and what stimuli reinforce us. Knowing these things, what we must do is to arrange them (the stimuli) so that behavior either occurs or does not occur. To develop better study habits, we should eliminate from our study situation those distracting stimuli that may in themselves be reinforcing but interfere with studying. If your roommate distracts you, even though you enjoy talking with him, remove yourself and your books to a remote corner of the library where the likelihood of encountering other people you might like to talk to becomes a remote possibility. Bring only the books and paper you need for a given study period.

A woman decided she was doing too much "cussing." She decided that each time she emitted a "cuss" word, she would take a dollar from the weekly allowance her husband gave her and place it in a safe place such as a piggy bank. At the end of each month, instead of spending the money on herself, she gave it to a worthwhile charitable organization. After a few months the "cussing" behavior had literally ceased.

Basically, we have learned that we respond in the presence of discriminative stimuli ($S^D$s) because we have been reinforced in some way in the past. If we can eliminate these discriminative stimuli, then it is impossible to respond to them. One way to give up smoking is not to buy, carry, or have around any cigarettes. However, as any reformed smoker will tell you, this is not an easy task. Smoking is associated with a great number of other stimuli besides cigarettes. We smoke when other

[4] C. B. Ferster, J. I. Nornberger, and C. B. Levitt, The control of eating, *Jour. Mathematics*, **1** (1962), 87–109.

people are around us who also smoke, after a meal, while having a cup of coffee or a drink. Simply not buying cigarettes may not be enough because there are always other people around who carry cigarettes.

TECHNIQUES OF CONTROL

**1.** *Aversive Control.*   Although we might wish it were otherwise, a good bit of our behavior is under the control of aversive or noxious stimuli. We have already discussed three basic techniques of aversive control: *escape, avoidance,* and *punishment.* Let us see how these aversive conditions apply in our everyday lives.

*Escape and Avoidance.*   We have already noted that we put on our sunglasses to escape from the bright rays of the sun, or kick off a shoe that pinches to escape from the pain that it produces. One may also avoid the sun by remaining in the shade, or the pain of shoe pinching by buying a pair of shoes that do not pinch. Unfortunately government, law, and education still use a great deal of these kinds of control. Does one pay his income taxes because he approves of reckless spending, graft, waste, special interests, or the support of unpopular wars? Not likely. We do so to *avoid* being fined or even being put behind bars. We obey the traffic laws to avoid getting a ticket. Students attend classes, read their assignments, and study for exams, not always because such behavior is positively reinforcing. Some teachers are dull and some subject matter uninteresting. Thus we do these things to avoid being dropped from a course, or failing it. Countless rules and regulations are set upon students. The rules are obeyed to avoid being punished. In the past the Church exerted a good bit of aversive control. One attended services, led the pure life, and obeyed the dictates of the clergy to avoid the possibility of eternal damnation. Many people today do not take the hell, fire, and brimstone threats very seriously, and to this extent the Church has lost its control.

Skinner has suggested that in one sense, *freedom* amounts to a condition in which one has been able to escape or avoid the aversive stimuli from his environment. We are not autonomous men with a free mind or will.

> Over the centuries, in erratic ways, men have constructed a world in which they are relatively free of many kinds of threatening or harmful stimuli— extremes of temperature, sources of infection, hard labor, danger, and even those minor aversive stimuli called discomfort.[5]

Escape and avoidance play a much more important role in the struggle for freedom when the aversive conditions are generated by other people. Other

[5] B. F. Skinner, *Beyond freedom and dignity,* op. cit., 27–28.

people can be aversive without so to speak, trying: they can be rude, dangerous, contagious or annoying, and one escapes from them or avoids them accordingly.[6]

The techniques of the old slave driver were effective. So long as a man worked, he escaped the whip. A child may behave properly to escape from a nagging parent, or if he continues to behave well, he will avoid further nagging. One can run away from home, drop out of school, defect from the army, or even drop out of a culture, as in the case of the hobo, the hermit, or the hippie.[7] Thus, the control is in the hands of those who have the power to present or withhold the aversive stimuli.

One of the great disadvantages of this kind of control is the possibility of reprisal. We may aggress against those who annoy us. A child may stand up to his parents. A multitude may overthrow a government, as in revolutions when the controlling agencies have been too aversive. Further, students may vandalize a school, or a dropout may attempt to destroy a culture.

**2.** *Punishment.*  Punishment has certainly been one of the most popular means of control because one can see the immediate effects in suppressing behavior which in the eyes of the punisher is undesirable. As we have already noted, if the punishment is strong enough, the behavior being punished may remain suppressed, at least for a while. So punishment may work if it is continuously applied to eliminate certain ongoing behavior. However, in many cases the effects of punishment are merely temporary, and if the behavior is positively reinforcing, when the punishment is ceased, the behavior will return to its full strength. So the effect of punishment results only in annoyance or harm to the organism. Also, there are a number of disadvantages to punishment. As we have just mentioned, it may only work temporarily. Of course, if punishment suppresses behavior until alternate or conflicting behaviors are established, these behaviors will interfere with the recovery of the punished response.

Other unfortunate consequences of punishment involve emotional side reactions in the form of anxiety and aggression. Mental hospitals and therapists' offices are filled with people who have been subjected to various forms of punishment. The juvenile delinquent and the mentally ill have at least one thing in common. Their past conditioning histories may have been filled with aversive stimulation, including threats or physically harmful stimuli which they can neither escape nor avoid.

In Skinner's *Walden Two*—a novel about a Utopian community in which the more appropriate techniques of behavioral engineering are being applied—Fraser, the founder of the fictitious community, speaks as follows regarding punishment:

[6] Ibid., 28.
[7] Ibid.

"It's temporarily effective, that's the worst of it. That explains several thousand years of bloodshed. Even nature has been fooled. We 'instinctively' punish a person who doesn't behave as we like—we spank him if he's a child or strike him if he's a man. A nice distinction! The immediate effect of the blow teaches us to strike again. Retribution and revenge are the most natural things on earth. But in the long run the man we strike is no less likely to repeat his act."

"But he won't repeat it if we hit him hard enough," said Castle.

"He'll still tend to repeat it. He'll want to repeat it. We haven't really altered his potential behavior at all. That's the pity of it. If he doesn't repeat it in our presence, he will in the presence of someone else. Or it will be repeated in the disguise of a neurotic symptom. If we hit him hard enough, we clear a little place for ourselves in the wilderness of civilization but we make the rest of the wilderness still more terrible." [8]

Although the circumstances under which these words were spoken are fictional, their significance for control is not. Governments who use force, sadistic parents, or frustrated authoritarians are only a few examples. However, governments that persistently use it do not last. The recurrent or eventual overthrow of these agencies illustrates the hostility engendered by the punished. On the individual level, delinquent personalities who have been brought up under conditions of chronic punishment commonly exhibit rebellion against authority. Faulty family relationships, unfortunate economic conditions, or disorganized communities are frequently the offending stimuli.

With regard to avoiding punishment on a personal level, Skinner has the following to say:

One may avoid occasions in which punishable behavior is likely to occur. A person who has been punished for drunkenness may "put temptation behind him" by staying away from places where he is likely to drink too much: a student who has been punished for not studying may avoid situations in which he is distracted from his work. Still another strategy is to change the environment so that behavior is less likely to be punished. We reduce natural punishing contingencies when we repair a broken stairway so that we are less likely to fall and we weaken punitive social contingencies by associating with more tolerant friends.[9]

3. *Emotional Conditioning.* Emotional conditioning involves both operant and respondent behavior. One example is seen in the pep talk to a team before going on the field or by cheerleaders who arouse the crowds at the appropriate times when the team needs their support. We can generate hostility toward the enemy by showing pictures of their atrocities or telling of their maltreatment of our loved ones. We persuade people to vote our way by telling them the good things our

---

[8] B. F. Skinner, *Walden Two* (New York: Macmillan, Inc., 1948), 217.
[9] B. F. Skinner, *Beyond freedom and dignity*, op. cit., 63.

candidate will do or has done. We may bring our sweetheart candy or send her roses, or we can give a good customer an elaborate Christmas gift. Emotional conditioning is involved in many of our present-day advertising which associates a product with a "pretty girl" or symbols of pleasure including springtime and sex, relaxation, social position, prestige, or acceptance.

Commercial agencies at Christmastime, for example, apply all sorts of conditioned emotionally arousing stimuli to elicit the emotions of joy or happiness—Christmas trees lighted and decorated, Santa Clauses, reindeer, brightly colored candles, and so forth—all of which are intended to get people in the Christmas buying spirit for the giving and receiving of gifts.

Techniques of propaganda also employ emotional conditioning—the instilling of prejudices, the hate campaigns, and the highly emotional speeches. The appeal of the emotional rather than the rational is by no means ineffective in gaining control. Whether or not these methods are the ones to be condoned is not the real question. The fact that they are effective is more to the point.

In some cases the application of emotional stimuli has to be done with some degree of subtlety. If one is too obvious or too ostentatious in the giving of a gift to arouse a positive disposition, the effect may be lost, and the recipient may suspect ulterior motives.

**4.** *Deprivation and Satiation.* The manipulation of primary as well as conditioned reinforcers in such a way as to deprive or satiate an organism has been known as long as man has had a recorded history. Armies have starved out their enemies, and whole nations have acquiesced to their opponents, not merely because the physical force of the opposition was greater, but because a constant engagement in war deprived them of all the necessities of survival. To cut off the lines of supply has been a basic military tactic.

Some business organizations today make use of the operation in various ways to control the behavior of their employees as well as their customers. Take the example of a young executive in a large American firm "on his way up." He is encouraged by his company to belong to expensive and fashionable country clubs, to send his children to the "right" schools, to live in a "good" neighborhood, and to drive a sleek automobile. Although his company may help in paying some of the bills, it encourages a way of life that is commonly known as "living beyond one's means." The man is constantly in a state of monetary deprivation. Yet these "good things in life" are very positively reinforcing. He cannot quit his job for risk of further and more intense deprivation, since he may find it difficult to find another job that pays as well. As William Whyte points out in *The Organization Man*,[10] the employee becomes

---

[10] W. Whyte, *The organization man* (Garden City, N.Y.: Doubleday, 1957).

bound to the company in numerous ways. His career, social life, family life, and indeed almost his entire existence, become centered around the company's control. At a more individual level, if one wishes to make another man susceptible to a bribe, arrange the contingencies, if possible, so that he is in a state of deprivation (monetary) which the bribe will alleviate.

Likewise, some advertising appeals are aimed at degrees of deprivation. They set up reinforcers (usually conditioned) as appeals for goods a person either does not have or cannot afford. This is often called "creating a need" in order to sell the product. What child would prefer a bland and rather tasteless breakfast cereal (even though sugar and spices could be added) when he could have "sugar, crispy crunchies." If you don't drive a "Zugar" automobile, you will be deprived of the social status (conditioned reinforcers) you may desire.

Frequently, automobile manufacturers these days appeal to economy (lack of deprivation). The little "Blitz" gets 30 miles to a gallon, costs less to buy and run. The technique relieves a person from a state of economic deprivation which he would find himself in if he bought the larger, more powerful automobile.

We have already mentioned the effects of food deprivation or satiation in the control of responding. If we wish to break the candy-eating "habit," we might "stuff him with candy until it comes out of his ears." Along the same lines, a few studies, mentioned earlier, indicated that satiation can be one way of breaking the cigarette smoking habit: "Continue to smoke until your mouth burns up."

We may control our drinking behavior at a cocktail party by eating several peanut butter sandwiches and drinking several glasses of milk beforehand. On the other hand, we may feed our guests salty hors d'œuvres, potato chips, and pretzels in order to increase the amount of highballs they will consume. If they "had a good time" and reciprocate, we have been reinforced by having a successful party.

**5.** *Drugs.*   Recent psychological literature is filled with studies illustrating the effects of drugs on behavior. The various tranquilizers have become one of the most popular medications prescribed today because of their effects in alleviating anxiety. The businessman facing the pressures of a tough sales convention, and the harassed housewife overcome by the frustrations of raising a family, are both able to control either their aggression or anxiety by taking a tranquilizer. Likewise, when we "ply a man with liquor" so that he will give us his business or let slip with some guarded information, we are applying drug control. Because of the dangers, control of alcohol, the "Noble Experiment" of the twenties and early thirties—better known as prohibition—was enacted. Because of unfortunate consequences in which criminals profited, the "experiment" failed. There were, of course, many other reasons. Some colleges forbid the use of alcohol by students and faculty or restrict its consumption to those places and circumstances that will be less dangerous to the individuals involved.

The frequent use of illicit drugs such as marijuana, "speed," and even heroin, has become a serious problem—particularly for the younger members of our society. People use these drugs because they find the "high" reinforcing. There is no question that these drugs alter behavior in one way or another. When one becomes addicted to such drugs as morphine or heroin—the so-called "hard" drugs—he will do just about anything for a "fix."

Drugs like chlorpromazine and reserpine have been effective in controlling the aggressive behavior of mentally disturbed people, both inside and outside mental hospitals. Drugs such as lithium reduce the manic behavior in manic excitement. We are told that the days of the closed ward, padded cells, and straightjackets are in the past. These methods of physical restraint have been replaced by the more modern methods of drug control.

Skinner[11] has suggested that we are now entering the age of chemical control by drugs and that in the not too distant future the emotional and motivational conditions of normal daily life may be maintained in any desired state through drugs. It is possible, through stimulants, to increase the frequency of responding, and through tranquilizers and depressants to reduce the same response rate.

**6.** *Extinction.* Often, one of the problems involved in control is to weaken or eliminate responses. We already mentioned punishment as one possibility. But punishment may not necessarily eliminate the behavior, and frequently leads to unfortunate consequences—not only for the individual who is punished, but also for the environment as well. The reader will recall that extinction involves the withholding of a positive reinforcer, either primary or conditioned, following a given response. In the case of responses that have been conditioned to high strength, the process may be a very slow one. In human responding such generalized reinforcers as attention and approval are common, not only for our verbal behavior, but for other kinds as well. In many cases we wish to eliminate undesirable behavior that has been maintained by these reinforcers. Perhaps the most simple way is to ignore these behaviors and the person making them. If one finds a particular person rather boring, one possibility is not to listen to him, for listening amounts at least to paying attention. Some people behave in irritating and obnoxious ways. Sometimes we find it easier to tell him to "shut up," but this basically is punishment and may not be effective. Instead

---

[11] B. F. Skinner, The control of human behavior, *Trans. New York Acad. Sci.*, **17**, no. 1, Series II (1955), 547–551.

of listening or paying attention to these undesirable behaviors, one might leave the room or pick up a newspaper or magazine and read it.

The temper tantrums or unnecessary crying of children, or even adults, are reinforced by those people who give in, thus reinforcing the behavior. If a child throws a temper tantrum and is merely left alone to continue his tantrums, the behavior will eventually die out, and the probability of the next tantrum is lessened. The parent who simply ignores this will find out that the child sooner or later will abandon this device to get his way. Some women have developed the technique of "turning on the tears" in order to get what they want (we might call this operant crying). The softhearted husband easily gives in because he simply cannot stand to see his wife cry. However, if he would refuse to give in to her tears and let his wife cry it out, she soon would find crying an ineffective way to control her husband. Likewise, the "cry baby" has been too frequently reinforced for his crying behavior.

Our discussion has centered mainly on withholding conditioned reinforcers in human conduct because so much of our behavior is maintained by them. However, the process of extinction, as we have learned, operates also for primary reinforcers. The author recalls as a child going to a Saturday matinée with another boy and his father. For some reason or other the boy threw a tantrum and behaved in a most obnoxious way. As a result, his father bought both of us double-decker ice cream cones. The obvious method should have been to withhold the ice cream cones, for in giving them, the obnoxious behavior was strengthened. Incidentally, the boy did not turn out very well. As an adult he has become a rather irresponsible psychopath. At the moment, he has been through seven divorces.

**7.** *Positive Reinforcement.* Our studies throughout this book have supported the principle that through the appropriate use of positive reinforcement we can control behavior that will not lead to unfortunate consequences. The proper use of reinforcement cannot only act for the better interests of the individual but for the whole society as well. Positive reinforcement is the most effective technique we have for the practical control of behavior. Through the selective reinforcement of a desired response or of approximations to it, we can shape out the best in all of us. We decide on the behavior we wish strengthened and reinforce it. Positive reinforcement does not lead to anxiety or hostility. What we refer to as the emotions of joy, happiness, or even love, refers to the presentation of some forms of positive reinforcement. Skinner has suggested that when we make a value judgment by calling something good or bad, it is to classify it in terms of its reinforcing effects.[12]

This is not to say that positive reinforcement is always good for the

12 B. F. Skinner, *Beyond freedom and dignity*, op. cit.

person. When we pay off the blackmailer, we are only encouraging him to blackmail again, or when we give in to the bully, we are only strengthening his bullying behavior. The fact is that positive reinforcement does work, and our behavioral engineers tell us that positive reinforcement is the most effective tool of control that we have.

It costs us nothing to give a word of praise or approval for a job well done.

In *Walden Two*, Fraser, after having explained to one of the community's visitors the unfortunate effects of punishment, goes on to explain how positive reinforcement can be used:

> "Now that we know how positive reinforcement works and why negative doesn't," he said at last, "we can be more deliberate and hence more successful in our cultural design. We can achieve a sort of control under which the controlled, though they are following a code more scrupulously than was the case under the old system, nevertheless feel free. They are doing what they want to do, not what they are forced to do. That's the source of the tremendous power of positive reinforcement. There's no restraint and no revolt. By a careful cultural design, we control not the final behavior, but the inclination to behave—the motives, the desires and the wishes."

Concerning the problem of freedom, Fraser goes on to say:

> "The question is: Can men live in freedom and peace? And the answer is: Yes, if we can build a social structure which will satisfy the needs of everyone and in which everyone will want to observe the supporting code. But so far this has been achieved only in *Walden Two*. Your ruthless accusation to the contrary, Mr. Castle, this is the freest place on earth. And it is free precisely because we make no use of force or threat of force. Every bit of our research, from the nursery through the psychological management of our adult membership is directed toward that end—to exploit every alternative to forcible control. By skillful planning, by a wise choice of techniques, we increase the feeling of freedom.[13]

By the appropriate use of positive reinforcement, either through withholding it in order to extinguish the "wrong" responses, or by selectively applying it to strengthen the "right" responses, we can go a long way in achieving the kind of control–including freedom that Skinner speaks of in *Walden Two*.

In the past 30 years we have seen the science of psychology develop along lines that have discovered the principles which govern human conduct. We have been able to learn many of the basic laws of behavior and the conditions in the environment that affect that behavior. By

[13] B. F. Skinner, *Walden Two*, op. cit., p. 219.

ing these independent (environmental) variables, it is possible p a way of life in which man can be free and happy.

All behavior as we can now discern it, is composed of variations on a basic themes. For the first time in mankind's saga, these themes are open to all who wish to see them in the steady light of science, rather than by the rare illuminations of intuitive minds. We are on the frontier of an enormous power; the power to manipulate our own behavior scientifically, deliberately, rationally. How this power will be used—whether for good or ill—no one of us can tell. Certain it is that whatever use is made of it will be determined by the character of the persons using it. But character itself is open to a science of behavior. We need to hasten and train a generation of men of good will. How this is to be done may be mankind's last desperate question of all. Without a science of psychology, no answer is possible; but psychology, while offering the methods, cannot ensure their use. It is to the latter that we finally commend our readers.[14]

[14] F. S. Kellet and W. N. Schoenfeld, *Principles of psychology* (New York: Appleton-Century-Crofts, 1950), 401.

# Bibliography

ADER, R., and R. TATUM. Free operant avoidance conditioning in humans, *Jour. Exp. Anal. Behav.* **4** (1961), 275–276.

ADLER, A. *Understanding human nature.* New York: Greenberg, 1927.

ADLER, A. *Social interest.* New York: Putnam, 1939.

ADORNO, T. W., E. FRENKEL-BRUNSWICK, D. J. LEVINSON, and R. N. SANFORD. *The authoritarian personality.* New York: Harper & Bros., 1950.

ALLEN, K. E., B. M. HART, J. S. BUELL, F. R. HARRIS, and M. M. WOLF. Effects of social reinforcement on isolate behavior of a nursery school child, *Child Dev.,* **35** (1964), 511–518.

ALLPORT, G. W. *Personality: A psychological interpretation.* New York: Holt, 1937.

ALLPORT, G., and A. S. ODBERT. Trait names: A psychological study, *Psychol. Monogr.,* **47** (1936), 1–171.

ALLPORT, G. W., P. E. VERNON, and G. LINDZEY. *A study of values.* Rev. ed. *Manual of directions.* Boston: Houghton Mifflin, 1951.

ANDERSON, O. E., and H. S. LIDDELL. Observations on experimental neurosis in sheep, *Arch. Neurol. Psychiat.,* **34** (1935), 330–354.

AYLLON, T. Intensive treatment of psychotic behavior by stimulus satiation and food reinforcement, *Behav. Res. Ther.,* **1** (1963), 53–61.

AYLLON, T., and N. H. AZRIN. Reinforcement and instructions with mental patients, *Jour. Exp. Anal. Behav.,* **7** (1964), 327–331.

AYLLON, T., and N. H. AZRIN. The measurement and reinforcement of behavior of psychotics, *Jour. Exp. Anal. Behav.,* **8** (1965), 357–383.

AYLLON, T., and N. AZRIN. *The token economy.* New York: Appleton-Century-Crofts, 1968.

AYLLON, T., and E. HAUGHTON. Control of the behavior of schizophrenic patients by food, *Jour. Exp. Anal. Behav.,* **5** (1962), 343–352.

AYLLON, T., and E. HAUGHTON. Modification of symptomatic verbal behavior of mental patients, *Behav. Res. Ther.,* **2** (1964), 87–97.

AYLLON, T., E. HAUGHTON, and H. B. HUGHES. Interpretation of symptoms: Fact or fiction, *Behav. Res. Ther.,* **3** (1965), 1–7.

AYLLON, T., and J. MICHAEL. The psychiatric nurse as a behavioral engineer, *Jour. Exp. Anal. Behav.*, **2** (1959), 323–334.

AZRIN, N. H. Some effects of noise on human behavior, *Jour. Exp. Anal. Behav.*, **1** (1958), 183–200.

AZRIN, N. H. Effects of punishment intensity during variable interval reinforcement, *Jour. Exp. Anal. Behav.*, **3** (1960), 123–142.

AZRIN, N. H. Suggested effects of punishment. In T. Verhave, (ed.), *The experimental analysis of behavior*. New York: Appleton-Century-Crofts, 1966.

AZRIN, N. H., W. C. HOLZ, and D. F. HAKE. Fixed ratio punishment, *Jour. Exp. Anal. Behav.*, **6** (1963), 141–148.

AZRIN, N. H., and W. C. HOLZ Punishment. In W. Honig, ed., *Operant behavior: Areas of research and applications*. New York: Appleton-Century-Crofts, 1966.

AZRIN, N. H., and O. R. LINDSLEY. The reinforcement of cooperation between children, *Jour. Abn. Soc., Psychol.*, **52** (1956), 100–102.

BACHRACH, A. J., W. J. ERWIN, and J. P. MOHR. The control of eating behavior in an anorexic by operant conditioning techniques. In L. P. Ullmann and L. Krasner, eds., *Case studies in behavior modification*. New York: Holt, Rinehart and Winston, 1965.

BAER, D. M. Escape and avoidance responses of pre-school children on two schedules of reinforcement, *Jour. Exp. Anal. Behav.*, **3** (1960), 155–159.

BAER, D. M. Effect of withdrawal of positive reinforcements on the extinguishing response in young children, *Child Dev.*, **32** (1932), 67–74.

BAER, D. M. Laboratory control of thumbsucking by withdrawal and representation of reinforcement, *Jour. Exp. Anal. Behav.*, **5** (1962), 525–526.

BAILEY, C. J., and N. E. MILLER. The effect of sodium amytal on approach–avoidance conflict in cats, *Jour. Comp. Physiol. Psychol.*, **45** (1952), 205–208.

BANDURA, A. *Principles of behavior modification*. New York: Holt, Rinehart and Winston, 1969.

BANDURA, A., J. GRUSEC, and P. MANLORE. Vicarious extinction of avoidance behavior, *Jour. Pers. and Soc. Psychol.*, **5** (1967), 16.

BANDURA, A., D. ROSS, and S. A. ROSS. Vicarious reinforcement and imitative learning. In A. W. Staats, ed., *Human learning*. Holt, Rinehart and Winston, 1964.

BANDURA, A., and R. WALTERS, *Social learning and personality development*. New York: Holt, Rinehart and Winston, 1963.

BARKER, R. G. An experimental study of the resolution of conflict in children: Time elapsing and amount of vicarious trial-end-error behavior occurring. In Q. Mc-Nemar and M. A. Merrill, eds., *Studies of personality*. New York: McGraw-Hill, 1942.

BARKER, R. G., T. DEMBO, and K. LEWIN. Frustration and regression. In R. G. Barker, J. S. Kouin, and H. F. Wright, eds., *Child development*. New York: Mc-Graw-Hill, 1943.

BARON, O. K., H. BROOKSHIRE, and R. H. LITTMAN. Effects of infantile and adult shock-trauma upon learning in the adult white rat, *Jour. Comp. Physiol. Psychol.*, **40** (1957), 530–534.

BARTLETT, C. L. Systematic desensitization vs. implosive therapy, *Jour. Abn. Psychol.*, **74** (1969), 587–592.

BARRETT, B. H. Reduction in rate of multiple tics by free operant conditioning methods, *Jour. Nerv. Ment. Dis.*, **135** (1962), 187–195.

BARTON, E. S., D. GUESE, E. CARCIA, and D. M. BAER. Improvement of retardates' mealtime behavior by time-out procedures using multiple baseline techniques, *Jour. Appl. Behav. Anal.*, **3** (1970), 77–84.

BEACH, F. A. and F. JAYNES. Effects of early experience on behavior, *Psychol. Bull.*, **51** (1954), 239–263.

BECHTEREV, V. M. *General principles of human reflexology*, trans. W. H. Gantt. New York: International Universities Press, 1932.

BELO, J. The Balinese temper, *Char. and Pers.*, **4** (1935), 120–126.

BIJOU, S. W. The development of a conditioning methodology for studying experimental neurosis in the rat, *Jour. Comp. Psychol.*, **34** (1942), 91–106.

BIJOU, S. W. A study of "experimental neurosis" in the rat by conditioned response techniques, *Jour. Comp. Psychol.*, **36** (1943), 1–20.

BIJOU, S. W. Patterns of reinforcement and resistance to extinction in young children, *Child. Dev.*, **28** (1957), 47–54.

BIJOU, S. W. Methodology for the experimental analysis of child behavior, *Psychol. Rep.*, **3** (1957), 243–250.

BIJOU, S. W. Operant extinction after fixed-interval reinforcement with young children, *Jour. Exp. Anal. Behav.*, **1** (1958), 35–40.

BIJOU, S., and D. M. BAER. Operant methods in child behavior and development. In W. Honig, ed., *Operant behavior: Areas of research and application*. New York: Appleton-Century-Crofts, 1966.

BINDRA, D., and L. CAMERON. Changes in experimentally produced anxiety with the passage of time: Incubation effect, *Jour. Exp. Psychol.*, **45** (1953), 197–203.

BLEULER, E. *Dementia praecox oder Gruppe der Schizophrenen*. Leipzig: Deuticke, 1911.

BLUM, G. S. *Psychoanalytic theories of personality*. New York: McGraw-Hill, 1953.

BOND, I. K., and Hutchison, H. C. Application of reciprocal inhibition therapy to exhibitionism, *Canad. Med. Assn. Jour.*, **83** (1960).

BRACKBILL, Y. Extinction of the smiling responses in infants as a function of reinforcement schedules, *Child Dev.*, **129** (1958), 115–124.

BRADY, J. P., and D. L. LIND. Experimental analysis of hysterical blindness. In L. P. Ullmann and L. Krasner, eds., *Case studies in behavior modification*. New York: Holt, Rinehart and Winston, 1965.

BRADY, J. V. The effect of electro-convulsive shock on a conditioned emotional response: The permanency of effect, *Jour. Comp. Physiol. Psychol.*, **44** (1951), 507–511.

BRADY, J. V. The effect of electro-convulsive shock on a conditioned emotional response: The significance of the interval between emotional conditioning and the electro-convulsive shock, *Jour. Comp. Physiol. Psychol.*, **45** (1952), 9–13.

BRADY, J. V. Assessment of drug effects on emotional behavior, *Science*, **123** (1956), 1033–1034.

BRADY, J. V. Ulcers in "executive" monkeys, *Scient. Amer.*, **199**, no. 4 (1958), 95–103.

BRADY, J. V., and H. F. HUNT. The effect of electro-convulsive shock on a conditioned emotional response: A control for impaired hearing, *Jour. Comp. Physiol. Psychol.*, **45** (1952), 180–182.

BRADY, J. V., and H. F. HUNT. An experimental approach to the analysis of emotional behavior, *Jour. Psychol.*, **40** (1955), 313–324.

BRADY, J. V., R. W. PORTER, D. G. CONRAD, and J. W. MASON. Avoidance behavior and the development of gastroduodenal ulcers, *Jour. Exp. Anal. Behav.*, **1** (1958), 69–72.

BREUER, J., and S. FREUD. Studies on hysteria. In *Standard ed.*, vol. II. London: Hogarth Press, 1955; first published in Germany, 1895.

BROWN, G. D., and V. O. TYLER. Time out from reinforcement: A technique for dethroning the "duke" of an institutionalized delinquent group, *Jour. Child. Psychol. and Psychiat.*, **9** (1969), 203–211.

BROWN, J. S. Factors determining conflict reactions in different discriminations, *Jour. Exp. Psychol.*, **31** (1942), 272–292.

BROWN, J. S. Generalized approach and avoidance responses in relation to conflict behavior. New Haven: Yale University, (dissertation). Reported by N. E. Miller in J. McV. Hunt, ed., *Personality and the behavior disorders.* New York: Ronald Press, 1944.

BROWN, J. S. Gradients of approach and avoidance responses and their relation to level of motivation, *Jour. Comp. Physiol. Psychol.*, **41** (1948), 450–465.

BUTTER, C. M., and D. R. THOMAS. Secondary reinforcement as a function of the amount of primary reinforcement, *Jour. Comp. Physiol. Psychol.*, **51** (1958), 346–348.

CAHOON, D. D., and C. CROSBY. A learning approach to chronic drug use: Sources of reinforcement, *Behav. Ther.*, **2** (1972), 64–71.

CAMERON, N. The functional psychoses. In J. McV. Hunt, ed., *Personality and the behavior disorders*, vol. II. New York: Ronald Press, 1944.

CAMERON, N. *The psychology of behavior disorders.* Boston: Houghton Mifflin, 1947.

CAMERON, N., and A. MAGARET. *Behavior pathology.* Boston: Houghton Mifflin, 1951.

CASEY, H. The effects of stress on the consumption of alcohol., *Quart. Jour. Stud. Alcohol.*, **21** (1960), 208–216.

CATTELL, R. B. The description of personality principles and findings in factor analysis, *Amer. Jour. Psychol.*, **58** (1945), 69–90.

CATTELL, R. B. The principal replicated factors discovered in objective personality tests, *Jour. Abn. Soc. Psychol.*, **50** (1955), 291–334.

CAUTELA, J. R. Treatment of compulsive behavior by covert sensitization, *Psychol. Rec.*, **16** (1966), 33–41.

CHILD, I. L. The relationship of somatotype to self-ratings on Sheldon's temperamental traits, *Jour. Pers.*, **18** (1950), 440–453.

COBB, S. Personality as affected by lesions in the brain. In J. McV. Hunt ed., *Personality and the behavior disorders.* New York: Ronald Press, 1944.

COBB, S. *Foundations of neuropsychiatry.* Baltimore: Williams & Wilkins, 1952.

Cobb, S. Contemporary problems in psychiatry. In *Theory and treatment of the psychoses: Some newer aspects.* St. Louis: Washington University, 1956.

Cohen, B. D., H. I. Kalish, J. R. Thurston, and E. Cohen. Experimental manipulation of verbal behavior, *Jour. Exp. Psychol.,* **47** (1954), 106–110.

Conger, J. The effects of alcohol on conflict behavior in the albino rat, *Quart. Jour. Stud. Alcohol.,* **12** (1951), 1–29.

Conger, J. C. The treatment of encopresis by management of social consequences, *Behav. Ther.,* **1** (1970), 386–390.

Cowles, J. T. Food-tokens as incentives for learning in chimpanzees, *Comp. Psychol. Monogr.,* **14,** no. 5 (1937).

D'Amato, M. R. Training of secondary reinforcement across the hunger and thirst drives, *Jour Exp. Psychol.,* **49** (1955), 352–355.

D'Amato, M. R. Secondary reinforcement and magnitude of primary reinforcement, *Jour. Comp. Physiol. Psychol.,* **48** (1955), 378–380.

Dennis, W. Infant reactions to restriction, *Trans. N. Y. Acad. Sci.,* **2** (1940), 202–218.

Diamond, S. *Personality and temperament.* New York: Harper & Bros., 1957.

Dinsmoor, J. A. The effect of hunger on discriminated responses, *Jour. Abn. Soc. Psychol.,* **47** (1952), 67–72.

Dinsmoor, J. A. Punishment: I; the avoidance hypothesis, *Psychol. Rev.,* **51** (1954), 34–46.

Dinsmoor, J. A., and L. H. Hughes. Training rats to press a bar to turn off shock, *Jour. Comp. Physiol. Psychol.,* **49** (1956), 235–238.

Diven, K. Certain determinants in the conditioning of anxiety reactions, *Jour. Psychol.,* **3** (1937), 291–308.

Dollard, J., L. W. Doob, N. E. Miller, O. H. Mowrer, and R. R. Sears. *Frustration and aggression.* New Haven: Yale University Press, 1939.

Dollard, J., and N. E. Miller. *Personality and psychotherapy.* New York: McGraw-Hill, 1950.

D'Zurlla, T. Recall efficiency and mediating cognitive events in "experimental repression," *Jour. Pers. and Soc. Psychol.,* **1** (1965), 253–257.

Ericksen, G. W., and J. L. Keuthe. Avoidance conditioning of verbs: Behavior without awareness, *Jour. Abn. Soc. Psychol.,* **53** (1956), 203–209.

Estes, W. K. An experimental study of punishment, *Psychol., Monogr.,* **57,** no. 263 (1944), iii–40.

Estes, W. K. A study of motivating conditions necessary for secondary reinforcement, *Jour. Exp. Psychol.,* **39** (1949), 306–310.

Estes, W. K., and B. F. Skinner. Some quantitative properties of anxiety, *Jour. Exp. Psychol.,* **29** (1941), 390–400.

Eysneck, H. J. *Dimensions of personality.* London: Routledge and Kegan Paul, 1947.

Eysenck, H. J., and S. Rachman. *The causes and cures of neurosis.* San Diego, Calif.: Knapp, 1965.

Farrar, C. Some origins in psychiatry, *Amer. Jour. Insan.,* **64** (1908), 523–552.

Feldman, M. P., and M. J. MacCulloch. Aversion therapy and the management of homosexuals, *Brit. Med. Jour.,* **1** (1967), 594.

FENICHEL, O. *The psychoanalytic theory of neurosis.* New York: Norton, 1945 (?).

FERSTER, C. B. Sustained behavior under delayed reinforcement, *Jour. Exp. Psychol.,* **45** (1953), 218–224.

FERSTER, C. B. The use of the free operant in the analysis of behavior, *Psychol. Bull.,* **50** (1953), 263–274.

FERSTER, C. B., and M. K. DE MEYER. A method for the experimental analysis of the behavior of autistic children, *Amer. Jour. Orthopsychiat.,* **32** (1962), 80–98.

FERSTER, C. B., J. I. NURNBERGER, and C. B. LEVITT. The control of eating, *Jour. Methetics,* **1** (1962), 87–109.

FERSTER, C. B., and J. SIMMONS. Behavior therapy with children, *Psychol. Rec.,* **16** (1966), 65–71.

FERSTER, C. B., and B. F. SKINNER. *Schedules of reinforcement.* New York: Appleton-Century-Crofts, 1957.

FINDLEY, J. D., and J. V. BRADY. Facilitation of large ratio performances by use of a conditioned reinforcement, *Jour. Exp. Anal. Behav.,* **8** (1965), 125–129.

FISKE, D. W. A study of relationships to somatotypes, *Jour. Psychol.,* **28** (1944), 504–519.

FLANAGAN, B., I. GOLDIAMOND, and N. AZRIN. Operant stuttering in the control of stuttering behavior through response contingent consequences, *Jour. Exp. Anal. Behav.,* **1** (1958), 173–178.

FLANAGAN, B., I. GOLDIAMOND, and N. AZRIN. Instatement of stuttering in normally fluent individuals through operant procedures, *Science,* **130** (1959), 979–981.

FORD, C. S., and F. A. BEECH. *Patterns of sexual behavior.* New York: Hoeber, 1952.

FRANKLIN, B. Operant reinforcement of prayer, *Jour. Appl. Behav. Anal.,* **2** (1969), 247.

FREUD, A. *The ego and the mechanisms of defense.* New York: International Universities Press, 1941.

FREUD, A., and D. T. BURLINGHAM. *War and children.* New York: Ernst Willard, 1943.

FREUD, S. *The standard edition of the complete psychological works,* ed. J. Strachey, London: Hogarth Press, 1953.

FREUD, S. Further remarks on the defense neuropsychoses. In *Collected Papers,* vol. 1. International Psychoanalytic Press, 1924; first pub. German, 1896.

FREUD, S. The interpretation of dreams. In *Standard ed.,* vols. IV and V. London: Hogarth Press, 1953; first German ed., 1900.

FREUD, S. The psychopathology of everyday life. In *The basic writings of Sigmund Freud.* New York: Random House, 1938; first German ed., 1904.

FREUD, S. Fragment of an analysis of a case of hysteria. In *Collected Papers,* vol. III. London Hogarth Press, 1933; first pub. Germany, 1905.

FREUD, S. Three essays on sexuality. In *Standard ed.,* vol. III. London: Hogarth Press, 1953; first German ed., 1905.

FREUD, S. *Leonardo da Vinci: A study of psychosexuality.* New York: Random House, 1947; first German ed., 1910.

FREUD, S. Psychoanalytic notes upon an autobiographical account of a case of paranoia (dementia praecox). In *Collected Papers,* vol. III. London: Hogarth Press, 1928; first pub. Germany, 1911.

FREUD, S. Instincts and their vicissitudes. In *Collected Papers,* vol. IV. London: Hogarth Press, 1925; first German ed., 1915.

FREUD, S. *A general introduction to psychoanalysis.* Garden City, N.Y.: Garden City Pub. Co., 1943; first German ed., 1917.

FREUD, S. Beyond the pleasure principle. In *Standard ed.,* vol. XVIII. London: Hogarth Press, 1955; first German ed., 1920.

FREUD, S. *The ego and the id.* London: Hogarth Press, 1947; first German ed., 1923.

FREUD, S. *Inhibitions, symptoms and anxiety.* London: Hogarth Press, 1936; first German ed., 1926.

FREUD, S. *Civilization and its discontents.* London: Hogarth Press, 1930; first German ed., 1930.

FREUD, S. *New introductory lectures on psychoanalysis.* New York: Norton, 1933; first German ed., 1933.

FREUD, S. *The problem of anxiety.* New York: Psychoanalytic Quarterly Press, 1936; first German ed., 1926.

FREUD, S. *An outline of psychoanalysis.* New York: Norton, 1949; first German ed., 1940.

FRICK, F. C. An analysis of operant discrimination, *Jour. Psychol.,* **26** (1948), 93–123.

FROMM, E. *Escape from freedom.* New York: Holt, Rinehart and Winston, 1941.

FULLER, P. R. Operant conditioning in a vegetative human organism. *Amer. Jour. Psychol.,* **62** (1949), 587–590.

GALLIMORE, R., R. THARP, and B. KEMP. Positively reinforcing function of "negative attention," *Jour. Exp. Child Psychol.,* **8** (1969), 140–146.

GELDER, M. G., and I. M. MARKS. Aversion treatment in transvestism and transexualaism. In R. Green, ed., *Transvetism and sex management.* Baltimore: Johns Hopkins Press, 1969.

GESELL, A., et al. *The first five years.* New York: Harper & Bros., 1940.

GESELL, A., and H. THOMPSON. Twins T and C from infancy to adolescence: A biogenic study of individual differences by the method of co-twin control, *Genet. Psychol. Monogr.,* **24** (1941), 3–122.

GEWITZ, J. L., and D. M. BAER. Deprivation and satiation of social reinforcers as drive conditions, *Jour. Abn. Soc. Psychol.,* **57** (1958), 165–172.

GODBEER, E. Factors introducing conflict in the choice of behavior of children. New Haven: Yale University (dissertation), 1940.

GOLDFARB, W. Effects of psychological deprivation in infancy and subsequent stimulation, *Amer. Jour. Psychiat.,* **102** (1945), 18–33.

GOLDIAMOND, I. Stuttering and fluency in manipulatable operant responses classes. In L. KRASNER and L. P. ULLMANN, eds., *Research in behavior modification.* New York: Holt, Rinehart and Winston, 1965.

GOLDIAMOND, I. Self-control procedures in personal behavior problems, *Psychol. Rep.,* **17** (1965), 851–858.

GOY, R. W. The effect of electro-convulsive shock on a conditioned emotional response: the relation between the amount of attenuation and the strength of the conditioned emotional response. Unpublished Ph.D. Dissertation, University of Chicago, 1953.

GRAHAM, P. K., W. A. CHARWAT, A. S. HONIG, and P. C. WELTZ. Aggression as a function of attack and attacker, *Jour. Abn. Soc. Psychol.*, **46** (1951), 512–520.

GREENSPOON, J. The reinforcing effects of two spoken words on the frequency of two responses, *Amer. Jour. Psychol.*, **68** (1955), 409–416.

GREENSPOON, J., and S. FOREMAN. Effect of delay of knowledge of results on learning a motor task, *Jour. Exp. Psychol.*, **51** (1956), 226–228.

GRINKER, R. R., and J. P. SPIEGEL. *Man under stress.* New York: Blakiston, 1945.

GRINKER, R. R., and J. P. SPIEGEL. *War neurosis.* New York: Blakiston, 1945.

GUTTMAN, N. Operant conditioning, extinction and periodic reinforcement in relation to concentration of sucrose used as a reinforcing agent, *Jour. Exp. Psychol.*, **46** (1953), 213–224.

GUTTMAN, N., and H. KALISH. Discriminability and stimulus generalization, *Jour. Exp. Psychol.*, **51** (1956), 79–88.

HALL, C. S. *A primer of Freudian psychology.* New York: World, 1954.

HALL, C. S., and G. LINDZEY. *Theories of personality.* New York: Wiley, 1957.

HALL, J. F. Studies in secondary reinforcement: I. Secondary reinforcement as a function of the frequency of primary reinforcement, *Jour. Comp. Physiol. Psychol.*, **44** (1951), 246–251.

HALVERSON, H. M. The acquisition of skill in infancy, *Jour. Genet. Psychol.*, **43** (1933), 3–48.

HARLOW, H. F. The heterosexual affectional response in monkeys, *Amer. Psychologist*, **17** (1962), 1–9.

HARLOW, H. F., and R. R. ZIMMERMANN. Affectional responses in infant monkeys, *Science*, **130** (1959), 421–432.

HARRIS, P. R., M. K. JOHNSON, C. S. KELLY, and M. M. WOLF. Effects of positive social reinforcement on regressed crawling of a nursery school child, *Jour. Educ. Psychol.*, **55** (1964), 35–41.

HART, B. M., K. E. ALLEN, J. S. BUELL, P. R. HARRIS, and M. M. WOLF. Effects of social reinforcement on operant crying, *Jour. Exp. Child. Psychol.*, **1** (1964), 145–153.

HATHAWAY, S. R., and J. C. McKINLEY. *Minnesota multiphasic personality inventory manual.* New York: The Psychological Corp., 1951.

HAUGHTON, E., and T. AYLLON. Production and elimination of symptomatic behavior. In L. P. Ullmann and L. Krasner, eds., *Case studies in behavior modification.* New York: Holt, Rinehart and Winston, 1965.

HEBB, D. O. *The organization of behavior.* New York: Wiley, 1949.

HEFFERLINE, R. F. Learning theory and clinical psychology: An eventual symbiosis. In A. J. Bachrach, ed., *Experimental foundation of clinical psychology.* New York: Basic Books, 1962.

HEFFERLINE, R. F., B. KEENAN, and R. HARFORD. Escape and avoidance conditioning in human subjects without their observation of the response, *Science*, **130** (1959), 1338–1339.

HERON, W. The pathology of boredom, *Scient. Amer.*, **196,** no. 1, 1957, 52–69.

HERON, W. T., and B. F. SKINNER. Changes in hunger during starvation, *Psychol. Rec.*, **1** (1937), 51–60.

Hess, E. H. Effects of meprobamate on imprinting in water fowl, *Ann. New York Acad. Sci.*, **67** (1957), 724–733.

Hess, E. H. "Imprinting" in animals, *Scient. Amer.*, **198**, no. 3 (1958), 81–90.

Hingten, J. N., and F. C. Frost. Shaping cooperative responses in early childhood schizophrenics, II. Reinforcement of mutual physical contact and vocal responses. In R. Ulrich, T. Stachnick, and J. Marby, eds., *Control of human behavior*. Glenview, Ill.: Scott, Foresman, 1966.

Hingten, J. N., B. J. Sanders, and M. K. DeMeyer. Shaping cooperative responses in early childhood schizophrenia. In L. P. Ullmann and L. Krasner, eds., *Case studies in behavior modification*. New York: Holt, Rinehart and Winston, 1965.

Hoch, P. H., and J. Zubin, eds., *Anxiety*. New York: Grune & Stratton, 1950.

Hoch, P. H., and Zubin, eds., *Experimental psychopathology*. New York: Grune & Stratton, 1957.

Holland, J. C. Human vigilance. *Science*, **128** (1958), 61–67.

Holz, W. C., and N. H. Azrin. A comparison of several procedures for eliminating behavior, *Jour. Exp. Anal. Behav.*, **6** (1963), 399–406.

Holz, W. C., N. H. Azrin, and T. Ayllon. Elimination of behavior of mental patients by response-produced extinction, *Jour. Exp. Anal. Behav.*, **6** (1963), 497–512.

Homme, L. Contingency theory and contingency management, *Psychol. Rec.*, **16** (1966), 233–241.

Homme, L. *How to use contingency contracting in the classroom*. Champaign: Ill.: Research Press, 1969.

Horney, K. *The neurotic personality of our time*. New York: Norton, 1937.

Horney, K. *Self-analysis*. New York: Norton, 1942.

Horney, K. *Our inner conflicts*. New York: Norton, 1945.

Hovland, C. I., and R. R. Sears. Experiments on motor conflict, I. Types of conflict and their modes of resolution. *Jour. Exp. Psychol.*, **23** (1930), 477–493.

Hovland, C. I., and R. R. Sears. Minor studies of aggression, VI. Correlation of lynchings with economic indices, *Jour. Psychol.*, **9** (1940), 301–310.

Hull, C. L. The rat's speed of locomotion gradient in the approach to food, *Jour. Comp. Psychol.*, **17** (1934), 398–422.

Hull, C. L. *Principles of behavior*. New York: Appleton-Century-Crofts, 1943

Hunt, H. F., and J. V. Brady. Some effects of electro-convulsive shock on a conditioned emotional response ("anxiety"), *Jour. Comp. Physiol. Psychol.*, **44** (1951), 88–98.

Hunt, J. McV. The effects of infant feeding frustration upon adult hoarding in the albino rat, *Jour. Abn. Soc. Psychol.*, **36** (1941), 338–360.

Hunt, J. McV. ed. *Personality and the behavior disorders*. 2 vols. New York: Ronald Press, 1944.

Isaacs, W., J. Thomas, and I. Goldiamond. Shaping vocal responses in mute catatonic schizophrenics, *Jour. Speech and Hear. Dis.*, **25** (1960), 8–12.

Itard, J. M. G. *The wild boy of Aveyron*, trans., G. and H. Humphery. New York: Appleton-Century, 1932.

Jacobson, E. The electrophysiology of mental activities, *Amer. Jour. Psychol.*, **44** (1932), 677–694.

JACOBSON, E. *Progressive relaxation,* Chicago: University of Chicago Press, 1938.

JAMES, W. *Principles of psychology.* 2 vols. New York: Holt, 1890.

JANET, P. *L'état mentale des hystériques.* Paris: Reuff, 1893–1894.

JAYNES, J. Imprinting: The interaction of learned and innate behavior, III. Practice effects on performance, retention and fear, *Jour. Comp. Physiol. Psychol.,* **51** (1958), 234–237.

JENKINS, J. G., and K. M. DALLENBACH. Oblivescence during sleep and waking, *Amer. Jour. Psychol.,* **35** (1924), 605–612.

JENKINS, W. O., and J. C. STANLEY. Partial reinforcement: A review and critique, *Psychol. Bull.,* **47** (1950), 193–234.

JONES, M. C. The elimination of children's fear, *Jour. Exp. Psychol.,* **7** (1924), 382–390.

JONES, M. C. A behavior study of fear: The case of Peter, *Jour. Genet. Psychol.,* **31** (1924), 508–515.

JUNG, C. G. *Studies in word association.* London: Heinemann, 1918.

JUNG, C. G. Symbols of transformation. In *Collected works,* vol. 5. London: Kegan Paul, 1956.

KALLMANN, F. *The genetics of schizophrenia.* New York: Augustin, 1938.

KALLMANN, F. *Heredity in health and mental disease.* New York: Norton, 1953.

KANTOR, J. R. *Principles of psychology.* 2 vols. New York: Knopf, 1924–1926.

KANTOR, J. R. *Problems in physiological psychology.* Bloomington, Ind.: Principia Press, 1947.

KANTOR, J. R. *Interbehavioral psychology.* Bloomington, Ind.: Principia Press, 1958.

KAPLAN, M. The effect of noxious stimulus intensity and duration during intermittent reinforcement escape behavior, *Jour. Comp. Physiol. Psychol.,* **45** (1952), 538–549.

KEISTER, M. E., and R. UPDEGRAF. A study of children's reactions to failure and an experimental attempt to modify them, *Child Dev.,* **8** (1937), 241–248.

KELLEHER, R. Schedules of conditioned reinforcement during experimental extinction, *Jour. Exp. Anal. Behav.,* **4** (1961), 1–5.

KELLER, F. S. Light-aversion in the white rat, *Psychol. Rec.,* **4** (1941), 235–250.

KELLER, F. S., and W. N. SCHOENFELD. *Principles of psychology.* New York: Appleton-Century-Crofts, 1950.

KELLOGG, W. N., and L. A. KELLOGG. *The ape and the child.* New York: Whittlesy House, McGraw-Hill, 1933.

KEYS, A. B., J. BROZEK, A. HENSHEL, O. MICKELSON, and H. L. TAYLOR. *The biology of human starvation.* Minneapolis: University of Minnesota Press, 1950.

KIMBLE, G. A. *Principles of general psychology.* 3rd ed. New York: Ronald Press, 1968.

KINSEY, A. C., W. B. POMEROY, and C. E. MARTIN. *Sexual behavior in the human male.* Philadelphia: Saunders, 1948.

KINSEY, A. C., W. B. POMEROY, C. E. MARTIN, and P. R. GEBHARD. *Sexual behavior in the human female.* Philadelphia: Saunders, 1953.

KLEBANOFF, S. G. An experimental analysis of approach–approach and avoidance–avoidance conflict. New Haven: Yale University (dissertation), 1939. Reported by N. E. Miller in Experimental studies of conflict. In J.

McV. Hunt, ed., *Personality and the behavior disorders*. Vol. 1. New York: Ronald Press, 1944), chapter xiv.

KOFFKA, K. *Principles of Gestalt psychology*. New York: Harcourt, Brace, 1935.

KRAEPELIN, E. *Psychiatrie: ein Lehrbuch fur Studierende und Arate*. 4 vols. Leipzig: Barth, 1909–1913.

KRETSCHMER, E. *Physique and character*. New York: Harcourt, Brace, 1925.

KRASNER, L., and L. P. ULLMANN, eds. *Research in behavior modification*. New York: Holt, Rinehart and Winston, 1965.

KUEHNER, M. The reduction of a long-standing fetish by means of aversive conditioning. In L. P. Ullmann, and L. Krasner, eds., *Case studies in behavior modification*. New York: Holt, Rinehart and Winston, 1965.

KUBZANSKY, P. E., and F. H. LEIDEMAN. Sensory deprivation: An overview. In P. Solomon, ed., *Sensory deprivation*. Cambridge, Mass.: Harvard University Press, 1961.

LANG, F. J., and A. D. LAZEVIC. The experimental desensitization of a phobia, *Jour. Abn. Soc. Psychol.*, **66** (1963), 319–325.

LANG, P. J., and B. G. MALAMED. Case report: Avoidance conditioning therapy in an infant with chronic ruminative vomiting, *Jour. Abn. Psychol.*, **74** (1969), 1–8.

LAVIN, N. I., J. G. THORPE, J. C. BARKER, C. S. BLAKEMORE, and C. G. CONWAY. Behavior therapy in the case of transvestism, *Jour. Nerv. Ment. Dis.*, **133** (1961), 346–353.

LAZARUS, A. The results of behavior therapy in 126 cases of severe neurosis, *Behav. Res. Ther.*, **1** (1963), 63–78.

LEIBNITZ, G. W. *Haupschriften zur Grundelung Philosophie*, vol. 2, E. Cassirer, ed., 1906.

LEMERE, F., and W. VOGTLIN. An evaluation of aversion treatment of alcoholism, *Quart. Jour. Stud. Alcohol*, **11** (1950), 199–204.

LEVY, D. M. Primary affect hunger, *Amer. Jour. Psychiat.*, **94** (1937), 643–652.

LEVY, D. M. *Maternal overprotection*. New York: Columbia University Press, 1943.

LEWIN, K. *Principles of topological psychology*. New York: McGraw-Hill, 1936.

LIBERMAN, R. P. *A guide to behavior analysis and therapy*. Elmsford, N.Y.: Pergamon Press, 1972.

LIDDELL, H. S. Conditioning and emotions, *Scient. Amer.*, **190** (1954), 48–57.

LIDDELL, H. S., and T. L. BAYNE. The development of "experimental neurasthenia" in sheep during the formation of difficult conditioned reflexes. *Amer. Jour. Psychol.*, **81** (1927), 494.

LIDDELL, H. S. Conditioned reflex method and experimental neurosis. In J. McV. Hunt, ed., *Personality and the behavior disorders*. Vol. 1. New York: Ronald Press, 1944, chapter xii.

LINDESMITH, A. R. *Opiate addiction*. Bloomington, Ind.: Principia Press, 1947.

LINDSLEY, O. R. Operant conditioning methods applied to research in chronic schizophrenia, *Psychiat. Res. Rep.*, **5** (1956), 140–153.

LINDSLEY, O. R. Progress Report I (an experimental analysis of psychotic behavior). Research Grant MH-977, National Institute of Mental Health, National Institute of Health, June 1956.

Lindsley, O. R. New techniques of analysis of psychotic behavior and final technical report for contract N-5-ori-07662, Annual Tech. Rep. III, Behavior Research Laboratory, Metropolitan State Hospital, Waltham, Mass., November 1956.

Lindsley, O. R. Report on the third and fourth years on *An experimental analysis of psychotic behavior* (Detailed progress report II) Behavior Research Laboratory, Metropolitan State Hospital, Waltham, Mass., June 1956–November 1958.

Lindsley, O. R. Characteristics of the behavior of chronic psychotics as revealed by free-operant conditioning methods. Paper read at annual meeting of Eastern Psychiatric Research Assn., October 24, 1959, New York.

Lindsley, O. R. Characteristics of the behavior of chronic psychotics as revealed by free-operant conditioning methods, *Dis. Nerv. Syst.* (Monogr. Sup.), **21** (1960), 1–13.

Locke, J. *An essay concerning human understanding.* London: A. and J. Churchel, 1694.

Lorenz, K. Z. *King Solomon's ring: A new light on animal ways.* New York: Crowell, 1952.

Lovaas, P. O., B. Schaeffer, and J. Q. Simmons. Building social behavior in autistic children by use of electric shock, *Jour. Exp. Res. Personal.*, **1** (1965), 99–109.

Lucero, R. J., and B. F. Meyer. A behavior rating scale suitable for use in mental hospitals, *Jour. Clin. Psychol.*, **7** (1951), 250–254.

Lundin, R. W. *An objective psychology of music.* Rev. ed. New York: Ronald Press, 1967.

Lundin, R. W. Musical learning and reinforcement theory, *Music Educ. Jour.*, **46** (1960), 46–50.

Lundin, R. W. *Principles of psychopathology.* Columbus, Ohio: Merrill Books, 1965.

MacCorquodale, K., and P. Meehl. "Cognitive" learning in the absence of competition of incentives, *Jour. Comp. Physiol. Psychol.*, **42** (1949), 383–390.

Madsen, O. H. Positive reinforcement in training a normal child: A case report. In L. P. Ullmann, and L. Krasner, eds., *Case studies in behavior modification.* New York: Holt, Rinehart and Winston, 1965.

Magaret, A. Generalization in successful psychotherapy, *Jour. Consult. Psychol.*, **14** (1950), 64–69.

Maier, N. R. F. *Frustration: A study of behavior without a goal.* New York: McGraw-Hill, 1940.

Mandel, K. N. Preliminary report on a new aversion therapy for homosexuals, *Behav. Res. and Ther.*, **8** (1970), 93–95.

Mandler, G., and W. K. Kaplan. Subjective evaluation and reinforcing effect of verbal stimuli, *Science*, **124** (1956), 582–583.

Marquis, J. N., W. G. Masgan, and G. W. Piaget. *A guidebook for systematic desensitization.* 2nd ed. Veterans Administration Workshop, Veterans Administration Hospital, Palo Alto, Calif., 1971, p. 45.

Marrone, R. I., M. A. Merksomer, and P. M. Salzberg. A short duration group treatment for smoking behavior by stimulus satiation, *Behav. Res. and Ther.*, **8** (1970), 347–352.

MARTIN, R. F. "Native" traits and regression in rats, *Jour. Comp. Psychol.*, **30** (1940), 1–16.

MARTIN, R. R., and S. K. HAROLDSON. Time out as punishment for stuttering during conversation, *Jour. Commun. Dis.*, **4** (1971), 15–19.

MASSERMAN, J. H. *Behavior and neurosis.* Chicago: University of Chicago Press, 1943.

MASSERMAN, J. H. *Principles of dynamic psychiatry.* Philadelphia: Saunders 1946.

MASSERMAN, J. H., and K. S. YUM. An analysis of the influence of alcohol in experimental neurosis in cats. *Psychosomat. Med.*, **8** (1946), 36–52.

MASTRON, A. R., and R. M. McFALL. Comparison of behavior modification approaches to smoking reduction, *Jour. Cons. and Clin. Psychol.*, **36** (1971), 153–162.

MAUSNER, B. Some comments on the failure of behavior therapy as a technique for modifying cigarette smoking, *Jour. Cons. and Clin. Psychol.*, **36** (1971), 167–170.

MAX, L. W. Experimental study of the motor theory of consciousness, IV. Action current responses in the deaf, awakening, kinesthetic imagery and abstract thinking, *Jour. Comp. Psychol.*, **23** (1937), 301–344.

McCLELLAND, D. C., and J. W. ATKINSON. The projective expression of needs: I. The effect of different intensities of hunger drive on perception, *Jour. Psychol.*, **25** (1948), 205–222.

McCLELLAND, D. C., and F. A. APICELLA. A functional classification of verbal reactions to experimentally induced failure, *Jour. Abn. Soc. Psychol.*, **40** (1945), 376–390.

McDOUGALL, W. *Outline of psychology.* New York: Scribner, 1923.

McDOUGALL, W. *Outline of abnormal psychology.* New York: Scribner, 1926.

McKELVEY, R. K., and M. H. MARX. Effects of infantile food and water deprivation on adult hoarding in the rat, *Jour. Comp. Physiol. Psychol.*, **44** (1951), 423–430.

McNAIR, D. M. Reinforcement of verbal behavior, *Jour. Exp. Psychol.*, **53** (1957), 40–46.

MEDNICK, M. T., and O. R. LINDSLEY. Some clinical correlates of operant behavior, *Jour. Abn. Soc. Psychol.*, **57** (1958), 13–16.

MEEHL, P., and K. MacCORQUODALE. Drive conditioning as a function of latent learning, *Jour. Exp. Psychol.*, **45** (1953), 20–24.

MELTZER, H. Individual differences in forgetting pleasant and unpleasant experiences, *Jour. Educ. Psychol.*, **21** (1930), 399–409.

MELZACK, R. The genesis of emotional behavior: An experimental study of the dog, *Jour. Comp. Physiol. Psychol.*, **47** (1954), 166–168.

MELZACK, R., and T. H. SCOTT. The effect of early experience on the response to pain, *Jour. Comp. Physiol. Psychol.*, **50** (1957), 155–161.

MERTENS, G. C., and G. B. FULLER. Conditioning of molar behavior in "regressed" psychotics, *Jour. Clin. Psychol.*, **19** (1963), 333–337.

MEYER, A. The nature and conception of dementia praecox, *Jour. Abn. Soc. Psychol.*, **21** (1910), 385–403.

MEYER, A. The psychobiological point of view. In M. Bentley and E. Cowdry, eds., *The problem of mental disorders.* New York: McGraw-Hill, 1934.

MEYER, A., and V. CRISP. Aversion therapy in two cases of obesity, *Behav. Res. and Ther.*, **2** (1964), 143–147.

MIKULAS, W. *Behavior modification: An overview.* New York: Harper & Row, 1972.

MILLER, N. E. Experimental studies of conflict. In J. McV. Hunt, ed., *Personality and the behavior disorders.* Vol. I. New York: Ronald Press, 1944, chapter xiv.

MILLER, N. E. Theory and experiment relating psychoanalytic displacement to stimulus-response generalization, *Jour. Abn. Soc. Psychol.*, **43** (1948), 155–178.

MILLER, N. E. Studies of fear as an acquirable drive: I. Fear as motivation and fear reduction as reinforcement in the learning of new responses, *Jour. Exp. Psychol.*, **38** (1948), 89–101.

MILLER, N. E., and B. BUGELSKI. Minor studies of aggression: II. The influence of frustrations imposed by the in-group on attitudes expressed toward the out-groups, *Jour. Psychol.*, **25** (1948), 437–442.

MILLER, N. E., J. S. BROWN, and H. LIPOFSKY. A theoretical and experimental analysis of conflict behavior, III. Approach–avoidance conflict as a function of the strength of drive. Reported by N. E. Miller, in J. McV. Hunt, ed., *Personality and the behavior disorders.* New York: Ronald Press, 1944.

MILLER, N. E., and J. DOLLARD. *Social learning and imitation.* New Haven: Yale University Press, 1941.

MILLS, K. C., M. B. SOBELL, and H. H. SCHAFFER. Training social drinking as an alternate to abstinence in alcoholics, *Behav. Ther.*, **2** (1971), 18–27.

MOWRER, O. H. Enuresis: A method for its study and treatment, *Amer. Jour. Orthopsychiat.*, **8** (1938), 436–459.

MOWRER, O. H. An experimental analogue of "regression" with incidental observations on "reaction formation," *Jour. Abn. Soc. Psychol.*, **35** (1940), 56–87.

MOWRER, O. H. Learning theory and the neurotic paradox, *Amer. Jour. Orthopsychiat.*, **18** (1948), 571–610.

MOWRER, O. H. *Learning theory and personality dynamics.* New York: Ronald Press, 1950.

MOWRER, O. H. "Q-technique" description, history and critique. In O. H. Mowrer, ed., *Psychotherapy, theory and research.* New York: Ronald Press, 1953.

MOWRER, O. H. *Psychotherapy, theory and research.* New York: Ronald Press, 1953.

MOWRER, O. H. *The crisis in psychiatry and religion.* New York: Van Nostrand, 1959.

MOWRER, O. H., and J. JONES. Extinction and behavior variability as a function of the effortfulness of task, *Jour. Exp. Psychol.*, **33** (1943), 369–386.

MOWRER, O. H., and R. R. LAMOREAUX. Avoidance conditioning and signal duration: A study of secondary motivation and reward, *Psychol. Monogr.*, **54**, no. 247 (1942), iii-34.

MURRAY, E. J., and N. E. MILLER. Displacement: Steeper gradient of generalization of avoidance than of approach with age of habit controlled, *Jour. Exp. Psychol.*, **43** (1952), 322–226.

MURRAY, H. A. *Manual for the thematic apperception test.* Cambridge, Mass.: Harvard University Press, 1943.

MUSSEN, P. H. Some personality and social factors related to changes in children's attitudes towards Negroes, *Jour. Abn. Soc. Psychol.*, **45** (1950), 423–441.

O'CONNOR, R. D. Modification of social withdrawal through symbolic modeling, *Jour. Appl. Beh. Anal.*, **2** (1969), 15–22.

O'KELLEY, L. I., and L. C. STECKLE. A note on long-enduring emotional responses in the rat, *Jour. Psychol.*, **8** (1939), 125–131.

OLDS, J. Pleasure centers in the brain, *Scient. Amer.*, **195** (1956), 108–118.

OLDS, J. Satiation effects on self-stimulation of the brain, *Jour. Comp. Physiol. Psychol*, **51** (1958), 675–678.

OLDS, J., and P. MILNER. Positive reinforcement produced by electrical stimulation of the ceptal area and other regions of the rat brain, *Jour. Comp. Physiol. Psychol.*, **47** (1954), 419–427.

ORLANSKY, J. Infant care and personality, *Psychol. Bull.*, **46** (1949), 1–48.

OPLER, M. K. Schizophrenia and culture, *Scient. Amer.*, **157,** no. 2 (1957).

ORLANDO, R., and S. BIJOU. Single and multiple schedules of reinforcement in developmentally retarded children. *Jour. Exp. Anal. Behav.*, **3** (1960), 339–358.

PALMER, S. Frustration, aggression and murder, *Jour. Abn. Soc. Psychol.*, **60** (1960), 430–432.

PAVLOV, I. P. *Conditioned reflexes,* trans. G. V. Anrep. London: Oxford University Press, 1927.

PAVLOV, I. P. *Lectures on conditioned reflexes,* trans. W. H. Gantt. New York: International Universities Press, 1928.

PEDILLA, S. G. Further studies on delayed pecking in chicks, *Jour. Comp. Psychol.*, **20** (1935), 413–445.

PERIN, C. T. Behavior potentiality as a joint function of the amount of training and the degree of hunger at the time of extinction, *Jour. Exp. Psychol.*, **30** (1942), 93–113.

POWELL, J., and N. AZRIN. The effects of shock as a punisher for cigarette smoking, *Jour. Appl. Behav. Anal.*, **1** (1968), 63–71.

PREMACK, D. Reinforcement theory. In D. Levine, ed., *Nebraska symposium on motivation.* Lincoln: University of Nebraska Press, 1965.

QUARTI, C., and J. RENAUD. A new treatment of constipation by conditioning: A preliminary report. In C. M. Franks, ed., *Conditioning techniques in clinical practice and research.* New York: Springer, 1964.

RACHMAN, S. Objective psychotherapy: Some theoretical considerations, *S. Afric. Med. Jour.* **33** (1958), 19–21.

RACHMAN, S. Sexual fetishism: An experimental analogue, *Psychol. Rec.*, **16** (1966), 293–296.

RACHMAN, S., and J. TEASDALE. *Aversion therapy and behavior disorders: An analysis.* Coral Gables, Fla. University of Miami Press, 1969.

RAIMY, V. C. Self-reference in counseling interviews, *Jour. Consult. Psychol.*, **12** (1948), 153–163.

RANK, O. *The trauma of birth.* New York: Harcourt, Brace, 1929.

RAYMOND, M. S. Case of fetishism treated by aversion therapy, *Brit. Med. Jour.*, **2** (1956), 854–857.

REDLICH, F. C. Some sociological aspects of the psychoses. In *Theory and treatment of the psychoses: Some newer aspects.* St. Louis: Washington University, 1956.

REESE, E. The analysis of human operant behavior. In J. Vernon, ed., *Introduction to psychology: A self-selection text.* Dubuque, Ia.: William C. Brown Co., 1966.

RHEINGOLD, H. L., J. L. GEWITZ, and H. E. ROSS. Social conditioning of vocalizations in the infant, *Jour. Comp. Physiol., Psychol.,* **52** (1959), 68–73.

RIBBLE, M. H. *The rights of infants.* New York: Columbia University Press, 1943.

RICE, H. K., and M. W. McDANIEL. Operant behavior in vegetative patients, *Psychol. Rec.,* **16** (1966), 279–281.

RICKARD, H. C., and M. B. MUNDY. Direct manipulation of stuttering behavior: An experimental-clinical approach. In L. P. Ullmann and L. Krasner, eds., *Case studies in behavior modification.* New York: Holt, Rinehart and Winston, 1965.

RIESEN, A. H. The development of visual perception in man and chimpanzee, *Science,* **106** (1946), 107–108.

ROGERS, C. R. *Counseling and psychotherapy.* Boston: Houghton Mifflin, 1942.

ROGERS, C. R. *Client-centered therapy: Its current practice, interpretations and theory.* Boston: Houghton Mifflin, 1951.

RORSCHACH, H. *Psychodiagnostics: A diagnostic test based on perception,* trans. P. Lamkau and B. Kronenberg. Bern: Huber, 1942; first German ed., 1921.

ROSENZWEIG, S. Preferences in the repetition· of successful and unsuccessful activities as a function of age and personality, *Jour. Genet. Psychol.,* **42** (1933), 423–441.

ROSENZWEIG, S. An outline of frustration theory. In J. McV. Hunt ed., *Personality and the behavior disorders.* New York: Ronald Press, 1944, chapter xi.

SALTER, A. *The case against psychoanalysis.* New York: Holt, 1952.

SALZINGER, K., R. S. FELDMAN, J. E. COWAN, and S. SALZINGER. Operant conditioning of verbal behavior in two speech-deficient boys. In L. Krasner and L. P. Ullmann, eds., *Research in behavior modification.* New York: Holt, Rinehart and Winston, 1965.

SANFORD, R. N. The effects of abstinence from food upon imaginal processes: A preliminary experiment, *Jour. Psychol.,* **2** (1936), 129–136.

SANFORD, R. N. The effects of abstinence from food upon imaginal processes: A further experiment, *Jour. Psychol.,* **3** (1937), 145–149.

SCHNAHL, D. P., E. LICHTENSTEIN, and D. E. HARRIS. Successful treatment of habitual smokers with warm, smokey air and rapid smoking, *Jour. Cons. and Clin. Psychol.,* **38** (1972), 105–111.

SCHOENFELD, W. N. An experimental approach to anxiety, escape and avoidance behavior. In P. H. Hoch and J. Zubin, eds., *Anxiety.* New York: Grune & Stratton, 1950.

SCHOENFELD, W. N., J. J. ANTONITIS, and P. J. BERSH. A preliminary study of learning conditions necessary for secondary reinforcement, *Jour. Exp. Psychol.,* **40** (1950), 40–50.

SCHWITZEGEBEL, R. *Street corner research.* Cambridge, Mass.: Harvard University Press, 1966.

SEARS, R. R., C. I. HOVLAND, and N. E. MILLER. Minor studies of aggression, I. Measurement of aggressive behavior, *Jour. Psychol.,* **9** (1940), 275–295.

SEARS, R. R., and P. S. SEARS. Minor studies of aggression, V. Strength of frustration reaction as a function of strength of drive, *Jour. Psychol.*, **9** (1940), 297–300.

SEEMAN, J. A study of the process of nondirective therapy, *Jour. Consult. Psychol.*, **13** (1949), 157–168.

SEEMAN, J. Research perspectives in psychotherapy. In O. H. Mowrer, ed., *Psychotherapy, theory and research.* New York: Ronald Press, 1953.

SHAFFER, L. F., and E. J. SHOBEN, JR. *The psychology of adjustment.* 2nd ed., Boston: Houghton Mifflin, 1956.

SHELDON, W. H., and S. S. STEVENS. *The varieties of human physique: An introduction to constitutional psychology.* New York: Harper & Brothers, 1940.

SHELDON, W. H., and S. S. STEVENS. *The varieties of human temperament, a psychology of constitutional differences.* New York: Harper & Brothers, 1942.

SHIRLEY, M. M. *The first two years.* Vol. I: *Postural and locomotor development.* Minneapolis: University of Minnesota Press, 1931.

SHIRLEY, M. M. *The first two years.* Vol. II: *Intellectual development.* Minneapolis: University of Minnesota Press, 1933.

SHOBEN, E. J., JR. Psychotherapy as a problem in learning theory, *Psychol. Bull.*, **46** (1959), 366–392.

SIDMAN, M. Avoidance conditioning with brief shock and no exteroceptive warning signal, *Science*, **118** (1953), 157–158.

SIDMAN, M. The temporal distribution of avoidance responses, *Jour. Comp. Physiol. Psychol.*, **47** (1954), 399–402.

SIDMAN, M. On the persistence of avoidance behavior, *Jour. Abn. Soc. Psychol.*, **50** (1955), 217–220.

SIDMAN, M. Technique for assessing the effects of drugs on timing behavior, *Science,* **122** (1955), 925

SIDMAN, M. A comparison of two types of warning stimulus in an avoidance situation, *Jour. Comp. Physiol. Psychol.*, **50** (1957), 282–287.

SIDMAN, M. Normal sources of pathological behavior, *Science*, **131** (1960), 61–68.

SIEGEL, F. S., and J. G. FORSHEE. The law of primary reinforcement in children. *Jour. Exp. Psychol.*, **45** (1953), 12–14.

SKINNER, B. F. On the rate of formation of a conditioned reflex, *Jour. Gen. Psychol.*, **7** (1932), 274–285.

SKINNER, B. F. On the rate of extinction of a conditioned reflex, *Jour. Gen. Psychol.*, **8** (1933), 51–60.

SKINNER, B. F. The rate of establishment of a discrimination, *Jour. Gen. Psychol.*, **9** (1933), 302–350.

SKINNER, B. F. Conditioning and extinction and their relation to the state of the drive, *Jour. Gen. Psychol.*, **14** (1936), 296–317.

SKINNER, B. F. *The behavior of organisms: An experimental analysis.* New York: Appleton-Century, 1938.

SKINNER, B. F. "Superstition" in the pigeon, *Jour. Exp. Psychol.*, **38** (1948), 168–172.

SKINNER, B. F. *Walden Two.* New York: Macmillan, Inc., 1948.

SKINNER, B. F. Are theories of learning necessary? *Psychol. Rev.*, **57** (1950), 193–216.

SKINNER, B. F. How to teach animals, *Scient. Amer.*, **185,** no. 6 (1951), 26–29.

SKINNER, B. F. Some contributions to an experimental analysis of behavior and to psychology as a whole, *Amer. Psycholog.*, **8** (1953), 69–78.

SKINNER, B. F. *Science and human behavior.* New York: Macmillan, Inc., 1953.

SKINNER, B. F. Critique of psychoanalytical concepts and theories, *Scient. Month.*, **79** (1954), 300–305.

SKINNER, B. F. The control of human behavior, *Trans., New York Acad. Sci.*, **17,** no. 7 (1955) (Series II), 547–551.

SKINNER, B. F. Freedom and the control of men, *Amer. Scholar.*, **25** (1955), 47–65.

SKINNER, B. F. What is psychotic behavior? In *Theory and treatment of the psychoses; Some newer aspects.* St. Louis: Washington University, 1956.

SKINNER, B. F. Psychology in the understanding of mental disease. In *Integrating the approaches to mental disease.* New York: Hoeber, 1957.

SKINNER, B. F. *Verbal behavior.* New York: Appleton-Century-Crofts, 1957.

SKINNER, B. F. Teaching machines, *Science*, **128** (1958), 969–977.

SKINNER, B. F. *Cumulative record.* New York: Appleton-Century-Crofts, 1959.

SKINNER, B. F. *Beyond freedom and dignity.* New York: Knopf, 1971.

SKINNER, B. F., H. C. SOLOMON, and O. R. LINDSLEY. A new method for the experimental analysis of the behavior of psychotic patients, *Jour. Nerv. Ment. Dis.*, **120** (1954), 403–406.

SKINNER, B. F., and W. H. MORSE. A second type of superstition in the pigeon, *Amer. Jour. Psychol.*, **70** (1957), 308–311.

SLOAN, W., and H. H. HARMAN. The constancy of the I-Q. in mental defectives, *Jour. Genet. Psychol.*, **71** (1947), 177–185.

SOLOMAN, R. L., and L. C. WYNNE. Traumatic avoidance learning acquisition in normal dogs, *Psychol. Monogr.*, **67** (1953), no. 4. (Whole No. 354).

SPEARMAN, C. "General intelligence," objectively defined and measured, *Amer. Jour. Psychol.*, **15** (1904), 201–293.

SPITZ, R. A. Hospitalism: An inquiry into the genesis of psychiatric conditions in early childhood, *Psychoanal. Stud. Child.*, **1** (1945), 53–74; **2** (1946), 113–117.

SPRAGG, S. D. S. Morphine addiction in chimpanzees, *Comp. Psychol. Monogr.*, **15** (1940), 1–132.

STAMPFF, T. G., and D. L. LEWIN. Essentials of implosive therapy: A learning theory based psychological therapy, *Jour. Abn. Psychol.*, **72** (1967), 496–503.

STEBBINS, W. C., R. W. LUNDIN, and D. LYON. The effect of alcohol on reaction time in the white rat, *Psychol. Rec.*, **10** (1960), 15–19.

STOCKARD, C. R. *The physical basis of personality.* New York: Norton, 1931.

STONE, C. P. Maturation and "instinctive" functions. In C. P. Stone, ed., *Comparative psychology.* 3rd ed. New York: Prentice-Hall, 1951.

TERMAN, L. M., and M. MERRILL. *Measuring intelligence.* Boston: Houghton Mifflin, 1937.

THOMPSON, W. R., and W. HERON. The effects of early restriction of activity in dogs, *Jour. Comp. Physiol. Psychol.*, **47** (1954), 77–92.

THOMPSON, W. R., and R. MELZACK. Early environment, *Scient. Amer.*, **194** no. 1 (1956), 38–42.

THORNDIKE, E. L. *Animal intelligence: Experimental studies.* New York: Macmillan, 1911.

THORNE, F. Directive and eclectic personality counseling. In J. L. McCary, ed., *Six approaches to psychotherapy*. New York: Dryden Press, 1955.

THURSTONE, L. L. Primary mental abilities, *Psychometr. Monogr.*, no. 1 (1938).

TITCHENER, E. B. *Systematic psychology*. New York: Macmillan, Inc., 1929.

TOLCOTT, M. A. Conflict: A study of some interactions between appetite and aversion in the white rat, *Genet. Psychol. Monogr.*, **38** (1948), 83–142.

TOLMAN, E. C. *Purposive behavior in animals and man*. New York: Century, 1932.

TOOLEY, J. T., and S. PRATT. An experimental procedure for the extinction of smoking behavior, *Psychol. Rec.*, **17** (1967), 209–218.

ULRICH, R. E., and N. H. AZRIN. Reflexive fighting in response to aversive stimulation, *Jour. Exp. Anal. Behav.*, **5** (1962), 511–520.

ULLMANN, L. P., and L. KRASNER, eds., *Case Studies in behavior modification*. New York: Holt, Rinehart and Winston, 1965.

VERNON, J. A., T. W. MCGILL, W. L. GULICK, and D. CANDLAND. The effect of human isolation upon some perceptual and motor skills. In P. Solomon, ed., *Sensory deprivation*. Cambridge, Mass.: Harvard University Press, 1961.

VERPLANCK, W. S. The control of the content of conversation: Reinforcement of statements of opinion, *Jour. Abn. Soc. Psychol.*, **51** (1955), 668–676.

VERPLANCK, W. S. The operant conditioning of human motor behavior, *Psychol. Bull.*, **53** (1956), 70–83.

VERPLANCK, W. S. A glossary of some terms used in the objective science of behavior, *Psychol. Rev. (suppl.)*, **64**, no. 6, pt. 2 (1957), 1–42.

VOEGLIN, W. L. The treatment of alcoholism by establishing a conditioned reflex, *Amer. Jour. Med. Sci.*, **119** (1940), 125–128.

VOEGLIN, W. L., and F. LEMERE. The treatment of alcohol addiction, *Quart. Jour. Stud. Alcohol*, **2** (1942), 717–803.

VON SENDEN, M. *Raum und Gestaltauffassung bei operierten Blindgeborenen vor und nach Operation*. Leipzig: Barth, 1932.

WARDEN, C. J. *Animal motivation studies: The albino rat*. New York: Columbia University Press, 1931.

WALTON, D. The application of learning theory to the treatment of a case of neurodermititis. In H. J. Eysenck, ed., *Behavior therapy and the neuroses*. London: Pergamon Press, 1960, 272–277.

WARNER, L. H. The association span of the white rat, *Jour. Genet. Psychol.*, **41** (1932), 51–90.

WARREN, A. B., and R. H. BROWN. Conditioned operant response phenomena in children, *Jour. Gen. Psychol.*, **28** (1943), 181–207.

WATERS, R. H., D. A. RETHLINGSHAFER, and W. E. CALDWELL eds., *Principles of comparative psychology*. New York: McGraw-Hill, 1960.

WATSON, J. B. Psychology as the behaviorist views it., *Psychol. Rev.*, **20** (1913), 158–177.

WATSON, J. B. The place of the conditioned reflex in psychology, *Psychol. Rev.*, **23** (1916), 89–116.

WATSON, J. B. *Psychology from the standpoint of a behaviorist*. Philadelphia: Lippincott, 1919.

WATSON, J. B. Experimental studies on the growth of the emotions. In *Psychologies of 1925*. Worcester, Mass.: Clark University Press, 1926.

WATSON, J. B. *Psychological care of infant and child.* New York: Norton, 1928.

WATSON, J. B. *Behaviorism.* New York: Norton, 1930.

WATSON, J. B., and R. RAYNOR. Conditioned emotional reactions, *Jour. Exp. Psychol.,* **3** (1920), 1–14.

WECHSLER, D. *Wechsler adult intelligence scale (manual).* New York: The Psychological Corp., 1955.

WEEKS, J. R. Experimental narcotic addiction, *Scient. Amer.,* **210** (1964), 46–52.

WEIR-MITCHELL, S. *Fat and blood.* 8th ed. Philadelphia: Lippincott, 1900.

WEISBERG, P., and P. B. WALDROP. Fixed interval work habits of Congress, *Jour. Appl. Behav. Anal.,* **5** (1972), 93–97.

WEISBERT, P. Social and non-social conditioning of infant vocalizations, *Child Dev.,* **34** (1963), 377–388.

WHITE, R. S. *The abnormal personality.* 2nd ed. New York: Ronald Press, 1956.

WHYTE, W. H., JR. *The organization man.* New York: Doubleday, 1957.

WIKLER, A. *The relation of pharmacology to psychiatry.* Baltimore: Williams & Wilkins, 1957.

WILLIAMS, C. D. The elimination of tantrum behavior by extinction procedures, *Jour Abn. Soc. Psychol.,* **59** (1959), 260.

WILLIAMS, S. B. Resistance to extinction as a function of the number of reinforcements, *Jour. Exp. Psychol.,* **23** (1938), 506–522.

WILSON, M. P. Periodic reinforcement: Interval and number of periodic reinforcements as parameters of response strength, *Jour. Comp. Physiol. Psychol.,* **47** (1954), 51–56.

WILSON, M. P., and F. S. KELLER. On the selective reinforcement of spaced responses, *Jour. Comp. Physiol. Psychol.,* **46** (1953), 190–193.

WINNICK, W. A. Anxiety indicators in an avoidance response during conflict and non-conflict, *Jour. Comp. Physiol. Psychol.,* **49** (1956), 52–59.

WOLF, M., T. RISLEY, and H. MEES. Application of operant conditioning procedures to the behavior problems of autistic children, *Behav. Res. Ther.,* **1** (1964), 305–312.

WOLF, S., and H. WOLFF. Evidence on the genesis of peptic ulcer in man. *Jour. Amer. Med. Assn.,* **120** (1942), 670–675.

WOLFE, J. B. Effectiveness of token rewards for chimpanzees, *Comp. Psychol. Monogr.,* **12,** no. 5 (1936).

WOLPE, J. *Psychotherapy by reciprocal inhibition.* Stanford, Calif.: Stanford University Press, 1958.

WOLPE, J. The prognosis in unpsychoanalyzed recovery from neurosis, *Amer. Jour. Psychiat.,* **117** (1961), 35–39.

WOLPE, J. Quantitative relationships in the systematic desensitization of a phobia, *Amer. Jour. Psychiat.,* **119** (1963), 1061–1068.

WOLPE, J. *The practice of behavior therapy.* Elmsford, N.Y.: Pergamon Press, 1969.

WOLPE, J., A. SALTER, and L. J. REYNA. *The conditioning therapies.* New York: Holt, Rinehart and Winston, 1964.

WUNDT, W. *Grundzuge der Physiologischen psychologie.* 2nd ed. Leipzig: Englemans, 1880.

YATES, A. J. *Frustration and conflict.* London: Methuen, 1962.

YUKL, G., K. N. WEXLEY, and J. SEYMORE. Effectiveness of pay incentives under variable ratio and continuous reinforcement schedules, *Jour. Appl. Psychol.*, **56** (1972), 10–23.

ZELLER, A. F. An experimental analogue of repression, I. Historical summary, *Psychol. Bull.*, **47** (1950), 39–51.

# Name Index

# Subject Index